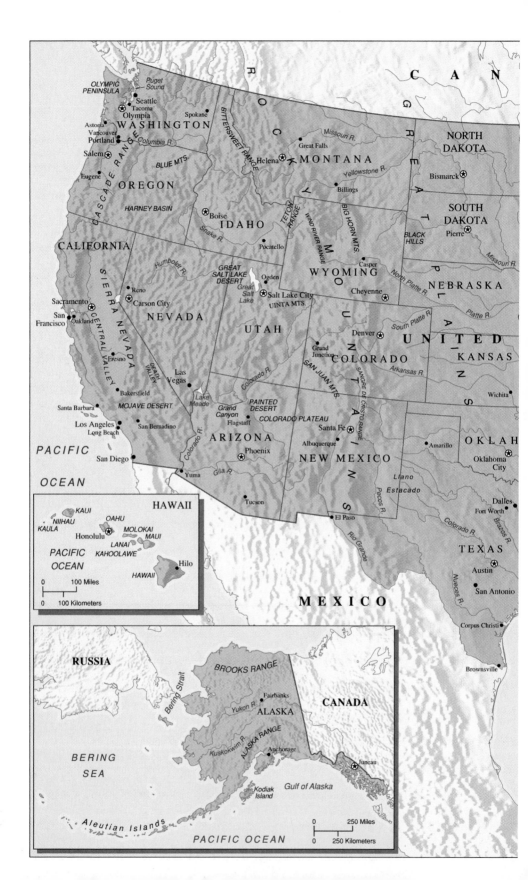

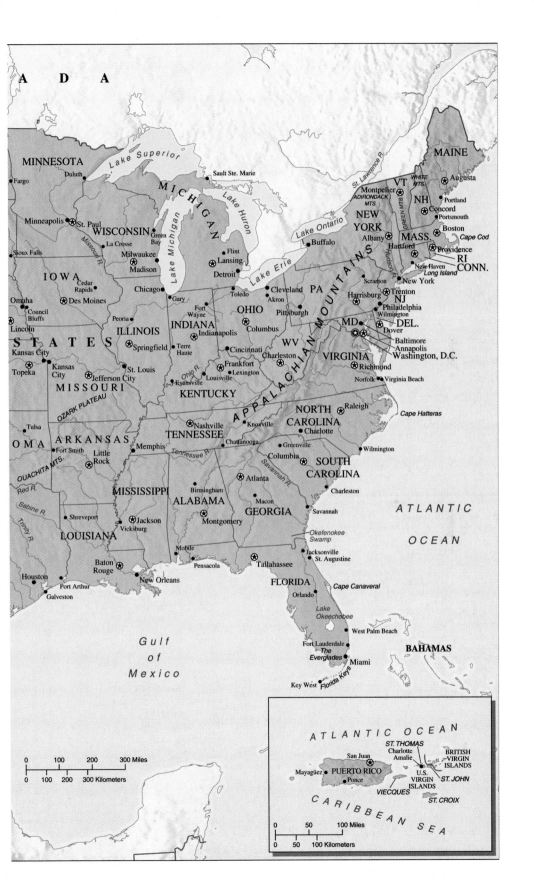

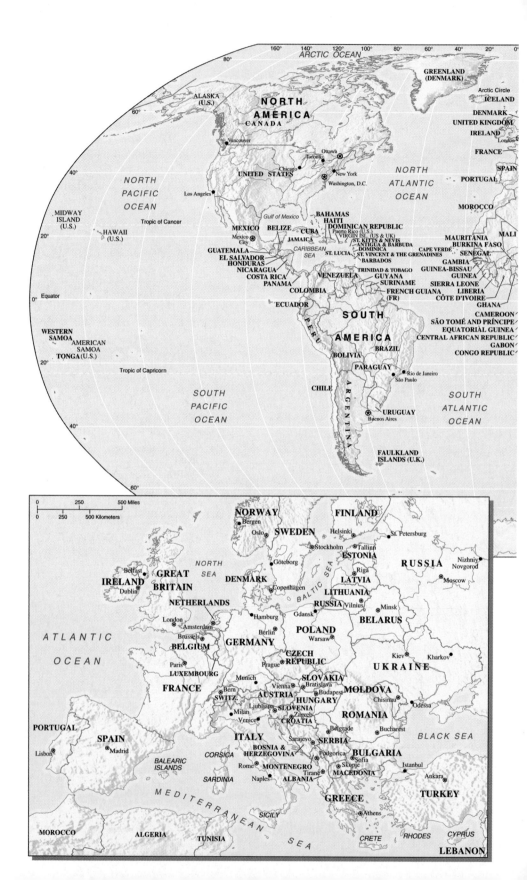

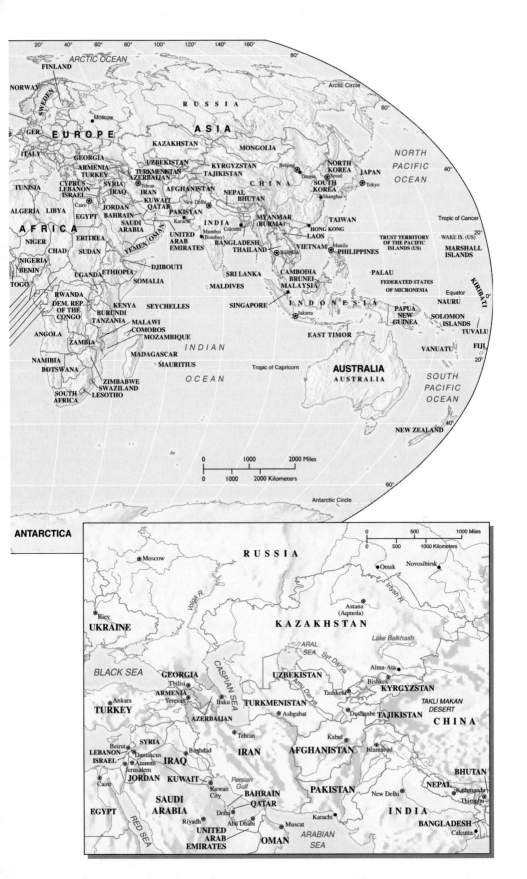

AMERICA

AMERICA

A NARRATIVE HISTORY

Brief Seventh Edition

Volume Two

GEORGE BROWN TINDALL

DAVID EMORY SHI

W · W · NORTON & COMPANY · NEW YORK · LONDON

FOR BRUCE AND SUSAN
AND FOR BLAIR

FOR
JASON AND JESSICA

Copyright © 2007, 2004, 2000, 1999, 1997, 1996, 1993, 1992, 1989, 1988, 1984
by W. W. Norton & Company, Inc.

Printed in the United States of America

Composition: TechBooks
Manufacturing: Quebecor, Taunton
Book design: Jo Anne Metsch
Editor: Karl Bakeman
Editorial assistant: Rebecca Arata
Manuscript editor: Abigail Winograd
Project editor: Carla L. Talmadge
Associate managing editor, College: Lory A. Frenkel
Director of Manufacturing, College: Roy Tedoff
Cartographer: CARTO-GRAPHICS/Alice Thiede and William Thiede

Acknowledgments and copyrights continue on page A104,
which serves as a continuation of the copyright page.

The Library of Congress has cataloged the one-volume edition as follows:

Tindall, George Brown.
America : a narrative history / George Brown Tindall,
David E. Shi.—Brief 7th ed.
    p.   cm.
Includes bibliographical references and index.
ISBN 13: 978-0-393-92734-4 (pbk.)
ISBN 10: 0-393-92734-2 (pbk.)
I. Shi, David E.   II. Title.

E178.1.T55 2007   2006046845
973—dc22
    ISBN 13: 978-0-393-92736-8 (pbk.)
    ISBN 10: 0-393-92736-9 (pbk.)

W. W. Norton & Company, Inc., 500 Fifth Avenue, New York, NY 10110
www.wwnorton.com

W. W. Norton & Company Ltd., Castle House, 75/76 Wells Street, London W1T 3QT

1 2 3 4 5 6 7 8 9 0

*W. W. Norton & Company has been independent since its founding in 1923,
when William Warder Norton and Mary D. Herter Norton first published
lectures delivered at the People's Institute, the adult education division of
New York City's Cooper Union. The Nortons soon expanded their program
beyond the Institute, publishing books by celebrated academics from America
and abroad. By mid-century, the two major pillars of Norton's publishing
program—trade books and college texts—were firmly established. In the 1950s,
the Norton family transferred control of the company to its employees, and
today—with a staff of four hundred and a comparable number of trade, college, and professional titles published each year—W. W. Norton & Company
stands as the largest and oldest publishing house owned wholly by its employees.*

CONTENTS

Part Six / M O D E R N   A M E R I C A

Part Seven / THE AMERICAN AGE

MAPS

PREFACE

Just as history is never complete, neither is a historical textbook. We have learned much from the responses of readers and instructors to the first six editions of *America: A Narrative History.* Perhaps the most important and reassuring lesson is that our original intention has proved valid: to provide a compelling narrative history of the American experience, a narrative animated by human characters, informed by analysis and social texture, and guided by the unfolding of events. Readers have also endorsed the book's distinctive size and format. *America* is designed to be read and to carry a moderate price. While the book retains its classic look, *America* sports a new color design for the Seventh Edition. We have added new eye-catching maps and included new art in full color. Despite these changes, we have not raised the price between the Sixth and the Seventh Editions.

As in previous revisions of *America,* we have adopted an overarching theme that informs many of the new sections we introduce throughout the Seventh Edition. In previous editions we have traced such broad-ranging themes as immigration, the frontier and the West, popular culture, and work. In each case we blend our discussions of the selected theme into the narrative, where they reside through succeeding editions.

The Seventh Edition of *America* highlights environmental history, a relatively new field that examines how people have shaped—and been shaped by—the natural world. Geographic features, weather, plants, animals, and diseases are important elements of environmental history. Environmental historians study how environments have changed as a result of natural processes such as volcanic eruptions, earthquakes, hurricanes, wildfires, droughts, floods, and climatic changes. They also study how societies have used and abused their natural environment through economic activities such as hunting, farming, logging and mining, manufacturing, building dams, and irrigation. Equally interesting is how different societies over time have perceived nature, as reflected in their religion, art, literature, and popular culture, and how they have reshaped nature according to those perceptions through the creation of parks, preserves, and designed landscapes. Finally, another major area of inquiry among environmental historians centers on the development of laws and regulations to govern the use of nature and maintain the quality of the natural environment.

Some of the new additions to the Seventh Edition related to environmental history are listed below.

- Chapter 1 includes discussions of the transmission of deadly infectious diseases from Europe to the New World and the ecological and social impact of the arrival of horses on the Great Plains.
- Chapter 3 examines the ways in which European livestock reshaped the New World environment and complicated relations with Native Americans.
- Chapters 5 and 6 describe the effects of smallpox on the American armies during the Revolution.
- Chapter 12 details the impact of early industrialization on the environment.
- Chapter 19 includes new material related to the environmental impact of the sharecrop-tenant farm system in the South after the Civil War, industrial mining in the Far West, and the demise of the buffalo on the Great Plains.
- Chapter 21 describes the dramatic rise of large cities after the Civil War and the distinctive aspects of the urban environment.
- Chapter 24 surveys the key role played by sportsmen in the emergence of the conservation movement during the late nineteenth century and details Theodore Roosevelt's efforts to preserve the nation's natural resources.
- Chapter 37 discusses President George W. Bush's controversial environmental policies and describes the devastation in Mississippi and Louisiana wrought by Hurricane Katrina.

Beyond these explorations of environmental history we have introduced other new material throughout the Seventh Edition. Fresh insights from important new scholarly works have been incorporated, and we feel confident that the book provides students with an excellent introduction to the American experience.

To enhance the pedagogical features of the text, we have added Focus Questions at the beginning of each chapter. Students can use these review tools to remind themselves of the key themes and central issues in the chapters. These questions are also available online as quizzes, the results of which students can e-mail to their instructors. In addition, the maps feature new enhanced captions designed to encourage students to think analytically about the relationship between geography and American history.

We have also revised the outstanding ancillary package that supplements the text. *For the Record: A Documentary History of America,* Third Edition, by David E. Shi and Holly A. Mayer (Duquesne University), is a rich resource with over 300 primary source readings from diaries, journals, newspaper articles, speeches, government documents, and novels. The *Study Guide,* by Charles Eagles (University of Mississippi), is another valuable resource. This edition contains chapter outlines, learning objectives, timelines, expanded vocabulary exercises, and many new short-answer and essay questions. *America: A Narrative History* Study Space is an online collection of tools for review and research. It includes chapter summaries, review questions and quizzes, interactive map exercises, timelines, and research modules, many new to this edition. *Norton Media Library* is a CD-ROM slide and text resource that includes images from the text, four-color maps, additional images from the Library of Congress archives, and audio files of significant historical speeches. Finally, the *Instructor's Manual and Test Bank,* by Mark Goldman (Tallahassee Community College) and Stephen Davis (Kingwood College) includes a test bank of short-answer and essay questions, as well as detailed chapter outlines, lecture suggestions, and bibliographies.

In preparing the Seventh Edition, we have benefited from the insights and suggestions of many people. Some of these insights have come from student readers of the text and we encourage such feedback. Among the scholars and survey instructors who offered us their comments and suggestions are: James Lindgren (SUNY Plattsburgh), Joe Kudless (Raritan Valley Community College), Anthony Quiroz (Texas A&M University – Corpus Christi), Steve Davis (Kingwood College), Mark Fiege (Colorado State University), David Head (John Tyler Community College), Hutch Johnson (Gordon College), Charles Eagles (University of Mississippi), Christina White and Eddie Weller at the South campus of San Jacinto College, Blanche Brick, Cathy Lively, Stephen Kirkpatrick, Patrick Johnson, Thomas Stephens, and others at the Bryan Campus of Blinn College, Evelyn Mangie (University of South Florida), Michael McConnell (University of Alabama – Birmingham), Alan Lessoff (Illinois State University), Joseph Cullon (Dartmouth University), Keith Bohannon (University of West Georgia), Tim Heinrichs (Bellevue Community College), Mary Ann Heiss (Kent State University), Edmund Wehrle (Eastern Illinois University), Adam Howard (University of Florida), David Parker

(Kennesaw State University), Barrett Esworthy (Jamestown Community College), Samantha Barbas (Chapman University), Jason Newman (Cosumnes River College), Paul Cimbala (Fordham University), Dean Fafoutis (Salisbury University), Thomas Schilz (Miramar Community College), Richard Frucht (Northwest Missouri State University), James Vlasich (Southern Utah University), Michael Egan (Washington State University), Robert Goldberg (University of Utah), Jason Lantzer (Indiana University), and Beth Kreydatus (College of William & Mary). Our special thanks go Tom Pearcy (Slippery Rock University) for all of his work on the timelines. Once again, we thank our friends at W. W. Norton, especially Steve Forman, Steve Hoge, Karl Bakeman, Neil Hoos, Lory Frenkel, Roy Tedoff, Dan Jost, Rebecca Arata, and Matt Arnold, for their care and attention along the way.

—George B. Tindall
—David E. Shi

18

RECONSTRUCTION: NORTH AND SOUTH

FOCUS QUESTIONS

· What were the different approaches to Reconstruction?

· How did Congress try to reshape southern society?

· What was the role of African Americans in the early postwar years?

· What were the main issues in national politics in the 1870s?

To answer these questions and access additional review material, please visit www.wwnorton.com/studyspace.

In the spring of 1865, the wearying war was over. At a frightful cost of over 600,000 lives and the destruction of the southern economy and much of its landscape, American nationalism had emerged triumphant, and some 4 million enslaved African-Americans were freed. Now the nation faced the imposing task of reuniting, providing for the freed slaves, and "reconstructing" a ravaged and resentful South.

THE WAR'S AFTERMATH

In the war's aftermath the victors faced important questions: Should the Confederate leaders be tried for treason? How should new governments be formed? How and at whose expense was the South's economy to be rebuilt? Should debts incurred by the Confederate state governments be honored?

Who should pay to rebuild the South's railroads and public buildings, dredge the clogged southern harbors, and restore damaged levees? What was to be done for the freed slaves? Were they to be given land? social equality? education? voting rights? Such complex questions required sober reflection and careful planning, but policy makers did not have the luxury of time or the benefit of consensus. Some wanted the former Confederate states returned to the Union with little or no changes in the region's social, political, and economic life. Others wanted southern society punished and transformed. At the end of 1865, the editors of the nation's foremost magazine, *Harper's Weekly,* expressed this vengeful attitude when they declared that "the forgive-and-forget policy . . . is mere political insanity and suicide."

ECONOMIC DEVELOPMENT IN THE NORTH   The Civil War was more truly a social revolution than the War of Independence, for it reduced the once-dominant power of the South's planter elite in national politics and elevated that of the northern "captains of industry." Government, both federal and state, grew more friendly to business leaders and more unfriendly to those who would probe into their activities. The wartime Congress had delivered on the major platform promises of the 1860 campaign, which had cemented the allegiance of northeastern businessmen and western farmers to the Republican party.

In the absence of southern members, Congress during the war had centralized national power and enacted the Republican economic agenda. It passed the Morrill Tariff, which doubled the average level of import duties. The National Banking Act created a uniform system of banking and banknote currency and helped finance the war. Congress also passed legislation confirming that the first transcontinental railroad would run along a north-central route, from Omaha to Sacramento, and donated public land and public bonds to ensure its financing. In the Homestead Act of 1862, moreover, Congress voted free federal homesteads of 160 acres to settlers, who had only to occupy the land for five years to gain title. The Morrill Land Grant Act of the same year conveyed to each state 30,000 acres of federal land per member of Congress from the state, the proceeds from the sale of which went to create colleges of "agriculture and mechanic arts." Such measures helped stimulate the North's economy in the years after the Civil War.

DEVASTATION IN THE SOUTH   The postwar South offered a sharp contrast to the victorious North. Along the path of General William T. Sherman's army, one observer reported in 1866, the countryside of Georgia and

A Street in the "Burned District"

Richmond, Virginia, Spring 1865.

South Carolina "looked for many miles like a broad black streak of ruin and desolation." Columbia, South Carolina, said another witness, was "a wilderness of ruins," Charleston a place of "vacant houses, of widowed women, of rotting wharves, of deserted warehouses, of weed-wild gardens, of miles of grass-grown streets, of acres of pitiful and voiceless barrenness."

Throughout the South, property values had collapsed. Confederate bonds and paper money were worthless; most railroads were damaged or destroyed. Cotton that had escaped destruction was seized as Confederate property or in forfeit of federal taxes. Emancipation wiped out $4 billion invested in human flesh and left the labor system in disarray. The great age of expansion in the cotton market was over. Not until 1879 would the cotton crop again equal the record harvest of 1860; tobacco production did not regain its prewar level until 1880; the sugar crop of Louisiana not until 1893; and the old rice industry of the Tidewater and the hemp industry of the Kentucky Bluegrass never regained their prewar status.

A TRANSFORMED SOUTH   The defeat of the Confederacy transformed much of southern society. The liberation of slaves, the destruction of property, and the free fall in land values left many planters destitute and homeless. After the Civil War many former Confederates were so embittered that they abandoned their native region rather than submit to "Yankee rule." Some migrated to Canada, Europe, Mexico, South America, or Asia. Others preferred the western territories and states. Still others moved to northern and midwestern cities on the assumption that their educational and economic opportunities would be better among the victors.

Most of those who remained in the South found their farms, homes, and communities transformed. One Confederate army captain reported that on his father's plantation "our negroes are living in great comfort. They were delighted to see me with overflowing affection. They waited on me as before, gave me breakfast, splendid dinners, etc. But they firmly and respectfully informed me: 'We own this land now. Put it out of your head that it will ever be yours again.'"

LEGALLY FREE, SOCIALLY BOUND   In the former Confederate states the newly freed slaves suffered most of all. According to the African-American abolitionist Frederick Douglass, the former slave remained dependent: "He had neither money, property, nor friends. He was free from the old plantation, but he had nothing but the dusty road under his feet. . . . He was turned loose, naked, hungry, and destitute to the open sky."

A few northerners argued that what the ex-slaves needed most was their own land. In 1865 Representative George Washington Julian of Indiana and Senator Charles Sumner of Massachusetts proposed to give freed slaves forty-acre homesteads carved out of Confederate lands taken under the Confiscation Act of 1862. But their plan for outright grants was replaced by a program of rentals, since under the law confiscation was effective only for the lifetime of the Confederate property owner. Discussions of land distribution, however, fueled rumors that freed slaves would get "forty acres and a mule," a slogan that swept the South at the end of the war. But even dedicated abolitionists shrank from taking land from whites to give to the freed slaves. Citizenship and legal rights were one thing, wholesale confiscation of property and land redistribution quite another.

Freedmen in Richmond, Virginia

According to a former Confederate general, freed blacks had "nothing but freedom."

Instead of land or material help, the freed slaves more often got advice about proper behavior.

THE FREEDMEN'S BUREAU On March 3, 1865, while the war was still raging, Congress set up within the War Department the Bureau of Refugees, Freedmen, and Abandoned Lands to provide "provisions, clothing, and fuel" to relieve "destitute and suffering refugees and freedmen and their wives and children." Agents of the Freedmen's Bureau were entrusted with negotiating labor contracts (a new practice for both African Americans and planters), providing medical care, and setting up schools, often in cooperation with such northern agencies as the American Missionary Association and the Freedmen's Aid Society. The bureau had its own courts to deal with labor disputes and land titles, and its agents were authorized to supervise trials involving blacks in other courts.

The failure to grasp the intensity of white intransigence and racial prejudice thwarted the efforts of Freedmen's Bureau agents to protect and assist the former slaves, however. Congress was not willing to strengthen the powers of the bureau to deal with such problems. Beyond temporary relief measures, no program of Reconstruction ever incorporated much more than constitutional and legal rights for freedmen. These were important in themselves, of course, but the extent to which even they should go was very uncertain, to be settled more by the course of events than by any clear-cut commitment to social and economic equality.

THE BATTLE OVER RECONSTRUCTION

The problem of reconstructing the South centered on deciding what governments would constitute authority in the defeated states. This problem arose first in Virginia at the very beginning of the Civil War, when the state's thirty-five western counties refused to go along with secession. In 1861 a loyal state government of Virginia was proclaimed at Wheeling, and that government in turn formed a new state, called West Virginia, which was admitted to the Union in 1863. As Union forces advanced into the South, President Lincoln in 1862 named military governors for Tennessee, Arkansas, and Louisiana. By the end of the following year, he had formulated a plan for regular civilian governments in those states and any others that might be liberated from Confederate rule.

LINCOLN'S PLAN AND CONGRESS'S RESPONSE   In late 1863 President Lincoln had issued a Proclamation of Amnesty and Reconstruction, under which any Confederate state could form a Union government whenever a number equal to 10 percent of those who had voted in 1860 took an oath of allegiance to the Constitution and Union and received a presidential pardon. Participants also had to swear support for laws and proclamations dealing with emancipation. Excluded from the pardon, however, were certain groups: civil, diplomatic, and high military officers of the Confederacy; judges, congressmen, and military officers of the United States who had left their federal posts to aid the rebellion; and those accused of failure to treat captured black soldiers and their officers as prisoners of war.

Under this plan, governments loyal to the Union appeared in Tennessee, Arkansas, and Louisiana, but Congress refused to recognize them. In the absence of specific provisions for Reconstruction in the Constitution, politicians disagreed as to where authority properly rested. A few conservative and most moderate Republicans supported Lincoln's program of immediate restoration. A small but influential group, known as Radical Republicans, demanded a sweeping transformation of southern society that would include making the freed slaves full-fledged citizens. The Radicals hoped to reconstruct southern society so as to dismantle the planter elite and the Democratic Party.

The Radical Republicans were talented, earnest leaders who maintained that Congress, not the president, should supervise the Reconstruction program. To this end in 1864 they helped pass the Wade-Davis bill, sponsored by Senator Benjamin Franklin Wade of Ohio and Representative Henry Winter Davis of Maryland. In contrast to Lincoln's 10 percent plan, the Wade-Davis bill required that a *majority* of white male citizens declare their allegiance and that only those who swore an "ironclad" oath that they had always remained loyal to the Union could vote or serve in the state constitutional conventions. The conventions, moreover, would have to abolish slavery, deny political rights to high-ranking civil and military officers of the Confederacy, and repudiate Confederate war debts. Passed during the closing days of the 1864 session, the bill went unsigned by Lincoln, and that "pocket veto" led the bill's sponsors to issue the Wade-Davis Manifesto, a blistering statement accusing the president of usurping power and attempting to use readmitted states to ensure his reelection.

Lincoln issued his final statement on Reconstruction in his last public address, on April 11, 1865. Speaking from the White House balcony, he dismissed the theoretical question of whether the Confederate states had technically remained in the Union as "good for nothing at all—a mere pernicious abstraction." Those states were simply "out of their proper practical relation with the Union," and the object was to get them "into their proper practical relation" as quickly as possible. Lincoln hoped to get new southern state governments in operation before Congress met in December. He worried that Congress might push through a harsher Reconstruction program. Lincoln wanted "no persecution, no bloody work," no dramatic restructuring of southern social and economic life.

On the evening of April 14, Lincoln went to Ford's Theater and his rendezvous with death. Shot in the head by John Wilkes Booth, a crazed actor and Confederate zealot, the president died the next morning. Pursued into Virginia, Booth was trapped and shot in a burning barn. His last words were "Tell mother I die for my country. I thought I did for the best." Three collaborators were tried and hanged, along with Mary Surratt, at whose boardinghouse they had plotted. Three other conspirators received life sentences, including a Maryland doctor who set the leg Booth had broken when he jumped from Lincoln's box onto the stage.

JOHNSON'S PLAN   Lincoln's death elevated to the White House Vice President Andrew Johnson of Tennessee, a man who lacked most presidential virtues. When General Ulysses Grant learned that Lincoln had died and Johnson was president, he said that he "dreaded the change" because the new commander in chief was vindictive toward his native South. Essentially illiterate, Johnson was provincial and bigoted. He was also short-tempered and lacking in self-control. At the inaugural ceremonies in early 1865, he had drunkenly slurred his address, embarrasing Lincoln and the nation. Johnson was a War (pro-Union) Democrat who had been put on the National Union ticket in 1864 as a gesture of unity. Of origins as humble as Lincoln's, Johnson had moved as a youth from his birthplace in Raleigh, North Carolina, to Greeneville, Tennessee, where he became the proprietor of a tailor shop. Self-educated with the help of his wife, Johnson grew prosperous, acquiring several slaves in the process.

Beginning in the 1830s, Johnson emerged as a leading Jacksonian Democrat. A bitter critic of the "swaggering" planter aristocracy "who are too lazy and proud to work," he promoted free land for the poor, defended slavery, and championed white supremacy. A notoriously stubborn man, he became a self-righteous, hot-tempered orator who enjoyed strong drink and employed abusive language to belittle his opponents. His fiery speeches and firm principles helped him win election as mayor, congressman, governor, and senator.

Like many other whites living in mountainous eastern Tennessee, Johnson ardently believed in the Union. In 1861 he was the only southern senator from a Confederate state to vote against secession, leading critics to denounce him as a "traitor" to the region. Yet his devotion to the Union did not include opposition to slavery. He hated the Confederacy because he hated the planter elite. "Damn the Negroes," Johnson bellowed to a friend during the war, "I am fighting those traitorous aristocrats, their masters."

Some of the Radical Republicans at first thought President Johnson, unlike Lincoln, was one of them. Johnson had, for example, asserted that treason "must be made infamous and traitors must be impoverished." But the Radicals would soon find Johnson to be as unsympathetic as Lincoln had been to their sweeping agenda, if for different reasons. Johnson's loyalty to the Union sprang from a strict adherence to the Constitution and a fervent belief in

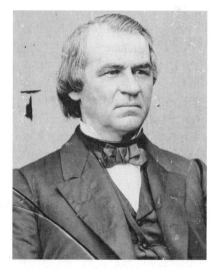

Andrew Johnson

A pro-Union Democrat from Tennessee.

limited government. He held that the rebellious states should be quickly brought back into their proper relation to the Union because the states and the Union were indestructible. In 1865 Johnson declared that "there is no such thing as Reconstruction. Those states have not gone out of the Union. Therefore Reconstruction is unnecessary."

Johnson's plan to restore the Union thus closely resembled Lincoln's. A new Proclamation of Amnesty, issued on May 29, 1865, excluded from pardon not only those Lincoln had excluded but also everybody with taxable property worth more than $20,000. Those wealthy planters and merchants were the people Johnson believed had led the South to secede. Those in the excluded groups might make special applications for presidential pardon, and before the year was out Johnson had issued some 13,000 pardons.

In each of the Rebel states not already organized by Lincoln, Johnson named a native Unionist provisional governor with authority to call a convention of men elected by loyal voters. Lincoln's 10 percent requirement was omitted. Johnson called upon the conventions to invalidate the secession ordinances, abolish slavery, and repudiate all debts incurred to aid the Confederacy. Each state, moreover, was to ratify the Thirteenth Amendment, which ended slavery. Like Lincoln, Johnson also endorsed limited voting rights for blacks. The state conventions for the most part met Johnson's requirements. Emboldened by the president's indulgence, however, southern whites ignored his advice to move cautiously in restoring their political and social traditions. Suggestions of black suffrage were scarcely raised in the state conventions and promptly squelched when they were.

SOUTHERN INTRANSIGENCE   When Congress met in December 1865, for the first time since the end of the war, it faced the fact that the new state governments in the former Confederacy were remarkably like the old ones. Among the new members presenting themselves to Congress were Georgia's Alexander Stephens, former vice president of the Confederacy, four Confederate generals, eight colonels, and six cabinet members. The Congress forthwith denied seats to all members from the eleven former Confederate states. It was too much to expect, after four bloody years, that the Unionists in Congress would welcome back ex-Confederates.

Furthermore, the new southern state legislatures, in passing repressive "black codes" restricting the freedom of blacks, baldly revealed that they intended to preserve the trappings of slavery as nearly as possible. As one southerner stressed, the "ex-slave was not a free man; he was a free Negro," and the black codes were intended to highlight the distinction.

The black codes varied from state to state, but some provisions were common. Existing black marriages, including common-law marriages, were recognized (although interracial marriages were prohibited), and testimony by blacks was accepted in legal cases involving them—in six states in all cases. Blacks could own property. They could sue and be sued in the courts. On the other hand, in Mississippi they could not own farmland, and in South Carolina they could not own city lots. They were required to enter into labor contracts with white employers, renewable annually, with provision for punishment in case of violation. Their dependent children were subject to compulsory apprenticeship and corporal punishment by the employer. "Vagrant" (unemployed) blacks were punished with severe fines, and if unable to pay, they were forced to work in the fields for whites who paid the courts for cheap labor. Slavery was thus revived in another guise.

THE RADICAL REPUBLICANS Faced with such evidence of southern intransigence, moderate Republicans drifted more and more toward the Radical camp. The new Congress set up a Joint Committee on Reconstruction, with nine members from the House and six from the Senate, to gather evidence and submit proposals for reconstructing the Southern states. As a parade of witnesses testified to the Rebels' impenitence, initiative on the committee fell to determined Radicals: Benjamin Wade of Ohio, George Julian of Indiana, Henry Wilson of Massachusetts, and most conspicuously of all, Thaddeus Stevens of Pennsylvania and Charles Sumner of Massachusetts.

Stevens, a crusty old bachelor with a chiseled face, thin, stern lips, and brooding eyes, was the domineering floor leader in the House. Driven by a genuine if at times fanatical idealism, he angrily insisted that the "whole fabric of southern society *must* be changed." Sumner, Stevens's counterpart in the Senate, agreed. Now recovered from "Bully" Brooks's 1856 assault, Sumner strove to see the South *reconstructed* rather than simply restored. This put him at odds with President Johnson. After visiting the White House, Sumner found the president "harsh, petulant, and unreasonable." He was especially disheartened by President Johnson's "prejudice, ignorance, and perversity" regarding the treatment of African Americans. Sumner and other Radicals now grew determined to take matters into their own hands. He argued that "Massachusetts could govern Georgia better than Georgia could govern herself." The southern plantations, seedbeds of aristocratic pretension and secession, he later added, "must be broken up, and the freedmen must have the pieces."

Most of the Radical Republicans had long been connected with the antislavery cause, and they approached the question of African-American rights with a sincere humanitarian impulse. Yet the Republicans also had political reasons for promoting civil rights. The Republicans needed black votes to maintain their control of Congress and the White House. They also needed to disenfranchise former Confederates to keep them from helping to elect Democrats who would restore the old ruling class to power. In public, however, the Radical Republicans rarely disclosed such partisan self-interest. Instead, they asserted that the Republicans, the party of Union and freedom, could best guarantee the fruits of victory and that extending voting rights to African Americans would be the best way to promote their welfare.

The growing conflict of opinion over Reconstruction policy brought about an inversion in constitutional reasoning. Secessionists—and Andrew Johnson—were now arguing that the Confederate states had in fact technically remained in the Union, and some Radical Republicans were contriving arguments that they had left the Union after all. Thaddeus Stevens argued that the Confederate states had indeed seceded and were now conquered provinces, subject to the absolute will of the victors. He added that the "whole fabric of southern society must be changed." Charles Sumner maintained that the southern states, by their acts of secession, had in effect committed suicide and reverted to the status of unorganized territories and thus were subject to the will of Congress. Most congressmen, however, embraced the "forfeited-rights theory," which held that the states continued to exist but by the acts of secession and war had forfeited "all civil and political rights under the Constitution." And Congress, not the president, was the proper authority to determine how and when such rights might be restored.

JOHNSON'S BATTLE WITH CONGRESS A long year of political battling remained, however, before this idea triumphed. By the end of 1865, the Radical Republicans' views had gained only a slight majority in Congress, insufficient to override presidential vetoes. The critical year of 1866 saw the gradual waning of Andrew Johnson's power, much of which was self-induced. Johnson first challenged Congress in February, when he vetoed a bill to extend the life of the Freedmen's Bureau. The measure, he said, assumed that wartime conditions still existed, whereas the country had returned "to a state of peace and industry." Since the Bureau was no longer valid as a war measure, Johnson believed it violated the Constitution. For the moment, Johnson's prestige remained sufficiently intact that the Senate upheld his veto.

Three days after the veto, however, on George Washington's Birthday, Johnson undermined his authority by launching an intemperate assault upon the Radical Republican leaders during an impromptu speech. From that point, moderate Republicans backed away from the president, and Radical Republicans went on the offensive.

In mid-March 1866 the Radical-led Congress passed the Civil Rights Act. A direct response to the black codes created by unrepentant state legislatures in the South, it declared that "all persons born in the United States . . . excluding Indians not taxed" were citizens entitled to "full and equal benefit of all laws." The granting of citizenship to native-born blacks, Johnson claimed, exceeded the scope of federal power. It would, moreover, "foment discord among the races." He vetoed the

The Cruel Uncle

A cartoon depicting Andrew Johnson leading two children, "Civil Rights" and "the Freedmen's Bureau," into the "Veto Wood."

measure, but this time, in April, Congress overrode the presidential veto. Then in July it enacted a revised Freedmen's Bureau bill, again overturning a veto. From that point on, Johnson's public and political support steadily eroded.

THE FOURTEENTH AMENDMENT   To remove all doubt about the validity of the new Civil Rights Act, the joint committee recommended a new constitutional amendment, which passed Congress in 1866 and was ratified by the states in 1868. The Fourteenth Amendment went far beyond the Civil Rights Act, however. The first section asserts four principles: it reaffirms the state and federal citizenship of all persons—regardless of race—born or naturalized in the United States, and it forbids any state (the word *state* would be important in later litigation) to "abridge the privileges and immunities of citizens," to deprive any *person* (again an important term) "of life, liberty, or property without due process of law," or to "deny any person . . . the equal protection of the laws."

These clauses have been the subject of lawsuits resulting in applications not foreseen at the time. The "due-process clause" has come to mean that state as well as federal power is subject to the Bill of Rights, and it has been used to protect corporations, as legal "persons," from "unreasonable" regulation by the states. Other provisions of the amendment had less far-reaching effects. One section specified that the debt of the United States "shall not be questioned" but declared "illegal and void" all debts contracted in aid of the Confederate rebellion. The final sentence specified the power of Congress to pass laws enforcing the amendment.

Johnson's home state was among the first to ratify the Fourteenth Amendment. In Tennessee, which had harbored more Unionists than any other Confederate state, the government had fallen under Radical Republican control. The rest of the South, however, steadfastly resisted the Radical challenge to Johnson's program. In 1866 bloody race riots in Memphis and New Orleans added fuel to the flames. Both incidents sparked indiscriminate massacres of blacks by local police and white mobs. The rioting, Radical Republicans argued, was the natural fruit of Johnson's foolish policy.

RECONSTRUCTING THE SOUTH

THE TRIUMPH OF CONGRESSIONAL RECONSTRUCTION   As 1866 drew to an end, the November congressional elections promised to be a referendum on the growing split between Johnson and the Radical Republicans. The president embarked on a speaking tour of the Midwest, a "swing around the circle," which provoked undignified shouting contests between the president and his audiences. In Cleveland he described the Radical Republicans as "factious, domineering, tyrannical" men. Various incidents tended to confirm his image as a "ludicrous boor," which Radical Republican newspapers eagerly promoted. When the election returns came in, the Republicans had more than a two-thirds majority in each house, a comfortable margin with which to override presidential vetoes.

Congress actually enacted a new reconstruction program even before the new members took office. On March 2, 1867, two days before the old Congress expired, it passed three basic laws of congressional Reconstruction over Johnson's vetoes: the Military Reconstruction Act, the Command of the Army Act, and the Tenure of Office Act.

The first of these acts prescribed conditions under which new southern state governments should be formed. The other two sought to block any effort by the president to obstruct the process. The Command of the Army Act required that all orders from the president as commander in chief go through the headquarters of the general of the army, then Ulysses Grant. The Tenure of Office Act required the Senate's permission for the president to remove any officeholder whose appointment the Senate had confirmed.

In large measure it was intended to retain Secretary of War Edwin Stanton, the one Radical Republican sympathizer in Johnson's cabinet. But an ambiguity crept into the wording of the act. Cabinet officers, it said, should serve during the term of the president who appointed them—and Lincoln had appointed Stanton, although, to be sure, Johnson was serving out Lincoln's term.

The Military Reconstruction Act was hailed—or denounced—as the triumphant victory of "Radical" Reconstruction. Originally intended by the Radical Republicans to give military commanders in the South ultimate control over law enforcement and to leave open indefinitely the terms of restoration, it was diluted by moderate Republicans until it boiled down to little more than a requirement that southern states accept African-American suffrage and ratify the Fourteenth Amendment.

Tennessee, which had already ratified the Fourteenth Amendment, was exempted from the application of the act. The other ten states were divided into five military districts, and the commanding officer of each was authorized to keep order and protect the "rights of persons and property." The Johnson governments remained intact for the time being, but new constitutions were to be framed "in conformity with the Constitution of the United States," in conventions elected by male citizens aged twenty-one and older "of whatever race, color, or previous condition." Each state constitution had to provide the same universal male suffrage. Then, once the constitution was ratified by a majority of voters and accepted by Congress, the state legislature had ratified the Fourteenth Amendment, and the amendment had become part of the Constitution, any given state would be entitled to renewed representation in Congress. Persons excluded from officeholding by the proposed amendment were also excluded from participation in the process. Before the end of 1867, new elections had been held in all the states but Texas.

Having clipped the president's wings, the Republican Congress moved a year later to safeguard its southern program from possible interference by the Supreme Court. On March 27, 1868, Congress simply removed the power of the Supreme Court to review cases arising under the Military Reconstruction Act, which Congress clearly had the constitutional right to do under its power to define the Court's appellate jurisdiction. The Court accepted this curtailment of its authority on the same day it affirmed the notion of an "indestructible Union" in *Texas v. White* (1869). In that case the Court also acknowledged the right of Congress to reframe state governments, thus endorsing the Radical Republican point of view.

THE IMPEACHMENT AND TRIAL OF JOHNSON   By 1868 Radical Republicans were convinced not only that the power of the Supreme Court and the president needed to be curtailed but also that Andrew Johnson himself had to be removed from office. Johnson, though hostile to the congressional Reconstruction program, had gone through the motions required of him. He continued to pardon former Confederates, however, and transferred several of the district military commanders who had displayed Radical Republican sympathies. Johnson lacked Lincoln's resilience and pragmatism, and he allowed his temper to get the better of his judgment. He castigated the Radical Republicans as "a gang of cormorants and bloodsuckers who have been fattening upon the country." During 1867 newspapers reported that the differences between Johnson and the Republicans had grown irreconcilable.

The Radical Republicans unsuccessfully tried to impeach Johnson early in 1867, alleging a variety of flimsy charges, none of which represented an indictable crime. Then Johnson himself provided the occasion for impeachment when he deliberately violated the Tenure of Office Act in order to test its constitutionality. Secretary of War Edwin Stanton had become a thorn in Johnson's side, refusing to resign despite his disagreements with the president's Reconstruction policy. On August 12, 1867, during a congressional recess, Johnson suspended Stanton and named General Ulysses Grant in his place. When the Senate refused to confirm Johnson's action, however, Grant returned the office to Stanton.

The Radical Republicans now saw their chance to remove the president, and they were explicit about their political purpose. As Charles Sumner declared, "Impeachment is a political proceeding before a political body with a political purpose." The debate in the House was clamorous and vicious. On February 24, 1868, the House passed eleven articles of impeachment by a party-line vote of 126 to 47.

Eight of the articles focused on the charge that Johnson had unlawfully removed Stanton. Article 9 accused the president of issuing orders in violation of the Command of the Army Act. The last two articles in effect charged him with criticizing Congress by "inflammatory and scandalous harangues." Article 11 also accused him of "unlawfully devising and contriving" to violate the Reconstruction Acts, contrary to his obligation to execute the laws. At the very least, it stated, Johnson had tried to obstruct Congress's will while observing the letter of the law.

The Senate trial began on March 5, 1868, and continued until May 26, with Chief Justice Salmon P. Chase presiding. Debate eventually focused on

Stanton's removal, the most substantive impeachment charge. Johnson's lawyers argued that Lincoln, not Johnson, had appointed Stanton, so the Tenure of Office Act did not apply to him. At the same time they claimed (correctly, as it turned out) that the law was unconstitutional.

As the five-week trial ended and the voting began in May 1868, the Senate Republicans could afford only six defections from their ranks to ensure the two-thirds majority needed to convict. In the end seven moderate Republicans and all twelve Democrats voted to acquit. The final tally was thirty-five to nineteen for conviction, one vote short of the two thirds needed for removal from office. The renegade Republicans offered two primary reasons for their controversial votes: they feared damage to the separation of powers among the branches of government if Johnson were removed, and they were assured by Johnson's attorneys that the president would stop obstructing congressional policy in the South.

Although the Senate failed to remove Johnson, the trial crippled his already weak presidency. During the remaining ten months of his term, he initiated no other clashes with Congress. In 1868 Johnson sought the Democratic presidential nomination but lost to New York governor Horatio Seymour, who then lost to the Republican, Ulysses Grant, in the general election. A bitter Johnson refused to attend Grant's inauguration. His final act as president was to issue a pardon to former Confederate president Jefferson Davis. In 1874, after failed bids for the Senate and the House, Johnson won a measure of vindication with election to the Senate, the only former president ever to do so, but he died a few months later. He was buried with a copy of the Constitution placed under his head.

As for the impeachment trial, only two weeks after it ended, a Boston newspaper reported that Americans were amazed at how quickly "the whole subject of impeachment seems to have been thrown into the background and dwarfed in importance" by other events. Moreover, impeachment of Johnson was in the end a great political mistake, for the failure to remove the president damaged Radical Republican morale and support. Nevertheless, the Radical cause did gain something: Johnson's agreement not to obstruct the process of Reconstruction. Thereafter Radical Reconstruction began in earnest.

RADICAL RULE IN THE SOUTH   In June 1868 Congress agreed that seven southern states had met the conditions for readmission to the Union, all but Virginia, Mississippi, and Texas. Congress rescinded Georgia's admission, however, when the state legislature expelled twenty-eight African-American members and seated former Confederate leaders. The federal military commander in Georgia then forced the legislature to reseat the black members and remove the Confederates, and the state was compelled to ratify the Fifteenth Amendment before being readmitted in July 1870. Mississippi, Texas, and Virginia had returned earlier in 1870, under the added requirement that they, too, ratify the Fifteenth Amendment. That amendment, ratified in 1870, forbade the states to deny any citizen the right to vote on grounds of "race, color, or previous condition of servitude."

Long before the new governments had been established, partisan Republican groups began to spring up in the South, promoted by the Union League, an organization founded in 1862 to rally support for the federal government. Its representatives enrolled blacks and loyal whites as members, initiated them into the secrets and rituals of the order, and instructed them "in their rights and duties." These Union Leagues became a powerful source of Republican political strength in the South and as a result drew the ire of unreconstructed whites.

The Reconstructed South

Throughout the South during Reconstruction, many former Confederates continued to harbor deeply ingrained racial prejudices. They adopted a militant stance against federally imposed changes in southern society. Whites used terror, intimidation, and violence to suppress black efforts to gain social and economic equality. In July 1866, for instance, a black woman in Clinch County, Georgia, was arrested and given sixty-five lashes for "using abusive language" in an encounter with a white woman. A month later another black woman suffered the same punishment. The Civil War had brought freedom to the enslaved, but it did not bring protection against exploitation or abuse.

THE FREED SLAVES   To focus solely on what white Republicans did to reconstruct the defeated South creates the false impression that the freed slaves were simply pawns in the hands of others. In fact, southern blacks were active agents in affecting the course of Reconstruction. Many former slaves found themselves liberated but destitute after the fighting ended. The mere promise of freedom, however, had raised their hopes for biracial democracy, equal justice, and economic opportunity. "Most anyone ought to know that a man is better off free than as a slave, even if he did not have anything," said the Reverend E. P. Holmes, a black Georgia preacher and former domestic servant. "I would rather be free and have my liberty."

Participation in the Union army or navy had provided many freedmen with training in leadership. Black military veterans would form the core of the first generation of African-American political leaders in the postwar South. Military service provided many former slaves with the first opportunities to learn to read and write. Army life also alerted them to alternative social choices and to new opportunities for economic advancement and social respectability. Fighting for the Union cause also instilled a fervent sense of nationalism. A Virginia freedman explained that the United States was "now *our* country—made emphatically so by the blood of our brethren."

Former slaves established independent churches after the war, churches that quickly formed the foundation of African-American community life. Blacks preferred Baptist churches over other denominations, in part because the decentralized structure allowed each congregation to worship in its own way. By 1890 over 1.3 million African Americans were worshipping in Baptist churches in the South, nearly three times as many as had joined any other denomination. In addition to forming viable new congregations, freed blacks organized thousands of fraternal, benevolent, and mutual-aid societies, clubs, lodges, and associations. Memphis, for example, had over 200 such organizations; Richmond boasted twice that number.

Freed slaves also hastened to reestablish and reaffirm their families. Marriages that had been prohibited were now legitimized through the assistance of the Freedmen's Bureau. By 1870 most former slaves were living in two-parent households.

Former slaves had little money or technical training and were thus faced with the prospect of becoming wage laborers to support themselves. To avoid this and retain as much autonomy as possible over their productive energies and those of their children, many freed slaves chose to become sharecroppers, tenant farmers who gained access to separate plots of land owned by whites. In payment for the use of the land and cabin, and sometimes even the tools, seed, and fertilizer needed to farm the land, they were required to give between one half and two thirds of the harvested crops to the white landowner. This arrangement gave them higher status than they would have had as wage laborers. It also gave them the freedom to set their own hours and work as much or as little as they pleased, and it enabled mothers and wives to devote time to domestic responsibilities while contributing to the family's income.

African-American communities in the postwar South also sought to establish schools. The antebellum planter elite had denied education to blacks because they feared that literate slaves would organize uprisings. After the war the white elite worried that formal education would encourage poor whites and poor blacks to leave the South in search of better social and economic opportunities. Economic leaders wanted to protect the competitive advantage afforded by the region's low-wage labor market. Yet white opposition to education for blacks made it all the more important to African Americans. South Carolina's Mary McLeod Bethune, the seventeenth child of former slaves and one of the first children in the household born after the Civil War, reveled in the opportunity to gain an education: "The whole world opened to me when I learned to read." She walked five miles to school as a child, earned a scholarship to college, and went on to become the first black woman to found a school that became a four-year college, Bethune-Cookman, in Daytona Beach, Florida.

The general resistance among the former slaveholding class to initiatives involving education forced the freed slaves to rely upon northern assistance or take their own initiative. African-American churches and individuals helped raise the money and often built the schools and paid the teachers. Soldiers who had acquired some literacy skills often served as the first teachers, and the classes included adults.

BLACKS IN SOUTHERN POLITICS   In the postwar South the new role of African Americans in politics caused the most controversy. If largely illiterate and inexperienced in the rudiments of politics, southern blacks were little different from the millions of whites enfranchised in the age of Jackson or immigrants herded to the polls by political bosses in New York and other cities after the war. Some freedmen frankly confessed their disadvantages. Beverly Nash, a black delegate to the South Carolina convention of 1868, told his colleagues: "I believe, my friends and fellow-citizens, we are not prepared for this suffrage. But we can learn. Give a man tools and let him commence to use them, and in time he will learn a trade. So it is with voting."

Several hundred African-American delegates participated in the statewide political conventions. Most had been selected by local political meetings or by churches, fraternal societies, Union Leagues, or black Federal army units, although a few simply appointed themselves. The African-American delegates "ranged all colors and apparently all conditions," but free mulattoes from the cities played the most prominent roles. At Louisiana's Republican state convention, for instance, nineteen of the twenty black delegates had been born free.

By 1867 former slaves had begun to gain political influence and vote in large numbers, and this development revealed emerging tensions within the African-American community. Some southern blacks resented the presence of northern brethren who moved south after the war, while others complained that few ex-slaves were represented in leadership positions. Northern blacks and the southern black elite, most of whom were urban dwellers, opposed efforts to redistribute land to the rural freedmen, and many insisted that political equality did not mean social equality. As an Alabama black leader stressed, "We do not ask that the ignorant and degraded shall be put on a social equality with the refined and intelligent." In general, however, unity rather than dissension prevailed, and African Americans focused on common concerns such as full equality under the law.

Brought suddenly into politics in times that tried the most skilled of statesmen, many African Americans served with distinction. Nonetheless, the derisive label "black Reconstruction" used by later critics exaggerates African-American political influence, which was limited mainly to voting, and overlooks the political clout of the large number of white Republicans, especially in the mountain areas of the upper South, who supported the congressional plan for Reconstruction. Only one of the new conventions, South

Freedmen Voting in New Orleans

The Fifteenth Amendment, passed in 1870, guaranteed at the federal level the right of citizens to vote regardless of "race, color, or previous condition of servitude." But former slaves had been registering to vote—and voting in large numbers—in state elections since 1867, as in this scene.

Carolina's, had a black majority, seventy-six to forty-one. Louisiana's was evenly divided racially, and in only two other conventions were more than 20 percent of the members black: Florida's, with 40 percent, and Virginia's, with 24 percent.

In the new state governments, any African-American participation was a novelty. Although some 600 blacks—most of them former slaves—served as state legislators, no black man was ever elected governor, and few served as judges. In Louisiana, however, Pinckney Pinchback, a northern black and former Union soldier, won the office of lieutenant governor and served as acting governor when the white governor was indicted for corruption. Several blacks were elected lieutenant governor, state treasurer, or secretary of state. There were two black senators in Congress during Reconstruction, Hiram Revels and Blanche K. Bruce, both from Mississippi, and fourteen black members of the House. Among them were some of the ablest congressmen of the time.

CARPETBAGGERS AND SCALAWAGS   The top positions in southern state governments went for the most part to white Republicans whom the opposition soon labeled carpetbaggers and scalawags, depending upon their place of birth. Northern opportunists who allegedly came south with all their belongings in carpetbags to reap political spoils were more often than not Union veterans who had arrived as early as 1865 or 1866, drawn south by the hope of economic opportunity. Others were lawyers, businessmen, editors, teachers, social workers, or preachers who came on missionary endeavors.

The scalawags, or southern white Republicans, were even more reviled and misrepresented. A Nashville newspaper editor called them the "merest trash that could be collected in a civilized community, of no personal credit or social responsibility." Most scalawags had opposed secession, forming a Unionist majority in mountain counties as far south as Georgia and Alabama and especially in the hills of eastern Tennessee. Though many were indeed crass opportunists who indulged in corruption at the public's expense, several were distinguished figures. They included the former Confederate general James Longstreet, who decided after Appomattox that the Old South must change its ways. To that end he became a successful cotton broker in New Orleans, joined the Republican party, and supported the Radical Reconstruction program. Others were former Whigs who found the Republican party's expansive industrial and commercial program in keeping with Henry Clay's earlier efforts to use the government to promote economic growth and industrial development.

THE RADICAL RECORD   Former Confederates not only resented carpetbaggers and scalawags, but they also objected to the new state constitutions, primarily because of their provisions allowing for black suffrage and civil rights. Nonetheless, most of the state constitutions remained in effect for some years after the end of Radical Republican control, and later constitutions incorporated many of their features. Conspicuous among the Radical innovations were steps toward greater democracy, such as requiring universal male suffrage, reapportioning legislatures more nearly according to population, and making more state offices elective.

Given the hostile circumstances in which the Radical Republican governments operated, their achievements were remarkable. They established the first state school systems, in which some 600,000 black pupils were enrolled by 1877. State governments under the Radical Republicans also paid more attention to the poor and to orphanages, asylums, and institutions for the disabled of both races. Public roads, bridges, railroads, and buildings were repaired or rebuilt. African Americans achieved new rights and opportunities that would never again be taken away, at least in principle: equality before the law and the right to own property, carry on business, enter professions, attend schools, and learn to read and write.

Yet several of the Republican state regimes also engaged on systematic corruption. Public money and public credit were often awarded to privately owned corporations, notably railroads, under conditions that invited influence peddling. Still, corruption was not invented by the Radical Republican regimes, nor did it die with them. In Mississippi the Republican Reconstruction governments were quite honest compared with those of their Democratic successors.

The Grant Years

THE ELECTION OF 1868   Ulysses S. Grant, who served as president during the collapse of Republican rule in the South, brought to the White House little political experience. But in 1868 northern voters supported the Lion of Vicksburg because of his brilliant record as a war leader. Both parties wooed Grant, but his falling-out with President Johnson pushed him toward the Republicans and built trust in him among the Radicals.

The Republican platform of 1868 endorsed Radical Reconstruction, cautiously defending black suffrage as a necessity in the South but a matter that each northern state should settle for itself. It also urged payment of the nation's war debt in gold rather than in the new "greenback" paper currency printed during the war. More important than the platform were the great expectations of a soldier-president, whose slogan was "Let us have peace."

The Democrats opposed the Republicans on both Reconstruction and the debt. The Republican Congress, the Democratic platform charged, had subjected ten states, "in the time of profound peace, to military despotism and Negro supremacy." As for the public debt the party endorsed the "Ohio idea" of Representative George H. Pendleton: since most war bonds had been bought with depreciated greenbacks, they should be paid off in greenbacks. With no conspicuously available candidate in sight, the convention turned to Horatio Seymour, wartime governor of New York and chairman of the convention. The Democrats ran a closer race than expected, attesting to the strength of traditional party loyalties. Although Grant swept the Electoral College by 214 to 80, his popular majority was only 307,000 out of 5.7 million votes. Over 500,000 African-American voters accounted for Grant's margin of victory.

Grant had proved himself a great leader in the war, but in the White House he was often blind to the political forces and influence peddlers around him. Shy and withdrawn, he was uncomfortable around intellectuals and impatient with idealists. Grant preferred watching horse races to reading about complex issues. Although personally honest, he was dazzled by men of wealth and unaccountably loyal to greedy subordinates who betrayed his trust. In the formulation of policy, he passively followed the lead of Congress. This approach initially endeared him to Republican party leaders, but it left him ineffective and caused others to grow disillusioned with his leadership. At the outset, Grant consulted nobody on his cabinet appointments. Some of his choices indulged personal whims; others simply reflected bad judgment. Secretary of State Hamilton Fish of New York turned out to be a fortunate exception; he masterfully guided foreign policy throughout the Grant presidency. Other than Fish, however, Grant's cabinet overflowed with incompetents.

THE GOVERNMENT DEBT   Financial issues dominated Grant's presidency. After the war the Treasury had assumed that the $432 million in greenbacks issued during the conflict would be retired from circulation and that the nation would revert to a "hard-money" currency—gold coins. Congress in 1866 granted the Treasury discretion to do so gradually. Many agrarian and debtor groups resisted this contraction of the money supply, believing that it would mean lower farm prices and harder-to-pay debts. They were joined by a large number of Radical Republicans who thought a combination of high tariffs and inflation would generate more rapid economic growth. In 1868 "soft-money" supporters in Congress halted the retirement of greenbacks, leaving $356 million outstanding. There matters stood when Grant took office.

The "sound-money" (or hard-money) advocates, mostly bankers, merchants, and other creditors, claimed that Grant's election was a mandate to save the country from the Democrats' "Ohio idea" of using greenbacks to repay government bonds. Quite influential in Republican circles, the sound-money advocates also had the benefit of agreeing with the deeply ingrained popular assumption that hard money was morally preferable to paper currency. Grant agreed as well, and in his inaugural address he endorsed payment of the national debt in gold as a point of national honor.

SCANDALS Within less than a year of his election, Grant had fallen into a cesspool of scandal. In the summer of 1869, two railroad entrepreneurs, the crafty Jay Gould and the flamboyant con man James Fisk, connived with the president's brother-in-law to corner the nation's gold market. That is, they would create a public craze for gold by purchasing massive quantities and convincing traders that the price would keep climbing. As more buyers joined the frenzy, the value of gold would soar. The only danger was the federal Treasury's selling large amounts of gold. Gould concocted an argument that the government should refrain from selling gold on the market because the resulting rise in gold prices would raise temporarily depressed farm prices. Grant apparently smelled a rat from the start, but he was seen in public with the speculators. As the rumor spread on Wall Street, gold rose from $132 to $163 an ounce. Finally, on Black Friday, September 24, 1869, Grant ordered the Treasury to sell a large quantity of gold, and the bubble burst. Fisk got out by repudiating his agreements and hiring thugs to intimidate his creditors. "Nothing is lost save honor," he said.

The plot to corner the gold market was only the first of several scandals that rocked the Grant administration. In 1872 the public learned about the financial crookery of the Crédit Mobilier, a construction company that had milked the Union Pacific Railroad for exorbitant fees to line the pockets of insiders who controlled both firms. Union Pacific shareholders were left holding the bag. This chicanery had transpired before Grant's election in 1868, but it now touched a number of prominent Republicans who had been given shares of Crédit Mobilier stock in exchange for favorable votes. Of the thirteen congressmen involved, only two were censured.

Even more odious disclosures soon followed, some involving the president's cabinet. Grant's secretary of war, it turned out, had accepted bribes from merchants who traded with Indians at army posts in the West. He was impeached, but he resigned in time to elude trial. Post-office contracts, it was revealed, went to carriers who offered the highest kickbacks. In St. Louis a "whiskey ring" bribed tax collectors to bilk the government of millions of dollars in revenue. Grant's private secretary was enmeshed in that scheme, taking large sums of money and other valuables in return for inside information. There is no evidence that Grant himself participated in any of the scandals, but his poor choice of associates and his gullibility earned him widespread censure.

WHITE TERROR   President Grant initially fought hard to enforce the federal efforts to reconstruct the postwar South. By the time he became president, southern resistance had turned violent, as unrepentant whites organized vigilante groups to terrorize blacks. Most white southerners remained so conditioned by the social prejudices embedded in the institution of slavery that they were unable to conceive of blacks as citizens. In some places, hostility to the new regimes turned violent. Said one unreconstructed Mississippian in 1875, "Carry the election peaceably if we can, forcibly if we must."

The prototype of all the terrorist groups was the Ku Klux Klan (KKK), first organized in 1866 by some young men of Pulaski, Tennessee, as a social club, with the costumes and secret rituals common to fraternal groups. At first a group of pranksters, its members soon began to intimidate blacks and white Republicans, and the KKK spread rapidly across the South in answer to the Republican party's Union League. Klansmen rode about the countryside, hiding behind masks and under robes, spreading horrendous rumors, harassing blacks, and wreaking violence and destruction.

Worse Than Slavery

This Thomas Nast cartoon chides the Ku Klux Klan and the White League for promoting conditions "worse than slavery" for southern blacks after the Civil War.

At the urging of President Grant, Congress struck back with three Enforcement Acts (1870-1871) to protect black voters. The first of these measures levied penalties on persons who interfered with any citizen's right to vote. A second placed the election of congressmen under surveillance by federal election supervisors and marshals. The third (the Ku Klux Klan Act) outlawed the characteristic activities of the Klan—forming conspiracies, wearing disguises, resisting law officers, and intimidating government officials. In 1871 the federal government singled out nine counties in up-country South Carolina and pursued mass prosecutions that brought an abrupt halt to Klan terrorism. In general, however, the federal acts designed to protect African Americans suffered from weak and inconsistent enforcement. Moreover, the South's strong tradition of states' rights and local autonomy resisted federal force.

CONSERVATIVE RESURGENCE   The Klan in fact could not take credit for the overthrow of Republican control in any state. Perhaps its most important effect was to weaken the morale of African Americans and Republicans in the South and strengthen in the North a growing weariness with the whole "southern question." Republican control in the South gradually loosened as "Conservative" parties—a name used by Democrats to mollify former Whigs—mobilized the white vote. Scalawags and many carpetbaggers drifted away from the Radical Republican ranks under pressure from their white neighbors. Few of them had joined the Republicans out of concern for black rights in the first place. And where persuasion failed to work, Democrats were willing to use chicanery. As one enthusiastic Democrat boasted, "The white and black Republicans may outvote us, but we can outcount them."

Such factors led to the collapse of Republican control in Virginia and Tennessee as early as 1869 and in Georgia and North Carolina in 1870. Reconstruction lasted longest in states with the largest black population, where whites abandoned Klan hoods for barefaced intimidation in paramilitary groups like the Mississippi Rifle Club and the South Carolina Red Shirts. In the 1873 elections in Yazoo County, Mississippi, the Republicans cast 2,449 votes and the Democrats 638; two years later the Democrats polled 4,049 votes, the Republicans 7. By 1876 Radical Republican regimes survived only in Louisiana, South Carolina, and Florida, and those collapsed after the elections of that year.

The erosion of northern interest in promoting civil rights in the postwar South reflected weariness as well as interest in other activities. Western expansion, Indian wars, new economic opportunities, and political debates over the tariff and the currency distracted attention from southern outrages. In addition, a business panic in 1873 led to a sharp depression and created both social problems and new racial tensions in the North and the South

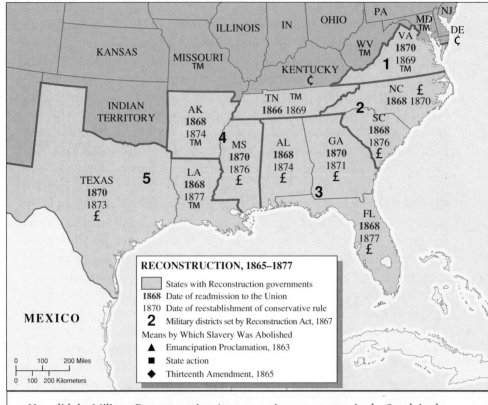

RECONSTRUCTION, 1865–1877

1868 Date of readmission to the Union
1870 Date of reestablishment of conservative rule
2 Military districts set by Reconstruction Act, 1867
Means by Which Slavery Was Abolished
▲ Emancipation Proclamation, 1863
■ State action
◆ Thirteenth Amendment, 1865

How did the Military Reconstruction Act reorganize government in the South in the late 1860s and 1870s? What did the former Confederate states have to do to be read-mitted to the Union? How did "Conservative" parties gradually regain control of the South from the Republicans in the 1870s?

that helped undermine already inconsistent federal efforts to promote racial justice in the former Confederacy.

REFORM AND THE ELECTION OF 1872   Long before Grant's first term ended, Republicans broke ranks with the administration. Their alienation was a reaction to Radical Reconstruction and the incompetence and corruption in the administration. A new faction, called Liberal Republicans, favored free trade, the redemption of greenbacks with gold, the removal federal troops from the South, the restoration of the rights of former Confederates, and civil service reform. Open revolt first broke out in Missouri, where Carl Schurz, a German immigrant and war hero, led a group of Liberal

What I Know about Raising the Devil

With the tail and cloven hoof of the devil, Horace Greeley (center) leads a small band of Liberal Republicans in pursuit of incumbent president Ulysses S. Grant and his supporters in this 1872 cartoon.

Republicans who, with Democratic help, elected a governor in 1870 and sent Schurz to the Senate.

In 1872 the Liberal Republicans held their own national convention, which produced a compromise platform condemning the Republican party's "vindictive" southern policy and favoring civil service reform but remaining silent on the protective tariff. The delegates stampeded to endorse an anomalous presidential candidate: Horace Greeley, editor of the *New York Tribune* and an enthusiastic reformer. During his long journalistic career, Greeley had promoted vegetarianism, brown bread, free thinking, socialism, and spiritualism. His image as a visionary eccentric was complemented by his open hostility to the Democrats, whose support the Liberals needed. The Democrats gave the nomination to Greeley as the only hope of beating Grant and the Radical Republicans. Greeley's promise to end Radical Reconstruction and restore "self government" to the South won over Democrats who otherwise despised the man and his beliefs.

The 1872 election result surprised no one. Republican regulars duly endorsed Radical Reconstruction and the protective tariff. Grant still had seven southern states in his pocket, generous aid from business and banking interests, and the stalwart support of the Radical Republicans. Above all he still evoked the glory of military heroism. Greeley carried only six southern and border states, none in the North. Devastated by his crushing defeat and the death of his wife, Greeley entered a saniatorium and died three weeks later.

PANIC AND REDEMPTION   A paralyzing economic panic followed closely upon the public scandals besetting the Grant administration. A contraction of the nation's money supply resulting from the Treasury's postwar withdrawal of greenbacks and the reckless overexpansion of the railroads into sparsely settled areas helped precipitate a financial panic. During 1873 some twenty-five strapped railroads defaulted on their interest payments. A financial panic in Europe forced many financiers to unload American stocks and bonds. Caught short of cash, the prominent investment bank of Jay Cooke and Company went bankrupt on September 18, 1873. The event so frightened investors that the New York Stock Exchange had to close for ten days. The panic of 1873 set off a depression that lasted six years. It was the longest and most severe depression that Americans had yet suffered, marked by widespread bankruptcies, chronic unemployment, and a drastic slowdown in railroad building.

Hard times and political scandals hurt Republicans in the midterm elections of 1874, allowing the Democrats to win control of the House of Representatives and gain seats in the Senate. The new Democratic House immediately launched inquiries into the Grant scandals and unearthed further evidence of corruption in high places. The financial panic, meanwhile, focused attention once more on greenback currency. Since the value of greenbacks was lower than that of gold, paper money had become the chief circulating medium. Most people spent greenbacks first and held their gold or used it to settle foreign accounts, thereby draining much gold out of the country. To relieve this deflationary spiral and stimulate business expansion, the Treasury reissued $26 million in greenbacks that had previously been withdrawn.

For a time the advocates of paper money were riding high. But Grant vetoed an attempt to issue more greenbacks in 1874, and in his annual message he called for their gradual withdrawal and resumption of specie—redeeming greenbacks in gold. Congress obliged the president by passing the specie Resumption Act of 1875. The resumption of payments in gold to customers who turned in greenbacks began on January 1, 1879, after the Treasury had built a gold reserve for the purpose and reduced the value of the greenbacks in circulation. This act infuriated those promoting an inflationary monetary policy and led to the formation of the National Greenback party. The much debated and very complex "money question" would remain one of the most divisive issues in American politics until the end of the century.

THE COMPROMISE OF 1877   Grant yearned to run for president again in 1876, but his scandal-ridden administration cost him Republican support. James Gillespie Blaine of Maine, a former Speaker of the House, emerged as the Republican front-runner, but he, too, bore the taint of scandal. Letters in the possession of James Mulligan of Boston linked Blaine to dubious railroad dealings. Newspapers soon published the "Mulligan letters," and Blaine's candidacy was dealt a hefty blow.

The Republican Convention therefore eliminated Blaine and several other hopefuls in favor of Ohio's favorite son, Rutherford B. Hayes. Three times governor of Ohio and an advocate of hard money, Hayes had a sterling reputation and had been a civil service reformer. But his chief virtue, as a journalist put it, was that "he is obnoxious to no one."

The Democratic Convention was abnormally harmonious from the start. The nomination went on the second ballot to Samuel J. Tilden, a millionaire corporation lawyer and reform governor of New York who had directed a campaign to overthrow first the corrupt Tweed ring that controlled New York City politics and then the canal ring in Albany, which had bilked New York State of millions.

The 1876 election campaign generated no burning issues. Both candidates favored the trend toward relaxing federal authority and restoring white conservative rule in the South. In the absence of strong differences, Democrats waved the Republicans' dirty linen. In response, Republicans waved "the bloody shirt," which is to say that they engaged in verbal assaults on former Confederates and the spirit of rebellion, linking the Democratic party to secession and the outrages committed against Republicans in the South.

Early election returns pointed to a Tilden victory. Tilden had a 254,000-vote edge in the popular vote and won 184 electoral votes, just one short of a majority. Hayes had 165 electoral votes, but Republicans also claimed 19 disputed votes from Florida, Louisiana, and South Carolina. The Democrats laid a counterclaim to 1 of Oregon's 3 votes. The Republicans had clearly carried Oregon, but the outcome in the South was less certain, and given the fraud and intimidation perpetrated on both sides, nobody will ever know the truth of the matter. In all three of the disputed southern states, rival canvassing boards sent in different returns. The Constitution offered no guidance in this unprecedented situation. Even if Congress were empowered to sort things out, the Democratic House and the Republican Senate proved unable to reach an agreement.

The impasse dragged on for months, and there was even talk of partisan violence. Finally, on January 29, 1877, the two houses set up a special Electoral Commission that would investigate and report its findings. It had fifteen members, five each from the House, the Senate, and the Supreme Court. Members were chosen such that there were seven from each major party, with Justice David Davis of Illinois as the swing vote. Davis, though appointed to the Court by Lincoln, was no party regular and in fact was thought to be leaning toward the Democrats. Thus the panel appeared to be stacked in favor of Tilden.

As it turned out, however, the panel got restacked the other way. Shortsighted Democrats in the Illinois legislature teamed up with minority Greenbackers to name Davis their senator. Davis accepted, no doubt with a sense of relief. From the remaining justices, all Republicans, the panel chose Joseph P. Bradley to fill the vacancy. The decision on each state went by a vote of eight to seven along party lines, in favor of Hayes. After much bluster and the threat of a filibuster by the Democrats, the House voted on March 2 to accept the report and declared Hayes elected by an electoral vote of 185 to 184.

Critical to this outcome was the defection of southern Democrats who had made several informal agreements with the Republicans. On February 26, 1877, a bargain was struck at Wormley's Hotel in Washington, D.C., between prominent Ohio Republicans (including James A. Garfield) and powerful southern Democrats. The Republicans promised that if elected, Hayes would withdraw federal troops from Louisiana and South Carolina, letting the Republican governments there collapse. In return, the Democrats pledged to withdraw their opposition to Hayes, accept in good faith the Reconstruction amendments, and refrain from partisan reprisals against Republicans in the South.

Southern Democrats could now justify deserting Tilden. This so-called Compromise of 1877 brought a final "redemption" from the Radicals and a return to "home rule," which meant rule by white Democrats. As a former slave observed in 1877, "The whole South—every state in the south—has got [back] into the hands of the very men that held us as slaves." Other, more informal promises, bolstered the secret agreement. Hayes's friends pledged more support for rebuilding Mississippi River levees and other internal improvements, including a federal subsidy for a transcontinental railroad along a southern route. Southerners extracted a further promise that Hayes would name a white southerner as postmaster general, the cabinet position with the most patronage jobs to distribute. In return, southerners would let the Republicans make James Garfield the Speaker of the new House. Such a deal illustrates the relative weakness of the presidency compared with Congress during the postwar era.

THE END OF RECONSTRUCTION   In 1877 President Hayes withdrew federal troops from Louisiana and South Carolina, and the Republican governments there soon collapsed—along with Hayes's claim to legitimacy. Hayes chose a Tennessean as postmaster general. But after southern Democrats failed to permit the choice of James Garfield as Speaker of the House, Hayes expressed doubt about any further subsidy for railroad building, and none was voted. Most of the other promises made at Wormley's Hotel were renounced or forgotten.

As for southern promises regarding the civil rights of blacks, only a few Democratic leaders remembered them for long. Over the next three decades the federal protection of civil rights crumbled under the pressure of restored white rule in the South and the force of Supreme Court decisions narrowing the application of the Fourteenth and Fifteenth Amendments. Radical Reconstruction never offered more than an uncertain commitment to racial equality. Yet it left an enduring legacy, the Thirteenth, Fourteenth, and Fifteenth Amendments—not dead but dormant, waiting to be revived. If Reconstruction did not provide social equality or substantial economic opportunities for African Americans, it did create the opportunity for future transformation. It was a revolution, sighed former North Carolina governor Jonathan Worth, and "nobody can anticipate the action of revolutions."

MAKING CONNECTIONS

- The political, economic, and racial policies of the conservatives who overthrew the Republican governments in the southern states are described in Chapter 19.

- Several of the political scandals mentioned in this chapter were related to the railroads, a topic discussed in greater detail in Chapter 20.

- This chapter ended with the election of Rutherford B. Hayes; for a discussion of Hayes's administration, see Chapter 22.

FURTHER READING

The most comprehensive treatment of Reconstruction is Eric Foner's *Reconstruction: America's Unfinished Revolution, 1863-1877* (1988). On Andrew Johnson, see Hans L. Trefousse's *Andrew Johnson: A Biography* (1989). An excellent brief biography of Grant is Josiah Bunting III's *Ulysses S. Grant* (2004).

Scholars have been fairly sympathetic to the aims and motives of the Radical Republicans. See, for instance, Herman Belz's *Reconstructing the Union: Theory and Policy during the Civil War* (1969) and Richard Nelson Current's *Those Terrible Carpetbaggers: A Reinterpretation* (1988). The ideology of the Radical Republicans is explored in Michael Les Benedict's *A Compromise of Principle: Congressional Republicans and Reconstruction, 1863–1869* (1974).

The intransigence of southern white attitudes is examined in Michael Perman's *Reunion without Compromise* (1973) and Dan T. Carter's *When the War Was Over: The Failure of Self-Reconstruction in the South, 1865–1867* (1985). Allen W. Trelease's *White Terror: The Ku Klux and Southern Reconstruction* (1971) covers the various organizations that practiced vigilante tactics. The difficulties former laborers had in adjusting to the new labor system are documented in James L. Roark's *Masters without Slaves: Southern Planters to the Civil War and Reconstruction* (1977). Books on southern politics during Reconstruction include Michael Perman's *The Road to Redemption: Southern Politics, 1869–1879* (1984), Terry L. Seip's *The South Returns to Congress: Men, Economic Measures, and Intersectional Relationships, 1868–1879* (1983), and Mark W. Summer's *Railroads, Reconstruction, and the Gospel of Prosperity: Aid under Radical Republicans, 1865–1877* (1984).

Numerous works feature the freed blacks' experience in the South. Start with Leon F. Litwack's *Been in the Storm So Long: The Aftermath of Slavery* (1979), which covers the transition from slavery to freedom. Joel Williamson's *After Slavery: The Negro in South Carolina during Reconstruction, 1861–1877* (1965) argues that South Carolina blacks took an active role in pursuing their political and economic rights. The Freedmen's Bureau is explored in William S. McFeely's *Yankee Stepfather: General O. O. Howard and the Freedmen* (1968). The situation of freed slave women is discussed in Jacqueline Jones's *Labor of Love, Labor of Sorrow: Black Women, Work, and the Family, from Slavery to the Present* (1985).

The politics of corruption outside the South is depicted in William S. McFeely's *Grant: A Biography* (1981). The political maneuvers of the election of 1876 and the resultant crisis and compromise are explained in C. Vann Woodward's *Reunion and Reaction: The Compromise of 1877 and the End of Reconstruction* (1951) and in William Gillette's *Retreat from Reconstruction, 1869–1879* (1979).

Part Five

GROWING

PAINS

1876

Granger movement brings about passage of Granger laws to help farmers (1870s)

No president wins a majority of the popular vote (1876–1896)

Rutherford B. Hayes serves as president after disputed election (1877–1881)

Bourbons (planter-merchant elite) dominate southern politics and use poll taxes, literacy tests, and the grandfather clause to disenfranchise blacks (1877–1890s)

Socialist Labor party is organized in America (1877)

Greenback party, which favors expansion of currency through additional paper money, elects 15 congressmen (1878)

Large numbers of Irish, British, and Germans immigrate to the U.S., including anarchists (1870s–1880s)

Japan industrializes and rises to world-power status (1870s–1890s)

Queen Victoria of England is proclaimed empress of India (1876)

Famine in China leads many Chinese men to immigrate to America (1877–1878)

First shipments of frozen meats arrive in Europe from Argentina and Australia (late 1870s)

Congress of Berlin gives Austria the right to "occupy and administer" the Ottoman provinces of Bosnia and Herzegovina (1878)

1880

Government services—such as water, sewers, street lighting, and fire and police protection—expand (1880s–1900)

Urban political machines help provide food, coal, money, and food for the poor (1880s–1910s)

James A. Garfield becomes president (1881)

Chester A. Arthur serves as president after Garfield is assassinated (1881–1885)

Civil Rights Act of 1875 is declared unconstitutional (1883)

Congress passes Pendleton Civil Service Reform Act to ensure distribution of government jobs based on merit (1883)

Grover Cleveland serves as president (1885–1889)

Greenback party disintegrates (1885)

European drive for raw materials and markets leads to scramble for colonies in Africa (1880s–1890s)

French company begins to dig a canal through Panama (1881–1887)

Pro-imperialist German colonial League established; British occupy Egypt (1882)

Austria, Germany, and Italy form the Triple Alliance (1882)

Germany enacts social security reform laws (1883–1889)

England's Reform Act gives vote to nearly all men (1884)

Berlin Conference meets to consider issues of imperialism (1884–1885)

Canadian Pacific, a transcontinental railroad, is completed (1885)

Indian National Congress is formed to foster Indian participation in government (1885)

Three Emperors' League (Germany, Russia, and Austria) collapses (1887)

Japan adopts a constitution (1889)

Second (Socialist) International attempts to strengthen the socialist movement (1889–1914)

African-American Exodusters move from the South to Kansas (1870s–1880s)

"Flood tide" of pioneers goes west; harsh life results in greater equality between men and women (1870s–1890s)

Vaudeville houses are established in cities across the U.S. (1870s–1890s)

Colleges and high schools organize football teams (1870s–1900s)

Andrew Carnegie invests $120 million in public libraries and education (1870s–1910s)

Indians defeat George A. Custer's forces in the Battle of Little Bighorn (1876)

Alexander Graham Bell patents the telephone, making possible unprecedented rapid communication over long distances (1876)

Thomas Edison's inventions of the phonograph (1877) and the first successful incandescent lightbulb drastically affect leisure and work (1879)

Atlanta Constitution heralds the advent of a "New South" (1880s)

Proponents of the New South espouse idea of "separate but equal" (1880s–1960s)

Baseball becomes national pastime (1880s)

Construction of taller buildings, made possible by iron and steel frames and electric elevators, allows more people to live and work in cities (1880s–1890s)

Immigrants from Europe and Asia settle in large numbers in the largest U.S. cities, providing much-needed labor; ethnic and racial tensions increase (1880s–1890s)

States hold referenda on the prohibition of alcoholic beverages (1880s–1890s)

Amusement parks appear in many major cities (1880s–1900s)

Number of employed women increases (1880s–1890s)

Chinese Exclusion Act prohibits immigration of Chinese for ten years (1882)

John D. Rockefeller consolidates oil-refining industry into Standard Oil Company of Ohio, which comes to control 90–95 percent of U.S. oil (1870s)

Second Industrial Revolution connects national transportation and communications networks, expanding the international market for U.S. goods (1870s)

Grangers promote farmer-owned cooperatives for buying and selling farm products (1870s)

Building of transcontinental railways and trunk lines extends miles of railways from 35,000 to 200,000 (1870s–1890s)

Mining, dry farming, and irrigation further open the West for settlement (1870s–1890s)

"Bonanza" farms, for mass production of crops and livestock, are established in the West (1870s–1890s)

Southern coal production increases from 5 million tons to 49 million tons (1875–1900)

Great Railroad Strike erupts when workers oppose wage cuts (1877)

Knights of Labor becomes a national movement (1878)

Andrew Carnegie consolidates steel industry in Pittsburgh (1880s)

George Westinghouse's improvements of the alternating-current motor enables factories to locate wherever they wish (1880s)

Textile production expands in the South; the number of mills increases from 161 to 400 (1880s–1900)

Sagging crop prices make it increasingly difficult to own land (1880s–1890s)

Rise of sheepherding and barbed-wire fencing disrupts cattle grazing, causing "barbed-wire wars" between small farmers and cattle barons (1880s)

Edison Electric Illuminating Company, the world's first public utilities company, is established in New York City (1882)

Foran Act is passed, penalizing employers who import contract labor from abroad (1885)

Strike at Chicago's International Harvester plant leads to the Haymarket bombing (1886)

American Federation of Labor is founded (1886)

1876

1880

In *Wabash Railroad v. Illinois*, U.S. Supreme Court denies states the right to regulate interstate commerce (1886)

Cleveland administration creates Interstate Commerce Commission (1887)

Dawes Severalty Act disrupts Indian culture by privatizing Indians' land (1887)

Farmers' Alliances turn to politics but fail to achieve significant gains for rural America (1880s–1890)

Benjamin Harrison serves as president (1889–1893)

1890

Mississippi constitutional convention effectively disenfranchises African Americans (1890)

National American Woman Suffrage Association is established, with Elizabeth Cady Stanton as its first president (1890)

People's party is established, otherwise known as the Populist party (1892)

Grover Cleveland serves as president for the second time (1893–1897)

Populists poll 1.5 million votes for congressional candidates (1894)

Supreme Court rules in *In re Debs* that force may be used to enforce federal law (1895)

Plessy v. Ferguson sanctions "separate but equal" segregation (1896)

William Jennings Bryan runs for president as Democratic-Populist-Silverite candidate on a free-silver platform (1896)

Struggle between urban and rural America culminates in 1896 election; collapse of the Populist party signals the failure of agrarian activism (1896)

1900

South Carolina becomes the first southern state to adopt a statewide primary, effectively excluding black voters (1896)

Eugene Debs organizes the Social Democratic party (1897)

William McKinley serves as president (1897–1901)

Bismarck is dismissed as prime minister of Germany (1890)

Doctrine of Social Darwinism fuels imperialism (1890s)

Large numbers of eastern and southern Europeans immigrate to in the U.S. (1890s–1900s)

France and Russia form the Dual Alliance (1894)

Sino-Japanese War furthers Japan's imperialism (1894–1895)

Spanish-American War (1898)

Hawaii is annexed by U.S.; Puerto Rico, Guam, and the Philippines become U.S. territories (1898)

Fashoda crisis in the Sudan brings British and French to brink of war (1898)

U.S. appoints military governor of Cuba (1898)

Beginning of Open Door trade policy in China (1899)

Boer War in South Africa (1899–1902)

Boxer Rebellion occurs in reaction to Western presence in China (1900)

Britain agrees to establishment of the Commonwealth of Australia (1900)

Foraker Act establishes a civil government in Puerto Rico (1900)

William Howard Taft is sent to the Philippines by McKinley to set up a civil government (1901)

Mark Twain publishes *The Adventures of Huckleberry Finn* (1884)

Depletion of buffalo and capture of Geronimo (1886) lead to collapse of Indian resistance movement (1880s)

Black players are banned from minor-league baseball teams (1887)

Andrew Carnegie's "Gospel of Wealth" is published (1889)

College enrollment increases from 52,000 (1870) to 157,000 (1890); professors increasingly have doctorates (1890s)

12 percent of whites and 50 percent of blacks are illiterate (1890)

Ghost Dance movement leads to bloodbath at Wounded Knee (1890)

"Streetcar suburbs" spring up as a result of transportation revolution, leading to exodus of middle and upper classes from city centers (1890s)

Annual lynchings average 187 with 82 percent occurring in the South (1890–1899)

Ongoing nativism leads to further immigration restrictions (1890s–1950s)

James Naismith invents basketball (1891)

Chinese Exclusion Act of 1882 is renewed for another 10 years (1892)

Ellis Island is opened as a reception center for new immigrants (1892)

Frederick Jackson Turner presents "The Significance of the Frontier in American History" (1893)

Stephen Crane publishes *The Red Badge of Courage* (1895)

Booker T. Washington's "Atlanta Compromise" urges blacks to accommodate white racism and domination (1895)

W.E.B. Du Bois calls for "ceaseless agitation" by blacks (1897)

Number of public schools in America increases from 800 (1880) to 6,000 (1900)

Nearly 100 settlement houses dot urban America (1900)

30 percent of residents of major cities are foreign-born (1900)

Texas Farmers' Alliance unsuccessfully promotes Alliance Exchange to free farmers from dependence on food processors and banks (1887)

Severe winters decimate the open range (1886, 1887), followed by 10 years of drought in the West (1890s)

Congress defeats the Farmers' Alliance sub-treasury plan for storage of crops and loans to farmers (1890)

Dependent Pension Act provides funds to veterans who cannot work (1890)

Five vertically integrated companies produce 90 percent of all meat shipped in interstate commerce (1890)

Tenant farmers and sharecroppers constitute a majority of farmworkers in the Deep South (1890)

Sherman Silver Purchase Act (1890)

McKinley Tariff raises duties on manufactured goods 49.5 percent (1890)

Sherman Anti-Trust Act prohibits businesses from monopolizing trade (1890)

U.S. surpasses Britain in iron and steel production (1890s)

Sears, Roebuck comes to dominate the mail-order industry (1890s)

Pittsburgh steelworkers stage Homestead strike (1892)

Ohio Supreme Court orders dissolution of Standard Oil Company (1892)

Depression destroys many small businesses (1893)

President Cleveland rescinds Sherman Silver Purchase Act, sharpening the debate regarding silver coinage (1893)

American Railway Union is founded by Eugene Debs (1893)

Employees of Pullman Palace Car Company in Illinois stage a major strike (1894)

J. P. Morgan and other financiers supply gold to buy up government bonds and stop demands on Treasury (1895)

Dingley Tariff raises duty to 57 percent of the value of imported goods, the highest in U.S. history (1897)

Gold Standard Act ends the silver movement (1900)

1890

1900

The Federal victory in 1865 restored the Union and in the process helped accelerate America's transformation into a modern nation-state. A distinctly national consciousness began to displace the sectional emphases of the antebellum era. During and after the Civil War the Republican-led Congress pushed through legislation to foster industrial and commercial development and western expansion. In the process the United States abandoned the Jeffersonian dream of a decentralized agrarian republic and began to forge a dynamic new industrial economy generated by an increasingly national market.

After 1865 many Americans turned their attention to the unfinished business of settling a continent and completing an urban-industrial revolution begun before the war. Huge national corporations based upon mass production and mass marketing began to dominate the economy. As the prominent sociologist William Graham Sumner remarked, the process of industrial development "controls us all because we are all in it. It creates the conditions of our own existence, sets the limits of our social activity, and regulates the bonds of our social relations."

The Industrial Revolution was not only an urban phenomenon; it transformed rural life as well. Those who got in the way of the new emphasis on large-scale, highly mechanized commercial agriculture and ranching were brusquely pushed aside. The friction between new market forces and traditional folkways generated political revolts and social unrest during the last quarter of the nineteenth century.

The clash between tradition and modernity peaked during the 1890s, one of the most strife-ridden decades in American history. A deep depression, agrarian unrest, and labor violence provoked fears of class warfare. This turbulent situation transformed the presidential election campaign of 1896 into a clash between rival visions of America's future. The Republican candidate, William McKinley, campaigned on behalf of modern urban-industrial values. By contrast, William Jennings Bryan, the nominee of the Democratic and Populist parties, was an eloquent defender of America's rural past. McKinley's victory proved to be a watershed in political and social history. By 1900 the United States would emerge as one of the world's greatest industrial powers, and it would thereafter assume a new leadership role in world affairs.

19

THE SOUTH AND THE WEST TRANSFORMED

FOCUS QUESTIONS

- What were the economic and political policies of the states in the post-Reconstruction South?
- How did segregation and disenfranchisement shape race relations in the New South?
- What were the experiences of the farmers, miners, and cowboys in the West?
- What were the consequences of late-nineteenth-century Indian policy?

To answer these questions and access additional review material, please visit www.wwnorton.com/studyspace.

After the Civil War the South and the West provided enticing opportunities for pioneers and entrepreneurs. Before 1860 most Americans had viewed the region between the Mississippi River and California as a barren landscape unfit for human habitation or cultivation, an uninviting land suitable only for Indians and animals. Half the state of Texas, for instance, was still not settled at the end of the Civil War. After 1865, however, the federal government encouraged western settlement and economic development. The construction of transcontinental railroads, the military conquest of the Indians, and a liberal land-distribution policy combined to help lure thousands of pioneers and expectant capitalists westward.

Although the first great wave of railroad building occurred in the 1850s, the most spectacular growth took place during the quarter century after the Civil War. From about 35,000 miles of track in 1865, the national rail network grew to nearly 200,000 miles by 1897. The transcontinental rail lines led the way, and they helped populate the plains and the Far West. Meanwhile, southern rail lines were rebuilt and supplemented with new branches. The defeated South, although not a frontier in the literal sense of the term, offered a fertile new ground for investment and industrial development. After 1865 proponents of a "New South" argued that the region must abandon its single-minded preoccupation with agriculture and pursue industrial and commercial development. As a result, the South as well as the West experienced dramatic social and economic changes during the last third of the nineteenth century. By 1900 the South and the West had been transformed in ways that few could have predicted, and fourteen new states were created out of the western territories.

THE NEW SOUTH

A FRESH VISION   After the Civil War many southerners looked wistfully to the plantation life that had characterized their region before the firing on Fort Sumter in 1861. A few prominent leaders, however, insisted that the postwar South must liberate itself from nostalgia and create a new society of small farms, thriving industries, and bustling cities. The major prophet of this New South was Henry W. Grady, the young editor of the *Atlanta Constitution*. Grady's compelling vision of a New South attracted many supporters, who preached the gospel of industry with evangelical fervor. The Confederacy, they reasoned, had lost because it had relied too much upon King Cotton. In the future the South must follow the North's example and industrialize. From that central belief flowed certain implications: that a more diversified and a more efficient agriculture would be a foundation for economic growth and that more widespread education, especially vocational training, would promote material success. By the late 1870s, with Reconstruction over and the panic of 1873 forgotten, a mood of progress permeated the editorials and speeches of the day.

ECONOMIC GROWTH   The chief accomplishment of the New South movement was an expansion of the region's textile production. From 1880 to 1900, the number of cotton mills in the South grew from 161 to 400, and the number of mill workers (among whom women and children outnumbered men) increased fivefold.

Tobacco growing also increased significantly after the Civil War. Essential to the rise of the tobacco industry was the Duke family of Durham, North Carolina. At the end of the Civil War, the story goes, Washington Duke took a load of tobacco and, with the help of his three sons, beat it out with hickory sticks, stuffed it into bags, hitched two mules to his wagon, and set out across the state, selling tobacco as he went. By 1872 the Dukes had a factory producing 125,000 pounds of tobacco annually, and Washington Duke prepared to settle down and enjoy success.

His son Buck (James Buchanan Duke), wanted even greater success, however. He recognized that the tobacco industry was "half smoke and half ballyhoo," so he poured large sums into advertising schemes. Duke also undersold competitors in their own market and cornered the supply of ingredients. In 1890 Duke brought most of his competitors into the American Tobacco Company, which controlled nine tenths of the nation's cigarette production. In 1911 the Supreme Court ruled that the company was in violation of the anti-trust laws and ordered it broken up, but by then Duke had found new worlds to conquer, in hydroelectric power and aluminum.

Systematic use of other natural resources helped revitalize the region along the Appalachian Mountain chain from West Virginia to Alabama. Coal production in the South grew from 5 million tons in 1875 to 49 million tons by 1900. At the southern end of the mountains, Birmingham, Alabama, sprang up during the 1870s as a major steel-producing center and soon tagged itself the Pittsburgh of the South.

Industrial growth created a need for wood-framed housing, and after 1870 lumbering became a thriving industry in the South. By the turn of the century, it had surpassed textiles in value. Tree cutting seemed to know no bounds, despite the resulting ecological devastation. In time the industry would be saved only by the warm climate, which fostered quick growth of re-planted forests, and the rise of scientific forestry.

Two forces that would impel an even greater industrial revolution were already on the southern horizon at the turn of the century: petroleum in the Southwest and hydroelectric power in the Southeast. In 1901 the Spindletop oil gusher in Texas brought a huge bonanza. Electrical power proved equally profitable, and local power plants dotted the South by the 1890s. Richmond, Virginia, developed the nation's first electric streetcar system in 1888, and Columbia, South Carolina, boasted the first electrically powered cotton mill in 1894. The greatest advance would begin in 1905 when Buck Duke's Southern Power Company set out to electrify entire river valleys in the Carolinas.

AGRICULTURE OLD AND NEW   At the start of the twentieth century, however, most of the South remained undeveloped, at least by northeastern standards. Despite the optimistic rhetoric of Henry Grady and other New South spokesmen, the typical southerner was less apt to be tending a textile loom than, as the saying went, facing the eastern end of a westbound mule. King Cotton survived the Civil War and expanded over new acreage even as its export markets leveled off. Louisiana cane sugar, probably the most war-devastated of all crops, was flourishing again by the 1890s.

The majority of southern farmers were not flourishing, however. A prolonged deflation in crop prices affected the entire Western world during the last third of the nineteenth century. Sagging prices for farm crops made it more difficult than ever to own land. Sharecropping and tenancy among poor blacks and whites became the norm. By 1890 most southern farms were worked by people who did not own the land.

How did the system work? Sharecroppers, who had nothing to offer the landowner but their labor, worked the owner's land in return for supplies and a share of the crop, generally about half. Tenant farmers, hardly better off, might have their own mule, a plow, and credit with the country store. They were entitled to claim a larger share of the crops. The sharecropper-tenant system was horribly inefficient; it was essentially a form of land slavery, and tenants and owners developed an intense suspicion of each other. The folklore of the rural South was replete with tales of tenants who remained stubbornly shiftless and scheming landlords who swindled farm-workers by not giving them a fair share of the crops.

The postwar South suffered an acute shortage of capital; people had to devise ways to operate without cash. One innovation was the crop-lien system: merchants furnished supplies in return for liens (or mortgages) on farmers' crops. To a few tenants and small farmers who seized the chance, such credit offered a way out of dependency, but to most it offered only a hopeless cycle of perennial debt. The merchant, who assumed great risks, generally charged interest that ranged, according to one journalist, "from 24 percent to grand larceny." The merchant required his farmer clients to grow a cash crop that could be readily sold at harvest time. Thus the routines of tenancy and sharecropping were geared to a staple crop, usually cotton. The resulting stagnation of rural life held millions, white and black, in bondage to privation and ignorance.

TENANCY AND THE ENVIRONMENT   The pervasive use of tenancy and sharecropping unwittingly caused profound environmental damage. Growing commercial row crops like cotton on the same land year after year

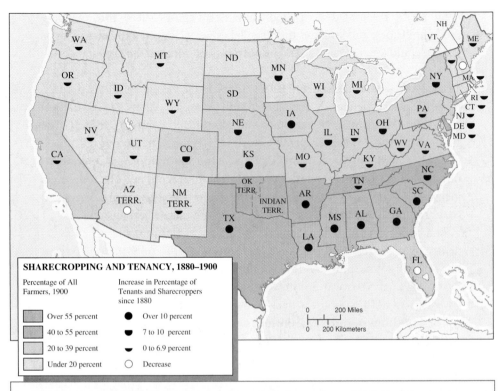

SHARECROPPING AND TENANCY, 1880–1900

Why was there a dramatic increase in sharecropping and tenancy in the late nineteenth century? Why did the South have more sharecroppers than other parts of the country? Why do you think the rate of sharecropping was lowest in western states like New Mexico and Arizona?

leached the nutrients from the soil. Tenants had no incentive to take care of farmland by manuring fields or rotating crops because it was not their own. They used fertilizer to accelerate the growing cycle, but the extensive use of phosphate fertilizers only accelerated soil depletion, by enabling multiple plantings each year. Fertilizer, said an observer, seduced southern farmers into believing that there was a "short cut to prosperity, a royal road to good crops of cotton year after year. The result has been that their lands have been cultivated clean year after year, and their fertility has been exhausted."

Once the soil had lost its fertility, the tenants moved on to another farm, leaving behind rutted fields whose topsoil washed away with each rain. The silt and mud flowed into creeks and rivers, swamping many lowland fields and filling millponds and lakes. By the early twentieth century much of the rural South resembled a ravaged land: deep gullies sliced through bare eroded hillsides, and streams and deep lakes were clogged with silt. As far as the eye could see, red clay devoid of nutrients dominated the landscape.

THE BOURBON REDEEMERS   In post–Civil War southern politics, habits of social deference and elitism still prevailed. After Reconstruction ended, in 1877, a planter-merchant elite dominated southern politics. The supporters of these postwar Democratic leaders referred to them as redeemers because they supposedly redeemed, or saved, the South from Yankee domination as well as from the limitations of a purely rural economy. The redeemers included a rising class of entrepreneurs eager to promote a more diversified economy based upon industrial development and railroad expansion.

The opponents of the redeemers labeled them Bourbons in an effort to depict them as reactionaries. Like the French royal family that, Napoléon had said, forgot nothing and learned nothing in the ordeal of revolution, the Bourbons of the postwar South were said to have forgotten nothing and to have learned nothing in the ordeal of the Civil War.

The Bourbons of the New South perfected a political alliance with northeastern conservatives and an economic alliance with northeastern capitalists. They generally pursued a government policy of frugality, except for the tax exemptions and other favors they offered business. They slashed expenditures and avoided political initiatives, making the transition from Republican rule to Bourbon rule less abrupt than is often assumed. The Bourbons' favorable disposition toward the railroads was not unlike that of the Radical Republicans. And despite their reputation for honesty, Bourbon officeholders were occasionally caught with their fingers in the till.

The Bourbons focused on cutting back the size and cost of government. This policy spelled austerity for public services, including the school systems started during Reconstruction. In 1871 the southern Atlantic states were spending $10.27 per pupil; by 1880 the figure was down to $6, and in 1890 it stood at only $7.63. In South Carolina in 1882, there were 3,183 schools but only 3,413 teachers. Illiteracy rates at the time were at about 12 percent among whites and 50 percent among blacks.

The Bourbons' urge to economize led them to adopt the degrading system of convict leasing. The destruction of prisons during the Civil War and the poverty of state treasuries afterward combined with the demand for cheap labor to make the leasing of convict workers a way for southern states to avoid penitentiary expenses and generate revenue. Convict leasing, in the absence of state supervision, allowed inefficiency, neglect, and disregard for human life to proliferate.

The Bourbons reduced not only state expenditures but also a vast amount of government debt. The corruption and extravagance of Radical Republican rule were commonly advanced as justification for the process, but repudiation of debts was not limited to debt incurred during Reconstruction. Altogether nine states repudiated more than half of what they owed bondholders and other creditors.

The penny-pinching Bourbon regimes did respond to the demand for commissions to regulate the rates charged by railroads for commercial transport. They also established boards of agriculture and public health, agricultural and mechanical colleges, teacher-training schools and women's colleges, and even state colleges for African Americans. Nor can any simplistic interpretation encompass the variety of Bourbon leaders. The Democratic party was then a mongrel coalition that threw old Whigs, Unionists, secessionists, businessmen, small farmers, hillbillies, planters, and even some Republicans together in an alliance against the Reconstruction Radicals. Democrats, therefore, even those who bore the Bourbon label, often marched to different drummers, and the Bourbon regimes never achieved complete unity in philosophy or government.

The Effects of Radical and Bourbon Rule in the South

This 1880 cartoon shows the South staggering under the oppressive weight of military Reconstruction (left) and flourishing under the "Let 'Em Alone Policy" of President Rutherford B. Hayes and the Bourbons (right).

Perhaps the ultimate paradox of the Bourbons' rule was that these paragons of white supremacy tolerated a lingering black voice in politics and showed no haste to raise legal barriers of racial separation. African Americans sat in Virginia's state legislature until 1890, in South Carolina's until 1900, and in Georgia's until 1908; some of them were Democrats. The South sent black congressmen to Washington in every election except one, until 1900, though they always represented gerrymandered districts into which most of a state's black voters had been thrown. Under the Bourbons the disenfranchisement of black voters remained inconsistent, a local matter brought about mainly by fraud and intimidation, although it occurred often enough to ensure white control of the southern states.

A like flexibility applied in other aspects of race relations. The color line was drawn less strictly immediately after the Civil War than it would be in the twentieth-century South. In some places, to be sure, racial segregation appeared before the end of Reconstruction, especially in schools, churches, hotels and rooming houses, and private social relations. In other public places, such as trains, depots, theaters, and soda fountains, however, segregation was more sporadic.

DISENFRANCHISING AFRICAN AMERICANS   During the 1890s the attitudes that permitted moderation in race relations evaporated. A violent "Negrophobia" swept across the South and much of the nation at the end of the century. Many whites had come to resent signs of black success and social influence. An Alabama newspaper editor declared that "our blood boils when the educated Negro asserts himself politically. We regard each assertion as an unfriendly encroachment upon our native superior rights, and a dare-devil menace to our control of the affairs of the state."

Education did bring enlightenment—as it was supposed to do. In 1889 the student newspaper at all-black Fisk University in Nashville predicted a profound change in race relations at the end of the century. It stressed that a new generation of young African Americans born since the end of the Civil War and educated in schools and colleges were determined to gain true equality. They were more assertive and less patient than their parents. A growing number of young white adults, however, were equally determined to keep "Negroes in their place."

Racial violence and repression surged to the fore during the last decade of the nineteenth century and the first two decades of the twentieth. By the end of the nineteenth century, the so-called New South had come to resemble the Old South. Ruling whites ruthlessly imposed their will over all areas of

African-American life. They prevented blacks from voting and enacted "Jim Crow" laws mandating public separation of the races. This development was not the logical culmination of the Civil War and emancipation but rather the result of a calculated campaign by white elites and thugs to limit African-American political, economic, and social life.

The political dynamics of the 1890s exacerbated racial tensions. The rise of Populism, a farm-based protest movement that culminated in the creation of a third political party in the 1890s, divided the white vote to such an extent that in some places the African-American vote became the balance of power. Some Populists courted black votes. In response the Bourbons revived the race issue, which they exploited with seasoned finesse, all the while controlling for their ticket a good part of the black vote in plantation areas. Nevertheless, during the 1890s the Bourbons began to insist that the black vote be eliminated completely from southern elections. Some farm leaders hoped that the disenfranchisement of African Americans would make it possible for whites to divide politically without raising the specter of "Negro domination."

But since the Fifteenth Amendment made it illegal simply to deny blacks the vote, racists accomplished their purpose indirectly, through such devices as poll taxes (or head taxes) and literacy tests. Mississippi led the way to near-total disenfranchisement of blacks—and many poor whites as well. The state called a constitutional convention in 1890 to change the suffrage provisions of the Radical Republican constitution of 1868. The resulting Mississippi plan set the pattern that seven more states would follow over the next twenty years. First, a residence requirement—two years in the state, one year in an election district—struck at those black tenant farmers who were in the habit of moving yearly in search of better opportunities. Second, voters were disqualified if convicted of certain crimes, many of them petty. Third, all taxes, including a poll tax, had to be paid by February 1 of each year. This proviso fell most heavily on the poor, most of whom were black. Finally, all voters had to be literate. The alternative, designed as a loophole for otherwise-disqualified whites, was an "understanding" clause. The voter, if unable to read the Constitution, could qualify by "understanding" it—to the satisfaction of the registrar. Fraud was thus institutionalized by "legal" disenfranchisement.

Other states added variations on the Mississippi plan. In 1898 Louisiana invented the "grandfather clause," which allowed illiterates to register to vote if their fathers or grandfathers had been eligible to vote on January 1, 1867, when African Americans were still disenfranchised. By 1910 Georgia, North

Carolina, Virginia, Alabama, and Oklahoma had adopted the grandfather clause. Every southern state, moreover, adopted a statewide Democratic primary, which became the only meaningful election outside isolated areas of Republican strength. With minor exceptions the Democratic primaries excluded African-American voters altogether. The effectiveness of these measures can be seen in a few sample figures: Louisiana in 1896 had 130,000 black voters registered and in 1900, 5,320. Alabama in 1900 had 121,159 literate black men over twenty-one, according to the census; only 3,742 were registered to vote.

THE SPREAD OF SEGREGATION   What came to be called Jim Crow social segregation followed disenfranchisement and in some states came first. From 1875 to 1883, in fact, any racial segregation violated a federal Civil Rights Act, which forbade discrimination in places of public accommodation. But in 1883 the Supreme Court ruled on seven civil rights cases involving discrimination against blacks by corporations or individuals. The Court held, with only one dissent, that the force of federal law could not extend to individual action because the Fourteenth Amendment, which provided that "no State" could deny citizens equal protection of the law, stood as a prohibition only against state action, not against individual action.

This interpretation left as an open question the validity of state laws *requiring* separate public facilities under the rubric of "separate but equal," a slogan popular with the New South prophets. In 1888 Mississippi required railway passengers to occupy the car set aside for their race. When Louisiana followed suit in 1890, the law was challenged in the case of *Plessy v. Ferguson*, which the Supreme Court decided in 1896.

The test case originated in New Orleans when Homer Plessy, an octoroon (a person of one-eighth African ancestry), refused to leave a whites-only railroad car when asked to do so. He was convicted of violating the segregation statute, and the case rose on appeal to the Supreme Court. The Court ruled that segregation laws "have been generally, if not universally recognized as within the competency of state legislatures in the exercise of their police power." Soon the principle of statutory racial segregation extended to every area of southern life, including streetcars, hotels, restaurants, hospitals, sports, and employment.

Violence accompanied the Jim Crow laws. From 1890 to 1899, lynchings in the United States averaged 188 per year, 82 percent of which occurred in the South; from 1900 to 1909, they averaged 93 per year, of which 92 percent occurred in the South. Whites constituted 32 percent of the victims during the former period but only 11 percent in the latter. A young Episcopal priest in Montgomery, Alabama, remarked that extremists had proceeded "from an undiscriminating attack upon the Negro's ballot to a like attack upon his schools, his labor, his life."

By the end of the nineteenth century, legalized racial discrimination—segregation of public facilities, political disenfranchisement, and vigilante justice punctuated by brutal public lynchings and race riots—had elevated government-sanctioned bigotry to an official way of life in the South. South Carolina senator Benjamin Tillman declared in 1892 that blacks "must remain subordinate or be exterminated."

How did African Americans respond to the resurgence of racism and statutory segregation? Some left the South in search of equality and opportunity, but the vast majority stayed in their native region. In the face of overwhelming force and prejudicial justice, survival in the South required blacks to wear a mask of deference and apply discretion. "Had to walk a quiet life," explained James Plunkett, a Virginia black. "The least little thing you would do, they [whites] would kill ya."

Yet accommodation did not mean total submission. Excluded from the dominant white world and eager to avoid confrontations, black southerners after the 1890s increasingly turned inward and constructed their own culture and nurtured their own pride. A young white visitor to Mississippi in 1910 noticed that nearly every black person he met had "two distinct social selves, the one he reveals to his own people, the other he assumes among the whites."

African-American churches continued to provide the hub for black community life. Often the only public buildings available for blacks, churches were used not only for worship but also for activities that had nothing to do with religion: social gatherings, club meetings, and political activities. For men especially, churches offered leadership roles and political status. Serving as a deacon was one of the most prestigious roles an African-American man could achieve. Churches enabled African Americans of all classes to interact and exercise roles denied them in the larger society. Religious life provided great comfort to people worn down by the daily hardships and abuses associated with segregation.

One irony of state-enforced segregation is that it opened up new economic opportunities for blacks. A new class of African-American entrepreneurs emerged to provide services—insurance, banking, funerals, barbering, hair salons—to the black community in the segregated South. At the same time, African Americans formed their own social and fraternal clubs and organizations, all of which helped bolster black pride and provide fellowship and opportunities for service. For example, the Independent Order of Odd Fellows, the largest of the African-American fraternal orders, had over 400,000 members in 1904.

Middle-class black women formed a network of thousands of racial-uplift organizations across the South and around the nation. The women's clubs were engines of social service in their communities. They cared for the aged and the infirm, the orphaned and the abandoned. They created homes for single mothers and provided nurseries for working mothers. They sponsored health clinics and classes in home economics for women. In 1896 the leaders of such women's clubs from around the country converged to form the National Association of Colored Women, an organization meant to combat racism and segregation. Its first president, Mary Church Terrell, told members that they had an obligation to serve the "lowly, the illiterate, and even the vicious to whom we are bound by the ties of race and sex, and put forth every effort to uplift and reclaim them."

WELLS   One of the most outspoken African-American activists of the time was Ida B. Wells. Born into slavery in 1862 in Mississippi, she attended a school staffed by white missionaries. In 1878 an epidemic of yellow fever killed both her parents as well as an infant brother. At age sixteen, Wells assumed responsibility for her five younger siblings and secured a job as a country schoolteacher. In search of greater economic security and opportunity, Wells moved to nearby Memphis, then fast emerging as a commercial hub and cultural center.

In 1883 Wells confronted the power of white supremacy. After being denied a seat on a railroad car because she was black, she became the first African American to file suit against such discrimination. The circuit court decided in her favor and fined the railroad, but the Tennessee Supreme Court overturned the ruling. Wells thereafter discovered her "first and [it] might be said, my only love"—journalism—and, through it, a weapon with which to promote civil rights. Writing under the pen name Iola, she became a prominent editor of *Memphis Free Speech,* a newspaper focusing on African-American issues.

In 1892, when three of her friends were lynched by a white mob, Wells launched a lifelong crusade against lynching. Angry whites responded by destroying her newspaper office and threatening to lynch her. She moved to New York and continued to use her fiery journalistic talent to criticize Jim Crow laws and demand that African Americans have their voting rights restored. Wells helped found the National Association for the Advancement of Colored People (NAACP) in 1909 and promoted women's suffrage. In demanding full equality, Wells often found herself in direct opposition to the accommodationist views of Booker T. Washington.

WASHINGTON AND DU BOIS

Booker T. Washington, born in Virginia of a slave mother and a white father, fought extreme adversity to get an education at Hampton Institute, one of the postwar missionary schools, and went on to build at Tuskegee, Alabama, a leading college for African Americans. By 1890 Washington had become the nation's foremost black educator.

Booker T. Washington

Founder of the Tuskegee Institute.

Washington argued that blacks should not antagonize whites by demanding social or political equality; instead, they should concentrate on establishing an economic base for their advancement. In a speech at the Atlanta Cotton States and International Exposition in 1895 that propelled him to fame, Washington advised African Americans: "Cast down your bucket where you are—cast it down in making friends . . . of the people of all races by whom we are surrounded. Cast it down in agriculture, mechanics, in commerce, in domestic service, and in the professions." He conspicuously omitted politics from that list and implied an endorsement of segregation: "In all things that are purely social we can be as separate as the five fingers, yet one as the hand in all things essential to mutual progress."

Some people bitterly criticized Washington, in his lifetime and after, for making a bad bargain: the sacrifice of broad education and civil rights for the dubious acceptance of white conservatives and the creation of economic opportunities for blacks. W.E.B. Du Bois led African Americans in this criticism. A native of Great Barrington, Massachusetts, and the son of free blacks, Du Bois first experienced southern racial practices as an undergraduate at Fisk University in Nashville. Later he earned a doctoral degree in history from Harvard and afterward attended the University of Berlin. In addition to an active career in racial protest, he left a distinguished record as a teacher and scholar. Trim and dapper in appearance, sporting a goatee, cane, and gloves, he possessed a combative, fiery spirit. Not long after he began his teaching career at Atlanta University in 1897, he began to assault

W.E.B. Du Bois

A fierce advocate for black education.

Booker T. Washington's accommodationist philosophy and put forward his own program of "ceaseless agitation."

Washington, Du Bois argued, preached "a gospel of Work and Money to such an extent" that it overshadowed "the higher aims of life." The education of African Americans, Du Bois maintained, should not be merely vocational but should nurture bold leaders willing to challenge segregation and discrimination through political action. He demanded that disenfranchisement and legalized segregation cease and that the laws of the land be enforced. Du Bois minced no words in criticizing Washington's "Atlanta Compromise" philosophy: "We refuse to surrender the leadership of this race to cowards."

THE NEW WEST

Like the South the region west of the Mississippi River has become wrapped in myths and constricting stereotypes. It is a land of extremes—majestic mountains, roaring rivers, searing deserts, dense forests, and fertile plains. For vast reaches of western America, the great epics of the Civil War and Reconstruction were remote events hardly touching the lives of Indians, Mexicans, Asians, and white trappers, miners, cowboys, traders, and Mormons scattered through the plains and mountains. There the march of settlement and exploitation continued, propelled by a lust for land and a passion for profit. On one level the settlement of the West beyond the Mississippi River constitutes a colorful drama of determined pioneers and cowboys overcoming all obstacles to secure their vision of freedom and opportunity amid the region's awesome vastness. On another level, however, the colonization of the Far West involved short-sighted greed and irresponsible behavior, a story of reckless exploitation that scarred the land, decimated its wildlife, and nearly exterminated the culture of Native Americans.

In the second tier of trans-Mississippi states—Iowa, Kansas, Nebraska—and in western Minnesota, farmers began spreading out onto the Great

Plains after the Civil War. From California, miners spread east through the mountains as scattered enclaves sprang up at one new strike after another. From Texas nomadic cowboys migrated northward onto the plains and across the Rocky Mountains into the Great Basin. As settlers moved west, they encountered a markedly different climate and landscape. The scarcity of water and timber on the Great Plains rendered obsolete the ax, the log cabin, the rail fence, and the usual methods of tilling the soil. For a long time the region had been called the Great American Desert; it was a barren barrier to cross on the way to the Pacific, unfit for human habitation and therefore, to white Americans, the perfect refuge for Indians. But that pattern changed in the last half of the nineteenth century as a result of newly discovered gold, silver, and other minerals, the completion of the transcontinental railroads, the destruction of the buffalo, the rise of the range-cattle industry, and the dawning realization that the arid region need not be a sterile desert. With the use of what water was available, techniques of dry farming and irrigation could make the land fruitful after all.

THE MIGRATORY STREAM   During the second half of the nineteenth century, an unrelenting stream of migrants flowed into the largely Indian and Latino West. Millions of Anglo-Americans, African Americans, Mexicans, and European and Chinese immigrants transformed the patterns of western society and culture. Most of the settlers were relatively prosperous white, native-born farming families. Because of the expense of transportation, land, and supplies, the very poor could not afford to relocate. Three quarters of the western migrants were men. The largest number of foreign immigrants came from northern Europe and Canada. In the northern plains, Germans, Scandinavians, and Irish were especially numerous.

AFRICAN-AMERICAN MIGRATION   In the aftermath of the collapse of Radical Republican rule in the South, thousands of African Americans began migrating west from Kentucky, Tennessee, Louisiana, Arkansas, Mississippi, and Texas. Some 6,000 southern blacks arrived in Kansas in 1879 alone, and as many as 20,000 may have come the following year. They came to be known as Exodusters, making their exodus from the South in search of a haven from racism and poverty.

The foremost promoter of African-American migration to the West was Benjamin "Pap" Singleton. Born a slave in Tennessee in 1809, he escaped and settled in Detroit. After the Civil War he returned to Tennessee, convinced that God was calling him to rescue his brethren. When Singleton learned that land in Kansas could be had for $1.25 an acre, he began distributing a

Nicodemus, Kansas

A colony founded by southern blacks in the 1860s.

recruiting pamphlet, *The Advantage of Living in a Free State,* to former slaves. In 1878 Singleton led his first party of 200 colonists to Kansas, bought 7,500 acres that had been an Indian reservation, and established the Dunlop community. Over the next several years, thousands of African Americans followed Singleton into Kansas, causing many southern leaders to worry about the loss of laborers. In 1879 white Mississippians closed access to the river and threatened to sink all boats carrying black colonists to the West.

The African-American exodus to the West died out by the early 1880s. Many of the settlers were unprepared for life on the plains. Their homesteads were not large enough to allow them to be self-sufficient, and most of the farmers were forced to supplement their income by hiring themselves out to white ranchers. Drought, grasshoppers, prairie fires, and dust storms led to crop failures. The sudden influx of so many people taxed resources and patience. Many of the black pioneers in Kansas soon abandoned their land and moved to the few cities in the state. Life on the frontier was not always the "promised land" that setters had been led to expect. Nonetheless, by 1890, some 520,000 African-Americans lived west of the Mississippi River. As many as 25 percent of the cowboys who participated in the Texas cattle drives were African Americans.

In 1866 Congress passed legislation establishing two "colored" cavalry units and dispatched them to the western frontier. Nicknamed buffalo soldiers by the Indians, they were mostly Civil War veterans from Louisiana and Kentucky. They built and maintained forts, mapped vast areas of the

Southwest, strung hundreds of miles of telegraph lines, protected railroad construction crews, subdued hostile Indians, and captured outlaws and rustlers. For this they were paid $13 a month. Eighteen of the buffalo soldiers won Congressional Medals of Honor for their service.

MINING THE WEST Valuable mineral deposits continued to lure people to the West after the Civil War. The mass migration of miners to California in 1849 (the forty-niners) set the typical pattern, in which the disorderly rush of prospectors was quickly joined by camp followers, a motley array of saloon keepers, prostitutes, cardsharps, hustlers, and assorted desperadoes out to mine the miners. An era of lawlessness eventually gave way to vigilante rule and, finally, to a stable community.

The drama of the 1849 gold rush was reenacted time and again in the following three decades. While nearly 100,000 early rushers were crowding around Pikes Peak in Colorado in 1859, miners discovered the Comstock Lode at Gold Hill, Nevada. The lode produced gold and silver and within twenty years had yielded more than $300 million from shafts that reached hundreds of feet into the mountainside. Yet in Arizona and Montana the most important mineral proved to be neither gold nor silver but copper.

The growing demand for orderly government in the West led to the hasty creation of new territories and eventually the admission of a host of new states. In 1861 Nevada became a territory, and in 1864 it was admitted to the Union in time to give its three electoral votes to Abraham Lincoln. After Colorado's admission in 1876, however, no new states entered the union for over a decade because of party divisions in Congress: Democrats were reluctant to create states out of territories that were heavily Republican. After the sweeping Republican victory of 1888, however, Congress admitted the Dakotas, Montana, and Washington in 1889 and Idaho and Wyoming in 1890, completing a tier of states from coast to coast. Utah entered the union in 1896 (after the Mormons abandoned the practice of polygamy) and Oklahoma in 1907, and in 1912 Arizona and New Mexico rounded out the forty-eight continental states.

MINING AND THE ENVIRONMENT During the second half of the nineteenth century, the nature of mining changed drastically. It became a mass-production industry as individual prospectors gave way to large companies. The first wave of miners who rushed to California in 1849 sifted gold dust and nuggets out of riverbeds by means of "placer" mining, or "panning." But once the placer deposits were exhausted, efficient mining required large-scale operations and huge investments. Companies shifted from surface digging to hydraulic mining, dredging, or deep-shaft "hard-rock" mining. Hydraulic mining used a powerful jet of water to excavate whole hillsides, washing the gravel through sluices that caught gold nuggets and disposed of the tailings (dirt and gravel debris). Dredging carved out whole riverbeds in order to sift gold from the surrounding sand and gravel.

Hydraulicking, dredging, and shaft mining transformed vast areas of vegetation and landscape. Huge hydraulic cannons shot enormous streams of water under high pressure, stripping the topsoil and gravel from the bedrock and creating steep-sloped barren canyons that could not sustain plant life. The tons of dirt and debris unearthed by the water cannons covered rich farmland downstream and created sandbars that clogged rivers and killed fish. In 1880 alone some 40,000 acres of farmland and orchards were destroyed by the effects of hydraulic mining while another 270,000 acres were severely damaged. All told, some 12 billion tons of earth were blasted out of the Sierra Nevadas and washed into local rivers. At the massive Malakoff Diggings in northeastern California, hydraulic mining removed an estimated 41 million cubic yards of soil and rock and left a lifeless canyon over a mile long and up to 350 feet deep. The mine used three huge nozzles and 30.5 million gallons of water, twice as much water as was used by the entire city of San Francisco. The sprawling complex had over 150 miles of ditches, dams, and associated reservoirs to supply its gigantic operations.

Irate California farmers in the fertile Central Valley bitterly protested the damage done downstream by the industrial mining operations. In 1878 they formed the Anti-Debris Association, with its own militia, to challenge the powerful mining companies. Efforts to pass state legislation restricting hydraulic mining repeatedly failed because mining companies controlled the votes. The Anti-Debris Association then turned to the courts. On January 7, 1884, the farmers won their case when federal judge Lorenzo Sawyer, a former miner, outlawed the dumping of mining debris where it could reach farmland or navigable rivers. Thus *Woodruff v. North Bloomfield Gravel Mining Company* became the first major environmental ruling in the nation. The town of Marysville, California, which in 1875 had been completely buried in silt and debris unleashed by upstream mines, threw a huge celebration upon learning of Judge Sawyer's decision. Similar parties occurred in farming communities across the state. As a result of the ruling, hydraulic mining dried up, leaving a legacy of abandoned equipment, ugly ravines, ditches, gullies, and mountains of discarded rock and gravel.

THE INDIAN WARS   As settlers pressed in from east and west, the Indians were forced into what was supposed to be their last refuge. Perhaps

INDIAN WARS,
1864–1890

What was the Great Sioux War? What happened at Little Bighorn, and what were
the consequences? Why were hundreds of Indians killed at Wounded Knee?

250,000 Indians on the Great Plains and in the mountain regions lived
mainly off the buffalo herds that provided food and, from their hides, clothing and shelter. In 1851 the chiefs of the Plains tribes had gathered at Fort
Laramie in what would become Wyoming Territory, where they had agreed
to accept definite tribal borders and leave settlers on their trails unmolested.
The treaty worked for a while, with wagon trains passing safely through Indian lands and the army building roads and forts without resistance. Fighting resumed, however, as the emigrants began to encroach upon Indian land
rather than merely pass through it. From 1850 to 1860, for example, 150,000
whites moved into Sioux territory in violation of treaty agreements.

From the early 1860s until the late 1870s, the frontier raged with Indian wars. In 1864 Colonel John Chivington's poorly trained militia assaulted an Indian camp along Sand Creek in Colorado Territory. Although the Indian camp displayed a white flag of truce, the soldiers slaughtered 200 Indians— men, women, and children. One general called the Sand Creek Massacre the "foulest and most unjustifiable crime in the annals of America."

With other scattered battles erupting, a congressional committee began to gather evidence on the grisly Indian wars and massacres. Its 1867 "Report on the Condition of the Indian Tribes" led to an act to establish an Indian Peace Commission charged with removing the causes of Indian wars in general. Congress decided that this would be best accomplished at the expense of the Indians, by persuading them to take up life on out-of-the-way reservations, a solution that perpetuated the encroachment on Indian hunting grounds.

In 1867 a conference at Medicine Lodge, Kansas, ended with the Kiowas, Comanches, Arapahos, and Cheyennes reluctantly accepting land in western Oklahoma. The following spring the Sioux agreed to settle within the Black Hills reservation in Dakota Territory. But Indian resistance on the southern plains continued until the Red River War of 1874–1875, when soldiers led by General Philip Sheridan, a hard-charging Civil War cavalryman, forced the Indians to disband in the spring of 1875. Seventy-two Indian chiefs were imprisoned for three years.

Meanwhile, trouble was brewing again in the north. In 1874 Lieutenant Colonel George A. Custer, a reckless, glory-seeking officer, led an exploratory expedition into the Black Hills, accompanied by gold seekers. Miners were soon filtering into the Sioux hunting grounds despite promises that the army would keep them out. The army had done little to protect Indian land, but when ordered to move against wandering bands of Sioux hunting on the range according to their treaty rights, it moved vigorously.

What became the Great Sioux War was the largest military event since the end of the Civil War. It lasted fifteen months and entailed some fifteen battles in a vast area of present-day Wyoming, Montana, South Dakota, and Nebraska. After several indecisive encounters, Custer found the main encampment of Sioux and their Northern Cheyenne allies on the Little Bighorn River. Separated from the main body of his men and surrounded by 2,500 warriors, Custer and 210 soldiers were annihilated.

Instead of following up their victory, the Indians threw away their advantage in celebration and renewed hunting. The army soon regained the offensive, and the Sioux were forced to give up their hunting grounds and the goldfields in return for payments. Forced onto reservations situated on the

The Battle of Little Bighorn

A painting by Amos Bad Heart Bull, an Oglala Sioux, 1876.

least valuable lands in the region, the Indians soon found themselves struggling to subsist under harsh conditions. Many died of starvation or disease.

In the Rocky Mountains and to the west, the same story of hopeless resistance was repeated. In Idaho the peaceful Nez Perces refused to surrender land along the Salmon River. Chief Joseph tried to avoid war, but when some unruly warriors started a fight, he directed a masterful campaign against overwhelming odds, one of the most spectacular feats in the history of Indian warfare. After a 1,500-mile retreat he was caught thirty miles short of the Canadian border and exiled to Oklahoma. In 1886 a generation of Indian wars virtually ended with the capture of Geronimo, a chief of the Chiricahua Apaches who had fought encroachments in the Southwest for fifteen years.

The epilogue, too, would be tragic. Late in 1888 Wovoka (or Jack Wilson), a Paiute in western Nevada, fell ill and in a delirium imagined he had visited the spirit world, where he learned of a deliverer coming to rescue the Indians and restore their lands. To hasten the day, he said, they had to take up a ceremonial dance at each new moon. The Ghost Dance craze fed upon old legends of a coming messiah and spread rapidly. In 1890 the Lakota Sioux took it up with such fervor that it alarmed white authorities. They banned the Ghost Dance on Lakota reservations, but the Indians defied the order, and a crisis erupted. On December 29, 1890, a bloodbath occurred at Wounded Knee, South Dakota. An accidental rifle discharge led nervous soldiers to fire into a group of Indians who had come to surrender. Nearly 200 Indians and 25 soldiers died in the Battle of Wounded Knee. The Indian wars had ended with characteristic brutality and misunderstanding.

THE DEMISE OF THE BUFFALO   Over the long run the collapse of Indian resistance in the face of white settlement on the Great Plains resulted as much from the decimation of the buffalo herds as from the actions of federal troops. In 1750 there were an estimated 30 million buffalo on the plains; by 1850 there were less than 10 million; by 1900 only a few hundred were left. What happened to them? The conventional story focuses on intensive harvesting of buffalo by white hunters after the Civil War. Americans east of the Mississippi River developed a voracious demand for buffalo robes and buffalo leather. The average white hunter killed 100 animals a day, and the hides and bones (to be ground into fertilizer) were shipped east on railroad cars. Some army officers encouraged the slaughter. "Kill every buffalo you can!" Colonel Richard Dodge told a sport hunter in 1867. "Every buffalo dead is an Indian gone."

This conventional explanation tells only part of a more complicated story, however. The buffalo disappeared from the western plains for a variety of environmental reasons, including a significant change in climate; competition with other grazing animals; and cattle-borne disease. A prolonged drought on the Great Plains during the late 1880s and 1890s, the same drought that would help spur the agrarian revolt and the rise of populism, also devastated the buffalo herds by reducing the grasslands upon which the animals depended. At the same time the buffalo had to compete for forage with an ever increasing number of horses, cattle, and sheep. By the 1880s over 2 million horses were grazing on buffalo lands. In addition, the Plains Indians themselves, empowered by horses and guns and spurred by the profits reaped from selling hides and meat to white traders, accounted for much of the devastation of the buffalo herds after 1840. White hunters who killed buffaloes by the millions in the 1870s and 1880s played a major role in the animal's demise, but only as the final catalyst. If there had been no white hunters, the buffalo would probably have lasted only another thirty years because their numbers had been so greatly reduced by other factors.

INDIAN POLICY   Most white westerners had little tolerance for moralizing on the Indian question, but many easterners decried the slaughter and mistreatment of Indians. Well-intentioned reformers sought to "Americanize" Indians by dealing with them as individuals rather than tribes. The

Dawes Severalty Act of 1887 proposed to introduce the communal Indians to individual land ownership and agriculture. Sponsored by Senator Henry Dawes of Massachusetts, the act permitted the president to divide the land of any tribe and grant 160 acres to each head of a family and lesser amounts to others. To protect the Indians' property, the government held it in trust for twenty-five years, after which the owner won full title and became a U.S. citizen. In 1901 citizenship was extended to the Five Civilized Tribes of Oklahoma and, in 1924, to all Indians.

But the more it changed, the more Indian policy remained the same. Although well-intended, the Dawes Act created new chances for more plundering of Indian land and disrupted what remained of the traditional culture. The Dawes Act broke up reservations and often led to the loss of Indian land to whites. Land not distributed to Indian families was sold, and some of the land the Indians did receive was lost to land speculators because of the Indians' inexperience with private ownership or simply because of their powerlessness in the face of fraud. Between 1887 and 1934 Indians lost an estimated 86 million of their 130 million acres. Most of what remained was unsuited for agriculture.

CATTLE AND COWBOYS   While the West was being taken from the Indians, cattle entered the grasslands where the buffalo had roamed. The cowboy enjoyed his brief heyday before fading into the folklore of the Wild West. From colonial times, especially in the South, cattle raising had been a common enterprise just beyond the fringe of settlement. In many cases, slaves took care of the livestock. Later, in the West, African-American cowboys were common.

Much of the romance of the open-range cattle industry derived from its Mexican roots. The Texas longhorns and the cowboys' horses had in large part descended from stock brought to America by the Spaniards, and many of the industry's trappings had been worked out in Mexico first: the cowboy's saddle, chaps (*chaparreras*) to protect the legs, spurs, and lariat.

For many years wild cattle competed with the buffalo in the Spanish borderlands. Natural selection and contact with Anglo-American scrub cattle produced the Texas longhorns: lean and rangy, they were noted more for speed and endurance than for yielding a choice steak. They had little value, moreover, because the largest markets for beef were too far away. At the end of the Civil War, as many as 5 million longhorns roamed the grasslands of Texas, still neglected—but not for long. In the upper Mississippi River valley, where herds had been depleted by the war, cattle were in great demand, and the Texas cattle could be had just for the effort of rounding them up.

The Cowboy Era

Cowboys herd cattle near Cimarron, Colorado, 1905.

New opportunities arose as railroads pushed farther west, where cattle could be driven through relatively vacant lands. Joseph G. McCoy, an Illinois livestock dealer, encouraged railroad executives to run a line from the prairies to Chicago, the meatpacking center. The Kansas-Pacific Railroad liked Mc-Coy's vision, and with its help he made Abilene, Kansas, the western terminus of a new line. In 1867 the first shipment of Texas cattle went to Chicago.

During the twenty years after the Civil War, some 40,000 cowboys roamed the Great Plains. They were young—the average age was twenty-four—and from diverse backgrounds. Some 30 percent were either Mexican or African American, and hundreds were Indians. Many others were Civil War veterans from the North and the South, and still others were immigrants from Europe. The life of a cowboy, for the most part, was rarely as exciting as has been depicted by motion pictures and television shows. Working as a ranch hand involved grueling wage labor interspersed with drudgery and boredom.

The thriving cattle industry spurred rapid growth, however. The population of Kansas increased from 107,000 in 1860 to 365,000 ten years later and reached almost 1 million by 1880. Nebraska witnessed similar increases. During the 1860s cattle would be delivered to rail depots, loaded onto freight cars, and shipped east. By the time the animals arrived in New York or Massachusetts, some would be dead or dying, and all would have lost significant weight. The secret to higher profits for the cattle industry was to devise a way to slaughter the cattle in the Midwest and ship the dressed carcasses east and west. That process required refrigeration to keep the meat from spoiling. In 1869 G. H. Hammond, a Chicago meat packer, shipped the first refrigerated beef in an air-cooled car from Chicago to Boston. Eight years later Gustavus Swift developed a more efficient system of mechanical refrigeration, an innovation that earned him a fortune and provided the cattle industry with a major stimulus.

The flush times of the cowtowns soon faded, however. The long cattle drives played out because they were economically unsound. The dangers of the trail, the wear and tear on men and cattle, the charges levied on drives that crossed Indian territory, and the advance of farms across the trails combined to persuade cattlemen that they could function best near railroads. As railroads spread out into Texas and across the plains, the cattle business spread with them as far as Montana and on into Canada.

In the absence of laws governing the open range, cattle ranchers at first worked out their own arrangements when rights and uses conflicted. As cattle wandered onto other ranchers' property, cowboys would "ride the line" to keep the strays off the adjoining ranches. In the spring they would "round up" the herds and sort out ownership by identifying the distinctive mark "branded" into the cattle. All that changed in 1873, when Joseph Glidden, an Illinois farmer, invented the first effective barbed wire, which ranchers used to fence off their claims at relatively low cost. Orders for the new fence poured in, and soon the open range was no more.

THE END OF THE OPEN RANGE   Yet a combination of factors put an end to the open range. Farmers kept crowding in and laying out homesteads. The boundless range was being overstocked by 1883, and expenses mounted as stock breeders formed associations to keep intruders off overstocked ranges, to establish and protect land titles, deal with railroads and buyers, to fight prairie fires, and cope with rustlers and wolves. The rise of sheepherding by 1880 caused still another conflict with the ranchers. A final blow to the open-range industry came with two unusually severe winters in 1886 and 1887, followed by ten long years of drought.

Surviving the hazards of the range required establishing legal title, fencing in the land, limiting the herds to a reasonable size, and providing shelter and hay during the rigors of winter. Moreover, as the long cattle drives gave way to more rail lines and refrigerated railcars, the cowboy settled into a more sedentary existence. Within merely two decades, from 1866 to 1886, the era of the cowboy had come and gone.

RANGE WARS   Conflicting claims over land and water rights ignited violent disputes between ranchers and farmers. Ranchers often tried to drive off neighboring farmers, and farmers in turn tried to sabotage the cattle barons, cutting their fences and spooking their herds. The cattle ranchers also clashed with sheepherders over access to grassland. A strain of ethnic and religious prejudice heightened the tension between ranchers and herders. In the Southwest, shepherds were typically Mexican Americans; in Idaho and Nevada, they were from the Basque region of Spain or Mormons. Many Anglo-American cattlemen and cowboys viewed those ethnic and religious groups as un-American and inferior, an attitude that helped them rationalize the use of violence against the sheepherders. Conflict faded, however, as the sheep for the most part found refuge in the high pastures of the mountains, leaving the grasslands of the plains to the ranchers.

Yet there also developed a perennial tension between large and small cattle ranchers. The large ranchers fenced in huge tracts of public land, leaving the smaller ranchers with too little pasture. To survive, the smaller ranchers cut the fences. In central Texas this practice sparked the Fence-Cutters' War of 1883–1884. Several ranchers were killed and dozens wounded before the state ended the conflict by passing legislation outlawing fence cutting.

FARMERS AND THE LAND   Among the legendary figures of the West, farmers projected an unromantic image in contrast to that of the cowboys, cavalrymen, and Indians. After 1865, on paper at least, the federal land laws offered farmers favorable terms. Under the Homestead Act of 1862, a farmer could realize the old dream of free land either by simply staking out a claim and living on it for five years or by buying the land at $1.25 an acre after six months.

As so often happens, however, environmental forces shaped development. The unchangeable fact of aridity, rather than land laws, influenced institutions in the West after the Civil War. Where farming was impossible, ranchers simply established dominance by control of the water, regardless of the law. Belated legislative efforts to develop irrigable land finally achieved a major success when the 1901 Newlands Reclamation Act (after the aptly named Senator Francis G. Newlands of Nevada) set up the Bureau of Reclamation. The proceeds of public land sales in sixteen states created a fund for irrigation works, and the Reclamation Bureau set about building such major projects as the Boulder (later the Hoover) Dam on the Nevada-Arizona line, the Roosevelt Dam in Arizona, and the Elephant Butte Dam in New Mexico.

The lands of the New West, like those on previous frontiers, passed to their ultimate owners more often from private hands than directly from the government. Many of the 274 million acres claimed under the Homestead Act passed quickly to cattle ranchers or speculators and thence to settlers. The land-grant railroads got some 200 million acres of the public domain between 1851 and 1871 and sold much of it to build towns along the lines. The West of ranchers and farmers was in fact largely the product of the railroads.

The first arrivals on the sod-house frontier of the Plains faced a grim struggle against danger, adversity, and monotony. Though land was relatively cheap, horses, livestock, wagons, wells, fencing, seed, and fertilizer were not. Freight rates and interest rates on loans seemed criminally high. As in the South, declining crop prices produced chronic indebtedness, leading strapped western farmers to embrace virtually any plan to inflate the money supply. The land itself, although fertile, resisted planting; the heavy sod broke many a plow. Since wood was almost nonexistent on the prairie, pioneer families used buffalo chips (dried dung) for fuel.

Farmers and their families also fought a constant battle with the elements: tornadoes, hailstorms, droughts, prairie fires, blizzards, and pests. Swarms of locusts would often cloud the horizon, occasionally covering the ground six inches deep and consuming everything in their path. A Wichita newspaper reported in 1878 that the grasshoppers devoured "everything green, stripping the foliage off the bark and from the tender twigs of the fruit trees, destroying every plant that is good for food or pleasant to the eyes, that man has planted."

As time passed and farmers were able to lay aside some money from their labor, farm families could leave their sod-houses and build frame houses with lumber carried from Chicago by the railroads. New machinery also provided fresh opportunities for farmers. In 1868 James Oliver, a Scottish immigrant living in Indiana, made a successful chilled-iron plow. With further improvements his "sodbuster" plow greatly eased the task of breaking the shallow but tough grass roots of the Plains. Improvements and new inventions lightened the burden of labor but added to the farmers' capital outlay.

To get a start on a family homestead required a minimum investment of $1,000. And while the overall value of farmland and farm products increased in the late nineteenth century, small farmers did not keep up with the march of progress. Their numbers grew but decreased in proportion to the population at large. The wheat produced on the eastern plains from Minnesota and North Dakota down to Texas, like cotton in the antebellum period, was the great export crop that evened America's balance of payments and spurred economic growth. For a variety of reasons, however, few small farmers prospered. And by the 1890s many were in open revolt against "greedy" bankers, railroads, and grain processors who seemed to thwart their efforts and deny their dreams.

PIONEER WOMEN   The West remained a largely male society throughout the nineteenth century. In Texas, for example, the ratio of men to women in 1890 was 110 to 1. Women continued to face traditional legal barriers and social prejudice. A wife could not sell property without her husband's approval. Texas women could not sue except for divorce, nor could they serve on juries, act as lawyers, or witness a will. But the fight for survival in the West often made husbands and wives more equal partners in everyday life than their eastern counterparts. Prairie life also allowed women more independence than could be had by leading domestic life back East.

"THE END OF THE FRONTIER HAS GONE"   American life reached an important juncture in the last decade of the nineteenth century. After the

Women of the Frontier

A woman and her family in front of their sod house. The difficult life on the prairie led to more egalitarian marriages than were found in most other regions of the country.

1890 population count, the superintendent of the national census noted that he could no longer locate a continuous frontier line beyond which population thinned out to fewer than two people per square mile. This fact inspired the historian Frederick Jackson Turner to develop the influential frontier thesis, first outlined in "The Significance of the Frontier in American History," a paper delivered to the American Historical Association in 1893. "The existence of an area of free land," Turner wrote, "its continuous recession, and the advance of American settlement westward, explain American development." The frontier, he added, had shaped the national character in striking ways. It was

> to the frontier [that] the American intellect owes its striking characteristics. That coarseness and strength combined with acuteness and acquisitiveness; that practical, inventive turn of mind, quick to find expedients; that masterful grasp of material things, lacking in the artistic but powerful to effect great ends; that restless, nervous energy; that dominant individualism, working for good and for evil, and with all that buoyancy and exuberance which comes with freedom—these are traits of the frontier, or traits called out elsewhere because of the existence of the frontier.

But, Turner ominously concluded in 1893, "the frontier has gone and with its going has closed the first period of American history."

Turner's "frontier thesis" guided several generations of scholars and students in their understanding of the distinctive characteristics of American history. His view of the frontier as the westward-moving source of the nation's democratic politics, open society, unfettered economy, and rugged individualism, far removed from the corruptions of urban life, gripped the popular imagination as well. But it left out much of the story. Turner's description of the frontier experience exaggerated the homogenizing effect of the environment and virtually ignored the role of women, African Americans, Indians, Mormons, Latinos, and Asians in shaping the diverse human geography of the western United States. Turner also implied that the West would be fundamentally different after 1890 because the frontier experience was essentially over. In many respects, however, that region has retained the qualities associated with the rush for land, gold, timber, and water rights during the post–Civil War decades. The mining frontier, as one historian has recently written, "set a mood that has never disappeared from the West: the attitude of extractive industry—get in, get rich, get out."

> ## MAKING CONNECTIONS
>
> · The problems of southern and western farmers described in this chapter set the stage for the rise of the Populists, as discussed in Chapter 22.
>
> · The late nineteenth century was a crucial period in the evolution of race relations in the South, bridging the antebellum period and the twentieth century.
>
> · This chapter closes with the observation that as of 1890, according to the superintendent of the census and the historian Frederick Jackson Turner, "the frontier has gone." Where would Americans now look to fulfill their expansionist urges?

FURTHER READING

The classic study of the emergence of the New South remains C. Vann Woodward's *Origins of the New South, 1877–1913* (1951). A more recent treatment of southern society after the end of Reconstruction is Edward L. Ayers's *Southern Crossing: A History of the American South, 1877–1906* (1995). A good survey of industrialization in the South is James C. Cobb's *Industrialization and Southern Society, 1877–1984* (1984).

C. Vann Woodward's *The Strange Career of Jim Crow*, 3rd ed. (2002), remains the standard on southern race relations at the end of the nineteenth century. Some of Woodward's points are challenged in Howard N. Rabinowitz's *Race Relations in the Urban South, 1865–1890* (1978). Leon Litwack's *Trouble in Mind: Black Southerners in the Age of Jim Crow* (1998) treats the rise of legal segregation, while Michael Perman's *Struggle for Mastery: Disfranchisement in the South, 1888–1908* (2001) surveys efforts to keep African Americans from voting. J. Morgan Kousser's *The Shaping of Southern Politics: Suffrage Restriction and the Establishment of the One-Party South, 1880–1910* (1974) handles disenfranchisement. An award-winning study of white women and the race issue is Glenda Elizabeth Gilmore's *Gender and Jim Crow: Women and the Politics of White Supremacy in North Carolina, 1896–1920* (1996).

For stimulating reinterpretations of the frontier and the development of the West, see William Cronon's *Nature's Metropolis: Chicago and the Great West* (1991), Patricia Nelson Limerick's *The Legacy of Conquest: The Unbro-*

ken *Past of the American West* (1987), Richard White's *"It's Your Misfortune and None of My Own": A New History of the American West* (1991), and Walter Nugent's *Into the West: The Story of Its People* (1999).

The role of African Americans in western settlement is the focus of William Laren Katz's *The Black West: A Documentary and Pictorial History of the African-American Role in the Westward Expansion of the United States* (1996) and Nell Irvin Painter's *Exodusters: Black Migration to Kansas after Reconstruction* (1977). The best account of the conflicts between Indians and whites is Robert Utley's *The Indian Frontier of the American West, 1846–1890* (1984). For a presentation of the Native American side of the story, see Peter Nabokov's *Native American Testimony: A Chronicle of Indian-White Relations from Prophecy to the Present, 1492–2000,* rev. ed. (1999).

On the demise of the buffalo herds, see Andrew C. Isenberg's *The Destruction of the Bison: An Environmental History, 1750–1920* (2000).

20

BIG BUSINESS AND ORGANIZED LABOR

FOCUS QUESTIONS

· What factors fueled the growth of the post–Civil War economy?

· What were the methods and achievements of major entrepreneurs?

· What led to the rise of large labor unions?

To answer these questions and access additional review material, please visit www.wwnorton.com/studyspace.

America emerged as an industrial and agricultural giant in the late nineteenth century. Between 1869 and 1899 the nation's population nearly tripled, farm production more than doubled, and the value of manufactures grew sixfold. Within three generations after the Civil War, the predominantly rural nation had became an urban-industrial society buffeted by the imperatives of mass production, mass consumption, and time-clock efficiency. Bigness became the prevailing standard of corporate life, and social tensions worsened with the rising scale of business enterprise.

THE RISE OF BIG BUSINESS

The Industrial Revolution created huge corporations that came to dominate the economy—as well as political and social life—during the late nineteenth century. As businesses grew, their owners sought to integrate all the processes of production and distribution into single companies, thus producing even larger firms. Others joined forces with their competitors in "pools" or "trusts" in an effort to dominate entire industries. This process of industrial combination and concentration transformed the nation's social order. It also aroused widespread dissent and the emergence of an organized labor movement.

Many factors converged to help launch the dramatic business growth after the Civil War. A nationwide shortage of labor served as a powerful incentive, motivating inventors and business owners to develop more efficient, labor-saving machinery. Technological innovations not only created new products but also brought about improved machinery and equipment, spurring dramatic advances in productivity. As the volume of production increased, the larger businesses and industries expanded into numerous states and in the process developed standardized machinery and parts, which became available nationwide. A group of shrewd, determined, and energetic entrepreneurs took advantage of fertile business opportunities to create huge enterprises. Federal and state officials after the Civil War actively encouraged the growth of big business by imposing high tariffs on foreign manufacturers as a means of blunting foreign competition and by providing government land and cash to finance railroads and other internal improvements.

The American agricultural sector, by 1870 the world's leader, fueled the rest of the economy by providing wheat and corn to be milled into flour and meal. With the advent of the cattle industry, the processes of slaughtering and packing meat themselves became major industries. So the farm sector directly stimulated the industrial sector of the economy. A national government-subsidized network of railroads connecting the East and West coasts played a crucial role in the development of related industries and in the evolution of a national market for goods and services. Industry in the United States also benefited from an abundance of power sources—water, wood, coal, oil, and electricity—that were inexpensive compared with those of the other nations of the world.

THE SECOND INDUSTRIAL REVOLUTION   The Industrial Revolution "controls us all," said Yale sociologist William Graham Sumner, "because we are all in it." Sumner and other Americans living during the second half of the nineteenth century experienced what economic historians have termed the Second Industrial Revolution. The First Industrial Revolution began in Britain during the late eighteenth century. It was propelled by the convergence of three new technologies: the coal-powered steam engine, textile machines for spinning thread and weaving cloth, and blast furnaces to produce iron.

The Second Industrial Revolution began in the mid–nineteenth century and was centered in the United States and Germany. It was sparked by an array of innovations and inventions in the production of metals, machinery, chemicals, and foodstuffs. While the First Industrial Revolution helped accelerate the growth of the early American economy, the second transformed the economy and the society into their modern urban-industrial form.

The Second Industrial Revolution involved three related developments. The first was the creation of an interconnected national transportation and communication network, which facilitated the emergence of new national and even international markets for American goods and services. Contributing to this development were the completion of the national telegraph and railroad systems, the emergence of steamships, and the laying of the under-sea telegraph cable, which spanned the Atlantic Ocean and connected the United States with Europe.

During the 1880s a second major breakthrough—the use of electric power—accelerated the pace of change. Electricity created dramatic advances in the power and efficiency of industrial machinery. It also spurred urban growth through the addition of electric trolleys and subways, and it greatly enhanced the production of steel and chemicals.

The third major aspect of the Second Industrial Revolution was the systematic application of scientific research to industrial processes. Laboratories

The Hand of Man (1902)

Photogravure by Alfred Stieglitz.

staffed by graduates of new research universities sprouted up across the country, and scientists and engineers discovered dramatic new ways in which to improve industrial processes. Researchers figured out, for example, how to refine kerosene and gasoline from crude oil. They also improved techniques for refining steel from iron and spawned new products—telephones, type-writers, adding machines, sewing machines, cameras, elevators, and farm ma-chinery—and lower consumer prices. These advances in turn expanded the scope and scale of industrial organizations. Capital-intensive industries such as steel and oil, as well as processed food and tobacco, took advantage of new technologies to gain economies of scale that emphasized maximum produc-tion and national as well as international marketing and distribution.

BUILDING THE TRANSCONTINENTAL RAILROADS   Railroads were the first big business, the first magnet for the great financial markets, and the first industry to develop a large-scale management bureaucracy. The railroads opened the trans-Mississippi West to economic development, con-nected raw materials to factories, and in so doing created an interconnected national market for the country's goods and produce. At the same time, the railroads were themselves gigantic consumers of iron, steel, lumber, and other capital goods.

The renewal of railroad building after the Civil War filled out the railway net-work east of the Mississippi River, but the most spectacular exploits were the transcontinental lines built across the Great Plains and the Rocky Mountains. Running through sparsely settled land, they served the purpose of binding the country together. The buccaneering executives and financiers directing the transcontinental railroads were shrewd entrepreneurs so driven by dreams of great wealth that they often cut corners and bribed legislators. They also ruth-lessly used federal troops to suppress the Plains Indians. But their shenanigans do not diminish the heroic efforts of the workers and engineers who built the rail lines, erected the bridges, and gouged out the tunnels under terrible weather conditions. Building the transcontinental railroads was an epic feat of daring engineering that tied a nation together, changed the economic and po-litical landscape, and enabled the United States to emerge as a world power.

Before the Civil War, sectional differences over routes had delayed the start of a transcontinental line. Secession and the departure of southerners from Congress finally permitted passage of the Pacific Railroads Act, which Abraham Lincoln signed into law in 1862, authorizing a line along a north-central route, to be built jointly by the Union Pacific Railroad westward from Omaha, Nebraska, and by the Central Pacific Railroad eastward from Sacramento, California.

Both railroads began construction during the war, but most of the work was done after 1865. The Union Pacific pushed across the plains at a rapid pace, avoiding the Rocky Mountains by going through Evans Pass in Wyoming. The work crews, including large numbers of ex-soldiers and Irish immigrants, had to cope with bad roads, water shortages, rugged weather, and Indian attacks.

The Central Pacific construction crews were mainly composed of Chinese workers lured to America first by the California gold rush and then by railroad jobs. Thousands of Chinese had emigrated, raising their numbers in the United States from 7,500 in 1850 to 105,000 in 1880. Most of these "coolie" laborers were single men intent upon accumulating money and returning to their homeland, where they could then afford to marry and buy a parcel of land. Their temporary status and dream of a good life back in China apparently made them more willing than American laborers to endure the dangerous working conditions and low pay of railroad work, as well as

The Union Pacific Meets the Central Pacific

The celebration of the completion of the first transcontinental railroad, Promontory, Utah, May 10, 1869.

the blatant racism. By 1867 the Central Pacific Railroad's 12,000 Chinese laborers represented 90 percent of its workforce.

Clearing trees, handling explosives, operating power drills, and working in snowdrifts were dangerous activities, and many Chinese died on the job. Fifty-seven miles east of Sacramento the construction crews encountered the towering Sierra Nevadas, through which they had to cut before reaching more level country in Nevada. The Union Pacific had built 1,086 miles to the Central Pacific's 689 when the race ended on the salt plains of Promontory, Utah, near Ogden. There, on May 10, 1869, Leland Stanford, former governor of California and one of the organizers of the Central Pacific, drove a gold spike symbolizing the railroad's completion.

The next transcontinental line, completed in 1881, linked the Atchison, Topeka, and Santa Fe Railroad with the Southern Pacific Railroad in southern California. The transcontinentals soon sprouted numerous trunk lines, which in turn encouraged the building of other transcontinentals. The result was a massive railroad-building boom that lasted into the 1890s and stimulated the rest of the economy.

FINANCING THE RAILROADS   The railroads were built by private companies that raised money for construction primarily by selling bonds to U.S. and foreign investors. While constitutional scruples over state sovereignty initially constrained the granting of federal aid for internal improvements, many states had subsidized the building of railroads within their borders. Finally, in 1850, Senator Stephen Douglas secured from Congress a federal grant of public lands to subsidize a north-south railroad connecting Chicago and Mobile, Alabama. Over the next twenty years transcontinental railroad companies received generous government aid in the form of federal land grants, as well as loans and tax breaks from federal, state, and local governments.

In the long run the federal government recovered much if not all of its investment. As farms, ranches, and towns sprouted around the rail lines, the value of the government land along the tracks skyrocketed. The railroads also hauled government freight, military personnel and equipment, and the mail. Moreover, by helping to accelerate the creation of a national market, the railroads spurred economic growth and thereby increased government revenues.

But that is only part of the story. The vast sums of money used to finance the building of the transcontinental lines generated shameless profiteering. Prince of the railroad robber barons was Jay Gould, a secretive trickster who mastered the art of buying rundown railroads, making cosmetic improvements, and

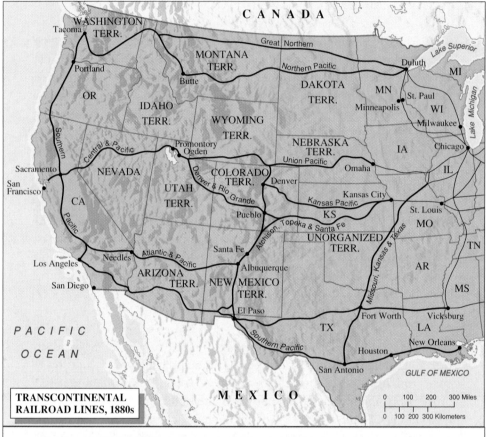

TRANSCONTINENTAL RAILROAD LINES, 1880s

What was the route of the first transcontinental railroad, and why was it not in the South? Who built the railroads? How were they financed?

selling out at a profit while using corporate funds for personal gain and political bribes. Nearly every enterprise he touched was compromised or ruined; Gould, meanwhile, built a fortune that amounted to $100 million upon his death.

Few railroad fortunes were built in those freewheeling times by purely ethical methods, but compared with opportunists such as Gould most railroad entrepreneurs were giants of honesty. They at least took some interest in the welfare of their companies, if not always in that of the public. Cornelius Vanderbilt, called Commodore by virtue of his early exploits in steamboating, stands out among the railroad barons. Already rich before the Civil War, he decided to give up the hazards of wartime shipping and move his money into land transport. His great achievement was consolidating separate trunk lines into a single powerful rail network led by the New York Central. After the Commodore's death, in 1877, his son William Henry extended the Vanderbilt lines to include more than 13,000 miles in the Northeast. The consolidation trend was nationwide: about two thirds of the nation's railroad mileage were under the control of only seven major groups by 1900.

INVENTIONS SPUR MANUFACTURING   Like the railroad industry, the story of manufacturing after the Civil War shows much the same pattern of expansion and merger in old and new industries. The U.S. Patent Office, which had recorded only 276 inventions during its first decade of existence, the 1790s, registered 234,956 in the 1890s. The list of innovations after the Civil War can be extended nearly indefinitely: barbed wire, farm implements, the air brake for trains, steam turbines, gas distribution and electrical devices, the typewriter (1867), the vacuum cleaner (1869), and countless others. Before the end of the century, the internal-combustion engine and the motion picture were spawning new industries that would blossom in the twentieth century.

These technological advances altered the lives of ordinary people far more than politics or intellectual developments. In no field was this truer than in the application of electricity to communications and power. Few if any inventions of the time could rival the importance of the telephone, which Alexander Graham Bell patented in 1876. To promote the new device, the inventor and his supporters formed the Bell Telephone Association, out of which grew in 1877 the Bell Telephone Company. In 1885 the Bell interests organized the American Telephone and Telegraph Company, which by 1899 was a huge holding company controlling forty-nine licensed subsidiaries and an operating company for long-distance lines.

In the development of electrical industries, the name Thomas Alva Edison stands above those of other inventors. Edison invented the phonograph in 1877 and the first successful incandescent lightbulb in 1879. At his laboratories in Menlo Park, New Jersey, he created or perfected hundreds of new devices and processes, including the storage battery, Dictaphone, mimeograph, electric motor, electric transmission, and the motion picture. In the process, Edison and his assistants demonstrated the significance of "research and development" activities.

In 1882, with the backing of the financier J. P. Morgan, the Edison Electric Illuminating Company began to supply current to eighty-five customers in New York City, beginning the great electric utility industry. A number of companies making lightbulbs merged into the Edison General Electric

Company in 1888. But the use of direct current limited Edison's lighting system to a radius of about two miles. To cover greater distances required an alternating current, which could be transmitted at high voltage and then stepped down by transformers. George Westinghouse, inventor of the air brake for railroads, developed the first alternating-current electric system in 1886 and set up the Westinghouse Electric Company to manufacture the equipment. Edison considered the new method too dangerous, but just as Edison's instrument supplanted Bell's first telephone, the Westinghouse system won the "battle of the currents," and the Edison companies had to switch over. After the invention of the alternating-current motor in 1888, Westinghouse improved upon it. This invention enabled factories to locate wherever they wished. Capable now of using electricity as a power source, they no longer had to cluster around waterfalls and coal deposits for a ready supply of energy.

ENTREPRENEURS

Thomas Edison and George Westinghouse were rare examples of inventors with the luck and foresight to get rich from the industries they created. Most of the architects of industrial growth—the great captains of industry—were not inventors but pure entrepreneurs, men skilled mainly in organizing and promoting industry. Called robber barons by critics because of their greed and ruthlessness, they helped create thousands of new jobs and supplied the nation with an array of new goods and services. Three post–Civil War business titans stand out for their enterprise: John D. Rockefeller, Andrew Carnegie, and J. Pierpont Morgan. Each of them in different ways replaced the small-scale economy of the early republic with vast new industries that forever altered the size and scope of the nation's business. Two other entrepreneurs, Richard Sears and Alvah Roebuck, perfected mail-order retailing.

ROCKEFELLER AND THE OIL TRUST   Born in New York State, the son of a flamboyant con man and a devout Baptist, John D. Rockefeller moved as a youth to Cleveland. Soon thereafter his father abandoned the family and started a new life under an assumed name with a second wife. Raised by his mother, John Rockefeller developed a passion for systematic organization and self-discipline. He was obsessed with precision, order, and tidiness. And early on he decided to bring order and rationality to the chaotic oil industry.

Cleveland's railroad and shipping connections made it a strategic location for servicing the oil fields of western Pennsylvania. In economic importance the Pennsylvania oil rush of the 1860s far outweighed the California gold rush of just ten years earlier. Well before the end of the Civil War, derricks checkered the area around Titusville, Pennsylvania, where the first oil well had been struck, and refineries sprang up in Pittsburgh and Cleveland.

John D. Rockefeller

His Standard Oil Company dominated the oil industry.

Of the two cities, Cleveland had the edge in transportation, and John Rockefeller made the most of the fast-growing commercial city's advantages. A man of icy efficiency and tenacious daring, Rockefeller moved aggressively into the oil business. In 1870 he incorporated his various interests, naming his enterprise the Standard Oil Company of Ohio. His goal was to eliminate all of his competitors. To do that, he hatched an ingenious scheme. In the early 1870s Rockefeller created the South Improvement Company, which he made the marketing agent for a large percentage of his oil shipments. By controlling this traffic, he gained clout with the railroads, which in turn gave him large rebates (or secret refunds) on the standard freight rates in order to keep his high-volume business. In some cases they even gave him information on competitors' shipments. Rockefeller then approached his Cleveland competitors and pressured them to sell out at his price. Most of them complied. Those who resisted were forced out. In less than six weeks, Rockefeller had taken over twenty-two of his twenty-six competitors. By 1879 Standard Oil was controlling 90 to 95 percent of the oil refined throughout the country.

Much of Rockefeller's success reflected his determination to "pay nobody a profit." Instead of depending upon the products or services of other firms, known as middlemen, Standard Oil started making its own barrels, cans, and whatever else it needed—in economic terms this is called vertical integration. The company kept large cash reserves to make it independent of banks in case of a crisis. Rockefeller also set out to control his transportation needs. With Standard Oil owning most of the pipelines leading to railroads, as well as the railroad tank cars and the oil-storage facilities, it was able to dissuade the railroads from serving its eastern competitors. Those rivals that insisted on holding out then faced a giant marketing organization capable of driving them to the wall with price wars.

Eventually, in order to consolidate scattered business interests under more efficient control, Rockefeller and his advisers resorted to the legal device of the trust. Long established in law to enable one or more persons to manage property belonging to others, such as children or the mentally incompetent, the trust was now used for another purpose: centralized control of business across state lines. Thus in 1882 Rockefeller organized the Standard Oil Trust. All thirty-seven stockholders in various Standard Oil enterprises conveyed their stock to nine trustees, getting "trust certificates" in return. The nine trustees were thus empowered to give central direction to the scattered Standard Oil companies.

But the trust device, widely copied in the 1880s, proved legally vulnerable to prosecution under state laws against monopoly or restraint of trade. In 1892 Ohio's supreme court ordered the Standard Oil Trust dissolved. For a while the company managed to unify control by the simple device of interlocking directorates, through which the board of directors of one company was made identical or nearly so to the boards of the others. Gradually, however, Rockefeller perfected the idea of the holding company, a company that controlled other companies by holding all or at least a majority of their stock. In 1899, Rockefeller brought his empire under the direction of the Standard Oil Company of New Jersey, a holding company. Though less vulnerable to prosecution under state law, some holding companies were broken up by the Sherman Anti-Trust Act of 1890.

Rockefeller not only made a colossal fortune, but he also gave much of it away, mainly to support advances in education and medicine. A man of simple tastes, who opposed the use of tobacco and alcohol and believed his fortune was a public trust awarded by God, Rockefeller became the world's leading philanthropist. He donated more than $500 million during his ninety-eight-year lifetime. "I have always regarded it as a religious duty," Rockefeller said late in life, "to get all I could honorably and to give all I could."

CARNEGIE AND THE STEEL INDUSTRY   Andrew Carnegie, like Rockefeller, experienced the atypical rise from poverty to riches that came to be known in those days as the typical American success story. Born in Scotland, he migrated with his family to Allegheny County, Pennsylvania, in 1848. Then thirteen, he started work in a textile mill at wages of $1.20 per week. At fourteen he was getting $2.50 per week as a telegraph messenger. Quick-witted, shrewd, and brilliant, he worked hard, and in 1853 he became personal secretary and telegrapher to the district superintendent of the Pennsylvania Railroad. When the superintendent became president of the line, Carnegie took his place, and the pace of his career accelerated. During the Civil War, Carnegie went to Washington, D.C., where he developed a military telegraph system.

Carnegie kept on moving—from telegraphy to railroading to bridge building, then to iron- and steel-making and investments. In 1872 he netted $150,000 on a trip to Great Britain, during which he met Sir Henry Bessemer, inventor of a new process of steelmaking. The next year, Carnegie resolved to concentrate on steel, the miracle material of the post–Civil War era, not because it was new but because it was suddenly cheap. Until the mid–nineteenth century, steel could be made only from wrought iron—itself expensive—and only in small quantities. Then, in 1855, Henry Bessemer invented what became known as the Bessemer converter, a process by which steel could be produced directly and quickly from pig iron (crude iron made in a blast furnace) by using forced air to heat the metal. As more steel was produced, its price dropped and use soared. In 1860 the United States had produced only 13,000 tons of steel. By 1880 production had reached 1.4 million tons.

Carnegie was never a technical expert on steel. He was a promoter, salesman, and organizer with a gift for hiring men of expert ability. Fiercely competitive and obsessed with efficiency and innovation, he insisted on up-to-date machinery and equipment. Carnegie retained a large portion of his annual profits during good times. During business depressions, when construction costs were low and competitors were forced to the wall, he used his surplus capital to buy out competitors and expand. He preached to his employees a philosophy of continual innovation in order to reduce operating costs.

Carnegie stood out from other business titans as a thinker who publicized a philosophy of big business, a conservative rationale that became deeply ingrained in the conventional wisdom of some Americans. Carnegie argued that the captains of industry were on the whole public benefactors. He believed that the best way to

Andrew Carnegie

Steel magnate and business icon.

dispense a fortune was to donate it during one's lifetime to causes promoting the public good: "The man who dies rich dies disgraced." Carnegie insisted that the wealthy should provide means for the less fortunate to help themselves by supporting universities, libraries, hospitals, parks, halls for meetings and concerts, and church buildings. Carnegie spent some $60 million on public libraries and another $60 million on higher education.

J. P. MORGAN, FINANCIER

Unlike Carnegie and Rockefeller, J. Pierpont Morgan was born to wealth, in Hartford, Connecticut, and increased it enormously through his bold financial innovations. Morgan's father was a partner in a London banking house, and his wealth enabled him to send young Pierpont to schools in Switzerland and Germany. After a brief apprenticeship, Morgan in 1857 began work in a New York firm that represented his father's London bank, and in 1860 he set himself up as its New York agent under the name J. Pierpont Morgan and Company. This firm, under various names, channeled European capital into the United States and grew into a financial power in its own right.

As an investment banker, Morgan bought corporate stocks and bonds wholesale and sold them at a profit. The growth of large corporations put investment firms such as Morgan's in an increasingly strategic position in the economy. Since the investment business depended upon the health of client companies, investment bankers became involved in the operation of their clients' firms, demanding seats on boards of directors so as to influence company policies.

J. Pierpont Morgan

A famous portrait by Edward Steichen (1903).

Like John Rockefeller, J. P. Morgan viewed competition as wasteful and chaotic. The solution was to consolidate rival firms into giant trusts. Morgan realized that railroads were the key to the times, so he bought and reorganized one rail line after another. After the panic of 1893, when hard times gutted the net worth of many railroads, Morgan bought many of them. By the 1890s he controlled one sixth of America's railway system.

Yet Morgan's crowning triumph was the consolidation of the steel industry. In 1901 he bought out Andrew Carnegie's huge steel and iron holdings. Carnegie set the price, nearly $500 million, of which Carnegie's personal share was nearly $300 million. After closing the deal, Morgan told the steel king, "Mr. Carnegie, I want to congratulate you on being the richest man in the world." Morgan's new United States Steel Corporation, a holding company for various steel interests, was a marvel of the new century, the first billion-dollar corporation, the climactic event in the age of corporate consolidation.

SEARS AND ROEBUCK   American inventors helped manufacturers after the Civil War produce a vast number of new products, but the most important challenge was extending the reach of modern commerce to the millions of people who lived on isolated farms and in small towns. In the aftermath of the Civil War, a traveling salesman from Chicago named Aaron Montgomery Ward decided that he could reach more people by mail than on foot and in the process could eliminate the middlemen whose services increased the retail price of goods. Beginning in the early 1870s, Montgomery Ward and Company began selling goods at a 40 percent discount through mail-order catalogs.

By the end of the century, a new retailer had come to dominate the mail-order industry: Sears, Roebuck and Company, founded by two young midwestern entrepreneurs, Richard Sears and Alvah Roebuck, who began offering a cornucopia of goods by mail in the early 1890s. The Sears, Roebuck catalog in 1897 was 786 pages long and was published in German and Swedish as well as English. It included groceries, drugs, tools, bells, furniture, iceboxes, stoves and household utensils, musical instruments, farm implements, boots and shoes, clothes, books, and sporting goods.

Cover of the 1897 Sears, Roebuck and Company Catalog

Sears's extensive mail-order business and discounted prices allowed its many products to reach customers in cities and the backcountry.

The Sears catalog helped create a truly national market and in the process transformed the lives of millions of people. With the advent of free rural mail delivery in 1898 and the widespread distribution of Sears catalogs, families on farms and in small towns and villages could purchase by mail the products that heretofore were either prohibitively expensive or available only to city dwellers. By the turn of the century, 6 million Sears catalogs were being distributed each year, and the catalog had become the single most widely read book in the nation after the Bible.

Labor Conditions and Organization

SOCIAL TRENDS   Accompanying the spread of giant corporations during the Gilded Age was a rising standard of living for most people. If the rich were still getting richer, a lot of other people were at least better off. The continuing demand for workers, meanwhile, was filled by new groups entering the workforce at the bottom: immigrants above all, but also growing numbers of women and children. Because of a long-term decline in prices and the cost of living, real wages and earnings in manufacturing went up about 50 percent between 1860 and 1890 and another 37 percent from 1890 to 1914. By latter-day standards, however, working conditions were dreary. At the turn of the century, the average hourly wage in manufacturing was about $3.50 in 2006 dollars. The average workweek was fifty-nine hours, which amounted to nearly six ten-hour workdays, but that was only an average. Most steelworkers put in a twelve-hour workday, and as late as the 1920s a great many worked a seven-day, eighty-four-hour workweek.

CHILD LABOR   A growing number of wage laborers in the late nineteenth century were children—boys and girls who worked full-time for meager wages amid unhealthy conditions. Young people had always worked in America: farms required everyone to pitch in. After the Civil War, however, many children took up work outside the home, operating machines, digging coal, stitching clothes, shucking oysters, peeling shrimp, canning food, blowing glass, and tending looms. Parents desperate for income believed they had no choice but to put their children to work. By 1880 one out of every six children was working full-time. By 1900 there were almost 2 million child laborers in the United States. In southern cotton mills, where few African Americans were hired, one fourth of the employees were below the age of fifteen, with half of the children below age twelve. Children as young as eight were laboring alongside adults twelve hours a day, six days a week. This meant they received little or no education and had little time for play or parental nurturance.

Factories, mills, mines, and canneries were dangerous places, especially for children. Throughout Appalachia, thousands of soot-smeared boys worked deep in the coal mines. In New England and the South, thousands of young girls worked in dusty textile mills. Foremen kept children awake by dousing them with water. Children suffered three times as many on-the-job accidents as adult workers, and respiratory diseases were common in the unventilated buildings. A child working in a textile mill was only half as likely to reach age twenty as a child outside a mill. Although some states passed laws limiting the number of hours children could work and establishing minimum-age requirements, they were rarely enforced and often ignored. By 1881 only seven states, mostly in New England, had laws requiring children to be at least twelve before they worked for wages. Yet the only proof required by employers in such states was a statement from a child's parents. Working-class and immigrant parents were often so desperate for income that they forged work permits for their children or taught their children to lie about their age to keep a job.

DISORGANIZED PROTEST   Under these circumstances it was difficult for workers to organize unions. Civic officials and business leaders respected property rights more than the rights of labor. Among workers recently removed from an agrarian world, the idea of permanent labor unions was slow to take hold. And much of the workforce was made up of immigrant workers from a variety of cultures. They spoke different languages and harbored ethnic animosities. Many, if not most, saw their jobs as transient, the first rung on the ladder to success. They hoped to move on to a homestead or return with their earnings to the old farms of their European homeland. Nonetheless, with or without unions, workers often staged impromptu strikes protesting long working hours and wage cuts. Such action often led to violent incidents during the 1870s, however, that colored much of the public's view of labor unions thereafter.

The decade's early years saw a reign of terror in the eastern Pennsylvania coalfields, attributed to an Irish group called the Molly Maguires. The Mollies took their name from an Irish patriot who had directed violent resistance against the British. They were motivated by the dangerous working conditions in the mines and the owners' brutal efforts to suppress union activity. Convinced of the justness of their cause, the Mollies aimed to right perceived wrongs against Irish workers by such methods as intimidation, beatings, and killings. Their terrorism reached its peak in 1874–1875. At trials in 1876, twenty-four of the Molly Maguires were convicted, and ten of them were hanged. The trials also resulted in a wage reduction in the mines.

THE RAILROAD STRIKE OF 1877   A more widespread labor incident was the Great Railroad Strike of 1877, the first major interstate strike in American history. After the panic of 1873 and the ensuing depression, the major rail lines in the East had cut wages. In 1877 they made another 10 percent cut, which provoked most of the railroad workers at Martinsburg, West Virginia, to walk off the job and block the tracks. Without organized direction, however, the group of picketers degenerated into a mob that burned and plundered railroad property.

Walkouts and sympathy demonstrations spread spontaneously from Maryland to San Francisco. The strike engulfed hundreds of cities and towns, leaving in its wake over 100 people dead and millions of dollars in property destroyed. Public sympathy for the strikers was so great at first that local militiamen, called out to suppress them, joined the workers instead. Militiamen from Philadelphia managed to disperse one crowd at the cost of twenty-six lives but then found themselves besieged in the railroad's roundhouse, where they disbanded and shot their way out.

Federal troops finally quelled the violence, but the looting, rioting, and burning went on for another day until the frenzy wore itself out. A reporter described the scene as "the most horrible ever witnessed, except in the carnage of war." Public opinion, sympathetic at first, began to blame the workers for the looting and violence. Eventually the strikers, lacking organized bargaining power, had no choice but to drift back to work. Everywhere the strikes failed.

For many Americans the Great Railroad Strike raised the specter of a worker-based social revolution. As a Pittsburgh newspaper warned, "This may be the beginning of a great civil war in this country between labor and capital." From the point of view of organized labor, however, the Great Railroad Strike demonstrated potential union strength and the need for tighter organization.

THE SAND-LOT INCIDENT   In California the railroad strike indirectly gave rise to a working-class political movement. At a San Francisco sand lot, a meeting to express sympathy for the strikers ended with attacks on some passing Chinese. Within a few days sporadic anti-Chinese riots had led to a mob attack on Chinatown. The depression of the 1870s had hit the

West Coast especially hard, and the Chinese were handy scapegoats for white laborers' frustrations.

Soon an Irish immigrant, Denis Kearney, had organized the Workingmen's Party of California, whose platform called for an end to further Chinese immigration. A gifted agitator, himself only recently naturalized, Kearney harangued the "sand lotters" about the "foreign peril" and assaulted the rich railroad barons for exploiting the poor—sometimes at gatherings outside their mansions on Nob Hill. In 1878 his new party won a hefty number of seats to a state constitutional convention but managed to incorporate into the state's basic law little more than ineffective attempts to regulate the railroads. The workingmen's movement peaked in 1879, when it elected many members to the state legislature and the mayor of San Francisco. Kearney lacked the gift for building a durable movement, but as his party went to pieces, his anti-Chinese theme became a national issue—in 1882 Congress voted to prohibit Chinese immigration for ten years.

TOWARD PERMANENT UNIONS   Meanwhile, efforts to build a permanent labor-union movement had begun to bear fruit. Earlier efforts, in the 1830s and 1840s, had largely been dominated by reformers with schemes that ranged from free homesteads to utopian socialism. But the 1850s witnessed the beginning of "job-conscious" unions in selected skilled trades. By 1860 there were about twenty such unions, and during the Civil War, because of the demand for labor, those craft unions grew in strength and number.

There was no overall federation of these groups until 1866, when the National Labor Union (NLU) convened in Baltimore. The NLU was composed of delegates from labor and reform groups more interested in political and social change than in bargaining with employers. The groups espoused such ideas as the eight-hour workday, workers' cooperatives, paper money, and equal rights for women and African Americans. But the organization lost momentum after the death of its president in 1869, and by 1872 it had entirely collapsed. The NLU was not a total failure, however. It was influential in persuading Congress to enact an eight-hour workday for federal employees and to repeal the 1864 Contract Labor Act, which allowed employers to bind immigrant (contract) laborers by paying for their passage from Europe. That immigrants were willing to work for low wages made them unpopular with American workers.

THE KNIGHTS OF LABOR   Before the National Labor Union collapsed, another labor group of national standing had emerged: the Noble

Order of the Knights of Labor, a name that evoked the aura of medieval guilds. The founder of the Knights of Labor, Uriah S. Stephens, a Philadelphia tailor, was a habitual "joiner" involved with several secret orders, including the Masons. Secrecy, he felt, along with a semireligious ritual, would protect members from retaliation by employers and create a sense of solidarity.

The Knights of Labor, started in 1869, grew slowly, but during the years of depression after 1873, as other unions collapsed it spread more rapidly. Throughout its existence the Knights emphasized reform measures and preferred boycotts to strikes as a way to put pressure on employers. It also had a liberal membership policy, welcoming all who had ever worked for wages, except lawyers, doctors, bankers, and those who sold liquor. Theoretically it was one big union of all workers, skilled and unskilled, regardless of race, color, creed, or sex. In the 1880s membership in the Knights grew rapidly, from about 100,000 to more than 700,000 in 1886. But the organization peaked in 1886 and went into rapid decline after the failure of a railroad strike.

ANARCHISM   The tensions between labor and management during the late nineteenth century in the United States and Europe helped generate

Members of the Knights of Labor

This national union was more egalitarian than most of its contemporaries.

interest in the doctrine of anarchism. Anarchists believed that government—any government—was in itself an abusive device used by the rich and powerful to oppress and exploit the working poor. Anarchists dreamed of the eventual disappearance of government altogether, and many of them believed that the transition to this stateless society could be hurried along by promoting revolutionary action among the masses. One favored tactic was the use of dramatic acts of violence against representatives of the government. A number of European anarchists emigrated to the United States during the last quarter of the nineteenth century, bringing with them their belief in the impact of "propaganda of the deed."

THE HAYMARKET AFFAIR Labor-related violence increased during the 1880s. On May 3, 1886, Chicago's International Harvester plant was the site of an unfortunate clash between strikers and policemen in which one striker was killed. Leaders of a minuscule anarchist movement in Chicago scheduled an open meeting the following night at Haymarket Square to protest the killing. Under a light drizzle the crowd listened to long speeches promoting socialism and anarchism and was beginning to break up when a group of policemen arrived and called upon the activists to disperse. At that point someone threw a bomb at the police, killing one officer and wounding others. The police fired on the demonstrators, killing four. Six more policemen were also killed. Subsequently, in a trial marked by prejudice and hysteria, seven anarchist leaders were sentenced to death despite the lack of any evidence linking them to the bomb thrower, whose identity was never established. Of the seven, two were reprieved, one committed suicide in prison, and four were hanged. All but one of the group were German speaking, and that one held a membership card in the Knights of Labor.

By the turn of the century, the Knights were but a memory. Several problems accounted for their decline: a leadership devoted more to ideas than to pragmatic organization, the failure of the Knights' cooperative enterprises, and a preoccupation with politics rather than negotiations with management. The Knights nevertheless attained some lasting achievements, among them the creation of the federal Bureau of Labor Statistics and the Foran Act of 1885, which penalized employers who imported contract laborers from abroad. The Knights also spread the idea of unionism and initiated a new type of union organization: the industrial union, an industrywide union of skilled and unskilled workers.

GOMPERS AND THE AFL The craft unions opposed the industrial unionism of the Knights. They organized workers who shared special skills, such as typographers or cigar makers. Leaders of the crafts unions feared that joining with unskilled laborers would mean a loss of their craft's identity and a loss of the skilled workers' bargaining power. In the summer of 1886, delegates from craft unions met at Columbus, Ohio, and organized the American Federation of Labor (AFL). In structure it differed from the Knights in that it was a federation of national craft organizations, each of which retained a large degree of autonomy and exercised greater leverage against management.

Samuel Gompers served as president of the AFL from its start until his death in 1924, with only one year's interruption. Born in London of Dutch Jewish ancestry, Gompers came to the United States as a teenager, joined the Cigarmakers' Union in 1864, and became president of his New York local in 1877. Gompers and other leaders of the union focused on concrete economic gains—higher wages, shorter hours, better working conditions—and avoided involvement with utopian ideas or politics.

Gompers had a thick hide, liked to talk and drink with workers in the back room, and advocated using the strike to achieve labor's objectives. His preference, though, was to achieve those objectives through agreements with management that included provisos for union recognition in the form of closed shops (which could hire only union members) or union-preference shops (which could hire others only if no union members were available).

The AFL at first grew slowly, but by 1890 it had already surpassed the Knights of Labor in membership. By the turn of the century, it claimed 500,000 members in affiliated unions; in 1914, on the eve of World War I, it had 2 million; and in 1920 it reached a peak of 4 million. But even then the AFL embraced less than 15 percent of the nation's non-agricultural workers. All unions, including the unaffiliated railroad brotherhoods, accounted for little more than 18 percent of those workers. Organized labor's strongholds were in transportation and the building trades. Most of the larger manufacturing industries—including textiles, tobacco, and packinghouses—remained almost untouched.

THE HOMESTEAD STRIKE   Two violent labor incidents in the 1890s scarred the emerging industrial-union movement and set it back for forty years: the Homestead steel strike of 1892 and the Pullman strike of 1894. The Amalgamated Association of Iron and Steel Workers, founded in 1876, had by 1891 a membership of more than 24,000 and was probably the largest craft union at the time. But it excluded unskilled steelworkers and had failed to organize the larger steel plants. The Homestead Works near Pittsburgh was an important exception. There the union had enjoyed friendly relations with Andrew Carnegie's company until Henry Clay Frick became its president in 1889. A showdown was delayed until 1892, however, when the union contract came up for renewal. Carnegie, who had expressed sympathy for unions in the past, had gone to Scotland and left matters in Frick's hands. Carnegie, however, knew what was afoot: a cost-cutting reduction in the number of workers and a deliberate attempt to smash the union. "Am with you to the end," he wrote to Frick.

As negotiations dragged on, the company announced it would deal with workers as individuals unless an agreement with the union was reached by June 29. A strike—or, more properly, a lockout of unionists—began on that date. Even before the negotiations ended, Frick had begun barricading the plant and had hired as plant guards 300 Pinkerton detectives whose specialty was union busting. On July 6, 1892, a battle erupted, in which nine workers and seven Pinkertons died. In the end the Pinkertons surrendered and marched away, taunted by crowds in the street. Six days later 8,000 state militiamen appeared at the plant to protect the strikebreakers hired to restore production. The strike dragged on until November, but by then the union was dead at Homestead. Its cause was not helped when an anarchist, a Lithuanian immigrant, tried to assassinate Frick. Much of the local sympathy for the strikers evaporated.

THE PULLMAN STRIKE   The Pullman strike of 1894 was perhaps the most notable walkout in American history. It paralyzed the economies of twenty-seven states and territories making up the western half of the nation. It grew out of a dispute at Pullman, Illinois, a model corporate town built on 4,000 acres outside Chicago, where workers of the Pullman Palace Car Company were housed in neat brick homes nestled on grassy lots along shaded streets. The town's idyllic appearance was deceptive, however. Employees were required to live there, pay rents and utility costs that were higher than those in nearby towns, and buy their goods from company stores. With the onset of the depression in 1893, George Pullman laid off 3,000 of 5,800 employees and cut wages 25 to 40 percent, but not his rents and other charges. After Pullman fired three members of a workers' grievance committee, a strike began on May 11, 1894.

During this tense period, Pullman workers had been joining the American Railway Union, founded the previous year by Eugene V. Debs. A charismatic man who led by example and the electric force of his convictions, Debs was a tireless spokesman for labor radicalism who launched a crusade to organize *all* railway workers—skilled and unskilled—into the American Railway Union. His earnest appeal generated a tremendous response, and soon he

Eugene V. Debs

Founder of the American Railway Union and later candidate for president as head of the Socialist Party of America.

was in charge of a powerful new labor organization. He quickly turned his attention to the Pullman controversy.

After George Pullman refused Debs's plea for arbitration, the union workers in June 1894 stopped handling Pullman railcars and by the end of July had tied up most of the railroads in the Midwest. The rail owners brought strikebreakers to connect mail cars to Pullman cars so that interference with Pullman cars would entail interference with the federal mail. U.S. attorney general Richard Olney, a former railroad attorney, swore in 3,400 special deputies to keep the trains running. When clashes occurred between the deputies and some of the strikers, lawless elements ignored Debs's plea for an orderly boycott and repeated some of the violent scenes of the 1877 strike.

Finally, on July 3, 1894, President Grover Cleveland answered an appeal from the railroads to send federal troops into the Chicago area, where the strike was centered. Illinois governor John Peter Altgeld issued a vigorous protest, insisting that the state could keep order, but Cleveland claimed authority and a duty to ensure delivery of the mail. "If it takes every dollar in the Treasury and every soldier in the United States to deliver a postal card in Chicago," he vowed, "that postal card should be delivered."

As strikers clashed with troops and burned hundreds of railcars, the federal district court granted an injunction forbidding any interference with the mail or any effort to restrain interstate commerce. On July 13 the union called off the strike, and a few days later the district court cited Debs for violating the injunction, and he served six months in jail. The Supreme Court upheld the decree in the case of *In re Debs* (1895) on broad grounds of national sovereignty. Debs served his term, during which he read deeply in socialist literature, and he emerged to devote the rest of his life to socialism.

SOCIALISM AND THE UNIONS   The major American unions, for the most part, never allied themselves with the socialists, as many European labor movements did. Although socialist ideas had been circulating in the country at least since the 1820s, the movement gained little notice before the rise of Daniel De Leon in the 1890s as the dominant figure in the Socialist Labor party. De Leon proposed to organize industrial unions with a socialist purpose and to build a political party that would abolish the state once it gained power. His ideas seem to have influenced Vladimir Lenin, leader of Russia's Bolshevik revolution of 1917, but De Leon preached revolution at the ballot box, not by violence.

To many, De Leon seemed doctrinaire and inflexible. Eugene Debs was therefore more successful at building a socialist movement in America. In 1897 Debs announced that he was a socialist and organized the Social Democratic party from the remnants of the American Railway Union; he received over 96,000 votes as its candidate for president in 1900. In 1901 his followers joined a number of secessionists from De Leon's party, led by Morris Hillquit of New York, to set up the Socialist Party of America. In 1904 Debs polled over 400,000 votes as the party's candidate for president and in 1912, more than doubled that, to more than 900,000 votes, or 6 percent of the popular vote.

By 1912 the Socialist party seemed well on the way to becoming a permanent fixture in American politics. Thirty-three cities had Socialist mayors. The Socialist party sponsored five English-language daily newspapers, eight foreign-language dailies, and a number of weeklies and monthlies. In the Southwest the party built a sizable grassroots following among farmers and tenants. But it reached its peak in 1912. It would be wracked by disagreements over America's participation in World War I and was split thereafter.

THE WOBBLIES   During the years of Socialist party growth, a parallel effort to revive industrial unionism emerged, led by the Industrial Workers of the World (IWW), nicknamed the Wobblies. The chief base for this group was the Western Federation of Miners, organized at Butte, Montana, in 1893. Like the Knights of Labor, it was designed to include all workers, skilled or unskilled. Its roots were in the mining and lumber camps of the West, where unstable conditions of employment created a large number of nomadic workers, to whom neither the AFL's pragmatic approach nor the socialists' political appeal held much attraction. The revolutionary goal of the Wobblies was an idea labeled syndicalism by its French supporters: the ultimate destruction of the state and its replacement by one big union. How that union would govern remained vague.

The Wobblies reached out to the fringe elements with the least power and influence, chiefly the migratory workers of the West and the ethnic groups of the East. Always ambivalent about diluting their revolutionary principles, Wobblies scorned the usual labor agreements even when they participated in them. They engaged in spectacular battles with employers but scored few victories. The largest was a textile strike at Lawrence, Massachusetts, in 1912; the strikers won wage raises, overtime pay, and other benefits. But the next year a strike of silk workers at Paterson, New Jersey, ended in disaster, and the IWW entered a rapid decline.

The fading of the movement was accelerated by the hysterical opposition it engendered. Its members branded as anarchists, bums, and criminals, the IWW was effectively destroyed during World War I, when most of its leaders were jailed for their militant opposition to the war. Nonetheless, the Wobblies left behind a rich folklore of nomadic working folk and a gallery of heroic agitators.

A Nation Transformed

By the end of the nineteenth century, the accelerating Industrial Revolution had transformed the nature of work and social life, generated a new urban consciousness and culture, and unleashed rising class tensions. With each passing year, more and more people jettisoned traditional rural folkways in favor of urban environs and enticing economic and social opportunities. As centers of production and consumption, the new industrial cities controlled the pace of national life.

The Industrial Revolution occurred at different rates and produced different effects across the expanding nation. Despite the energetic efforts of New South boosters, the states of the former Confederacy, burdened by a chronic shortage of capital and a poorly educated populace, lagged well behind the rest of the nation in industrial development, urban expansion, and per capita income.

The recurring theme of American life after the Civil War was an acute sense of accelerated social and intellectual change. The velocity and scope of change at midcentury and after was bewildering. Some believed that the United States had lost much of its stability and cohesion as a result of urban-industrial development and western expansion. It had become a loose aggregate of competing individuals, separated from one another by economic differences and ethnic, racial, and class prejudices. How to restore a sense of community and cohesion would become the collective challenge of all Americans.

MAKING CONNECTIONS

- The Darwinian ideas implicit in the attitudes of many leading entrepreneurs, especially Andrew Carnegie, are described in greater detail in the next chapter.

- In response to the growth of the railroads, reformers in the 1880s and 1890s began to push for government regulation of industry, a trend explored in Chapter 22.

- The economic and industrial growth described in this chapter was an important factor in America's "new imperialism" of the late nineteenth century, as shown in Chapter 23.

- The socialist approach to reform was a significant influence on the Progressive movement, covered in Chapter 24.

FURTHER READING

For a masterful synthesis of post–Civil War industrial development, see Walter Licht's *Industrializing America: The Nineteenth Century* (1995). On the growth of railroads, see Albro Martin's *Railroads Triumphant: The Growth, Rejection, and Rebirth of a Vital American Force* (1992). A monumental study of the transcontinental railroad is David Haward Bain's *Empire Express: Building the First Transcontinental Railroad* (1999). On the 1877 railroad strike, see David O. Stowell's *Streets, Railroads, and the Great Strike of 1877* (1999).

On entrepreneurship in the iron and steel sector, see Thomas J. Misa's *A Nation of Steel: The Making of Modern America, 1865–1925* (1995). The best biographies of the leading business tycoons are Ron Chernow's *Titan: The Life of John D. Rockefeller, Sr.* (1998) and Jean Strouse's *Morgan, American Financier* (1999). Nathan Rosenberg's *Technology and American Economic Growth* (1972) documents the growth of invention during the period.

Much of the scholarship on labor stresses the traditional values and the culture of work that people brought to the factory. Herbert G, Gutman's *Work, Culture, and Society in Industrializing America: Essays in American Working-Class History* (1975) best introduces these themes. Also see David Montgomery's *The Fall of the House of Labor: The Workplace, the State, and American Labor Activism, 1865–1925* (1987).

For the role of women in the changing workplace, see Alice Kessler-Harris's *Out to Work: A History of Wage-Earning Women in the United States* (1982) and Susan E. Kennedy's *If All We Did Was to Weep at Home: A History of White Working-Class Women in America* (1979).

As for the labor unions, Gerald N. Grob's *Workers and Utopia: A Study of Ideological Conflict in the American Labor Movement, 1865–1900* (1961) examines the difference in outlook between the Knights of Labor and the American Federation of Labor. For the Knights, see Leon Fink's *Workingmen's Democracy: The Knights of Labor and American Politics* (1983). Also useful is Susan Levine's *Labor's True Woman: Carpet Weavers, Industrialization, and Labor Reform in the Gilded Age* (1984), on the role of women in the Knights. To trace the rise of socialism among organized workers, see Nick Salvatore's *Eugene V. Debs: Citizen and Socialist* (1982). Strikes are discussed in Paul Avrich's *The Haymarket Tragedy* (1984) and Paul Krause's *The Battle for Homestead, 1880–1892: Politics, Culture, and Steel* (1992).

21

THE EMERGENCE OF
URBAN AMERICA

FOCUS QUESTIONS

· How did immigration affect the growth of the modern city?

· What led to the rise of powerful reform movements?

· What was the impact of Darwinian thought on the social sciences?

· What were the literary and philosophical trends of the late nineteenth century?

To answer these questions and access additional review material, please visit www.wwnorton.com/studyspace.

During the second half of the nineteenth century, the United States experienced an urban transformation unparalleled in world history. The late nineteenth century, declared an economist in 1899, was "not only the age of cities, but the age of great cities." Between 1860 and 1910 the urban population of the United States mushroomed from 6 million to 44 million. By 1920 more than half the population lived in urban areas.

The rise of big cities during the nineteenth century created a distinctive urban culture. People from different ethnic and religious backgrounds and representing every walk of life poured into the high-rise apartment buildings and congested tenements springing up in every major city. They came in search of jobs, wealth, and excitement.

Not surprisingly, the rise of metropolitan America created an array of social problems. Rapid urban development produced widespread poverty and political corruption. It also produced dirt and disease, crowded housing, and unsafe working conditions in factories, mines, mills, and slaughterhouses. People needed basic services, such as education, transportation, sewers, fresh water, inoculations against disease, and factory inspections to prevent unsafe working conditions. Broadened access to public education and to public health services would eventually improve literacy and lower infant mortality rates. Breakthroughs in medical science would bring cures for tuberculosis, typhoid, and diphtheria—although those infectious diseases would remain the century's leading killers. But in the meantime, the question of how to feed, clothe, shelter, and educate the new arrivals taxed the imagination and patience of many urban leaders.

AMERICA'S MOVE TO TOWN

The prospect of good jobs and social excitement lured people to the cities from the countryside and overseas. City people and laborers became recognizably urban in demeanor and outlook. The contrasts between farm and city life grew more vivid with each passing year.

EXPLOSIVE URBAN GROWTH   The frontier was a safety valve for urban unrest, the historian Frederick Jackson Turner said in his influential thesis on American development. Its cheap lands afforded a release for the population pressures mounting in the cities. If there were such a thing as a safety valve in his own time, however, he had it exactly backward. The flow of population toward cities was greater than the flow toward the West.

Much of the westward migration in fact was itself an urban movement, spawning new towns near the mining digs or at the railheads. The Pacific coast boasted a greater urban proportion of the population in the West than anywhere else; its major concentrations were first around San Francisco Bay and then in Los Angeles, which became a boomtown after the arrival of the Southern Pacific and Santa Fe Railroads in the 1880s. In the Northwest, Seattle also grew quickly, first as the terminus of three transcontinental railroad lines and, by the end of the century, as the staging area for the Yukon gold rush. Minneapolis, St. Paul, Omaha, Kansas City, and Denver were no longer the mere villages they had been in 1860. The South, too, produced new cities: Durham, North Carolina, and Birmingham, Alabama, which were centers of tobacco and iron manufactures, and Houston, Texas, which handled cotton and cattle and, later, oil. The industrial explosion powered the growth of new cities during this period.

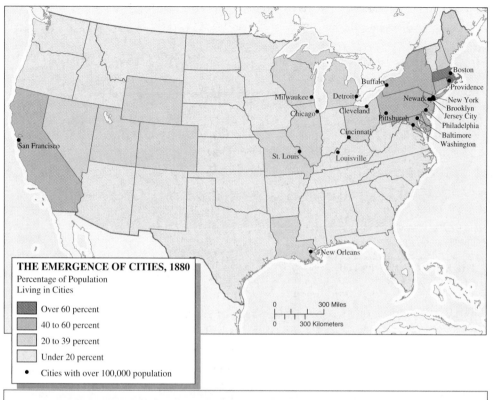

THE EMERGENCE OF CITIES, 1880
Percentage of Population
Living in Cities

- Over 60 percent
- 40 to 60 percent
- 20 to 39 percent
- Under 20 percent
- Cities with over 100,000 population

Which states had the largest population in 1880? What drove the growth of western cities? How were western cities different from eastern cities?

Several technological innovations enabled cities to expand vertically to accommodate their surging populations. In the 1870s innovations in heating, such as steam circulating through pipes and radiators, contributed to the building of multiple-apartment dwellings, since fireplaces were no longer needed. In 1889 the Otis Elevator Company installed the first electric elevator, which made possible the erection of taller buildings—before the Civil War few structures had risen higher than three or four stories. During the 1880s engineers developed cast-iron and steel-frame construction, which was stronger than brick and thereby enabled the construction of "skyscrapers," which depend on steel frames and girders.

Cities also expanded horizontally after the introduction of important transportation innovations. Before the 1890s the chief power sources of urban transport were either animals or steam. Horse- and mule-drawn streetcars had

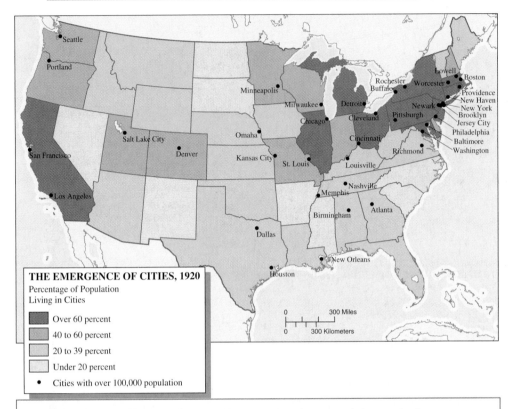

THE EMERGENCE OF CITIES, 1920

Percentage of Population Living in Cities

- Over 60 percent
- 40 to 60 percent
- 20 to 39 percent
- Under 20 percent
- • Cities with over 100,000 population

How did technology change life in cities in the early twentieth century? What was the role of mass transit in expanding the urban population? How did the demographics of these new cities change between 1880 and 1920?

appeared in antebellum cities, but they were slow and cumbersome, and cleaning up manure from the streets added to their cost. In 1873 San Francisco became the first city to use cars pulled by steam-driven cables. Some cities used steam-powered commuter trains on elevated tracks, but by the 1890s electric trolleys were preferred. Mass transportation received an added boost around the turn of the century, when subway systems began to operate in Boston, New York, and Philadelphia.

The spread of mass transit allowed large numbers of people to become commuters, and a growing middle class retreated to quieter, tree-lined "streetcar suburbs," whence they could travel into the central city for business or entertainment (though laborers generally stayed put, unable to afford even the nickel fare). Urban growth often became a sprawl, since it

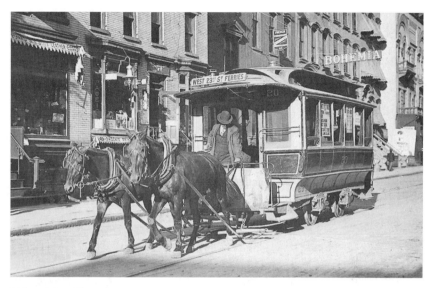

Urban Mass Transit

A horse-drawn streetcar moving along rails in New York City.

usually took place without plan, in the interest of a fast buck, and without thought to the need for parks and public services.

THE ALLURE AND PROBLEMS OF THE CITIES   The wonder of the cities—their glittering new electric lights, their streetcars, telephones, department stores, vaudeville shows and other amusements, newspapers and magazines, and a thousand other attractions—cast a magnetic lure on rural youth. The new cities threw into stark contrast the frustration of unending toil and the isolation of country life. In times of rural depression, thousands left farms for the cities in search of opportunity and personal freedom.

Yet those who moved to the city often traded one set of problems for another. Workers in the big cities often had no choice but to live in crowded apartments, most of which were poorly designed. In 1900 Manhattan's 42,700 tenements housed almost 1.6 million people. Such unregulated urban growth created immense problems of health and morale.

During the last quarter of the nineteenth century, cities became so cramped and land so scarce that architects were forced to build upward. In New York City this resulted in "dumbbell" tenement houses. These structures, usually six to eight stories tall and jammed tightly against one another,

Urbanization and the Environment

A garbage cart retrieves trash in New York City, ca. 1890

derived their name from the fact that housing codes required a two-foot-wide air shaft between buildings. The fronts and the backs of adjoining buildings abutted each other, but the midsections were narrower, giving the structures the appearance of dumbbells when viewed from overhead. Twenty-four to thirty-two families would cram into each building. Some city blocks housed almost 4,000 people. The tiny air shaft provided little ventilation; instead, it proved to be a fire hazard, fueling and conveying flames from building to building.

The early tenements were poorly heated and had communal toilets outside in a yard or alley. Shoehorned into their quarters, families had no privacy, free space, or sunshine; children had few places to play except in the streets; infectious diseases and noxious odors were rampant. Not surprisingly, the mortality rate among the urban poor was much higher than that of the general population. In one poor Chicago district at the end of the century, three out of five babies died before their first birthday.

CITY POLITICS   The sheer size of the cities helped create a new form of politics. Because local government was often fragmented and beset by parochial rivalries, a need grew for a central organization to coordinate citywide services such as public transportation, sanitation, and utilities. Urban political machines developed, consisting of local committeemen, district captains, and culminating in a political boss. While the bosses granted patronage favors and engaged in graft, buying votes and taking kickbacks, they also provided needed services. They distributed food, coal, and money to the poor; found jobs for those who were out of work; sponsored English-language classes for immigrants; organized sports teams, social clubs, and neighborhood gatherings; fixed problems at city hall; and generally helped newcomers adjust to their new life. In return the political professionals felt entitled to some reward for having done the grubby work of the local organization.

CITIES AND THE ENVIRONMENT Nineteenth-century urban communities were filthy and disease ridden, noisy and smelly. They overflowed with garbage, contaminated water, horse manure, roaming pigs, and untreated sewage. Providing clean water was a chronic problem, and raw sewage was dumped into streets and waterways. Epidemics of water-related diseases such as cholera, typhoid fever, and yellow fever ravaged populations. Animal waste was pervasive. In 1900, for example, there were over 3.5 million horses in American cities, each of which generated 20 pounds of manure and several gallons of urine daily. In Chicago alone, 82,000 horses produced 300,000 tons of manure each year. The life expectancy of urban draft horses was only two years, which meant that thousands of horse carcasses had to be disposed of each year. In New York City alone, 15,000 dead horses were removed annually.

During the late nineteenth century, municipal reformers organized to clean up the cities. Their goal was not only to improve the appearance of metropolises but also to remove the environmental causes of disease. The "sanitary reformers"—public health officials and municipal engineers—persuaded city governments to banish hogs and cattle, mount cleanup campaigns, establish water and sewage systems, institute trash collection, and replace horses with electric streetcars. By 1900, 94 percent of American cities had developed regular trash-collection services.

Yet such improvements in public health had important social and ecological trade-offs and caused unanticipated problems. Waste that once had been put into the land was now dumped into waterways. Urban populations had to deal with the waste dumped upstream; rural populations had to deal with the urban waste sent downstream.

Similarly, solving the horse-manure problem involved trade-offs. The manure dropped on city streets did cause stench and bred countless flies, many of which carried diseases such as typhoid fever. But urban horse manure also had benefits. Farmers living on the outskirts of cities used it to fertilize hay and vegetable crops. City-generated manure was the agricultural lifeblood of the vegetable farms outside New York, Baltimore, Philadelphia, and Boston. Likewise, human waste was used on farm fields. In the nineteenth century most cities converted the "night soil" from outhouses into agricultural fertilizer.

Ultimately, however, the development of public water and sewer systems and flush toilets separated urban dwellers and their waste from the agricultural cycle at the same time that the emergence of refrigerated railcars and massive meatpacking plants separated most people from their sources of food. While the advances provided great benefits, a flush-and-forget-it mentality emerged. Well into the twentieth century, people presumed that running water purified itself, and consequently they dumped massive amounts of untreated waste into rivers and bays. What they failed to calculate was the carrying capacity of the waterways. And the high phosphorous content of bodily waste dumped into streams led to algae blooms that sucked the oxygen out of the water and unleashed a string of environmental reactions that suffocated fish and affected marine ecology. By the 1930s, Lake Erie was coated with algae; the fish population had plummeted.

THE NEW IMMIGRATION

The Industrial Revolution during the second half of the nineteenth century brought to American shores waves of immigrants from every part of the globe. By 1900 nearly 30 percent of the residents of major cities were foreign-born. These newcomers provided much-needed labor, but their arrival also generated ugly racial and ethnic tensions.

AMERICA'S PULL   The migration of foreigners to the United States has been one of the most powerful forces shaping American history, and this was especially true after the Civil War. The tide of immigration rose from just under 3 million in the 1870s to more than 5 million in the 1880s then fell to a little over 3.5 million in the depression decade of the 1890s and rose to its high-water mark of 8.8 million in the first decade of the new century. European immigrants moved from the great agricultural areas of eastern and southern Europe directly to the foremost cities of America. They wanted to live with others of like language, customs, and religion, and they lacked the means to go west and settle on farms.

This nation of immigrants continued to draw new inhabitants for much the same reasons as always and from much the same segments of society. Immigrants took flight from famine, cholera, or the lack of economic opportunity in their native lands. They fled racial, religious, and political persecution and compulsory military service.

Yet more immigrants were probably pulled by America's opportunities than were pushed out by conditions at home. American industries, seeking cheap labor, sent recruiters abroad. Railroads, eager to sell land and build up the traffic on their lines, distributed tempting propaganda in a medley of languages. Many of the western and southern states set up official bureaus and agents to attract immigrants. Under the Contract Labor Act of 1864, the federal government itself encouraged immigration: it allowed companies to recruit foreign workers by paying for their passage and then recouping the money from the immigrants' wages. The law was repealed in 1868, but not until 1885 did the government forbid companies to import contract labor, a practice that put immigrants under the control of their employers.

A NEW WAVE   Before 1880 immigrants were mainly from northern and western Europe. By the 1870s, however, that pattern had begun to change. The proportion of people from southern and eastern Europe rose sharply. After 1890 they made up a majority of the newcomers, and by the first decade of the new century they formed 70 percent of the immigrants to the United States. Among these new immigrants were Italians, Hungarians, Czechs, Slovaks, Poles, Serbs, Croats, Russians, Romanians, and Greeks—all people whose culture and language were markedly different from those of western Europe and whose religion for the most part was Judaism or Catholicism.

ELLIS ISLAND   As the number of immigrants passing through the port of New York soared during the late nineteenth century, the state-run Castle Garden receiving center overflowed with corruption. With reports of abuses filling the newspapers, Congress ordered an investigation, which resulted in the closure of Castle Garden, in 1890. Thereafter the federal government's new Bureau of Immigration took responsibility for admitting newcomers to New York City.

To launch this effort, Congress funded the construction of a new reception center on a tiny island off the New Jersey coast, a mile south of Manhattan, near the Statue of Liberty. In 1892 Ellis Island opened its doors to the "huddled masses" of the world. In 1907, the reception center's busiest year, more than 1 million new arrivals passed through the receiving center, an average of about 5,000 per day; in one day alone, immigration officials processed some 11,750.

Steerage Deck of the S.S. *Pennland*, 1893

These immigrants are about to arrive at Ellis Island in New York Harbor. Many newcomers to America settled in cities because they lacked the means to take up farming.

MAKING THEIR WAY   Once on American soil, immigrants felt exhilaration, exhaustion, and usually a desperate need for work. Many were greeted by family and friends who had arrived earlier, others by representatives of the many immigrant-aid societies or by agents offering the men jobs in mines, mills, or sweatshops. Since most immigrants knew little if any English and nothing about American employment practices, they were easy subjects for exploitation.

In exchange for some whiskey and a job, obliging recruiters claimed a healthy percentage of their wages. Among Italians and Greeks these agents were known as padrones, and they came to dominate the labor market in New York. Other contractors provided train tickets to cities such as Buffalo, Pittsburgh, Cleveland, Chicago, Milwaukee, Cincinnati, and St. Louis.

Strangers in a new land, most of the immigrants gravitated to neighborhoods populated by their own kind. The immigrant enclaves—nicknamed Little Italy, Little Hungary, Chinatown, and so on—served as crucial transitional communities between the newcomers' Old World past and their New World future. In such kinship communities, immigrants practiced

The Registry Room at Ellis Island

Inspectors asked arriving passengers twenty-nine probing questions, including "Are you a polygamist?"

their religion and clung to their native customs, conversed in their native tongue, and filled an aching loneliness. But they paid a price for such community solidarity. When the "new immigrants" moved into an area, older residents typically moved out, taking with them whatever social prestige and political influence they had achieved. The quality of living quickly deteriorated as housing and sanitation codes then went unenforced.

THE NATIVIST RESPONSE   Many native-born Americans saw the new immigration as a threat, and the undercurrent of nativism so often present in American culture surfaced during the late nineteenth century, mainly expressed in anti-Catholic and anti-Semitic sentiments. But more than religious prejudice underlay hostility toward the latest newcomers. Cultural differences confirmed in the minds of nativists the assumption that the Nordic peoples of the old immigration were superior to the Slavic and Latin peoples of the new immigration. Many of the new immigrants were illiterate, and more appeared so because they could not speak English. Some resorted to crime, and political and social radicals turned up in sufficient numbers to encourage nativists to blame labor disputes on alien elements.

Nativism led to a movement to restrict immigration, but it had mixed success beyond the exclusion of certain individuals deemed undesirable. In 1891 Representative Henry Cabot Lodge of Massachusetts took up the cause of excluding illiterates, a measure that would have affected much of the new wave of immigrants even though literacy in English was not required. Bills embodying the restriction passed Congress several times during the next twenty-five years but were vetoed by Presidents Grover Cleveland, William H. Taft, and Woodrow Wilson. In 1917, however, Congress overrode Wilson's veto.

Advocates of immigration restriction during the late nineteenth century did succeed in excluding the Chinese, who were victims of every act of discrimination that the new European immigrants suffered and color prejudice as well. By 1880 there were some 75,000 Chinese in California, about one ninth of the state's population. Railroad owners found them hardworking. Many white workers, however, resented them for accepting lower wages, but their greater sin, a New York newspaper editor stressed, was perpetuating "those disgusting habits of thrift, industry, and self-denial."

Exclusion of the Chinese began in 1880, when the urgent need for railway labor had ebbed. A new treaty with China permitted the United States to "regulate, limit, and suspend" Chinese immigration, and in 1882 Congress passed a bill authorizing a ten-year suspension of Chinese immigration. The legislation closing the doors to Chinese immigrants received overwhelming support. The Chinese Exclusion Act was periodically renewed before being extended indefinitely in 1902. Not until 1943 were barriers to Chinese immigration finally removed.

The West Coast counterpart to Ellis Island was the Immigration Station on rugged Angel Island, six miles offshore from San Francisco. Opened in 1910, it served as a processing center for tens of thousands of Asian immigrants, most of them Chinese. Although the Chinese Exclusion Act had sharply reduced the flow of Chinese immigrants, it did not stop the influx completely. Those arrivals who could claim a Chinese-American parent were allowed to enter, as were certain officials, teachers, merchants, and students. The powerful prejudice the Chinese immigrants encountered helps explain why over 30 percent of the arrivals at Angel Island were denied entry.

POPULAR CULTURE

The sprawling new cities created new patterns of recreation and leisure. Popular culture took on new or greatly expanded dimensions that endowed life with a more cosmopolitan quality. For example, traveling circuses brought entertainment to large cities and small towns. Creative promoters such as Phineas T. Barnum and James A. Bailey made the circus the most eclectic form of entertainment. In the congested metropolitan areas, politics became as much a form of public entertainment as it was a means of providing civic representation and public services. People flocked to hear visiting candidates give speeches in cavernous halls, on outdoor plazas, or from railway cars. In cities such as New York, Philadelphia, Boston, and Chicago, membership in a political party was akin to belonging to a social club. In addition, labor unions provided activities that were more social than economic in nature, and members often visited the union hall as much to socialize as to discuss working conditions. The sheer number of people congregated in cities also helped generate a market for new forms of mass entertainment, such as traveling Wild West shows, vaudeville shows, and spectator sports.

VAUDEVILLE   Growing family incomes and innovations in urban transportation—cable cars, subways, electric streetcars and streetlights—enabled more people to take advantage of urban cultural life. By far the most popular—and most diverse—form of theatrical entertainment in the late nineteenth century was vaudeville. The term derives from a French word for a play accompanied by music. It emerged in the United States in saloons whose owners sought to attract more customers by offering a free show.

Early "variety" shows were held in seedy beer halls and featured comedians, singers, musicians, blackface minstrels, farcical plays, animal acts, jugglers, gymnasts, dancers, mimes, and magicians. Vaudeville houses became popular gathering places for all social classes and types—men, women, and children—all of whom were expected to behave according to middle-class standards of gentility and decorum.

OUTDOOR RECREATION   The congestion and disease associated with city life led many people to participate in forms of outdoor recreation intended to restore their vitality and improve their health. People sought places within the city to escape the tenements and the factories and offices. New York City in the 1850s set up a park commission, which hired Frederick Law Olmsted to design and plan Central Park. Olmsted viewed city parks as much more than recreational centers; he sought to create oases of culture that would promote social stability and cohesion. He was convinced that Central Park would exercise "a distinctly harmonizing and refining influence upon the most unfortunate and lawless classes of the city—an influence favorable to courtesy, self-control, and temperance." Olmsted went on to design parks for Boston, Brooklyn, Chicago, Philadelphia, and San Francisco.

Although originally intended as places where people could walk and commune with nature, parks soon offered more vigorous forms of exercise and recreation. Croquet lawns and tennis courts were among the first additions to city parks because they took up little space and required little maintenance. Because croquet could be played by both sexes, it combined the virtues of sport with the opportunities of courtship. Croquet as a public sport suffered a setback in the 1890s, however, when Boston clergymen lambasted the drinking, gambling, and licentious behavior associated with it.

Even more popular than croquet or tennis was cycling, or "wheeling." In the 1870s bicycles began to be manufactured in the United States, and by the end of the century a bicycle craze had swept the country. Bicycles were especially popular with women who chafed at the restricting conventions of the

Tandem Tricycle

In spite of the danger and discomfort of early bicycles, "wheeling" became a popular form of recreation and mode of transportation.

Victorian era. The new vehicles offered exercise, freedom, and access to the countryside. Female cyclists were able to discard their cumbersome corsets and full dresses in favor of "bloomers" and split skirts.

The urban working poor could not afford to acquire a bicycle or join a croquet club, however. Nor did they have as much free time as the affluent. They toiled long hours six days a week, and at the end of their long days and on Sundays they eagerly sought recreation and fellowship on street corners or on the front stoops of their apartment buildings. Organ grinders and musicians would perform on the sidewalks among the food vendors. Many ethnic groups, especially the Germans and the Irish, formed male singing, drinking, or gymnastic clubs. Working folk also attended bare-knuckle boxing matches or baseball games and on Sundays would gather for picnics. By the end of the century, large-scale amusement parks such as Brooklyn's Coney Island provided entertainment for the entire family. Yet many inner-city youth could not afford the trolley fare, so the crowded streets and dangerous alleys remained their playgrounds.

SALOON CULTURE   The most popular destinations for working-class Americans with free time were saloons and dance halls. The saloon was the poor-man's social club during the late nineteenth century. By 1900 there were more saloons in the United States than there were grocery stores and meat markets. New York City alone had 10,000, or one for every 500 residents. Chicago had one saloon for every 335 people; Houston, one for every 300; San Francisco, one for every 215. Often sponsored by beer brewers and frequented by local politicians, saloons offered a free lunch to encourage patrons to visit and buy 5¢ beer or 15¢ whiskey.

Saloons provided much more than food and drink, however; they were in effect public homes, offering haven and fellowship to people who often worked ten hours a day, six days a week. Saloons were especially popular among male immigrants seeking friends and companionship in a new land. Saloons served as busy social hubs and were often aligned with local political machines. In New York City in the 1880s, most of the primary elections and local political caucuses were conducted in saloons.

Saloons were defiantly male enclaves. Although women and children occasionally entered a saloon—through a side door—in order to carry home a pail of beer (called "rushing the growler") or to drink at a backroom party, the main bar at the front of the saloon was for men only. Some saloons provided "snugs," small separate rooms for female patrons.

Saloons aroused intense criticism. Anti-liquor societies such as the Women's Christian Temperance Union and the Anti-Saloon League charged that saloons contributed to alcoholism, divorce, crime, and absenteeism from work. The reformers demanded that saloons be closed down. Yet drunkenness in saloons was the exception rather than the rule. Most patrons of working-class saloons had little money to waste, and recent studies have revealed that the average amount of money spent on liquor was no more than 5 percent of a man's annual income. Saloons were the primary locus of the workingman's leisure time and political activity. As a journalist observed, "The saloon is, in short, the social and intellectual center of the neighborhood."

WORKINGWOMEN AND LEISURE   In contrast to the male public culture centered in saloons, the leisure activities of working-class women, many of them immigrants, were more limited at the end of the nineteenth century. Married women were so encumbered by housework and maternal responsibilities that they had little free time. Married working-class women could not afford domestic help or sitters for their children, so they tended to combine entertainment with their work and often used the streets as their public space. Washing clothes, supervising children, or shopping at the local market provided opportunities for fellowship with other women.

Single women had more opportunities for leisure and recreation than did working mothers. As the average workday gradually declined from twelve hours in the 1880s to nine or ten hours in 1914, all working people had more free time. In the cities young factory hands, domestic servants, office workers, and retail clerks eagerly sought access to urban pleasures. City amusements enticed women from their congested and drab tenements. Women flocked to dance halls, theaters, amusement parks, and picnic grounds. On hot summer days many working-class folk went to public beaches. For young workingwomen in and around New York City, for example, an excursion to Coney Island was a special treat. Not only could they swim, but they could also experience the sideshow attractions, vaudeville shows, dance pavilions, restaurants, and boardwalk. By 1900 as many as 500,000 people converged on Coney Island on Saturdays and Sundays.

With the advent of movie theaters during the second decade of the twentieth century, the cinema became the most popular form of entertainment for women. As a promotional flyer for a movie theater promised, "If you are tired of life, go to the movies. If you are sick of troubles rife, go to the picture show. You will forget your unpaid bills, rheumatism and other ills, if you stow your pills and go to the picture show." Although some parents and social reformers tried to restrict young single women's freedom to engage in urban recreation and entertainment, many young women followed their own wishes and in so doing helped carve out their own social sphere.

Steeplechase Park, Coney Island, Brooklyn, New York

Members of the working class could afford the inexpensive rides at this popular amusement park.

SPECTATOR SPORTS   In the last quarter of the nineteenth century, new spectator sports such as college football and basketball and professional baseball gained mass popularity, reflecting the growing urbanization of life. People could gather easily for sporting events in the large cities. And news of the games could be conveyed quickly by newspapers and specialized sports magazines that relied upon telegraph reports. Saloons also posted the scores. Athletic rivalries between distant cities were made possible by the network of railroads spanning the continent. Spectator sports became urban extravaganzas, unifying the diverse ethnic groups in the large cities and attracting people with the leisure time and ready cash to spend on watching others perform—or bet on the outcome.

Football emerged as a modified form of soccer and rugby. The College of New Jersey (Princeton) and Rutgers played the first college football game in 1869. Some 200 students and other spectators saw Rutgers win, six to four. By the end of the century, dozens of colleges and high schools had football teams, and some college games attracted more than 50,000 spectators.

Basketball was invented in 1891, when Dr. James Naismith, a physical-education instructor, nailed two peach baskets to the walls of the Young Men's Christian Association training school in Springfield, Massachusetts. Naismith wanted to create an indoor winter game that could be played between the fall football and spring baseball seasons. Basketball quickly grew in popularity among boys and girls. All-female Vassar and Smith Colleges added the sport in 1892. In 1893, Vanderbilt University in Tennessee became the first college to field a men's team.

Baseball laid claim to being America's national pastime at midcentury. Contrary to popular opinion, Abner Doubleday did not invent the game. Instead, Alexander Cartwright, a New York bank clerk and sportsman, is recognized as the father of organized baseball. In 1845 he gathered a group of merchants, stockbrokers, and physicians to form the Knickerbocker Base Ball Club of New York.

The first professional baseball team was the Cincinnati Red Stockings, which made its appearance in 1869. In 1900 the American League was organized, and two years later the first World Series was held. Baseball became the national pastime and the most democratic sport in America. People from all social classes (mostly men) attended the games, and ethnic immigrants were among the most faithful fans. Cheering for a city baseball team gave uprooted people a common loyalty and a sense of belonging. Only white players were allowed in the major leagues, however. African Americans played on "minor-league" teams or in all-black Negro leagues.

By the end of the nineteenth century, sports of all kinds had become a major cultural phenomenon in the United States. A writer for *Harper's Weekly* announced in 1895 that "ball matches, football games, tennis tournaments, bicycle races, [and] regattas, have become part of our national life." They "are watched with eagerness and discussed

Baseball Card, 1887

The excitement of rooting for the home team united all classes.

with enthusiasm and understanding by all manner of people, from the day-laborer to the millionaire."

EDUCATION AND THE PROFESSIONS

THE SPREAD OF PUBLIC EDUCATION   The growth of public education, spurred partly by the determination to "Americanize" immigrant children, helped quicken the emergence of a new urban society after the Civil War. In 1870 there were 7 million pupils in public schools; by 1920 the number had more than tripled. Despite such progress, leaders in education struggled to overcome a pattern of political appointments, corruption, and incompetence in the public schools.

The spread of secondary schools accounted for much of the increased enrollment. In antebellum America private academies had prepared those who intended to enter college. At the beginning of the Civil War, there were only about 100 public high schools in the whole country, but their number grew to about 800 in 1880 and to 6,000 at the turn of the century.

HIGHER EDUCATION   Colleges at this time sought to instill discipline and morality, with a curriculum heavy on mathematics and the classics (and, in church-related schools, theology), along with ethics and rhetoric. History, modern languages and literature, and some science courses were tolerated, although laboratory work was usually limited to a professor's demonstration in class.

The college-student population rose from 52,000 in 1870 to 157,000 in 1890 and 600,000 in 1920. During those years the number of institutions rose from 563 to about 1,000. To accommodate the diverse needs of these growing numbers, colleges moved from rigidly prescribed courses toward an elective system. The new approach allowed students to favor their strong points and colleges to expand their scope. But as Senator Henry Cabot Lodge complained, it also allowed students to "escape without learning anything at all by a judicious selection of unrelated subjects taken up only because they were easy or because the burden imposed by those who taught them was light."

Colleges remained largely male enclaves, but women's access to higher education did improve markedly in the late nineteenth century. Before the Civil War a few colleges had already become coeducational, and state universities in the West were commonly open to women from the start. But colleges in the South and the East fell in line very slowly. Vassar, opened in 1865, was the first women's college to teach by the same standards as the best of the men's colleges. In the 1870s two more excellent women's schools appeared in Massachusetts: Wellesley and Smith, the latter being the first to set the same admission requirements as men's colleges. Thereafter the older women's colleges rushed to upgrade their standards in the same way.

The dominant new trend in American higher education after the Civil War was the rise of the graduate school. Heretofore most professors had a knowledge more broad than deep. With some notable exceptions they engaged in little research, nor were they expected to advance the frontiers of knowledge. Gradually, however, more and more American scholars studied at German universities, where training was more systematic and focused. After the Civil War the German system became the basis for the modern American graduate university. By the 1890s the doctorate degree was fast becoming a requirement to become a professor.

REALISM IN THOUGHT, CULTURE, AND LITERATURE

Much as popular culture was transformed as a result of the urban-industrial revolution, intellectual life adapted to new social realities. Before the Civil War various forms of idealism dominated American thought. Although quite diverse in motive and method, idealists shared a basic conviction that fundamental truths rested in the unseen world of ideas and spirit or in the distant past rather than in the tangible world of fact and contemporary experience. The most prominent writers, artists, and philosophers were more concerned with Romantic or biblical themes than with common aspects of "real" life.

At midcentury and after, however, a more realistic sensibility began to challenge this idealistic tradition. This realistic movement matured into a full-fledged cultural force during the second half of the nineteenth century. More and more thinkers, writers, and artists focused on the emerging realities of scientific research and technology, factories and railroads, cities and immigrants, wage labor and social tensions.

The rise of realism resulted from a transformed social, intellectual, and moral landscape. The horrors of the Civil War led many people to adopt a more realistic outlook, as did the growing influence of a modern scientific belief that empirical evidence constituted the only admissible basis for knowledge.

The prestige of empirical science increased enormously during the second half of the nineteenth century as researchers explored electromagnetic induction, the conservation of matter, the laws of thermodynamics, and the relationship between heat and energy. Breakthroughs in chemistry led to new understandings of the formation of compounds and the nature of reactions. Discoveries of fossils opened up new horizons in geology and paleontology, and greatly improved microscopes enabled zoologists to decipher cell structures.

DARWINISM AND SOCIAL DARWINISM   Every field of thought in the post–Civil War years felt the impact of Charles Darwin's *On the Origin of Species* (1859). In that seminal work Darwin argued that existing species, including humanity itself, had evolved through a long process of "natural selection" from less complex forms of life: those species that adapted to survival by reason of quickness, shrewdness, or other advantages reproduced their kind, while others died away. This idea of evolution shocked people who held conventional religious views in that it contradicted a literal interpretation of the creation stories in the biblical Book of Genesis. Heated arguments arose between scientists and clergymen. Some of the faithful rejected Darwin's doctrine while others found their faith severely shaken. Many people, however, eventually came to reconcile science and religion, viewing evolution as a natural process created by God.

The temptation to apply evolutionary theory to the social (human) world proved irresistible. Darwin's fellow Englishman Herbert Spencer became the first major prophet of what came to be called social Darwinism, and he exerted an important influence on American thought. Spencer argued that human society and institutions, like plant and animal species, passed through the process of natural selection, which resulted in what he called the "survival of the fittest."

If, as Spencer believed, society naturally evolved for the better, then individual freedom was inviolable, and any government interference with the competitive process of social evolution was a serious mistake. Social Darwinism thus endorsed a hands-off government policy, then known as laissez-faire; it decried the government regulation of business, the proposals for a graduated income tax, sanitation and housing regulations, and even protection of consumers against medical quacks. Such initiatives, no matter how well intended, would only help the "unfit" survive and thereby impede progress. The only acceptable charity for social Darwinists was voluntary, and even that was of dubious value. Spencer warned that "fostering the good-for-nothing at the expense of the good, is an extreme cruelty."

For Spencer and his many supporters, successful businessmen and corporations were the engines of social progress. If small businesses were crowded out by trusts and monopolies, that, too, was part of the evolutionary process.

Corporate titan John D. Rockefeller told his Baptist Sunday-school class that the "growth of a large business is merely a survival of the fittest."

REFORM DARWINISM   Herbert Spencer's use of Darwin to promote "rugged individualism" did not go without challenge. Reform found its major philosopher in an obscure civil servant, Lester Frank Ward, who fought his way up from poverty and never lost his empathy for the underdog. Ward's book *Dynamic Sociology* (1883) singled out one product of evolution that Spencer and others had neglected: the human brain. Humans, unlike animals, had a mind that could plan for and shape the future. Far from being the helpless pawn of powerful evolutionary forces, Ward argued, humanity could actively shape the process of societal improvement. The competition extolled by Spencer and other social Darwinists was in fact highly wasteful, as was the natural competitive process: plant or cattle breeding, for instance, could actually improve on the results of natural selection.

Ward's so-called reform Darwinism held that cooperation, not competition, would better promote progress. Government could become the agency of progress by striving to ameliorate poverty, which impeded the development of the mind, and to promote the education of the masses. "Intelligence, far more than necessity," Ward wrote, "is the mother of invention," and "the influence of knowledge as a social factor, like that of wealth, is proportional to the extent of its distribution." Intellect, rightly informed by science, could plan successfully. In the benevolent "sociocracy" of the future, Ward argued, legislatures would function mainly to sanction decisions worked out in the sociological laboratory.

PRAGMATISM   Around the turn of the century, the concept of evolutionary human and social development found expression in a philosophical principle set forth in mature form by Harvard professor William James in his book *Pragmatism: A New Name for Some Old Ways of Thinking* (1907). James shared Lester Frank Ward's concern with the role of ideas in the process of evolution. Pragmatists, said James, believed that ideas gain their validity not from their inherent truth but from their social consequences and practical applications. Thus, scientists could test the validity of their ideas in the laboratory and judge their import by their applications. Pragmatism reflected a quality often looked upon as genuinely American: the inventive, experimental spirit, which recognized that science—and society—are characterized by change rather than fixity.

John Dewey, who would become the chief philosopher of pragmatism after James, preferred the term *instrumentalism*, by which he meant that ideas were instruments for action, especially for promoting social reform. Dewey, unlike James, threw himself into movements for the rights of labor and women, the promotion of peace, and the reform of education. He believed that education was the process through which society would gradually progress toward greater social equality and harmony.

REALISM IN FICTION AND NONFICTION

Literature also felt the impact of new scientific ideas and the modern urban scene. A rebellious group of young writers discarded the Romanticism and sentimentalism of antebellum culture in favor of fiction and poetry that depicted contemporary reality without moralizing.

CLEMENS   Samuel Langhorne Clemens (Mark Twain) was a transitional figure between Romanticism and Realism. A native of Missouri, he was impelled to work at age twelve, becoming first a printer and then a Mississippi riverboat pilot. When the Civil War shut down the river traffic, he briefly joined a Confederate militia company, then left with his brother for Nevada, where he wrote for a local newspaper. He moved on to California in 1864 and first gained widespread notice with his tall tale of the gold country, "The Celebrated Jumping Frog of Calaveras County" (1865). With the success of *Roughing It* (1872), an account of his western years, he moved to Hartford, Connecticut, and was able to set himself up as a full-time author and hilarious lecturer.

Clemens was the first significant writer born and raised west of the Appalachian Mountains. His early writings accentuated his western background, but for his greatest books he drew heavily upon his boyhood in the border slave state of Missouri and the tall-tale tradition of southwestern humor. In *The Adventures of Tom Sawyer* (1876), he evoked the prewar Hannibal, Missouri, where his own boyhood was cut so short. Clemens's masterpiece, *The Adventures of Huckleberry Finn* (1884), created unforgettable characters in Huck Finn, his shiftless father, the runaway slave Jim, the Widow Douglas, "the King," and "the Duke." Huck Finn embodied the instinct of every red-blooded boy to "light out for the territory" whenever polite society set out to civilize him. Huck's effort to help his friend Jim escape bondage expressed well the moral dilemmas imposed by slavery on everyone.

LITERARY NATURALISM   Realism grew into a powerful literary movement during the 1880s, but during the 1890s it took on a new character in the writings of the so-called naturalists. This group of young literary rebels imported scientific determinism into literature, viewing people as prey to natural forces and internal drives without control or full understanding of them. Frank Norris thus pictured in *McTeague* (1899) the descent into madness of a San Francisco dentist and his wife, driven by greed, violence, and lust. Stephen Crane in *Maggie: A Girl of the Streets* (1893) and *The Red Badge of Courage* (1895) portrayed people caught up in environments that were beyond their control. *Maggie* depicts a tenement girl driven to prostitution and death amid scenes so grim and sordid that Crane had to finance the book's publication himself. *The Red Badge of Courage,* his masterpiece, evokes fear, nobility, and courage amid the carnage of the Civil War.

Two naturalists, Jack London and Theodore Dreiser, achieved a degree of popular success. London was both a professed socialist and a believer in the German philosopher Friedrich Nietzsche's doctrine of the superman. In adventure stories such as *The Call of the Wild* (1903) and *The Sea Wolf* (1904), London celebrated the triumph of brute force and the will to survive.

Theodore Dreiser did not celebrate the overwhelming power of social and biological forces; he dissected them for the reader. The result was powerfully disturbing to readers accustomed to more genteel fare. Dreiser shocked the public probably more than the others with protagonists who sinned without remorse and without punishment. *Sister Carrie* (1900), for example, shows Carrie Meeber surviving illicit loves and going on to success on the stage.

SOCIAL CRITICISM   Behind their dogma of determinism, several of the naturalists harbored intense outrage at human misery and social injustice. Their indignation was shared by an increasing number of journalists and social critics who addressed themselves more directly to protest and reform. One of the most influential of these reformers was Henry George, a journalist who vowed to seek out the cause of poverty in the midst of the industrial progress he saw around him. The basic social problem, George reasoned, was the "unearned increment" in wealth that came to those who owned land. He published the fruit of his thought in *Progress and Poverty* (1879), a thick, rambling, and difficult book whose earnest moralism and sympathetic tone helped it sell 2 million copies in several languages.

George held that everyone had a basic right to the use of the land, since it was provided by nature to all. Nobody had a right to the increasing value that accrued from it, however, since that was created by the community, not by its owner. He proposed simply to tax the "unearned" increment in the value of the land, or the rent. George's "single-tax" idea generated much discussion, but his influence centered on the paradox he posed in his title, *Progress and Poverty,* and his plea for social cooperation and equality.

Another social critic, Thorstein Veblen, brought to his work a background of formal training in economics and the purpose of making that subject into an evolutionary or historical science. In his best-known work, *The Theory of the Leisure Class* (1899), he examined the pecuniary values of the affluent and introduced phrases that have since become commonplace in our language: *conspicuous consumption* and *conspicuous leisure.* With the advent of industrial society, Veblen argued, the showy display of money and property became the conventional basis of social status. For the upper classes, moreover, it became necessary to spend time nonproductively as evidence of the ability to afford a life of leisure.

THE SOCIAL GOSPEL

While novelists, journalists, and commentators were writing about the rising social tensions and injustices of late-nineteenth-century America, more and more people were addressing these problems through social action. Some reformers focused on legislative solutions to social problems; others stressed philanthropy or organized charity. A few militants promoted socialism or anarchism. Whatever the method or approach, however, social reformers were on the march at the turn of the century, and their activities gave American life a new urgency and energy.

THE RISE OF THE INSTITUTIONAL CHURCH Churches responded slowly to the mounting social concerns, for American Protestantism had become one of the main props of the established order. The Reverend Henry Ward Beecher, for instance, pastor of the fashionable Plymouth Congregational Church in Brooklyn, preached material success, social Darwinism, and the unworthiness of the poor.

As the middle classes moved out to the streetcar suburbs, their churches followed. From 1868 to 1888, for instance, seventeen Protestant churches abandoned the area south of Fourteenth Street in Manhattan. In the center of Chicago, 60,000 residents had no church, Protestant or Catholic. Where churches became prosperous, they fell under the spell of complacent respectability and do-nothing social Darwinism. Some prominent clergymen expressed open disdain for the lower classes. Not surprisingly, more and more working-class people felt out of place in churches where affluence was both worshipped and flaunted.

A Salvation Army Group

In Flint, Michigan, 1894.

Gradually, however, some religious leaders realized that Protestantism was in danger of losing its working-class constituency unless it reached out to the urban poor. Two organizations were created expressly for that purpose. The Young Men's Christian Association (YMCA) entered the United States from England in the 1850s and grew rapidly after 1870; the Salvation Army, founded in London in 1878, entered the United States a year later. Individual urban churches also began to develop institutional features that were more social than strictly religious in function. Church leaders acquired gymnasiums, libraries, lecture rooms, and other facilities in an effort to attract working-class people back to organized religion.

RELIGIOUS REFORMERS   Church reformers who feared that Christianity was becoming irrelevant to the needs and aspirations of the working poor began preaching what came to be called the social gospel. Washington Gladden of Columbus, Ohio, professed the social gospel from the pulpit of a middle-class Congregational church. The new gospel in fact expressed the social conscience of the middle class. Gladden maintained that true Christianity resided not in rituals, dogmas, or even the mystical experience of God, but in the principle that "thou shalt love thy neighbor as thyself." Christian law should therefore govern the workplace, with laborer and employer united in serving each other's interests. The "law of greed and strife," he insisted, "is not a natural law; it is unnatural; it is a crime against nature; the law of brotherhood is the only natural law." In attacking the premises of social Darwinism, Gladden thus argued for labor's right to organize, supported maximum-hours laws and factory inspections, and endorsed anti-trust legislation.

EARLY EFFORTS AT URBAN REFORM

THE SETTLEMENT-HOUSE MOVEMENT   While preachers of the social gospel dispensed inspiration, other dedicated reformers attacked the problems of the slums from community centers called settlement houses. By 1900 perhaps 100 settlement houses existed in America, some of the best known being Jane Addams and Ellen Starr's Hull-House in Chicago and Lillian Wald's Henry Street Settlement in New York City.

The settlement houses were staffed mainly by idealistic middle-class young people, a majority of them college-trained women who had few other outlets for meaningful work. Settlement workers sought to broaden the horizons and improve the lives of slum dwellers in diverse ways. At Hull-House, for instance, staff members recruited the neighborhood children into clubs and kindergartens and set up a nursery for the infant children of working mothers. Settlement houses were also meant to provide workingmen with an alternative to the saloon as a place of recreation and an alternative to the neighborhood political boss as a source of social services. Their programs gradually expanded to include health clinics, lectures, music and art studios, employment bureaus, men's clubs, gymnasiums, and savings banks.

Jane Addams

One of the heroic leaders of the settlement house movement.

Settlement-house leaders realized, however, that the spreading slums made their work as effective as bailing out the ocean with a teaspoon. They therefore organized political support for tenement laws, public playgrounds, juvenile courts, mothers' pensions, workers' compensation laws, and legislation prohibiting child labor.

WOMEN'S SUFFRAGE   Settlement-house workers, insofar as they were paid, made up but a fraction of all gainfully employed women. With rapid population growth in the late nineteenth century, the number of employed women steadily increased, as did the percentage of women in the labor force. These changes in occupational status had little connection with the women's rights movement, however, which increasingly focused on the issue of suffrage. Immediately after the Civil War, Susan B. Anthony, a seasoned veteran of the movement, demanded that the Fifteenth Amendment guarantee the vote for women as well as black men. But she made little impression on those who insisted that women belonged solely in the home.

In 1869 the unity of the women's movement disintegrated in a manner reminiscent of the anti-slavery rift three decades before. The question once again was whether the movement should concentrate on one overriding issue or broaden its focus. Susan B. Anthony and Elizabeth Cady Stanton founded the National Woman Suffrage Association to promote a women's suffrage amendment to the Constitution, but they looked upon suffrage as but one among many feminist causes to be promoted. Later that same year, Lucy Stone, Julia Ward Howe, and other leaders formed the American Woman Suffrage Association, which focused single-mindedly on the vote as the first and most basic reform.

In 1890, after three years of negotiation, the rival groups united as the National American Woman Suffrage Association, with Elizabeth Cady Stanton as president for two years, followed by Susan B. Anthony until 1900. The work thereafter was carried on by a new generation of activists led by Anna Howard Shaw and Carrie Chapman Catt. Over the years the movement achieved some local and partial victories as a few states granted women suffrage in school-board or municipal elections. In 1869 the territory of Wyoming provided full suffrage to women and after 1890 retained women's suffrage when it became a state. Three other western states soon followed suit, but not until New York acted in 1917 did a state east of the Mississippi River adopt universal suffrage.

Despite the focus on the vote, women did not confine their public activism to that issue. In 1866 the Young Women's Christian Association, a parallel to the YMCA, appeared in Boston and spread elsewhere. The New England Women's Club, started in 1868 by Julia Ward Howe and others, was an early example of the women's clubs that proliferated to the extent that a General Federation of Women's Clubs tied them together nationally in 1890. Many women's clubs confined themselves to "literary" and social activities, but others became deeply involved in charities and reform. The New York Consumers' League, formed in 1890, and the National Consumers' League,

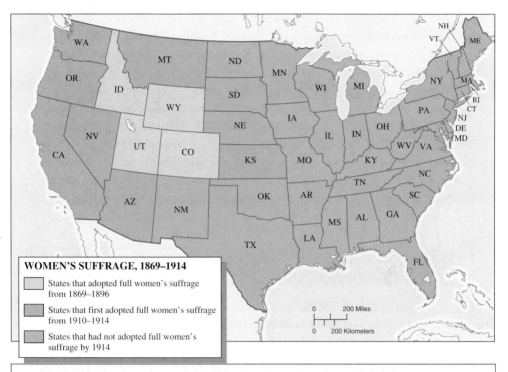

WOMEN'S SUFFRAGE, 1869–1914

States that adopted full women's suffrage from 1869–1896

States that first adopted full women's suffrage from 1910–1914

States that had not adopted full women's suffrage by 1914

0   200 Miles

0   200 Kilometers

Which states first gave women the right to vote? Why did it take fifty-one years, from Wyoming's grant of full suffrage to women until Congress's ratification of the Nineteenth Amendment, for women to receive the right to vote? How was suffrage part of a larger women's reform movement?

established nine years later, sought to make the buying public, chiefly women, more aware of degrading labor conditions.

TOWARD A WELFARE STATE   Even without the support of voting women in most places, the states adopted rudimentary measures to regulate big business and labor conditions in the public interest. They passed laws to regulate railroads and working conditions, but the laws were generally poorly enforced or overturned by the courts. In the meantime, it was often the local political machines that stepped in to help those who were suffering. While local and federal governments lacked a bureaucracy to assist those who had fallen on hard times, the political machines in the cities supplied temporary jobs, food, or other necessities. The machines, then, were the precursor to the modern welfare state.

At the end of the nineteenth century, opinion in the country stood poised between conservative rigidities and a growing sense that new conditions imposed new personal and government responsibilities. The last two decades of the nineteenth century had already seen a slow erosion of free-market values, which had found their most secure home in the courts. There emerged instead a concept of the general-welfare state, which called upon the government to act on behalf of the whole society rather than allow rugged individualism to run rampant. The conflict between government intervention and laissez-faire values spilled over into the new century, but by the mid–twentieth century, after the Progressive movement and the New Deal, the nation would be firmly committed to the premises of the general-welfare state.

MAKING CONNECTIONS

- As the next chapter shows, the presidential election of 1896 was in many ways a contest between the new urban values discussed in this chapter and those of a more traditional rural society.

- The reform impulse discussed in this chapter finds voice again in the discussion of the Progressive movement in Chapter 24.

- The nativist thinking discussed in this chapter fueled the restrictive immigration laws of the 1920s, discussed in Chapter 26.

FURTHER READING

For a survey of urbanization, see David, R. Goldfield's *Urban America: A History*, 2nd ed. (1989) Gunther Barth discusses the emergence of a new urban culture in *City People: The Rise of Modern City Culture in Nineteenth-Century America* (1980). John Bodnar offers a synthesis of the urban immigrant experience in *The Transplanted: A History of Immigrants in Urban America* (1985). See also Roger Daniels's *Guarding the Golden Door: American Immigration Policy and Immigrants since 1882* (2004). Walter Nugent's *Crossings: The Great Transatlantic Migrations, 1870–1914* (1992) provides a wealth of demographic information and insight.

On urban environments and sanitary reforms, see Martin v. Melosi's *The Sanitary City: Urban Infrastructure in America from Colonial Times to the Present* (2000), Joel A. Tarr's *The Search for the Ultimate Sink: Urban Pollution in Historical Perspective* (1996), and Suellen Hoy's *Chasing Dirt: The American Pursuit of Cleanliness* (1995).

For the growth of urban leisure and sports, see Roy Rosenzweig's *Eight Hours for What We Will: Workers and Leisure in an Industrial City, 1870–1920* (1983) and Steven A. Riess's *City Games: The Evolution of American Urban Society and the Rise of Sports* (1989). Saloon culture is examined in Medelon Powers's *Faces along the Bar: Lore and Order in the Workingman's Saloon, 1870–1920* (1998).

Richard Hofstadter's *Social Darwinism in American Thought,* rev. ed. (1969) and Cynthia Eagle Russett's *Darwin in America: The Intellectual Response, 1865–1912* (1976) examine the impact of evolutionary theory on thought and culture. On the rise of realism in thought and the arts during the second half of the nineteenth century, see David E. Shi's *Facing Facts: Realism in American Thought and Culture, 1850–1920* (1995).

Eleanor Flexner and Ellen Fitzpatrick's *Century of Struggle: The Woman's Rights Movement in the United States* (1996) surveys the condition of women in the late nineteenth century. The best study of the settlement-house movement is Jean Bethke Elshtain's *Jane Addams and the Dream of American Democracy: A Life* (2002).

22

GILDED AGE POLITICS AND AGRARIAN REVOLT

FOCUS QUESTIONS

- What were the political developments of the Gilded Age?
- What problems, real and perceived, affected farmers of the era?
- What factors precipitated the agrarian revolt and the rise of the Populists?
- What was significant about the election of 1896?

To answer these questions and access additional review material, please visit www.wwnorton.com/studyspace.

In 1873 the writers Mark Twain and Charles Dudley Warner created an enduring label for the post-Civil War era when they collaborated on a novel titled *The Gilded Age.* The book depicts an age of widespread political corruption, personal greed, and social vulgarity. Perspectives on the times would eventually change, but generations of political scientists and historians have since reinforced the two novelists' judgment. As a young college graduate in 1879, Woodrow Wilson described the state of the post-Civil War political system: "No leaders, no principles; no principles, no parties."

PARADOXICAL POLITICS

Throughout the last third of the nineteenth century, political inertia reigned at the national level. A close balance between Republicans and Democrats in Congress created a sense of stalemate. Neither party was willing to embrace controversial issues or take bold initiatives because neither had a commanding advantage with the electorate. Timidity prevailed. The Gilded Age has long been viewed as a time of political mediocrity, in which the parties refused to confront "real issues" such as the runaway growth of an unregulated economy and its attendant social injustices.

Voters of the time nonetheless thought politics was very important. Voter turnout during the Gilded Age was commonly about 70 to 80 percent, even in the South, where the disenfranchisement of African Americans was not yet complete. (By contrast, the turnout for the 2004 presidential election was 56 percent.) The paradox of such a high rate of voter participation in the face of the inertia at the national political level raises an obvious question: How was it that leaders who failed to address the "real issues" of the day presided over the most highly organized and politically active electorate in U.S. history?

The answer is partly that the politicians and the voters believed that they *were* dealing with crucial issues: tariff rates, the initial efforts to regulate corporations, monetary policy, Indian disputes, civil service reform, and immigration. But the answer also reflects the extreme partisanship of the times and the essentially local nature of political culture during the Gilded Age.

PARTISAN POLITICS   Most Americans after the Civil War were intensely loyal to the Democratic or Republican party. Political parties gave people an anchor for their activity and loyalty in an unstable world. Local party officials took care of those who voted their way and distributed appointive public offices and other favors to party loyalists. These "city machines" used patronage and favoritism to retain the loyalty of business supporters while providing jobs, food, or fuel to working-class voters who had fallen on hard times. The party faithful eagerly took part in rallies and picnics, deriving a sense of camaraderie as well as an opportunity for recreation that offered a welcome relief from their usual workday routine.

Party loyalties and voter turnout in the late nineteenth century reflected religious and ethnic divisions as well as geographic differences. The Republican party attracted mainly Protestants of British descent. Their base was New England, and their other strongholds were New York and the upper Midwest, both of which were populated with Yankee stock. The Republicans, the party of Abraham Lincoln, could rely upon the votes of African Americans and Union veterans of the Civil War.

The Democrats, by contrast, tended to be a heterogeneous, often unruly coalition embracing southern whites, immigrants and Catholics of any origin, Jews, freethinkers, skeptics, and all those repelled by the "party of morality." As one Chicago Democrat explained, "A Republican is a man who wants you t' go t' church every Sunday. A Democrat says if a man wants to have a glass of beer on Sunday he can have it."

Republicans pressed nativist causes, calling for restrictions on both immigration and the employment of foreigners and greater emphasis on the teaching of the "American" language in the schools. Prohibitionism revived along with nativism in the 1880s. Among the immigrants who crowded into the growing cities were many Irish, Germans, and Italians who enjoyed alcoholic beverages. Republicans increasingly saw saloons as the central social evil around which all others revolved, including vice, crime, political corruption, and neglect of families, and they associated these problems with the ethnic groups that frequented saloons.

POLITICAL STALEMATE AT THE NATIONAL LEVEL   Between 1869 and 1913, from the presidency of Ulysses S. Grant through that of William Howard Taft, Republicans monopolized the White House except for the two nonconsecutive terms of Democrat Grover Cleveland, but Republican domination was more apparent than real. Between 1872 and 1896 no president won a majority of the popular vote. In each of those presidential elections, sixteen states invariably voted Republican and fourteen voted Democratic, leaving a pivotal six states whose results might change. The important swing-vote role played by two of those states, New York and Ohio, helps explain the election of eight presidents from those states from 1872 to 1912.

Lackluster presidents also contributed to the political stalemate. No chief executive between Abraham Lincoln and Theodore Roosevelt could be described as a "strong" president. None challenged the prevailing view that Congress, not the White House, should formulate policy. Senator John Sherman of Ohio expressed the widely held notion that the legislative branch should take initiative in a republic: "The President should merely obey and enforce the law."

Republicans controlled the Senate and Democrats controlled the House during the Gilded Age. Only during 1881–1883 and 1889–1891 did a Republican president coincide with a Republican Congress, and only between 1893 and 1895 did a Democratic president enjoy a Democratic majority in Congress.

The counterbalancing strength of the parties in Congress and the fear in each party of alienating key factions deterred any vigorous initiatives in Congress. Because most bills required bipartisan support to pass both houses and because legislators tended to vote along party lines, the Democrats and the Republicans pursued a policy of evasion on the national issues of the day. Only the tariff provoked clear-cut divisions between protectionist

Republicans and low-tariff Democrats, but there were individual exceptions even on that. On the important questions of the money supply, regulation of big business, farm problems, civil service reform, and immigration, the parties differed very little. As a result, they primarily became vehicles for seeking office and dispensing patronage in the form of government jobs and contracts.

STATE AND LOCAL INITIATIVES   Unlike today, Americans during the Gilded Age expected little direct support from the federal government; most significant political activity occurred at the state and local levels. Residents of the western territories were largely forced to fend for themselves rather than rely upon federal authorities. They formed towns, practiced vigilante justice, and made laws on their own. Once incorporated into the Union, the former territories retained much of their autonomy.

Thus state governments after the Civil War were the primary centers of political activity and innovation. Over 60 percent of the nation's spending and taxing were exercised by state and local authorities. Then, unlike today, the large cities spent far more on local services than did the federal government. And three fourths of all public employees worked for state and local governments. Local issues such as prohibition, Sunday closing laws, and parochial-school funding often generated more excitement than complex debates over tariffs and monetary policies. It was the state and local governments that first sought to curb the power and restrain the abuses of corporate interests.

CORRUPTION AND REFORM

During the Gilded Age, states attempted to regulate big business; most of those efforts were overturned by the courts, however. A close alliance developed between business owners and political leaders. Railroad passes, free entertainment, and a host of other favors were freely provided to politicians, newspaper editors, and other leaders in positions to influence public opinion or affect legislation.

On the local level the exchange of favors for votes was not perceived as improper either. People voted for their party out of intense partisan loyalty. Although they looked to their parties to supply them with favors and even jobs, they did not see themselves as "selling their vote." This was simply the age-old practice of patronage democracy, in which local officials awarded party loyalists with contracts and public jobs, such as heading custom houses and post offices.

The Bosses of the Senate

This 1875 cartoon bitingly portrays the period's alliance between big business and politics.

Both Republican and Democratic leaders squabbled over the "spoils" of office, the appointive offices at the local and national levels. After each election it was expected that the victorious party would throw out the defeated party's appointees and appoint their own men to office. Each party had its share of corrupt officials willing to buy and sell government appointments or congressional votes, yet each also witnessed the emergence of factions promoting honesty in government. The struggle for cleaner government soon became one of the foremost issues of the day.

HAYES AND CIVIL SERVICE REFORM   In the aftermath of Reconstruction, President Rutherford B. Hayes admirably embodied the "party of morality." Hayes brought to the White House in 1877 a new style of uprightness, in sharp contrast to the corruption of the Grant administration. The son of an Ohio farmer, Hayes was wounded four times in the Civil War and was promoted to the rank of major general. Elected governor of Ohio in 1867, he served three terms. Honest and respectable, competent and dignified, he lived in a modest style with his wife, who was nicknamed Lemonade Lucy because of her refusal to serve alcohol at White House functions.

Yet Hayes's presidency suffered from the supposedly secret deal that awarded him victory over the Democrat Samuel Tilden in the 1876 election. Snide references to Hayes as "His Fraudulence" denied him any chance at a second term, which he renounced from the beginning. Hayes's Republican party was split between so-called Stalwarts and Half-Breeds, led respectively by senators Roscoe Conkling of New York and James G. Blaine of Maine. The difference between these Republican factions was even murkier than that between the parties. The Stalwarts had been stalwart in their support of President Grant during the furor over the misbehavior of his cabinet members. They also promoted Radical Reconstruction of the South and the "spoils system" of distributing federal political jobs to party loyalists. The Half-Breeds acquired their name because they were only half loyal to Grant and half committed to reform of the spoils system.

Hayes aligned himself with the growing public discontent over the corruption that had undermined the Grant administration. In promoting civil service reform, he issued an executive order in 1877 declaring that those already in office (for the most part Grant's appointees) would be dismissed only for the good of the government and not for political reasons. His cabinet tried to carry out the new policy. Secretary of the Treasury John Sherman revealed that both New York customs collector Chester A. Arthur and naval officer Alonzo Cornell were guilty of "laxity" and of using the customhouse to reward political favors on behalf of Conkling's organization. Hayes removed Arthur and Cornell and thereby won Conkling's lasting hatred.

For all of Hayes's efforts to clean house, he retained a limited vision of government's role in society. On the economic issues of the day, he held to a conservative line that would guide his successors for the rest of the century. His solution to labor troubles, demonstrated during the Great Railroad Strike of 1877, was to send in federal troops and break the strike. His answer to the demands of farmers and debtors that he expand the currency was to veto the Bland-Allison Act, which provided for a limited expansion of silver currency through the government's purchase of $2 million to $4 million in silver coins per month. (The bill was passed when Congress overrode Hayes's veto.)

GARFIELD AND ARTHUR   With Hayes out of the running for a second term, the Republicans were forced to look elsewhere in 1880. The Stalwarts, led by Conkling, brought Ulysses S. Grant forward for a third time, still a strong contender despite the tarnish of his administration's scandals. For two days the Republican Convention in Chicago was deadlocked, with Grant holding a slight lead over James G. Blaine and John Sherman. When

Wisconsin's delegates suddenly switched their votes to former House Speaker (now Senator-elect) James A. Garfield, the convention stampeded to the dark-horse candidate. As a sop to the Stalwarts, the convention tapped Chester A. Arthur, of customhouse notoriety, for vice president.

The Democrats named Winfield Scott Hancock, a Union general during the Civil War, to counterbalance the Republicans' "bloody-shirt" attacks on their party as the vehicle of secession. In the close election, Garfield eked out a plurality of only 39,000 votes, or 48.5 percent of the vote, but with a comfortable margin of 214 to 155 in the Electoral College.

On July 2, 1881, after only four months in office, President Garfield was walking through the Washington, D.C., railroad station when a deranged man, Charles Guiteau, shot him in the back. "I am a Stalwart," Guiteau shouted to the arresting officers. "Arthur is now President of the United States." Two months later, Garfield died of complications resulting from the shooting.

Chester Arthur, one of the chief henchmen of Stalwart leader Roscoe Conkling, was now president. Little in his past suggested that he would rise above spoils politics. But Arthur, a wealthy, handsome widower who loved fine wines and sported a lavish wardrobe and billowing sideburns, demonstrated surprising leadership qualities as president. He distanced himself from Conkling and the Stalwarts and established a genuine independence. As Arthur noted, "For the vice-presidency I was indebted to Mr. Conkling, but for the presidency of the United States my debt is to the Almighty."

Most startling of all was Arthur's emergence as something of a civil service and tariff reformer, despite the Stalwarts' expectations that he would oppose such changes. The assassin Guiteau had unwittingly galvanized public support of political reform. A civil service reform bill sponsored by "Gentleman George" Pendleton, a Democratic senator from Ohio, passed in 1883, setting up a three-member federal Civil Service Commission independent of the cabinet departments, the first such agency established on a permanent basis. About 14 percent of all government jobs would now be filled on the basis of competitive examinations rather than political connections. What was more, the president could enlarge the class of jobs based on merit at his discretion, as many presidents later did.

Meanwhile, the tariff continued to be the most controversial national political issue. The high tariff, a heritage of the Civil War, had by the early 1880s raised federal revenues to a point where the government was enjoying a surplus that drew money into the Treasury and out of circulation, thus impeding economic growth. Some argued that lower tariff rates would reduce consumer prices by enabling foreign competition, and at the same time leave more money in circulation. In 1882 Arthur named a special tariff commission, which recommended a 20 to 25 percent rate reduction, but Congress's effort to enact the proposal was marred by logrolling (the trading of votes to benefit different legislators' local interests). The result was the "mongrel tariff" of 1883, so called because of its different rates for different commodities. Overall the new tariff provided for a slight rate reduction, but it also raised the duty on some articles.

THE SCURRILOUS CAMPAIGN   As the 1884 presidential election neared, Chester Arthur's record as an unexpected reformer might have commended him to the voters, but it did not please the leaders of his party. The Republicans dumped Arthur and turned to the majestic senator James G. Blaine of Maine, leader of the Half-Breeds. Blaine was the consummate politician. He never forgot a name or a face, he inspired the party faithful with his oratory, and at the same time he knew how to wheel and deal in the back rooms.

During the campaign, however, letters surfaced that linked Blaine to efforts to exchange his influence for selfish gain. For the reform element of the Republican party, this was too much, and many bolted the ticket. Party regulars scorned the idealists as goo-goos—the good-government crowd who ignored partisan realities—and one newspaper editor jokingly tagged them mugwumps, after an Algonquian word for a self-important chieftain. To the party regulars, in what soon became a stale joke, mugwumps were unreliable Republicans who had their mugs on one side of the fence and their "wumps" on the other.

The rise of the mugwumps influenced the Democrats to nominate the New Yorker Stephen Grover Cleveland as a reform candidate. Elected mayor of Buffalo in 1881, Cleveland first attracted national attention for battling corruption in that city. In 1882 he was elected governor of New York, and he continued to build a reform record by fighting New York City's corrupt Tammany Hall organization. As mayor and as governor, he repeatedly vetoed what he considered special-privilege bills serving selfish interests. Cleveland possessed little charisma but impressed the public with his stubborn integrity. He was a crusader against corruption, and as such he drew many of those making up the growing chorus of political reformers.

Senator James G. Blaine of Maine

The Republican candidate in 1884.

But a scandal erupted when the *Buffalo Evening Telegraph* revealed that as a bachelor Cleveland had had an affair with an attractive Buffalo widow, Maria Halpin. Mrs. Halpin had named Cleveland as the father of a boy born to her in 1874. Cleveland had responded by providing financial support when the child was placed in an orphanage. The respective personal escapades of Blaine and Cleveland provided the 1884 campaign with some of the most colorful battle cries in political history: "Blaine, Blaine, James G. Blaine, the continental liar from the state of Maine," Democrats chanted; Republicans countered with "Ma, ma, where's my pa? Gone to the White House, ha, ha, ha!"

Near the end of the mudslinging campaign, Blaine and his supporters committed two fateful blunders. The first occurred at New York's fashionable Delmonico's restaurant, where Blaine attended a lavish fund-raising dinner with a clutch of millionaire bigwigs. Cartoons and accounts of this "Belshazzar's feast" festooned the opposition press for days.

The second fiasco occurred when a Protestant minister visiting the Republican headquarters in New York City insolently referred to the Democrats as the party of "rum, Romanism, and rebellion." Blaine let pass the implied insult to Irish Catholics—a fatal oversight, since he had always cultivated Irish-American support with his anti-British talk and public reminders that his mother was Catholic. Democrats spread the word that Blaine was anti-Irish and anti-Catholic. The two incidents may have tipped the election. The electoral vote, in Cleveland's favor, stood at 219 to 182, although the popular vote ran far closer: Cleveland's plurality nationwide was fewer than 30,000 votes.

CLEVELAND AND THE SPECIAL INTERESTS   For all of Cleveland's hostility to the spoils system and politics as usual, he represented no sharp break with the conservative public policies of his Republican predecessors, except in opposing government favors to business. He held to a strictly limited view of government's role in both economic and social matters, a rigid philosophy illustrated by his 1887 veto of a bill to aid drought-stricken farmers. Back to Congress it went with a lecture on the need to limit the powers and functions of government. "Though the people support the government, the government should not support the people," Cleveland asserted.

Despite his strong convictions, Cleveland had a mixed record on civil service. He harbored good intentions, but as the first Democratic president since James Buchanan's term from 1856 to 1860, he also led a party hungry for partisan appointments. Before his inauguration he repeated his support for the Pendleton Civil Service Reform Act: he pledged not to remove able government workers simply on partisan grounds. Yet party pressures gradually forced Cleveland's hand. When he left office, about two thirds of federal officeholders were Democrats, but he had almost doubled the number of jobs subject to civil service regulation. Cleveland thereby satisfied neither mugwumps nor spoilsmen; indeed, he managed to antagonize both.

Cleveland also incurred the wrath of many Union war veterans by his firm stand against expanded pensions. Congress had passed the first Civil War pension law in 1862 to provide for Union veterans disabled in service and for the widows, orphans, and dependents of veterans. By 1882 the Grand Army of the Republic, an organization of Union veterans and a powerful pressure group, was trying to get pensions paid for any disability, no matter how it was incurred. Meanwhile, many veterans succeeded in getting legislators to pass private pension bills. Insofar as time permitted, Cleveland examined the bills critically and vetoed the dubious ones. Although he signed more pension bills than any of his predecessors, he also vetoed more. The issue reached a climax in 1887 when Cleveland vetoed a new dependent pension bill containing more liberal benefits to veterans and their families. Cleveland argued that it would become a refuge for frauds rather than a "roll of honor."

In about the middle of his term, Cleveland advocated an important new policy: railroad regulation. Since the late 1860s states had adopted laws regulating railroads and from the early 1870s Congress had debated federal legislation. In 1886 a Supreme Court decision spurred action. Reacting to the case of *Wabash, St. Louis, and Pacific Railroad Company v. Illinois,* in which the Court had ruled that a state could not regulate rates on interstate traffic, Cleveland urged that since this "important field of control and regulation [has] thus been left entirely unoccupied," Congress should act.

It did, and in 1887 Cleveland signed into law an act creating the Interstate Commerce Commission (ICC), the first independent federal regulatory commission. The law required that all freight and passenger railroad rates be "reasonable and just," and it empowered the ICC to investigate railroads and prosecute violators. Railroads were also forbidden to grant secret rebates to preferred shippers; discriminate against persons, places, and commodities; or enter into pools (agreements among competing companies to fix rates). The commission's actual powers proved to be weak, however, when first tested in the courts. Though creating the ICC seemed to conflict with Cleveland's fear of big government, it accorded with his wariness of the growing influence of big business. The Interstate Commerce Act, to his mind, was a legitimate exercise of sovereign power.

THE TARIFF Cleveland's most dramatic challenge to special interests focused on tariff reform. Why was the tariff such an important and controversial issue? By the late nineteenth century, Republican party officials and business leaders had come to assume that national prosperity and high tariffs were closely linked. Others disagreed. Many observers concluded that the formation of huge corporate "trusts" was not a natural development of a maturing capitalist system. Instead, critics charged that government tariff policies had fostered big business at the expense of small producers and retailers by effectively shutting out foreign imports, thereby enabling American corporations to dominate their markets and charge higher prices for their products.

Grover Cleveland

As president, he made the issue of tariff reform central to the politics of the late 1880s.

By shielding manufacturers from foreign competition, critics argued, the tariff made it easier for them to combine into ever-larger entities.

Cleveland agreed. Having decided that the rates were too high and too often inequitable, he devoted his entire annual message in 1887 to the subject. He did so with the full knowledge that he was walking onto a political minefield on the eve of an election year. "What is the use of being elected if you don't stand for something?" he asked skeptical advisers.

Cleveland's annual message noted that tariff revenues had bolstered the federal surplus, making the Treasury "a hoarding place for money needlessly withdrawn from trade and the people's use." The high tariff, he added, pushed up prices for everybody and benefited only a few politically powerful manufacturing interests. The wise solution was to spur Congress to look at the items on the tariff list, more than 4,000 of them, with an eye to eliminating as many as possible and lowering all the remaining duties.

The House soon passed a bill calling for modest tariff reductions, from an average of about 47 percent of the value of imported goods to about 40 percent. But the bill stalled in the Republican Senate and finally died a lingering death, the victim of committee debate. If Cleveland's tariff proposal accomplished his purpose of drawing party lines more firmly, it also confirmed the fears of his advisers. A presidential election, for the first time in years, highlighted a sharp difference between the major parties on an issue of substance.

THE ELECTION OF 1888   In 1888 Cleveland was the nominee of his party. The Republicans, now calling themselves the GOP (Grand Old Party), turned to the obscure Benjamin Harrison. Grandson of a former president, Harrison was a lawyer in Indiana, a pivotal state in national elections. He also boasted a good war record, and little in his political record would offend any voter. The Republican platform accepted Cleveland's challenge to make the protective tariff the chief issue; it also promised generous pensions to Civil War veterans.

The campaign thus became the first one waged mainly on the tariff issue. To ensure against tariff reduction, manufacturers obligingly filled up Harrison's campaign fund, which was used to denounce Cleveland's un-American "free-trade" stance and his vetoes of veterans' pension bills.

On the eve of the election, Cleveland suffered a devastating blow from a dirty campaign trick. Posing as an English immigrant and using the false name Charles F. Murchison, a California Republican had written the British ambassador, Sir Lionel Sackville-West, asking his advice on how to vote. Sackville-West hinted in reply that the man should vote for Cleveland. Published two weeks before the election, the "Murchison letter" aroused a storm of protest against foreign intervention and suggested a link between Cleveland and British free traders.

Still, the outcome in the 1888 election was very close. Cleveland won the popular vote by 5,538,000 to 5,447,000, but that was little comfort. The distribution of votes was such that Harrison, with the key states of Indiana and New York on his side, carried the Electoral College by 233 to 168.

REPUBLICAN REFORM UNDER HARRISON   As president, Benjamin Harrison was a competent and earnest figurehead overshadowed by his flamboyant secretary of state, James G. Blaine. Harrison's first step was to reward those responsible for his victory. He owed a heavy debt to the Union war veterans, which he discharged by naming the head of the veterans' group to the office of federal pension commissioner. The new commissioner proceeded to approve veterans' pensions with such abandon that the secretary of the interior removed him from office six months later. In 1890 Congress passed, and Harrison signed, the Dependent Pension Act, substantially the same measure that Cleveland had vetoed three years earlier. Any war veteran unable to make a living by manual labor for whatever reason was granted a monthly pension. The pension rolls almost doubled by 1893.

During the first two years of Harrison's term, the Republicans controlled the presidency and both houses of Congress for the first time between 1875 and 1895. They made the most of their clout. During 1890 several significant pieces of legislation made their way to the White House for Harrison's signature. In addition to the Dependent Pension Act, Congress and the president approved the Sherman Anti-Trust Act, the Sherman Silver Purchase Act, the

McKinley Tariff Act, and the admission of Idaho and Wyoming as new states, following the admission of the Dakotas, Montana, and Washington in 1889.

Both parties had pledged during the campaign to address the growing power of trusts and monopolies. The Sherman Anti-Trust Act, named for Ohio senator John Sherman, chairman of the committee that drafted it, forbade contracts, combinations, or conspiracies in restraint of trade or in the effort to establish monopolies in interstate or foreign commerce. A broad consensus put the vague law through, but its passage turned out to be largely symbolic. During the next decade successive administrations rarely enforced the new law, in part because of confusion about what constituted "restraint of trade." From 1890 to 1901, the Justice Department instituted only eighteen anti-trust suits, and four of those were against labor unions.

Congress, meanwhile, debated currency legislation against the backdrop of growing distress in the farm regions of the West and the South. Hard-pressed farmers demanded increased coinage of silver to inflate the currency supply and raise commodity prices, making it easier for them to earn the money with which to pay their debts. The silverite forces were also strengthened, especially in the Senate, by members from new western states with silver-mining interests. Congress thus passed the Sherman Silver Purchase Act replacing the Bland-Allison Act of 1878. It required the Treasury to purchase 4.5 million ounces of silver each month and to issue in payment paper money redeemable in gold or silver. Although it doubled the amount of silver purchased, that was still too little to inflate the nation's overall money supply. The stage was thus set for the currency issue to eclipse all others during the financial panic that would sweap the country three years later.

Republicans viewed their victory over Cleveland in 1888 as a mandate not just to maintain the protective tariff but to raise it. Piloted through Congress by the prominent Ohio representative William McKinley, the McKinley Tariff of 1890 raised duties on manufactured goods to the highest level ever. The absence of a public consensus for higher tariffs became clearly visible in the 1890 midterm elections. The voters repudiated the Republican-sponsored McKinley Tariff with a landslide of Democratic votes. In the new House, Democrats outnumbered Republicans by almost three to one; in the Senate the Republican majority was reduced to eight. One of the election casualties was Congressman William McKinley himself. But there was more to the election than the tariff. Voters also reacted to the baldly partisan measures of the Harrison administration and its extravagant expenditures on military pensions and other programs.

The large Democratic vote in 1890 may also have been a reaction to Republican efforts to legislate on a local level against government-supported

Catholic (parochial) schools. In many districts with a high percentage of Catholic constituents, Democratic legislators had defied the principle of separation of church and state by allocating local tax revenues to help support parochial schools. In 1889 Wisconsin Republicans pushed through a law that struck at parochial schools and turned large numbers of outraged Catholic immigrants into Democratic activists. Protestant Republicans also sought to prohibit alcoholic beverages. Between 1880 and 1890 sixteen out of twenty-one states outside the South held referenda on a constitutional prohibition of alcoholic beverages, although only six states actually voted for prohibition. With this assault on drinking, Republicans were playing a losing game, arousing anti-prohibitionists on the Democratic side. In 1890 the Democrats swept state after state.

AGRARIAN PROTEST MOVEMENTS

The 1890 election reflected more than a reaction against the Republican tariff, patronage politics, extravagant spending, and moralizing. The Democratic victory revealed a deep-seated unrest in the farming communities of the South and the West. As the congressional Democrats took power, the beginnings of an economic crisis appeared on the horizon. Farmers' debts mounted as crop prices plummeted.

Frustrated by the unwillingness of Congress to meet their demands and ease their plight, disgruntled farmers began to organize their political efforts. Like so many of their counterparts laboring in urban factories, they realized that social change required demonstrations of power, and power lay in numbers—and organization. Unlike labor unions, however, the farm organizations faced a complex array of economic variables affecting their livelihood. They had to deal with more than just management. Bankers, food processors, railroad and grain-elevator operators, as well as the world commodities market, all affected the agricultural sector. So, too, did the unpredictable forces of nature: droughts, blizzards, insects, and erosion.

There were also important obstacles to collective action by farmers. Farmers' rugged individualism and physical isolation made communication and organization especially difficult. Another hurdle was the fact that after the Civil War agricultural interests had diverged and in some cases conflicted with one another. On the Great Plains, for example, the railroads were the largest landowners. In addition, there were large absentee landowners, some foreign, who leased out vast tracts of land. There were also huge "bonanza" farms that employed hundreds of seasonal workers.

Yet the majority of farmers were simple rural folk in the South and West who were small landowners, tenant farmers, and hourly wage workers. It was the middle-size landowners who were most affected by rapidly rising land values and rising indebtedness. Those farmers were concerned with land values and crop prices, while tenants, sharecroppers, and farmhands supported land-distribution schemes that would give them access to their own land.

Given such a diversity of interests within the agricultural sector, farm activists discovered that it was often difficult to develop and maintain a cohesive political organization. Yet for all the difficulties, they persevered, and the results were dramatic, if not completely successful. Thus, for example, the deep-seated unrest in the farming communities of the South and the West began to find voice in the Granger movement, the Farmers' Alliances, and the new People's party (also known as the Populist party), agrarian movements of considerable political and social significance.

ECONOMIC CONDITIONS   For some time, farmers in the South and Midwest had been subject to worsening economic and social conditions. The source of their problems was a long decline in commodity prices, from 1870 to 1898, the product of domestic increases in production and growing international competition for world markets. Considerations of abstract economic forces puzzled many farmers, however. How could one speak of overproduction when so many remained in need? Instead, many farmers assumed, there must be a screw loose somewhere in the system.

The railroads and the food processors who handled the farmers' products were seen as the villains. Farmers resented the high railroad freight rates that prevailed in farm regions with no alternative forms of transportation. High tariffs operated to the farmers' disadvantage because they protected manufacturers from foreign competition, allowing them to raise the prices of factory goods upon which farmers depended. Farmers, however, had to sell their wheat, cotton, and other staples in foreign markets, where competition lowered prices. Tariffs inflicted a double blow on farmers because insofar as they hampered imports, they indirectly hampered exports by making it harder for foreign buyers to get the currency or exchange necessary to purchase American crops.

Debt, too, had been a perennial agricultural problem. After the Civil War, farmers grew ever more enmeshed in debt: western farmers incurred mortgages to cover the costs of land and machinery, while southern farmers were forced to pledge their crops to the local merchant in exchange for food and supplies. As commodity prices dropped, the debt burden grew because

"I Feed You All!"

This 1875 poster shows the farmer at the center of society.

farmers had to cultivate more wheat or cotton to raise the same amount of money. By growing more, they furthered the vicious cycle of surpluses and price declines.

THE GRANGER MOVEMENT   When the Department of Agriculture sent Oliver H. Kelley, a former Minnesota farmer and post-office clerk, on a tour of the South in 1866, it was the farmers' isolation that most impressed him. Resolving to do something about it, Kelley in 1867 founded the National Grange of the Patrons of Husbandry, better known as the Grange (an old word for granary). In the next few years the Grange mushroomed, reaching a membership as high as 1.5 million by 1874. While the Grange started out as a social and educational response to the isolation of farm folk, as it grew, it began to promote farmer-owned cooperatives for the buying and selling of crops. The Grangers' goal was to free farmers from the conventional "middlemen" to whom they were forced to pay high fees.

The Grange soon became indirectly involved in politics, through independent third parties, especially in the Midwest during the early 1870s. The Grangers' chief political goal was state regulation of the rates charged by railroads and crop warehouses. In five states they brought about the passage of "Granger laws," which were challenged in the courts. In a key case involving warehouse regulation, *Munn v. Illinois* (1877), the Supreme Court affirmed that the state, according to its "police powers," had the right to regulate property when that property was clothed in a public interest.

Although such legal victories bolstered the Granger cause, the movement gradually declined as members' energies were drawn off into cooperatives, whereby farmers would make collective agreements about the storage and sale of their crops. Other former Grange members focused on political action. Out of the independent political movements of the time, there grew in 1875 the Greenback party, which favored expansion of the money supply with more paper money. In the 1878 midterm elections it polled over 1 million votes and elected fifteen congressmen. But in 1880 the party's fortunes declined, and it disintegrated after 1884.

FARMERS' ALLIANCES   As the Grange lost energy, another consortium of farm organizations grew in size and significance: the Farmers' Alliances. Like the Grange, the Farmers' Alliances offered social and recreational opportunities for their members, but they also emphasized political action. Farmers throughout the South and Midwest, where tenancy rates were highest, rushed to join the Alliance movement. They saw in collective action a way to seek relief from the hardships created by chronic indebtedness, declining crop prices, and devastating droughts. Yet unlike the Grange, which was a national organization that tended to attract larger and more prosperous farmers, the Alliance was a grassroots local organization representing marginal farmers.

The Alliance movement swept across the Southern cotton belt and established strong positions in Kansas and the Dakotas. In 1886 a white minister in Texas, which had one of the largest and most influential Alliance movements, responded to the appeals of African-American farmers by organizing the Colored Farmers' National Alliance. The white leadership of the Alliance movement in Texas endorsed this development because the Colored Alliance stressed that its objective was economic justice, not social equality. By 1890 the Alliance movement had members from New York to California, numbering about 1.5 million, and the Colored Farmers' National Alliance claimed over 1 million members.

A powerful attraction for many isolated, struggling farmers and their families was the sense of community provided by the Alliance network. The Alliance movement welcomed rural women and men over sixteen years of age who displayed a "good moral character," believed in God, and demonstrated "industrious habits." Women eagerly embraced the opportunity to engage in economic and political issues. An Alliance publication made the point explicitly: "The Alliance has come to redeem woman from her enslaved condition, and place her in her proper sphere." The number of women in the movement grew rapidly, and many assumed key leadership roles in the "grand army of reform."

The Alliance movement sponsored an ambitious social and educational program and about 1,000 affiliated newspapers. Unlike the Grange, however, the Alliance proposed an elaborate economic program. In 1890 Alliance agencies and exchanges in some eighteen states claimed a business of $10 million, but they soon went the way of the Granger cooperatives, victims of both discrimination by wholesalers, manufacturers, railroads, and bankers and their own inexperienced management and overextended credit.

In 1887 Charles W. Macune, the new Alliance president, proposed that Texas farmers create their own Alliance Exchange in an effort to free themselves from their dependence upon grain processors and banks. Members of the exchange would sign joint notes (to be used to get cash), borrow money from banks, and purchase their goods and supplies from a new corporation created by the Alliance in Dallas. The exchange would also build its own warehouses to store and market members crops. While their crops were being stored, member farmers would be able to obtain credit from the warehouse cooperative so that they could buy household goods and supplies.

This grand cooperative scheme collapsed when Texas banks refused to accept the joint notes from Alliance members. Macune and others then focused their energies on what Macune called a "subtreasury plan." Under this scheme, farmers would be able to store their crops in new government warehouses and obtain government loans for up to 80 percent of the value of their crops at 1 percent interest. Besides providing immediate credit, the plan would allow the farmer the leeway to hold a crop for a better price later, since he would not have to sell it immediately at harvest time to pay off debts. The plan would also promote inflation because the loans to farmers would be made in new legal-tender notes.

The subtreasury plan went before Congress in 1890 but was never adopted. Its defeat as well as setbacks to other Alliance proposals convinced many farm leaders that they needed more political power in order to secure railroad regulation, currency inflation, state departments of agriculture, anti-trust laws, and farm credit.

FARM POLITICS   In the West, where hard times had descended after the blizzards of 1887, farmers demanded third-party political action. In the South, however, white Alliance members hesitated to bolt the Democratic party, seeking instead to influence or control it. Both approaches gained startling success. Independent parties under various names upset the political balance in western states. In the South, the Alliance forced the Democrats to nominate candidates pledged to their program. In 1890 the southern states elected four pro-Alliance governors, seven pro-Alliance legislatures, forty-four pro-Alliance congressmen,

Mary Elizabeth Lease, 1890

A charismatic leader in the farm protest movement.

and several senators. Among the most respected of the southern Alliance leaders was Thomas E. Watson of Georgia. The son of prosperous slaveholders who had lost everything during and after the Civil War, Watson became a successful lawyer and colorful orator on behalf of the Alliance cause. He took the lead in urging African-American tenant farmers and sharecroppers to join with their white counterparts in ousting the white political elite. "You are kept apart," he told black and white farmers, "that you may be separately fleeced of your earnings."

THE POPULIST PARTY AND THE ELECTION OF 1892

As economic conditions worsened, many agrarian activists began promoting the formation of a new national political party. In 1891 delegates from farm, labor, and reform organizations met in Cincinnati to discuss the creation of the People's party. Few southerners attended, but many delegates endorsed the third-party idea after their failure to win over the Democratic party to the subtreasury plan. In 1891 William Peffer of Kansas and Tom Watson of Georgia were the first People's party candidates elected to the Senate. In 1892 a larger meeting in St. Louis proposed a national convention of the People's party at Omaha to adopt a platform and choose national candidates.

The 1892 Populist platform focused on issues of finance, transportation, and land. Its financial program demanded implementation of the subtreasury plan, unlimited coinage of silver, an increase in the amount of money in circulation, and a graduated income tax, whose rates would rise with personal levels of income. As for transportation, the party called for the government to nationalize the railroads, as well as the telephone and telegraph systems. It also called for the government to reclaim from railroads and other corporations lands "in excess of their actual needs" and forbid land ownership by immigrants who were not citizens. Finally, the platform endorsed the eight-hour workday and laws restricting immigration, taking these positions to win support from urban workers, whom Populists looked upon as fellow "producers." The party's platform turned out to be more exciting than its candidate, Iowa's James B. Weaver. Though an able, prudent man, Weaver carried the stigma of his defeat on the Greenback ticket twelve years before. To attract southern voters who might be distracted by Weaver's service as a Union general, the party named a former Confederate general for vice president.

The Populist party was the startling new feature of the 1892 campaign. The Democrats renominated Grover Cleveland, and Republicans turned again to Benjamin Harrison. The tariff remained the chief issue between them. The outcome, however, was different. Both major candidates polled over 5 million votes, but Cleveland carried a plurality of the popular vote and a majority of the Electoral College. Weaver gained over 1 million votes, 10 percent of the total, and carried Colorado, Kansas, Nevada, and Idaho, for a total of twenty-two electoral votes. In Kansas the Populists won the governor's office, four congressional seats, and control of the state senate. In neighboring Nebraska the Populists won control of both statehouses.

THE ECONOMY AND THE SILVER SOLUTION

INADEQUATE CURRENCY   While agitated farmers were funneling their discontent into politics and businessmen were consolidating their holdings, a fundamental weakness in the economy was about to manifest itself in a major economic collapse. The nation's money supply in the late nineteenth century lacked the flexibility to grow along with the expanding economy. From 1865 to 1890, the amount of currency in circulation per capita decreased about 10 percent. Currency deflation raised the cost of borrowing money, as a tight money supply caused bankers to hike interest rates on loans.

Metallic currency dated from the Mint Act of 1792, which authorized free and unlimited coinage of silver and gold at a ratio of 15 to 1, meaning that the amount of precious metal in a silver dollar weighed fifteen times as much as that in a gold dollar, a reflection of the relative value of gold and silver at the time. "Free and unlimited coinage" simply meant that owners of precious metals could have any quantity of their gold or silver coined free, except for a nominal fee to cover costs.

A fixed ratio of the values of gold and silver did not reflect fluctuations in the market value of the metals, however. When gold rose to a market value higher than that reflected in the official ratio, owners ceased to present it for coinage. The country was actually on a silver standard until 1837, when Congress changed the ratio to 16 to 1, which soon reversed the situation. Silver became more valuable in the open market than in coinage, and the country drifted to a gold standard. This state of affairs prevailed until 1873, when Congress passed a general revision of the coinage laws and dropped the then-unused provision for the coinage of silver.

This occurred just when silver production in the western states began to increase, however, reducing its market value through the growth in supply. Under the old laws that development would have induced owners of silver to present it at the mint for coinage. Soon advocates of currency inflation began to denounce the "crime of '73," which they had scarcely noticed at the time. Gradually suspicion grew that bankers and merchants had conspired in 1873 to ensure a scarcity of money. But the pro-silver forces had little more legislative success than the advocates of greenback inflation. The Bland-Allison Act of 1878 and the Sherman Silver Purchase Act of 1890 provided for some silver coinage, but too little in each case to offset the overall contraction of the nation's money supply.

THE DEPRESSION OF 1893   Just before Grover Cleveland started his second presidential term in 1893 (the only non-consecutive second term of a president in U.S. history), one of the most devastating business panics in history erupted when the Philadelphia and Reading Railroad declared bankruptcy, setting off a national financial panic. Not only was business affected, but entire farm regions were also devastated by the spreading depression. One quarter of the cities' unskilled workers lost their jobs, and by the fall of 1893 over 600 banks had closed. By 1894 the economy had reached bottom. That year some 750,000 workers went on strike, millions found themselves unemployed, and railroad construction workers, laid off in the West, began tramping east and talked of marching on Washington, D.C.

Few of them, however, made it to the capital. One protest group that did reach Washington was "Coxey's Army," led by Jacob S. Coxey, a wealthy Ohio quarry owner turned Populist who demanded that the federal government provide the unemployed with meaningful work. Coxey, his wife, and their son, Legal Tender Coxey, rode in a carriage ahead of some 400 hardy protesters who finally straggled into Washington. There Coxey was arrested for walking on the grass. Although his ragtag army dispersed peacefully, the march on Washington, as well as the growing political strength of Populism, struck fear into the hearts of many Americans. Critics portrayed Populists as "hayseed socialists" whose election would endanger property rights and the entire capitalist system.

The 1894 congressional elections taking place amid this climate of anxiety represented a severe setback for the Democrats, who paid politically for the economic downturn, and the Republicans were the chief beneficiaries. The third-party Populists emerged with six senators and seven representatives. They had polled 1.5 million votes for their congressional candidates and expected the festering discontent to carry them to national power in 1896.

SILVERITES VERSUS GOLDBUGS   The course of events would dash that hope, however. In the mid-1890s national attention focused on the currency issue. One of the causes of the 1893 depression was the failure of a major British bank, which had led many British investors to unload their American stocks and bonds in return for gold. Soon after Grover Cleveland's inauguration the U.S. gold reserve had fallen below $100 million. To plug the drain on the Treasury, by stopping the issuance of silver notes redeemable in gold, the president sought repeal of the Sherman Silver Purchase Act. Cleveland won the repeal in 1893, but at the cost of irreparable division in his own party. One embittered pro-silver Democrat labeled the president a traitor.

Western silver interests now escalated their demands for silver coinage, presenting a strategic dilemma for Populists: Should the party promote the long list of varied reforms it had originally advocated, or should it try to ride the silver issue into power? The latter seemed the practical choice. As a consequence, the Populist leaders decided, over the protests of more radical members, to hold their 1896 nominating convention last, confident that the two major parties would at best straddle the silver issue, and they would then reap a harvest of bolting silverite Republicans and Democrats.

THE ELECTION OF 1896   Contrary to those expectations, the major parties took opposing positions on the currency issue. The Republicans, as expected, chose Ohioan William McKinley on a gold-standard platform. On the Democratic side the pro-silver forces gathered to wrest control of the party from Cleveland and the fiscal conservatives. In William Jennings Bryan the silver Democrats found a crusading, charismatic leader. A fervent Baptist and advocate of the free coinage of silver, Bryan was a two-term congressman from Nebraska who had been defeated in the senate race in 1894. At the 1896 convention the self-assured Bryan delivered a galvanizing speech that had most of the 20,000 delegates on their feet and many in tears. Like a revivalist at a camp meeting, he galvanized the audience with the emotion of his appeal. Bryan spoke for silver and the new West, for the "hardy pioneers" and against the "financial magnates" of the urban East as well as Cleveland's "do-nothing" response to the depression. He directly challenged Republicans as well as Cleveland and the gold Democrats with a compelling metaphor:

William Jennings Bryan

His "cross of gold" speech at the 1896 Democratic Convention roused the delegates and secured him the party's presidential nomination.

"You shall not press down upon the brow of labor this crown of thorns. You shall not crucify mankind upon a cross of gold!"

The next day the heroic Bryan was nominated on the fifth ballot, and in the process the Democratic party was fractured beyond repair. Disappointed pro-gold Cleveland Democrats were so disgusted by Bryan's inflationary program and Populist rhetoric that they walked out of the convention and nominated their own candidate, who then announced, "Fellow Democrats, I will not consider it any great fault if you decide to cast your vote for [the Republican] William McKinley."

When the Populists met in St. Louis two weeks later, they faced an impossible choice. "If we fuse [with the Democrats]," one Populist admitted, "all the silver men we have will leave us for the more powerful Democrats." But if the Populists named their own candidate, they would divide the silver vote with Bryan and give the election to McKinley. In the end the delegates backed Bryan but chose their own vice presidential candidate, Georgia's Thomas Watson, and invited the Democrats to drop their vice-presidential nominee, an action Bryan refused to countenance.

During the 1896 campaign, the thirty-six-year-old Bryan crisscrossed the country, using his spellbinding eloquence to support "the struggling masses" of workers, farmers, and small-business owners and promising the panacea of the unlimited coinage of silver. McKinley, meanwhile, conducted a "front-porch campaign," receiving selected delegations of supporters at his home in Canton, Ohio, and giving only prepared responses. His campaign manager, Mark Hanna, shrewdly portrayed Bryan as a radical whose "communistic spirit" would ruin the capitalist system. Many observers agreed with the portrait.

By preying upon such fears, the McKinley campaign raised vast sums of money to finance an army of Republican speakers who stumped the country in his support. In the end the Democratic-Populist-Silverite candidates were overwhelmed. McKinley won the popular vote by 7.1 million to 6.5 million and the Electoral College vote by 271 to 176.

Bryan carried most of the West and the South but garnered little support in the metropolitan centers east of the Mississippi and north of the Ohio and

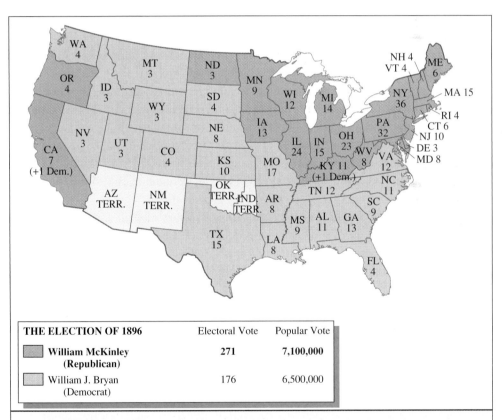

THE ELECTION OF 1896	Electoral Vote	Popular Vote
William McKinley (Republican)	**271**	**7,100,000**
William J. Bryan (Democrat)	176	6,500,000

How did Bryan's "cross of gold" speech divide the Democratic party? How was McKinley's strategy different from Bryan's? Why was Bryan able to carry the West and the South but unable to win in cities and the North?

Potomac rivers. Urban workers saw little to gain from the inflation promoted by Bryan and the silverites. Factory workers in the cities found it easier to identify with McKinley's "full dinner pail" campaign slogan than with Bryan's free silver. Moreover, in the critical midwestern battleground, from Minnesota and Iowa eastward to Ohio, Bryan carried not a single state. Many ethnic voters, normally drawn to the Democrats, were repelled by Bryan's evangelical style. Farmers in the East and the Midwest, moreover, were hurting less than those in the wheat and cotton belts. With less tenancy and a greater diversity of crops in those farm regions, prospering farmers saw little attraction in agrarian radicalism.

A NEW ERA

The election of 1896 was a climactic political struggle between rural and metropolitan America, and metropolitan America won. As its first important act the McKinley administration called a special session of Congress to raise the tariff again. The Dingley Tariff of 1897 became the highest ever. By 1897 prosperity was returning, helped along by inflation of the currency, which bore out the arguments of the greenbackers and silverites. But the inflation came, in one of history's many ironies, not from silver but from a new flood of gold onto the market and into the mints. During the 1880s and 1890s discoveries of gold in South Africa, Canada, and Alaska led to spectacular new gold rushes, a return to the gold standard, and an end to the free-silver movement.

At the close of the nineteenth century, the old issues of tariff and currency policy, which had dominated national politics since the Civil War, gave way to global concerns: the outbreak of the Spanish-American War and the acquisition of territories outside the Western Hemisphere. At the same time, the advent of a new century brought new social and political developments. Although the Populist movement faded with William Jennings Bryan's defeat, most of the policies promoted by Bryan Democrats and Populists, dismissed as too radical and controversial in 1896, would be implemented over the next two decades. Bryan's impassioned candidacy helped transform the Democratic party into a vigorous instrument of "progressive" reform during the early twentieth century. Democrats began to promote anti-trust prosecutions, state laws to limit the working hours of women and children, the establishment of a minimum wage, and measures to support farmers and protect labor-union organizers. As the United States looked ahead to a new century, it began to place more emphasis on the role of national government in society and the economy.

> ## MAKING CONNECTIONS
>
> · The laissez-faire policies of the Gilded Age were challenged by progressive reform activists, as will be discussed in Chapter 24.
>
> · William Jennings Bryan was one of the most prominent figures in American politics and political culture over some thirty years. He will be discussed again in Chapters 24 and 26.

FURTHER READING

A good overview of the Gilded Age is Vincent P. De Santis's *The Shaping of Modern America, 1877–1920* (1973). Nell Irvin Painter's *Standing at Armageddon: The United States, 1877–1919* (1987) focuses on the experience of the working class.

Excellent presidential biographies include Hans L. Trefousse's *Rutherford B. Hayes* (2002), Zachary Karabell's *Chester Alan Arthur* (2004), Henry F. Graff's *Grover Cleveland* (2002), and Kevin Phillips's *William McKinley* (2003).

Scholars have also examined various Gilded Age issues and interest groups. Gerald W. McFarland's *Mugwumps, Morals, and Politics, 1884–1920* (1975) explores the issue of reforming the civil service. Tom E. Terrill's *The Tariff, Politics, and American Foreign Policy, 1874–1901* (1973) lends clarity to that complex issue. The complex finances of the Gilded Age are covered in Walter T. K. Nugent's *Money and American Society, 1865–1880* (1968).

One of the most controversial works on populism is Lawrence Goodwyn's *The Populist Movement: A Short History of the Agrarian Revolt in America* (1978). A more balanced account in Robert C. McMath Jr.'s *American Populism: A Social History, 1877–1898* (1992).

Part Six

MODERN AMERICA

1900
William McKinley is reelected president (1900)

Progressives promote efficiency, regulation, and reform legislation (1900–1917)

Commission system of municipal government is implemented for the first time (1901)

McKinley is assassinated; Theodore Roosevelt serves as president (1901–1909)

Government reforms continue as more states adopt direct primaries and direct elections (1900s–1920s)

City-manager plan of municipal government is implemented (1908)

William Howard Taft serves as president (1909–1913)

1910
Ballinger-Pinchot controversy over conservation leads to reform of committee system in the House (1910)

Roosevelt forms "Bull Moose" party after split with Taft (1912)

Seventeenth Amendment is ratified, establishing direct election of senators (1913)

Woodrow Wilson serves as president (1913–1921)

U.S. enters World War I on side of Britain, France, and Russia (1917)

Espionage and Sedition Acts outlaw criticism of government leaders and war policies (1917, 1918)

Wilson delivers his Fourteen Point peace plan to Congress (1918)

Congress rejects Wilson's Fourteen Points and the League of Nations (1919)

Secretary of State A. Mitchell Palmer leads witch hunts against suspected liberals, launching the first Red Scare in the U.S. (1919)

1920
Nineteenth Amendment grants women the right to vote (1920)

Warren G. Harding serves as president (1921–1923)

Hay-Pauncefote Treaty establishes mutual consent of Britain and U.S. to construction of Central American canal (1901)

Panama wins independence from Colombia with support of U.S. troops (1903); U.S. constructs Panama Canal (1904–1914)

Roosevelt Corollary to the Monroe Doctrine aims to curtail European interference in the Americas (1904)

Russo-Japanese War (1904–1905)

U.S. accepts Japanese control of Korea with Taft-Katsura Agreement (1905)

Bloody Sunday Massacre leads to revolt in Russia (1905)

Great White Fleet circles the globe, brandishing U.S. naval might (1907–1909)

U.S. troops intervene in Honduras (1907, 1911, 1912, 1919, 1924)

Root-Takahira Agreement reaffirms Open Door policy in China (1908)

Revolution takes place in China (1911)

U.S. troops occupy Nicaragua (1912–1925; 1926–1933)

Panama Canal opens (1914)

Wilson sends troops to Mexico, Haiti, and Dominican Republic (1914–1916)

Serbian nationalist murders Austrian archduke Franz Ferdinand, precipitating World War I (1914)

German U-boat sinks the British liner *Lusitania* (1915)

Albert Einstein publishes *The Foundations of the General Theory of Relativity* (1916)

Bolsheviks seize power in Russia (1917)

Russians withdraw from war after separate peace with Germany in Treaty of Brest-Litovsk (1918)

Treaty of Versailles ends World War I (1919)

League of Nations is in effect (1920–1946)

Washington Conference attempts to ward off conflicts in the Pacific (1921)

Benito Mussolini seizes power in Italy (1922)

Muckrakers use the press to arouse America's social conscience (1900s)

Baseball's first World Series is played (1903)

National Child Labor Committee is founded to combat employment of young children (1904)

Upton Sinclair's *The Jungle* depicts horrors of meatpacking industry (1906)

Gentlemen's Agreement halts influx of Japanese laborers to U.S. (1907)

Angel Island is established as West Coast reception center for immigrants, mainly Asians (1910)

Civil rights activists establish NAACP (1910)

Triangle Shirtwaist Company fire leads to increased regulation of the workplace (1911)

Frederick W. Taylor publishes *The Principles of Scientific Management* (1911)

U.S. drafts 4 million men; women, blacks, and other ethnic minorities are employed in munitions factories (1916–1919)

Great Migration of southern blacks to northern cities takes place (1916–1920s)

Influenza epidemic kills 500,000 Americans (1918–1919)

Nationwide race riots result in hundreds of dead and injured (1919)

Eighteenth Amendment launches Prohibition (1919)

1900

Discovery of Spindletop gusher in Texas brings oil rush to Southwest (1901)

Roosevelt's intervention (1902) leads to settlement of coal strike (1903)

Congress creates Department of Commerce and Labor (1903)

Northern Securities Company is broken up in the first of 25 successful Roosevelt-administration anti-trust suits (1904)

Industrial Workers of the World (Wobblies) is established (1905)

Swift and Company v. U.S. establishes "stream-of-commerce" doctrine, making meat packers subject to federal legislation (1905)

Hepburn Act, Meat Inspection Act, and Pure Food and Drug Act increase federal regulatory authority over the economy (1906)

1910

Mann-Elkins Act extends federal regulation to telephone and telegraph industries (1910)

Supreme Court dissolves Standard Oil and the American Tobacco Company (1911)

AFL membership increases 37 percent (1913–1918)

Sixteenth Amendment creates income tax (1913)

Federal Reserve Act creates regional reserve banks (1913)

Underwood-Simmons Tariff reduces average duty from 37 percent to 29 percent (1913)

Federal Trade Commission is created to prevent unfair trade practices (1914)

Clayton Anti-Trust Act tightens 1890 Sherman Anti-Trust Act (1914)

War in Europe causes economic boom in U.S. (1915)

War mobilization results in widespread civilian rationing (1916–1919)

Federal Highways Act provides funds for national road network (1916)

War Industries Board sets priorities and plans industrial production (1917)

Widespread strikes partially paralyze U.S. economy (1919)

1920

Marcus Garvey promotes Negro nationalism (1920s)

Gangsters make fortunes illegally producing and distributing alcohol (1920s)

KKK leads nativist campaign (1920s)

Jazz music becomes popular (1920s)

National Woman's party proposes equal rights amendment (1923)

Harding administration is plagued with corruption; Teapot Dome scandal unfolds (1923–1924)

Calvin Coolidge serves as president after Harding dies in office (1923–1929)

Progressive party is organized and nominates Robert La Follette for president (1924)

1930 Herbert Hoover serves as president (1929–1933)

Hoover signs Emergency Relief Act to provide funds to states to relieve suffering (1932)

Franklin D. Roosevelt serves as president (1933–1945)

FDR pushes through New Deal relief measures to combat Great Depression (1933)

FDR's stalemate with Congress brings New Deal legislation to a halt (1935)

FDR launches his Second New Deal to break stalemate with Congress and radicals (1935)

1940

FDR proposes lend-lease bill to Congress, pledging to make America the "arsenal for democracy" (1941)

U.S. funds Manhattan Project, which builds the atomic bomb (1942–1945)

1945 FDR is elected to a fourth term (1944)

Harry S. Truman serves as president after FDR dies in office (1945–1953)

Kellogg-Briand Pact renounces war as "an instrument of national policy" (1928)

Nationalists rule in China under Chiang Kai-shek (1928–1949)

Japanese occupy Manchuria (1931)

U.S. annouces formal diplomatic recognition of Soviet Union (1933)

Hitler becomes chancellor of Germany (1933)

U.S. troops are withdrawn from Nicaragua, Haiti, and Cuba as part of the "Good Neighbor" policy (1934)

Spanish Civil War (1936–1939)

Chinese and Japanese troops begin full-scale war in the Pacific (1937)

Germany annexes Austria (1938)

France and Britain abandon Czechoslovakia with the Munich Pact (1938)

Germany invades Czechoslovakia (1939)

Germany signs nonaggression pact with Soviets, then invades Poland, leading to World War II in Europe (1939)

Japan, Italy, and Germany sign the Tripartite Pact, a defensive alliance (1940)

Nazi troops begin blitzkrieg (1940)

Germany invades Russia (1941)

Atlantic Charter sets forth Allied war aims (1941)

Japanese attack Pearl Harbor; U.S. enters the war (1941)

Allies take control of North Africa, then attack Italy (1943)

D-day invasion is launched (1944)

Allies "leapfrog" toward Japan (1944–1945)

Soviets set up puppet regimes in Eastern Europe (1944–1945)

Big Three meet at Yalta to discuss the postwar world (1945)

Germany surrenders (1945)

U.S. drops atomic bombs on Hiroshima and Nagasaki, ending the war (1945)

50 million people die in World War II (1939–1945)

Modernist literary movement includes F. Scott Fitzgerald, Ernest Hemingway, Thomas Wolfe, William Faulkner (1920s–1930s)

Harlem Renaissance epitomizes black cultural movement (1920s–1930s)

Scopes "monkey trial" debates teaching of evolution in public schools (1925)

95 million people attend 23,000 movie theaters weekly (1930)

Unemployed veterans demonstrate in Washington, D.C. (1932)

800,000 dust-bowl migrants flee to California (1932–1935)

Twenty-first Amendment ends Prohibition (1933)

Poverty delays 800,000 marriages in the 1930s; marriages decline by one fourth (1930s)

John Steinbeck and Richard Wright write about displacement and racism during the Great Depression (1930s–1940s)

NAACP membership rises from 50,000 to 450,000 during the war (1941–1945)

FDR orders internment of Japanese Americans (1942)

Bracero program brings over 200,000 Mexican farmworkers to U.S. (1942–1945)

One third of eligible Native American men (25,000) serve in the war (1941–1945)

6 million women enter the labor force during the war (1941–1945)

15 million Americans serve in World War II (1941–1945)

Nonfarm wages increase 20 percent; wages for farmers increase only 10 percent (1921–1928)

Membership in labor unions declines from 5 million to 3.5 million (1920–1929)

McNary-Haugen bill calls for tariffs to protect farmers (1924)

Speculative investment in stocks and real estate sets stage for depression (1925–1929)

Stock market crashes (1929)

1930

Great Depression causes personal income to plummet, unemployment rises from 3 percent to 25 percent, 9,000 banks close, and runs on banks occur (1929–1933)

Hawley-Smoot Tariff establishes high rates on imports (1930)

Roosevelt declares a 4-day banking holiday and establishes the Emergency Banking Relief Act (1933)

FERA, AAA, NIRA, and CCC are some of the Hundred Days measures enacted under the New Deal (1933)

Johnson Debt Default Act prohibits private loans to countries that have defaulted on World War I debts (1934)

1940

Wagner Act legalizes collective bargaining for labor (1935)

AFL expels CIO unions (1936)

Social Security Act (1935)

Office of Price Administration enacts wartime rationing (1942)

Servicemen's Readjustment Act (G.I. Bill) earmarks $13 billion for veterans (1944)

1945

National Security Industrial Association forges permanent peacetime alliance between industry and military (1944)

National debt reaches $260 billion, 6 times what it was in 1941 (1945) he United States entered the twentieth century on a wave of unrelenting change. In 1800 the nation was a rural, agrarian society largely detached from the concerns of international affairs. By 1900 the United States had become a highly industrialized urban culture with a growing involvement in world politics and commerce. In other words, the nation was on the threshold of modernity.

The prospect of modernity both excited and scared Americans. Old truths and beliefs clashed with unsettling scientific discoveries and social practices. People debated the legitimacy of Darwinism, the existence of God, the dangers of jazz, and the federal effort to prohibit the sale of alcoholic beverages. The automobile and airplane helped shrink distances, and communications innovations such as radio and film contributed to a national consciousness. In the process the United States began to emerge from its isolationist shell.

Noninvolvement in foreign wars and nonintervention in the internal affairs of foreign governments formed the pillars of foreign policy until the end of the century. During the 1890s, however, expanding commercial interests around the world led Americans to extend the horizons of their concerns. Imperialism was the order of the day among the great European powers, and a growing number of American expansionists demanded that the United States also adopt a global ambition and join in the hunt for new territories and markets. Such motives helped spark the Spanish-American War of 1898 and helped justify the resulting acquisition of colonies outside the continental United States. Entangling alliances with European powers soon followed.

The outbreak of the Great War in Europe in 1914 posed an even greater challenge to the American tradition of isolation and nonintervention. The prospect of a German victory over the French and the British threatened the European balance of power, which had long ensured the security of the United States. By 1917 it appeared that Germany might emerge triumphant and begin to menace the Western Hemisphere. Woodrow Wilson's crusade to use American intervention in World War I to transform the world order in accordance with his idealistic principles severed U.S. foreign policy from its isolationist moorings. It also spawned a prolonged debate about the role of the United States in world affairs, a debate that World War II would resolve for a time on the side of internationalism.

While the United States was entering the world stage as a formidable military power, it was also settling into its role as a great industrial power. Cities and factories sprouted across the landscape. An abundance of new jobs served as a magnet attracting millions of immigrants. They were not always welcomed, nor were they readily assimilated. Ethnic and racial strife, as well as labor agitation, increased after 1900. In the midst of such social turmoil and unparalleled economic development, reformers made their first sustained attempt to adapt their political and social institutions to the realities of the industrial age. The worst excesses and injustices of urban-industrial development—corporate monopolies, child labor, political corruption, hazardous working conditions, urban ghettos—were finally addressed in a comprehensive way. During the Progressive Era (1900–1917) local, state, and federal governments sought to rein in the excesses of industrial capitalism and develop a more efficient public policy.

A conservative Republican resurgence challenged the notion of the new regulatory state during the 1920s. Free enterprise and corporate capitalism witnessed a dramatic revival. But the stock market crash of 1929 helped propel the United States and the world into the worst economic downturn in history. The unprecedented severity of the Great Depression renewed public demands for federal programs to protect the general welfare. "This nation asks for action," declared President Franklin D. Roosevelt in his 1933 inaugural address. The many New Deal initiatives and agencies instituted by Roosevelt and his Democratic administration created the framework for a welfare state that has since served as the basis for American public policy.

The New Deal helped revive public confidence and put people back to work, but it did not end the Great Depression. It took a world war to restore full employment. The necessity of mobilizing the nation in support of the Second World War also served to accelerate the growth of the federal government. And the incredible scope of the war helped catapult the United States into a leadership role in world politics. The creation and use of nuclear bombs ushered in a new era of atomic diplomacy that held the fate of the world in the balance.

For all of the new creature comforts associated with modern life, Americans in 1945 found themselves living amid an array of new anxieties, not the least of which was a global "cold war" against Communism.

23

AN AMERICAN EMPIRE

FOCUS QUESTIONS

- What were the circumstances that led to America's "new imperialism"?
- What were the causes of the Spanish-American War?
- What were the main tenets of Theodore Roosevelt's foreign policy in Asia and Latin America?

To answer these questions and access additional review material, please visit www.wwnorton.com/studyspace.

Throughout the nineteenth century most Americans displayed what one senator called "only a languid interest" in foreign affairs. The overriding priorities of the time were industrial development, western settlement, and domestic politics. Foreign relations simply were not important to the vast majority of people. After the Civil War an isolationist mood swept across the United States as the country basked in its geographic advantages: wide oceans as buffers, the British navy situated between America and the powers of Europe, and militarily weak neighbors in the Western Hemisphere.

Yet the notion of America's having a Manifest Destiny ordained by God to expand its territory and its influence remained alive in the decades after the Civil War. Several prominent political and business leaders argued that the rapid industrial development of the United States required the acquisition of foreign territories to gain easier access to vital raw materials. In addition, as their exports grew, American companies and farmers became increasingly intertwined in the world economy. This, in turn, required an expanded naval presence to protect the global shipping lanes. And a modern steam-powered navy needed bases where its ships could replenish their supplies of coal and water. For these reasons and others the United States during the last quarter of the nineteenth century began to expand its military presence beyond the Western Hemisphere.

TOWARD THE NEW IMPERIALISM

By the late nineteenth century, European powers had already unleashed a new surge of imperialism in Africa and Asia, where they had seized territory, established colonies, and promoted economic exploitation and Christian evangelism. Writing in 1902, the British economist J. A. Hobson declared that imperialism was "the most powerful factor in the current politics of the Western world."

IMPERIALISM IN A GLOBAL CONTEXT   Western imperialism had economic roots; it was above all a quest for markets and raw materials. The Second Industrial Revolution generated such dramatic increases in production that business leaders felt compelled to find new markets for their burgeoning supply of goods and new sources of investment for their growing supply of capital. Manufacturers, on the other hand, were eager to find new sources of raw materials to supply their expanding needs. At the same time, the aggressive nationalism and bitter rivalries of the European powers made all of them compete with one another as they expanded their farflung empires.

The result was a widespread process of imperial expansion into Africa and Asia. Beginning in the 1880s, the British, French, Belgians, Italians, Dutch, Spanish, and Germans used military force and political guile to conquer those continents. Each of the imperial nations, including the United States, dispatched Christian missionaries to convert native peoples. By 1900 some 18,000 Christian missionaries were scattered around the world. Often the conversion to Christianity was the first step in the loss of a culture's indigenous traditions. The Western religious activities also influenced the colonial power structure. As a British nationalist explained such global ambitions, "Today, power and domination rather than freedom and independence are the ideas that appeal to the imagination of the masses—and the national ideal has given way to the imperial." This imperial outlook set in motion clashes among the Western powers that would lead to unprecedented conflict in the twentieth century.

AMERICAN IMPERIALISM As the European nations expanded their control over much of the rest of the world, the United States also began to acquire territories outside the North American continent. Most Americans became increasingly aware of world markets as developments in transportation and communication quickened the pace of commerce and diplomacy. From the first, agricultural exports had been the basis of economic growth. Now the conviction grew that American manufacturers had matured to the point where they could outsell foreign competitors in the world market. But should the expansion of markets lead to territorial expansion as well? or to intervention in the internal affairs of other countries? On such points, Americans disagreed, but a small yet influential group of public officials embraced the idea of overseas possessions, regardless of the implications. These expansionists included Senators Albert J. Beveridge of Indiana and Henry Cabot Lodge of Massachusetts, Theodore Roosevelt, and not least of all, naval captain Alfred Thayer Mahan.

During the 1880s Captain Mahan had become a leading advocate of sea power and Western imperialism. In 1890 he published *The Influence of Sea Power upon History, 1660–1783*, in which he argued that national greatness and prosperity flowed from sea power. Modern economic development called for a powerful navy, a strong merchant marine, foreign commerce, colonies, and naval bases. Mahan championed America's "destiny" to control the Caribbean, build an isthmian canal, and spread Western civilization in the Pacific. His ideas were widely circulated in popular journals and within the U.S. government.

Yet even before Mahan's writings became influential, a gradual expansion of the navy had begun. In 1880 the nation had fewer than 100 seagoing vessels, many of them rusting or rotting at the docks. By 1896 eleven powerful new battleships had been built or authorized.

IMPERIALIST THEORY Claims of racial superiority bolstered the new imperialist spirit. Spokesmen in each Western country, including the United States, used the arguments of social Darwinism to justify economic exploitation and territorial conquest. Among nations as among individuals, expansionists claimed, the fittest survive and prevail. John Fiske, a historian and popular lecturer on Darwinism, developed racial corollaries from Darwin's ideas. In *American Political Ideas Viewed from the Standpoint of Universal History* (1885), he stressed the superior character of "Anglo-Saxon" institutions and peoples. The English "race," he argued, was destined to dominate the globe in the institutions, traditions, language—even in the blood—of the world's peoples. Josiah Strong, a Congregationalist minister, added the sanction of religion to theories of racial and national superiority. In his book *Our Country: Its Possible Future and Its Present Crisis* (1885), Strong asserted that "Anglo-Saxons" embodied two great ideas: civil liberty and "a pure spiritual Christianity." The Anglo-Saxon was "divinely commissioned to be, in a peculiar sense, his brother's keeper."

EXPANSION IN THE PACIFIC

For Josiah Strong and other expansionists, Asia offered an especially alluring temptation. President Andrew Johnson's secretary of state, William H. Seward, believed that the United States must inevitably exercise commercial domination "on the Pacific Ocean, and its islands and continents." Eager for American manufacturers to exploit Asian markets, Seward believed the United States first had to remove all foreign interests from the northern Pacific coast and gain access to that region's valuable ports. To that end, Seward cast covetous eyes on the British crown colony of British Columbia, sandwiched between Russia's possessions in Alaska and the Washington Territory.

Late in 1866, while encouraging British Columbians to consider making their colony a U.S. territory, Seward learned of Russia's desire to sell Alaska. He leaped at the opportunity, and in 1867 the United States bought Alaska for $7.2 million, less than 2¢ an acre. "Seward's folly" of buying the Alaskan "icebox" proved in time to be the biggest bargain since the Louisiana Purchase.

SAMOA AND HAWAII   Seward's successors at the State Department sustained his expansionist vision. During the post–Civil War years the United States sought coaling stations and trading posts in the Pacific Ocean, and it laid claim to various small islands and atolls. Two of those island groups were especially strategic: Samoa and Hawaii (also known as the Sandwich Islands). In 1878 the Samoans signed a treaty granting the United States a naval base on one of its islands. The following year the German and British governments worked out similar arrangements on other Samoan islands. In Hawaii the Americans had a clearer field to exploit. The islands, a united kingdom since 1795, hosted a sizable settlement of American missionaries and planters. The Hawaiian Islands were strategically more important to the United States than

Samoa was, since their occupation by another major power might have posed a threat to American sugar interests and even to defense of the continent.

In 1875 the Hawaiians signed a reciprocal trade agreement, according to which their sugar entered the United States duty-free. Twelve years later they granted the United States a naval base at Pearl Harbor, near Honolulu. These agreements prompted a boom in sugar growing, and American settlers in Hawaii came to dominate the economy. In 1887 the Americans forced Hawaii's king to create a constitutional government, which they controlled.

Hawaii's political climate changed sharply when the king's sister, Queen

Queen Liliuokalani

The Hawaiian queen sought to preserve her nation's independence.

Liliuokalani, ascended the throne in 1891 and tried to reclaim power. Shortly before that the McKinley Tariff had destroyed Hawaii's favored position in the sugar trade by putting the sugar of all countries on the duty-free list and granting growers in the United States a 2¢ subsidy per pound of sugar. The resultant economic crisis and discontent in Hawaii led the white population to revolt early in 1893 and seize power. U.S. marines supported the coup. Within a month the new American-dominated government sent a delegation to Washington and signed a treaty annexing Hawaii to the United States.

These events occurred just weeks before President Benjamin Harrison left office, however, and Democratic senators blocked the treaty's ratification. President Cleveland withdrew the treaty and sent a special commissioner to Hawaii to investigate the situation. The commissioner ordered the marines home and reported that Americans on the islands had acted improperly. Most Hawaiians opposed annexation, said the commissioner, who thought the revolution had been engineered mainly by U.S. sugar planters hoping for annexation in order to be eligible for the new subsidy for sugar grown in the United States. Cleveland therefore proposed to restore the queen in return for amnesty to the revolutionists. The provisional government refused to step down, however, and on July 4, 1894, it proclaimed the islands the Republic of Hawaii, which included in its constitution a standing provision for annexation to the United States.

When William McKinley became president in 1897, he was looking for an excuse to annex the Hawaiian Islands. This excuse was found when the Japanese, also hoping to take over the islands, sent warships to Hawaii. McKinley responded by sending U.S. warships and asking the Senate to annex the territory. When the Senate could not muster the two-thirds majority needed to approve the treaty, McKinley used a joint resolution of the House and the Senate to achieve his aims. The resolution passed by simple majorities in both houses, and the United States annexed Hawaii in the summer of 1898.

THE SPANISH-AMERICAN WAR

Until the 1890s a nagging ambivalence about acquiring overseas territories had checked America's drive to expand. Suddenly, in 1898 and 1899, the inhibitions collapsed, but not in a quest for bases and trade. Rather, the chief motive was a sense of outrage at another country's imperialism.

"CUBA LIBRE" Throughout the second half of the nineteenth century, Cubans had repeatedly revolted against Spanish rule, only to be ruthlessly put down. Cuba was one of Spain's oldest colonies and had become a major export market for the mother country. Yet American investments in Cuba, mainly in sugar and mining, were steadily increasing. The United States in fact traded more with Cuba than Spain did. The growing economic interest in their island neighbor made Americans sympathetic to the idea of Cuban independence. So when Cubans revolted against Spanish rule on February 24, 1895, public feeling in the United States was with the rebels.

Events in Cuba supplied exciting copy for the press. William Randolph Hearst's *New York Journal* and Joseph Pulitzer's *New York World* were at the time locked in a monumental competition for readers. "It was a battle of gigantic proportions," one journalist wrote, "in which the sufferings of Cuba merely chanced to furnish some of the most convenient ammunition." The sensationalism in covering events in Cuba came to be called yellow journalism, and Hearst emerged as the undisputed champion.

PRESSURE FOR WAR American neutrality in the Cuban struggle for independence changed sharply when William McKinley entered office in 1897. His platform had endorsed Cuban independence as well as U.S. control of Hawaii and the construction of an isthmian canal. Knowing that the Cuban rebels enjoyed American support, Spain offered autonomy (self-government without formal independence) in return for peace: The Cubans rejected the offer. Spain was impaled on the horns of a dilemma, unable to end the rebellion and unready to give up Cuba.

Early in 1898 events moved rapidly to arouse American opinion against Spain. On February 9 Hearst's *New York Journal* released the text of a letter from a Spanish official, Depuy de Lôme, to a friend in Havana. In the letter, which had been stolen from the post office by a Cuban spy, de Lôme called President McKinley "weak and a bidder for the admiration of the crowd." The breach in diplomatic etiquette was such that de Lôme resigned to prevent further embarrassment to his government.

Six days later, during the night of February 15, 1898, the U.S. battleship *Maine* exploded and sank in Havana Harbor with a loss of 260 men. The ship's captain, one of only 84 survivors, scribbled a telegram to Washington: "*Maine* blown up in Havana Harbor at nine forty tonight and destroyed. Many wounded and doubtless more killed or drowned. . . . Public opinion should be suspended until further report." But those eager for a war with Spain saw no need to withhold judgment; they demanded an immediate declaration of war. Theodore Roosevelt, assistant secretary of the navy, called the sinking "an act of dirty treachery on the part of the Spaniards." The United States, he declared, "needs a war."

A naval court of inquiry reported that an external mine had sunk the ship. Lacking hard evidence, the court made no effort to fix the blame, but the yellow press had no need of evidence. The *New York Journal* gleefully reported: "The Whole Country Thrills with War Fever." The outcry against Spain rose in a crescendo with the words "Remember the *Maine!* To Hell with Spain!" Few of those promoting war wrestled with the obvious fact that the Spanish government was determined to avoid a confrontation with the United States and therefore had nothing to gain from sinking the *Maine*. A comprehensive study in 1976 concluded that the sinking of the *Maine* was an accident, the result of an internal explosion triggered by a fire in its coal bunker.

The weight of outraged public opinion and the influence of militant Republicans such as Theodore Roosevelt and Henry Cabot Lodge eroded President McKinley's neutrality. On March 9, 1898, the president pushed through Congress a $50-million defense appropriation. The Spanish government, sensing the growing militancy in the United States, announced a unilateral cease-fire in early April. On April 10 the Spanish ambassador gave the U.S. State Department a message that amounted to a surrender. But the message came too late. The following day, McKinley sent Congress his war message. He asked for the power to use armed forces in Cuba to protect U.S. property and trade. On April 20 a joint resolution of Congress declared

The Sinking of the *Maine* in Havana Harbor

The uproar created by the incident and its coverage in the "yellow press" pushed President William McKinley to declare war.

Cuba independent and demanded withdrawal of Spanish forces. The Teller Amendment, added on the Senate floor, disclaimed any American designs on Cuban territory. McKinley signed the resolution and sent a copy to the Spanish government. On April 22 the president announced a blockade of Cuba, an act of war under international law. Rather than give in to an ultimatum, the Spanish government declared war on April 24. Determined to be first, Congress declared war the next day, making the declaration retroactive to April 21, 1898.

Why such a rush to war after the message from Spain had indicated that it was ready for an armistice? No one knows for sure, but it seems apparent that too much momentum and popular pressure had built up for a confidential message to change the course of events. Also, leaders of the business community were demanding a quick resolution of the problem. Many of them lacked faith in the willingness or ability of the Spanish government to resolve the crisis. Still, it is fair to ask why McKinley did not take a stronger stand for peace. He might have defied Congress and public opinion, but in the end he deemed the political risk too high. The ultimate blame for war, if blame must be levied, belongs to the American people for letting themselves be whipped into such a hostile frenzy.

MANILA   The war itself lasted only 114 days. The American victory marked the end of Spain's once-great New World empire and the emergence of the United States as a world power. But if war with Spain saved many lives by ending the insurrection in Cuba, it also led to U.S. involvement in another insurrection, in the Philippines, and it created a host of commitments in the Caribbean and the Pacific that would haunt American policy makers during the twentieth century.

The Spanish-American War was barely under way before the U.S. navy produced a spectacular victory in an unexpected quarter: Manila Bay. While public attention centered on Cuba, young Theodore Roosevelt focused on the Spanish-controlled Philippines. As assistant secretary of the navy, he ordered Commodore George Dewey to engage Spain's ships in the Philippines in case of war. President McKinley approved the orders. Arriving late on April 30, 1898, Dewey's squadron destroyed or captured all the Spanish warships in Manila Bay. Dewey, without an occupation force, was now in awkward possession of the bay. Once reinforcements arrived, the American forces, with the help of Filipino insurrectionists under Emilio Aguinaldo, liberated Manila from Spanish control on August 13.

THE CUBAN CAMPAIGN   While these events transpired halfway around the world, the fighting in Cuba reached a surprisingly quick climax. The U.S. Navy blockaded the Spanish fleet at Santiago while an invasion force of some 17,000 American troops was hastily assembled at Tampa, Florida. One significant unit was the First Volunteer Cavalry, better known as the Rough Riders and best remembered because Lieutenant Colonel Theodore Roosevelt was second in command. Eager to get "in on the fun" and "act up to my preachings," Roosevelt had quit the Navy Department after war was declared. He ordered a custom-fitted uniform with yellow trim, grabbed a dozen pairs of spectacles, and rushed to help organize a colorful volunteer regiment of Ivy League athletes, leathery ex-convicts, Indians, and southwestern sharpshooters.

The major land action of the Cuban campaign occurred on July 1. While a much larger American force attacked Spanish positions at San Juan Hill, a smaller unit, including the dismounted Rough Riders—most of whose horses were still in Florida—and two African-American regiments, seized the enemy position atop nearby Kettle Hill. Theodore Roosevelt later claimed that he "would rather have led that charge than serve . . . three terms in the U.S. Senate." A friend wrote to Roosevelt's wife that her husband was "revelling in victory and gore."

The two battles put U.S. forces atop heights from which they could bring Santiago and the Spanish fleet under siege. On July 3 the Spanish ships made a gallant run for it, but the aging vessels were little match for the newer American fleet. The casualties were one-sided: 474 Spanish were killed or wounded and 1,750 were taken prisoner, while only one American was killed and one wounded. Santiago surrendered on July 17. On July 25 an American force moved onto the Spanish-held island of Puerto Rico.

The next day the Spanish government sued for peace. After discussions lasting two weeks, negotiators signed an armistice on August 12, 1898, less than four months after the war's start and the day before American troops entered Manila. The peace protocol specified that Spain should give up Cuba and that the United States should annex Puerto Rico and occupy the city, bay, and harbor of Manila pending the transfer of power in the Philippines.

And so the "splendid little war," as the future secretary of state John Hay called it in a letter to Roosevelt, officially ended. It was splendid only in the sense that its cost was relatively slight. Of the more than 274,000 Americans who served during the war and the ensuing demobilization, 5,462 died, but only 379 in battle. Most succumbed to malaria, typhoid, dysentery, or yellow fever. At such a cost the United States was launched onto the world stage as a great power, with all the benefits—and burdens—of that new status.

THE DEBATE OVER ANNEXATION The United States and Spain signed the Treaty of Paris on December 10, 1898, but the status of the Philippines remained in limbo. President McKinley, who claimed that at first he could not locate the Philippines on a map, gave ambiguous signals to the peace commission, which itself was divided. There had been no demand for annexation of the Philippines or other Spanish possessions before the war, but Commodore Dewey's victory at Manila Bay quickly kindled expansionist fever. Business leaders began thinking of the commercial possibilities in the nearby continent of Asia, such as oil for the lamps of China and textiles for its millions of people. Missionary societies yearned to convert "the little brown brother" to Christianity. Although most of these Filipino candidates for conversion were already Catholic, the word went forth that the Philippines should be taken for the sake of their souls. Spanish negotiators raised

"Well, I Hardly Know Which to Take First."

At the end of the nineteenth century, it seemed that Uncle Sam had developed a considerable appetite for foreign territory.

the delicate point that U.S. forces had no claim by right of conquest and had even taken Manila after the armistice. American negotiators finally offered the Spanish $20 million as compensation for possession of the Philippines, as well as Puerto Rico in the Caribbean and Guam in the Pacific.

Meanwhile, Americans had taken other giant steps in the Pacific. Hawaii had been annexed in the midst of the war. In 1899, after another outbreak of fighting over the royal succession in Samoa, Germany and the United States agreed to partition the Samoa Islands. The United States annexed the easternmost islands; Germany took the rest.

The Treaty of Paris was opposed by most Democrats and Populists and some Republicans. Anti-imperialists argued that the unprecedented acquisition of the Philippines would undermine democracy. They appealed to traditional isolationism, American principles of self-government, the inconsistency of liberating Cuba and annexing the Philippines, the involvement in foreign entanglements that would undermine the logic of the Monroe Doctrine, and the danger that the Philippines would be expensive if not impossible to defend. The prospect of incorporating so many alien peoples was also troubling. "Bananas and self-government cannot grow on the same piece of land," one senator claimed.

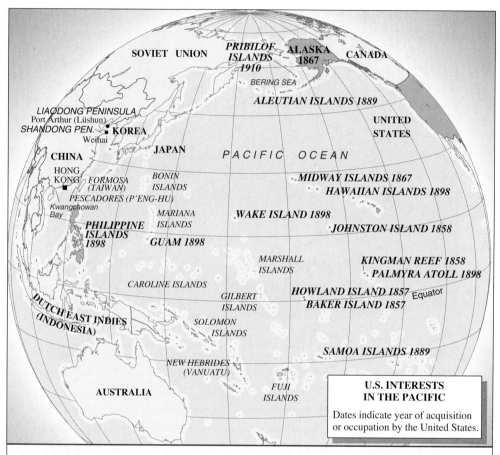

SOVIET UNION
PRIBILOF ISLANDS 1910
ALASKA 1867
CANADA
BERING SEA
ALEUTIAN ISLANDS 1889
UNITED STATES
LIAODONG PENINSULA
Port Arthur (Lüshun)
SHANDONG PEN.
Weihai
KOREA
JAPAN
PACIFIC OCEAN
CHINA
HONG KONG
FORMOSA (TAIWAN)
PESCADORES (P'ENG-HU)
Kwangchowan Bay
BONIN ISLANDS
MIDWAY ISLANDS 1867
HAWAIIAN ISLANDS 1898
WAKE ISLAND 1898
MARIANA ISLANDS
JOHNSTON ISLAND 1858
PHILIPPINE ISLANDS 1898
GUAM 1898
KINGMAN REEF 1858
PALMYRA ATOLL 1898
MARSHALL ISLANDS
CAROLINE ISLANDS
GILBERT ISLANDS
HOWLAND ISLAND 1857
BAKER ISLAND 1857
Equator
DUTCH EAST INDIES (INDONESIA)
SOLOMON ISLANDS
NEW HEBRIDES (VANUATU)
SAMOA ISLANDS 1889
AUSTRALIA
FUJI ISLANDS

U.S. INTERESTS IN THE PACIFIC

Dates indicate year of acquisition or occupation by the United States.

Why was McKinley eager to acquire territory in the Pacific and the Caribbean? What kind of political system did the U.S. government create in Hawaii and in the Philippines? How did Filipinos and Hawaiians resist the Americans?

The opposition may have been strong enough to kill the treaty had not the populist Democrat William Jennings Bryan influenced the vote for approval. A formal end to the war, he argued, would open the way for the future independence of Cuba and the Philippines. Ratification finally came on February 6, 1899.

By that time U.S. troops had already clashed with Filipino insurrectionists near Manila. The Filipino rebel leader, Emilio Aguinaldo, had been in exile until Commodore Dewey brought him back to Luzon to make trouble for the Spanish. Since Aguinaldo's forces were more or less in control of the islands

Turmoil in the Philippines

Emilio Aguinaldo (seated third from right) and other leaders of the Filipino insurgence.

outside Manila, what followed over the next two years was largely an American war of conquest. It was a sordid conflict, with massacres and torture on both sides. In the end it took 63,000 U.S. troops, 4,300 American deaths, and almost three years to suppress the revolt. Organized Filipino resistance collapsed by the end of 1899, but even after the American capture of Aguinaldo in 1901, sporadic guerrilla action lasted until mid-1902.

Against the backdrop of this nasty guerrilla war, the great debate over annexation continued in the United States. The treaty debates inspired a number of anti-imperialist groups, which united in 1899 as the American Anti-Imperialist League. The league attracted members representing many shades of opinion; the main characteristic they had in common was that most belonged to an older generation. Andrew Carnegie footed the bills; on imperialism, at least, the union leader Samuel Gompers agreed with him. The usually soft-spoken philosopher William James exploded in voicing his opposition to the expansionists: "God damn the United States for its vile conduct in the Philippine Isles!" The selfish proponents of imperialism, he declared, had caused the nation to "puke up its ancient soul."

ORGANIZING THE ACQUISITIONS   Such criticism, however, did not faze the expansionists. McKinley quickly moved to set up a civil government in the Philippines. On July 4, 1901, the U.S. military government came to an end, and under an act of Congress, Judge William Howard Taft became the civil governor. The Philippine Government Act, passed by Congress on July 1, 1902, declared the Philippine Islands an "unorganized territory." In 1934 the Tydings-McDuffie Act offered independence after ten more years. Independence finally took effect on July 4, 1946.

Closer to home, Puerto Rico had been acquired in part to serve as a U.S. outpost guarding the approach to the Caribbean and any future isthmian canal. In 1900 the Foraker Act established a civil government on the island. Residents of the island were declared citizens of Puerto Rico; they were not made citizens of the United States until 1917. In 1952 Puerto Rico became a commonwealth with its own constitution and elected officials, a unique status. Like a state, Puerto Rico is free to change its constitution insofar as it does not conflict with the U.S. Constitution.

Liberated Cuba, American authorities soon learned, posed problems at least as irksome as those in the new possessions. After the American occupation forces had restored order, started schools, and improved sanitary conditions, they began handing the reins of power to the Cubans. The Platt Amendment to the army-appropriations bill passed by Congress in 1901 sharply restricted the new government's independence, however. The amendment required that Cuba never impair its independence by signing a treaty with a third power, that it keep its debt within the government's power to repay it out of ordinary revenues, and that it acknowledge the right of the United States to intervene in Cuba for the preservation of Cuban independence and the maintenance of "a government adequate for the protection of life, property, and individual liberty." Finally, Cuba was called upon to sell or lease to the United States lands to be used for coaling or naval stations, a proviso that led to a U.S. naval base at Guantánamo Bay, which is still in operation.

Imperial Rivalries in East Asia

THE "OPEN DOOR" During the 1890s not only the United States but also Japan emerged as a world power. Commodore Matthew Perry's voyage of 1853–1854 had opened Japan to Western ways, and the island nation had begun modernization in earnest after the 1860s. Flexing its new muscles, Japan defeated China's stagnant empire in the First Sino-Japanese War (1894–1895) and as a result acquired the island of Formosa (modern-day Taiwan). China's weakness, demonstrated in the war, led Russia, England, France, and Germany to renew their scramble for "spheres of influence" on that remaining frontier of imperialist expansion.

The possibility that those competing powers would carve up China and erect tariff barriers in their own spheres of influence dimmed the bright prospect of American trade with China. The British had much to lose in a tariff war, for they already enjoyed substantial trade with China. Fearful of such a development, the British suggested in 1899 that the United States join them in preserving China's commercial and territorial integrity. The State Department agreed that something must be done, but Secretary of State John Hay preferred to act alone rather than in concert with the British.

In its origins and content, what came to be known as the Open Door policy resembled the Monroe Doctrine. In both cases the United States unilaterally proclaimed a hands-off policy that the British had earlier proposed as a joint statement. The policy outlined in Hay's Open Door Note, dispatched in 1899 to London, Berlin, and St. Petersburg and a little later to Tokyo, Rome, and Paris, proposed to keep China open to trade with all countries on an equal basis. None except Britain accepted Hay's principles, but none rejected them either, so Hay simply announced that all powers had accepted the policy.

The Open Door policy was rooted in the self-interest of American businesses eager to exploit Chinese markets. Yet it also tapped the deep-seated sympathies of those who opposed imperialism, especially as it endorsed China's territorial integrity. But it had little legal standing. When the Japanese, concerned about Russian pressure in Manchuria, asked how the United States intended to enforce the Open Door policy, Hay replied that the United States was "not prepared" to do so. So it would remain for forty years, a hollow but dangerous commitment, until continued Japanese expansion would bring about war with America in 1941.

THE BOXER REBELLION   A new Asian crisis arose in 1900 when a group of Chinese nationalists known to the Western world as Boxers ("Fists of Righteous Harmony") rebelled against foreign involvement in China, surrounding the foreign embassies in Peking (Beijing). The British, Germans, Russians, Japanese, and Americans quickly mounted a military expedition to relieve the embassy compound. Hay, fearful that the intervention might become an excuse to dismember China, seized the chance to further refine his Open Door policy. The United States, he declared in a circular letter of July 3, 1900, sought a solution that would "preserve Chinese territorial and administrative integrity" as well as "equal and impartial trade with all parts of the Chinese Empire." Six weeks later the expedition reached Peking and broke the Boxer Rebellion.

Big-Stick Diplomacy

More than any other American political leader of his time, Theodore Roosevelt transformed the role of the United States in world affairs. The nation had emerged from the Spanish-American War a world power, and he insisted that this status entailed major new responsibilities. To ensure that the country accepted its international obligations, Roosevelt stretched both the Constitution and executive power to the limit. In the process he pushed a reluctant nation onto the center stage of world affairs.

ROOSEVELT'S RISE   In the fall elections of 1898, Republicans benefited from the euphoria of military victory, increasing their majority in Congress. That hardly amounted to a mandate for imperialism, however, since the election preceded most of the debates on the issue. But in 1900 the Democrats turned once again to William Jennings Bryan, who sought to make imperialism the "paramount issue" of the campaign. The Democratic platform condemned the Philippine conflict as "an unnecessary war" that had "placed the United States, previously known . . . throughout the world as the champion of freedom, in the false and un-American position of crushing with military force the efforts of our former allies to achieve liberty and self-government." The Republicans welcomed the opportunity to disagree. They renominated William McKinley and named as his running mate Theodore Roosevelt, who had been elected governor of New York after his self-inflated role in the Spanish-American War.

The trouble with Bryan's idea of a solemn referendum on imperialism was the near impossibility of making any presidential contest so simple. Bryan himself complicated his message by insisting once again on the free coinage of silver, and the tariff became an issue again as well. The Republicans' biggest advantage was probably the return to national prosperity, which they were fully ready to take credit for. Those who opposed imperialism but also opposed free silver or tariff reduction faced a bewildering choice.

The outcome was a victory for McKinley greater than his last, 7.2 million to 6.4 million popular votes and 292 to 155 electoral votes. There had been no clear-cut referendum on annexations, but the question was settled nonetheless, although it would take another year and a half to subdue the Filipino rebels. The job would be finished under the direction of another president, however.

On September 6, 1901, at a reception at the Pan-American Exposition in Buffalo, an anarchist named Leon Czolgosz (pronounced chole-gosh) approached McKinley, a pistol concealed in his bandaged hand, and fired at point-blank range. McKinley died six days later, thereby elevating Theodore Roosevelt to the White House. "Now look," Republican senator Mark Hanna erupted. "That damned cowboy is President of the United States!"

Six weeks short of his forty-third birthday, Roosevelt was the youngest man ever to take charge of the White House, but he had more experience in public affairs than most and more vitality than any. Born in 1858, the son of a wealthy New York merchant and a Georgia belle, Roosevelt had grown up in Manhattan in cultured comfort, had visited Europe as a child, spoke German fluently, and had graduated from Harvard Phi Beta Kappa in 1880. Rigorous exercise and outdoor adventure were two of his many passions. Boxer, wrestler, and outdoorsman, he was also an omnivorous reader, a renowned historian and essayist, and a zealous moralist.

Roosevelt studied law briefly and within two years of graduation from college won election to the New York legislature. That same year he published *The Naval War of 1812,* the first of numerous historical, biographical, and other works to flow from his pen. He seemingly had the world at his feet—and then disaster struck. In 1884 his beloved mother, only forty-eight years old, died. Eleven hours later, in the same house, his twenty-two-year-old wife struggled with kidney failure before dying in his arms, having recently given birth to their only child. Roosevelt was distraught and bewildered. "The light has gone out of my life," he wrote in his diary. The double funeral was so wrenching that the officiating minister wept throughout his prayer. In an attempt to recover from this "strange and terrible fate," Roosevelt turned his baby daughter over to his sister, quit his political career, sold the family house, and moved west to take up the cattle business in the Dakota Territory. The blue-blooded New Yorker relished hunting, leading roundups, capturing outlaws, fighting Indians—and reading novels by the campfire. Although his western career lasted only two years, he never quite got over being a cowboy.

Back in New York City, Roosevelt remarried and ran unsuccessfully for mayor; and he later served six years as civil service commissioner in Washington, D.C., and two years as New York City's police commissioner. After President McKinley appointed him assistant secretary of the navy in 1897, Roosevelt did all he could to promote the war with Spain over Cuba. "A just war," he insisted, "is in the long run far better for a man's soul than the most prosperous peace."

Roosevelt combined his boundless energy with an unshakable righteousness that led him to cast every issue in moral and patriotic terms. He saw the presidency as his "bully pulpit," and he was eager to preach fist-smacking

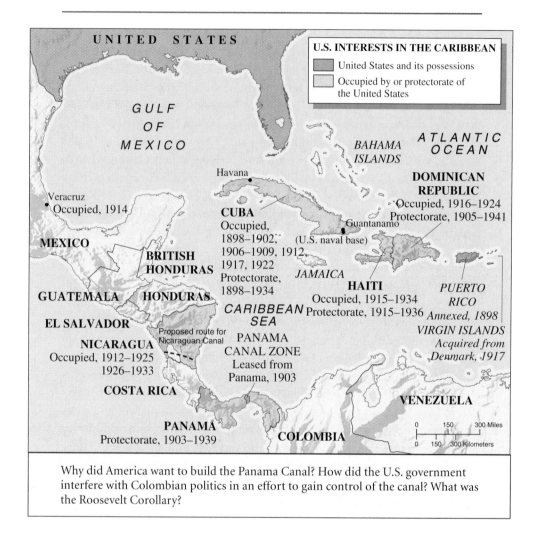

UNITED STATES

U.S. INTERESTS IN THE CARIBBEAN
United States and its possessions
Occupied by or protectorate of
the United States

GULF
OF
MEXICO

BAHAMA
ISLANDS

ATLANTIC
OCEAN

Havana

DOMINICAN
REPUBLIC
Occupied, 1916–1924
Protectorate, 1905–1941

Veracruz
Occupied, 1914

CUBA
Occupied,
1898–1902,
1906–1909, 1912,
1917, 1922
Protectorate,
1898–1934

Guantanamo
(U.S. naval base)

MEXICO

BRITISH
HONDURAS

JAMAICA

GUATEMALA HONDURAS

HAITI
Occupied, 1915–1934
Protectorate, 1915–1936

PUERTO
RICO
Annexed, 1898

EL SALVADOR

CARIBBEAN
SEA

NICARAGUA
Occupied, 1912–1925
1926–1933

Proposed route for
Nicaraguan Canal

PANAMA
CANAL ZONE
Leased from
Panama, 1903

VIRGIN ISLANDS
Acquired from
Denmark, 1917

COSTA RICA

VENEZUELA

PANAMA
Protectorate, 1903–1939

COLOMBIA

0   150   300 Miles
0   150   300 Kilometers

Why did America want to build the Panama Canal? How did the U.S. government
interfere with Colombian politics in an effort to gain control of the canal? What was
the Roosevelt Corollary?

sermons on the virtues of honesty, civic duty, and the strenuous life to his
national flock. But appearances were deceiving. His energy left a false impression of impulsiveness, and the talk of morality cloaked a cautious pragmatism. Roosevelt could get carried away, but as he said of his foreign-policy
actions, this was likely to happen only when "I am assured that I shall be able
eventually to carry out my will by force."

THE PANAMA CANAL   After the Spanish-American War the United
States became more deeply involved than ever in the Caribbean, where one

issue overshadowed every other: the Panama Canal. The narrow isthmus of Panama, a part of Colombia, had long excited dreams of an interoceanic canal. After America's victory over Spain, Secretary of State John Hay commenced talks with the British ambassador to revise the Clayton-Bulwer Treaty of 1850, which prohibited either nation from constructing a transoceanic canal. The negotiations led to the Hay-Pauncefote Treaty of 1901, in which Britain gave its consent to the American plan for a canal across Panama.

Other obstacles remained, however. From 1881 to 1887, a French company had spent nearly $300 million and sacrificed some 20,000 lives to dig less than one third of a canal

Digging the Canal

President Theodore Roosevelt operating a steam shovel during his 1906 visit to the Panama Canal.

through Panama. The company now offered to sell its holdings to the United States. Meanwhile, Secretary of State Hay had opened negotiations with Ambassador Tomás Herrán of Colombia to build a canal across Panama, which was then a reluctant province of Colombia. In return for a Canal Zone six miles wide, the United States agreed to pay $10 million in cash and a rental fee of $250,000 a year. The United States Senate ratified the Hay-Herrán Treaty in 1903, but the Colombian senate held out for $25 million in cash.

Colombia's rejection of the treaty heightened the desire of Panamanian rebels for independence. An employee of the French canal company then hatched a plot in collusion with the company's representative, Philippe Bunau-Varilla. Bunau-Varilla visited Roosevelt and Hay and then, apparently with inside information, informed the Panamanian rebels that the U.S.S. *Nashville* would arrive at Colón, Panama, on November 2, 1903.

An army of some 500 Panamanians revolted against Colombian rule the next day. Colombian troops, who could not penetrate the overland jungle, found U.S. ships blocking the sea-lanes. On November 7 the Roosevelt administration made good on its collusion with the revolutionaries by recognizing Panama's independence, and on November 18 Roosevelt and the new Panamanian ambassador, who happened to be Bunau-Varilla, signed a treaty extending the Canal Zone from six to ten miles in width. For $10 million down and $250,000 a year, the United States received "in perpetuity the use, occupation and control" of the Canal Zone. Colombia eventually got its $25 million, in 1921, but only after America's interest in Colombian oil had lubricated the wheels of diplomacy. There was no apology, but the payment was made to remove "all misunderstandings growing out of the political events in Panama, November, 1903." The canal opened on August 15, 1914, two weeks after the outbreak of World War I in Europe. It was a tribute to American engineering and a boon to American commerce and the Panamanian economy.

THE ROOSEVELT COROLLARY   Even without the canal the United States would have been concerned with the stability of the Caribbean region, and particularly with the activities of any hostile power there. A prime excuse for intervention in those days was to force the collection of debts owed to foreigners. In 1904 a crisis over the Dominican Republic's debts gave Roosevelt an opportunity to formulate U.S. policy. In his annual address to Congress in 1904, he set forth what came to be known as the Roosevelt Corollary to the Monroe Doctrine: the principle, in short, that since the Monroe Doctrine prohibited European intervention in the region, the United States was justified in intervening first to forestall the actions of outsiders. Roosevelt suggested that the United States could exercise an "international police power" in its own sphere of influence. As put into practice by mutual agreement with the Dominican Republic in 1905, the Roosevelt Corollary called for the United States to install and protect a collector of customs, who would apply a portion of the nation's revenues to debt payments owed

The World's Constable

President Theodore Roosevelt wields "the big stick," symbolizing his approach to diplomacy.

foreign nations. The principle, applied peaceably in 1905, became the basis for military interventions later on.

THE RUSSO-JAPANESE WAR   In east Asia, meanwhile, the principle of equal trading rights embodied in the Open Door policy received a serious challenge when tensions between Russia and Japan flared into a fight over China and Korea. On February 8, 1904, war broke out when the Japanese launched a surprise attack that devastated the Russian fleet. The Japanese then occupied Korea and drove the Russians back across the Yalu River into Manchuria. But neither side could score a knockout blow, and neither relished a prolonged war. When the Japanese signaled President Roosevelt that they would welcome a negotiated settlement, he agreed to sponsor a peace conference, held in Portsmouth, New Hampshire. In the Treaty of Portsmouth (1905), the concessions all went to the Japanese. Russia acknowledged Japan's "predominant political, military, and economic interests in Korea" (Japan would annex the kingdom in 1910), and both powers agreed to evacuate Manchuria.

RELATIONS WITH JAPAN   Japan's show of strength in the war with Russia raised doubts about the security of the Philippines. During the Portsmouth talks, Roosevelt sent Secretary of War William Howard Taft to meet with the Japanese foreign minister in Tokyo. The two men arrived at the Taft-Katsura Agreement of July 29, 1905, in which the United States accepted Japanese control of Korea and Japan disavowed any designs on the Philippines. Three years later the Root-Takahira Agreement, negotiated by Secretary of State Elihu Root and the Japanese ambassador, promised to respect the other's possessions and reinforced the Open Door policy by supporting "the independence and integrity of China" and "the principle of equal opportunity for commerce and industry in China."

Behind the diplomatic facade of goodwill, however, lay simmering mutual distrust. For many Americans the Russian threat in east Asia now gave way to distrust of Japan's "yellow peril" (a term apparently coined by Germany's kaiser Wilhelm II). Racial animosities on the West Coast helped sour relations with Japan. In 1906 San Francisco's school board ordered students of Chinese, Japanese, and Korean descent to attend a separate public school. The Japanese government sharply protested the show of ethnic prejudice, and President Roosevelt managed to talk the school board into changing its policy. For its part, Japan agreed to limit sharply its issuance of visas to the United States. This "Gentleman's Agreement" of

1907, the precise terms of which have never been revealed, halted the influx of Japanese immigrants and brought some respite to racial agitation in California.

THE UNITED STATES AND EUROPE   During these years of expansionism the United States cast its gaze mainly westward and southward. But events in Europe also required attention. While Roosevelt was mediating the Russo-Japanese War in 1905, another crisis was brewing in Morocco, where the Germans and French fought for control. Roosevelt felt that the United States had something at stake in preventing the outbreak of a major war. At the kaiser's behest he talked the French and the British into attending an international conference at Algeciras, Spain, with American delegates present. Roosevelt then maneuvered the Germans into accepting his lead. The Act of Algeciras, signed in 1906, affirmed the independence of Morocco and guaranteed an open door for trade there. Roosevelt received the Nobel Peace Prize in 1906 for his work at Portsmouth and Algeciras. For all his bellicosity on other occasions, he had earned it.

Before Roosevelt left the White House in March 1909, he celebrated America's rise to the status of a world power with one great flourish. In late 1907 he sent the entire U.S. Navy, by then second in strength only to the British fleet, on a grand tour around the world. It was the first such display of American naval might in the Pacific, and many feared the reaction of the Japanese, for whose benefit Roosevelt had in fact staged the show. They need not have worried, for in Japan the flotilla got the greatest welcome of all. Thousands of schoolchildren turned out, waving tiny American flags and singing "The Star-Spangled Banner" in English. The triumphal procession continued home by way of the Mediterranean and steamed back into American waters in 1909, just in time to close out Roosevelt's presidency on a note of success.

Yet it was a success that would have mixed consequences. Roosevelt's ability to project American power abroad was burdened by a racist ideology shared by many prominent political figures of the time. He once told the graduates of the Naval War College that all "the great masterful races have been fighting races, and the minute that a race loses the hard fighting virtues . . . it has lost the right to stand as equal to the best." On another occasion he called war the best way to promote "the clear instinct for race selfishness" and insisted that "the most ultimately righteous of all wars is a war with savages." Such a belligerent and bigoted attitude would come back to haunt the United States in world affairs—and at home.

MAKING CONNECTIONS

· The Spanish-American War marked a turning point in U.S. foreign policy. America's emergence as a global power is a central theme of the twentieth century.

· Theodore Roosevelt's foreign policy displayed an activist approach to the presidency. The next chapter describes connections between his foreign policies and his approach to domestic affairs.

FURTHER READING

An excellent survey of the diplomacy of the era is Charles Soutter Campbell's *The Transformation of American Foreign Relations, 1865–1900* (1976). For background on the events of the 1890s, see Walter LaFeber's *The American Search for Opportunity, 1865–1913* (1993) and D. Healy's *U.S. Expansionism: The Imperialist Urge in the 1890s* (1970). The dispute over American policy in Hawaii is covered in Thomas J. Osborne's *"Empire Can Wait": American Opposition to Hawaiian Annexation, 1893–1898* (1981).

Ivan Musicant's *Empire by Default: The Spanish-American War and the Dawn of the American Century* (1998) is the most comprehensive volume on the conflict. For the war's aftermath in the Philippines, see Stuart Creighton Miller's *"Benevolent Assimilation": The American Conquest of the Philippines, 1899–1903* (1982). Robert L. Beisner's *Twelve against Empire: The Anti-Imperialists, 1898–1900* (1968) handles the debate over annexation.

A good introduction to American interest in China is Michael H. Hunt's *The Making of a Special Relationship: The United States and China to 1914* (1983). Kenton J. Clymer's *John Hay: The Gentleman as Diplomat* (1975) examines the role of this key secretary of state in forming policy.

For U.S. policy in the Caribbean and Central America, see Walter LaFeber's *Inevitable Revolutions: The United States in Central America*, 2nd ed. (1993). David McCullough's *The Path between the Seas: The Creation of the Panama Canal, 1870–1914* (1977) presents the fullest account of how the United States secured the Panama Canal.

24

THE PROGRESSIVE ERA

FOCUS QUESTIONS

- What were the basic elements of Progressive reform?
- What were the central issues confronting the presidencies of Theodore Roosevelt, William H. Taft, and Woodrow Wilson?
- What was the significance of the election of 1912?

To answer these questions and access additional review material, please visit www.wwnorton.com/studyspace.

Theodore Roosevelt's emergence as a national leader coincided with the onset of what historians have labeled the Progressive Era (1900–1917). The Progressive movement arose in response to many societal changes, the most powerful of which were the devastating depression of the 1890s and its attendant social unrest. The depression brought hard times to the cities, deepened distress in rural areas, and provoked both the fears and the conscience of the rapidly growing middle and upper-middle classes. By the turn of the century, so many outraged activists were at work seeking to improve social conditions and political abuses that people began to speak of a Progressive Era, a time of fermenting idealism, moral and religious fervor, and constructive social, economic, and political change.

ELEMENTS OF REFORM

Progressivism was a reform movement so varied and comprehensive in its goals and motives that it almost defies definition. Political Progressives crusaded against the abuses of urban political bosses and corporate robber barons. Their goals were greater democracy, honest and efficient government, more effective regulation of big business and "special interests," and greater social justice for working people.

The Progressive movement represented the animating spirit of the times rather than a single organized group or party. What reformers shared was a common assumption that the complex social ills and tensions generated by the urban-industrial revolution required expanding the scope of local, state, and federal government authority so as to elevate the public interest over private greed. Many Progressives were motivated by religious beliefs that led some of them to concentrate on moral reforms such as the prohibition of alcoholic beverages and Sunday closing laws.

The "real heart of the movement," declared one reformer, was "to use the government as an agency of human welfare." Governments were now called upon to extend a broad range of direct services: schools, good roads (a movement propelled first by cyclists and then by automobilists), conservation of natural resources, public health and welfare, care of the disabled, and farm loans and farm demonstration agents (county workers who visited farms to demonstrate new technology), among others. Such initiatives represented the first tentative steps toward what would become known during the 1930s and thereafter as the welfare state.

THE ANTECEDENTS OF PROGRESSIVISM The Progressive impulse began at the local level in the 1880s as a response to problems caused by industrialization and urbanization and only gradually emerged on the national level. Beginning in the large cities of the East and the Midwest, private citizens worked to improve basic public services such as sewerage, housing, and transportation. Reformers of local government believed in greater efficiency, less favoritism, and more expertise. They wanted to reorder government itself through detailed budgets, audits, and a more rationalized structure of government offices. Early efforts to improve public health, education, and factory conditions grew out of a desire to improve the administration and enforcement of local and state laws.

Another significant force in fostering the spirit of Progressivism was the growing prominence of socialist critiques of living and working conditions. The Socialist party of the time, small but earnest and vocal, served as the left wing of Progressivism. Most Progressives found socialist remedies unacceptable, and the main Progressive reform impulse grew in part from a desire to counter the growing appeal of socialist doctrines.

THE MUCKRAKERS   Poverty, unsafe working conditions, infectious diseases, and child labor in unhealthy factories were complex social issues; remedying them would take more than an idealistic desire to effect change in government, public health, and working conditions. Public consciousness needed to be raised, a process that required publicizing both scandals and festering social ills. A group of journalists dubbed muckrakers rose to the challenge. These writers, who thrived on exposing corruption and social injustice, got their name when Theodore Roosevelt compared them to a character in John Bunyan's *Pilgrim's Progress:* "A man that could look no way but downwards with a muckrake in his hands." "Muckrakers are often indispensable to ... society," Roosevelt said, "but only if they know when to stop raking the muck."

Henry Demarest Lloyd is sometimes cited as the first of the muckrakers, for his critical examination of the Standard Oil Company and other monopolies in his book *Wealth against Commonwealth* (1894). Lloyd exposed the growth of corporate giants responsible to none but themselves, able to corrupt if not control governments. Lincoln Steffens likewise revealed the prevalence of municipal corruption in a series of articles later collected into a book, *The Shame of the Cities* (1904).

Another early muckraker was Jacob Riis, a Danish immigrant who exposed slum conditions in *How the Other Half Lives* (1890). The chief outlets for social critics were the popular middle-class magazines that began to flourish in the 1890s, such as the *Arena* and *McClure's*.

Without the muckrakers, Progressivism would never have achieved widespread popular support. In feeding a growing public appetite for facts about modern social problems, the muckrakers demonstrated one of the salient features of the Progressive movement, and one of its central failures. The Progressives were stronger on diagnosis than on remedy. They harbored a naive faith in the power of democracy. Reveal the facts, expose corruption, arouse public indignation, and bring government closer to the people, they assumed, and the correction of evils would follow automatically. The cure for the ills of democracy was, to Progressive reformers, simply a more enlightened and more engaged democracy.

FEATURES OF PROGRESSIVISM

DEMOCRACY   The most important Progressive reform intended to democratize government was the direct primary, in which candidates would be nominated by the vote of all party members rather than by a few political bosses who selected candidates for the parties. After South Carolina adopted the first statewide primary in 1896, the concept spread within two decades to nearly every other state.

The primary was but one expression of a broad movement for greater public participation in the political process. In 1898 South Dakota became the first state to adopt the initiative and referendum, procedures that allow voters to enact laws directly. If a designated number of voters petitioned to have a measure put on the ballot (the initiative), the electorate could then vote it up or down (the referendum). Oregon also adopted a spectrum of reform measures, including a voter-registration law (1899), the initiative and referendum (1902), the direct primary (1904), a sweeping corrupt-practices act (1908), and the recall (1910), whereby public officials could be removed by a public petition and vote. By 1920 nearly twenty states had adopted the initiative and referendum, and nearly a dozen had adopted the recall. The direct election of U.S. senators by the people, rather than by the state legislatures, was another Progressive political reform. The popular election of senators required a constitutional amendment, and by 1912 the Senate finally agreed to the Seventeenth Amendment, which was ratified by the states in 1913.

EFFICIENCY   A second major theme of Progressivism was the "gospel of efficiency." In the business world at the turn of the century and after, Frederick W. Taylor, the original "efficiency expert," developed an array of scientific management techniques designed to cut manufacturing costs and enhance productivity. Taylorism, as scientific management came to be known, promised to reduce waste through the careful analysis of labor processes. By meticulously studying the time it took each worker to perform a task, Taylor prescribed the optimal technique for the average worker and established detailed performance standards for each job classification. The promise of higher wages, he believed, would motivate workers to exceed the "average" expectations.

Instead, many workers resented Taylor's innovations. They saw in scientific management a tool to make employees work faster than was healthy or fair. Yet Taylor's controversial efficiency system brought concrete improvements in productivity, especially among those industries whose production processes

Robert M. La Follette

A proponent of expertise in government.

were highly standardized and whose jobs were precisely defined.

In government the efficiency movement called for nonpartisan "experts" to replace bureaucrats and demanded the reorganization of agencies to prevent redundancy, establish clear lines of authority, and assign accountability to specific officials. The most ardent disciple of the principle of government by experts was Wisconsin governor Robert M. La Follette, "Fighting Bob," who established a Legislative Reference Bureau staffed by professors and specialists to provide research, advice, and help in the drafting of legislation designed to curb the power of special interests and promote social justice. This "Wisconsin idea" of efficient government was widely publicized and copied by other states.

Two ideas for making municipal government more efficient gained headway in the first decade of the new century. The commission system was first adopted by Galveston, Texas, in 1901, when local government collapsed in the aftermath of a devastating hurricane that killed 6,000 people and destroyed half the town. It placed ultimate authority in a board composed of elected administrative heads of city departments, commissioners of sanitation, police, utilities, and so on. By 1914 more than 400 towns and small cities across the country had adopted the commission system. The more durable idea, however, was the city-manager plan, under which a professional administrator ran the municipal government in accordance with policies set by the elected council and mayor. Staunton, Virginia, first adopted the plan in 1908. By 1914 the National Association of City Managers had heralded the arrival of a new profession.

REGULATION   Of all the problems facing American society at the turn of the century, one engaged a greater diversity of reformers and elicited more solutions than any other: the regulation of giant corporations, which became a third major theme of Progressivism. Beginning in the 1870s, states had tried to regulate the freight rates of railroads and the working conditions in other businesses, only to be thwarted by Supreme Court rulings. The judges declared that only the federal government could regulate companies involved in interstate commerce. By the 1890s the growth of monopolistic corporations had spurred reformers to act on a national level. While some Progressives believed that the problems of concentrated economic power and its abuses should be left to business to work out for itself, a policy known as laissez-faire, others advocated an active government policy of trust-busting in the belief that restoring old-fashioned competition was the best way to prevent economic abuses.

Efforts to restore the competitiveness of small firms proved unworkable, however, in part because breaking up large corporations was fraught with difficulty. As a consequence, the main thrust of Progressive reform over the years was toward regulation, rather than dissolution, of big businesses. To some extent, regulation and "stabilization" won acceptance among business leaders because whatever respect they paid to competition in principle, they preferred not to face it in practice. As time passed, however, regulatory agencies often came under the influence or control of those they were supposed to regulate.

SOCIAL JUSTICE   A fourth important feature of the Progressive spirit was the impulse toward social justice, which motivated diverse actions, from the promotion of private charities to campaigns against child labor and liquor. Led by women, the settlement-house movement of the late nineteenth century had spawned a corps of social workers and genteel reformers animated by religious ideals and devoted to the uplift of slum dwellers. But with time it became apparent that social evils extended beyond the reach of private charities and demanded government intervention.

Labor legislation was perhaps the most significant reform to emerge from the drive for social justice. It emerged first at the state level. The National Child Labor Committee, organized in 1904, led a movement for state laws banning the still-widespread employment of young children. Within ten years the committee

Child Labor

A young girl working as a spinner in a cotton mill in Vermont, 1910.

helped foster in most states new laws banning the labor of underage children (the minimum age varying from twelve to sixteen) and limiting the hours older children might work.

Closely linked to the child-labor reform movement was a concerted effort to regulate the hours of work for women. Spearheaded by Florence Kelley, the head of the National Consumers' League, this Progressive crusade promoted the passage of state laws addressing the distinctive hardships that long working hours imposed on women who were wives and mothers.

The Supreme Court pursued a curiously erratic course in ruling on new state labor laws. In *Lochner v. New York* (1905), the Court voided a ten-hour workday law because it violated workers' "liberty of contract" to accept any terms they chose. Then in *Muller v. Oregon* (1908), the high court upheld a ten-hour-workday law for women. The justices relied largely on sociological data that attorney Louis D. Brandeis presented regarding the adverse effects of long hours on the health and morals of women. In *Bunting v. Oregon* (1917), the Court accepted a ten-hour workday for both men and women but for twenty more years held out against state minimum-wage laws.

Legislation to protect workers against avoidable accidents gained momentum from disasters such as the 1911 fire at the Triangle Shirtwaist Company in New York City, in which 146 people, mostly young women, died because the owner kept the stairway doors locked to prevent theft. Workers trapped on the three upper floors of the ten-story building died in the fire or leaped to their death. Stricter building codes and factory-inspection acts followed.

PROHIBITION For many Progressive activists with strong religious convictions, the cause of liquor prohibition was the foremost societal concern. The Women's Christian Temperance Union had been battling the sale of alcoholic beverages since 1874, but the most successful political action followed the formation in 1893 of the Anti-Saloon League, an organization that pioneered the strategy of the single-issue pressure group. In 1913 the league endorsed an amendment to the Constitution prohibiting the sale of all alcoholic beverages, which was adopted by Congress in 1917. By the time it was ratified two years later, state and local action had already dried up areas occupied by nearly three fourths of the nation's population.

ROOSEVELT'S PROGRESSIVISM

While most Progressive initiatives originated at the state and local levels, calls for national Progressive efforts began to appear around 1900. Theodore

Roosevelt brought to the White House in 1901 an expansive vision of the presidency that well suited the cause of Progressive reform. In one of his first addresses to Congress, he stressed the need for a new political approach. When the Constitution was first drafted, he explained, the nation's social and economic conditions were quite unlike those at the dawn of the twentieth century. Modern urban-industrial society required more active government involvement.

More than any other president since Lincoln, Roosevelt possessed an activist bent. Still, his initial approach to reform was cautious. He sought to avoid the extremes of socialism on the one hand and laissez-faire individualism on the other. A skilled political maneuverer, he broke the tradition of the Gilded Age presidents by serving as a very active chief executive. Roosevelt greatly expanded the role and visibility of the presidency, as well as the authority and scope of the federal government. His capacity for hard work was boundless; his boyish energy was infectious. He thrived on crises and took the leadership role in negotiating major legislation and labor disputes. Always a self-promoter, he effectively managed publicity and news about the White House. Roosevelt craved the spotlight. As one of his sons explained, "Father always wanted to be the bride at every wedding and the corpse at every funeral." He also cultivated party leaders in Congress and steered away from such divisive issues as the tariff and regulation of the banks. And when he did approach the explosive issue of the trusts, he took care to reassure the business community. For him politics was the art of the possible. Unlike the more radical Progressives and the doctrinaire "lunatic fringe," as he called it, he would take half a loaf rather than none at all.

THE TRUSTS   On the issue of huge business trusts, Roosevelt endorsed the "sincere conviction that combination and concentration should be, not prohibited, but supervised and within reasonable limits controlled." In 1902 he proposed a "square deal" for all, calling for enforcement of existing antitrust laws and stricter controls on big business. Effective regulation, he insisted, was better than a futile effort to restore small business by breaking up all giant corporations, which might be achieved only at a cost to the efficiencies of scale gained in larger operations.

Because Congress balked at regulatory legislation, Roosevelt forced the issue by a more vigorous federal prosecution of the Sherman Anti-Trust Act of 1890. He chose his target carefully. In the case against the sugar trust (*United States v. E. C. Knight and Company,* 1895), the Supreme Court had declared manufacturing strictly an *intrastate* activity. Most railroads, however, were beyond question engaged in *interstate* commerce and thus subject to federal authority. Consequently, in 1902 Roosevelt moved against the Northern

Roosevelt's Duality

Theodore Roosevelt as an "apostle of prosperity" (top) and as a Roman tyrant (bottom). Roosevelt's energy, spirit, self-righteousness, and impulsiveness elicited sharp reactions.

Securities Company, a holding company merging the competing Great Northern and Northern Pacific Railroads. Roosevelt attacked the trust for essentially forming a monopoly, and in 1904, in *United States v. Northern Securities Company*, the Supreme Court ordered the combination dissolved. Roosevelt continued to use his executive powers to enforce the Sherman Anti-Trust Act, but he avoided conflict in Congress by proposing no further anti-trust legislation. Altogether, his administration brought about twenty-five anti-trust suits.

THE 1902 COAL STRIKE   Support for Roosevelt's use of the "big stick" against corporations was strengthened by the stubbornness of mine owners in the anthracite coal strike of 1902. On May 12 some 150,000 members of the United Mine Workers (UMW) walked off the job in West Virginia and Pennsylvania. They demanded a 20 percent wage increase, a reduction in daily working hours from ten to nine, and formal recognition of their union by management. The operators dug in their heels and shut down the mines in an effort to starve out the miners, many of whom were immigrants from eastern Europe. One mine owner revealed the social prejudices of the era when he asserted, "The miners don't suffer—why, they can't even speak English."

Presidents such as Hayes and Cleveland had responded to labor unrest by dispatching federal troops. But the coal strike had not become violent when Roosevelt aggressively intervened. He was concerned about the approach of winter amid a nationwide coal shortage and the effects of the strike on the fall congressional elections—he told a friend that the public would blame the Republicans if coal were in short supply. By October 1902 the price of coal had soared, and hospitals and schools reported empty coal bins. Roosevelt thus decided upon a bold move: he invited leaders of both sides to a conference in Washington, where he appealed to their "patriotism, to the spirit that sinks personal considerations and makes individual sacrifices for the public good." The mine owners attended the conference but refused even to speak to the UMW leaders. The "extraordinary stupidity and temper" of the "wooden-headed" owners infuriated Roosevelt. With the conference deadlocked, the president threatened to take over the mines and send in the army to run them. Militarizing the mines would have been an act of dubious legality, but the owners feared that Roosevelt might do it and that public opinion would support him.

The coal strike ended on October 23, 1902, with an agreement to submit the issues to an arbitration commission named by the president. The agreement enhanced the prestige of both Roosevelt and the union's leader, although it produced only a partial victory for the miners. By the arbitrators' decision in 1903, the miners won a nine-hour workday but only a 10 percent wage increase and no union recognition.

AN EXPANDING GOVERNMENT   In 1903 Congress strengthened both anti-trust enforcement and government regulation by creating a new federal agency, the Department of Commerce and Labor, and passing the Elkins Act, which made it illegal for corporations to take, as well as to give, secret rebates to their preferred customers. The Bureau of Corporations had no direct regulatory powers, but it did have a mandate to report on the activities of interstate corporations. Its findings could lead to anti-trust suits, but its purpose was rather to help corporations correct malpractices and avoid the need for lawsuits. Many companies cooperated, but others held back. When Standard Oil refused to turn over its records, the government brought an anti-trust suit that resulted in the campany's dissolution in 1911. The Supreme Court ordered the American Tobacco Company broken up at the same time.

ROOSEVELT'S SECOND TERM

Roosevelt's energy and policies built a coalition of Progressive- and conservative-minded voters who assured his election in his own right in 1904. The Democrats, having twice lost with William Jennings Bryan, turned to Alton B. Parker, who as chief justice of New York's supreme court, had upheld labor's right to the closed shop (requiring that all employees be union members) and the state's right to limit hours of work. Despite Parker's liberal record, party leaders presented him as a safe conservative. Yet the effort to portray their Democratic candidate as more conservative than Roosevelt proved a futile gesture for the party that had twice nominated Bryan. Despite Roosevelt's trust-busting, most business leaders, according to the *New York Sun,* preferred the "impulsive candidate of the party of conservatism to the conservative candidate of the party which the business interests regard as permanently and dangerously impulsive."

An invincible popularity and the sheer force of his personality swept Roosevelt to an impressive victory of 7.6 million votes to Parker's 5.1 million, with 336 electoral votes for Roosevelt and 140 for Parker. Parker carried only the Solid South of the former Confederacy and two border states, Kentucky and Maryland. On election night, Roosevelt announced that he would not run again, a statement he later would regret.

LEGISLATIVE LEADERSHIP   Elected in his own right, Roosevelt approached his second term with heightened confidence and a stronger commitment to Progressive reform. In 1905 he devoted most of his annual message to the need for greater regulation and control of big business. The independent Roosevelt took aim at the railroads first.

Roosevelt asked Congress to extend the authority of the Interstate Commerce Commission to give it more effective control over railroad rates. He had to mobilize all the pressure and influence at his disposal to push through the bill introduced by Representative Peter Hepburn of Iowa. Enacted in 1906, the Hepburn Act gave the ICC power to set maximum freight rates. The commission no longer had to go to court to enforce its decisions. The Hepburn Act also extended the ICC's regulatory reach beyond railroads, to pipelines, freight companies, sleeping-car companies, bridges, and ferries.

On the very day after passage of the Hepburn Act, a growing movement for the regulation of meat packers, food processors, and makers of drugs and patent medicines reached fruition. Discontent with abuses in the processing of food and drugs had grown rapidly as a result of the muckrakers' disclosures. The chief chemist of the Agriculture Department, for example, supplied telling evidence of harmful additives used in the preparation of "embalmed meat" and other food products. Others reported on dangerous ingredients in some patent medicines.

Perhaps the most telling blow against such abuses was struck by Upton Sinclair's novel *The Jungle* (1906), which graphically portrayed the filthy conditions in Chicago's meatpacking industry. Roosevelt read *The Jungle*—and reacted quickly. He sent two federal agents to Chicago to investigate, and their report confirmed all that Sinclair had said. Soon Roosevelt and Congress were hammering out a bill to address the problems.

The Meat Industry

Pigs strung up along the hog-scraping rail at Armour's packing plant in Chicago, ca. 1909.

The Meat Inspection Act of 1906 required federal inspection of meats destined for interstate commerce and empowered officials in the Agriculture Department to impose sanitary standards. The Pure Food and Drug Act, enacted the same day, placed restrictions on the makers of prepared foods and patent medicines and forbade the manufacture, sale, or transportation of adulterated, misbranded, or harmful foods, drugs, and liquors.

With the achievements of 1903 and 1906, Theodore Roosevelt's campaign for regulatory legislation reached its chief goals and in the process moved the federal government a great distance from the laissez-faire policies that had prevailed before the turn of the century.

CONSERVATION   One of the most enduring legacies of Roosevelt's leadership was his energetic support for the emerging conservation movement. Roosevelt was the first president to challenge the long-standing myth of America's having inexhaustible natural resources. In fact, Roosevelt came to believe that conservation of natural resources was the "great material question of the day." He and other early conservationists were convinced that the tradition of freewheeling individual and corporate exploitation of the environment must be supplanted by the scientific management of the nation's natural resources for the *long-term* public benefit. "The things that will destroy America," he said, "are prosperity at any price, peace at any price, safety first instead of duty first, the love of soft living and the get-rich-quick theory of life."

After the Civil War a growing number of organizations and individuals had begun to oppose the unregulated exploitation of natural resources and sought to preserve wilderness areas. Timber companies stripped forests and moved on, leaving debris and erosion behind. Ranchers abused the native grasslands by overgrazing their herds, and farmers depleted the soil by excessive planting. Commercial hunters, trappers, and fishermen decimated game animals. Industries polluted streams, rivers, and air.

Such reckless abuse of the environment eventually generated intense concern and organized opposition. George Perkins Marsh, a Vermont diplomat and one of the first advocates of government conservation efforts, published a best-selling book, *Man and Nature* (1864), in which he observed that man was "everywhere a disturbing agent. Wherever he plants his foot, the harmonies of nature are turned to discords." Marsh urged Americans to intervene to protect the long-term health of the environment.

By the end of the nineteenth century, many Americans were heeding Marsh's warning. Just as reformers promoted the regulation of business and industry for the public welfare, activists championed efforts to manage and preserve the natural environment for future generations. Among the first promoters of resource conservation were ardent sport hunters and fishermen among the social elite (including Theodore Roosevelt), who worried that rapacious commercial hunters and trappers were killing game animals to the point of extermination. In 1886, for example, the sportsman-naturalist George Bird Grinnell, editor of *Forest and Stream*, founded the Audubon Society to protect wild birds from being decimated for their plumage. Two years later Grinnell, Roosevelt, and a dozen other recreational hunters formed the Boone and Crockett Club, named in honor of Daniel Boone and Davy Crockett, the legendary frontiersmen. The club's goal was to ensure that big-game animals and fish were protected for posterity, a goal shared by national monthly newspapers such as *American Sportsman, Forest and Stream,* and *Field and Stream.* By 1900 most states had enacted laws regulating game hunting and had created game refuges and wardens to enforce the new rules, much to the chagrin of local hunters, including Indians, who now were forced to abide by state laws designed to protect the interests of wealthy recreational hunters.

Along with industrialists concerned about water quality, Roosevelt and the sportsmen conservationists formed a powerful coalition promoting the rational government management of natural resources: rivers and streams, forests, minerals, and natural wonders. Those concerns, as well as the desire of railroad companies to transport tourists to destinations featuring majestic scenery, led the federal government to displace Indians in order to establish the 2-million-acre Yellowstone National Park in 1872 at the junction of the Montana, Wyoming, and Idaho territories (the National Park Service would be created in 1916 after other parks had been established). In 1881 Congress created a Division of Forestry (now the U.S. Forest Service) within the Department of the Interior. At the same time, New York State officials established a Forest Commission in 1885 to manage timber in the vast state-owned acreage of the Adirondack Mountains. Seven years later the legislature created the 5-million-acre Adirondack Park. The legislature also imposed restrictions on hunting in state forests and created a "forest police" to enforce the new regulations. As president, Theodore Roosevelt created fifty federal wildlife refuges, approved five new national parks, and designated as national monuments unfit for economic use such natural treasures as the Grand Canyon.

In 1898 Roosevelt, while serving as vice president, had endorsed the appointment of Gifford Pinchot, a close friend and the nation's first professional forester, as the head of the Division of Forestry. Pinchot and Roosevelt believed that conservation entailed the scientific management of natural resources to serve the public interest. In his first State of the Union address, delivered in 1901, Roosevelt explained that conservationists were concerned not simply with protecting national forests for their beauty; their foremost objective was utilitarian: to ensure that there would always be forests to "increase and sustain the resources of our country and the industries which depend upon them." Pinchot explained that the conservation movement sought to promote the "greatest good for the greatest number for the longest time."

Roosevelt and Pinchot championed the Progressive notion of efficiency and government regulation. They were not romantics about nature, nor were they ecologists; they did not understand the complex interdependence of trees, plants, insects, and animals, nor did they appreciate the environmental benefits of natural fires. Instead, they were utilitarian Progressives determined to ensure that entrepreneurs and industrialists exploited nature in appropriate ways. As Pinchot insisted, "The first principle of conservation is development." He sought to ensure the wisest "use of the natural resources now existing on this continent for the benefit of the people who live here now."

The president and Pinchot were especially concerned about the millions of acres of public land still owned by the government. Over the years vast tracts of federal land had been given away or sold at discount prices to large business enterprises. Roosevelt and Pinchot were determined to end such carelessness. They championed the systematic management of natural resources by government experts trained to promote the most efficient public use of the environment. This meant, for example, that commercial loggers must abide by Forestry regulations; otherwise there would be no trees for future generations to exploit. "Forestry," Pinchot explained, "is handling trees so that one crop follows another." He and Roosevelt opposed the mindless clear-cutting of entire forests for short-term profit and sought to restrict particular forests from any economic development. In fact, Roosevelt as president used the Forest Reserve Act (1891) to exclude from settlement or harvest some 172 million acres of federal timberland. Lumber companies were furious, but Roosevelt held firm. As he bristled, "I hate a man who skins the land."

FROM ROOSEVELT TO TAFT

Toward the end of his second term, Roosevelt crowed: "I have had a great time as president." But he was ready to move on, and he held to his 1904 decision not to run again. Instead he sought to have his secretary of war, William Howard Taft, replace him, and the Republican Convention ratified the choice on its first ballot in 1908. The Democrats, whose conservative strategy had backfired in 1904, decided to give William Jennings Bryan one more chance. Still vigorous at forty-eight, Bryan retained a faithful following, but once again it was not enough. In the end, voters opted for Roosevelt's chosen successor, leaving Bryan only the southern states plus Nebraska, Colorado, and Nevada. The real surprise of the election was the strong showing of the Socialist party candidate, labor hero Eugene V. Debs, who attracted over 400,000 votes, illustrating the mounting intensity of working-class unrest.

Born to a prominent Cincinnati family, Taft boasted more experience in public service than any other president since Martin Van Buren. After graduating second in his class at Yale, he had progressed through appointive offices, from assistant prosecutor, tax collector, and judge in Ohio to solicitor in the Justice Department, federal judge, governor general in the Philippines, and secretary of war. The presidency was the only elective office he ever held. Later he would be appointed chief justice of the Supreme Court (1921–1930), a job more suited to his temperament.

Taft never felt comfortable in the White House. He once observed that whenever someone said "Mr. President," he looked around for Roosevelt. The political dynamo in the family was his wife, Helen, who had wanted the presidency more than he. One of the major tragedies of Taft's presidency was

William Howard Taft

Speaking at Manassas, Virginia, in 1911.

that Helen Taft suffered a debilitating stroke soon after they entered the White House, and for most of his term she remained unable to serve as his political adviser.

TARIFF REFORM   A former student of the social Darwinist William Graham Sumner, Taft had absorbed the laissez-faire views of his mentor and therefore differed with orthodox Republican protectionism. Against Roosevelt's advice he had promised a tariff reduction during the campaign, and true to his word he called a special session of Congress to consider his proposal eleven days after his inauguration. But if Taft seemed bolder in pressing an issue that Roosevelt had skirted, he proved less adroit in shepherding legislation through Congress.

A reduced tariff passed the House with surprising ease. Before the Senate passed the bill, however, it made more than 800 changes, most of which raised tariff rates. Outraged by the obvious catering to special state and local interests, a group of ten Progressive Republicans joined the Democrats in an unsuccessful effort to defeat the bill. Taft at first agreed with them but then, fearful of a party split, backed the Republican majority and agreed to an imperfect bill. Temperamentally conservative, inhibited by scruples about interfering too much with the legislative process, Taft drifted into the orbit of the Republican Old Guard and quickly alienated the Progressive wing of his party, whom he tagged "assistant Democrats."

BALLINGER AND PINCHOT   In 1910 Taft's policies drove the wedge deeper between the conservative and Progressive Republican factions. What came to be known as the Ballinger-Pinchot controversy made Taft appear to be a less reliable custodian of Roosevelt's conservation policies than he actually was. The controversy arose after Taft's secretary of the interior, Richard A. Ballinger, turned over coal-rich federal lands in Alaska to a group of investor friends. Apparently without Ballinger's knowledge, this group had already agreed to sell part of the land to a mining syndicate. When Gifford Pinchot, chief of forestry, revealed the scam, Taft fired Pinchot for insubordination. A joint congressional investigation later exonerated Ballinger from all charges of fraud or corruption, but conservationist suspicions created such pressure that he resigned in 1911.

In firing Pinchot, Taft had acted according to the strictly legal view that his training had taught him to value. But the unsavory circumstances surrounding the incident tarnished Taft's public image. Events had conspired to cast the president in a conservative role at a time when Progressive sentiment was riding high. The result was a sharp setback in the congressional elections of 1910, first by the widespread defeat of pro-Taft candidates in the Republican primaries, then by the election of a Democratic majority in the House and enough Democrats in the Senate to allow Progressive Republicans to wield the balance of power.

TAFT AND ROOSEVELT   In 1910 Theodore Roosevelt returned from his extended travels abroad. With news accounts highlighting the Taft "betrayal" of Roosevelt's programs, the former president's followers urged him to take action. After hesitating for several months, Roosevelt again entered the political arena. At a speech in Kansas, he issued a stirring call for an array of new federal regulatory laws, a federal social-welfare program, and new measures of direct democracy, including the old Populist demands for the initiative, recall, and referendum on a nationwide basis. Thereafter, Roosevelt intensified his criticism of the Taft administration.

Equally critical of Taft was Senator Robert La Follette of Wisconsin, who in 1911 helped organize the National Progressive Republican League and soon became its leading candidate for the Republican party nomination. A militant reformer fiercely committed to greater government regulation of business and civil rights for all Americans, La Follette was more of a crusader than a politician. Complicating matters for the Republicans, Roosevelt officially threw his hat into the ring in 1912. Even though many of La Follette's supporters rushed to embrace the ex-president, the Wisconsin idealist stubbornly refused to give way. He felt that Roosevelt was not genuinely committed to the sweeping reforms necessary for a truly progressive America.

The rebuke implicit in Roosevelt's decision to run against Taft, his chosen successor, was in many ways undeserved. During Taft's first year in office, one political tempest after another had left his image irreparably damaged. The three years of solid achievement that followed could not restore its luster or reunite his divided party. Taft had at least attempted tariff reform, which

The Bull Moose Candidate in 1912

A skeptical view of Theodore Roosevelt.

Roosevelt had never dared. And in the end his administration set aside more public land for conservation in four years than Roosevelt's had in nearly eight and brought more anti-trust suits, by a score of eighty to twenty-five. Taft also established the Bureau of Mines and the federal Children's Bureau (1912). He supported both the Sixteenth Amendment (1913), which authorized a federal income tax, and the Seventeenth Amendment (1913), which provided for the popular election of senators instead of state legislatures appointing them.

Despite Taft's Progressive record, Roosevelt now hastened the demise of his former friend and lieutenant. Brusquely pushing aside La Follette's claim to the Progressive Republican mantle, Roosevelt won most of the Republican primaries in 1912, even in Taft's Ohio. But such popular support was no match for Taft's advantages as president and party leader. The Taft forces nominated their man at the national convention by the same steamroller tactics that had nominated Roosevelt in 1904. Outraged at such "naked theft," the Roosevelt delegates issued a call for a Progressive party convention, which assembled in Chicago on August 5. The new third-party supporters were a curious mixture of social-gospel clergymen and laymen, college presidents, professors, journalists, liberal businessmen, and social workers. Roosevelt told the group he felt "fit as a bull moose" in accepting their nomination. Now it was the Democrats' turn.

WOODROW WILSON'S PROGRESSIVISM

WILSON'S RISE   The emergence of Thomas Woodrow Wilson as the Democratic nominee in 1912 climaxed a political rise even more rapid than that of Grover Cleveland. In 1910, before his entering the race for election as governor of New Jersey, Wilson had been president of Princeton University but had never run for public office. Born in Staunton, Virginia, in 1856, the son of a stern Presbyterian minister, he had grown up in Georgia and the Carolinas during the Civil War and Reconstruction.

Driven by a sense of destiny and duty, Wilson was resolute, humane, rigid, and self-exacting to a fault. He nurtured a righteous commitment to principle, and his fits of tenacious inflexibility would prove to be his greatest weakness. Running as a reform candidate, Wilson was elected governor of New Jersey. After his election he pressured New Jersey lawmakers to enact a workers' compensation law, a corrupt-practices law, measures to regulate public utilities, and ballot reforms. Such strong leadership in a state known as the home of the trusts because of its lenient in-corporation laws brought Wilson to national attention.

In the spring of 1911, a group of southern Democrats in New York opened a Wilson presidential-campaign headquarters, and Wilson set forth on strenuous tours to all regions of the country, denouncing special privilege and political bossism. Wilson believed that the president of the country should be as active in directing legislation as in the administration and enforcement of laws. In calling for a strong presidency, Wilson expressed views closer to Roosevelt's than to Taft's. He likewise shared Roosevelt's belief that politicians should promote the general welfare rather than narrow special interests. And like Roosevelt he was critical of big business, organized labor, socialism, and agrarian radicalism.

Despite a fast start the Wilson campaign seemed headed for defeat by convention time, and House Speaker Champ Clark of Missouri seemed destined to win the nomination. On the fourteenth ballot, however, William Jennings Bryan, having decided that party conservatives were behind Clark, went over to Wilson; others followed, and Wilson captured the nomination.

THE ELECTION OF 1912 The 1912 presidential election involved four candidates: Wilson and Taft represented the two major parties, while Eugene Debs ran as a Socialist, and Roosevelt headed the Progressive party ticket. No sooner did the campaign open than Roosevelt's candidacy almost ended. While stepping into a car in Milwaukee, he was shot by a crazed man. The bullet went through his overcoat, spectacles case, and fifty-page speech, then fractured a rib before lodging just below his right lung. Roosevelt demanded that he be driven to the auditorium to deliver his speech. In a dramatic gesture he showed the audience his bloodstained shirt and punctured text and vowed, "It takes more than this to kill a bull moose."

With Taft and Debs trailing, the campaign settled down to a debate over the competing ideologies of the two front-runners: Roosevelt's New Nationalism and Wilson's New Freedom. The fuzzy ideas that Roosevelt fashioned into his New Nationalism had first been presented systematically in *The Promise of American Life* (1909), a widely influential book by Herbert Croly, a New York journalist. Its central point was that Progressives must give up Jeffersonian prejudices against big government and use the power of government to achieve democratic ends in the public interest.

Roosevelt's New Nationalism would enable government to promote social justice and enact such reforms as graduated income and inheritance taxes, workers' compensation for disabling injuries or illnesses, regulation of the labor of women and children, and a stronger Bureau of Corporations. These ideas and more went into the platform of his Progressive party, which called for a federal trade commission with sweeping authority over business and a tariff commission to set rates on a "scientific basis."

Before the end of his administration, Wilson would be swept into the current of such New Nationalism, too, but initially he adhered to the decentralizing anti-trust traditions of his party. Wilson relied heavily for his political stances on Louis D. Brandeis, a Progressive lawyer from Boston who focused Wilson's thought much as Croly had focused Roosevelt's. Brandeis's design for Wilson's New Freedom differed from Roosevelt's New Nationalism in its belief that the federal government should restore competition rather than regulate monopolies. This required eliminating all trusts, lowering tariffs, and breaking up the concentration of financial power on Wall Street. Brandeis and Wilson also dreamed of turning over most federal social programs to the states and cities. In this sense they saw the vigorous expansion of federal power as only a temporary necessity, not a permanent condition. Having restored competition and the diffusion of power and programs, the national government would revert to its aloof heritage. Roosevelt, who was convinced that both corporate concentration and an expanding federal government were permanent developments, dismissed the New Freedom as mere nostalgia.

The Republican schism between Taft and Roosevelt opened the way for Woodrow Wilson to win by 435 electoral votes to 88 for Roosevelt and 8 for Taft. The 1912 election was significant in a number of respects. First, it was a high-water mark for Progressivism. The candidates debated the basic issues in a campaign unique in its focus on vital alternatives and its highly philosophical tone. And the Socialist party, the left wing of Progressivism, polled over 900,000 votes for Eugene V. Debs, about 6 percent of the total vote, its highest proportion ever.

Second, the election gave the Democrats effective national power for the first time since the Civil War. For two years during the second administration of Grover Cleveland, 1893–1895, they had held the White House and majorities in both houses of Congress, but they had quickly fallen out of power during the severe depression of the 1890s. Now, under Wilson, the Democrats again held the presidency and enjoyed majorities in the House and Senate.

Wilson's Reforms

Woodrow Wilson campaigning from a railroad car.

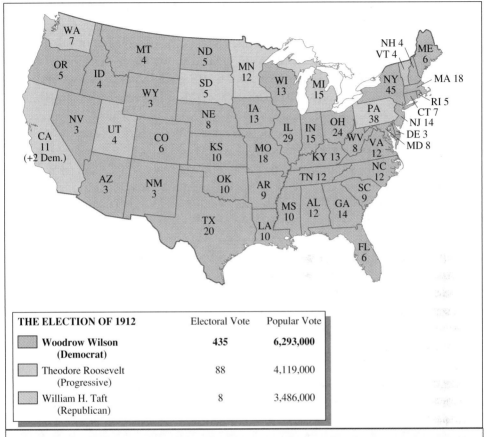

THE ELECTION OF 1912	Electoral Vote	Popular Vote
Woodrow Wilson (Democrat)	**435**	**6,293,000**
Theodore Roosevelt (Progressive)	88	4,119,000
William H. Taft (Republican)	8	3,486,000

Why was Taft so unpopular? How did the division between Roosevelt and Taft give Wilson the victory? Why was Wilson's victory in 1912 significant?

Third, Wilson's election brought southerners back into the orbit of national and international affairs in a significant way for the first time since the Civil War. Five of Wilson's ten cabinet members were born in the South, and William Jennings Bryan, the secretary of state, was an idol of the southern masses. At the president's right hand, and one of the most influential members of the Wilson circle, was "Colonel" Edward M. House of Texas. Wilson described House as "my second personality." Southern legislators, by virtue of their seniority, held most committee chairmanships. As a result, much of the Progressive legislation of the Wilson era would bear the names of the southerners who guided the bills through Congress.

WILSONIAN REFORM   Wilson's 1913 inaugural address vividly expressed the ideals of economic reform that inspired many Progressives. "We have been proud of our industrial achievements," he observed, "but we have not hitherto stopped thoughtfully enough to count the human cost." He promised specifically a lower tariff and a new banking system.

Whereas Roosevelt had been a strong president by force of personality, Wilson became a strong president by force of conviction. The president, he argued, must become the dynamic voice in national affairs. Wilson courted popular support, but he also courted members of Congress through personal contacts, invitations to the White House, and speeches to Congress. He used patronage power to reward friends and punish enemies. Though he might have acted through a bipartisan Progressive coalition, he chose instead to rely upon party loyalty.

THE TARIFF   The new president's leadership met its first test on the issue of tariff reform. Tariffs were originally needed to protect infant American industries from foreign competition. Now, however, Wilson believed, tariffs were being abused by corporations to suppress foreign competition and keep consumer prices high. He often claimed that the "tariff made the trusts," believing that tariffs had encouraged the growth of monopolies and degraded the political process by spawning armies of paid lobbyists who invaded Congress each year. In attacking high tariffs, Wilson sought to strike a blow for consumers and honest government. He acted quickly and boldly, summoning Congress to a special session and addressing it in person—the first president to do so since John Adams. In response to Wilson's request for lower tariff duties to promote competition, Congress voted for tariff reductions, with only four Democrats crossing the party line, and the bill passed the House easily. The opposition centered in the Senate, the traditional graveyard of tariff reform. In the end, Louisiana's two "sugar senators" were the only Democrats to vote against the bill. The Underwood-Simmons Tariff of 1913 reduced the overall average duty from about 37 percent to about 29 percent. The Wilson administration lowered tariff rates but raised revenues with the first federal income tax levied under the newly ratified Sixteenth Amendment.

THE FEDERAL RESERVE ACT   Before the new tariff had cleared the Senate, the administration proposed the first major banking and currency reform since the Civil War. Ever since Andrew Jackson had killed the second Bank of the United States in the 1830s, the nation had been without a central bank. Instead, the country's money supply was provided by hundreds of private banks. Such a decentralized system fostered instability and inefficiency. It also gave disproportionate influence to banks centered in New York City. By 1913 virtually everyone agreed that the banking system needed restructuring. Wilson told Congress that a federal banking system was needed to ensure that "the banks may be the instruments, not the masters, of business and of individual enterprise and initiative."

The Federal Reserve Act of 1913 created a new national banking system with twelve regional Federal Reserve banks, each owned by member banks in its district. All national banks became members of the new Federal Reserve system; state banks could join if they wished. Each member bank had to subscribe 6 percent of its capital to the Federal Reserve bank and deposit a portion of its reserve there.

This arrangement made it possible to expand both the money supply and bank credit in times of high business activity or as the level of borrowing increased. A Federal Reserve Board exercised general supervision over the activities of the member banks and adjusted interest rates to fight inflation or stimulate business. It is hard to exaggerate the significance of the passage of the Federal Reserve Act. Through Wilson's skillful leadership, Congress took a major step in providing the nation with a sound yet flexible currency system and at the same time helped decentralize the money supply.

ANTI-TRUST LAWS Wilson made trust-busting the central focus of the New Freedom because the concentration of economic power had continued to grow despite the Sherman Anti-Trust Act and the federal watchdog agency, the Bureau of Corporations. During the summer of 1914, Wilson decided to make a strong Federal Trade Commission (FTC) the cornerstone of his anti-trust program. Created in 1914, the five-member commission replaced Roosevelt's Bureau of Corporations and assumed new powers to

Reading the Death Warrant

Woodrow Wilson's plan for banking and currency reform spells the death of the "money trust," according to this cartoon.

define "unfair trade practices" and issue "cease-and-desist" orders when it found evidence of unfair competition.

Henry D. Clayton, an Alabama Democrat, drafted an Anti-trust Act, passed in 1914, that outlawed practices such as price discrimination (charging different customers different prices for the same goods); "tying" agreements, which limited the right of dealers to handle the products of competing manufacturers; and corporations' acquisition of stock in competing corporations. In every case, however, conservative forces in the Senate qualified these provisions by tacking on the weakening phrase "where the effect may be to substantially lessen competition" or words of similar effect. And conservative southern Democrats and northern Republicans amended the Clayton Anti-Trust Act to allow for broad judicial review of the FTC's decisions, further weakening its freedom of action. In accordance with the president's recommendation, however, corporate officials were made personally responsible for any violations.

Agrarian reformers, allied with organized labor won a stipulation in the Clayton Act declaring that farm and labor organizations were not per se unlawful combinations in restraint of trade. Injunctions in labor disputes, moreover, were not to be handed down by federal courts unless "necessary to prevent irreparable injury to property." President Wilson himself admitted that the act did little more than affirm the right of unions to exist by forbidding their dissolution for being in restraint of trade.

Administration of the anti-trust laws generally proved disappointing to the more vehement Progressives under Wilson. The Justice Department offered advice to business owners interested in arranging matters so as to avoid anti-trust prosecutions. The appointment of conservatives to the Interstate Commerce Commission and the Federal Reserve Board won plaudits from the business world and profoundly disappointed Progressives.

SOCIAL JUSTICE   Wilson had in fact never been a strong Progressive of the social-justice persuasion. He had carried out his promises to lower the tariff, reorganize the banking system, and strengthen the anti-trust laws, but he was not inclined to go much further. The New Freedom was now complete, he wrote late in 1914; the future would be "a time of healing because [it would be] a time of just dealing."

The sweep of events and the pressures of more far-reaching Progressives pushed Wilson beyond where he intended to go on some points. Yet Wilson retained several social blind spots. Although he endorsed state action for women's suffrage, he declined to support a federal suffrage amendment because his party platform had not done so. He withheld support from federal child-labor legislation because he regarded it as a state matter, and he opposed a bill providing federal loans for strapped farmers on the grounds that it was "unwise and unjustifiable to extend the credit of the government to a single class of the community."

PROGRESSIVISM FOR WHITES ONLY   Like many other Progressives, Woodrow Wilson showed little interest in the plight of African Americans. In fact, he shared many of the racist attitudes prevalent at the time. Although Wilson never joined the Ku Klux Klan and he denounced its "reign of terror," he sympathized with its motives of restoring white rule in the postwar South and relieving whites of the "ignorant and hostile" power of the black vote. As a student at Princeton, Wilson had detested the enfranchisement of blacks, arguing that Americans of Anglo-Saxon origin would always resist domination by "an ignorant and inferior race."

Later, as a politician, Wilson courted black voters, but he rarely consulted African-American leaders and repeatedly avoided opportunities to associate with them in public. Many of the southerners he appointed to his cabinet were uncompromising racists who systematically segregated the employees in their agencies. When black leaders protested these actions, Wilson replied that such racial segregation was intended to eliminate "the possibility of friction" in the federal workplace.

PROGRESSIVE RESURGENCE   The need to weld a winning coalition in 1916 pushed Wilson back on the road of reform. Progressive Democrats were restless, and after war broke out in Europe in 1914, further divisions in the party arose over defense and foreign policy. At the same time the Republicans were repairing their own rift. The Progressive party showed little staying power in the 1914 midterm election, and Roosevelt showed little will to preserve it. Most observers recognized that Wilson could gain reelection only by courting Progressives of all parties. In 1916 Wilson scored points with them when he nominated Louis D. Brandeis to the Supreme Court. Conservatives waged a vigorous battle against Brandeis, but Senate Progressives rallied to win confirmation of the social-justice champion as the first Jewish member of the Supreme Court.

Wilson, meanwhile, began to embrace the broad program of farm and labor reforms he had earlier spurned. The agricultural sector continued to suffer from a shortage of capital. To address the problem, Wilson supported a proposal to set up land banks to sponsor farm loans. With this boost the Federal Farm Loan Act became law in 1916. It created twelve Federal Land banks that paralleled the Federal Reserve banks and offered low-interest loans to farmers.

Farmers with automobiles had more than a passing interest as well in the Federal Highways Act of 1916, which provided dollar-matching contributions to states with highway departments that met certain federal standards. The measure authorized distribution of $75 million over five years and marked a sharp departure from Jacksonian opposition to internal improvements at federal expense, just as the Federal Reserve System departed from Jacksonian banking principles. Although the argument that highways were one of the nation's defense needs had weakened constitutional scruples against the act, the Highways Act still restricted support to "post roads" used for the delivery of mail. A renewal act in 1921 would mark the beginning of a systematic network of numbered U.S. highways.

The Progressive resurgence of 1916 broke the logjam on labor reforms as well. Advocates of child-labor legislation persuaded Wilson to overcome doubts about its constitutionality and sign the Keating-Owen Act, which excluded from interstate commerce goods manufactured by children under the age of fourteen. But the Supreme Court soon ruled it unconstitutional on the grounds that regulation of interstate commerce could not extend to the conditions of labor. On the other hand, the Supreme Court upheld the Adamson Act of 1916, which mandated the eight-hour workday for railroad workers.

In Wilson's first term, Progressive government reached its zenith. Progressivism had conquered the old premise that the government is best that governs least. Progressivism, a loose amalgam of agrarian, business, government, and social reform, amounted in the end to a movement for active government on behalf of the public interest.

LIMITS OF PROGRESSIVISM

Like all great historic movements, Progressivism contained elements of paradox and irony. Despite all the talk of greater democracy at the turn of the century, it was also the age of disenfranchisement of African Americans in the South and xenophobic reactions to "new" immigrants. The initiative and referendum, supposedly democratic reforms, proved subject to manipulation by well-financed publicity campaigns. And much of the public policy of the time came to be formulated by experts and members of appointed boards, not by broad segments of the population. There is a fine irony in the fact that the drive to increase the political role of ordinary people paralleled efforts to strengthen executive leadership and exalt professional expertise.

This age of much-ballyhooed efficiency and expertise, in business as well as government, generated a situation in which more and more key decisions were made by faceless policy makers.

Progressivism was largely a middle-class movement in which the poor and unorganized had little influence. It is surprising that a movement so dedicated to democratic rhetoric should experience so steady a decline in voter participation. In 1912, the year of the Bull Moose campaign, voting dropped off by almost 7 percent. The new politics of issues and charismatic leaders proved to be less effective in turning out voters than traditional party organizations and bosses had been. And by 1916 the optimism of an age that looked to infinite progress was already confronted by a vast slaughter. Europe had stumbled into war, and America would soon be drawn in. The twentieth century, which had dawned with such bright hopes, held in store episodes of unparalleled horror.

MAKING CONNECTIONS

- Many of the Progressive reforms described in this chapter—particularly business regulation and the growth of the welfare state—provided the seeds for the New Deal reforms of the 1930s, the focus of Chapter 28.

- After World War I, the Progressive impulse manifested itself in reforms such as Prohibition and women's suffrage, but the moralistic strain in Progressivism would take an ugly turn in the Red Scare and immigration restriction.

- The next chapter shows how Wilson's foreign policy in Latin America and Europe reflected the same moralism that guided his domestic policy.

FURTHER READING

A splendid analysis of Progressivism is John Whiteclay Chambers II's *The Tyranny of Change: America in the Progressive Era, 1890–1920* (1992). The evolution of government policy toward business is examined in Martin J. Sklar's *The Corporate Reconstruction of American Capitalism, 1890–1916: The Market, the Law, and Politics* (1988). Mina Carson's *Settlement Folk:*

Social Thought and the American Settlement Movement, 1885–1930 (1990) and Jack M. Holl's *Juvenile Reform in the Progressive Era: William R. George and the Junior Republic Movement* (1971) examine social problems in the cities. An excellent study of the role of women in Progressivism's emphasis on social justice is Kathryn Kish Sklar's *Florence Kelley and the Nation's Work: The Rise of Women's Political Culture, 1830–1900* (1995). On the tragic fire at the Triangle Shirtwaist Company, see David Von Drehle's *Triangle: The Fire That Changed America* (2003).

There is a rich body of scholarship focused on the conservation movement. See especially Rebecca Conard's *Places of Quiet Beauty: Parks, Preserves, and Environmentalism* (1997), Samuel P Hays's *Conservation and the Gospel of Efficiency: The Progressive Conservation Movement, 1890–1920* (1959), Karl Jacoby's *Crimes against Nature: Squatters, Poachers, Thieves, and the Hidden History of American Conservation* (2001), John F. Reiger's *American Sportsmen and the Origins of Conservation* (1975), and Ted Steinberg's *Down to Earth: Nature's Role in American History* (2002). Robert Kanigel's *The One Best Way: Frederick Winslow Taylor and the Enigma of Efficiency* (1997) highlights the role of efficiency in the Progressive Era.

On the pivotal election of 1912, see James Chace's *1912: Wilson, Roosevelt, Taft, and Debs—The Election That Changed the Country* (2004) Excellent biographies include Kathleen Dalton's *Theodore Roosevelt: A Strenuous Life* (2002) and H. W. Brands's *Woodrow Wilson* (2003). For banking developments, see Allan H. Meltzer's *A History of the Federal Reserve, vol. 1, 1913–1951* (2003).

25

AMERICA AND
THE GREAT WAR

FOCUS QUESTIONS

· How did Wilson's foreign policy lead to American involvement in Latin America?

· What were the causes of the Great War in Europe?

· Why did the United States enter the Great War, and what was its role?

· How did Wilson promote his peace plan?

· What were the consequences of the war?

To answer these questions and access additional review material, please visit www.wwnorton.com/studyspace.

Throughout the nineteenth century the United States reaped the benefits of its geographic distance from the wars that plagued Britain and Europe. The Atlantic Ocean provided a welcome buffer. During the early twentieth century, however, events combined to end the nation's comfortable isolation. Expanding world trade entwined American interests with the fate of Europe. In addition, the development of steam-powered ships and submarines meant that foreign navies could threaten American security. At the same time the election of Woodrow Wilson in 1912 brought to the White House a stern moralist determined to impose his standards for right conduct on renegade nations. This combination of circumstances made the outbreak of war in Europe in 1914 a profound crisis for the United States, a crisis that would transform the nation's role in international affairs.

WILSON AND FOREIGN AFFAIRS

Woodrow Wilson brought to the presidency little background in foreign relations. The former college professor admitted before taking office that "it would be an irony of fate if my administration had to deal chiefly with foreign affairs." But events in Latin America and Europe were to make the irony all too real. From the summer of 1914, when a catastrophic world war erupted in Europe, foreign relations increasingly preoccupied Wilson's attention.

Although lacking in international experience, Wilson did not lack ideas or convictions about global issues. He saw himself as a man of destiny who would help create a new world order governed by morality and idealism rather than crass national interests. Both he and Secretary of State William Jennings Bryan believed that America had a religious duty to promote democracy and moral progress in the world. How to foster such democratic idealism and self-determination abroad, however, remained a thorny issue, as Wilson soon discovered in responding to rapidly changing events on his own continent.

INTERVENTION IN MEXICO   Between 1876 and 1910, Porfirio Díaz had dominated Mexico. As military dictator he had suppressed opposition and showered favors upon wealthy allies and foreign investors, who piled up holdings in Mexican mines, petroleum, railroads, and agriculture. Eventually, however, the dictator's grip slipped, and in 1910 popular resentment boiled over in revolt. Revolutionary armies occupied Mexico City, and in 1911 Díaz fled.

The leader of the rebellion, Francisco Madero, a charismatic dreamer, proved unable to manage the tough customers attracted to the revolt by the scramble for power. In 1913 Madero's chief of staff, General Victoriano Huerta, assumed power, and Madero was murdered soon afterward. Confronted with a military dictatorship across the nation's southern border, Wilson challenged the legitimacy of Huerta's violent coup but expressed sympathy with a revolutionary faction led by Venustiano Carranza and began to put diplomatic pressure on Huerta. "I am going to teach the South American republics to elect good men," he vowed to a British diplomat.

Early in 1914 Wilson removed an embargo on arms to Mexico in order to help Carranza's forces, and he stationed warships off Veracruz (formerly Vera Cruz)

Pancho Villa (center)

Villa and his followers rebelled against the president of Mexico and antagonized the United States with violent attacks against "gringos."

to halt foreign arms shipments to Huerta. On April 9, 1914, several American sailors gathering supplies at Tampico strayed into a restricted area and were arrested. The Mexican officials quickly released them and sent an apology to the U.S. naval commander. There the incident might have ended, but the naval officer demanded that the Mexicans salute the American flag. Wilson backed him up and won from Congress authority to use force to bring Huerta to terms. Before the Tampico incident could be resolved, Wilson sent a naval force to Veracruz. U.S. marines and sailors went ashore on April 21, 1914, occupying the city at a cost of 19 American lives. At least 200 Mexicans were killed.

In Mexico the U.S. occupation aroused the opposition of all factions, and Huerta tried to rally support against a foreign invasion. At this juncture, Wilson accepted a mediation offer by the ABC powers (Argentina, Brazil, and Chile). In 1914 they proposed a withdrawal of U.S. forces, the removal of Huerta, and the installation of a provisional government. Huerta refused to step down, but the moral effect of the proposal, his isolation abroad, and the growing strength of his foes soon forced him to leave office. The Carranzistas entered Mexico City, and the Americans left Veracruz. Wilson's "missionary diplomacy" seemed to have worked. In 1915 the United States and several Latin American governments recognized Carranza as president of Mexico.

But no sooner had the Carranzistas taken power than they began to squabble among themselves for the spoils of office. The most incendiary confrontation occurred between Carranza and his foremost general, the popular Pancho Villa, a violent former bandit who shrewdly claimed to represent "the people" behind the revolution. Enraged by America's recognition of Carranza as the de facto leader of Mexico, Villa, in early 1916, led an attack that murdered sixteen American mining engineers. It was a deliberate attempt to provoke U.S. intervention, discredit Carranza, and build up Villa as an opponent of the "gringos." Two months later Villa's band of renegades entered Columbus, New Mexico, burned the town, and killed seventeen Americans.

A furious Woodrow Wilson sent General John J. Pershing and a force of 11,000 soldiers deep inside Mexico. For nearly a year, Pershing's troops chased Villa through northern Mexico, but missing their quarry, they returned home in 1917. Carranza then pressed his own war against the bandits and in 1917 put through a new liberal constitution. Mexico was establishing a more orderly government, almost in spite of Wilson's actions rather than because of them.

PROBLEMS IN LATIN AMERICA   In the Caribbean, Wilson found it as hard to act on his ideals as it had been in Mexico. During President Taft's term, from 1909 to 1913, the United States had practiced "dollar diplomacy." The policy had its origin in 1909, when Taft had personally cabled the Chinese government on behalf of American investors interested in forming an international consortium to finance railroad lines in China. In Latin America "dollar diplomacy" worked differently and with somewhat more success. The idea was to encourage American bankers to help prop up the finances of shaky Caribbean governments.

One of the first applications of Wilsonian idealism to foreign policy came when the president renounced dollar diplomacy. The government, he declared, was not supporting any "special groups or interests." Despite Wilson's public stand against using military force to back up American investments, however, he kept the marines in Nicaragua, where they had been sent by President Taft in 1912 to prevent renewed civil war. There they would stay almost continuously until 1933. In 1915 Wilson dispatched more marines, this time to Haiti, after the country experienced two successive revolutions and subsequent government disarray. The U.S. forces stayed until 1934. Turmoil in the Dominican Republic brought U.S. marines to that country in 1916, where they remained until 1924. The presence of U.S. military force in the region only worsened the already prevalent irritation at "Yankee imperialism."

An Uneasy Neutrality

During the summer of 1914, problems in Mexico and Central America loomed larger in Wilson's thinking than the gathering storm in Europe. When the thunderbolt of war struck Europe in August 1914, Americans were stunned. Whatever the troubles in Mexico, whatever disorders and interventions agitated other countries, it seemed unreal that civilized Europe could

WORLD WAR I IN EUROPE, 1914

Central powers (Triple Alliance)
Allied powers (Triple Entente)
Neutral countries

How did the European system of alliances spread conflict across all of Europe? How was World War I different from previous wars? How did the war in Europe lead to ethnic tensions in the United States?

descend into such an orgy of destruction. But the assassination of the Austrian archduke Franz Ferdinand by a Serbian nationalist, Austria-Hungary's determination to punish Serbia, and Russia's military mobilization in sympathy with Slavic Serbia suddenly triggered a conflict between the two major European system of alliances: the Triple Alliance, or Central powers (Germany, Austria-Hungary, and Italy), and the Triple Entente, or Allied powers (France, Great Britain, and Russia). The sequence of decisions leading to World War I had unfolded with little thought to their consequences. When Russia refused to stop its army's mobilization, Germany, which backed Austria-Hungary, declared war on Russia on August 1, 1914, and on Russia's ally France two days later. Germany then invaded Belgium to get at France, which brought Great Britain into the war on August 4. Japan, eager to seize German holdings in the Pacific, declared war on August 23, and Turkey entered on the side of the Central powers on October 29. Although allied with the Central powers, Italy initially stayed out of the war and in 1915 struck a bargain by which it joined the Allied powers.

As the fighting unfolded, it quickly became apparent that the First World War was unlike any previous conflict in its scope and carnage. Machine guns, high-velocity rifles, aerial bombing, poison gas, flame throwers, land mines, long-range artillery, and armored tanks changed the nature of warfare and produced massive casualties and widespread destruction. Over 61 million men served in the armed forces on both sides, and over 9 million combatants were killed in action. Another 19 million were wounded.

The battlefields of World War I were surreal in their horrors. During the Battle of Verdun, in France, which lasted from February to December 1916, some 32 million artillery shells were fired—1,500 shells for every square meter of the battlefield. Such devastating firepower ravaged the landscape, turning farmland and forests into wasteland.

Trench warfare gave the First World War its lasting character. Most of the great battles of the war involved hundreds of thousands of men crawling out of their muddy, rat-infested trenches and then crossing a no-man's-land to attack enemy positions, only to be pushed back a day or a week later. The 475 miles of trenches provided protection and living space as well as a jumping-off point for large- and small-scale attacks by day or night. Life in the trenches was miserable. In addition to the dangers of enemy fire, soldiers were forced to deal with flooding and such diseases as trench fever and trench foot, which could lead to amputation. Lice and rats were constant companions. The stench was unbearable. Soldiers on both sides ate, slept, and fought among the dead and amid the reek of death.

Fighting on the Western Front

A gun crew firing on entrenched German positions, 1918.

INITIAL REACTIONS   As the trench war along the western front in Belgium and France stalemated, the casualties soared and pressure for U.S. intervention increased. On the first day of the Battle of the Somme, on July 1, 1916, 20,000 British soldiers were killed and 40,000 others were wounded—all in less than twenty-four hours. Shock in the United States over the sudden outbreak of war in Europe gave way to gratitude that an ocean stood between America and the killing fields. President Wilson repeatedly urged Americans to remain "neutral in thought as well as in action."

That was more easily said than done. More than one third of Americans were first- or second-generation immigrants who retained close ties to their old country. Among the 13 million immigrants from the countries at war, the 8 million German Americans were by far the largest group, and the 4 million Irish Americans harbored a deep-rooted enmity toward Britain. These groups instinctively leaned toward the Central powers.

Old-line Americans, largely of British origin, supported the Allied powers. Americans identified also with France, which had contributed to American culture and ideas and to independence itself. Britain and France, if not their ally Russia, seemed the custodians of democracy, while Germany seemed the embodiment of autocracy and militarism. If not a direct threat to the United States, Germany would pose at least a potential threat if it destroyed the balance of power in Europe. High officers of the U.S. government were pro-British in thought from the outset of the war.

A STRAINED NEUTRALITY   At first the war in Europe brought a slump in American exports and the threat of a depression, but by the spring of 1915 the Allies' demand for food and military supplies generated an economic boom. France and Britain bought so much from the United States that they soon needed loans to continue making purchases. Early in the war, Secretary of State William Jennings Bryan declared that loans to any warring nation were "inconsistent with the true spirit of neutrality." Technically he was correct, but Wilson, for all his public professions of neutrality, was in fact determined to aid Great Britain. He quietly began approving credit to sustain trade with the Allies. American investors would advance over $2 billion to the Allies before the United States entered the war, and only $27 million to Germany.

The administration nevertheless clung to its official stance of neutrality through two and a half years of warfare in Europe and tried to uphold the traditions of "freedom of the seas," which had guided American policy since the Napoleonic Wars of the early nineteenth century. Trade on the high seas assumed a new importance as the German army's advance through Belgium toward Paris ground down into the stalemate of trench warfare. In a war of attrition, survival depended upon access to supplies, and in such a war British naval power counted for a great deal. In November 1914 the British declared the whole North Sea a war zone and sowed it with mines. Four months later they announced that they would seize ships carrying goods produced by or intended for their enemies.

NEUTRAL RIGHTS AND SUBMARINES   British actions, including the blacklisting of companies that traded with the enemy and censoring the mail, raised some old issues of neutral rights, but the German reaction introduced an entirely new question. In the face of the British blockade, whereby only submarines could venture out to harass the enemy, the German government proclaimed a war zone around the British Isles. Enemy ships in those waters were liable to sinking by submarines, the Germans declared. As the chief advantage of U-boat (*Unterseeboot*) warfare was in surprise, it violated the established international procedure of stopping an enemy vessel on the high seas and providing for the safety of passengers and crew before sinking it. Since the British sometimes flew neutral flags as a ruse, neutral ships in this war zone would also be in danger.

The United States pronounced the German policy "an indefensible violation of neutral rights" and warned that Germany would be held to "strict accountability" for any destruction of American lives and property. Then, on May 7, 1915, a German U-boat torpedoed the passenger liner *Lusitania*, which exploded and sank within eighteen minutes. Before the ship's departure from New York, bound for Liverpool, the German embassy had published warnings in American newspapers against travel to the war zone, but 128 Americans were nevertheless among the 1,198 persons lost.

Americans were outraged. To quiet the uproar, Wilson urged patience: "There is such a thing as a man being too proud to fight. There is such a thing as a nation being so right that it does not need to convince others by force that it is right." But his previous demand for "strict accountability" forced him to make a stronger response. On May 13 Secretary of State Bryan reluctantly signed a note demanding that the Germans abandon unrestricted submarine warfare, disavow the sinking of the *Lusitania*, and pay reparations. The Germans responded that the passenger ship was armed (which it was not) and carried a secret cargo of small arms and ammunition (which it did). A second note on June 9 repeated American demands in stronger terms. Bryan, unwilling to risk war over the issue, resigned in protest. His successor, Robert Lansing, signed the note.

In response to the uproar over the *Lusitania*, the German government had secretly ordered U-boat captains to avoid sinking large passenger vessels. When, despite the order, two American lives were lost in the sinking of the New York-bound British liner *Arabic*, the German government declared on September 1, 1915, "Liners will not be sunk by our submarines without

The *Lusitania*

Americans were outraged when a German torpedo sank the *Lusitania* on May 7, 1915.

warning and without safety of the lives of non-combatants, provided that the liners do not try to escape or offer resistance." With this *Arabic* pledge, Wilson's resolute stand seemed to have won a victory for his policy.

THE DEBATE OVER PREPAREDNESS   The *Lusitania* incident and, more generally, the quarrels over protecting neutral commerce during wartime contributed to a growing demand for a stronger U.S. army and navy. After the *Lusitania* sinking the outcry from preparedness advocates grew into a clamor. In his annual message in 1915, Wilson alerted Congress to his plans for war preparedness. The response was far from unanimous. Progressives and pacifists, especially in the rural South and the West, opposed military expansion.

Wilson eventually accepted a compromise between advocates of an expanded force under federal control and advocates of a traditional citizen army. The National Defense Act of 1916 expanded the regular army from 90,000 to 175,000 and permitted a gradual enlargement to 223,000. It also increased the national guard to 440,000. The Naval Construction Act of 1916 authorized between $500 and $600 million for a three-year shipbuilding program.

Forced to relent on military preparedness, progressive opponents of a buildup insisted that the financial burden should rest upon the wealthy people they held responsible for pushing the nation toward war. The income tax became their weapon. Supported by a groundswell of popular support, they wrote into the Revenue Act of 1916 changes that doubled the basic income tax from 1 to 2 percent, lifted the surtax on income over $2 million to 13 percent, added an estate tax graduated up to a maximum of 10 percent, levied a 12.5 percent tax on gross receipts of munitions makers, and added a new tax on corporations. The new taxes amounted to the most clear-cut victory of radical Progressives in the entire Wilson period, a victory that Wilson supported in preparation for the upcoming presidential election.

THE ELECTION OF 1916   As the 1916 election approached, Republicans hoped to regain their normal electoral majority, and Theodore Roosevelt hoped to be their leader again. But in 1912 he had committed the deadly sin of bolting his party, and what was more his eagerness for the United States to enter the war scared many voters. Needing somebody who would draw Bull Moose Progressives back into the fold, the Republican regulars turned to Justice Charles Evans Hughes, a Progressive governor of New York from 1907 to 1910. On the Supreme Court since then, he had neither endorsed a candidate in 1912 nor spoken out on foreign policy.

The Democrats, as expected, chose Wilson once again and in their platform endorsed a program of social legislation, neutrality regarding the war

Peace with Honor

Woodrow Wilson's policies of neutrality proved popular in the 1916 campaign.

in Europe, and reasonable military preparedness. The party further commended women's suffrage to the states and pledged support for a postwar league of nations to enforce peace with collective-security measures against aggressors. The Democrats' most popular issue was a pledge to keep the nation out of the war in Europe. The peace theme, refined in the slogan "He kept us out of war," became the rallying cry of the Wilson campaign.

The candidates in the 1916 presidential election were remarkably similar. Both Wilson and Hughes were the sons of preachers; both were attorneys and former professors; both had been Progressive governors; both were known for their pristine integrity. Theodore Roosevelt highlighted the similarities between them when he called the bearded Hughes a "whiskered Wilson." Wilson, however, proved to be the better campaigner. In the end, Wilson's twin pledges of peace and Progressivism, a unique combination of issues forged in the legislative and diplomatic crucibles of 1916, brought victory. The final vote showed a Democratic sweep of the Far West and the South, enough for victory in the Electoral College, by 277 to 254, and in the popular vote, by 9 million to 8.5 million. Wilson also carried many social-justice Progressives who in 1912 had supported the Bull Moose campaign.

LAST EFFORTS FOR PEACE   Immediately after the election, Wilson offered to mediate an end to the European war, but neither side was willing to abandon its major war aims. Wilson then decided to make one more appeal, in the hope that public opinion would force the hands of the warring governments. Speaking before the Senate, he asserted that this would have to be a "peace without victory," for only a "peace among equals" could endure.

Although Wilson did not know it, he was already too late. Exactly two weeks before he spoke, German military leaders had decided to wage unrestricted submarine warfare on all shipping in the Atlantic. Faced with weakening resources in a war of attrition, the Germans took the calculated risk of provoking American anger in the hope of scoring a quick knockout. On January 31, 1917, Germany announced the new policy, effective the next day: all vessels would be sunk without warning.

On February 3, 1917, Wilson informed a joint session of Congress that the United States had broken diplomatic relations with the German government. He added that he still did not believe the Germans would do what they said they felt at liberty to do—only overt acts would persuade him that they intended to sink neutral ships. In case of such acts, he would take measures to protect American seamen and citizens.

Then, on March 1, news of the so-called Zimmermann telegram broke in the American press. The British had intercepted and decoded an important message from German foreign secretary Arthur Zimmermann to his ambassador in Mexico. The note instructed the envoy to offer an alliance and financial aid to Mexico in case of war between the United States and Germany. In return for diversionary action against the United States, Mexico would recover "the lost territory in Texas, New Mexico, and Arizona." All this was contingent on war with the United States, but an electrified public read in it an aggressive intent. Later in March another bombshell burst when a revolution overthrew Russia's czarist government and established the provisional government of a Russian republic. The fall of the czarist autocracy allowed Americans the illusion that all the major Allied powers were now fighting for constitutional democracy. Not until November 1917 was that illusion shattered, when the Bolsheviks, led by Vladimir Lenin, seized power in Russia and began establishing a Communist dictatorship.

AMERICA'S ENTRY INTO THE WAR

In March 1917 German submarines did the unthinkable: they sank five American merchant vessels. On March 20 Wilson's cabinet unanimously endorsed a declaration of war, and the following day the president called a special session of Congress. When it met on April 2, Wilson asked Congress to recognize the war that imperial Germany was already waging against the United States. The German government had revealed itself as a natural foe of liberty, and Wilson argued in the rhetoric of Progressivism, "the world must be made safe for democracy." The war resolution passed the Senate by a vote of 82 to 6 on April 4. The House concurred, 373 to 50, and Wilson signed the measure on April 6.

How had matters come to this, less than three years after Wilson's proclamation of neutrality? Prominent among the various explanations of America's entrance into the war were the effects of British propaganda and America's deep involvement in trade with the Allies, which some observers then and later credited to the intrigues of war profiteers and munitions makers. Some Americans thought German domination of Europe would be a threat to U.S. security, especially if it meant the destruction or capture of the British navy. Whatever the influence of such factors, they likely would not have been decisive without the issue of submarine warfare. This issue need not have become decisive, either, since such neutrals as Norway, Sweden, and Denmark took relatively heavier losses yet stayed out of the war. But once Wilson had taken a stand for the traditional rights of neutrals and noncombatants, he was to some extent at the mercy of decisions by the German high command.

AMERICA'S EARLY ROLE   The scope of America's role in the European war remained unclear for a time. Few on either side of the Atlantic expected more from the United States than a token military effort. Despite Congress's preparedness measures, the army remained small and untested. The navy also was largely undeveloped. But the U.S. Navy made a major contribution when it persuaded the Allies to adopt a convoy system of escorting merchant ships in groups, resulting in an impressive decrease in Allied shipping losses to German submarines.

Within a month of America's declaration of war, the British and French requested money for supplies, a request Congress had anticipated in the Liberty Loan Act, which added $5 billion to the national debt in "liberty bonds." Of this amount, $3 billion could be lent to the Allied powers. The United States was also willing to furnish naval support, financial credits, supplies, and munitions. But to raise and train a large army, equip it, and send it across a submarine-infested ocean seemed out of the question.

The United States agreed to send a token military force to bolster Anglo-French morale, and on June 26, 1917, the first American contingent, about 14,500 men commanded by General John J. Pershing, began to disembark

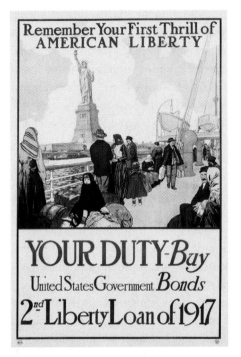

Remember Your First Thrill of AMERICAN LIBERTY

YOUR DUTY-Buy United States Government **Bonds** 2ⁿᵈ Liberty Loan of 1917

The Thrill of American Liberty

This Liberty Loan poster urges immigrants to do their duty for their new country by buying government bonds.

on the French coast. After reaching Paris, Pershing decided that the war-weary Allies would be unable to mount an offensive by themselves. He therefore requested that Wilson send 1 million American troops by the following spring, and the president obliged.

When the United States entered the war, the combined strength of the regular army and national guard was only 379,000; at the end it would be 3.7 million. The need for such large numbers of troops converted Wilson to the idea of conscription. Under the Selective Service Act of May 18, 1917, all men aged twenty-one to thirty (later, eighteen to forty-five) had to register to be drafted for military service. By July 1917, when the first lottery was held to determine who would actually be drafted to fight in the war, almost 24 million men were registered. In the course of the war, about 2 million Americans crossed the Atlantic, and about 1.4 million of them saw some combat.

MOBILIZING A NATION Complete economic mobilization on the home front was also necessary to conduct the war efficiently. In 1916 Congress had created a Council of National Defense, which in turn set up other wartime agencies. The U.S. Shipping Board, organized in 1917, within two years was constructing more than forty steel and ninety wooden ships monthly. In 1917 Congress created a Food Administration, headed by Herbert Hoover, a future president who sought to raise crop production while reducing civilian use of foodstuffs. "Food will win the war" was the slogan. Hoover directed a propaganda campaign that "Hooverized" the country with "meatless Tuesdays," "wheatless Wednesdays," "porkless Saturdays," the planting of victory gardens, and the creative use of leftovers. The Fuel Administration introduced the country to daylight saving time and "heatless Mondays" to save fuel.

The War Industries Board (WIB), established in 1917, soon became the most important of all the mobilization agencies. Wilson summoned Bernard Baruch, a brilliant Wall Street investor, to head the board, giving him a virtual dictatorship over the economy. The WIB could allocate raw materials, tell manufacturers what to produce, order construction of new plants, and with presidential approval, fix prices.

A NEW LABOR FORCE   The closing off of foreign immigration from Europe during the war and the movement of almost 4 million men into the armed services created a labor shortage. To meet it, women, African Americans, and other ethnic minorities were encouraged to enter industries and agricultural activities heretofore dominated by white men. Northern businesses sent recruiting agents into the Deep South to find workers for their factories and mills, and over 400,000 southern blacks began the Great Migration northward during the war years, a mass movement that continued unabated through the 1920s. Mexican Americans followed the same migratory pattern. Recruiting agents and newspaper editors portrayed the North as the "land of promise" for southern blacks suffering from their region's depressed agricultural economy and rising racial intimidation and violence. By 1930 the number of African Americans living in the North was triple that of 1910.

But the newcomers were not always welcomed above the Mason-Dixon line. Many native white workers resented the new arrivals, and racial tensions sparked riots in cities across the country. In 1917 over forty African Americans and nine whites were killed during a riot over employment in a defense plant in East St. Louis. Two years later the toll of a Chicago race riot was nearly as high, with twenty-three African Americans and fifteen whites left dead. In these and other incidents of racial violence, the pattern was the same: whites angered by the influx of blacks into their communities would seize upon an incident as an excuse to rampage through black neighborhoods, killing, burning, and looting while white policemen looked the other way or encouraged the mobs.

For women, American intervention in World War I had more positive effects. Initially women supported the war effort in traditional ways. They helped organize war-bond and war-relief drives, conserved foodstuffs and war-related materials, supported the Red Cross, and joined the army nurse corps. But as the scope of the war widened, both government and industry sought to mobilize women workers for service on farms, loading docks, and railway crews, as well as in armaments industries, machine shops, steel and lumber mills, and chemical plants. Many women leaders saw such opportunities as a breakthrough. "At last, after centuries of disabilities and discrimination," said a speaker at a Women's Trade Union League meeting in 1917, "women are coming into the labor [force] and festival of life on equal terms with men."

In fact, however, war-generated changes in female employment were limited and brief. About 1 million women participated in "war work," but they usually were young, single, and already working outside the home. Most returned to their previous jobs once the war ended. In fact, male-dominated unions encouraged women to revert to their stereotypical domestic roles after the war. The Central Federated Union of New York baldly insisted that "the same patriotism which induced women to enter industry during the war should induce them to vacate their positions after the war." The anticipated gains of women in the workforce failed to materialize. In fact, in 1920 the 8.5 million working women made up a smaller percentage of the labor force than women had in 1910. Still, one tangible result of women's contributions to the war effort was Woodrow Wilson's decision to endorse women's suffrage. In the fall of 1918, he told the Senate that giving women the vote was "vital to the winning of the war."

WAR PROPAGANDA   The exigencies of winning the war also led the government to mobilize public opinion. On April 14, 1917, eight days after the declaration of war, Wilson established the Committee on Public Information. Its executive director, George Creel, a Denver journalist, sold Wilson on the idea that the best approach to influencing public opinion was "expression, not repression"—propaganda instead of censorship. Creel organized a propaganda machine to convey the Allies' war aims to the people and, above all, to the enemy, where it might encourage public pressure to end the fighting.

CIVIL LIBERTIES   By arousing public opinion to such a frenzy, the war effort channeled the zeal of Progressivism into grotesque campaigns of "Americanism" and witch hunting. Wilson had foreseen these consequences. "Once lead this people into war," he told a newspaper editor, "and they'll forget there ever was such a thing as tolerance." Popular prejudice equated anything German with disloyalty. Schools even dropped German-language courses.

While mobs hunted spies and chased rumors, the federal government stalked bigger game, with results often as absurd. The Espionage and Sedition Acts of 1917 and 1918 effectively outlawed criticism of government leaders and war policies. These laws led to more than 1,500 prosecutions and 1,000 convictions. Such repression disillusioned many Progressives. Senator Robert La Follette declared that those engaged in such a "witch-hunt" were trying "to throw the country into a state of terror, to coerce public opinion, stifle criticism, suppress discussion of the issues of the war, and put a quietus on all opposition. It is time for the American people to assert and maintain their rights."

The impact of these acts fell with most severity upon radicals. Eugene V. Debs, who had polled over 900,000 votes as the Socialist candidate for president in 1912, was arrested and eventually sentenced to ten years in prison for encouraging draft resistance. In 1920, still in jail, he polled nearly 1 million votes for president.

In an important decision just after the war, the Supreme Court upheld the Espionage and Sedition Acts. *Schenck v. United States* (1919) sustained the conviction of a man for circulating anti-draft leaflets among members of the armed forces. In this case, Justice Oliver Wendell Holmes observed, "Free speech would not protect a man in falsely shouting fire in a theater, and causing a panic." The Sedition Act applied where there was "a clear and present danger" that free speech in wartime might create evils Congress had a right to prevent.

"THE DECISIVE POWER"

American troops played little more than a token role in the European fighting until the end of 1917, when the Allied position turned desperate. In October the Italian lines collapsed in the face of the Austrian offensive. In November, having suffered some 5.5 million casualties and widespread food and ammunition shortages, the Russian provisional republican government succumbed to a revolution led by Vladimir Lenin and his Bolshevik party, which promised the Russian people "peace, land, and bread." With German troops then deep in Russian territory and with armies of "White" Russians organizing to resist the Bolsheviks, Lenin concluded a separate peace with the Germans in the Treaty of Brest-Litovsk (March 3, 1918). The Central powers were then free to concentrate their forces on the western front, and the American war effort became a "race for France," to restore the balance of strength in that arena. French premier Georges Clemenceau appealed to the Americans to accelerate their mobilization. "A terrible blow is imminent," he predicted to an American journalist. "Tell your Americans to come quickly."

THE WESTERN FRONT   On March 21, 1918, Clemenceau's prediction came true when the Germans began the first of several offensives in France and Belgium to try to end the war before the Americans arrived in force. On May 27 the Germans began their next drive along the Aisne River, took Soissons, and pushed on to the Marne River along a forty-mile front. By May

America at War

U.S. soldiers fire an artillery gun in Argonne, France.

1918 there were 1 million fresh U.S. troops in Europe, and for the first time they made a difference. In a counterattack, American forces retook Cantigny on May 28 and held it. During early June a marine brigade blocked the Germans at Belleau Wood, and army troops took Vaux and opposed the Germans at Château-Thierry. Though these actions had limited military significance, their effect on Allied morale was immense. Each was a solid American success, and together they reinforced General Pershing's demand for a separate U.S. army.

Before that could come to pass, the Second Battle of the Marne erupted on July 15, 1918, and proved to be the turning point in the western campaign. On both sides of Reims, the Germans assaulted the French lines. Within three days, however, they had stalled, and the Allies began to roll the German front back into Belgium. On September 12 an army of more than 500,000 staged the first strictly American offensive of the war, aimed at German forces at St.-Mihiel. Within three days the Germans had pulled back. Two weeks later the massive Meuse-Argonne offensive employed U.S. divisions in a drive toward the rail center at Sedan, which supplied the entire German front. The largest American action of the war resulted in 117,000 American casualties, including 26,000 dead. All along the front from Sedan to Flan-

**WORLD WAR I,
THE WESTERN FRONT, 1918**

- - - Western front, March 1918
—— German offensive, spring 1918
⟶ Allied counteroffensive
—— Western front, November 1918

Why was the war on the western front a stalemate for most of World War I? What was the effect of the arrival of the American troops? Why was the Second Battle of the Marne the turning point of the war?

ders, the Germans were in retreat. "America," wrote a German commander, "thus became the decisive power in the war."

Meanwhile, in an effort to prevent Allied supplies stockpiled in Russia from falling into German hands and to encourage the counter-revolutionary Russian "Whites" in their civil war against the "Reds," fourteen Allied nations sent troops into eastern Russia. On August 2, 1918, some 8,000 Americans joined the expedition and remained on Russian soil until April 1920. But the Allied intervention in Russia was a colossal failure. The Bolsheviks were able to consolidate their power and defeat the Whites. Lenin and the Soviets never forgave the West for attempting to thwart their revolution.

THE FOURTEEN POINTS   As the conflict in Europe was ending, neither the Allies nor the Central powers, despite Wilson's prodding, had stated openly what they hoped to gain through the bloodletting. Wilson insisted that the Americans had no selfish ends. "We desire no conquest, no dominion," he stressed in his war message. Unfortunately for his idealistic purpose, the Bolsheviks later published copies of secret treaties in which the Allies had promised territorial gains in order to win Italy, Romania, and Greece to their side. When an Interallied Conference in Paris late in 1917 failed to agree on a statement of aims, Wilson formulated his own.

With advice from a panel of experts, Wilson drew up a peace plan that would be labeled the Fourteen Points. These he delivered to a joint session of Congress on January 8, 1918, "as the only possible program" for peace. The first five points called for open diplomacy, freedom of the seas, removal of trade barriers, armaments reduction, and an impartial adjustment of colonial claims based upon the interests of the populations involved. Most of the remaining points called upon the Central powers to evacuate occupied lands and allow self-determination for various nationalities, a crucial principle for Wilson. Point 14, the capstone in Wilson's thinking, called for the formation of a "league" of nations to guarantee the independence and territorial integrity of all countries, great and small.

Wilson sincerely believed in the Fourteen Points, but they also served important political purposes. One of their aims was to keep Russia in the war by a more liberal statement of purposes—a vain hope, as it turned out. Another was to reassure the Allied peoples that they were involved in a noble cause. A third was to drive a wedge between the governments of the Central powers and their people by offering a reasonable peace. But the chaos into which Central Europe descended in 1918, as Germany and Austria-Hungary verged on starvation and experienced socialist uprisings, took matters out of Wilson's hands.

THE END OF THE WAR   On September 29, 1918, German general Erich Ludendorff advised his government to seek the best peace terms possible. On October 3 a new chancellor made the first German overtures for peace on the basis of the Fourteen Points. The Allies, after a month of diplomatic fencing, accepted the Fourteen Points as a basis of peace but with two significant reservations: the right to discuss freedom of the seas further and the demand for reparations (financial compensation to the victors) for war damages.

Meanwhile, German morale plummeted, culminating in a naval mutiny. Germany's allies, Bulgaria, Turkey, and Austria-Hungary, dropped out of the war during the early fall of 1918. On November 9 the kaiser, head of the German Empire, abdicated, and a German republic was proclaimed. Two days later, on November 11, 1918, an armistice was signed, ceasing the hostilities. Under the armistice the Germans agreed to evacuate occupied territories, pull back behind the Rhine River, and surrender their navy, railroad equipment, and other matériel. The Germans were assured that the Fourteen Points would be the basis of the peace conference.

During its nineteen months of participation in the war, the United States saw 126,000 of its servicemen killed. Germany's war dead totaled over 2 million, including civilians; France lost 1,375,000 combatants, the United Kingdom had 703,000 military deaths, and Russia lost 1.7 million. The new Europe emerging from the conflagration would be much different: more violent, more polarized, more cynical, less sure of itself, and less capable of decisive action. The United States, for good or ill, would be sucked into the vacuum of power created by the destructiveness of the Great War.

THE FIGHT FOR PEACE

DOMESTIC UNREST   Woodrow Wilson made a fateful decision to attend the Paris Peace Conference, which convened on January 18, 1919, and would last almost six months. A president had never left the country for so long, and doing so dramatized all the more Wilson's messianic vision and his desire to ensure his goal of a lasting peace. From one viewpoint it was a shrewd move, for his prestige and determination made a difference in Paris. But during his prolonged trip abroad, he lost touch with political developments at home, where his political coalition was already unraveling under the pressures of wartime discontent. Western farmers complained about the government's control of wheat prices while eastern business leaders chafed at revenue policies designed, according to the *New York Sun,* "to pay for the war out of taxes raised north of the Mason and Dixon Line." Organized labor, despite real gains, groused about inflation and the problems of reconversion to a peacetime economy.

In the midterm elections of 1918, Wilson made matters worse when he defied his advisers and urged voters to elect a Democratic Congress to support his foreign policies. Republicans, who for the most part had supported his war measures, took affront. So, too, did many voters. In elections held a week before the armistice, the Democrats lost control of both houses of

Congress. With an opposition majority in the new Congress, Wilson further weakened his standing by failing to include a single prominent Republican in the American delegation headed for Paris and the treaty negotiations. Former President Taft suggested that Wilson's real intention in going to Paris was "to hog the whole show."

When Wilson reached Europe in December 1918, enthusiastic demonstrations greeted him in Paris. At the conference table, however, he had to deal with some tough-minded statesmen who did not share his utopian zeal. The Paris conference included delegates from all countries that had declared war or broken diplomatic relations with Germany. But it was dominated by the Big Four: the prime ministers of Britain, France, and Italy and the president of the United States. British prime minister David Lloyd George was a gifted politician fresh from electoral victory following a campaign whose slogan declared, "Hang the kaiser." Italy's prime minister, Vittorio Orlando, was there to pick up the spoils promised his country in the secret Treaty of London (1915). French premier Georges Clemenceau, a stern realist, insisted on severe measures to weaken Germany and guarantee French security.

The Big Four

Woodrow Wilson (second from left) with Georges Clemenceau of France and Arthur Balfour of Great Britain at the Paris Peace Conference.

THE LEAGUE OF NATIONS   Woodrow Wilson insisted that his cherished League of Nations come first in the conference and in the treaty. Whatever compromises he might have to make regarding territorial boundaries and financial claims, whatever mistakes might result, Wilson believed that a league of nations committed to collective security would maintain international stability.

Wilson presided over the commission to draft a league charter. Article Ten of the charter, which he called "the heart of the League," pledged members to consult on military and economic sanctions against aggressors. The use of armed force would be a last resort. The League structure would allow each member an equal voice in the Assembly; the Big Five (Britain, France, Italy, Japan, and the United States) and four rotating members would make up the Council; the administrative staff, in Geneva, would make up the Secretariat; and a Permanent Court of International Justice (set up in 1921 and usually called the World Court) could "hear and determine any dispute of an international character."

On February 14, 1919, Wilson delivered the finished draft of the League charter and departed the next day for a month-long visit home. Already he faced rumblings of opposition. Republican Henry Cabot Lodge, chairman of the Senate Foreign Relations Committee, claimed that the League's covenant was unacceptable. His statement of March 4 bore the signatures of thirty-nine Republican senators or senators-elect, more than enough to block ratification.

TERRITORY AND REPARATIONS   Back in Paris, Wilson grudgingly acceded to French demands for territorial concessions and reparations from Germany. The Allied statesmen also agreed that the Allies would occupy a demilitarized German Rhineland for fifteen years and that the League of Nations would administer Germany's coal-rich Saar Basin. France could use Saar mines for fifteen years, after which the region's voters would determine whether to join Germany or France.

In other territorial matters, Wilson had to compromise his principle of national self-determination. There was in fact no way to make Europe's boundaries correspond to ethnic divisions because mixed populations were scattered through Central Europe. In some areas, moreover, national self-determination yielded to other interests, such as trade and defense. The result was a reorganized map of Central Europe in which portions of the former Austro-Hungarian Empire became independent, most notably Czechoslovakia and Yugoslavia, and portions were attached to Poland, Romania, and Italy.

EUROPE AFTER THE TREATY OF VERSAILLES, 1918

······· 1914 boundaries

New nations

Plebiscite areas

Occupied area

Why was self-determination difficult for states in Central Europe? How did territorial concessions weaken Germany? Why might territorial changes like the creation of the Polish Corridor or the concession of the Sudetenland to Czechoslovakia have created problems in the future?

Ethnic and nationalist tensions continued and would contribute to the crisis that culminated in World War II.

The discussion of reparations was among the longest and most bitter at the conference. Despite a pre-armistice agreement that Germany would be liable only for civilian damages, Clemenceau and Lloyd George proposed reparations for the entire cost of the war. On this point, Wilson made perhaps his most fateful concessions. He agreed to a clause in the treaty by which Germany accepted responsibility for starting the war and for its entire cost. The "war guilt" clause offended Germans and provided a source of persistent bitterness upon which Adolf Hitler would later capitalize.

On May 7, 1919, the victorious powers presented the treaty to the German delegates, who returned three weeks later with 443 pages of criticism protesting that the terms violated the Fourteen Points. A few small changes were made, but when the Germans still refused to sign, the French prepared to move their army across the Rhine River. Finally, on June 28, 1919, the Germans gave up and signed the treaty at Versailles.

WILSON'S LOSS AT HOME   The force of Woodrow Wilson's idealism struck deep, and on July 8, 1919, he returned home with the Versailles Treaty amid a great clamor of popular support. One third of the state legislatures had endorsed the League, as had thirty-three of the nation's forty-eight governors. Wilson called upon the Senate to accept the "great duty" of ratifying the treaty.

Senator Henry Cabot Lodge, however, doubted that the Paris negotiators could make "mankind suddenly virtuous by a statute or written constitution." A powerful Republican who nourished an intense dislike for Wilson, Lodge relished a fight. He knew the undercurrents already stirring up opposition to the treaty: the resentment felt by German, Italian, and Irish groups, the disappointment of liberals with Wilson's compromises on reparations and boundaries, the distractions of demobilization and resulting domestic problems, and the revival of isolationism. Lodge's close friend Theodore Roosevelt, still a popular figure, lambasted Wilson and the League, noting that he keenly distrusted a "man who cares for other nations as much as his own."

Others agreed. In the Senate a group of "irreconcilables," fourteen Republicans and two Democrats, opposed U.S. participation in

The League of Nations Argument in a Nutshell

J. N. "Ding" Darling's summation of the League controversy.

the League on any terms. They were mainly western and midwestern Progressives who feared that new foreign commitments would threaten domestic programs and reforms. The irreconcilables would be useful to Lodge's purpose, but he belonged to a larger group of "reservationists," who insisted upon limiting U.S. involvement in the League. Wilson said that he had already amended the covenant to these ends, pointing out that with a veto in the League Council, the United States could not be obligated to do anything against its will.

Lodge, who set more store by the old balance of power than by the new idea of collective security, offered a set of amendments, or reservations. Wilson responded by agreeing to interpretive reservations but to nothing that would reopen the negotiations with Germany and the Allies. He especially opposed the amendments weakening Article Ten of the League of Nations covenant, which provided for collective action by the signatory governments against aggression.

By September, with momentum for the treaty slackening, Wilson decided to go directly to the people. Against the advice of doctors and friends, he set forth on a railroad tour through the Midwest to the West Coast, pounding out speeches on his typewriter between stops. In all he traveled 8,000 miles in twenty-two days, giving thirty-two major addresses and voicing dire warnings of the consequences if the treaty were not approved.

For a while, Wilson seemed to be regaining the initiative, but on October 2, 1919, he suffered a severe stroke, leaving him paralyzed on his left side and an invalid for the rest of his life. For seventeen months his protective wife, Edith, kept him isolated from all but the most essential business. The illness intensified his stubbornness. He might have done better to have secured the best compromise possible, but he refused to yield. As he scoffed to an aide, "Let Lodge compromise."

Lodge was determined to amend the treaty before it was ratified. Between November 7 and 19, the Senate adopted fourteen of Lodge's reservations to the Versailles Treaty, most having to do with the League. Wilson refused to make any compromises or concessions. As a result, the Wilsonians found themselves thrown into an unlikely combination with the irreconcilables, who opposed the treaty under any circumstances. The Senate vote on the treaty with Lodge's reservations was thirty-nine for and fifty-five against. On the question of taking the treaty without reservations, irreconcilables and reservationists combined to defeat ratification again, with thirty-eight for and fifty-three against.

In the face of strong public criticism, however, the Senate voted to reconsider. On March 19, 1920, twenty-one intransigent Democrats deserted Wilson and joined the reservationists, but the treaty once again fell short of a two-thirds majority, by a vote of forty-nine yeas and thirty-five nays. The real winners were the smallest of the three groups in the Senate, neither the Wilsonians nor the reservationists but the irreconcilables.

When Congress declared the war at an end by joint resolution on May 20, 1920, Wilson vetoed the action; it was not until after he left office that a joint resolution officially ended the state of war with Germany and Austria-Hungary, on July 2, 1921. Peace treaties with Germany, Austria, and Hungary were ratified on October 18, 1921, but by then Warren Gamaliel Harding was president of the United States.

LURCHING FROM WAR TO PEACE

The Versailles Treaty, for all the time it spent in the Senate before being defeated, was but one issue clamoring for public attention in the turbulent period after the war. Demobilization of the armed forces and the government's war effort proceeded in haphazard fashion. The War Industries Board closed shop on January 1, 1919, and the sudden cancellation of war contracts left workers and business leaders to cope with reconversion to a peacetime economy on their own. Wilson's leadership was missing. He had been preoccupied by the war and the League, and once bedridden by his illness, he became strangely grim and peevish. His rudderless administration floundered through rough waters during its last two years.

THE SPANISH FLU   Amid the initial confusion of postwar life, many Americans confronted a virulent menace that produced far more casualties than the war itself. It became known as the Spanish flu, and its contagion spread around the globe. Erupting in the spring of 1918 and lasting a year, the pandemic killed more than 22 million people throughout the world, twice as many as died in World War I. In the United States alone the flu accounted for over 675,000 deaths, seven times the number of combat deaths in France.

American servicemen returning from France brought the flu with them, and it raced through the congested army camps and naval bases. By September 1918 the epidemic had spread to the civilian population. In that month 10,000 Americans died from the disease. Municipal health officers began fining people for spitting on the sidewalks or sneezing without a handkerchief. Millions of people began wearing surgical masks to work. Phone booths were locked up, as were other public facilities, such as dance halls, poolrooms, and theaters. Even churches and saloons in many communities were declared off-limits. Still the death toll rose. From September 1918 to June 1919, one quarter of the population contracted the illness.

By the spring of 1919, the pandemic had run its course. It ended as suddenly—and as inexplicably—as it had begun. Although another outbreak occurred in the winter of 1920, the population had grown more resistant to its assaults. No disease, plague, war, famine, or natural catastrophe in world history had killed so many people in such a short time.

THE ECONOMIC TRANSITION The problems of postwar readjustment were worsened by widespread labor unrest. Prices continued to rise steeply after the war, and discontented workers, released from wartime constraints, were more willing to strike for their demands. In 1919 more than 4 million workers walked out in thousands of disputes. After a general strike in Seattle, public opinion of militant workers began to turn hostile.

The most celebrated postwar labor confrontation was the Boston police strike, which inadvertently launched a presidential career. On September 9, 1919, most of Boston's police force went out on strike, demanding recognition of their union. Massachusetts governor Calvin Coolidge mobilized the national guard to arrest looters and restore order. After four days the strikers were ready to return, but the police commissioner fired them all. When labor leader Samuel Gompers appealed for their reinstatement, Coolidge responded in words that suddenly turned him into a national figure: "There is no right to strike against the public safety by anybody, anywhere, anytime."

RACIAL FRICTION The summer of 1919 also brought a season of violent race riots, in the North and the South. Whites invaded the black section of Longview, Texas, in search of a teacher who had allegedly accused a white woman of a liaison with a black man. They burned shops and houses and ran several African Americans out of town. A week later in Washington, D.C., reports of black assaults on white women aroused white mobs, and for four days gangs of white and black rioters waged race war in the streets until soldiers and driving rains ended the fighting.

These were but preliminaries to the Chicago riot of late July, in which 38 people were killed, 537 injured, and 1,000 left homeless. It all started on the shores of Lake Michigan, when a black youth's raft drifted into the whites' beach area, and whites started stoning him. The climactic disorders of the summer occurred in the rural area around Elaine, Arkansas, where African-American tenant farmers tried to organize a union. According to official reports, 5 whites and 25 blacks were killed in the violence, but whites told one reporter in the area that in fact more than 100 blacks had died. Altogether twenty-five race riots erupted in 1919.

THE RED SCARE   Public reaction to the wave of labor strikes and race riots reflected the impact of Russia's Bolshevik revolution. A minority of radicals thought America's domestic turbulence, like that in Russia, was the first scene in a drama of world revolution. A much larger public was persuaded that they might be right. After all, Lenin's tiny faction in Russia had exploited confusion to impose its will on the entire nation. Wartime hysteria against all things German was thus readily transformed into a postwar Red Scare.

Fears of revolution in America might have remained latent except for the actions of a lunatic fringe. In April 1919 the postal service intercepted nearly forty homemade mail bombs addressed to prominent citizens. One slipped through and blew off the hands of a Georgia senator's maid. In June another bomb destroyed the front of Attorney General A. Mitchell Palmer's house in Washington.

In June 1919 the Justice Department decided to deport radicals, and Attorney General Palmer set up as the head of the department's new General Intelligence Division the young J. Edgar Hoover, who began to collect files on radicals. Raids began on November 7, 1919, when agents swooped down on the Union of Russian Workers in twelve cities. Many of those arrested were deported without a court hearing. On January 2, 1920, police raids in dozens of cities swept up some 5,000 suspects, many taken from their homes without search warrants. About half of those seized were kept in custody. That same month the New York State legislature expelled five duly elected Socialist members.

Basking in popular approval, Palmer continued to warn of the Red menace, but like other fads and alarms, the ugly mood of intolerance passed. By the summer of 1920, the Red Scare had begun to evaporate. Communist revolutions in Europe died out, leaving Bolshevism isolated in Russia. Bombings tapered off; the wave of strikes and race riots receded. The reactionary attorney general began to seem more threatening to civil liberties than a handful of radicals were to the social order. By September 1920, when a bomb explosion at the corner of Broad and Wall Streets in New York City killed thirty-eight people, Americans were ready to take it for what it was: the work of a crazed mind and not the start of a revolution.

The Red Scare nevertheless left a lasting mark on American life. Part of its legacy was the continuing crusade for "100 percent Americanism" and restrictions on immigration. It also left a stigma on labor unions (already weakened by their internal ethnic and racial tensions) and contributed to the anti-union open-shop campaign—the American plan, its sponsors called it. But for many thoughtful Americans the chief residue of the Great War, President Wilson's physical collapse, and its chaotic aftermath was a profound disillusionment.

MAKING CONNECTIONS

- The Red Scare at the end of World War I led to a wave of nativism and to immigration restriction, outlined in the next chapter.

- This chapter ended by noting the "profound disillusionment" Americans felt with efforts to reform the world. The political aspect of that disillusionment—the return to "normalcy" in the 1920s—is discussed in Chapter 27.

- The treaty ending World War I was designed to cripple Germany's military strength. But as Chapter 29 shows, within two decades Adolf Hitler was leading a rebuilt German military force into World War II.

FURTHER READING

A lucid overview of international events covered in this chapter is Robert H. Ferrell's *Woodrow Wilson and World War I, 1917–1921* (1985). On Wilson's stance toward war, see Ross Gregory's *The Origins of American Intervention in the First World War* (1971). An excellent brief biography is H. W. Brands's *Woodrow Wilson* (2003).

Edward M. Coffman's *The War to End All Wars: The American Military Experience in World War I* (1968) is a detailed presentation of America's military involvement. David M. Kennedy's *Over Here: The First World War and American Society* (1980) surveys the impact of the war on the home front. Maurine Weiner Greenwald's *Women, War, and Work: The Impact of World War I on Women Workers in the United States* (1980) discusses the role of women. Ronald Schaffer's *America in the Great War: The Rise of the War Welfare State* (1991) shows the effect of war mobilization on business organization. Richard Polenberg's *Fighting Faiths: The Abrams Case, the Supreme*

Court, and Free Speech (1987) examines the prosecution of a case under the 1918 Sedition Act.

How American diplomacy fared in the making of peace has received considerable attention. Thomas J. Knock interrelates domestic affairs and foreign relations in his explanation of Wilson's peacemaking in *To End All Wars: Woodrow Wilson and the Quest for a New World Order* (1992).

The problems of the immediate postwar years and chronicled by a number of historians. On the Spanish flu, see John M. Barry's *The Great Influenza: The Epic Story of the Deadliest Plague in History* (2004). Labor tensions are examined in David E. Brody's *Labor in Crisis: The Steel Strike of 1919* (1965) and Francis Russell's *A City in Terror: The 1919 Boston Police Strike* (1975). On racial strife, see William M. Tuttle Jr.'s *Race Riot: Chicago in the Red Summer of 1919* (1970). The fear of Communists is analyzed in Robert K. Murray's *Red Scare: A Study in National Hysteria, 1919–1920* (1955).

26

THE MODERN TEMPER

FOCUS QUESTIONS

· What issues mobilized the reactionary groups of the 1920s?

· How did the new social trends in the 1920s challenge traditional attitudes?

· How did modernism influence American culture?

To answer these questions and access additional review material, please visit www.wwnorton.com/studyspace.

The horrors of World War I dealt a shattering blow to the widespread belief that Western civilization was steadily progressing, a myth that had dominated the public consciousness for a century and had been a powerful stimulus of Progressivism. The editors of *Presbyterian* magazine announced in 1919 that the "world has been convulsed . . . and every field of thought and action has been disturbed. . . . The most settled principles and laws of society . . . have been attacked."

The war's unimaginable carnage produced a postwar disillusionment among young intellectuals that challenged traditional values. A new "modernist" sensibility emerged among artists, writers, and journalists. At once a mood and a movement, as well as a label for a historical era and a cultural style, modernism appeared first in Europe at the end of the nineteenth century and had become a pervasive international force by 1920. It arose out of a widespread recognition that Western civilization had entered an era of bewildering change. New technologies, new modes of transportation and communication, and new scientific discoveries such as quantum mechanics and relativity theory combined to rupture perceptions of reality and generate new forms of artistic expression. Modernism manifested itself in a cluster of diverse intellectual and artistic movements: impressionism, futurism, Dadaism, surrealism, Freudianism. As the French painter Paul Gauguin acknowledged, the upheavals of modernism produced "an epoch of confusion."

At the same time that the war provided an accelerant for modernism, it stimulated volatile social tensions and political radicalism. The postwar wave of strikes, bombings, anti-Communist hysteria, and race riots convinced many Americans that the country had entered a frightening new era of turmoil and turbulence. Conflict abounded. Defenders of tradition located the germs of radicalism in the polyglot cities teeming with immigrants and foreign ideas. The defensive mood of the 1920s fed on a growing tendency to connect American nationalism with nativism, Anglo-Saxon racism, and militant Protestantism.

REACTION IN THE TWENTIES

NATIVISM   That so many political radicals in the United States were immigrants strengthened the suspicion that the seeds of sedition were foreign-born. In the early 1920s over half the white men and one third of the white women working in manufacturing and industry were foreign-born, most of them from central or eastern Europe. That socialism and anarchism were prevalent in those regions made such immigrant workers especially suspicious in the eyes of "old stock" Americans.

The most celebrated case of nativist prejudice involved two Italian-born anarchists, Nicola Sacco and Bartolomeo Vanzetti. Arrested in 1920 for a robbery and murder in South Braintree, Massachusetts, they were tried by a judge who privately referred to them as "anarchist bastards." People then and since have insisted that Sacco and Vanzetti were sentenced more for their political beliefs and their ethnic origin than for any crime they had committed. The case became a great radical and liberal cause of the 1920s, but despite pleas for mercy and worldwide demonstrations on behalf of the two men, Sacco and Vanzetti were sent to the electric chair in 1927. Recent investigations have pointed to their likely guilt.

The surging postwar nativism generated new efforts to restrict immigration. Congress, alarmed at the influx of foreigners after 1919, passed the Emergency Immigration Act of 1921, which restricted European arrivals each year to 3 percent of the foreign-born of any nationality as shown in the 1910 census. A quota law in 1924 reduced the number to 2 percent based on the 1890 census, which included fewer of the "new" immigrants from southern and eastern Europe. This law set a permanent limitation, which became effective in 1929, of slightly over 150,000 immigrants per year based on the "national origins" of the U.S. population as of 1920. In signing the law, President Calvin Coolidge pledged, "America must be kept American."

However inexact the quotas, their purpose was clear: to tilt the balance in favor of the old immigration from northern and western Europe, which was assigned about 85 percent of the total. The law completely excluded people from east Asia. Yet it left the gate open to immigrants from Western Hemisphere countries, so that an ironic consequence was a substantial increase in the Hispanic Catholic population. People of Latin American descent (chiefly Mexicans, Puerto Ricans, and Cubans) became the fastest growing ethnic minority in the country.

THE KLAN   During the postwar years the nativist tradition took on a new form, a revived Ku Klux Klan modeled on the group founded in the South after the Civil War. The new Klan was devoted to "100 percent Americanism" rather than to the old Confederacy, and it restricted its membership to native-born white Protestants. It was determined to protect its warped notion of the American way of life not only from blacks but also from Roman Catholics, Jews, and immigrants. In going nativist, the new Klan spread far outside the South. Its appeal reached areas as widely scattered as Oregon and Maine. It thrived in small towns and cities in the North and especially in the Midwest. And it was preoccupied with the defense of white ("native") women and Christian morals.

Klan Rally

In 1925 40,000 Klan members paraded down Pennsylvania Avenue in Washington, D.C.

The Klan represented a vicious reflex against the modern and the alien, against shifting moral standards, the declining influence of churches, and the social permissiveness of cities and colleges. In the Southwest the Klan became more than anything else a moral crusade. "It is going to drive the bootleggers forever out of this land," declared a Texan. "It is going to bring clean moving pictures . . . clean literature . . . break up roadside parking . . . enforce the laws . . . protect homes." Instead, the Klan terrorized and assaulted blacks and immigrants. Estimates of its peak membership, probably inflated, range from 3 million to 8 million, but the Klan's influence diminished as quickly as its numbers grew. Nativist excitement declined after passage of the 1924 immigration law. The Klan also suffered from recurrent factional quarrels and schisms. And its willing use of violence tarnished its moral pretensions.

FUNDAMENTALISM   While the Klan saw a threat mainly in the "alien menace," many adherents of the old-time religion saw threats from modernism in the churches: new ideas that the Bible should be studied in the light of modern scholarship (the "higher criticism") or that it could be reconciled with scientific theories of evolution. Fearing that such modernist notions had infected schools and even pulpits, fundamentalism, grounded in a literal interpretation of the Bible, took on a new militancy.

Among the rural fundamentalist leaders only William Jennings Bryan, the former presidential candidate and secretary of state, had the following, prestige, and eloquence to make the movement a popular crusade. By 1920 Bryan was showing signs of age, but he remained as silver-tongued as ever. In 1921 he sparked a drive for laws prohibiting the teaching of Darwinian evolution in the public schools. Anti-evolution bills began to appear in legislatures, but the only victories came in the South—and there were few of those.

The climax came in Tennessee, where in 1925 the legislature outlawed the teaching of evolution in public schools and colleges. A young teacher at a high school in Dayton, Tennessee, John T. Scopes, accepted an offer from the American Civil Liberties Union to defend a test case. It soon was a case heard round the world. Before the opening day of the "monkey trial," the streets of Dayton swarmed with publicity hounds, curiosity seekers, evangelists and atheists, hucksters, and a mob of reporters.

The two stars of the show were Bryan, who led the prosecution of Scopes for teaching evolution in violation of Tennessee law, and Clarence Darrow, a renowned Chicago trial lawyer and confessed agnostic, who defended Scopes by challenging the anti-evolution law. The trial quickly became a debate between fundamentalism and modernism. When the judge (a

Courtroom Scene during the Scopes Trial

The media, food vendors, and others flocked to Dayton, Tennessee, for the case against John Scopes, the teacher who taught evolution.

practicing evangelist) damaged Darrow's case by ruling out scientific testimony on evolution, most observers assumed the trial was over.

But the defense rebounded by calling Bryan as an expert witness on biblical interpretation. Darrow, who had once supported Bryan as a presidential candidate, now relentlessly entrapped the statesman in literal-minded interpretations and exposed Bryan's ignorance of biblical history and scholarship. Bryan insisted that a "great fish" had swallowed Jonah, that Joshua had made the sun stand still, that the world was created in 4004 B.C.—all, according to Darrow, "fool ideas that no intelligent Christian on earth believes." It was a bitter scene. At one point the two men, their patience exhausted in the broiling summer heat, lunged at each other, shaking their fists, leading the judge to adjourn the court.

The next day the testimony ended. The only issue before the court, the judge ruled, was whether Scopes had in fact taught evolution. He was found guilty, but the Tennessee Supreme Court, while upholding the law, overruled the $100 fine on a legal technicality. The chief prosecutor accepted the higher court's advice against "prolonging the life of this bizarre case" and dropped the issue. With more prescience than he knew, Bryan had described the trial as a "duel to the death." A few days after it closed, he died of a heart condition aggravated by heat and fatigue.

PROHIBITION   Prohibition of alcoholic beverages offered another example of reforming zeal channeled into a drive for moral righteousness and conformity. Moralists had been campaigning against excessive drink since the eighteenth century. Around 1900, however, the leading temperance organizations, the Women's Christian Temperance Union and the Anti-Saloon League, shifted their efforts from reforming individuals to campaigning for a national prohibition law. The Anti-Saloon League became one of the most effective pressure groups in history, mobilizing Protestant churches behind its single-minded battle to elect "dry" candidates.

The 1916 elections produced in both houses of Congress two-thirds majorities suffering an amendment to the Constitution prohibiting alcoholic beverages. Soon the wartime spirit of sacrifice, the need to use grain for food, and wartime hostility to German-American brewers transformed the cause into a virtual test of patriotism. On December 18, 1917, Congress sent to the states the Eighteenth Amendment, which one year after ratification, on January 16, 1919, banned the manufacture, sale, and transportation of intoxicating liquors nationwide.

Prohibition

A 1926 police raid on a speakeasy.

The new amendment did not keep people from drinking, however. Congress never supplied adequate enforcement, if such were even possible given the public thirst, the spotty support of local officials, and the profits to be made in bootlegging. In Detroit, across the river from Ontario, Canada, where booze was legal, the liquor industry during Prohibition was second in size only to the auto industry. Speakeasies, hip flasks, and cocktail parties were among the social innovations of the era, along with increased drinking by women.

It would be too much to say that Prohibition gave rise to organized crime, for systematic vice, gambling, and extortion had long been practiced and were often tied in with saloons. But Prohibition supplied ruthless, flamboyant criminals, such as "Scarface" Al Capone, with a new, enormous source of income, while the automobile and the submachine gun provided greater mobility and greater firepower. Gangland leaders showed remarkable gifts for exploiting loopholes in the law when they did not simply bribe policemen and politicians.

Capone was by far the most celebrated criminal of the 1920s. In 1927 he pocketed $60 million from his bootlegging, prostitution, and gambling empire, and he flaunted his wealth as well as his open disregard for legal authorities. He bludgeoned to death several conspiring police lieutenants and ordered the execution of dozens of his criminal competitors. Law-enforcement officials began to smash his bootlegging operations in 1929, but they were unable to pin anything on him until a Treasury agent infiltrated his gang and uncovered evidence that was used to convict him later that year of tax evasion. He was sentenced to eleven years in prison.

In the light of the illegal activities of Capone and other members of organized-crime syndicates, it came as no great surprise when a commission in 1931 reported evidence that enforcement of Prohibition had broken down. Still, the commission voted to extend Prohibition, and President Herbert Hoover chose to stand by what he called the "experiment, noble in motive and far-reaching in purpose."

THE ROARING TWENTIES

In many ways the reactionary temper of the 1920s and the repressive movements to which it gave rise seemed the dominant trends of the decade. But they arose in part as reactions to disruptive social and intellectual currents. During those years a new cosmopolitan, urban America confronted provincial small-town and rural America, and cultural conflict reached new levels of tension.

Young urban intellectuals developed an active disdain for the old-fashioned values of the hinterlands. Sinclair Lewis's novel *Main Street* (1920) caricatured the stifling life of the prairie town, depicting a "savorless people, gulping tasteless food, and sitting afterward, coatless and thoughtless, in rocking chairs prickly with inane decorations, listening to mechanical music, saying mechanical things about the excellence of Ford automobiles, and viewing themselves as the greatest race in the world." The banality of small-town life became a pervasive theme in much of the literature of the time, and the heartland responded with counterimages of cities infested with vice, crime, corruption, and foreigners.

THE JAZZ AGE   Writer F. Scott Fitzgerald dubbed the postwar era the Jazz Age because young people were willing to experiment with new forms of recreation and sexuality. The new jazz music bubbling up in New Orleans, Kansas City, Memphis, New York City, and Chicago blended African and European traditions to form a distinctive sound characterized by improvisation, "blue notes," and polyrhythm. The syncopated rhythms of jazz were immensely popular among rebellious young adults and helped spawn carefree new dance steps such as the Charleston and the black bottom, gyrations that shocked guardians of morality.

Frankie "Half Pint" Jackson and His Band at the Sunset Cafe, Chicago, 1920s

Jazz emerged in the 1920s as an especially American expression of the modernist spirit. African-American artists bent musical conventions to give fuller rein to improvisation and sensuality.

If people were not listening to ragtime or jazz or to the family radio shows that became the rage in the 1920s, they were frequenting movie theaters. By 1930 there were more than 23,000 theaters around the country, and they drew more than 95 million customers each week. In Muncie, Indiana, a small city of 35,000, nine movie theaters were operating seven days a week. Films became even more popular after the introduction of sound in 1927.

THE NEW MORALITY   Much of the shock to traditionalists during the Jazz Age came from the changes in manners and morals evidenced first among young people and especially on college campuses. In *This Side of Paradise* (1920), a novel of student life at Princeton, F. Scott Fitzgerald wrote of "the great current American phenomenon, the 'petting party.'" None of the Victorian mothers, he said, "had any idea how casually their daughters were accustomed to be kissed." From such novels and from magazines and movies, many Americans learned about the cities' wild parties, illegal drinking, promiscuity, and speakeasies.

Sex came to be discussed with surprising frankness during the 1920s. Much of the talk derived from a spreading awareness of Dr. Sigmund Freud, the Viennese father of psychoanalysis. By the 1920s his ideas had begun to infiltrate popular awareness, and in society and literature there was talk of libido, Oedipus complexes, sublimation, and repression.

The "New Woman" of the 1920s

Two flappers dance atop the Sherman Hotel in Chicago, 1926.

Fashion also reflected the rebellion against prudishness and a loosening of inhibitions. In 1919 women's skirts were typically six inches above the ground; by 1927 they were at the knees, and the "flapper," with her bobbed hair, rolled stockings, cigarettes, lipstick, and sensuous dancing, was providing a shocking model of the new feminism. The name *flapper* derived from the way female rebels allowed their galoshes to flap around their ankles. Conservative moralists saw the flappers as just another sign of a degenerating society. Others saw in the "new woman" an expression of rugged American individualism.

By 1930, however, the thrill of rebellion was waning; the revolution against Victorian morality had run its course. Its extreme expressions in time aroused doubts that the indulgence of lust equaled liberation. And the much-discussed revolution in morals was also greatly exaggerated. The twenties roared for only a small proportion of the population. F. Scott Fitzgerald reminded Americans in 1931 that the Jazz Age was jazzy for only the "upper tenth" of the population. Still, some new folkways had come to stay. In the late 1930s a survey disclosed that among college women almost half had had sexual relations before marriage.

THE WOMEN'S MOVEMENT   At the same time that many women were embracing new sexual mores, all women were being liberated politically. The suffrage movement, which had been in the doldrums since 1896, sprang back to life in the second decade of the new century. In 1912 Alice

Votes for Women

Suffragettes march in New York City in 1912, their children by their side.

Paul, a Quaker social worker, returned from an apprenticeship with the militant suffragists of England to chair the National American Woman Suffrage Association's Congressional Committee. Paul instructed female activists to picket state legislatures, target and "punish" politicians who failed to endorse suffrage, chain themselves to public buildings, provoke police to arrest them, and undertake hunger strikes. By 1917 Paul and her followers were picketing the White House and deliberately inviting arrest, after which they went on hunger strikes in prison.

In 1915 Carrie Chapman Catt had once again become head of the National Woman Suffrage Association (NWSA). For several years, President Woodrow Wilson had evaded the issue of a suffrage amendment, but he supported a plank in the 1916 Democratic platform endorsing state action for women's suffrage. He addressed the NWSA that year, and thereafter he worked closely with its leaders. On June 4, 1919, the Senate finally adopted the Nineteenth Amendment, by a bare two-thirds majority, and after fourteen months the states ratified the women's suffrage amendment on August 21, 1920, the climactic achievement of the Progressive Era.

Women thereafter entered politics in growing numbers, but this development did not suddenly release women from deeply embedded social customs and legal discrimination. Women tended to vote like men on most issues. One group, however, wanted something more. Alice Paul set a new goal, first introduced in Congress in 1923: an equal rights amendment that would eliminate any remaining legal distinctions between the sexes, including the special legislation for the protection of working women put on the books in the previous fifty or so years. It would be another fifty years before Alice Paul would see Congress adopt her amendment in 1972; she did not live to see it fall short of ratification, however.

The sharp increase in the number of women in the workforce during World War I proved short-lived, but in the longer view a steady increase in the number of employed women occurred in the 1920s and 1930s. Working women remained concentrated in traditional occupations: they were mostly domestics, office workers, teachers, clerks, salespeople, dressmakers, milliners, and seamstresses. On the eve of World War II, women's work was little more diversified than it had been at the turn of the century, but by 1940 it would be on the eve of a major transformation.

THE "NEW NEGRO" The discriminations experienced by African Americans and women display many parallels, and their struggles for equality have frequently coincided. The most significant development in African-American life during the early twentieth century was the Great Migration northward. A massive movement of blacks from the South to the North began in 1915–1916, when rapidly expanding war industries were experiencing a labor shortage, leaving openings for African Americans in the North. Altogether between 1910 and 1920 the Southeast lost some 323,000 blacks, or 5 percent of the 1920 native black population, and by 1930 it had lost another 615,000, or 8 percent of the 1920 African-American population. The migration north led to a slow but steady growth in black political influence. African Americans were freer to speak and act in a northern settling, and they gained political leverage by settling in large cities in states with many electoral votes.

Along with political activity came a bristling spirit of protest, a spirit that received cultural expression in a literary and artistic movement labeled the Harlem Renaissance. Claude McKay, a Jamaican immigrant, was the first significant writer of the movement, which sought to rediscover black folk culture. Poems collected in McKay's *Harlem Shadows* (1922) expressed defiance in such titles as "If We Must Die" and "To the White Fiends." Other emergent black writers included Langston Hughes, Zora Neale Hurston, Countee Cullen, Jean Toomer, and James Weldon Johnson.

The spirit of the "New Negro" also found an outlet in what came to be called Negro nationalism, which exalted blackness, black cultural expression, and at its most extreme, black exclusiveness. The leading spokesman for such views was the flamboyant Marcus Garvey. Racial bias, Garvey said, was so ingrained in whites that it was futile to appeal to their sense of justice. He advised blacks to liberate themselves from the surrounding white culture. "We have outgrown slavery," he declared, "but our minds are still enslaved to the thinking of the Master Race."

Garvey endorsed the "social and political separation of all peoples to the extent that they promote their own ideals and civilization." Such a separatist message appalled other African-American leaders. W.E.B. Du Bois, for example, labeled Garvey "the most dangerous enemy of the Negro race." Garvey and his aides created their own black version of Christianity, organized their own fraternal lodges and community cultural centers, started their own businesses, and published their own newspaper. Garvey's message of racial pride and self-reliance appealed to many blacks who had arrived in the northern cities during the Great Migration and had grown embittered with the hypocrisy of American democracy during the postwar economic slump. Garvey declared that the only lasting hope for blacks was to flee America and build their own republic in Africa.

In 1916 Garvey brought to New York the Universal Negro Improvement Association, which he had started in his native Jamaica two years before. He quickly

Marcus Garvey

Garvey was the founder of the
Universal Negro Improvement
Association and a leading spokesman
for "Negro nationalism" in the 1920s.

enlisted 500,000 members in his association, and claimed as many as 6 million by 1923. At the peak of his popularity, however, Garvey was convicted
of mail fraud. He was imprisoned from
1925 until pardoned and deported to
Jamaica in 1927 by President Calvin
Coolidge. Garvey died in obscurity in
London in 1940, but the memory of his
movement kept alive an undercurrent
of racial pride that would reemerge
later under the slogan of black power.

Even more influential in promoting black rights was the National Association for the Advancement of
Colored People. Founded in 1910, it
was led by northern white liberals
and black leaders such as Du Bois. Its
main strategy focused on getting the
federal government to enforce the
Fourteenth and Fifteenth Amendments. In 1919, the NAACP launched
a campaign against lynching, still a common atrocity in many parts of the
country, most of whose victims were black. An anti-lynching bill making
mob murder a federal offense passed the House in 1922 but lost to a filibuster by southern senators. Nonetheless, the bill stayed before the House
until 1925, and continuing agitation of the issue helped to reduce lynchings,
which declined to one third of what they had been the previous decade.

THE CULTURE OF MODERNISM

After 1920 changes in the realms of science and social thought were
perhaps even more dramatic than those affecting women and African Americans. As the twentieth century advanced, the easy faith in progress and reform
expressed by Progressives fell victim to a series of frustrations and disasters,
including the Great War, the failure of the League of Nations to win approval
in the United States, Woodrow Wilson's physical and political collapse, and
the failure of Prohibition. Startling new findings in physics further shook
prevailing assumptions.

SCIENCE AND SOCIAL THOUGHT   Physicists of the early twentieth century altered the image of the cosmos in bewildering ways. Since Isaac Newton's research in the late seventeenth century, conventional wisdom had held that the universe was governed by laws that the scientific method could ultimately uncover. A world of such certain order and rationality had bolstered hopes of infinite progress in human knowledge.

This rational world of order and certainty disintegrated at the turn of the century when Albert Einstein, a young German physicist, announced his theory of relativity, which maintained that space, time, and mass were not absolutes but were relative to the location and motion of the observer. Newton's eighteenth-century mechanics, according to Einstein's relativity theories, worked well enough at relatively slow speeds, but the more nearly one approached the velocity of light (about 186,000 miles per second), the more all measuring devices would change accordingly, so that yardsticks would become shorter, clocks and heartbeats would slow down, even the aging process would ebb.

Relativity was not the only disconcerting concept that Einstein discovered. The farther one reached out into the universe and the farther one reached down into the minute world of the atom, the more certainty dissolved. The discovery of radioactivity in the 1890s showed that atoms were not irreducible units of matter and that some of them emitted particles of energy. This meant, Einstein noted, that mass and energy were not separate phenomena but interchangeable.

Meanwhile, the German physicist Max Planck had discovered that electromagnetic emissions of energy, whether as electricity or light, came in little bundles that he called quanta. The development of quantum theory suggested that atoms were far more complex than once believed. In 1927 the pioneering German physicist Werner Heisenberg announced that the activities within an atom were ultimately indescribable. One could never know both the position and the velocity of an electron, Heisenberg concluded, because the very process of observation would affect the behavior of the particle, altering its position or velocity.

Heisenberg's "uncertainty principle" meant that human knowledge had limits. Just as Enlightenment thinkers drew on Isaac Newton's principles of gravitation two centuries before to formulate their views on the laws governing society, the ideas of relativity and uncertainty in the twentieth century convinced some people to deny the relevance of absolute values in any sphere of society, thus undermining the concepts of personal responsibility and absolute standards. Anthropologists aided the process by transforming the word *culture,* which had before meant "refinement," into a term for the whole system of ideas, folkways, and institutions within which any group lived. Even the most primitive societies had cultures, and all things being relative, one culture should not impose its value judgments upon another. Two anthropologists, Ruth Benedict and Margaret Mead, were especially effective in spreading this viewpoint.

MODERNIST ART AND LITERATURE   The cluster of scientific ideas associated with Charles Darwin, Sigmund Freud, and Albert Einstein helped inspire a modernist revolution in the minds of many intellectuals and creative artists during the early twentieth century. The modernist world was one in which, as Karl Marx said, "all that is solid melts into air." Modernism arose out of a widespread recognition that Western civilization was entering an era of bewildering change. New technologies, new modes of transportation and communication, and new scientific discoveries combined to transform the nature of everyday life and to generate dramatic new forms of artistic expression and architectural design.

Whereas nineteenth-century writers and artists took for granted an accessible world that could be readily observed and accurately represented, self-willed modernists viewed reality as something to be created rather than copied, expressed rather than reproduced. As a consequence, they concluded that the subconscious regions of the psyche were more interesting and more potent than reason, common sense, and logic.

In the various arts such concerns spawned abstract painting, atonal music, free verse in poetry, stream-of-consciousness narrative, and interior monologues in stories and novels. Writers showed an intense concern with new forms of expression in an effort to violate expectations and shock their audiences.

The chief American prophets of modernism were living in Europe: Ezra Pound and T. S. Eliot in London and Gertrude Stein in Paris. All were deeply concerned with creating new and often difficult styles of modernist expression. Pound, as foreign editor of *Poetry,* served as the conduit through which many American poets achieved publication in the leading journals and magazines promoting experimentalism. At the same time he became the leader of the imagist movement, a revolt against the ornamental verbosity of Victorian poetry in favor of the concrete image.

Ezra Pound's brilliant protégé was the St. Louis–born Harvard graduate T. S. Eliot, who in 1915 contributed to *Poetry* his first major poem, "The Love Song of J. Alfred Prufrock," the musings of an ineffectual man who "after tea and cakes and ices" could never find "the strength to force the moment to its crisis." Eliot went to Oxford in 1913 and soon decided to make England his home and poetry his career. He rejected the nineteenth century's "cheerfulness, optimism, and hopefulness," as well as the traditional notion of poetry as the literal representation of a beautiful world. The modern poet, he insisted, must "be able to see beneath both beauty and ugliness; to see the boredom, and the horror and the glory." Eliot's *The Waste Land* (1922) made few concessions to readers in its obscure allusions, its juxtaposition of unexpected metaphors, its deep sense of postwar disillusionment and melancholy, and its suggestion of a burned-out civilization. The poem became for an alienated younger generation almost the touchstone of the modern temper.

Gertrude Stein, another voluntary exile, settled in Paris in 1903 and became an early champion of experimentalism and a collector of modern art. Long regarded as no more than the literary eccentric who wrote "a rose is a rose is a rose is a rose," she would later be recognized as one of the chief promoters of the modernist prose style. At the time she was known chiefly through her influence on such literary expatriates of the 1920s as Sherwood Anderson and Ernest Hemingway, whom she told, "All of you young people who served in the war, you are the lost generation."

The earliest chronicler of that "lost" generation, F. Scott Fitzgerald, blazed up brilliantly and then quickly flickered out like the tinseled, carefree, sad young characters in his novels. Successful and famous at age twenty-four, having published *This Side of Paradise* in 1920, he, along with his wife, Zelda, experienced and depicted the "greatest, gaudiest spree in history." What gave depth to the best of Fitzgerald's work was what a character in *The Great Gatsby* (1925), his finest novel, called "a sense of the fundamental decencies" amid all the surface gaiety—and almost always a sense of impending doom.

Ernest Hemingway suffered even more from a psychic wound inflicted by an uncaring world. For him literature was a means of defense, a way to strike back, and in the process find a meaning for himself rather than accept one imposed by society. Hemingway's novels *The Sun Also Rises* (1926) and *A Farewell to Arms* (1929) depict a desperate search for "real" life and the doomed, war-tainted love affairs of Americans of the "lost generation." Hundreds of writers tried to imitate Hemingway's terse style, but few had his gift, which lay less in what he had to say than in the way he said it.

THE SOUTHERN RENAISSANCE   As modernist literature arose in response to the changes taking place in the United States and Europe, so southern literature of the 1920s reflected a regional world in the midst of rebirth. A southern renaissance in writing emerged from the conflict between the dying world of tradition and the modern commercial world struggling to come to life in the aftermath of the Great War. While in the South the conflict of values aroused the Ku Klux Klan and fundamentalist furies that tried desperately to bring back the world of tradition, it also inspired the creativity of the South's young writers.

Two of the most notable of the new southern writers were Thomas Wolfe and William Faulkner. Fame rushed in first on Wolfe and his native Asheville, North Carolina, which he wrote about in his first novel, *Look Homeward,*

Angel. "Against the Victorian morality and the Bourbon aristocracy of the South," Wolfe had "turned in all his fury," wrote newspaper editor Jonathan Daniels, a former classmate. Despite his lust for experience and knowledge, his demonic drive to escape the encircling hills for the "fabled" world outside, and his agonized search for some "lost lane-end into heaven," Wolfe never completely severed his roots in the South.

William Faulkner's achievement, more than Wolfe's, was rooted in the coarsely textured social world that produced him. Born near Oxford, Mississippi, he grew up there and transmuted his hometown into the fictional Jefferson, in Yoknapatawpha County. In writing *Sartoris* (1929), he began to discover that his "own little postage stamp of native soil was worth writing about" and that he "would never live long enough to exhaust it." With *Sartoris* and the creation of his mythical land of Yoknapatawpha, Faulkner kindled a blaze of creative energy. Next, as he put it, he wrote his gut into *The Sound and the Fury* (1929). It was one of the triumphs of the modernist style, but most early readers, taking their cue from the title instead of the critics, believed that its complex prose and themes signified nothing.

Modernism and the southern literary renaissance, both of which emerged from the crucible of the Great War and its aftermath, were products of the 1920s. But the widespread alienation felt by the writers and artists of the 1920s did not survive the decade. The onset of the Great Depression in 1929 sparked a renewed sense of commitment and affirmation in the arts, as if people could no longer afford the art-for-art's-sake emphasis of the 1920s. Alienation would give way to social purpose in the decade to come.

MAKING CONNECTIONS

- The next chapter discusses the growing consumer culture of the 1920s, an economic offshoot of the Roaring Twenties described in this chapter.

- Chapter 28 touches on the changes in literary culture wrought by the Great Depression, from the modernism discussed in this chapter to a recognition of the social role of literature and the cultural "rediscovery of America" in the 1930s.

- The status of women in the workforce did not improve in the 1920s despite the successes of the women's movement. That status changed, at least temporarily, during World War II. In Chapter 30 the rise of Rosie the Riveter is discussed.

Further Reading

For a lively survey of the interwar period, start with William E. Leuchtenburg's *The Perils of Prosperity, 1914–32,* 2nd ed. (1993). The best introduction to the culture of the 1920s remains Loren Baritz's *The Culture of the Twenties* (1970). See also Lynn Dumenil's *The Modern Temper: American Culture and Society in the 1920s* (1995).

John Higham's *Strangers in the Land: Patterns of American Nativism, 1860–1925,* 2nd ed. (1988) details the story of immigration restriction. The controversial Sacco and Vanzetti case is thoroughly explored in *Kill Now, Talk Forever: Debating Sacco and Vanzetti,* edited by Richard Newby (2002). For analysis of the revival of Klan activity, see Nancy MacLean's *Behind the Mask of Chivalry: The Making of the Second Ku Klux Klan* (1994).

Women's suffrage is treated extensively in Eleanor Flexner's *Century of Struggle: The Woman's Rights Movement in the United States,* enlarged ed. (1996). See Charles F. Kellogg's *NAACP: A History of the National Association for the Advancement of Colored People* (1967) for his analysis of the pioneering court cases against racial discrimination. Nathan Irvin Huggin's *Harlem Renaissance* (1971) assesses the cultural impact of the Great Migration on New York. On the migration to Chicago see James R. Grossman's *Land of Hope: Chicago, Black Southerners, and the Great Migration* (1989). Nicholas Lemann's *The Promised Land: The Great Black Migration and How It Changed America* (1991) is a fine exposition of the changes brought about by the migration in the both the South and the North.

On southern modernism, see Daniel Joseph Singal's *The War Within: From Victorian to Modernist Thought in the South, 1919–1945* (1982). Stanley Coben's *Rebellion against Victorianism: The Impetus for Cultural Change in 1920s America* (1991) surveys the appeal of modernism among writers, artists, and intellectuals.

27

REPUBLICAN RESURGENCE AND DECLINE

FOCUS QUESTIONS

· How did the conservatism of Harding, Coolidge, and Hoover shape their policies?

· What drove the growth of the American economy in the 1920s?

· What were the causes of the Great Depression?

To answer these questions and access additional review material, please visit www.wwnorton.com/studyspace.

The Progressive political coalition that reelected Woodrow Wilson in 1916 proved to be quite fragile, and by 1920 it had fragmented. It began to show signs of fissure during the war, when radicals and other reformers were disaffected by America's involvement. After the war, Wilson's support continued to erode as his health problems incapacitated him. Organized labor resented the administration's unsympathetic attitude toward the strikes of 1919–1920, and western farmers complained that wartime price controls had discriminated against them. While prominent intellectuals grew disillusioned with the popular support for Prohibition and religious fundamentalism, many among the middle class lost interest in political activism. They instead channeled their energies into building a new business civilization based upon mass production and mass consumption, greater leisure, and the introduction of labor-saving electrical appliances in the home. Moreover, Progressivism's final triumphs at the national level crystallized before the war's end: the Eighteenth Amendment, which outlawed alcoholic beverages, was ratified in 1919, and the Nineteenth Amendment, which extended women's suffrage to the entire country, became law a year later.

Progressivism did not completely disappear in the 1920s, however. Although smaller in number, reformers remained active in Congress during much of the decade even while the White House was in conservative Republican hands. The Progressive impulse for "good government" and extended public services remained strong, especially at the state and local levels, where movements for good roads, education, public health, and social welfare gained momentum during the decade. At the same time, however, the reactionary temper of the times gave rise to the grassroots drive for moral righteousness and conformity, animating the Ku Klux Klan and the fundamentalist and prohibitionist movements.

"NORMALCY"

THE ELECTION OF 1920   After World War I most Americans grew weary of idealistic crusades and suspicious of leaders promoting reform. Woodrow Wilson himself recognized the reactionary temper. "It is only once in a generation," he remarked, "that a people can be lifted above material things. That is why conservative government is in the saddle two-thirds of the time."

When the Republicans met in Chicago in 1920, the Old Guard party regulars found their man in the affable Ohio senator Warren Gamaliel Harding, who had set the tone of his campaign when he told a Boston audience, "America's present need is not heroics, but healing; not nostrums, but normalcy; not revolution, but restoration; not agitation, but adjustment; not surgery, but serenity; not the dramatic, but the dispassionate; not experiment, but equipoise; not submergence in internationality, but sustainment in triumphant nationality." Harding caught the mood of the times—a longing for "normalcy" and contentment with the status quo.

Harding's promise of a "return to normalcy" reflected his own conservative values and folksy personality. The son of an Ohio farmer, he described himself not as an intellectual or a crusader but "just a plain fellow" who was "old-fashioned and even reactionary in matters of faith and morals." Such a description, however, suggests a certain puritan regimen that Harding never practiced. Far from being an old-fashioned moralist in his personal life, he drank bootleg liquor in the midst of Prohibition, smoked and chewed tobacco, relished weekly poker games, and had numerous liaisons with women other than his austere wife, whom he called Duchess. The general public, however, remained unaware of Harding's escapades. Instead, voters saw him as a handsome, charming, gregarious, and lovable politician. A man of self-confessed limitations in vision, leadership, and intellectual power, he once admitted that "I cannot hope to be one of the great presidents, but perhaps I may be remembered as one of the best loved." He got his wish.

The Democrats in 1920 hoped that Harding would not be president at all. James Cox, former newsman and former governor of Ohio, won the presidential nomination of a fragmented Democratic party on the forty-fourth ballot. For vice president the convention named Franklin D. Roosevelt, who as assistant secretary of the navy occupied the same position his Republican cousin Theodore Roosevelt had once held.

The Democrats suffered from the breakup of the Wilsonian coalition and the conservative postwar mood. In the words of the Progressive journalist William Allen White, Americans in 1920 were "tired of issues, sick at heart of ideals, and weary of being noble." The country voted overwhelmingly for Harding's promised "return to normalcy." Harding got 16 million votes to 9 million for Cox, who carried no state outside the Democratic Solid South.

EARLY APPOINTMENTS AND POLICY   Harding in office had much in common with Ulysses Grant. His cabinet, like Grant's, mixed some of the best men in the party with some of the worst. Charles Evans Hughes became a distinguished secretary of state. Herbert Hoover in the Commerce Department, Andrew W. Mellon in the Treasury Department, and Henry A. Wallace in the Agriculture Department were also efficient, forceful figures. Of the others, Secretary of the Interior Albert B. Fall landed in prison and Attorney General Harry M. Daugherty only narrowly escaped prosecution. Many lesser offices went to members of the soon notorious "Ohio gang," headed by Daugherty, a group of Harding's Ohio friends with whom the president met regularly for poker games lubricated with illegal liquor.

Harding and his friends set about dismantling or neutralizing as many components of Progressivism as they could. Harding's four appointments to the Supreme Court were all conservatives, including Chief Justice William Howard Taft, who announced that he had been "appointed to reverse a few decisions." During the 1920s the Taft court struck down a federal child-labor law and a minimum-wage law for women, issued numerous injunctions against striking unions, and made rulings limiting the powers of federal regulatory agencies.

The Harding administration established a pro-business tone reminiscent of the McKinley White House. To sustain economic growth, Secretary of the Treasury Mellon promoted government spending cuts and federal tax reductions. As Ronald Reagan would argue sixty years later, Mellon insisted that tax cuts should go mainly to the rich, on the assumption that wealth in the hands of the few would promote the general welfare through increased capital investment.

At Mellon's behest, Congress first repealed the wartime excess-profits tax and lowered the maximum rate on personal income from 65 percent to 50 percent. Subsequent revenue acts eventually lowered the maximum tax rate to 20 percent. The Revenue Act of 1926 extended further benefits to high-income individuals by lowering estate taxes and repealing the gift tax. Much of the tax money released to the wealthy by these acts seems to have fueled the speculative excess of the late 1920s as much as it boosted consumer spending and entrepreneurial activity. Mellon, however, did balance the federal budget for a time. Government expenditures fell, as did the national debt.

In addition to tax cuts, Mellon favored the time-honored Republican policy of high tariffs. So, too, did spokesmen for several emerging industries. Wartime innovations in chemical and metal processing revived the argument for protection of infant American industries from foreign competition. The Fordney-McCumber Tariff of 1922 dramatically increased rates on chemical and metal products as a safeguard against the revival of German industries that had previously commanded the field. To please the farmers, the new act further extended the duties on imported farm products.

Higher tariffs had unexpected consequences, however. During the war the United States had been transformed from a debtor nation to a creditor nation. Foreign capital had long flowed into the United States, playing an important role in fueling economic expansion. But the private and public credits given the Allies to purchase American supplies during the war had reversed the pattern. Mellon now insisted that the European powers repay all that they had borrowed during the war, but the American tariff walls erected against imports made it all the harder for other nations to sell their products in the United States and thereby acquire dollars with which to repay their war debts. For nearly a decade further extensions of U.S. loans and investments sent more dollars abroad, postponing the settling of accounts.

Rounding out the Republican economic program was a more lenient attitude toward government regulation of corporations. Neither Harding nor his successor, Calvin Coolidge, could dissolve the regulatory agencies created by Progressivism, but they named commissioners who promoted "friendly" government regulation. Harding appointed advocates of big business to the Interstate Commerce Commission, the Federal Reserve Board, and the Federal Trade Commission. One senator characterized the new appointments as "the nullification of federal law by a process of boring from within." Republican senator Henry Cabot Lodge agreed, noting, "We have torn up Wilsonism by the roots."

A CORRUPT ADMINISTRATION   Republican conservatives such as Lodge, Mellon, Coolidge, and Hoover were operating out of a sincere philosophical conviction intended to benefit the nation. By contrast, the crass members of Harding's "Ohio gang" used their White House connections to line their own pockets. In 1923 Harding learned that the head of the Veterans Bureau was systematically looting the government's medical and hospital supplies. The corrupt administrator resigned and fled to Europe, and Harding's general counsel committed suicide.

Not long afterward a close crony of Attorney General Daugherty's also shot himself. The man held no federal appointment, but he had set up an office in the Justice Department from which he peddled influence for a fee. Daugherty himself was implicated in the fraudulent handling of German assets seized after the war. When investigated, he refused to testify on the grounds that he might incriminate himself. Twice brought to court, he was never indicted; possibly the lack of evidence was a result of his destruction of pertinent records. These were but the most visible of the many scandals that touched the Justice Department, the Prohibition Bureau, and other agencies under Harding.

But one major scandal rose above all others. Teapot Dome, like the Watergate break-in fifty years later, became the catchword for an era of government corruption. An oil deposit on federal land in Wyoming, Teapot Dome had been set aside to be administered by the Interior Department under Albert Fall. Fall let private companies exploit the oil deposits, arguing that such contracts were in the government's interest. Yet he acted in secret, without allowing competitive bids.

Suspicion grew when Fall's personal standard of living suddenly skyrocketed. It turned out that he had taken "loans" of about $400,000 (which came in "a little black bag") from oil executives. For the rest of his life, Fall insisted that the loans were unrelated to the oil leases and that he had contrived a good deal for the government, but at best the questionable circumstances revealed his fatal blindness to propriety.

Harding himself avoided public disgrace. How much he knew of the scandals swirling around him remains unclear, but he knew enough to give the

Juggernaut

This 1924 cartoon alludes to the dimensions of the Teapot Dome scandal.

appearance of being troubled. "My God, this is a hell of a job!" he confided to a journalist. "I have no trouble with my enemies, I can take care of my enemies all right. But my damn friends, my God-damn friends. . . . They're the ones that keep me walking the floor nights!" In 1923 Harding left on what would be his last journey, a western speaking tour and a trip to the Alaska Territory. In Seattle he suffered an attack of food poisoning, recovered briefly, then died in a San Francisco hotel.

Not since the death of Lincoln had there been such an outpouring of grief for a "beloved President," for the kindly, ordinary man who found it in his heart (as Wilson had not) to pardon Eugene Debs, the former Socialist candidate who had been jailed for opposing U.S. intervention in World War I. As Harding's funeral train moved toward Washington, D.C., then back to Ohio, millions stood by the tracks to honor their lost leader.

Eventually, however, grief yielded to scorn and contempt. For nearly a decade after Harding's death, scandalous revelations concerning his administrative officials were paraded before congressional committees and then the courts. Harding's extramarital affairs also came to light. As a

result of the amorous detours and corrupt associates, Harding's foreshort-
ened administration came to be viewed as one of the worst in history.
More recently, however, scholars have suggested that the scandals obscured
several accomplishments. Some historians credit Harding with leading the
nation out of the turmoil of the postwar years and creating the foundation
for the decade's remarkable economic boom. They also stress that he was a
hardworking president who played a far more forceful role in shaping economic and foreign policies than was previously believed. Harding also
promoted diversity and civil rights. He appointed Jews to key federal positions and criticized the Klan as well as other "factions of hatred and prejudice and violence." No previous president had promoted women's rights as
forcefully as Harding did. Still, even Harding's foremost scholarly defender
admits that he lacked good judgment and "probably should never have
been president."

"SILENT CAL"   The news of Harding's death came when Vice President
Calvin Coolidge was visiting his father in the mountain village of Plymouth,
Vermont, his birthplace. There, at 2:47 A.M. on August 3, 1923, by the light of
a kerosene lamp, Colonel John Coolidge administered the oath of office to

Conservatives in the White House

Warren Harding (left) and Calvin Coolidge (right).

his son. The rustic simplicity of Plymouth, the very name itself, evoked just the image of traditional values and solid integrity that the country would long for amid the wake of the Harding scandals.

Coolidge brought to the White House a clear conviction that the presidency should revert to its passive stance of the Gilded Age and defer to the leadership of Congress. Americans embraced the unflappability of Silent Cal and his conservatism. Even more than Harding, Coolidge identified the nation's welfare with the success of big business. "The chief business of the American people is business," he intoned. "The man who works there worships there." Where Harding had sought to balance the interests of labor, agriculture, and industry, Coolidge focused on industrial development at the expense of the other two areas. He sought to unleash the free-enterprise system, and even more than Harding, he sought to end government regulation and reduce taxes.

THE ELECTION OF 1924   In filling out Harding's unexpired term, Calvin Coolidge successfully distanced himself from the scandals and put two lawyers of undoubted integrity in charge of the prosecutions. A man of honesty and ability, a good administrator who delegated well and managed Republican factions adroitly, he quietly took control of the Republican party machinery and seized the initiative in the campaign for the 1924 nomination, which he won with only token opposition.

The Coolidge luck held as the Democrats again fell victim to internal dissension, prompting humorist Will Rogers's classic statement that "I am a member of no organized political party. I am a Democrat." The party's divisions reflected the deep rift between the new urban culture of the twenties and the more traditional hinterland, a gap that the party could not bridge. It took 103 ballots to bestow a tarnished nomination on John W. Davis, a Wall Street lawyer from West Virginia who could nearly outdo Coolidge in conservatism.

While the Democrats bickered, a new farm-labor coalition mobilized a third-party effort. Meeting in Cleveland on July 4, 1924, farm and labor groups reorganized the Progressive party and nominated Wisconsin senator Robert M. La Follette for president. La Follette also won the support of the Socialist party and the American Federation of Labor.

In the campaign, Coolidge focused on La Follette, whom he called a dangerous radical who would turn America into a "communistic and socialistic state." The country preferred to "keep cool with Coolidge," who swept both the popular and the electoral votes by decisive majorities. Davis took only the solid Democratic South, and La Follette carried only his native Wisconsin.

THE NEW ERA

Business executives interpreted the 1924 Republican victory as a vindication of their leadership, and Coolidge saw in the decade's surging prosperity a confirmation of his pro-business philosophy. In fact, the prosperity and technological achievements of the time had much to do with Coolidge's victory over the Democrats and Progressives. Those in the large middle class who before had formed an important part of the Progressive coalition were now absorbed instead into the new corporate and consumer world created by advances in communications, transportation, and business organization. As more and more commentators stressed, the United States was entering a "new era" of advanced capitalism.

THE CONSUMER CULTURE   The economy was changing markedly during the 1920s. Dramatic increases in efficiency meant that the marketplace was flooded with new consumer delights. Goods once available only to the wealthy were now accessible to the general public. Middle-class consumers could own cameras, wristwatches, cigarette lighters, vacuum cleaners, and washing machines. But those enticing new goods would produce economic havoc if people did not abandon their traditional notions of frugality and go on a buying spree. Hence, business leaders, salespersons, and public relations experts began a concerted effort to eradicate what was left of the original Protestant ethic's emphasis on plain living.

The public had to be taught the joys of carefree consumerism, and the new industry of mass advertising obliged. By portraying impulse buying as a therapeutic measure to bolster self-esteem, advertisers shrewdly helped undermine notions of frugality. In his popular novel *Babbitt*, Sinclair Lewis recognized advertising's impact upon middle-class life: "These standard advertised wares—toothpastes, socks, tires, cameras, instantaneous hot water heaters—were the symbols and proofs of excellence."

Inventions in communications, such as motion pictures, radio, and telephones, were also transforming social life and creating a more homogeneous national culture. In 1905 the first movie house opened, in Philadelphia, and within three years there were nearly 10,000 movie theaters nationwide. During the next decade, Hollywood became the center of movie production, spinning out Westerns and the timeless comedies of Mack Sennett's Keystone Company, in which slapstick comedians, most notably Charlie Chaplin, perfected their art, transforming it into a powerful form of social criticism. By the mid-1930s every large city and most small towns had movie theaters, and films replaced oratory as the chief mass entertainment, growing into a multimillion-dollar industry that catered to the working poor as well as to the affluent. In the mid-1920s motion pictures were attracting 50 million people weekly, equal to half the national population.

Radio broadcasting had an even more spectacular growth. The first radio commercial aired in 1922. By the end of that year, there were over 500 stations and some 3 million receivers in action. In 1927 Congress established a Federal Radio Commission to regulate the industry; in 1934 it became the Federal Communications Commission, with authority over other forms of communication as well. Calvin Coolidge was the first president to address the nation by radio, and he did so each month, paving the way for Franklin Roosevelt's popular and influential "fireside chats."

A nationwide mass culture replaced the local and regional economies of the nineteenth century. The leading advertising agency explained in 1926 that the advent of nationally circulated magazines, chain stores,

The Rise of Radio

The radio brings this farm family together and connects them to the outside world. By the end of the 1930s, millions would tune in to newscasts, soap operas, sports events, and church services.

syndicated news features, motion pictures, national brand names, and radio programs was creating "a nation which lives to [the same] pattern everywhere." Nonetheless, even though working-class folk could buy brand goods, phonographs, and radios, as well as movie tickets, the new consumer culture did not erase social distinctions. "Participating in mass culture," as one historian stressed, "made them feel no more mainstream or middle class, no less ethnic, religious, or working class than they already felt."

AIRPLANES, AUTOMOBILES, AND THE ECONOMY   Advances in transportation were equally startling. Wilbur and Orville Wright, owners of a Dayton, Ohio, bicycle shop, built the first airplane, which they flew on a beach near Kitty Hawk, North Carolina, in 1903. The use of planes advanced slowly until the outbreak of war in Europe in 1914. An American aircraft industry developed during the war but foundered in the postwar demobilization. In 1925 the government began to subsidize the industry through airmail contracts, and the following year it started a program of federal aid to air transport and navigation, making available funds for the construction of airports.

Aviation received a psychological boost in 1927 when Charles A. Lindbergh Jr. flew the first transatlantic solo flight, traveling from New York to Paris in thirty-three and a half hours. The scope of the New York City parade honoring

Ford Motor Company's Highland Park Plant, 1913

Gravity slides and chain conveyors contributed to the mass production of automobiles.

Lindbergh surpassed even the celebration of victory in World War I. The accomplishments of Lindbergh and other aviators helped catapult the aviation industry into prominence. By 1930 there were forty-three airline companies in operation in the United States.

Nevertheless, by far the most significant transportation development of the twentieth century was the automobile. The first motor car had been manufactured for sale in 1895, but the founding of the Ford Motor Company in 1903 revolutionized the industry. Ford's reliable Model T (the celebrated Tin Lizzie) appeared in 1908 at a price of $850 (in 1924 it would sell for $290). Henry Ford aimed "to democratize the automobile. When I'm through everybody will be able to afford one, and about everyone will have one." He was right. In 1916 the number of cars manufactured passed 1 million; by 1920 more than 8 million were registered, and in 1929 there were more than 23 million. The production of automobiles stimulated the whole economy by consuming large amounts of steel, rubber, glass, and textiles. It gave rise to a gigantic market for oil products just as the Spindletop gusher heralded the opening of vast southwestern oilfields. The automotive revolution also quickened the movement for good roads, introduced efficient mass-production assembly-line techniques to other industries, speeded transportation and tourism, encouraged the sprawl of suburbs, and sparked real-estate booms in California and Florida.

STABILIZING THE ECONOMY   During the 1920s the efficiency craze, which had been a prominent feature of the Progressive impulse, powered the wheels of mass production and consumption and became a cardinal belief of Republican leaders. As Harding's and Coolidge's dynamic secretary of commerce, Herbert Hoover transformed the trifling Commerce Department into the most active agency of those two Republican administrations. During a period of government retrenchment, Hoover promoted expansion. He sought out new markets for business and sponsored more than 1,000 conferences on product design, production, and distribution. He also extended the wartime emphasis on standardization to include, for example, automobile tires and paving bricks, bedsprings and toilet paper.

Most of all Hoover endorsed the burgeoning trade-association movement. The organization of business trade associations became his favorite instrument for "stabilization," to avoid the waste inherent in competition. Through such associations, executives in a given field would share information on sales, purchases, shipments, production, and prices. The information allowed them to plan with more confidence, the advantages of which included predictable costs, prices, and markets, as well as more stable employment and wages. Sometimes abuses crept in as the associations skirted the edge of legality by engaging in price-fixing and other monopolistic practices, but the Supreme Court in 1925 held the practice of sharing information as such to be within the law.

THE BUSINESS OF FARMING   During the Harding and Coolidge administrations, agriculture remained the weakest sector in the economy, in many ways as weak as it had been during the 1890s, when cities flourished and much of rural America languished. For a brief time after the war, farmers' hopes soared on wings of prosperity. The wartime boom lasted into 1920, and then commodity prices collapsed as European farmers resumed high levels of production. Low prices persisted into 1923, especially in the wheat and corn belts. A bumper cotton crop in 1926 resulted in a price collapse and an early taste of depression in much of the South, where foreclosures and bankruptcies spread.

In some ways, farmers shared the business outlook of the so-called New Era. Many commercial farms, like corporations, were getting larger, more efficient, and more mechanized. By 1930 about 13 percent of all farmers had tractors, and the proportion was even higher on the western plains. Better plows and other new machines were part of the mechanization process that accompanied improved crop yields, fertilizers, and methods of animal breeding.

Farm organizations of the 1920s moved from the attempted alliance with urban labor that had marked the Populist era toward a new view of farmers as profit-conscious business owners. During the postwar farm depression, farm groups formed regional commodity-marketing associations, which enabled them to negotiate ironclad contracts with producers for the delivery of their crops over a period of years. These associations also brought order to the marketing of farm products, requiring uniform standards and grades, efficient handling and advertising, and a business-like organization with professional technicians and executives.

But if concern with marketing co-ops and other business-like approaches drew farmers further from populist traditions, nagging problems still invited political solutions. The most effective political response to the collapse of farm prices of the early 1920s was the formation of the farm bloc, a congressional coalition of western Republicans and southern Democrats that put through a program of agricultural legislation from 1921 to 1923. During that period the farm bloc passed bills exempting farm cooperatives from anti-trust laws and creating new credit banks that could lend to cooperative producing and marketing associations.

In the spring of 1924, Senator Charles L. McNary of Oregon and Representative Gilbert N. Haugen of Iowa introduced a bill to secure "equality for agriculture in the benefits of the protective tariff." Their plan sought to dump American farm surpluses on the world market in order to raise commodity prices in the home market. The goal was to achieve "parity"—that is, to raise domestic farm prices to a point where farmers would have the same purchasing power relative to other commodity prices that they had enjoyed between 1909 and 1914, a time viewed in retrospect as a golden age of American agriculture. A McNary-Haugen bill finally passed both houses of Congress in 1927 and again a year later, only to be vetoed both times by President Coolidge, who criticized the measure as an unsound effort at price-fixing and un-American and unconstitutional to boot. Nonetheless, the bill catapulted the farm problem into the arena of national debate, defined it as a problem of crop surpluses, and revived the political alliance between the South and the West.

SETBACKS FOR UNIONS   Urban workers more than farmers shared in the affluence of the 1920s. "A workman is far better paid in America than anywhere else in the world," a French visitor wrote in 1927, "and his standard of living is enormously higher." Nonfarmworkers gained about 20 percent in real wages between 1921 and 1928, while farm income rose only 10 percent. The benefits of this rise were distributed unevenly, however. Miners and textile workers suffered a decline in real wages. In these and other trades, technological unemployment followed the introduction of new production methods and more efficient machines, because technology eliminated as well as created jobs.

Organized labor did no better than organized agriculture in the 1920s. Even though President Harding had supported the practice of collective bargaining and tried to reduce the twelve-hour workday and the six-day workweek so that laborers "may have time for leisure and family life," he ran into stiff opposition in Congress. Overall, unions suffered a setback after the growth years of the war as the Red Scare and the strikes of 1919 left the uneasy impression that unions practiced political subversion. The brief postwar depression of 1921 further weakened the unions, as did the popularity of open-shop associations. While the open shop in theory implied only the employer's right to hire anyone, in practice it often meant discrimination against unionists and the refusal to recognize unions even in shops where most of the workers belonged to one. Prosperity, propaganda, welfare capitalism, and active hostility combined to cause union membership to drop from about 5 million in 1920 to 3.5 million in 1929.

The Gastonia Strike

These female textile workers pit their strength against that of a national guardsman during the strike at the Loray Mill in Gastonia, North Carolina, in 1929.

PRESIDENT HOOVER, ENGINEER

HOOVER VERSUS SMITH   On August 2, 1927, while on vacation in the Black Hills of South Dakota, President Coolidge passed to reporters slips of paper with the curious statement "I do not choose to run for President in 1928." Exactly what he meant puzzled observers and has since perplexed historians. Apparently he at least half hoped to be drafted at the convention, but his statement cleared the way for Herbert Hoover to mount an active campaign for the Republican nomination. Well before the 1928 Republican Convention in Kansas City, Hoover was too far in the lead to be stopped. The party platform took credit for postwar prosperity, debt and tax reduction, and the high protective tariff that had been in operation since 1922 ("as vital to American agriculture as it is to manufacturing"). It rejected the McNary-Haugen program but promised a farm board to manage crop surpluses more efficiently.

The Democratic nomination went to Governor Alfred E. Smith of New York. The Democratic party had had its fill of factionalism in 1924, and all remained fairly harmonious until Smith revealed in his acceptance speech a desire to liberalize Prohibition. Hoover, by contrast, had pronounced the outlawing of alcoholic beverages "a great social and economic experiment, noble in motive and far-reaching in purpose," and he called for improved enforcement.

The two candidates projected sharply different images. Hoover was the Quaker son of middle America, the successful engineer and businessman from rural Iowa, the brilliant architect of Republican prosperity, a simple man who dressed plainly, spoke tersely, and followed his strong conscience. Smith was the prototype of those things that rural and small-town America distrusted: the son of Irish immigrants, Catholic, and a critic of Prohibition. Outside the large cities such qualities were handicaps he could scarcely surmount, for all his affability and wit. The religious right launched a furious attack on him. The Klan mailed out thousands of postcards proclaiming that the Catholic New Yorker was the Antichrist.

In the third consecutive Republican landslide, Hoover won 21 million popular votes to Smith's 15 million and an even more top-heavy electoral majority of 444 to 87. Hoover even cracked the Solid South, leaving Smith only six Deep South states plus Massachusetts and Rhode Island. The election was above all a vindication of Republican prosperity, but the shattering defeat of the Democrats concealed a major political realignment in the making. Smith had nearly doubled the vote for the Democratic candidate of four years before. Smith's image, though a handicap in the hinterlands, swung big northern cities back into the Democratic column. In the agricultural states of the West, there were signs that some disgruntled farmers had switched over to the Democrats. A coalition of urban workers and unhappy farmers was in the making, and the Great Depression of the 1930s would solidify it.

HOOVER IN CONTROL   The milestone year of 1929 dawned with high hopes. The economy seemed solid, income was rising, and the chief architect of Republican prosperity was about to enter the White House. "I have no fears for the future of our country," Hoover told his inauguration audience. "It is bright with hope."

Forgotten in the rush of later events would be Hoover's credentials as a progressive, humanitarian president. Over the objection of Treasury Secretary Mellon, he announced a plan for tax reductions in the low-income brackets. He shunned corrupt patronage practices, and he refused to countenance "Red hunts" or interference with peaceful picketing of the White

Herbert Hoover

"I have no fears for the future of our country," Hoover told the nation at his inauguration in 1929.

House. He also defended his wife's right to invite prominent blacks to the White House, and he sought more money for all-black Howard University.

Hoover showed greater sympathy than Coolidge for the struggling agricultural sector. In 1929 he pushed through Congress the Agricultural Marketing Act, which established both a Federal Farm Board with a revolving loan fund of $500 million to help farm cooperatives market commodities and a program in which the Farm Board could set up "stabilization corporations" empowered to buy surpluses. To open up glutted markets, he also proposed higher tariffs on imported farm products. After a fourteen-month struggle with competing interests, however, Hoover settled for a generally upward revision of Tariffs on manufactures as well as farm goods. The Hawley-Smoot Tariff of 1930 carried duties to a new high. Average rates went from about 32 to 40 percent. More than 1,000 economists petitioned Hoover to veto the bill because, they predicted, it would raise prices paid by consumers, damage the export trade and thus hurt farmers, promote inefficiency, and provoke foreign reprisals. Events proved them right, but Hoover felt that he had to go along with his party in an election year. That proved to be a disastrous mistake, for it only exacerbated the growing economic depression.

THE ECONOMY OUT OF CONTROL   Depression? Most Americans during the 1920s had come to assume that there would never be another depression. Their misguided optimism proved to be an important factor in generating the economic free fall after 1929. Throughout the 1920s the idea grew that American business had entered a new era of *permanent* growth. Such naive talk helped promote an array of get-rich-quick schemes.

Until 1927 stock values had risen with profits, but then they began to soar on wings of fanciful speculation. Mellon's tax reductions had released money that, with the help of aggressive brokerage houses, found its way to Wall Street. One could now buy stock on margin—that is, make a small down payment (usually 10 percent) and borrow the rest from a broker, who held the stock as security against a down market. If the stock price fell and the buyer failed to provide more cash, the broker could sell the stock to cover his loan.

Gamblers in the market ignored warning signs. By 1927 residential construction and automobile sales were catching up to demand, business inventories had risen, and the rate of consumer spending had slowed. By mid-1929 production, employment, and other gauges of economic activity were declining. Still the stock market rose, driven by excessive confidence and perennial greed. By 1929 the stock market had become a fantasy world. Conservative financiers and brokers who counseled caution went unheeded. Hoover worried, too, and he sought to discourage speculation, but to no avail. On September 4 stock prices wavered, and the next day they dropped. The great bull market staggered on into October, trending downward but with enough good days to keep hope alive. On October 22 a leading bank president told reporters, "I know of nothing fundamentally wrong with the stock market or with the underlying business and credit structure."

THE CRASH AND ITS CAUSES   The next day, stock values tumbled, and the day after that a wild scramble to unload stocks lasted until word arrived that leading bankers had formed a pool to buy stocks and halt the slide. For the rest of the week, stock prices steadied, but after a weekend to think the situation over, stockholders began to unload their portfolios. On Tuesday, October 29, the most devastating single day in the market's history to that point, the index dropped almost 13 percent. The plunge in prices fed on itself as brokers sold the shares they held for buyers who failed to come up with more cash. During October the value of stocks on the New York Stock Exchange fell by an average of 37 percent.

Business and government leaders initially expressed hope. According to President Hoover, "the fundamental business of the country" was sound. Some speculators who got out of the market went back in for bargains but found themselves caught in a slow erosion of values. By 1933 the value of stocks on the New York Stock Exchange was less than 20 percent of the value at the market's 1929 peak.

Caution was now the watchword for consumers and business leaders. Buyers held out for lower prices, orders fell off, wages fell or ceased altogether, and the decline in purchasing power brought further cutbacks in business activity. From 1929 to 1932, personal income declined by more than half, from $82 million to $40 million. Unemployment continued to rise dramatically, from 1.6 million in 1929 to 12.8 million in 1933, from 3 percent to 25 percent of the labor force. Farmers, already in trouble, faced catastrophe as commodity prices were cut in half. More than 9,000 banks closed during this period, hundreds of factories and mines shut down, entire towns were abandoned, and thousands of farms were sold to pay debts. A cloud of gloom spread across the nation.

The stock market crash alone did not cause the Great Depression, but it did reveal major structural flaws in the economy and in government policies. Too many businesses during the 1920s had maintained prices and taken profits while holding down wages. As a result, about one third of the nation's personal income went to only 5 percent of the population. By plowing profits back into expansion rather than raising wages, business brought on a growing imbalance between rising productivity and declining purchasing power. As the demand for goods declined, the rate of investment in new plants and equipment also began to decline. For a time the softness of purchasing power was concealed by an increase in installment buying, and the deflationary effects of high tariffs were concealed by the volume of foreign loans and investments, which supported foreign demand for American goods. But the flow of American capital abroad began to dry up when the stock market became a more attractive investment. Swollen profits and dividends enticed the rich into market speculation. When trouble came, the bloated corporate structure collapsed.

Government policies also contributed to the debacle. Treasury Secretary Mellon's tax reductions led to oversaving by the consuming public, which helped diminish the demand for consumer goods. The growing money supply fed the fever of speculation by lowering interest rates. Hostility toward unions discouraged collective bargaining and may have worsened the prevalent imbalances in income. High tariffs discouraged foreign trade. Lax enforcement of anti-trust laws encouraged concentration, monopolies, and high prices.

Another culprit was the gold standard. The world monetary system remained fragile throughout the 1920s. When economic output, prices, and savings began dropping in 1929, policy makers—certain that they had to keep their currencies tied to gold at all costs—either did nothing or tightened money supplies, thus exacerbating the downward spiral. The only way to restore economic stability within the constraints of the gold standard was to let prices and wages continue to fall. The best policy, Andrew Mellon advised, would be to "liquidate labor, liquidate stocks, liquidate the farmers, liquidate real estate," allowing the downturn to "purge the rottenness out of the system." Such passivity helped turn a recession into the world's worst depression.

THE HUMAN TOLL OF THE DEPRESSION   The devastating collapse of the economy caused immense social hardships across the nation. By 1933 over 13 million people were out of work, and many more found themselves working fewer hours. African Americans and Mexicans were usually the first laid off. Factories shut down, banks closed, and farms went bankrupt; millions of people found themselves not only jobless but also homeless and penniless. Hungry people lined up at churches and soup kitchens; others rummaged through trash cans behind restaurants. Local welfare agencies were swamped with appeals for charity and quickly ran out of funds. Many of the destitute slept on park benches or in back alleys. Others congregated in makeshift shelters in vacant lots. Thousands of desperate men in search of jobs rode the rails. These hobos or tramps, as they were derisively called, sneaked onto empty railway cars and rode from town to town looking for work. During the winter homeless people wrapped themselves in newspapers to keep warm, sarcastically referring to their coverings as Hoover blankets. Some grew weary of their grim fate and ended their lives. Suicide rates soared during the 1930s. America had never before experienced social distress on such a scale.

HOOVER'S EFFORTS AT RECOVERY   Although the policies of public officials helped bring on economic collapse, few political or economic leaders acknowledged the severity of the crisis: all that was needed, they thought, was a slight correction of the market. Those who held to the theory of limited government, such as Andrew Mellon, thought the economy would cure itself. Hoover, however, was unwilling to sit by and let events take their course. In fact, he did more than any previous president had ever done in such dire economic circumstances. Still, his own philosophy, now hardened into dogma, set strict limits on action by the federal government, and he refused to set his philosophy aside even to meet the unprecedented emergency.

Hoover believed that the country's main need was confidence. In speech after speech, he exhorted the public to keep up hope. He asked business and labor leaders to keep the mills and shops open, maintain wage levels, and spread out the work to avoid layoffs—in short, to let the shock fall on corporate profits rather than on purchasing power. In return, union leaders, who had little choice, agreed to refrain from making wage demands and staging strikes.

While reassuring the public, however, Hoover also accelerated the commencement of government construction projects in order to provide jobs, but state and local cutbacks more than offset the new federal spending. At

Hoover's demand the Federal Reserve returned to an easier credit policy, and Congress passed a modest tax reduction to put more purchasing power into people's pockets. The high Hawley-Smoot Tariff, proposed at first to help farmers, brought reprisals abroad, devastating foreign trade.

As always, depression hurt the political party and president in power. Near the city dumps and along railroad tracks, the dispossessed huddled in shacks of tar paper and galvanized iron, in old packing boxes and abandoned cars. These squalid settlements were labeled Hoovervilles; a Hoover flag was an empty pocket turned inside out. Such scornful labels reflected the quick erosion of Hoover's political support. In 1930 the Democrats gained their first national victory since 1916, winning a majority in the House and enough gains in the Senate to control it in coalition with farm state Republicans in the West.

CONGRESSIONAL INITIATIVES   With a new Congress in session, demands for federal action impelled Hoover to stretch his philosophy of

Impact of the Depression

Two children set up shop in a Hooverville in Washington, D.C.

government to its limits. He was ready now to use government resources to at least shore up the financial institutions. In early 1932 the new Congress responded to pleas from the desperate banking sector by setting up the Reconstruction Finance Corporation (RFC) to provide emergency loans to banks, life-insurance companies, building-and-loan societies, farm mortgage associations, and railroads. The RFC staved off some bankruptcies, but Hoover's critics charged that it favored business at the expense of workers. The RFC nevertheless remained a key federal agency through the decade and during World War II.

Further help to the financial structure came with the Glass-Steagall Act of 1932, which increased the availability of commercial loans. It also released about $750 million in gold formerly used to back Federal Reserve notes, countering the effect of foreign withdrawals and domestic hoarding of gold at the same time that it enlarged the supply of credit. For homeowners the Federal Home Loan Bank Act of 1932 created with Hoover's blessing a series of discount banks for home mortgages. They provided savings-and-loan associations with a service much like the one that the Federal Reserve System provided to commercial banks.

Hoover's critics argued that all these measures reflected a dubious "trickle-down" theory. If government could help banks and railroads, asked New York senator Robert F. Wagner, "is there any reason why we should not likewise extend a helping hand to that forlorn American, in every village and every city of the United States, who has been without wages since 1929?" The contraction of credit devastated such debtors as farmers and those who made purchases on the installment plan or held balloon mortgages, whose monthly payments increased over time.

By 1932 members of Congress were filling the hoppers with bills to provide federal relief directly to distressed people. At that point, Hoover might have pleaded "dire necessity," taken the leadership of the relief movement, and salvaged his political fortunes. Instead, he held back and only grudgingly edged toward federal humanitarian relief. On July 21, 1932, he signed the Emergency Relief Act, which avoided a federal dole (direct cash payments to individuals) but gave the RFC $300 million for relief loans to the states, authorized loans of up to $1.5 billion for state and local construction projects, and appropriated $322 million for federal construction.

FARMERS AND VETERANS IN PROTEST   Government relief for farmers had long since been abandoned. Faced with total loss, some farmers began to defy the law. Angry mobs stopped foreclosures and threatened to lynch bankers and judges. In Nebraska, farmers burned corn to keep warm;

Anger and Frustration

Unemployed veterans, members of the Bonus Expeditionary Force, clash with Washington, D.C., police at Anacostia Flats in July 1932.

dairy farmers dumped milk into roadside ditches in an effort to raise prices. Like voluntary efforts to reduce the number of acres cultivated, these strikes generally failed, but they vividly dramatized the farmers' frustration and anger.

Fears of organized revolt arose when unemployed World War I veterans converged on Washington, D.C., in the spring of 1932. The "Bonus Expeditionary Force" grew quickly to more than 15,000. Their purpose was to get immediate payment of the cash bonus to war veterans that Congress had voted in 1924 in the form of life insurance payable in 1945 (earlier to heirs of deceased veterans). The House approved a bonus bill, but when the Senate voted it down, most of the veterans went home. The rest, having no place to go, camped in vacant government buildings and in a shantytown within sight of the Capitol. The chief of the Washington police gave the squatters a friendly welcome and won their trust, but a fearful White House fretted. Eager to disperse the destitute veterans, Hoover persuaded Congress to vote funds to buy their tickets home. More left, but others stayed even after Congress adjourned, hoping at least to meet with the embattled president.

Late in July the administration ordered the shantytown razed. In the ensuing melee a policeman panicked, fired into the crowd, and killed two veterans. The secretary of war then dispatched about 700 soldiers under General Douglas MacArthur, who was aided by junior officers Dwight D. Eisenhower and George S. Patton. The soldiers easily drove out the unarmed veterans and their families and burned the shacks. MacArthur self-righteously explained in his report that when dealing with "riotous elements," a show of "obvious strength gains a moral ascendancy." General MacArthur claimed that the "mob," spurred by "the essence of revolution," was about to seize control of the government. To most Americans the Bonus Army was more pathetic than threatening. The spectacle of army troops using tanks to dislodge unarmed veterans did not help Hoover's eroding image.

The stress took its toll on Hoover's health and morale. "I am so tired," he sometimes sighed, "that every bone in my body aches." As the months passed, presidential news conferences grew more strained and less frequent. When friends urged Hoover to seize the reins of leadership, he replied, "I can't be a Theodore Roosevelt" or "I have no Wilsonian qualities." His gloom and growing sense of futility were apparent to the country. In a mood more despairing than rebellious, Americans waited impatiently to see what the next presidential campaign would bring.

MAKING CONNECTIONS

- This chapter discussed setbacks suffered by labor unions during the Republican administrations of the 1920s. In the next chapter, unions win new protections under Franklin Roosevelt's New Deal.

- An element of the "normalcy" discussed in this chapter was American isolation from global affairs. Chapter 29 discusses that isolationism in the context of the coming of World War II.

- The characteristics of American society in the 1920s may be compared with the postwar society and culture of the 1950s, discussed in Chapter 32.

Further Reading

A fine synthesis of events immediately following the First World War is Ellis W. Hawley's *The Great War and the Search for a Modern Order: A History of the American People and Their Institutions, 1917–1933* (1979).

On Harding, see Robert K. Murray's *The Harding Era: Warren G. Harding and His Administration* (2000). On Coolidge, see Robert H. Ferrell's *The Presidency of Calvin Coolidge* (1998). On Hoover, see Martin L. Fausold's *The Presidency of Herbert C. Hoover* (1985).

Overviews of the depressed economy are found in Charles P. Kindleberger's *The World in Depression, 1929–1939*, rev. and enlarged ed. (1986) and Peter Fearon's *War, Prosperity, and Depression: The U.S. Economy, 1917–1945* (1987). John A. Garraty's *The Great Depression: An Inquiry into the Causes, Course, and Consequences of the Worldwide Depression of the Nineteen Thirties* (1986) describes how people survived the Depression.

28

NEW DEAL AMERICA

FOCUS QUESTIONS

- What were the social effects of the Great Depression and Franklin Roosevelt's efforts at relief, recovery, and reform?

- Why did the New Deal arouse criticism from both the right and the left?

- How did the New Deal expand the federal government's authority and responsibilities?

- What were the major cultural changes of the 1930s?

To answer these questions and access additional review material, please visit www.wwnorton.com/studyspace.

Upon arriving in the White House in March 1933, Franklin Delano Roosevelt (FDR) inherited a nation mired in the third year of an unprecedented economic depression. No other business slump had been so deep, so long, so baffling, or so painful. One out of every four Americans was unemployed, and in many large cities nearly half the adults were out of work. Some 500,000 Americans had lost homes or farms because they could not make their mortgage payments. Thousands of banks had failed; millions of depositors had lost their life savings. The global depression had also helped accelerate the rise of fascism and communism. Totalitarianism was on the march in Europe and Asia—and democratic capitalism was on the defensive. President Roosevelt and a supportive Congress immediately adopted bold measures to relieve the human suffering, restore confidence, and promote economic recovery. Such initiatives provided the foundation for what came to be called welfare capitalism.

From Hooverism to the New Deal

On June 14, 1932, while the ragtag Bonus Army was still encamped in Washington, D.C., Republicans gathered in Chicago to renominate Herbert Hoover. The delegates went through the motions in a mood of defeat. The Democrats, in contrast, converged on Chicago later in the month confident that they would nominate the next president. New York governor Franklin D. Roosevelt had already lined up most of the delegates, and he won the nomination on the fourth ballot.

In a dramatic gesture, Roosevelt appeared in person to accept the nomination instead of awaiting formal notification. He told the expectant delegates, "I pledge you, I pledge myself to a new deal for the American people." What the New Deal would be in practice Roosevelt had little idea as yet, but he was much more flexible and willing to experiment than Hoover. What was more, his upbeat personality communicated joy and hope, as did his campaign song, "Happy Days Are Here Again."

FRANKLIN ROOSEVELT   Born in 1882 into a wealthy family, educated by governesses and tutors at his father's rambling Hudson River estate, Franklin Roosevelt led the cosmopolitan life of a young patrician. After attending an elite Connecticut boarding school, he earned degrees from Harvard and Columbia Law School. While a law student, he married Anna Eleanor Roosevelt, a niece of President Theodore Roosevelt, his own distant cousin.

In 1910 Franklin Roosevelt won a Democratic seat in the New York State Senate. As a freshman legislator he displayed the contradictory qualities that would characterize his political career: he was an aristocrat with a sincere empathy for common folk, a traditionalist with a penchant for experimenting, an affable charmer with an infectious smile and upturned chin who harbored profound convictions, and a skilled political tactician with a shrewd sense of timing and a distinctive willingness to listen to and learn from others.

In 1912 Roosevelt had backed Woodrow Wilson, and for both of Wilson's terms he served as his assistant secretary of the navy. Then, in 1920, largely on the strength of his name, he gained the Democratic vice-presidential nomination. Political defeat was followed by personal crisis when in 1921, at the age of thirty-nine, Roosevelt contracted polio, which left him permanently crippled, unable to stand or walk without braces. But his prolonged struggle with this disability transformed the snobbish young aristocrat. A friend recalled that Roosevelt emerged from his struggle with polio "completely warm-hearted, with a new humility of spirit" that led him to identify with the poor and the suffering. For seven years, aided by his talented wife, Eleanor, Roosevelt strengthened his body, and in 1928 he ran for governor of New York and won. Reelected by a whopping majority of 700,000 in 1930, he became the Democratic front-runner for the presidency in 1932.

Behind the public facade of a cheery and self-confident politician, Roosevelt was at times a crass manipulator of people and power. Obsessed with gaining the highest office in the land, he was willing to sacrifice all else in his life—marriage, health, staff, friends—to that end. Roosevelt occasionally inflated his own accomplishments and took credit for those of others, but his own strengths and achievements were considerable. A born leader, he had a talent for surrounding himself with capable people and getting the most out of them. Most important, however, was his bulldog determination to succeed, to overcome all obstacles, to triumph over despair and adversity, and in the process to achieve greatness.

THE 1932 CAMPAIGN   Partly to dispel doubts about his health, Roosevelt set forth on a grueling campaign tour in 1932. He blamed the Depression on Hoover and the Republicans, and he began to define what he meant by his New Deal. Like Hoover, Roosevelt made the requisite pledge to balance the budget, but he left open the loophole that he would incur short-term deficits to prevent starvation. He was evasive on the tariff, and on farm policy he offered several options pleasing to farmers but ambiguous enough not to alarm city dwellers. He came out unequivocally for strict regulation of electric companies, and he consistently stood by his party's pledge to repeal the Prohibition amendment. Perhaps most important, he recognized that a mature economy would require imaginative national planning. "The country needs, and, unless I mistake its temper, the country demands bold, persistent experimentation." What came across to voters, however, was less the content of his speeches than his irrepressible confidence.

The dour Hoover, by contrast, had no confidence. Democrats, he argued, ignored the international causes of the Depression. Roosevelt's reckless proposals, Hoover warned, "would destroy the very foundations of our

The "New Deal" Candidate

Governor Franklin D. Roosevelt, the Democratic nominee for president in 1932, campaigning in Topeka, Kansas. Roosevelt's confidence inspired voters.

American system." But few were listening. Frustrated by the persistent Depression, the country wanted a new course, a new leadership, a new deal.

Some voters took a dim view of both major candidates. Those who believed that only a radical departure would suffice supported the Socialist party candidate, Norman Thomas, who polled 882,000 votes, and a few went on to support the Communist party candidate, who won 103,000 votes. The wonder is that a desperate people did not turn in greater numbers to such radical alternatives. Instead, they swept Roosevelt into office by a whopping margin.

THE INAUGURATION For the last time the country waited four months, until March 4, for a new president and Congress to take office. The Twentieth Amendment, ratified on January 23, 1933, provided that the president would thereafter take office on January 20 and the newly elected Congress on January 3.

Amid spreading destitution and misery, unemployment continued to rise during the bleak winter of 1932–1933, and panic struck the banking system. As bank after bank collapsed, frantic people rushed to their own banks to remove their savings. The run on the banks exacerbated the crisis and paralyzed

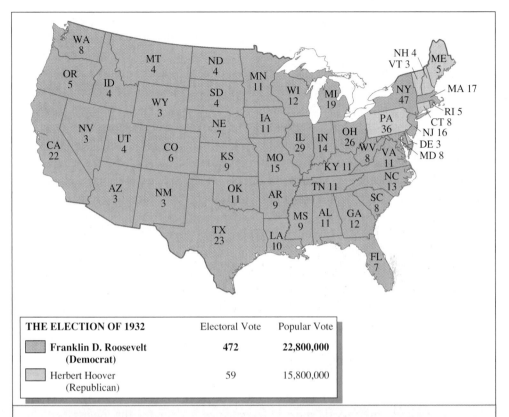

THE ELECTION OF 1932	Electoral Vote	Popular Vote
Franklin D. Roosevelt (Democrat)	472	22,800,000
Herbert Hoover (Republican)	59	15,800,000

Why did Roosevelt appeal to voters struggling during the Depression? What were Hoover's criticisms of Roosevelt's "New Deal"? What policies defined Roosevelt's New Deal during the presidential campaign?

the economy. When the Hoover administration left office, four fifths of the nation's banks were closed, and the country was on the brink of economic paralysis.

The profound crisis of confidence that greeted Roosevelt when he took office on March 4, 1933, gave way to a mood of expectancy. The new president promised vigorous action. He asserted "that the only thing we have to fear is fear itself." He would not merely exhort, he promised: "This nation asks for action, and action now!" He called for "broad executive power to wage a war" against the economic crisis. It was exactly what a distraught nation wanted to hear. One citizen wrote Roosevelt that the speech was "the finest thing this side of heaven. It seemed to give the people, as well as myself, a new hold on life."

COMPETING SOLUTIONS   When Roosevelt and the New Dealers arrived in Washington, they were confronted by three major challenges: reviving the devastated economy, relieving the human misery brought on by the Great Depression, and alleviating the desperate plight of farmers and their families. Roosevelt's "brain trust" of advisers developed conflicting opinions about how best to turn the economy around. Some promoted vigorous enforcement of the anti-trust laws as a means of restoring business competition; others argued for the opposite, saying that anti-trust laws should be suspended so as to enable large corporations to collaborate with the federal government in "managing" the economy. Still others called for a massive expansion of welfare programs and a prolonged infusion of government spending to address the profound human crisis and revive the economy.

For his part, Roosevelt vacillated among these three schools of thought. In part his approach reflected the political reality that conservative southern Democrats controlled the Congress and the president could not risk alienating these powerful proponents of balanced budgets and limited government. Roosevelt's inconsistencies also reflected his own outlook. He was a pragmatist rather than an ideologue. As he once explained, "Take a method and try it. If it fails admit it frankly and try another." Roosevelt's New Deal would therefore take the form of a series of trial-and-error actions.

Roosevelt and his advisers initially settled on a three-pronged strategy to address the problems facing the nation. First, they sought to remedy the financial crisis and provide short-term emergency relief for the jobless. Second, they tried to promote industrial recovery through increased federal spending and cooperative agreements between management and organized labor. Third, they attempted to raise commodity prices (and thereby farm income) by paying farmers to reduce the size of crops and herds. By reducing the overall supply of farm products, prices for grain and meat would eventually rise. None of these initiatives worked perfectly, but their combined effect was to restore hope and energy to a nation paralyzed by fear and uncertainty.

STRENGTHENING THE MONETARY SYSTEM   On his second day in office, Roosevelt followed through on his pledge to act decisively: he called a special session of Congress and declared a four-day bank holiday to halt hysteria and restore confidence in the financial system. It took the Democratic-controlled Congress only seven hours to pass the Emergency Banking Relief Act, which permitted sound banks to reopen and provided managers for those still in trouble. On March 12, 1933, in the first of his radio-broadcast "fireside chats," the president insisted that it was safer to "keep your money in a reopened bank than under the mattress." The following day, deposits in reopened banks exceeded withdrawals. Having ended the bank panic, Roosevelt slashed military pensions and government payrolls and then urged Congress to pass the Twenty-first Amendment, which ended Prohibition.

Those measures were but the beginning of an avalanche of executive and legislative action. Between March 9 and June 16, 1933, the so-called Hundred Days, Congress passed more than a dozen of Roosevelt's major proposals, legislation whose scope was unprecedented in American history.

With the banking crisis over, an acute debt problem continued to paralyze farmers and homeowners as did, along with a lingering distrust of the banks. By early 1933 banks were foreclosing on farm mortgages at the rate of 20,000 per month. By executive decree, Roosevelt reorganized all farm credit agencies into the Farm Credit Administration. Congress then authorized the extensive refinancing of farm mortgages at lower interest rates to stem the tide of foreclosures. The Home Owners' Loan Act provided a similar service to city dwellers through the Home Owners' Loan Corporation, which refinanced mortgage loans at lower monthly payments for strapped homeowners. The Banking Act further shored up confidence in the banking system, by creating the Federal Deposit Insurance Corporation to insure personal bank deposits up to $5,000. It also required commercial banks to separate themselves from investment-brokerage operations.

Roosevelt and Congress also tightened the regulation of Wall Street. The Federal Securities Act required that new stock and bond issues register with the Federal Trade Commission and, later, with the Securities and Exchange Commission, a new agency that regulated the chaotic stock and bond markets.

Throughout 1933 Roosevelt tinkered with devaluation of the currency as a way to raise stock and commodity prices and ease the debt burden on strapped investors and farmers. With the government's official abandonment of the gold standard on April 19, the decline in the value of the dollar increased the prices of commodities and stocks at home.

The Galloping Snail

A vigorous Roosevelt drives Congress to action in this *Detroit News* cartoon from March 1933.

RELIEF MEASURES Another urgent priority in 1933 was relieving the widespread personal distress caused by the Depression. Hoover had steadfastly resisted using federal funds to provide direct relief for the unemployed. Roosevelt had fewer qualms.

Congress took a first step toward relief with the creation of the Civilian Conservation Corps (CCC), which provided useful jobs to working-class men age eighteen to twenty-five. Nearly 3 million CCC workers thereafter performed a variety of jobs in forests, parks, and recreational areas and on soil-conservation projects. They built roads, bridges, campgrounds, and fish hatcheries; planted trees; taught farmers how to control soil erosion; and fought fires. Directed by army officers and foresters, they worked under military discipline and were perhaps the most direct analogue of an army at war in the whole New Deal. Like the military at the time, CCC camps were racially segregated.

The Federal Emergency Relief Administration (FERA) addressed the broader problems of human distress. Designed as a shared undertaking of the federal government and the state and city governments, it was in fact shaped and directed by the Roosevelt administration. Harry L. Hopkins, a tireless social worker from Iowa who had directed Roosevelt's relief program in New York State, headed the new effort and became the second most powerful figure in the administration. He pushed the FERA with a boundless energy, spending $5 million within two hours of taking office. FERA funds created jobs by financing state construction of over 5,000 public buildings and 7,000 bridges, organized adult literacy programs, financed college education for poor students, and set up day-care centers for low-income families. The FERA also helped local agencies dispense food and clothing to the needy.

The first large-scale experiment with *federal* work relief, which put people directly on the government payroll at competitive wages, came with the formation of the Civil Works Administration (CWA). Created in November 1933, when it had become apparent that the state-sponsored programs funded by the FERA were inadequate, the CWA provided federal jobs and wages to those unable to find work that winter. It was hastily conceived and implemented but during its four-month existence put to work over 4 million people. The agency organized a variety of useful projects: from making highway repairs and laying sewer lines, constructing or improving more than 1,000 airports and 40,000 schools, and providing 50,000 teaching jobs that helped keep rural schools open. As the number of people employed by the CWA soared, the program's costs skyrocketed to over $1 billion. Roosevelt balked at the expenditures and worried that people would become dependent upon federal jobs. So in the spring of 1934, he ordered the CWA dissolved. By April some 4 million workers were again unemployed.

Roosevelt nevertheless continued to favor work relief over the dole (direct cash payment to individuals); he thought the dole was an addictive "narcotic, a subtle destroyer of the human spirit." Real jobs, however, nurtured "self-respect and self-reliance." In 1935, he asked, therefore, for an array of new federal job programs, and Congress responded by passing a $4.8-billion bill providing work relief for the jobless. To manage these programs, Roosevelt created the Works Progress Administration (WPA), headed by Harry Hopkins. Hopkins was told to provide millions of jobs quickly, and as a result some of the new jobs appeared to be make-work or mere "leaning on shovels." But before the WPA died during World War II, it left permanent monuments on the landscape in the form of buildings, bridges, hard-surfaced roads, airports, and schools.

The WPA also employed a wide range of talented Americans in the Federal Theatre Project, the Federal Art Project, the Federal Music Project, and the Federal Writers' Project. Talented writers such as Ralph Ellison, John Cheever, and Saul Bellow found work writing travel guides to the United States, and Orson Welles directed Federal Theatre Project productions. Critics charged that these programs were frivolous, but Hopkins replied that writers and artists needed "to eat just like other people." The National Youth Administration (NYA), also under the WPA, provided part-time employment to students, set up technical training programs, and aided jobless youths. Twenty-seven-year-old Lyndon Johnson was director of an NYA program in Texas, and Richard Nixon, a penniless Duke University law student, found work through the NYA at 35¢ an hour. Although the WPA took care of only about 3 million out of some 10 million jobless at any one time, in all it helped some 9 million Americans weather desperate times before it expired in 1943.

RECOVERY THROUGH REGULATION

In addition to rescuing the banks and providing immediate relief for the unemployed, Roosevelt and his advisers promoted the recovery of the agricultural and industrial sectors. Roosevelt's brain trust of university-trained experts, lawyers, and professors initially believed that the trend toward economic concentration was inevitable: big businesses were not going to disappear. The brain trust also believed that the mistakes of the 1920s showed that the only way to operate an integrated economy at full capacity and in the public interest was through stringent regulation and organized central planning in cooperation with big business, not by breaking up huge corporations. The success of gevernment-led economic planning during World War I reinforced such ideas. New recovery programs sprang from those beliefs.

AGRICULTURAL RECOVERY   The sharp decline in crop prices after 1929 meant that many farmers could not afford to plant or harvest their crops. The Agricultural Adjustment Act of 1933 created the Agricultural Adjustment Administration (AAA), which sought to help raise commodity prices by paying farmers to cut back production. The money for the benefits payments made to farmers would be raised from a "processing tax" levied on the businesses that processed farm products for sale (such as cotton gins, flour mills, and meatpacking plants).

As a complement to the AAA, Roosevelt created the Commodity Credit Corporation. This CCC extended loans to farmers above the market price of their crops, which were kept off the market in federal warehouses. If crop prices rose over time, a farmer could repay the loan, retrieve the crops, and sell them. If prices did not rise, the government kept the crops in storage, and the farmer kept the loaned money.

By the time Congress acted on the farm bills in 1933, the growing season was already under way, and the prospect of another bumper cotton crop created an urgent problem. The AAA reluctantly sponsored a plow-under program. To destroy a growing crop was a "shocking commentary on our civilization," Agriculture Secretary Henry Wallace lamented. "I could tolerate it only as a cleaning up of the wreckage from the old days of unbalanced production." In addition to plowing under ripening crops, the AAA encouraged farmers to destroy young livestock as a means of raising prices by reducing supply.

For a while these farm measures worked. By the end of 1934, Wallace could report significant declines in wheat, cotton, and corn production and a simultaneous increase in commodity prices. Farm income increased by 58 percent between 1932 and 1935. The AAA was only partially responsible for the gains, however. The devastating drought that settled over the Great Plains between 1932 and 1935 played a major role in reducing production and creating the epic "dust-bowl" migrations so poignantly evoked in John Steinbeck's novel *The Grapes of Wrath*. Many migrant families had actually been driven off the land by AAA benefit programs that encouraged large farmers to take land worked by tenants and sharecroppers out of cultivation.

Although it created unexpected problems, the AAA achieved successes in boosting the overall farm economy. Many conservatives, however, opposed its sweeping powers, and on January 6, 1936, the Supreme Court, in *United States v. Butler,* ruled the AAA's tax on food processors unconstitutional. The administration hastily devised a new plan to achieve crop reduction indirectly, with the Soil Conservation and Domestic Allotment Act (1936), which it pushed through Congress in six weeks. The new act omitted processing taxes and acreage quotas but provided benefit payments to farmers who engaged in soil-conservation practices and cut back on soil-depleting staple crops. Since the money to pay benefits came out of general funds and not from taxes, the approach was not vulnerable to lawsuits.

The act was an almost unqualified success as an engineering and educational project because it helped heal the scars of erosion and the plague of dust storms. But soil conservation nevertheless failed as a device for limiting production. With their worst lands taken out of production, farmers cultivated their fertile acres more intensively. In response, Congress passed the Agricultural Adjustment Act of 1938, which reestablished the earlier programs but left out the processing taxes. Benefit payments to farmers would come from general federal funds. Increasingly federal farm programs came to dominate the nation's agricultural economy.

INDUSTRIAL RECOVERY   The industrial counterpart to the AAA was the National Industrial Recovery Act (NIRA), passed in 1933. The NIRA had two major components. One created the Public Works Administration (PWA), granting $3.3 billion for public buildings, highway programs, flood control, bridges, tunnels, and aircraft carriers. Under the direction of Interior Secretary Harold L. Ickes, the PWA indirectly served the purpose of work relief. Ickes focused on well-planned permanent improvements, and he used private contractors rather than workers on the government payroll. PWA workers built Virginia's Skyline Drive, New York's Triborough Bridge, the Overseas Highway from Miami to Key West, and Chicago's subway system.

The more controversial and ambitious part of the NIRA created the National Recovery Administration (NRA), headed by the colorful former army general Hugh S. Johnson. Modeled on the War Industries Board of 1917–1918, its purpose was twofold: to stabilize the business sector by reducing chaotic competition through the implementation of codes that set wages and prices and to generate more purchasing power for consumers by providing jobs, defining labor standards, and raising wages. The NRA raised trade-union hopes for the protection of basic hour and wage standards and liberal hopes for comprehensive government planning for the economy.

In each industry, committees representing management, labor, and government drew up fair-practice codes. The labor standards were quite progressive. Every code set a forty-hour workweek and minimum weekly wages of $13 ($12 in the South, where living costs were considered lower), which more than doubled earnings in some cases. Child labor under the age of sixteen was prohibited.

Labor unions, already hard pressed by the economic downturn and a loss of members, were understandably concerned about the NRA's efforts to reduce competition by allowing businesses to cooperate in fixing wages and prices as well as production levels. To gain their support, the NRA included a provision that guaranteed the right of workers to organize unions. While prohibiting employers from interfering with labor-organizing efforts, however, the NRA did not create adequate enforcement measures, nor did it require employers to bargain in good faith with labor representatives.

For a time the NRA worked, and an air of confidence began to replace the depression blues as the downward spiral of wages and prices subsided. But as soon as economic recovery began, critics charged that the larger companies were dominating the code negotiations, that they were using the codes to stifle competition by dividing up markets and entrenching their own positions, and that price-fixing among industry giants was robbing small producers of the chance to compete. The NRA wage codes also excluded agricultural and domestic workers—three out of every four employed African Americans. The effort to develop detailed codes for every industry in the nation proved an administrative nightmare, and the daily annoyances of code enforcement inspired growing hostility among business executives.

By 1935 the NRA had developed more critics than friends, and a full economic recovery was nowhere in sight. In 1935, when the Supreme Court declared the NRA unconstitutional, few mourned. Yet the NRA experiment left an enduring mark. With dramatic suddenness the industry codes had set important new workplace standards, such as the forty-hour workweek and the abolition of child labor. The NRA's endorsement of collective bargaining also spurred union growth.

REGIONAL PLANNING   The wide-ranging scope of the New Deal embraced more than the centralized planning approaches of the NRA. The creation of the Tennessee Valley Authority (TVA) was a truly bold venture to revitalize one of the most underdeveloped and poverty-stricken regions of the country, where disease and illiteracy were rampant.

In May 1933 Congress created the TVA as a multipurpose public corporation. The TVA sought to bring cheap electricity to the Tennessee River valley, build fertilizer plants, provide jobs and recreation, and educate rural folk in the ways of modern life. By 1936 the TVA had six dams completed or under way, and the agency had developed a plan to build nine high dams on the Tennessee River, which would create the "Great Lakes of the South." The TVA, moreover, opened the rivers to navigation, fostered soil conservation and forestry, experimented with fertilizers, and drew new industry to the region.

The TVA's success at generating greater power consumption and lower electricity rates awakened private utilities to the mass consumer markets. It also transported farmers of the valley from the age of kerosene to the age of electricity. Although 90 percent of urban dwellers had electricity by 1930, only ten percent of rural Americans did. Through loans of more than $321 million to rural cooperatives, the Rural Electrification Administration paved the way to the electrification of 288,000 rural households in the Tennessee valley and across the nation.

THE SOCIAL COST OF THE DEPRESSION

Although New Deal programs helped ease the devastation wrought by the Depression, they did not restore prosperity or end the widespread human suffering. Throughout the 1930s the Depression continued to take a toll on ordinary Americans who remained in the throes of a shattered economy that was only slowly working its way back to health.

CONTINUING HARDSHIPS   As late as 1939, some 9.5 million workers (17 percent of the labor force) remained unemployed. Prolonged economic hardship continued to create personal tragedies and tremendous social strains. Poverty led desperate people to do desperate things. Petty theft soared during the 1930s, as did street-corner begging and prostitution. Although the divorce rate dropped, in part because couples could not afford to live separately or pay the legal fees to obtain a divorce, all too often husbands down on their luck simply deserted their wives. A 1940 survey revealed that 1.5 million husbands had left home.

With their future uncertain, married couples often decided not to have children; the birthrate plummeted during the 1930s. Couples with children sometimes could not support them. In 1933 the Children's Bureau reported that one out of every five children was not getting enough to eat. Struggling parents often sent children to live with relatives or friends. Some 900,000 children left home and joined the army of homeless "tramps."

Dust Storm Approaching, 1930s

When a dust storm blew in, it brought utter darkness, as well as the sand and grit that soon covered every surface, both indoors and out.

DUST BOWL MIGRANTS   In the southern plains of the Midwest and the Mississippi River valley, a decade-long drought during the 1930s helped produce an environmental and human catastrophe known as the dust bowl. Colorado, New Mexico, Kansas, Nebraska, Texas, and Oklahoma were the hardest hit. As crops withered, income plummeted. Unrelenting winds swept across the treeless plains, scooping up millions of tons of parched topsoil into billowing dark clouds that floated east across entire states, engulfing farms and towns in what were called black blizzards. A massive dust storm in May 1934 darkened skies from Colorado to the Atlantic seaboard, depositing silt on porches and rooftops as well as on ships in the Atlantic Ocean. In 1937 there were seventy-two major dust storms. The worst of them killed livestock and people and caused railroads to derail and automobiles to careen off roads. By 1938 over 25 million acres of prairie land had lost most of its topsoil.

What made these dust storms worse than normal was the transition during the early twentieth century from scattered subsistence farming to widespread industrial agriculture, in which "factory farms" used dry-farming techniques to plant vast acres of wheat, corn, and cotton. The advent of powerful tractors, deep-furrow plows, and mechanical harvesters greatly increased the scale and intensity of farming—and the indebtedness of farmers.

The mercurial cycle of falling crop prices and rising indebtedness led farmers to plant as much and as often as they could. Overfarming and overgrazing disrupted the fragile ecology of the plains by decimating the native prairie grasses that stabilized the nutrient-rich topsoil. Constant plowing loosened vast amounts of dirt that were easily swept up by powerful winds during the devastating drought of the 1930s. Hordes of grasshoppers followed the gigantic dust storms and devoured what meager crops were left standing.

Human misery paralleled the environmental devastation. The dust storms penetrated windows and doors. A Kansas woman reported that the grit "got into cupboards and clothes closets; our faces were as dirty as if we had rolled in the dirt; our hair was gray and stiff and we ground dirt between our teeth." Parched farmers could not pay mortgages, and banks foreclosed on their property. Suicides and divorces soared in the "Dust Bowl" states. With each year, millions of people abandoned their farms.

Uprooted farmers and their families formed a migratory stream rushing from the blighted South and Midwest toward California, buoyed by currents of hope and desperation. The West Coast was rumored to have plenty of jobs. So off they went on a cross-country trek in search of new opportunities. Although frequently lumped together as "Okies," most of the dust-bowl refugees were from cotton belt communities in Arkansas, Texas, and Missouri, as well as Oklahoma. During the 1930s and 1940s, some 800,000 people left those four states and headed to the Far West. Not all were farmers; many were white-collar workers and retailers whose jobs had been tied to the health of the agriculture sector. Most of the dust-bowl migrants were white, and most were young adults in their twenties and thirties who relocated with spouses and children. Some traveled on trains or buses; others hopped a freight train or hitched a ride; most rode in their own cars, the trip taking four to five days on average.

The dust-bowl migrants who had come from cities gravitated to California's urban areas—Los Angeles, San Diego, or San Francisco. Many of the newcomers, however, moved into the San Joaquin Valley, the agricultural heartland of the state. There they discovered that California was no paradise. Only a few of the migrants could afford to buy land. Most found themselves competing with local Latinos and Asians for seasonal work as pickers in the cotton fields or orchards of large corporate farms. Living in tents or crude cabins and frequently on the move, they suffered from exposure and poor sanitation.

They also felt the sting of social prejudice. The writer John Steinbeck explained that "Okie us'ta mean you was from Oklahoma. Now it means you're a dirty son-of-a-bitch. Okie means you're scum. Don't mean nothing in itself, it's the way they say it." Such hostility toward the migrants drove one third of them to return to their home states. Most of the farmworkers who stayed tended to fall back upon their old folkways rather than assimilate into their new surroundings. These gritty "plain folk" had brought with them their own prejudices, against blacks and ethnic minorities, as well as a potent tradition of evangelical Protestantism and a distinctive style of music variously labeled country, hillbilly, or cowboy. This "Okie" subculture remains a vivid part of California society.

MINORITIES AND THE NEW DEAL   The Depression was especially traumatic for the most disadvantaged groups. However progressive Franklin Roosevelt was on social issues, he failed to assault long-standing patterns of racism and segregation for fear of alienating conservative southern Democrats in Congress. As a result, many of the New Deal programs were for whites only. The Federal Housing Administration, for example, refused to guarantee mortgages on houses purchased by blacks in white neighborhoods. Both the CCC and the TVA practiced racial segregation.

The efforts of the Roosevelt administration to raise crop prices by reducing production proved especially devastating for African Americans and Mexican Americans. To earn the federal payments for reducing crops as provided by the AAA and other New Deal agriculture programs, many farm owners would first take out of cultivation the marginal lands worked by tenants and sharecroppers, many of whom were blacks or Latinos. The effect was to drive the landless off farms and eliminate the jobs of many migrant workers. Over 200,000 African-American tenant farmers nationwide were displaced by the AAA.

Mexican Americans suffered even more. Thousands of Mexicans had migrated to the United States during the 1920s, most of them settling in California, New Mexico, Arizona, Colorado, Texas, and the midwestern states. But because many Mexican Americans were unable to prove their citizenship, either out of ignorance of the regulations or because their migratory work hampered their ability to meet residency requirements, they were denied access to the many new federal relief programs under the New Deal. As economic conditions worsened, government officials called for the deportation of Mexican-born Americans to avoid the cost of providing them with public services and relief. By 1935 over 500,000 Mexican Americans and their American-born children had returned to Mexico. The state of Texas alone returned over 250,000 people.

Native Americans were also devastated by the Great Depression. They initially were encouraged by Roosevelt's appointment of John Collier as the commissioner of the Bureau of Indian Affairs (BIA). Collier steadily increased the number of Native Americans employed by the BIA and strove to ensure that Indians gained access to the various New Deal relief programs. Collier's primary objective, however, was passage of the Indian Reorganization Act. He wanted the new legislation to replace the provisions of the 1887 Dawes Act, which had sought to "Americanize" the Indians by breaking up their tribal land and allocating it to individuals. Collier insisted that the Dawes Act had produced only widespread poverty and demoralization. He hoped to reinvigorate Indian cultural traditions by restoring land to tribes, granting Indians the right to charter business enterprises and establish self-governing constitutions, and providing federal funds for vocational training and economic development. The act that Congress finally passed was a much-diluted version of Collier's original proposal, however.

Culture in the Thirties

In view of the celebrated—if exaggerated—alienation of writers, artists, and intellectuals rebelling against the materialism of the 1920s, one might have expected the onset of the Great Depression to have deepened their despair. Instead, it brought a renewed sense of militancy and affirmation, as if society could no longer afford the art-for-art's-sake outlook of the 1920s.

In the summer of 1932, even the "golden boy" of the lost generation, the writer F. Scott Fitzgerald, had declared that "to bring on the revolution, it may be necessary to work within the Communist party." But few remained Communists for long. Being a notoriously independent lot, most left-wing writers rebelled at demands to hew to a shifting party line. And many abandoned communism upon learning that the Soviet leader Joseph Stalin practiced a tyranny more horrible than anything under the czars.

LITERATURE AND THE DEPRESSION Among the Depression-era writers who addressed themes of immediate social significance two novelists deserve special notice: John Steinbeck and Richard Wright. The single piece of fiction that best captured the ordeal of the Depression, Steinbeck's *The Grapes of Wrath* (1939), treated workers as people rather than ideological tools. Steinbeck had traveled with displaced "Okies" fleeing the Oklahoma dust bowl to pursue jobs in the fields of California's Central Valley. This firsthand experience allowed him to create a vivid tale of the Joad family's painful journey west from Oklahoma.

Among the most talented of the young novelists emerging in the 1930s was Richard Wright, an African American born near Natchez, Mississippi. The grandson of former slaves and the son of a sharecropper who deserted his family, Wright ended his formal schooling in the ninth grade (as valedictorian of his class). He then worked in Memphis and greedily devoured books he borrowed on a white friend's library card, all the while saving up to go north to escape the racism of the segregated South. In Chicago, where he arrived on the eve of the Depression, the Federal Writers' Project gave him a chance to develop his talent. His period as a Communist, from 1934 to 1944, gave him an intellectual framework that did not overpower his fierce independence.

Native Son (1940), Wright's masterpiece, is set in the Chicago he had come to know before moving to New York. It tells the story of Bigger Thomas, a product of the ghetto, a man hemmed in, and finally impelled to murder, by forces beyond his control. Somehow Wright managed to transform into literary power his own bitterness and rage at what he called "the Ethics of Living Jim Crow."

POPULAR CULTURE   While many writers and artists dealt directly with the human suffering and social tensions spawned by the Great Depression, the more popular cultural outlets, such as radio programs and movies, provided patrons with a welcome escape from the decade's grim realities.

By the 1930s radio had become a major source of family entertainment. More than 10 million families owned a radio, and by the end of the decade the number had tripled. Millions of housewives listened to radio "soap operas," ongoing dramas that were broadcast daily in fifteen-minute episodes and derived their name from their sponsors, soap manufacturers.

Late-afternoon radio programs were directed at children home from school. In the evening after supper, families would gather around the radio to listen to newscasts; comedies such as *Amos 'n' Andy* and the husband-and-wife team of George Burns and Gracie Allen; adventure dramas such as *Jack Armstrong, The Lone Ranger, Dick Tracy,* and *The Green Hornet;* and big-band musical programs, all interspersed with commercials. On Sundays most radio stations broadcast church services. Fans could also listen to baseball and football games or boxing matches. Franklin Roosevelt was the first president to take full advantage of the popularity of radio broadcasting. He hosted sixteen "fireside chats" to generate public support for his New Deal initiatives.

Movies were even more popular than radio shows. In the late 1920s what had been silent films were transformed by the introduction of sound. The "talkies" made movies the most popular form of entertainment during the 1930s—much more popular than they are today. The introduction of double features in 1931 and the construction of outdoor drive-in theaters in 1933 also boosted interest and attendance. More than 60 percent of the population—70 million people—saw at least one movie each week.

The movies of the 1930s rarely dealt directly with hard times. Exceptions were film versions of *Gone with the Wind* (1939) and *The Grapes of Wrath* (1940). Much more common were movies intended for pure entertainment; they transported viewers into the realm of adventure, spectacle, humor, and fantasy. People relished shoot-'em-up gangster films, animated cartoons, spectacular musicals, "screwball" comedies, and horror films such as *Dracula* (1931), *Frankenstein* (1931), *The Mummy* (1932), and *Werewolf of London* (1935).

The best way to escape the daily troubles of the Depression was to watch one of the zany comedies of the Marx Brothers, former vaudeville performers.

The Marx Brothers

In addition to their vaudeville antics, the Marx Brothers satirized social issues such as Prohibition.

As one Hollywood insider explained, the movies of the 1930s were intended to "laugh the big bad wolf of the depression out of the public mind." *The Cocoanuts* (1929), *Animal Crackers* (1930), and *Monkey Business* (1931) introduced Americans to the anarchic antics of Chico, Groucho, Harpo, and Zeppo Marx, who combined slapstick humor with verbal wit to create plotless masterpieces of irreverent satire.

The Second New Deal

During Roosevelt's first year in office, his programs and his personal charms generated massive support. The president's travels and speeches, his twice-weekly press conferences, and his radio-broadcast fireside chats brought vitality and warmth from a once-remote White House. In the congressional elections of 1934, the Democrats increased their strength in both the House and the Senate, an almost unprecedented midterm victory for a party in power. Only seven Republican governors remained in office throughout the country.

ELEANOR ROOSEVELT One of the reasons for Roosevelt's popularity was his wife, Eleanor, who became an enormous political asset and would prove to be one of the most influential and revered leaders of the time. From an early age, Eleanor Roosevelt had embraced social service. Her compassion resulted in part from the loneliness she experienced as she was growing up and in part from the sense of betrayal she felt upon learning in 1918 that her husband was engaged in an extramarital affair with Lucy Mercer, her secretary. In the face of personal troubles, Eleanor Roosevelt "lived to be kind." Compassionate without being maudlin, more stoical than sentimental, she exuded warmth and sincerity, and she challenged the complacency of the comfortable and the affluent.

The First Lady

An intelligent, principled, and candid woman, Eleanor Roosevelt became a political figure in her own right. Here she is serving as guest host for a radio program, ca. 1935.

Eleanor Roosevelt was an activist who redefined the role of the presidential spouse. She was the first woman to address a national political convention, to write a nationally syndicated column, and to hold regular press conferences. A tireless advocate and agitator, Eleanor crisscrossed the nation, representing the president and the New Deal, defying local segregation ordinances to meet with African-American leaders, supporting women's causes and organized labor, highlighting the plight of unemployed youth, and imploring Americans to live up to their egalitarian and humanitarian ideals.

CRITICISM   Public criticism of the New Deal during Franklin Roosevelt's first year in office was muted. But not for long. The Depression's downward slide had been halted, but unemployment remained high (10 million were out of work in 1935, more than 20 percent of the workforce), and prosperity remained elusive. "We have been patient and long suffering," said a farm leader in October 1933. "We were promised a New Deal. Instead we have the same old stacked deck." Even more unsettling to some was the dramatic growth of executive power and the emergence of welfare capitalism, whereby workers developed a sense of entitlement to federal support programs. In 1934 a group of conservative businessmen and politicians, including Alfred E. Smith and John W. Davis, two former Democratic presidential candidates, formed the American Liberty League to oppose New Deal measures as violations of personal and property rights.

More potent threats to Roosevelt came from the hucksters of social panaceas. The most flamboyant of the group was Louisiana's "Kingfish," Senator Huey P. Long. A short, strutting man, Long sported pink suits and pastel shirts, red ties, and two-toned shoes. He was a brilliant but unscrupulous reformer driven by a relentless urge for power and attention. First as Louisiana's governor, then as political boss of the state, Long had delivered tax favors, roads, schools, free textbooks, charity hospitals, and better public services. That he had become a sort of state dictator in the process, using bribery, physical intimidation, and blackmail to achieve his ends, seemed irrelevant to many of his ardent supporters.

In 1933 Long joined Roosevelt in Washington as a Democratic senator. He initially supported the New Deal but quickly grew suspicious of the NRA's collusion with big business. He had also grown jealous of Roosevelt's mushrooming popularity, having developed his own aspirations for the Oval Office. Promoting himself as a true if self-indulgent friend of the people, Long had his own plan for dealing with the Great Depression.

Long's Share-the-Wealth program proposed to confiscate large personal fortunes, guarantee every family a cash grant of $5,000 and every worker an annual income of $2,500, provide pensions to the aged, reduce working hours, pay veterans' bonuses, and ensure a college education for every qualified student. It did not matter to him that his figures failed to add up or that his program offered little to promote an economic recovery. Whether he had a workable plan or not, by early 1935 the charismatic Long was claiming 7.5 million supporters across the country.

Another popular social scheme was hatched by a gray-haired California doctor, Francis E. Townsend. Outraged by the sight of three elderly women raking through garbage cans in Long Beach, Townsend proposed government pensions for the aged. In 1934 he began promoting the Townsend Recovery Plan, which would pay $200 a month to every citizen over sixty who retired from employment and promised to spend the money within the month. The plan had the lure of providing financial security for the aged and stimulating economic growth. Critics noted that the cost of his program for 9 percent of the population would be more than half the national income. Yet Townsend was indifferent to details. "I'm not in the least interested in the cost of the plan," he blandly told a House committee.

A third huckster of panaceas, Father Charles E. Coughlin, the Roman Catholic "radio priest," founded the National Union for Social Justice in 1935. In broadcasts over the CBS network, he promoted schemes for the coinage of silver and made attacks on bankers that increasingly hinted at anti-Semitism.

"The Kingfish"

Huey Long, governor of Louisiana. Although he often led people to believe he was a country bumpkin, Long was a shrewd lawyer and consummate politician.

Coughlin, Townsend, and Long drew support largely from desperate lower-middle-class Americans. Of the three, Long had the widest following. A 1935 survey showed that he could draw 5 million to 6 million votes as a third-party candidate for president in 1936, perhaps enough to undermine Roosevelt's chances of reelection. Beset by pressures from both ends of the political spectrum, Roosevelt hesitated for months before deciding to "steal the thunder" from the left by instituting new programs of reform and social security. "I'm fighting Communism, Huey Longism, Coughlinism, Townsendism," Roosevelt told a reporter in early 1935. He needed "to save our system, the capitalist system," from such "crackpot ideas." Political pressures impelled Roosevelt to move to the left, but so did the growing influence within the administration from Supreme Court justices Louis Brandeis and Felix Frankfurter. These powerful advisers urged Roosevelt to be less cozy with big business and to push for restored competition and heavy taxes on large corporations.

OPPOSITION FROM THE COURT   A series of Supreme Court decisions finally spurred the president to act. On May 27, 1935, the Court killed the National Industrial Recovery Act by a unanimous vote. The defendants in *Schechter Poultry Corporation v. United States,* quickly tagged the "sick-chicken" case, had been convicted of selling an "unfit chicken" and violating other NRA code provisions. The high court ruled that Congress had delegated too much power to the executive branch when it granted the code-making authority to the NRA. Congress had also exceeded its power under the commerce clause by regulating intrastate commerce. The poultry in question, the Court decided, had "come to permanent rest within the state," although earlier it had been moved across state lines. In a press conference soon afterward, Roosevelt fumed: "We have been relegated to the horse-and-buggy definition of interstate commerce." The same line of reasoning, he warned, might endanger other New Deal programs.

LEGISLATIVE ACHIEVEMENTS OF THE SECOND NEW DEAL
To rescue his legislative program from such judicial and political challenges, Roosevelt in 1935 ended the stalemate in Congress and launched the second phase of the New Deal. He demanded several pieces of "must" legislation, most of which Congress passed within a few months.

The National Labor Relations Act, often called the Wagner Act for its sponsor, New York senator Robert Wagner, gave workers the right to bargain with employers through unions of their own choice and prohibited employers from interfering with union activities. A National Labor Relations Board of five members could supervise plant elections and certify unions as bargaining agents where a majority of the workers approved. The board could also investigate the actions of employers and issue "cease-and-desist" orders against specified unfair practices.

The Social Security Act of 1935, Roosevelt announced, was the New Deal's "cornerstone" and "supreme achievement." Indeed, it has proved to be the most significant and far-reaching of all the New Deal initiatives. The concept was by no means new. Progressives during the early 1900s had proposed a federal system of social security for the aged, indigent, disabled, and unemployed. Other nations had already enacted such programs, but the United States remained steadfast in its tradition of individual self-reliance. The Great Depression revived the idea, however, and Roosevelt masterfully guided the legislation through Congress.

The Social Security Act included three major provisions. Its centerpiece was a federally-administered pension fund for retired people over the age of sixty-five and their survivors. Beginning in 1937, workers and employers contributed payroll taxes to establish the fund. Benefit payments started in 1940 and averaged $22 per month, a modest sum even for those depressed times. Roosevelt stressed that the pension program was not intended to guarantee a comfortable retirement; it was designed to supplement other sources of income and protect the elderly from some of the "hazards and vicissitudes of life." Only later did American come to perceive of Social Security as the *primary* source of retirement income for most of the aged.

Social Security

A poster distributed by the government to educate the public about the new Social Security Act.

The Social Security Act also set up a shared federal-state unemployment-insurance program, financed by a payroll tax on employers. In addition, the new legislation committed the national government to a broad range of social-welfare activities based upon the assumption that "unemployables"—people who were unable to work—would remain a state responsibility while the national government would provide work relief for the able-bodied. To that end the law inaugurated federal grants-in-aid for three state-administered public-assistance programs—old-age assistance, aid for dependent children, aid to the blind—and further aid for maternal, child-welfare, and public health services.

Relatively speaking, the new federal program was quite conservative. It was the only government pension program in the world financed by taxes on the earnings of workers: most other countries funded such programs out of general revenues. The Social Security payroll tax was also a regressive tax in that it entailed a single fixed rate for all, regardless of income level. It thus hurt the poor more than the rich, and it also impeded Roosevelt's efforts to revive the economy because it removed from circulation a significant amount of money: the new Social Security tax took money out of workers' pockets and placed it in a pension trust fund, exacerbating the shrinking money supply that was one of the main causes of the Depression. By taking discretionary income away from workers, the government blunted the sharp increase in public consumption needed to restore the health of the economy. In addition, the Social Security system initially excluded 9.5 million workers who most needed the new program: farm laborers, domestic workers, and the self-employed, a disproportionate percentage of whom were African Americans.

Roosevelt regretted the limitations, but he knew that they were necessary compromises in order to see the Social Security Act through Congress and enable it to withstand court challenges. As he replied to an aide who criticized funding the pension program through employee contributions:

> I guess you're right on the economics, but those taxes were never a problem of economics. They are politics all the way through. We put those payroll contributions there so as to give the contributors a moral, legal, and political right to collect their pensions and their unemployment benefits. With those taxes in there, no damn politician can ever scrap my Social Security program.

The last of the major bills making up the second phase of the New Deal was the Revenue Act of 1935, sometimes called the Wealth-Tax Act but popularly known as the soak-the-rich tax. The Revenue Act raised tax rates on income above $50,000. Estate and gift taxes also rose, as did the corporate tax on all but small corporations (those with an annual income below $50,000).

Business leaders fumed over Roosevelt's tax and spending policies. The wealthy resented their loss of status and the growing power of government and labor. They railed against the New Deal and Roosevelt, whom they called a traitor to his own class. Visitors at the home of J. P. Morgan Jr. were cautioned not to mention Roosevelt's name lest it raise Morgan's blood pressure. By "soaking" the rich, Roosevelt stole much of the thunder from the political left, although the results of his tax policy fell short of the promise. The new soak-the-rich tax failed to increase federal revenue significantly, nor did it result in a significant redistribution of income. Still, the prevailing view was that the president had moved in a radical direction. Roosevelt countered by stressing his basic conservatism and asserting that he had no love for socialism: "I am fighting communism. . . . I want to save our system, the capitalistic system." Yet he added that to save it from revolutionary turmoil required a more equal distribution of wealth.

ROOSEVELT'S SECOND TERM

On June 27, 1936, Roosevelt accepted the Democratic party's presidential nomination for a second term. He promised to continue to promote a government motivated by a "spirit of charity" rather than a government "frozen in the ice of its own indifference."

THE ELECTION OF 1936   The popularity of Roosevelt and the New Deal impelled the Republican Convention in 1936 to avoid candidates too closely identified with the "hate-Roosevelt" contingent. The party chose Governor Alfred M. Landon of Kansas, a former Bull Moose Progressive who had endorsed many New Deal programs. He was probably more liberal than most of his backers and clearly more so than the party's platform, which accused the New Deal of usurping power.

The Republicans hoped that the followers of Huey Long, Charles Coughlin, Francis Townsend, and other dissidents would combine to draw enough votes away from Roosevelt to throw the election to them. But that possibility faded when an assassin, the son-in-law of a Louisiana judge whom Long had sought to remove, gunned down the Kingfish in 1935. Coughlin, Townsend, and a remnant of the Long movement supported Representative William Lemke of North Dakota on a Union party ticket, but it was a forlorn effort, polling only 882,000 votes.

In 1936 Roosevelt forged a new electoral coalition that would affect national politics for years to come. While holding the support of most traditional Democrats in the North and the South, the president made strong gains among beneficiaries of New Deal farm programs in the West. In the northern cities he held on to the ethnic groups helped by New Deal welfare measures. Middle-class voters, whose property had been saved by New Deal initiatives, flocked to support him, as did intellectuals stirred by the ferment of new ideas coming from the government. The revived labor movement threw its support to Roosevelt, and in the most profound departure of all African-American voters for the first time cast the majority of their ballots for a Democratic president. "My friends, go home and turn Lincoln's picture to the wall," a Pittsburgh journalist told black Republicans. "That debt has been paid in full." The final tally revealed that 81 percent of those with an income under $1,000 a year opted for Roosevelt, as did 79 percent of those earning between $1,000 and $2,000. By contrast, only 46 percent of those earning over $5,000 voted for FDR.

In his acceptance speech to the Democratic Convention, Roosevelt abandoned efforts to reassure corporate leaders. As the Americans of 1776 had sought freedom from political autocracy, he noted, the Americans of 1936 sought freedom from the "economic royalists." He later claimed that never before had business leaders been "so united against one candidate." They were "unanimous in their hate for me—and I welcome their hatred." Roosevelt campaigned with tremendous buoyancy, and he wound up carrying every state except Maine and Vermont, with a popular vote of 27.7 million to Landon's 16.7 million. Democrats would also dominate Republicans in the new Congress, by 77 to 19 in the Senate and 328 to 107 in the House. After the lopsided victory, Roosevelt rode a wave of popularity into his second term.

THE COURT-PACKING PLAN   Soon after his landslide reelection, however, Roosevelt found himself deluged in a sea of troubles. His second inaugural address, delivered on January 20, 1937, promised even greater reforms. The challenge to American democracy, he maintained, was that millions of citizens "at this very moment are denied the greater part of what the very lowest standards of today call the necessities of life. . . . I see one-third of a nation ill-housed, ill-clad, ill-nourished." He viewed the election of 1936 as a mandate for even more extensive government action, and the overwhelming Democratic majorities in Congress ensured the passage of new legislation to buttress the Second New Deal. But one major roadblock stood in the way: the Supreme Court.

By the end of its 1936 term, the Court had ruled against New Deal programs in seven of the nine major cases it reviewed. Suits against the Social Security and Wagner Acts were pending. Given the conservative bent of the Court, the Second New Deal seemed in danger of being nullified, just as much of the original New Deal had been.

For that reason, Roosevelt resolved to change the Court's philosophy by enlarging the Court, a move for which there was ample precedent and power. Congress, not the Constitution, determines the size of the Court, which at different times has numbered six, seven, eight, nine, and ten justices and in 1937 numbered nine. On February 5 Roosevelt sent his plan to enlarge the Court to Congress, without having consulted congressional leaders. He wanted to create up to fifty new federal judges, including six new Supreme Court justices, and diminish the power of the judges who had served ten or more years or reached the age of seventy.

But the Court-packing maneuver, as opponents quickly tagged the president's scheme, backfired. It was a shade too contrived, much too brazen, and far too political. By implying that some judges were impaired by senility, Roosevelt affronted the elder statesmen of Congress and the Court, especially Justice Louis D. Brandeis, who was both the oldest and the most liberal of the Supreme Court judges. Roosevelt's scheme also ran headlong into a deep-rooted public veneration of the courts and aroused fears that another president might use the precedent for quite different purposes.

As it turned out, unforeseen events derailed Roosevelt's drive to change the Court. A sequence of Court decisions during the spring of 1937 reversed previous judgments in order to uphold the Wagner and Social Security Acts. In addition, a conservative justice resigned, and Roosevelt named to the vacancy one of the most consistent New Dealers, Senator Hugo Black of Alabama.

Roosevelt later claimed he had lost the battle but won the war. The Court had reversed itself on important New Deal legislation, and the president was able to appoint justices in harmony with the New Deal. But the episode created dissension within the Democratic party and blighted Roosevelt's prestige. For the first time, Democrats in large numbers deserted the president, and the Republican opposition found a powerful issue to use against the administration. During the first eight months of 1937, the momentum of Roosevelt's 1936 landslide victory was lost. As Secretary of Agriculture Henry Wallace later remarked, "The whole New Deal really went up in smoke as a result of the Supreme Court fight."

A NEW DIRECTION FOR LABOR   Rebellions meanwhile erupted on other fronts while the Court-packing bill pended. Under the impetus of the New Deal, the labor-union movement stirred anew. John L. Lewis, head of the United Mine Workers, increased membership from 150,000 to 500,000 within a year. Spurred by the mine workers' example, Sidney Hillman of the Amalgamated Clothing Workers and David Dubinsky of the International Ladies Garment Workers joined Lewis in promoting a campaign to organize workers in the mass-production industries. As leaders of some of the few industrial unions (made up of all types of workers) in the American Federation of Labor, they found the smaller, more restrictive craft unions (made up of male workers, with each union limited to a single skilled trade) to be obstacles to organizing the basic industries.

In 1935, with passage of the Wagner Act, the industrial unionists formed a Committee for Industrial Organization (CIO), and craft unionists (in the AFL) began to fear submergence by the mass unions of unskilled workers. Jurisdictional disputes spread among the unions, and in 1936 the AFL expelled the CIO unions, which then formed a permanent structure, called after 1938 the Congress of Industrial Organizations (also known by the initials CIO). The rivalry spurred both groups to greater unionizing efforts.

The CIO's major organizing drives in the automobile and steel industries began in 1936, but they were thwarted by management's use of blacklisting, private detectives, labor spies, vigilante groups, and other forms of intimidation to suppress the unions. Early in 1937 automobile workers spontaneously adopted a new technique, the "sit-down strike," in which workers refused to leave a plant until employers granted collective bargaining rights to their union.

Led by the fiery young autoworker and union organizer Walter Reuther, thousands of employees at the General Motors assembly plants in Flint, Michigan, occupied the factories and stopped all production. Management refused to recognize the union efforts, and the standoff lasted over a month before the company finally relented and signed a contract recognizing the United Automobile Workers. Other automobile manufacturers soon followed suit. And the following month, U. S. Steel capitulated to the Steel Workers Organizing Committee (later the United Steelworkers of America), granting it recognition, a 10 percent wage hike, and a forty-hour workweek.

Having captured two giants of heavy industry, the CIO went on in the next few years to organize much of industrial America: the rubber, oil, and electronics industries and a good part of the textile industry, in which unionists had to fight protracted struggles to organize scattered plants. The slow pace of labor organizing in textiles denied the CIO a major victory in the South comparable to its swift conquest of automobiles and steel in the North, but even down South a labor movement gained a foothold. Union membership in the United States grew from under 3 million in 1933 to 8.5 million in 1940. Wages rose and working conditions improved because of their efforts. Whether by design or accident, union members became solid Democrats.

A SLUMPING ECONOMY   During the years 1935 and 1936 the economy finally showed signs of recovery. By the spring of 1937, economic output had moved above the 1929 level. But worried about deficits and rising inflation, Roosevelt ordered sharp cuts in federal spending. At the same time the Treasury began to reduce disposable income by collecting $2 billion in Social Security from employee paychecks. Private spending could not fill the gap left by reductions in government spending, and big business still lacked the faith to risk large capital investments. The result was the slump of 1937, which was sharper than that of 1929 but was called by the press a recession to distinguish it from the depression. By the end of 1937, an additional 4 million people had been thrown out of work; grim scenes of the earlier depression reappeared. The 1937 recession ignited a fierce debate within the administration. One group, led by Treasury Secretary Henry Morgenthau, favored less federal spending and a balanced budget. The other group, which included Harry Hopkins and Harold Ickes, argued for renewed government spending and stricter enforcement of anti-trust laws.

ECONOMIC POLICY AND LATER REFORMS   Roosevelt seemed bewildered by the recession, but he eventually endorsed the ideas of the spenders. In the spring of 1938, he asked Congress to adopt a large-scale spending program intended to increase mass purchasing power, and Congress voted almost $3.3 billion, mainly for public works projects. In a short time the increase in spending reversed the economy's decline, but the recession and Roosevelt's reluctance to adopt massive, sustained government spending forestalled the achievement of full recovery. Only the massive crisis of World War II would return the U. S. economy to full production and full employment.

The 1937 recession further eroded Roosevelt's prestige and dissipated the mandate of the 1936 elections. The only major reforms enacted in Roosevelt's second term were the Wagner-Steagall National Housing Act, the Bankhead-Jones Farm Tenant Act, and the Fair Labor Standards Act. The Housing Act of 1937 set up the U.S. Housing Authority (USHA) in the Department of the Interior, which extended long-term loans to local agencies willing to assume part of the cost of slum clearance and public housing. The agency also subsidized rents for low-income residents.

The Farm Tenant Act, passed in 1937, was to be administered by a new agency, the Farm Security Administration (FSA). The program offered loans to prevent marginally profitable farm owners from sinking into tenancy. It also offered loans to tenants to help them purchase their own farms. But by the late 1930s the idea of small homesteads was doomed to failure. American mythology still exalted the family farm, but in reality the ever-larger agricultural unit predominated. In the end the FSA proved to be little more than another relief operation that tided a few farmers over difficult times. Sadly, a more effective answer to the problem awaited national mobilization for war, which moved many tenants into the military services or defense industries, broadened their horizons, and taught them skills that enabled them to leave the farm altogether.

The Fair Labor Standards Act of 1938 applied only to employees in enterprises that operated in or affected interstate commerce. It set a minimum wage of 40¢ an hour and a maximum workweek of forty hours, to be put into effect over several years. The act also prohibited child labor under the age of sixteen. Southern congressmen howled in opposition to the bill because it raised wages in their region and thus increased employers' expenses.

THE LEGACY OF THE NEW DEAL

SETBACKS FOR THE PRESIDENT   Although critics were unable to defeat the Fair Labor Standards Act, their stiff resistance revealed that an effective opposition to the New Deal was emerging within the president's own party, especially in the conservative southern wing. Southern Democrats were at best uneasy bedfellows of organized labor and African Americans, and more and more of them drifted toward closer cooperation with conservative Republicans. By the end of 1937, a formidable anti-New Deal bloc had developed in Congress.

In 1938 the conservative opposition stymied Roosevelt's proposal to reorganize the executive branch amid cries that it would lead to dictatorship. As the political season of 1938 advanced, Roosevelt unfolded a new idea as momentous as his Court-packing plan: a proposal to reshape the Democratic party in the image of the New Deal. He announced his plan to campaign in Democratic primaries as the party leader with the goal of seeing his own supporters nominated. Instead of succeeding, however, the effort to shape the state elections backfired and broke the spell of presidential invincibility, or what was left of it. As in the Court-packing fight, Roosevelt had risked his prestige while handing his adversaries a combustible issue to use against him. His opponents tagged his intervention in the primaries an attempt to "purge" the Democratic party of its southern conservatives; the word evoked visions of Adolf Hitler and Joseph Stalin, tyrants who had purged their Nazi and Communist parties with blood.

The elections of November 1938 resulted in another setback for the administration, caused in part by the friction among the Democrats. FDR had failed in his efforts to liberalize the party by ousting southern conservatives. The Democratic dominance in the House fell from 229 to 93, in the Senate from 56 to 42. The margins remained large, but the president now headed an increasingly divided party. In his State of the Union message in 1939, Roosevelt for the first time proposed no new reforms. He did manage, however, to put through his plan to reorganize the executive branch. Under the Administrative Reorganization Act of 1939, the president could "reduce, coordinate, consolidate, and reorganize" the agencies of government. With that, Roosevelt's domestic innovations feebly ended.

A HALFWAY REVOLUTION   The New Deal had lost momentum, but it had wrought several enduring changes. By the end of the 1930s, the power of the national government was vastly enlarged over what it had been in 1932, and hope had been restored to people who had grown disconsolate. But the New Deal entailed more than just bigger government and revived public confidence. It also constituted a significant change from the older liberalism embodied in the Progressivism of Theodore Roosevelt and Woodrow Wilson. Those reformers, despite their sharp differences, had assumed that the function of progressive government was to use aggressive regulation to ensure that the people had an equal opportunity to pursue their notions of happiness.

Franklin Roosevelt and the New Dealers went beyond this concept of a regulatory state by insisting that the government not simply *respond* to social crises but also take positive steps to *avoid* them. To this end, the New Deal's various welfare and benefit programs conferred on the government the responsibility to ensure a minimum level of well-being for all Americans. The New Deal had established minimum qualitative standards for labor conditions and public welfare and helped middle-class Americans hold on to their savings, their homes, and their farms. The protection afforded by bank-deposit insurance, unemployment pay, and Social Security pensions would come to be universally accepted as a safeguard against future depressions.

The old Progressive formulation of regulation versus trust-busting was now superseded by the rise of the "broker state," a powerful federal government that mediated among major interest groups. Government's role was to act as an honest broker protecting a variety of interests, not just big business but workers, farmers, consumers, small business, and the unemployed.

In implementing his domestic program, Roosevelt steered a zigzag course between the extremes of laissez-faire capitalism and socialism. The first New Deal had experimented for a time with a managed economy under the NRA but had abandoned that experiment for a turn toward enforcing competition through regulation and priming the economy with increased government spending. This tactic finally produced full employment during World War II.

Roosevelt himself, impatient with political theory, was flexible in developing policy: he kept what worked and discarded what did not. The result was, paradoxically, both profoundly revolutionary and profoundly conservative.

Roosevelt sharply increased the regulatory functions of the federal government and laid the foundation for what would become an expanding welfare system. Despite what his critics charged, however, his initiatives fell far short of socialism; they left the basic capitalist structure in place. In the process of such bold experimentation and dynamic preservation, the New Deal represented a "halfway revolution" that permanently altered the nation's social and political landscape.

MAKING CONNECTIONS

- In the mid-1930s, just as Roosevelt was getting the New Deal into place, the growing conflict in Europe began to consume more and more of his (and America's) attention; Chapter 29 shows how Roosevelt went from combating the Depression to leading the United States into World War II.

- Harry Truman, Roosevelt's successor in the White House, tried unsuccessfully to expand the idea of the New Deal into new areas (national health insurance and federal aid to education, for example), topics covered in Chapter 31.

FURTHER READING

The best recent interpretive survey of the 1930s is David M. Kennedy's *Freedom from Fear: The American People in Depression and War, 1929–1945* (1999). Michael E. Parrish's *Securities Regulation and the New Deal* (1970) and Ellis W. Hawley's *The New Deal and the Problem of Monopoly: A Study in Economic Ambivalence* (1966) analyze government attempts to forestall another market crash.

Alan Brinkley's *The End of Reform: New Deal Liberalism in Recession and War* (1995) suggests that the New Deal reformers did not go far enough in their efforts to curb big business. On the critics of the New Deal, see Alan Brinkley's *Voices of Protest: Huey Long, Father Coughlin, and the Great Depression* (1982). James N. Gregory's *American Exodus: The Dust Bowl Migration and Okie Culture in California* (1989) describes the migratory movement's effect on American culture. On the environmental and human causes of the dust bowl, see Donald Worster, *Dust Bowl: The Southern Plains in the 1930s* (1979).

29

FROM ISOLATION TO GLOBAL WAR

FOCUS QUESTIONS

· What was the impact of isolationism and peace movements on national politics between the two world wars?

· How did the United States respond to German aggression in Europe?

· How did events in Asia lead to Japan's attack on Pearl Harbor and America's entry into the global war?

To answer these questions and access additional review material, please visit www.wwnorton.com/studyspace.

In the late 1930s the winds of war swept across Asia and Europe, abruptly shifting the focus of American politics from domestic to foreign affairs. Another Democratic president had to turn his attention from social and economic reform to military preparedness and war. And the public again had to wrestle with a painful choice: involve the country in volatile world affairs or remain aloof and officially neutral.

POSTWAR ISOLATIONISM

THE LEAGUE AND THE UNITED STATES Between Woodrow Wilson and Franklin Roosevelt lay two decades of relative isolation from foreign entanglements. The post–World War I mood of indifference to global affairs set the pattern. The voters in 1920 expressed their resistance to international commitments, and President-elect Harding lost little time in disposing of American membership in the League of Nations. The spirit of isolation found other expressions as well: higher tariffs, the Red Scare, and restrictive immigration laws, with which the nation all but shut the door to newcomers.

The United States may have felt the urge to insulate itself from a wicked world, but it could hardly ignore its substantial global interests. American business had expanding worldwide connections. Investments and loans abroad put in circulation the dollars that purchased American exports. America's overseas possessions, moreover, directly involved the country in world affairs, especially in the Pacific. Even the League of Nations was too great an organization to ignore. After 1924 the United States gradually entered into joint efforts with the League on such tasks as policing the international trade in drugs and arms, and American diplomats took part in a variety of economic, cultural, and technical conferences.

WAR DEBTS AND REPARATIONS   Probably nothing did more to heighten American isolationism during the 1920s and 1930s—or anti-American feeling in Europe—than the war-debt tangle. When in 1917 the Allies had begun to exhaust their sources of private credit in the United States, the U.S. government advanced them millions of dollars, first for the war effort and then for postwar reconstruction.

To Americans the repayment of the war debts seemed a simple matter of obligation, but Europeans commonly had a different perception. The French and the British had insisted that they could pay America only as they collected reparations from defeated Germany. Twice during the 1920s the resulting strain on Germany brought the structure of international payments to the verge of collapse, and both times the Reparations Commission called in American bankers to work out rescue plans.

The whole structure finally did collapse during the Great Depression. In 1931 President Hoover negotiated a moratorium on both German reparations and Allied payment of war debts. At the end of 1932, after Hoover's debt moratorium ended, most of the European countries defaulted on their war debts to the United States. In retaliation, Congress passed the Johnson Debt Default Act of 1934, which prohibited private loans to any defaulting government.

ATTEMPTS AT DISARMAMENT   After World War I many Americans decided that the armaments race had caused the war and that arms limitations treaties would bring lasting peace. The United States had no intention of maintaining a large army, but under the naval building program begun in 1916, it had constructed a fleet second only to that of Britain.

Neither the British nor the Americans relished a naval armaments race, but both shared a concern about the alarming growth of Japanese military power. Since 1914 Japanese-American relations had grown increasingly strained as the United States objected to continued Japanese encroachments in Asia. During World War I, Japan had taken China's Shan-tung Peninsula and the islands of Micronesia from its enemy, Germany. In 1917, after the United States entered the war, Viscount Kikujiro Ishii visited Washington to secure American recognition of Japan's expanded position in Asia, dropping hints that Germany had several times tried to get Japan to quit the war. To forestall the loss of an ally in the war, Secretary of State Robert Lansing had signed an ambiguous agreement saying that "Japan has special interests in China." Americans were unhappy with the Lansing-Ishii Agreement, but it was viewed as the only way to keep Japan in the war.

After the war ended, Japanese-American relations deteriorated. To address the problem, President Warren Harding invited eight key countries to the Washington Conference of 1921. It opened with a surprise announcement by the U.S. secretary of state, Charles Evans Hughes, who laid out a disarmament plan to destroy most of the world's navies. Delegates from the United States, Britain, Japan, France, and Italy signed a Five-Power Treaty

The Washington Conference, 1921

The Big Five at the conference were (from left) Kijuro Shidehara (Japan), Arthur Balfour (Great Britain), Charles Evans Hughes (United States), Aristide Briand (France), and Carlo Schanzer (Italy).

(1922), incorporating Hughes's plan for tonnage limits on their navies and a moratorium of ten years, during which no battleships would be built. The five powers also agreed to refrain from further fortification of their Pacific possessions. The agreement in effect partitioned the world: U.S. naval power became supreme in the Western Hemisphere, Japanese power in the western Pacific, and British power from the North Sea to Singapore.

Two other major agreements emerged from the Washington Conference. With the Four-Power Treaty, the United States, Britain, Japan, and France agreed to respect one another's possessions in the Pacific. The Nine-Power Treaties for the first time pledged the signers to support the principle of the Open Door enunciated by Secretary of State John Hay at the turn of the century. The Open Door enabled all nations to compete for trade and investment opportunities in China on an equal footing rather than allow individual nations to create economic monopolies in particular regions of that country. The signers of the Nine-Power Treaties also promised to respect the territorial integrity of China. The powers, in addition to those signing the Five-Power Treaty, were China, Belgium, Portugal, and the Netherlands.

With these agreements in hand, President Harding's supporters could boast of a brilliant diplomatic stroke that relieved citizens of the need to pay for an enlarged navy and defused potential conflicts in the Pacific. Yet the agreements were without obligation and without teeth. The signers of the Four-Power Treaty agreed only to consult, not to help one another. The formal endorsement of the Open Door in the Nine-Power Treaties was just as ineffective, for the United States remained unwilling to use force to uphold the principle. Moreover, the naval-disarmament treaty set tonnage limits only on battleships and aircraft carriers; the race to build cruisers, destroyers, submarines, and other smaller craft continued.

THE KELLOGG-BRIAND PACT   During and after World War I the fanciful ideal of simply abolishing war seized the American imagination. Peace societies thrived, and the glorious vision of ending war by the stroke of a pen culminated in the Kellogg-Briand Pact of 1928. This unique treaty originated when the French foreign minister Aristide Briand proposed to President Calvin Coolidge's secretary of state, Frank B. Kellogg, an agreement whereby the two countries would never go to war with each other. Kellogg countered with a scheme to have all nations sign the pact, an idea all the more acceptable to the many peace organizations of the day.

The Pact of Paris (its official name), signed on August 27, 1928, declared that the signatories "condemn recourse to war . . . and renounce it as an instrument of national policy." Eventually sixty-two nations joined the pact, but all reserved "self-defense" as an escape hatch. The U.S. Senate included a reservation declaring the Monroe Doctrine necessary to America's self-defense and then ratified the agreement by a vote of eighty-five to one. A Virginia senator who voted for "this worthless, but perfectly harmless peace treaty" wrote a friend that he feared it would "confuse the minds of many good people who think that peace may be secured by polite professions of neighborly and brotherly love."

THE "GOOD NEIGHBOR" POLICY   In Latin America the spirit of peace and noninvolvement helped allay long-festering resentments against the United States, which had freely intervened in the Caribbean during the first two decades of the century. In 1924 American marines left the Dominican Republic after an eight-year occupation. U.S. troops left Nicaragua a year later but returned in 1926 with the outbreak of disorder and civil war. In 1927 the Coolidge administration negotiated an agreement for U.S.-supervised elections, but one rebel leader, César Augusto Sandino, held out, and the marines stayed until 1933.

In 1930 President Hoover improved America's image in Latin America by permitting publication of a memorandum that denied that the Monroe Doctrine justified U.S. intervention in Latin America. It stopped short of repudiating intervention on any grounds, but that fine point hardly blunted the celebration in Latin America. Although Hoover never endorsed this so-called Clark memorandum, named for American diplomat Reuben Clark, he never ordered military intervention in the region. Before he left office, steps had been taken to withdraw American forces from Nicaragua and Haiti.

Franklin D. Roosevelt likewise embraced the policy of the "good neighbor" and soon advanced it in practice. In 1933, at the Seventh Pan-American Conference, the United States supported a resolution declaring that no nation "has the right to intervene in the internal or external affairs of another." Under President Roosevelt the marines completed their withdrawal from Nicaragua and Haiti, and in 1934 the president negotiated with Cuba a treaty that abrogated the Platt Amendment (1901), which had given the United States a formal right to intervene in Cuba.

WAR CLOUDS

JAPANESE INCURSIONS INTO CHINA   Improving U.S. relations in the Western Hemisphere during the 1930s proved an exception in an otherwise dismal world scene as war clouds darkened over Europe and Asia. Actual conflict erupted first in Asia, where unsettled social and political conditions in China had attracted foreign encroachments since before the turn of the century. In 1929 Chinese nationalist aspirations and China's subsequent clashes with Russia convinced the Japanese that their own extensive investments in Manchuria, including the South Manchurian Railway, were in danger.

Japanese military occupation of Manchuria began with the Mukden incident of 1931, when an explosion destroyed a section of railroad track near that city. The Japanese army based in Manchuria to guard the railway blamed the incident on the Chinese and used it as a pretext to occupy all of Manchuria. In 1932 the Japanese converted Manchuria into the puppet empire of Manchukuo.

The Manchuria incident, as the Japanese called their undeclared war, flagrantly violated the Nine-Power Treaties, the Kellogg-Briand Pact, and Japan's pledges as a member of the League of Nations. But when China asked the League and the United States for help, neither obliged. President Herbert Hoover refused to invoke military or economic sanctions.

In early 1932 Japan's indiscriminate bombing of civilians in Shanghai, China's great port city, aroused Western indignation but no action. When the League of Nations condemned Japanese aggression in 1933, Japan withdrew from the League. Thereafter, hostilities in Manchuria gradually subsided and ended with a truce. An uneasy peace settled upon east Asia for four years, during which time Japan's military leaders extended their political sway in Tokyo.

ITALY AND GERMANY   The rise of the Japanese militarists paralleled the rise of totalitarian dictators in Italy and Germany. In 1922 Benito Mussolini had seized power in Italy after organizing the Fascist movement, a composite of superheated nationalism and socialism. The party's program, and above all Mussolini's promise to restore order and pride in a country fragmented by dissension and self-doubts, enjoyed a wide appeal. Once in power, Mussolini largely abandoned the socialist part of his platform and gradually suppressed all opposition. By 1925 he was wielding dictatorial power as Il Duce (the Leader).

There was always something ludicrous about the strutting Mussolini. Italy, after all, was a minor European power. But Germany was another matter, and most Americans were not amused, even at the beginning, by Il Duce's German counterpart, Adolf Hitler. Hitler's National Socialist German Workers' (Nazi) party duplicated the major features of Italian fascism, including the ancient Roman salute. Hitler capitalized on the weakness of Germany's postwar government, the poverty and despair caused by a severe economic depression, and festering German resentment toward the Versailles Treaty.

Named chancellor on January 30, 1933, Hitler swiftly won dictatorial powers and in 1934 assumed the title of Reichsführer (national leader). The Nazi police state cranked up the engines of tyranny, persecuting Jews, whom Hitler blamed for Germany's troubles, and rearming in defiance of the Versailles Treaty. Hitler flouted international agreements, pulled Germany out of the League of Nations in 1933, and threatened to extend control over all German-speaking peoples. Despite one provocation after another, the European democracies lacked the will to resist.

RUSSIAN RECOGNITION   Isolationist sentiment in the United States grew even more potent during the early 1930s, but one significant exception to American insularity was Roosevelt's decision to favor official recognition of Soviet Russia. By 1933 the reasons for America's refusal to recognize the Bolshevik regime had grown stale. Seen as an expansive market for U.S. goods, the Soviet Union stirred fantasies of an American trade boom, much

Axis Leaders

Mussolini and Hitler in Munich, June 1940.

as China had at the turn of the century. Japanese expansionism in Asia, moreover, gave the Soviet Union and the United States a common foreign-policy concern. Given an opening by the shift of opinion, Roosevelt invited the Soviet commissar for foreign affairs to visit Washington, D.C. After nine days of talks, a formal exchange of notes on November 16, 1933, signaled the renewal of diplomatic relations. The Soviet commissar promised that his country would abstain from promoting communist propaganda in the United States, extend religious freedom to Americans in the Soviet Union, and reopen the question of unpaid Russian debts to the United States.

THE MARCH OF AGGRESSION   After 1932 a catastrophic chain of events in Asia and Europe sent the world hurtling toward disaster. In 1934 Japan renounced the Five-Power Treaty. The next year, Mussolini commenced Italy's conquest of Ethiopia. That same year a referendum in Germany's Saar Basin, held in accordance with the Versailles Treaty, delivered the coal-rich region into the hands of Hitler. In 1936 Hitler's armed forces reoccupied the Rhineland, a direct violation of the Versailles Treaty. The French did nothing to oust the German force, however.

The year 1936 also brought the Spanish Civil War, which began with an uprising of the Spanish armed forces in Morocco, led by General Francisco Franco, against the democratically elected Spanish republic. Over the next three years, Franco established a fascist dictatorship with help from Hitler and Mussolini while the European democracies left the Spanish republic to its fate.

On July 7, 1937, Japanese and Chinese troops clashed at the Marco Polo Bridge, west of Peking, and the incident quickly developed into a full-scale war. World War II had begun in Asia two years before it would erupt in Europe. That same year, Japan joined Germany and Italy in establishing an alliance known as the Rome-Berlin-Tokyo "Axis."

By 1938 the peace of Europe trembled in the balance. Having rebuilt the German military force, Hitler forced the *Anschluss* (union) of Austria with Germany in March 1938. Six months later British and French leaders, recognizing the situation's severity but failing to comprehend Hitler's ruthlessness, sought to appease the German leader by agreeing to abandon the Sudetenland in Czechoslovakia, a country that had probably the second strongest army in central Europe. Germany promptly took the mountainous Sudetenland, largely German in population, which had been given to Czechoslovakia at the Paris Peace Conference in 1919 because of its strategic importance to that new nation's defense.

After promising that the Sudetenland would be his last territorial demand, Hitler in 1939 brazenly broke his pledge. He occupied the remainder

Keeping in mind the terms of the Treaty of Versailles (see page 725), explain why Hitler began his campaign of expansion by invading the Rhineland and the Sudetenland. Why would Hitler have wanted to retake the Polish Corridor? Why did the attack on Poland begin World War II whereas Hitler's previous invasions of his European neighbors did not?

of Czechoslovakia and seized former German territory from Lithuania. In quick succession the Spanish republic collapsed on March 28, and Mussolini seized the kingdom of Albania on April 7. On September 1, 1939, Hitler launched his conquest of Poland. A few days before, he had signed a nonaggression pact with Soviet Russia. Having deserted Czechoslovakia, Britain and France now honored their commitment to go to war if Poland were invaded.

DEGREES OF NEUTRALITY During these years of deepening crisis, the Western democracies seemed paralyzed, hoping in vain that each concession would appease the appetites of fascist dictators. Americans retreated more deeply into isolation. The neutrality laws of the 1930s sought to keep the United States insulated from the quarrels of Europe. But while Americans wanted to steer clear of war altogether, their sympathies were more strongly than ever with the Western democracies, and the triumph of fascist aggression in Europe aroused fears for national security. The Neutrality Act of 1935 forbade the sale of arms and munitions to all belligerents (warring nations) whenever the president proclaimed that a state of war existed, and it declared that Americans who traveled on belligerents' ships did so at their own risk. Roosevelt would have preferred discretionary authority to levy an embargo only against aggressors, but he reluctantly accepted the act because it was to be effective for only six months.

Yet on October 3, 1935, just weeks after Roosevelt signed the legislation, Italy invaded Ethiopia, and Roosevelt invoked the act. When Congress reconvened in 1936, it extended the arms embargo and added a provision forbidding loans to belligerents. Then, in July 1936, while Italian troops mopped up the last resistance in Ethiopia, the Spanish Civil War broke out. Roosevelt now became more isolationist than some of the most extreme isolationists. Although the Spanish Civil War involved a fascist uprising against a recognized democratic government, Roosevelt accepted the French and British position that only their nonintervention would keep the fight from spreading to the rest of Europe.

The conflict in Spain led Roosevelt to seek a "moral embargo" on the arms trade, and he encouraged Congress to extend the neutrality laws to cover civil wars. Congress did so in 1937 with only one dissenting vote. The Western democracies then stood by as German and Italian soldiers, planes, and armaments supported Franco's overthrow of Spanish democracy.

In the spring of 1937, Congress passed another neutrality law, which continued restraints on arms sales and loans, forbade Americans to travel on the ships of nations at war, and prohibited the arming of American merchant ships trading with warring nations. The new law also empowered the president to require that goods other than arms or munitions exported to belligerents be sold on a cash-and-carry basis (that is, the nation purchasing the goods would have to pay cash and transport the cargo in its own ships). This was an ingenious scheme to preserve a profitable trade without running the risk of war.

The new law had its first test in July 1937, when Japanese and Chinese forces clashed at the Marco Polo Bridge. Since neither side declared war,

Roosevelt was able to avoid invoking the neutrality law, which would have favored the Japanese, since China had greater need of American arms but few means to get supplies past the Japanese navy. A flourishing trade in munitions to China flowed around the world as ships carried American military equipment across the Atlantic to England, where it was reloaded onto British ships bound for Hong Kong. Roosevelt, by his refusal to invoke the neutrality laws, had challenged strict isolationism.

Roosevelt soon ventured a step further. In Chicago on October 5, 1937, he denounced the "reign of terror and international lawlessness" whereby 10 percent of the world's population threatened the peace of the other 90 percent. He called for a "quarantine" against those nations "creating a state of international anarchy and instability from which there is no escape through mere isolation or neutrality." Public reaction to the speech was mixed, but the president nevertheless quickly backed off from its implications and refused to spell out any program for dealing with aggression.

After the German occupation of Czechoslovakia in 1939, Roosevelt no longer pretended impartiality in the deepening European struggle. He began to educate the public about the menace of unchecked fascism. He urged

Neutrality

A 1938 cartoon shows U.S. foreign policy entangled by the serpent of isolationism.

Congress to repeal the munitions embargo and permit the United States to sell arms on a cash-and-carry basis to Britain and France, but to no avail. "You haven't got the votes," Vice President John Nance Garner told him, "and that's all there is to it." When the Germans attacked Poland on September 1, Roosevelt proclaimed official neutrality but in a radio talk stressed that he would not, like Woodrow Wilson in 1914, ask Americans to remain neutral in thought because "even a neutral has a right to take account of the facts."

Roosevelt summoned Congress into special session and asked again for amendments to the Neutrality Act. "I regret the Congress passed the Act," he confessed. "I regret equally that I signed the Act." Under the Neutrality Act of 1939, Britain and France could buy supplies with cash and take away in their own ships weapons or anything else they wanted. American ships, on the other hand, were excluded from the ports of warring nations and from specified war zones. Roosevelt then designated as a war zone the Baltic Sea and the waters around Great Britain and Ireland, from Norway south to the coast of Spain. One unexpected effect of this move was to relieve Hitler of any inhibitions about using unrestricted submarine warfare to blockade Britain.

Once the great democracies of western Europe faced war, American public opinion, appalled at Hitler's tyranny, rallied to aid its allies without being drawn into the war itself. For a time it seemed that the Western Hemisphere could remain insulated. After the Nazis overran Poland in less than a month, the war settled into a stalemate in early 1940 that began to be called the phony war. What lay ahead, it seemed, was a long war of attrition—much like World War I—in which Britain and France would have the resources to outlast Hitler. That illusion lasted from October 1939 until the spring of 1940.

THE STORM IN EUROPE

BLITZKRIEG   In the spring of 1940 the long winter lull in the European fighting suddenly erupted into Blitzkrieg—lightning war. At dawn on April 9, without warning, Nazi troops occupied Denmark and landed along the Norwegian coast. Denmark fell in a day, Norway within a few weeks. On May 10 Hitler unleashed dive bombers and tank divisions on neutral Belgium and the Netherlands. On May 21 German troops moving down the valley of the Somme River reached the English Channel, cutting off a British force sent to help the Belgians and the French. A desperate evacuation from the French beaches at Dunkirk enlisted every available boat, from warship to tug. Amid the chaos some 338,000 soldiers, about one third of them French, escaped to England.

The Blitz

In London, St. Paul's Cathedral looms above the destruction wrought by German bombs during the Blitz. Churchill's response: "We shall never surrender."

Having outflanked France's heavily fortified defense perimeter, the Maginot Line, the German forces rushed ahead, cutting the French armies to pieces and spreading panic by strafing refugees. On June 14 the Nazi swastika flew over Paris.

AMERICA'S GROWING INVOLVEMENT Britain now stood alone, but its new prime minister, Winston Churchill, breathed defiance. "We shall go on to the end," he pledged; "we shall never surrender." Nevertheless, America seemed suddenly vulnerable as Hitler unleashed his air force against Britain. President Roosevelt called for a military buildup and the production of 50,000 combat planes a year. In 1940 Congress voted more than $17 billion for defense. In response to Churchill's appeal for military supplies, the War and Navy Departments began releasing stocks of arms, planes, and munitions to the British.

The world crisis transformed Roosevelt. Having been stalemated for much of his second term by congressional opposition to his domestic program, he was revitalized by the war in Europe. Nervous cabinet officers, military leaders, and diplomats now encountered a decisive, forceful president willing to exert executive authority on behalf of Britain. Roosevelt acted with remarkable boldness in the face of an American public that still held staunchly to the doctrine of isolationism.

The summer of 1940 brought the desperate Battle of Britain, in which the Royal Air Force finally forced the Germans to give up plans to invade the British Isles. Submarine warfare meanwhile strained the resources of the battered Royal Navy. To relieve the pressure, Churchill urgently requested the transfer of American destroyers to help protect convoys from submarines. Secret negotiations led to an executive agreement under which fifty "overaged" destroyers went to the British in return for ninety-nine-year leases on naval and air bases in Newfoundland, Bermuda, and islands in the

Caribbean. Roosevelt disguised the action as necessary for defense of the hemisphere. Two weeks later, on September 14, 1940, Congress adopted the first peacetime conscription in American history. All 16 million men aged twenty-one to thirty-five were required to register for a year's military service within the United States.

The new state of affairs prompted vigorous debate between "internationalists," who believed national security demanded aid to Britain, and isolationists, who charged that Roosevelt was drawing the United States into an unnecessary war. In 1940 internationalists organized the nonpartisan Committee to Defend America by Aiding the Allies, drawing its strongest support from the East and West Coasts and the South. Two months later isolationists formed the America First Committee. The isolationists argued that a Nazi victory, while distasteful, would pose no threat to American national security.

FDR'S THIRD TERM   In the midst of these profound global crises, the quadrennial presidential campaign came due. Isolationist sentiment was strongest in the Republican party, yet their nominee took a different stance. Wendell L. Willkie was a former Democrat who had voted for Roosevelt in 1932. An Indiana farm boy whose disheveled charm inspired strong loyalty, he openly supported aid to the Allies.

The Nazi victory in France ensured that Roosevelt would decide to run for an unprecedented third term. The president cultivated party unity with his foreign policy and kept a sphinxlike silence about his intentions. The world crisis reconciled southern conservatives to the man whose foreign policy, at least, they supported. At the convention in Chicago, Roosevelt won nomination for a third term with only token opposition. For his new running mate, he tapped his secretary of agriculture, Henry Wallace, a devoted supporter who would appeal to farm voters.

Throughout the summer, Roosevelt assumed the role of a man above the political fray, busy rather with urgent matters of defense and diplomacy. Because Willkie's foreign-policy ideas mirrored Roosevelt's, the Republican nominee was reduced to attacking New Deal red tape and promising to run the programs better. Roosevelt won the election by a comfortable margin of 27 million votes to Willkie's 22 million and by a wider margin, 449 to 82, in the Electoral College. Though the popular vote was closer than in any presidential election since 1916, the dangerous world situation had persuaded a majority of voters to back the Democrats' slogan: "Don't switch horses in the middle of the stream."

THE "ARSENAL OF DEMOCRACY"   Bolstered by the mandate for a third term, Roosevelt moved quickly to provide greater aid to besieged Britain, whose cash was running out. Since direct government loans would arouse memories of earlier war-debt defaults—the Johnson Debt Default Act of 1934 forbade such loans anyway—the president created an ingenious device to bypass that issue and yet supply British needs: the "lend-lease" program. In a fireside chat, Roosevelt told the nation that it must become "the great arsenal of democracy" to help prevent Britain's fall, and to do so it must make new efforts to help the British purchase American supplies. The lend-lease bill, introduced in Congress on January 10, 1941, authorized the president to sell, lend, or lease arms and other equipment and supplies to "any country whose defense the President deems vital to the defense of the United States."

For two months a bitter debate over the lend-lease bill raged in Congress and around the country. Isolationists saw it as the point of no return. Administration supporters denied that lend-lease would lead to American involvement in the war, but they knew that it did increase the risk. Lend-lease became law in early 1941, and Britain and China were the first beneficiaries.

While the nation debated, the war intensified. Italy had officially entered the European war as Hitler's ally in June 1940. In late 1940, as the American presidential campaign approached its climax, Mussolini launched attacks on Greece and, from Italian-controlled Libya, assaulted the British in Egypt. But his troops had to fall back in both cases, and in the spring of 1941 German forces under General Erwin Rommel joined the Italians in Libya, forcing the British to withdraw into Egypt, their resources having been drained to help Greece. In April 1941 Nazi armored divisions overwhelmed Yugoslavia and Greece, and by the end of May airborne forces had subdued the Greek island of Crete, putting Hitler in a position to menace the entire Middle East.

With Hungary, Romania, and Bulgaria forced into the Axis fold, Hitler controlled nearly all of Europe, but his ambition was unbounded. On June 22, 1941, Nazi troops suddenly fell upon the Soviet Union, their ally, hoping to use another lightning stroke to eliminate the potential threat on Germany's eastern front. The Nazis massed 3.6 million soldiers on a 2,000-mile front from the Arctic to the Black Sea. After retreating for four months, however, Russian soldiers and civilians rallied to defend Leningrad, Moscow, and Sevastopol. During the winter of 1941–1942, a ferocious Soviet counterattack proved to be the most important development of the war in Europe. Still, in the summer of 1941 the Nazi juggernaut appeared unstoppable.

Winston Churchill had already decided to provide British support to the Soviet Union in case of such an attack. Roosevelt adopted the same policy, offering American aid to Russia two days after the German invasion in late June 1941. Stalinist Russia, so long as it held out against the Germans, ensured Britain's survival. American aid was now indispensable to Europe's defense, and the logic of lend-lease led to deeper American involvement. To deliver aid to Britain, supply ships had to maneuver through the German submarine "wolf packs" in the North Atlantic. So in April 1941 Roosevelt informed Churchill that the U.S. Navy would extend its patrol areas in the North Atlantic nearly to Iceland.

In August 1941 Roosevelt and Churchill held a secret meeting off the coast of Newfoundland. There they drew up a statement of international principles known as the Atlantic Charter. Their joint statement called for the self-determination of all peoples, economic cooperation, freedom of the seas, and a new international system of collective security. The Soviet Union later endorsed the charter.

Having entered into a joint statement of war aims with the anti-Axis powers, the United States soon became involved in shooting incidents in the North Atlantic. After a German submarine attacked an American battleship, the president ordered American ships to "shoot on sight" any German or Italian raiders ("rattlesnakes of the Atlantic") that ventured into American waters. Five days later the U.S. Navy announced that it would convoy British-bound merchant ships all the way to Iceland.

Further attacks prompted Congress to make the changes in the 1939 Neutrality Act that had been requested by the president. On November 17 Congress removed the bans on arming merchant vessels and allowed them to enter combat zones and belligerent ports. Step-by-step the United States was giving up neutrality and embarking on naval warfare against Germany. Still, Americans hoped to avoid the final step of all-out war. The decision to go to war would be made in response to aggression in an unexpected quarter—the Pacific.

THE STORM IN THE PACIFIC

JAPANESE AGGRESSION   After the Nazi victories in Europe during the spring of 1940, America's relations with Japan took a turn for the worse. Japanese militarists, bogged down in the vastness of China, now eyed new temptations in Southeast Asia. They wanted to incorporate into their "Greater East Asia Co-Prosperity Sphere" the oil, rubber, and other strategic materials that their crowded homeland lacked. As it was, Japan depended upon the United States for important supplies, including 80 percent of its fuel.

On September 27, 1940, the Tokyo government signed a Tripartite Pact with Germany and Italy, by which each pledged to declare war on any nation

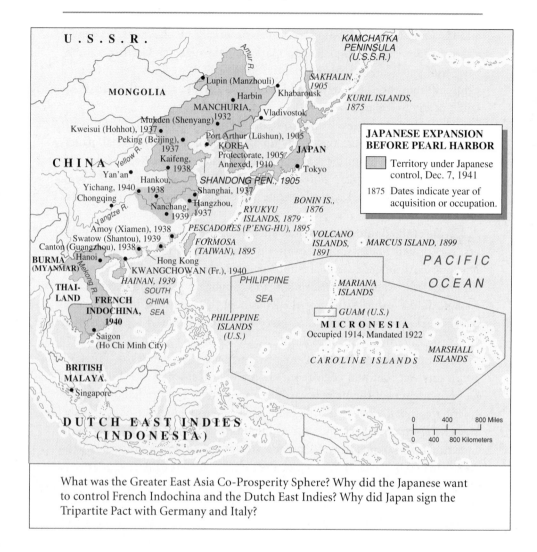

What was the Greater East Asia Co-Prosperity Sphere? Why did the Japanese want to control French Indochina and the Dutch East Indies? Why did Japan sign the Tripartite Pact with Germany and Italy?

that attacked any of them. On April 13, 1941, while the Nazis were sweeping through the Balkans, Japan signed a nonaggression pact with the Soviet Union, and once the Nazis invaded Russia in June, the Japanese were freed of any threat from the north.

In July 1941 Japan announced that it was creating a protectorate over all of French Indochina. Responding to this latest act of aggression, Roosevelt froze all Japanese assets in the United States, he restricted exports of oil to Japan, and he took the armed forces of the Philippines into the U.S. Army and put their commander, General Douglas MacArthur, in charge of all U.S. forces in the Far East. By September 1941 the oil restrictions had tightened into a complete embargo. Forced to secure oil supplies elsewhere, the Japanese army and navy began planning attacks on the Dutch and British colonies in Southeast Asia.

Actions by both sides put the United States and Japan on a collision course leading to war. In his regular talks with the Japanese ambassador, Secretary of State Cordell Hull insisted that Japanese withdrawal from French Indochina and China was the price of renewed trade with the United States. A more flexible position might have strengthened the moderates in Japan. Prime Minister Fumimaro Konoe, however, while known as a man of liberal principles who preferred peace, caved in to pressures from the militants. Perhaps he had no choice.

The Japanese warlords, for their part, seriously misjudged the United States. The desperate wish of the Americans to stay out of the war might still have enabled the Japanese to conquer the British and Dutch colonies in the Pacific. But the warlords decided that they dared not leave the U.S. Navy intact and the Philippines untouched on the flank of their new lifeline to the south.

TRAGEDY AT PEARL HARBOR   Thus a tragedy began to unfold with a fatal certainty, mostly out of sight of the American people, whose attention was focused on the Nazi submarine threat in the Atlantic. Late in August 1941 Prime Minister Konoe proposed a meeting with President Roosevelt. Secretary of State Hull urged the president not to meet unless agreement on fundamental issues could be reached in advance. On September 6 the Japanese government approved a surprise attack on Hawaii and gave Konoe six more weeks in which to reach a settlement.

The Japanese emperor's concern about the risk of an attack afforded the prime minister one last chance to pursue a compromise, but the presence of Japanese troops in China remained a stumbling block to any American agreement. In October, Konoe urged War Minister Hideki Tōjō to consider withdrawal of Japanese forces while saving face by keeping some troops in north China. Instead, the inflexible Tōjō forced Konoe to resign in October. Tōjō became prime minister the next day. The war party was now in complete control of the Japanese government.

By late November, Washington officials knew that war was imminent. Reports of Japanese troop transports moving south from Formosa prompted U.S. officials to send warnings to Pearl Harbor and Manila and to the British government. The massive Japanese movements southward clearly signaled attacks on the British and the Dutch. American leaders had every reason to expect war in the southwest Pacific, but none expected that Japan would

The Attack on Pearl Harbor

This view from an army airfield shows the destruction and confusion brought on by the surprise attack.

commit most of its aircraft carriers to another attack 5,000 miles away, at Pearl Harbor, the major American base in the Pacific.

On the morning of December 7, 1941, American Servicemen decoded the last part of a secret Japanese message breaking off the diplomatic negotiations in Washington. Tōjō instructed Japan's ambassador to deliver the message at 1 P.M. (7:30 A.M. in Honolulu), about a half hour before the attack was to begin, but delays held up delivery by more than an hour. The War Department sent out an alert at noon that something was about to happen, but the message, which went by commercial wire because radio contacts were broken, arrived in Hawaii eight and a half hours later. Even so, the decoded Japanese message did not mention Pearl Harbor specifically, and U.S. military leaders there would probably have assumed the attack was to come in Southeast Asia.

It was still a sleepy Sunday morning in Hawaii when the first Japanese planes roared down the west coast and the central valley of Oahu to begin their assault. For nearly two hours the Japanese planes kept up their fierce attack. Of the eight U.S. battleships in Pearl Harbor, three were sunk, and the others were badly battered. Altogether nineteen ships were sunk or disabled. At the airfields on the island, the Japanese destroyed about 180 planes. Before it was over, the raid had killed more than 2,400 American military personnel and civilians.

The surprise attack fulfilled the dreams of its planners, but it fell short of total success in two ways. The Japanese ignored oil-storage tanks in Hawaii, without which the surviving U.S. ships might have been forced back to the West Coast, and they missed the American aircraft carriers that had fortuitously left port a few days earlier. In the naval war to come, those aircraft carriers would be decisive.

Later that day (December 8 in the western Pacific), Japanese forces invaded the Philippines, Guam, Midway, Hong Kong, and the Malay Peninsula. With one stroke the Japanese had silenced America's debate on neutrality—a suddenly unified and vengeful nation resolutely prepared for the struggle.

The day after the attack on Pearl Harbor, President Roosevelt told Congress that December 7 was "a date which will live in infamy," and he asked for a declaration of war. It was approved with only one dissenting vote, by Representative Jeanette Rankin of Montana, a pacifist who was unable in good conscience to vote for war in 1917 or 1941. On December 11 Germany and Italy impetuously declared war on the United States. The separate wars in Asia and Europe had become one global conflict—and American isolationism was cast aside.

MAKING CONNECTIONS

- During the 1930s the United States tried to stake out a neutral position in the growing world conflict. Compare that effort with earlier American attempts at neutrality, from the Napoleonic Wars of Jefferson's administration onward.

- The American alliance with the Soviet Union described in this chapter proved to be temporary; after the war the Americans and the Soviets would be adversaries in a prolonged cold war, the beginnings of which are outlined in Chapter 31.

- The Japanese conquest of French Indochina would play an important role in the events leading to American involvement in that region, a topic discussed in Chapter 34.

FURTHER READING

The best overview of interwar diplomacy remains Selig Adler's *The Uncertain Giant, 1921–1941: American Foreign Policy between the Wars* (1965). Joan Hoff's *American Business and Foreign Policy, 1920–1933* (1971) highlights the efforts of Republican administrations during the 1920s to promote international commerce. Robert Dallek's *Franklin D. Roosevelt and American Foreign Policy, 1932–1945* (1979) provides a judicious assessment of Roosevelt's foreign policy during the 1930s.

A noteworthy study of America's entry into World War II is Waldo Heinrichs's *Threshold of War: Franklin D. Roosevelt and American Entry into World War II* (1988). See also David Reynolds's *From Munich to Pearl Harbor: Roosevelt's America and the Origins of the Second World War* (2001). Bruce M. Russett's *No Clear and Present Danger: A Skeptical View of the United States Entry into World War II* (1972) provides a critical account of American actions.

On Pearl Harbor, see Gordon W. Prange's *Pearl Harbor: The Verdict of History* (1986). Japan's perspective is described in Akira Iriye's *The Origins of the Second World War in Asia and the Pacific* (1987).

30

THE SECOND
WORLD WAR

FOCUS QUESTIONS

· What were the social and economic effects of World War II,
  especially in the West?

· How did the Allied forces win the war?

· What efforts did the Allies make to shape the postwar world?

To answer these questions and access additional review material, please visit
www.wwnorton.com/studyspace.

The Japanese attack on Pearl Harbor ended a period of uneasy
neutrality for the United States, and it plunged the nation
into a global conflict that would cost the lives of over 400,000
Americans. The war would also transform social and economic life, as well as
international affairs. The Second World War would become the most destructive and far-reaching conflict in history. It was so terrible in its intensity
and obscene in its cruelties that it altered the image of war itself. Devilish new
instruments of destruction were invented—plastic explosives, flame throwers, proximity fuses, rockets, jet airplanes, and atomic weapons—and systematic genocide emerged as an explicit war aim of the Nazis. Racist propaganda
flourished on both sides, and intense hatred of the enemy caused many military and civilian prisoners to be executed. The scorching passions of such a
total war blanched many moral scruples. Over 50 million deaths resulted
from the war, and the physical destruction was incalculable. Whole cities were
leveled, nations dismembered, and societies transformed. The world is still
coping with the consequences.

AMERICA'S EARLY BATTLES

SETBACKS IN THE PACIFIC   For months after Pearl Harbor, the news from the Pacific was "all bad," as President Roosevelt confessed. The Japanese captured a string of Allied outposts in the three months before the end of December, 1941: Guam, Wake Island, the Gilbert Islands, Hong Kong, Singapore, and Java. The Japanese capture of Rangoon, in Burma (Yangon in present-day Myanmar), in March 1942 cut off the Burma Road, the main supply route to China. By May the Japanese had ousted U.S. forces from the Philippines, and they controlled a new empire that stretched from Burma eastward through the Dutch East Indies and extended to Wake Island and the Gilbert Islands.

The Japanese might have consolidated an almost impregnable empire with the resources they had seized. But the Japanese navy succumbed to what one of its admirals later called victory disease: they decided to push farther into the South Pacific, isolate Australia, and strike again at Hawaii. Japanese planners hoped to destroy the American navy before the productive power of the United States could be brought to bear on the war effort.

Early Defeats

U.S. prisoners of war, captured by the Japanese in the Philippines, 1942.

CORAL SEA AND MIDWAY American forces finally halted the Japanese advance toward Australia in two decisive naval clashes. The Battle of the Coral Sea (May 7–8, 1942) stopped a fleet convoying Japanese troop transports toward New Guinea. Planes from the *Lexington* and the *Yorktown* sank one Japanese aircraft carrier, damaged another, and destroyed smaller ships. American losses were greater, but the Japanese designs on Australia were thwarted.

Less than a month after the Coral Sea conflict, Admiral Isoroku Yamamoto, the Japanese naval commander, led his fleet toward Midway Island, from which he hoped to render Pearl Harbor helpless. This time it was the Japanese who were the victims of surprise. American cryptanalysts had by then broken the Japanese naval code, and Admiral Chester Nimitz, commander of the central Pacific, knew their plan of attack. He reinforced Midway with planes and the carriers *Enterprise, Hornet,* and *Yorktown.*

The first Japanese foray against Midway, on June 4, 1942, severely damaged the American installations on the island, but at the cost of about one third of the Japanese planes. Meanwhile, American torpedo planes and dive bombers caught three of the four Japanese carriers in the process of servicing their planes. The decks of the Japanese ships were cluttered with bombs, gasoline, and planes. Dive bombers sank three of them during the first assault. Later the Japanese lost another carrier, but not before its planes had disabled the *Yorktown.* The only other major American loss was a destroyer. The Japanese defeat at Midway was the turning point of the Pacific war. It demonstrated that aircraft carriers, not battleships, would decide the naval conflict.

SETBACKS IN THE ATLANTIC   Early Allied setbacks in the Pacific were matched by losses in the Atlantic. Since the blitzkrieg of 1940, German submarine "wolf packs" had wreaked havoc in the North Atlantic. In 1942, German U-boats appeared off American shores and began to attack coastal ships, most of them tankers. Nearly 400 ships were lost in American waters before effective countermeasures brought the problem under control. The naval command hastened the building of small escort vessels, meanwhile pressing into patrol service all kinds of surface craft and planes, some of them civilian. During the second half of 1942, these efforts sharply reduced American losses.

MOBILIZATION AT HOME

The attack on Pearl Harbor ended not only the long public debate on isolation and intervention but also the long economic depression that had ravaged the country during the 1930s. The war effort required all of America's immense productive capacity and full employment of the workforce. For 1942 alone the government ordered 60,000 planes, 45,000 tanks, and 8 million tons of merchant shipping. The next year's goals were even higher. Mobilization was in fact already further along than preparedness had been in 1916–1917. The draft had been in effect for more than a year, and the army had grown to more than 1.4 million men by July 1941. Congress quickly extended the term of military service to last until six months after the war's end. Men between the ages of eighteen and forty-five were now subject to conscription. Altogether more than 15 million American men and women would serve in the armed forces during the war. The average soldier or sailor was twenty-six years old, stood five feet eight inches, and weighed 144 pounds, an inch taller and eight pounds heavier than the average recruit in World War I. Less than half the servicemen had finished high school.

ECONOMIC CONVERSION   The economy, too, was already partially mobilized for war, by lend-lease and the defense buildup. Congress had authorized the president to reshuffle government agencies and to allot materials and facilities as needed for defense, with penalties for any agency that failed to comply. The War Production Board, created in 1942, directed the conversion of manufacturing to war production. The Office of Scientific Research and Development mobilized thousands of scientists to design the many technologies and devices that contributed to the war effort, which would include radar, sonar, the proximity fuse, and the bazooka.

The pressure of wartime needs and the stimulus of government spending more than doubled the gross national product between 1940 and 1945. Government expenditures during the war years soared. The total was about 10 times what America spent in World War I and 100 times the expenditures during the Civil War. The massive infusion of government capital into the economy also encouraged greater centralization and consolidation in private industry. Larger companies tended to win the most government contracts, and the more they won, the larger they became. Conversely, those without government contracts withered and died. In 1942 alone 300,000 businesses shut down.

America's basic economic problem during the war years was no longer creating jobs but finding workers for the booming shipyards, aircraft factories, and munitions plants. Millions of people who had lived on the margins of the economic system, especially women, were now brought fully into the workforce. Pockets of stubborn poverty did not disappear, but for most civilians the war spelled neither severe hardship nor suffering but a better life than ever before, despite shortages and rationing of consumer goods. Labor unions benefited directly from the dramatic growth of the civilian workforce. Union membership increased significantly during the war years, from about 11 million to 15 million.

ECONOMIC CONTROLS   Increased family income and government spending during the war raised fears of inflation. Some of the available money went into taxes and war bonds, but even so, more purchasing power was sent chasing scarce consumer goods just as industrial production was converting to war needs. Consumer durables such as cars, washing machines, and nondefense housing in fact ceased to be produced at all. In the face of such wartime shortages, only strict restraints would keep prices from soaring out of sight. In 1941 Roosevelt created the Office of Price Administration, and the following year Congress authorized it to set price ceilings. With prices frozen, basic consumer goods had to be allocated through rationing, which began with tires and was gradually extended to other scarce items such as sugar, coffee, meat, and gasoline.

At first, however, wages and farm prices were not tightened, and this complicated matters. War prosperity offered farmers a chance to recover from two decades of distress, and farm-state legislators raised both floors and ceilings on farm prices. Higher food prices reinforced workers' demands for higher wages. To relieve this inflationary pressure, the president won new authority to control wages and farm prices. Businesses and workers chafed at the new controls, and on occasion the government was forced to seize industries threatened by strikes. The coal mines and railroads were nationalized for a short time in 1943. Despite these problems the government's program to stabilize the war economy succeeded. By the end of the war, consumer prices had risen by only about 31 percent, a far better record than the World War I rise of 62 percent.

To make the economic controls work, the government launched a program to encourage conservation of resources. As one popular slogan had it, "Use it up, wear it out, make it do or do without." People collected scrap metal and grew their own food in backyard "victory gardens." In 1942, when the war plants faced a rubber shortage, President Roosevelt asked citizens to turn in "old tires, old rubber raincoats, old garden hoses, rubber shoes, bathing caps, gloves—whatever you have that is made of rubber."

DOMESTIC CONSERVATISM   Despite the government's efforts to encourage sacrifices for the war effort, Americans expressed their discontent with price controls, labor shortages, rationing, and a hundred other petty vexations. They manifested those concerns in a reaction against Roosevelt liberalism at the polls that indicated a growing political conservatism. In 1942 the congressional elections registered a national swing against the New Deal. Republicans gained forty-six seats in the House and nine in the Senate, chiefly in the farm areas of the midwestern states. Democratic losses outside the South strengthened the southern delegation's position within the party, and the delegation itself reflected conservative victories in southern primaries. A coalition of conservatives dismantled "nonessential" New Deal agencies, including the National Youth Adminstration, the Civilian Conservation Corps, and the Farm Security Administration.

Organized labor, despite substantial gains during the war, felt the impact of the conservative trend. In the spring of 1943, when John L. Lewis led the coal miners out on strike, Congress passed the Smith-Connally War Labor Disputes Act, which authorized the government to seize plants useful to the war effort. In 1943 a dozen states adopted laws restricting picketing and other union activities, and in 1944 Arkansas and Florida set in motion a wave of "right-to-work" legislation that outlawed the closed shop (requiring that all employees be union members).

SOCIAL EFFECTS OF THE WAR

MOBILIZATION AND THE DEVELOPMENT OF THE WEST   The dramatic expansion of defense production after 1940 and the mobilization of millions of people in the armed forces accelerated economic development and a population boom in the western states. Nearly 8 million people moved into the states west of the Mississippi River between 1940 and 1950. The Far West experienced the fastest rate of urban growth in the country. Small cities such as Phoenix and Albuquerque mushroomed while Seattle, San Francisco, Los Angeles, and San Diego witnessed dizzying growth. San Diego's population, for example, increased by 147 percent between 1941 and 1945. The migration of workers to new defense jobs in the West had significant demographic effects. Communities with few African Americans witnessed an influx of blacks. Lured by news of job openings and higher wages, African Americans from Texas, Oklahoma, Arkansas, and Louisiana headed west. During the war years, Seattle's African-American population jumped from 4,000 to 40,000, Portland's from 2,000 to 15,000.

CHANGING ROLES FOR WOMEN   The war marked an important watershed in the changing status of women. With millions of men going into military service, the demand for labor shook up old prejudices about sex roles in the workplace—and in the military. Nearly 200,000 women served in the Women's Army Corps (WAC) and the navy's equivalent, Women Accepted for Volunteer Emergency Services (WAVES). Lesser numbers joined the Marine Corps, the Coast Guard, and the Army Air Force.

Over 6 million women entered the workforce during the war, an increase of more than 50 percent and in manufacturing alone an increase of some 110 percent. By 1944 over one third of all American women were in the labor force. Old barriers fell overnight as women became toolmakers, machinists, riveters, crane operators, lumberjacks, stevedores, blacksmiths, and railroad workers. Desperate for laborers, the government launched an intense publicity campaign to draw women into traditional male jobs. "Rosie the Riveter," a beautiful model dressed in overalls, served as the cover girl for the recruiting campaign.

One striking feature of the wartime economy was the larger proportion of older, married women in the workforce. In 1940 about 15 percent of married women were employed outside the home; by 1945, 24 percent were. In the workforce as a whole, married women for the first time outnumbered single women. Many women were

Women in the Military

This navy recruiting poster urged women to join the WAVES (Women Accepted for Volunteer Emergency Service).

eager to get away from the grinding routine of domestic life. One female welder remembered that her wartime job "was the first time I had a chance to get out of the kitchen and work in industry and make a few bucks. This was something I had never dreamed would happen." And it was something that many women did not want to relinquish after the war.

AFRICAN AMERICANS IN WORLD WAR II   The most volatile issue ignited by the war was African-American participation in the defense effort. From the start black leaders demanded equality in the armed forces and defense industries. Eventually about 1 million African Americans served in the armed forces, but most were assigned to segregated units. The most important departure from this pattern came with a 1940 decision to integrate officer-candidate schools, except those for air force cadets. A separate military flight school at Tuskegee, Alabama, trained about 600 African-American pilots, many of whom distinguished themselves in combat.

War industries were even less hospitable to integration. "We will not employ Negroes," said the president of North American Aviation. In 1941 A. Philip Randolph, the brilliant head of the Brotherhood of Sleeping Car Porters, organized a March on Washington movement to demand an end to racial discrimination in defense industries. The Roosevelt administration, alarmed at the prospect of a mass descent on the capital, struck a bargain. Randolph called off the march in return for an executive order prohibiting racial discrimination in companies that received federal defense contracts.

African-American leaders quickly broadened their drive for wartime participation into a more inclusive and open challenge to all kinds of discrimination, including racial segregation itself. Membership in the NAACP soared during the war, from 50,000 to 450,000. African Americans could look forward to greater political participation after the Supreme Court, in *Smith v. Allwright* (1944), struck down Texas's whites-only primary on the grounds that Democratic primaries were part of the election process and thus subject to the Fifteenth Amendment.

LATINOS IN THE LABOR FORCE   As rural folk moved to the western cities, many farm counties across the nation experienced a labor shortage. In an ironic about-face, local and federal government authorities who before

Tuskegee Airmen, 1942

One of the last segregated military training schools, the flight school at Tuskegee trained African-American men for combat during World War II.

the war had forced undocumented Mexican laborers back across the border now recruited them to harvest crops. Before it would assist in providing the needed workers, the Mexican government insisted that the United States ensure minimum working and living conditions. The result was the creation of the bracero program in 1942. Mexico agreed to provide seasonal farmworkers in exchange for a promise by the U.S. government not to draft them into military service. The workers were hired on year-long contracts, and American officials provided transportation from the border to their job sites. Under the bracero program some 200,000 Mexican farmworkers entered the western United States. At least that many more crossed the border as undocumented workers.

The rising tide of Mexican Americans in Los Angeles provoked a growing stream of anti-Latino editorials and incidents. Even though Mexican Americans fought in the war with great valor, earning seventeen Congressional Medals of Honor, there was constant conflict between servicemen and Mexican-American gang members and teenage "zoot-suiters" in southern California. In 1943 several thousand off-duty sailors and soldiers, joined by hundreds of local white civilians, rampaged through downtown Los Angeles streets, assaulting Latinos, African Americans, and Filipinos. The violence lasted a week and came to be labeled the zoot-suit riots. (Zoot suits were the flamboyant suits popular in the 1940s and worn by some young Mexican-American men.)

NATIVE AMERICANS AND THE WAR EFFORT   Indians supported the war effort more fully than any other group in American society. Almost one third of eligible Native American men, over 25,000 people, served in the armed forces. Another one fourth worked in defense-related industries. Thousands of Indian women volunteered as nurses or joined the WAVES. As was the case with African Americans, Indians benefited from the experiences afforded by the war. Those who left reservations to work in defense plants or to join the military gained new vocational skills as well as a greater awareness of opportunities available in the larger American society.

Why did so many Native Americans fight in such high numbers for a nation that had stripped them of their land and decimated their heritage? Some felt that they had no choice. Mobilization for the war effort ended many New Deal programs that had provided Indians with jobs. Reservation Indians thus faced the necessity of finding new jobs elsewhere. Others viewed the Nazis and the Japanese warlords as threats to their own homeland. The most common sentiment animating Indian involvement in the war effort, however, seems to have been a genuine sense of patriotism.

Whatever the reasons, Indians distinguished themselves in the military. Unlike their African-American counterparts, Indian servicemen were integrated into regular units. Perhaps the most distinctive activity performed by Indians was their service as "code talkers": every military branch used Indians to encode and decipher messages using their native languages.

INTERNMENT OF JAPANESE AMERICANS   The record on civil liberties during World War II was on the whole better than that during World War I, if only because there was virtually no domestic opposition to the war effort after the attack on Pearl Harbor. Neither German Americans nor Italian Americans faced the harassments meted out to their counterparts in the previous war; few had much sympathy for Hitler or Mussolini. The shameful exception to an otherwise improved record was the treatment accorded to Americans of Japanese descent in the months following the attack on Pearl Harbor. One California barbershop offered "free shaves for Japs" but noted that it was "not responsible for accidents." Others were even blunter. Idaho's governor declared: "A good solution to the Jap problem would be to send them all back to Japan, then sink the island. They live like rats, breed like rats, and act like rats." Such attitudes were widespread, and the government finally succumbed to demands that it force all Japanese, citizens or not, into "war relocation camps" in the interior.

Caught up in the war hysteria and racial prejudice unleashed by the attack on Pearl Harbor, President Roosevelt initiated the removal and confinement of Japanese Americans when he issued Executive Order 9066 on February 19, 1942. More than 60 percent of the internees were U.S. citizens; one third were under the age of nineteen. More than 100,000 people were eventually removed from their homes and businesses. Forced to sell their farms and businesses at great losses, the internees lost both their liberty and their property. Not until 1983 did the government acknowledge the injustice of the internment policy. Five years later Congress voted to give $20,000 and an apology to each of the 60,000 former internees who were still living.

THE ALLIED DRIVE TOWARD BERLIN

In mid-1942 the "home front" had begun to get news from the war fronts that some of the lines were holding at last. By midyear a fleet of American air and sea subchasers was suppressing German U-boats off the Atlantic coast. This event was all the more important because Allied war plans called for the defeat of Germany first.

WAR AIMS AND STRATEGY   There were good reasons for giving top priority to defeating Hitler: Nazi forces in western Europe and the Atlantic posed a more direct threat to the Western Hemisphere than did Japan, and Germany's war potential exceeded Japan's. Yet Japanese attacks involved Americans directly in the Pacific war from the start, and as a consequence more Americans went to the Pacific than crossed the Atlantic during the first year of fighting.

The Pearl Harbor attack brought British prime minister Winston Churchill to Washington, D.C. for talks about a common war plan. Thus began a successful but not always harmonious wartime alliance between the United States and Great Britain. The meetings in Washington in 1942 affirmed the priority of winning the war against Germany. Agreement on war aims did not bring agreement on strategy, however. When Roosevelt and Churchill met at the White House a second time in 1942, they could not agree on the location of the first attack against the Nazis. American strategists wanted to strike German-held France directly across the English Channel before the end of 1942. With vivid memories of the last war, the British feared a mass bloodletting in trench warfare if they struck prematurely. The Soviets, bearing the brunt of the German attack in the east, insisted that the Western Allies must do something to relieve the pressure along the Russian front. Finally, the Americans accepted Churchill's proposal to invade French North Africa, now allied with Germany .

THE NORTH AFRICAN CAMPAIGN   On November 8, 1942, British and American units commanded by General Dwight D. Eisenhower landed in Morocco and Algeria. Completely surprised, French forces under the Vichy government (which collaborated with the Germans) had little will to resist. Farther east, British forces were pushing German armies back across Libya. Before spring the Germans were caught in a gigantic pair of pincers. By April the British had linked up with American forces. Hammered from all sides and unable to retreat across the Mediterranean, an army of more than 200,000 Germans surrendered on May 12, 1943, leaving all of North Africa in Allied hands.

While the Battle of Tunisia was still unfolding, Roosevelt and Churchill met at Casablanca, Morocco. Stalin declined to leave beleaguered Russia for the meeting but continued to press for the opening of a second front in western Europe. Since the German invasion of Russia in 1941, over 90 percent of German military casualties had occurred on the Russian front. The British and American engagements with German forces in North Africa were minuscule in comparison with the scope and fury of the fighting in Russia.

Churchill and Roosevelt spent eight days at Casablanca, hammering out key strategic decisions. The Americans wanted to launch a massive Allied invasion of German-occupied France as soon as possible, but the British still insisted that such a major assault was premature. They convinced the Americans that they should follow up a victory in North Africa with an assault on Sicily and Italy. Roosevelt and Churchill also decided to step up the bombing of Germany and to increase shipments of military supplies to the Soviet Union and the Nationalist Chinese forces fighting the Japanese.

Before leaving Casablanca, Roosevelt announced, with Churchill's endorsement, that the war would end only with the "unconditional surrender" of all enemies. This demand was designed to reassure Stalin that the Western Allies would not negotiate separately with the Germans. The West desperately needed Soviet cooperation in defeating Germany, and Roosevelt and Churchill were eager to reassure Stalin of their good intentions.

THE BATTLE OF THE ATLANTIC While fighting raged in North Africa, the more crucial Battle of the Atlantic reached its climax on the high seas. Several factors contributed to the success of the Allied effort. Scientists had perfected a variety of detection devices: radar, which the British had already used to advantage in the Battle of Britain, bounced radio waves off objects and registered their position on a screen; sonar detected sound waves from submerged U-boats; sonobuoys, dropped from planes, radioed back their findings; and advanced magnetic equipment enabled aircraft to detect objects underwater.

By early 1943 in the western portion of the North Atlantic, there were at any given time an average of 31 convoys with 145 escorts and 673 merchant ships, as well as a number of heavily escorted troopships. None of the troopships going to Britain or the Mediterranean was lost. The U-boats kept up the Battle of the Atlantic until the war's end, but their commander later admitted that the battle had been lost by the end of May 1943. He credited the difference largely to radar. What he did not know then was that the Allies had a secret weapon: by early 1943 their cryptanalysts were routinely decoding secret messages and telling their subhunters where to look for German U-boats.

SICILY AND ITALY On July 10, 1943, after the Allied victory in the North African campaign, about 250,000 British and American troops landed on Sicily, scoring a complete surprise. The German-Italian collapse in Sicily ended Mussolini's twenty years of Fascist rule. On July 25, 1943, Italy's king notified the dictator of his dismissal as prime minister. A new regime startled the Allies when it offered not only to surrender but also to switch sides in the war. Unfortunately, mutual suspicions prolonged talks until September 3, while the Germans poured reinforcements into Italy. In the confusion the Italian army disintegrated, although most of the navy escaped to Allied ports. A few army units later joined the Allied effort. Mussolini, plucked from imprisonment by a daring German airborne raid, became head of a puppet government in northern Italy.

Therefore the Allied assault on the Italian mainland did not turn into an easy victory. The main landing at Salerno on September 9 encountered heavy German resistance. The Americans, joined by British troops, nevertheless secured beachheads within a week and captured Naples. After a five-month siege of Rome, the Americans finally took the fabled city on June 4, 1944. Yet they enjoyed only a brief moment of glory, for the long-awaited cross-Channel landing in France, begun two days later, quickly became the focus of attention.

THE STRATEGIC BOMBING OF EUROPE   Behind the long-postponed landings on the Normandy beaches lay months of preparation. While waiting, the U.S. Army Air Force and the Royal Air Force (RAF) had attacked Hitler's "Fortress Europe." By 1943 American strategic bombers were full-fledged partners of the RAF in the effort to pound Germany into submission. Yet despite the widespread damage it caused, the strategic air offensive ultimately failed to dismantle German production or, as later studies found, break civilian morale. By the end of 1943, however, new jettisonable gas tanks permitted Allied escort fighters to fly as far as Berlin and back, protecting the bomber groups. Thereafter, heavy losses of both planes and pilots forced the German Luftwaffe to conserve its strength and cease challenging every Allied mission.

With air supremacy assured, the Allies were free to concentrate on their primary urban and industrial targets and, when the time came, to provide cover for the Normandy landings. On April 14, 1944, General Eisenhower assumed control of the Strategic Air Forces for the invasion of German-controlled France. On D-day, June 6, 1944, he told the troops, "If you see fighting aircraft over you, they will be ours."

THE TEHRAN MEETING   Late in November 1943 Churchill and Roosevelt had met with Stalin in Tehran, Iran, to coordinate plans for the invasion of France and a Soviet offensive from the east. After Churchill and Roosevelt assured Stalin that a cross-Channel invasion was finally coming, the Soviet premier in return promised to enter the war against Japan after Germany's defeat. The Allied leaders also agreed to begin plans for a new international

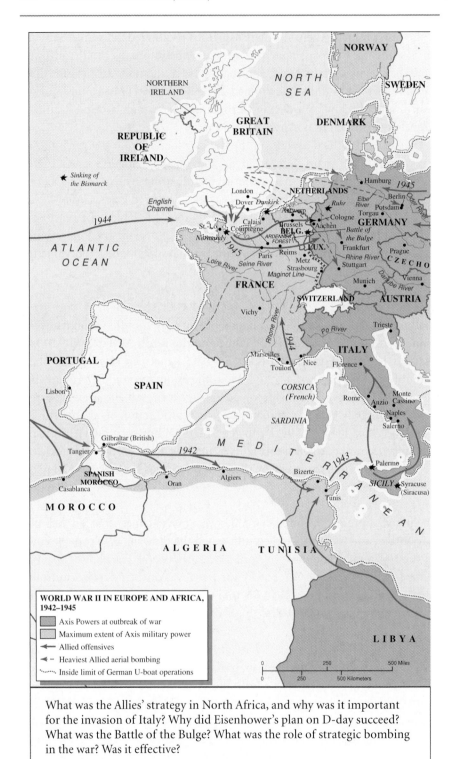

WORLD WAR II IN EUROPE AND AFRICA, 1942–1945

- Axis Powers at outbreak of war
- Maximum extent of Axis military power
- Allied offensives
- Heaviest Allied aerial bombing
- Inside limit of German U-boat operations

What was the Allies' strategy in North Africa, and why was it important for the invasion of Italy? Why did Eisenhower's plan on D-day succeed? What was the Battle of the Bulge? What was the role of strategic bombing in the war? Was it effective?

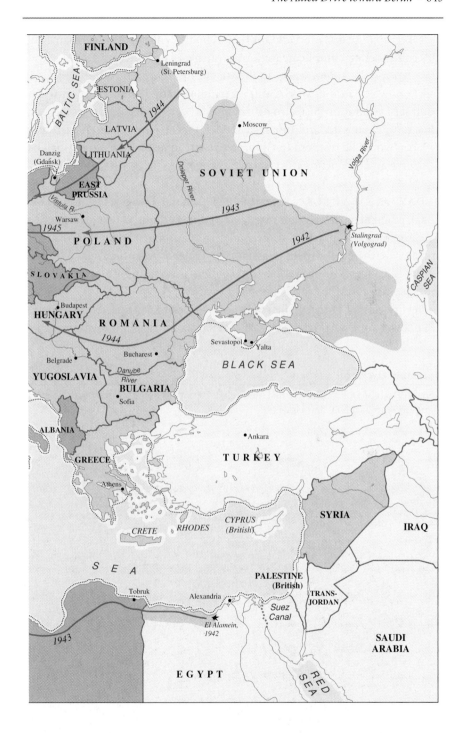

peacekeeping organization and for the occupation of postwar Germany. Politics continued to complicate military strategy.

Earlier in November, while on the way to the Tehran meeting, Churchill, and Roosevelt had met with China's general Chiang Kai-shek in Cairo. The resulting Declaration of Cairo affirmed that war against Japan would continue until Japan's unconditional surrender, that all Chinese territories taken by Japan would be restored to China, and that "in due course Korea shall become free and independent."

D-DAY AND AFTER   In early 1944 General Dwight D. Eisenhower, smart, efficient, and well organized, arrived in London to take command at the Supreme Headquarters of the Allied Expeditionary Force (SHAEF) and prepare for the cross-Channel assault on Hitler's "Atlantic Wall." Within a few months over 1 million American soldiers were training along England's southern coast for the cross-Channel invasion.

The invasion of France, called Operation Overlord, surprised the Germans. Eisenhower fooled Hitler's generals into believing that the invasion would

Operation Overlord

General Dwight D. Eisenhower instructing paratroopers before they board their airplanes to launch the D-day assault.

come at Pas de Calais, on the French-Belgian border. Instead, the landings occurred in Normandy, about 200 miles south. Airborne forces dropped behind the beaches during the night while planes and battleships pounded the coastal defenses.

At dawn on June 6, 1944, D-day, the invasion fleet of some 4,000 ships carrying and 150,000 men (57,000 Americans) filled the horizon off the Normandy coast. Overhead, thousands of Allied planes supported the invasion force. Sleepy German soldiers awoke to see the vast armada arrayed before them. Despite Eisenhower's meticulous planning and the imposing array of Allied troops and firepower, the D-day invasion almost failed. Cloud cover and German anti-aircraft fire caused many of the paratroopers and glider pilots to miss their landing zones. Oceangoing landing craft delivered their troops to the wrong locations. Low clouds led the Allied planes to drop their bombs too far inland. The naval bombardment was equally ineffective. In addition, rough seas made many soldiers seasick and capsized dozens of landing craft.

The Landing at Normandy

D-day, June 6, 1944. Before they could huddle under a seawall and begin to root out the region's Nazi defenders, soldiers on Omaha Beach had to cross a fifty-yard stretch that exposed them to bullets fired from machine guns housed in concrete pillboxes.

Over 1,000 men drowned. Waterlogged radios failed to work, and the deafening noise of the artillery and gunfire made oral communication impossible.

On Utah Beach the American troops made it in against relatively light opposition, but farther east, on a four-mile segment designated Omaha Beach, bombardment failed to take out the German defenders, and the Americans were caught in heavily mined water. In just ten minutes 197 of the 205 men in one rifle company were killed or wounded. By nightfall the bodies of some 5,000 killed or wounded Allied soldiers were strewn across Normandy's beaches. German losses were even heavier. Entire units were decimated or captured. Operation Overlord was the greatest military invasion in the annals of warfare and the climactic battle of World War II. With the beachhead secured, the Allied leaders knew that victory was now in their grasp.

Within two weeks after D-day, the Allies had landed 1 million troops, 556,000 tons of supplies, and 170,000 vehicles. They had seized a beachhead sixty miles wide and five to fifteen miles deep. They continued to pour men and supplies onto the beaches and to edge inland through the marshes and hedgerows. A stubborn Hitler issued disastrous orders to contest every inch of land. Field Marshal Erwin Rommel, convinced that all was lost, began to intrigue for a separate peace. Other like-minded German officers, sure that the war was hopeless, tried to kill Hitler at his headquarters on July 20, 1944, but the Führer survived the bomb blast, and hundreds of conspirators and suspects were tortured to death. General Rommel was granted the option of suicide, which he took.

Meanwhile, Hitler's tactics brought calamity to the German forces in western France. On July 25 American units broke out westward into Brittany and eastward toward Paris. On August 15 a joint American-French invasion force landed on the French Mediterranean coast and raced up the Rhône Valley. German resistance in France collapsed. A division of the Free French resistance, aided by American forces, had the honor of liberating Paris on August 25. Hitler's forces retreated toward the German border, and by mid-September most of France and Belgium were cleared of enemy troops.

LEAPFROGGING TO TOKYO

Even in the Pacific, relegated to a lower priority, Allied forces had brought the war within reach of the enemy's homeland by the end of 1944. The war's first American offensive, in fact, had been in the southwest Pacific. There the Japanese, stopped at Coral Sea and Midway, had thrust into the southern Solomon Islands and were building an airstrip on Guadalcanal, from which they would be able to attack Allied transportation routes to Australia. On August 7, 1942, two months before the North Africa landings, the First Marine Division landed on Guadalcanal and seized the airstrip.

MACARTHUR IN NEW GUINEA   Meanwhile, American and Australian forces under General Douglas MacArthur had begun to push the Japanese out of their positions on New Guinea's northern coast. These costly battles, fought through some of the hottest, most humid, and most mosquito-infested swamps in the world, secured the eastern tip of New Guinea by the end of January 1943.

At this stage, American war planners were confronted with two propositions by the leaders of rival branches of the armed service, the army and the navy. The vainglorious MacArthur, sometimes accused of being a legend in his own mind, proposed to move his forces westward along the northern coast of New Guinea toward the Philippines and ultimately to Tokyo. Naval admiral Chester Nimitz argued for a sweep through the islands of the central Pacific to Formosa and China. The combined chiefs of staff agreed to pursue both plans.

During the Battle of the Bismarck Sea (March 2–3, 1943), American bombers sank eight Japanese troopships and ten warships carrying reinforcements. Thereafter the Japanese dared not risk sending transports to reinforce points under siege, making it possible for the Allies to use the tactic of neutralizing Japanese strongholds with air and sea power and moving on, leaving them to die on the vine. Some called it leapfrogging or island-hopping, and it was a major factor contributing to the Allied victory. By the end of 1943, MacArthur's forces controlled the northern coast of New Guinea.

NIMITZ IN THE CENTRAL PACIFIC   Admiral Nimitz's advance through the central Pacific had as its first target Tarawa in the Gilbert Islands. Tarawa was one of the most heavily protected islands in the Pacific. In a pitched battle nearly 1,000 U.S. soldiers, sailors, and marines lost their lives rooting out 4,000 Japanese soldiers who refused to surrender. The Gilbert Islands provided airfields from which the Seventh Air Force began softening up strong points in the Marshall Islands to the northwest. Japanese planes completely abandoned the region.

In the Battle of the Philippine Sea, fought mostly in the air on June 19–20, 1944, the Japanese lost 3 more carriers, 2 submarines, and over 300 planes, at a cost of only 17 U.S. planes. The battle secured the Mariana Islands, and soon large B-29 bombers were winging their way to the first systematic bombing of the Japanese homeland. Defeat in the Marianas convinced General Tōjō that the war was lost. On July 18, 1944, he and his entire cabinet resigned.

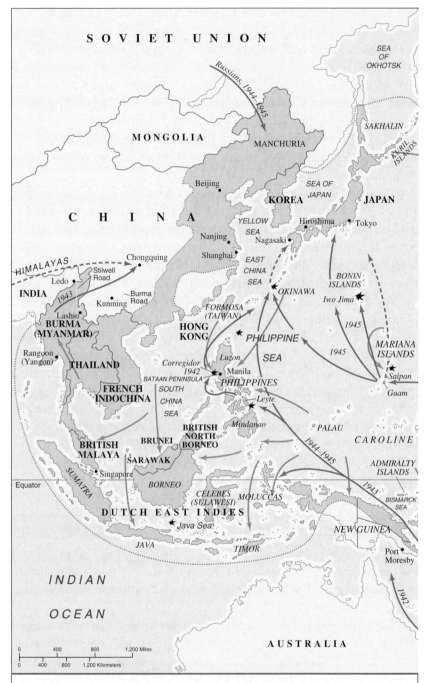

What was "leapfrogging"? Why were the battles in the Marianas a major turn-
ing point in the war? What was the significance of the Battle of Leyte Gulf?
How did the battle at Okinawa affect how both sides proceeded in the war?
Why did Truman decide to drop atomic bombs on Hiroshima and Nagasaki?

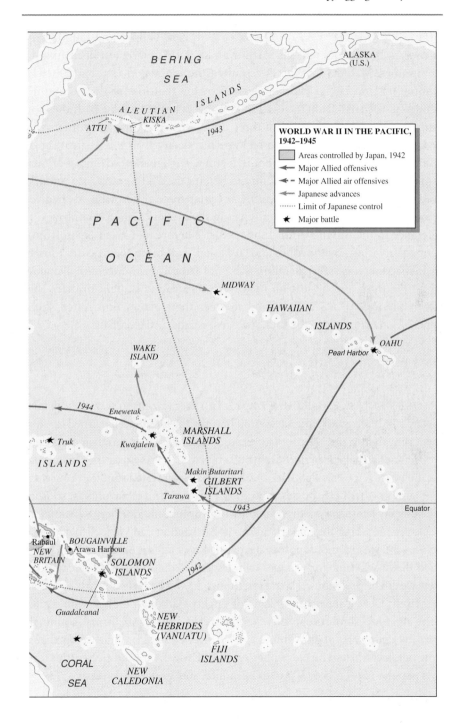

BERING SEA

ALASKA (U.S.)

ISLANDS

ALEUTIAN
KISKA
ATTU
1943

PACIFIC OCEAN

MIDWAY

HAWAIIAN
ISLANDS

WAKE ISLAND

OAHU
Pearl Harbor

1944
Enewetak

Truk
Kwajalein
MARSHALL ISLANDS

ISLANDS

Makin Butaritari
GILBERT ISLANDS
Tarawa
1943
Equator

Rabaul
NEW BRITAIN
BOUGAINVILLE
Arawa Harbour
SOLOMON ISLANDS
1942

Guadalcanal
NEW HEBRIDES (VANUATU)

FIJI ISLANDS

CORAL SEA
NEW CALEDONIA

WORLD WAR II IN THE PACIFIC, 1942–1945

Areas controlled by Japan, 1942
Major Allied offensives
Major Allied air offensives
Japanese advances
Limit of Japanese control
Major battle

THE BATTLE OF LEYTE GULF   With New Guinea and the Mariana Islands all but conquered, MacArthur and Nimitz focused on liberating the Philippines. MacArthur's forces assaulted the islands on October 20, 1944, landing first on Leyte. The Japanese, knowing that loss of the Philippines would cut them off from the essential resources of the Dutch East Indies (Indonesia), brought in fleets from three directions. The three encounters that resulted on October 25 came to be known collectively as the Battle of Leyte Gulf, the largest naval engagement in history. The Japanese lost most of their remaining sea power and the ability to defend the Philippines. Also remarkable was the first use of suicide attacks by Japanese pilots, who crash-dived into American ships, killing themselves in the process. Called "kamikazes" (a reference to the "divine wind" that centuries before had saved Japan from a Mongol invasion) by the Allies and "tokkotai" (meaning special attack force) by the Japanese, most of the pilots were not fanatical volunteers. The majority of the thousand or so who died were very young student draftees (between the ages of 17–24) ordered to steer their planes into Allied ships. Whatever their motives, the tokkotai caused substantial damage.

A New Age Is Born

ROOSEVELT'S FOURTH TERM   In 1944, war or no war, the calendar dictated another presidential election. This time the Republicans turned to a former crime fighter and New York governor, Thomas E. Dewey, as their candidate. No Democrat challenged Roosevelt, but a fight did develop over the second spot on the ticket. Vice President Henry Wallace had aggravated southern conservatives and northern city bosses, who feared his ties with labor unions, so Roosevelt finally chose the relatively unknown Missouri senator Harry S. Truman.

Dewey ran under the same handicap as Alf Landon and Wendell Willkie had before him. He did not propose to dismantle Roosevelt's programs; rather, he argued that it was time for younger men to replace the "tired" old leaders of the New Deal. The problem was that even though he was considerably younger than Roosevelt, Dewey showed few signs of vitality. Although blessed with a silky voice and a stylish wardrobe, he was ill at ease in public, stiff, formal, seemingly arrogant, and worst of all—dull. Roosevelt showed signs of illness and exhaustion, but nevertheless, on November 7, 1945, he was once again elected, this time by a popular vote of 25.6 million to 22 million and an electoral vote of 432 to 99.

CONVERGING MILITARY FRONTS   Meanwhile, Allied forces were mired in war in Europe; complete victory remained elusive. After the quick sweep across France, the Allies lost momentum in the fall of 1944 and settled down to slugging it out along the border of Germany. The armies would fight along this line all winter, but first, on December 16, 1944, the Germans sprang a surprise in the rugged Ardennes Forest, where the Allied line was thinnest. The Nazis advanced along a fifty-mile bulge in the Allied lines in Belgium and Luxembourg (hence the name the Battle of the Bulge) before they stalled at Bastogne. Reinforced by the Allies just before it was surrounded, Bastogne held out for six days against relentless attacks. The American situation remained desperate until December 23, when the weather improved, allowing Allied air power to drop supplies and attack the Germans. On December 26, the besieged American army at Bastogne was relieved.

Germany's sudden counterattack upset Eisenhower's timetable and made continued coordination with the Soviet army even more crucial. The Nazis poured resources into the battle at Bastogne but were unable to hold the eastern front when in January 1945 the Soviets began their final offensive. The destruction of Hitler's last reserve units at the Battle of the Bulge also left open the door to Germany's heartland. The western offensives began in February, and by early March Allied forces were crossing the Rhine River into Germany. By that time the Soviet offensive on the eastern front had also reached the German border.

YALTA AND THE POSTWAR WORLD   As the final offensives against Germany got under way, the Big Three leaders met again, in early February 1945 at Yalta, a resort in southern Russia. While the focus at Tehran in 1943 had been on wartime strategy, the leaders now discussed the shape of the postwar world. Stalin was self-confident, demanding, and sarcastic. He knew that the Soviet forces' control of key areas would ensure that his demands would be met. Two aims loomed large in Roosevelt's thinking. One was the need to ensure that the Soviet Union would join the war against Japan. The other was based upon the lessons he had drawn from the previous world war. Chief among the mistakes to be remedied were the failures of the United States to join the League of Nations and of the Allies to maintain a united front in negotiations with the German aggressors after the war.

The Yalta meeting thus began by calling for a conference to create a new world organization, called the United Nations. The conferees also decided that substantive decisions in the new organization's Security Council would require the agreement of its five permanent members: the United States, Britain, the Soviet Union, France, and China.

GERMANY AND EASTERN EUROPE   With Hitler's Reich stumbling to its doom, the leaders at Yalta had to make arrangements for the postwar governance of Germany. The war map dictated the basic pattern of occupation

The Yalta Conference

Churchill, Roosevelt, and Stalin confer on the shape of the postwar world in February 1945.

zones: the Soviet Union would control eastern Germany, and the Western Allies would control the rich industrial areas of the west. Berlin, isolated within the Soviet zone, would be jointly occupied. Churchill and Roosevelt insisted that liberated France receive a zone along its border with Germany and one in Berlin. Austria was similarly divided, with Vienna, like Berlin, under joint occupation within the Soviet zone. Russian demands for reparations of $20 billion to the Allies, half of which would go to the Soviet Union, were referred to a reparations commission. That commission never reached agreement, although the Soviets took untold amounts of German machinery and equipment from their occupation zone.

With respect to Eastern Europe, where Soviet forces were advancing on a broad front, there was little the Western Allies could do to influence events. Poland became the main focus of Western concern. Britain and France had gone to war in 1939 to defend it, and now, six years later, the course of the war had ironically left Poland's fate in the hands of the Soviets. Events had long foreshadowed the outcome. When they entered Poland in 1944, the Soviets allowed a puppet regime in Lublin to take control of civil administration. The Soviets refused to recognize the legitimacy of Poland's government-in-exile in London, formed by officials who had fled the country following Hitler's invasion in 1939. With Soviet troops at the gates of Warsaw, the underground resistance in the city rose up against the Nazi occupiers. But because the Polish underground supported the Polish government-in-exile, the Soviet armies idled for two months while the Nazis killed thousands of Poles in Warsaw, potential rivals of the Soviets' Lublin puppet government.

At Yalta the Big Three promised to sponsor free elections, democratic governments, and constitutional safeguards of freedom throughout the rest of Europe. The Yalta Declaration of Liberated Europe reaffirmed faith in the principles of the Atlantic Charter and the Declaration of the United Nations, but in the end it made little difference. It may have postponed Communist takeovers in Eastern Europe for a few years, but before long Communist members of coalition governments had purged the opposition. Russia, twice invaded by Germany in the twentieth century, was determined to create compliant buffer states between it and the German state.

YALTA'S LEGACY   Critics later attacked the Yalta agreements for "giving" Eastern Europe over to Soviet domination. Some argued that Roosevelt's declining health allowed him to buckle under Stalin's insistent demands. Yet the course of the war shaped the actions at Yalta, not personal diplomacy. The Soviets had the upper hand in Eastern Europe. Perhaps the most bitterly criticized of the Yalta accords was a secret agreement on the Far East, made public after the war. The combined chiefs of staff estimated that Japan could hold out for eighteen months after the defeat of Germany. Costly campaigns thus lay ahead, and the atomic bomb was still an expensive and untested gamble.

Roosevelt thus believed he had no choice but to accept Stalin's demands on postwar arrangements in the Far East, subject technically to agreement later by China's general Chiang Kai-shek. Stalin wanted continued Soviet control of Outer Mongolia through its puppet People's Republic, acquisition of the Kuril Islands from Japan, and recovery of rights and territory lost after the Russo-Japanese War of 1905. Stalin in return promised to enter the war against Japan two or three months after the German defeat, recognize Chinese sovereignty over Manchuria, and conclude a treaty of friendship and alliance with the Chinese Nationalists. Roosevelt's concessions would later appear in a different light, but given their geographic advantages in Asia, as in Eastern Europe, the Soviets were in a position to get what they wanted in any case.

THE COLLAPSE OF THE THIRD REICH   By 1945 the collapse of Nazi resistance was imminent, but President Roosevelt did not live to join the celebrations. Throughout 1944 his health had been declining, and on April 12, 1945, while drafting a speech, he died from a cerebral hemorrhage.

Hitler's Germany collapsed less than a month later. The Allied armies rolled up almost unopposed to the Elbe River, where they met advance detachments of Soviets on April 25. Three days later Italian partisans captured and brutally killed Mussolini as he tried to flee. In Berlin, which was under siege by the Soviets, Hitler married his mistress, Eva Braun, in an underground bunker on April 30, just before killing her and himself. On May 2 Berlin fell to the Soviets. That day, German forces in Italy surrendered. On May 7 the Germans signed an unconditional surrender in the Allied headquarters at Reims.

Massive victory celebrations on V-E Day, May 8, 1945, were tempered by the tragedies that had engulfed the world: mourning for the lost president and the death and mutilation of untold millions. Most shocking was the Allied armies' confirmation of the existence of the death camps in which Nazis had sought to apply their "final solution" to the "Jewish problem": the wholesale extermination of some 6 million Jews, along with more than 1 million others from occupied countries.

May 8, 1945

The celebration in New York's City's Times Square on V-E Day.

During the war, reports from Red Cross and underground sources had amassed growing evidence of Germany's systematic genocide against European Jews. Stories appeared in major American newspapers as early as 1942, but they were nearly always buried on inside pages. Reports of such horror seemed beyond belief. In addition, American government officials, even some Jewish leaders, dragged their feet on the question for fear that relief efforts for Jewish refugees might stir latent anti-Semitism at home. Finally Roosevelt had set up a War Refugees Board in 1944. It managed to rescue about 200,000 European Jews and some 20,000 others. But more might have been done. The Allies rejected a plan to bomb the rail lines leading to the largest death camp, Auschwitz, in Poland, although American planes hit industries five miles away. Moreover, few refugees were accepted into the United States. The Allied handling of the Holocaust was inept at best and disgraceful at worst.

A GRINDING WAR AGAINST JAPAN   The sobering thought that Japan must still be defeated cast a further pall over the victory celebrations. American forces continued to assault the Japanese Empire in the early months of 1945, but at a heavy cost. On February 19, 1945, U.S. marines invaded Iwo Jima, a volcanic island 760 miles from Tokyo that was needed to provide a fighter escort for bombers over Japan and a landing strip for disabled B-29 bombers. It took nearly six weeks to secure the site from Japanese defenders hiding in caves, and the cost was high: more than 20,000 American casualties, including nearly 7,000 dead.

The fight for Okinawa, beginning on Easter Sunday, April 1, was even bloodier. The island was large enough to afford a staging area for the planned invasion of the Japanese islands, and its capture required the largest amphibious operation of the Pacific war, involving some 300,000 troops. The fight raged until late June, incurring nearly 50,000 American casualties. The Japanese lost an estimated 140,000, including about 42,000 Okinawans. When resistance on Okinawa collapsed, the Japanese emperor instructed his new prime minister to seek peace.

THE ATOMIC BOMB   In 1939 physicist Albert Einstein had alerted President Roosevelt to German research on nuclear fission. In response the president in 1940 had launched the $2-billion top-secret Manhattan Project, involving over 120,000 scientists and technicians in several locations. In a laboratory in Los Alamos, New Mexico, under the direction of J. Robert Oppenheimer, a group of physicists worked out the scientific and technical problems of the bomb's construction. On July 16, 1945, the first atomic fireball rose from the desert. Oppenheimer said later that in the bunker where observers watched the test blast, "a few people laughed, a few people cried, most people were silent." President Harry S. Truman, thrust into the presidency upon Roosevelt's death in April, wrote in his diary, "We have discovered the most terrible bomb in the history of the world."

Word of the new weapon changed all strategic calculations. How to use this awful weapon posed profound problems. Some scientists favored a demonstration explosion for the Japanese in a remote area, but that idea was vetoed because only two bombs were available, and even those might misfire. The choice of targets received more consideration. After deciding against Kyōto, Japan's ancient capital and repository of national and religious treasures, priority went to Hiroshima, a port city of 400,000 people in southern Japan, which was a center of war industries, headquarters of the Japanese Second General Army, and command center for the homeland's defenses.

On July 25, 1945, President Truman ordered the atomic bomb dropped if Japan did not surrender before August 3. Although an intense scholarly debate has emerged over the decision to drop the bomb, it is clear that Truman believed that the atomic bomb would save lives by avoiding an American invasion against defenders who would fight like "savages, ruthless, merciless, and fanatic."

The ferocious Japanese defense of Okinawa had convinced military planners that an amphibious invasion of Japan itself, scheduled to begin on November 1, 1945, could cost as many as 250,000 Allied casualties and even more Japanese losses. Moreover, some 100,000 Allied prisoners of war being held in Japan were to be executed when an invasion began. It is important to remember as well that the bombing of cities and the consequent killing of civilians had become accepted military practice during 1945. Once the Japanese navy was destroyed, American ships had roamed the Japanese coastline, shelling targets onshore. American planes had bombed at will and mined the waters of the Inland Sea. Tokyo, Nagoya, and other major cities had been devastated by firestorms created by incendiary bombs. The firebomb raids on Tokyo on a single night in March 1945 killed 100,000 civilians and left over 1 million people homeless. By July more than sixty of Japan's largest cities had been firebombed, resulting in 500,000 deaths and 13 million civilians left homeless. The use of atomic bombs on Japanese cities was thus seen as a logical next step to end the war without an invasion of Japan. As it turned out, American scientists greatly underestimated the physical effects of the atomic bomb. They predicted that 20,000 people would be killed. The number would be much higher.

On July 26 the heads of the American, British, and Chinese governments issued the Potsdam Declaration, demanding that Japan surrender or face "prompt and utter destruction." The deadline passed, and at 8:15 A.M. on

August 6, flying at 31,600 feet, a B-29 bomber named *Enola Gay* released the five-ton uranium bomb nicknamed Little Boy. Forty-three seconds later, as the *Enola Gay* turned sharply to avoid the blast, the bomb tumbled to an altitude of 1,900 feet, where it exploded as planned with the force of 20,000 tons of TNT. A blinding flash of light was followed by a fireball towering to 40,000 feet. The tail gunner on the *Enola Gay* described the scene: "It's like bubbling molasses down there . . . the mushroom is spreading out . . . fires are springing up everywhere . . . it's like a peep into hell."

The shock wave, firestorm, cyclonic winds, and radioactive rain killed some 80,000 people. Dazed survivors wandered the streets, so badly burned that their skin peeled off in large strips. By the end of the year, the death toll had reached 140,000 as the effects of radiation burns and infection took their toll. In addition, 70,000 buildings were destroyed, and four square miles of the city turned to rubble.

Two days after the Hiroshima bombing an opportunistic Soviet Union, eager to share the spoils of victory, hastened to enter the war in Asia. Truman and his aides, frustrated by the stubborn refusal of Japanese military and political

The Bomb

This image shows the wasteland that remained after the atomic bomb "Little Boy" decimated Hiroshima in 1945.

leaders to surrender and fearful that the Soviet Union's entry into the war would complicate negotiations, ordered the second atomic bomb dropped. On August 9 a B-29 aircraft named *Bockscar,* carrying a bomb dubbed Fat Man, flew over its primary target, Kokura. The city was so shrouded in haze and smoke from an earlier air raid, however, that *Bockscar* turned to its secondary target, Nagasaki, where at 11:02 A.M. it dropped its terrifying bomb, killing 36,000 people. That night the Japanese emperor urged his cabinet to surrender on the sole condition that he remain as sovereign. The next day the U.S. government announced its willingness to let the emperor keep his throne, but under the authority of an Allied supreme commander. Frantic exchanges ended with Japanese acceptance of the terms on August 14, 1945, when the emperor himself delivered a radio message announcing the surrender to his people. On September 2, 1945, General MacArthur and other Allied representatives accepted Japan's formal surrender on board the battleship *Missouri.*

THE FINAL LEDGER

Thus ended the most deadly conflict in human history. One estimate has it that 70 million fought in the war, at a cost of some 50 million military and civilian dead, including those murdered in concentration camps. The Soviet Union suffered the greatest losses of all: over 13 million military deaths, more than 7 million civilian deaths, and at least 25 million left homeless. World War II was more costly for the United States than any other foreign war: 292,000 battle deaths and 114,000 other deaths. But in proportion to its population, the United States suffered a loss far smaller than any of the other major Allies or their enemies, and American territory escaped the devastation inflicted on so many other parts of the world.

World War II had profound effects on American life and society. Mobilization for the war stimulated a phenomenal increase in productivity and brought full employment, thus ending the Great Depression and laying the foundation for an era of unprecedented prosperity. New technologies and products developed for military purposes—radar, computers, electronics, plastics and synthetics, jet engines, rockets, atomic energy—began to transform the private sector as well. And new opportunities for women as well as for African Americans and other minorities set in motion changes that would culminate in the civil rights movement of the 1960s and the feminist movement of the 1970s.

The Democratic party benefited from the war effort by solidifying its control of both the White House and Congress. The dramatic expansion of the federal government occasioned by the war continued after 1945. Presidential authority and prestige increased enormously at the expense of congressional and state power. The isolationist sentiment in foreign relations that had been so powerful in the 1920s and 1930s disintegrated as the United States emerged from the war with far-flung global responsibilities and interests. Thus the war's end opened a new era for the United States in the world arena. It accelerated the growth of American power while devastating all other world powers, leaving the United States economically and militarily the strongest nation on earth.

MAKING CONNECTIONS

- The impact of World War II on the home front was much more extensive than that of World War I, especially in the effects of war on race and gender relations.

- The growing domestic conservatism of the war years continued into the 1950s, a topic discussed in the next chapter.

- Dwight D. Eisenhower's success as a military commander and the Allied leader led to his nomination and election as president in 1952. Compare Eisenhower's political experience to the experience of Ulysses S. Grant and other American military leaders.

FURTHER READING

John Keegan's *The Second World War* (1989) surveys the European conflict, while Charles B. MacDonald's *The Mighty Endeavor: The American War in Europe* (1986) concentrates on U.S. involvement. Roosevelt's wartime leadership is analyzed in Eric Larrabee's *Commander in Chief: Franklin Delano Roosevelt, His Lieutenants, and Their War* (1987).

Books on specific European campaigns include Stephen E. Ambrose's *D-Day, June 6, 1944: The Climactic Battle of World War II* (1994) and Charles B. MacDonald's *A Time for Trumpets: The Untold Story of the Battle of the Bulge* (1995). On the Allied commander, see Carlo D'Este's *Eisenhower: A Soldier's Life* (2002).

For the war in the Far East, see John Costello's *The Pacific War, 1941–1945* (1981), Ronald H. Spector's *Eagle against the Sun: The American War with Japan* (1985), John W. Dower's award-winning *War without Mercy: Race and Power in the Pacific War* (1986), and Dan van der Vat's *The Pacific Campaign: The U.S.-Japanese Naval War, 1941–1945* (1991).

An excellent overview of the war's effects on the home front is Michael C. C. Adams's *The Best War Ever: America and World War II* (1994). On economic effects, see Harold G. Vatter's *The U.S. Economy in World War II* (1985).

Susan M. Hartmann's *The Home Front and Beyond: American Women in the 1940s* (1982) treats the new working environment for women. Neil A. Wynn looks at the participation of blacks in *The Afro-American and the Second World War* (1976). The story of the oppression of Japanese Americans is told in Peter Irons's *Justice at War: The Story of the Japanese American Internment Cases* (1983).

A sound introduction to U.S. diplomacy during the conflict can be found in Gaddis Smith's *American Diplomacy during the Second World War, 1941–1945* (1965). To understand the role that Roosevelt played in policy making, consult Warren F. Kimball's *The Juggler: Franklin Roosevelt as Wartime Statesman* (1991).

The issues and events that led to the deployment of atomic weapons are addressed in Martin J. Sherwin's *A World Destroyed: The Atomic Bomb and the Grand Alliance* (1975).

Part Seven

THE
AMERICAN
AGE

1945

Harry Truman serves as president
(1945–1953)

George Kennan outlines the rationale of
containment in *Foreign Affairs* (1947)

National Security Act makes permanent
the Joint Chiefs of Staff, creates the Central Intelligence Agency and the National
Security Council (1947)

Truman Doctrine establishes plan to help
postwar Europe (1947)

Dixiecrats nominate Strom Thurmond for
president; Truman unexpectedly wins
reelection (1948)

House Un-American Activities Committee
keeps lists on possible subversives, eventually fueling the outbreak of a second
Red Scare (1940s–1950s)

11 top Communist party leaders are convicted under the Smith Act (1949)

1950

Alger Hiss is convicted for lying about espionage; Congress passes McCarran Internal Security Act; Senator Joseph McCarthy begins witch hunt for
Communists (1950)

Twenty-second Amendment limits presidents after Truman to two terms (1951)

Dwight D. Eisenhower serves as president
(1953–1961)

U.S. executes Julius and Ethel Rosenberg
for espionage (1953)

McCarthy hearings are held; Congress votes
to censure Senator McCarthy (1954)

1960

Civil Rights Acts do little to achieve equality for black citizens (1957, 1960)

John F. Kennedy serves as president
(1961–1963)

Black employment in the upper ranks of
the federal civil service increases 88 percent (1961–1963)

Lyndon B. Johnson serves as president following JFK's assassination (1963–1969)

Lyndon Johnson defeats Barry Goldwater
in landslide (1964)

Voting Rights Act ends literacy tests in the
South (1965)

Johnson decides not to run for reelection;
Democratic Convention in Chicago is
accompanied by violence (1968)

Martin Luther King Jr. and Robert
Kennedy are killed by assassins (1968)

United Nations is created (1945)

Communists take over governments in
Eastern Europe (1946–1948)

Civil war erupts in Greece (1946–1947)

India achieves independence (1947)

Marshall Plan funnels $13 billion to
Europe (1948–1951)

Soviets blockade West Berlin; U.S. and Allies respond with Berlin airlift (1948)

State of Israel is declared; Arabs begin war
to destroy it (1948)

Soviets lift blockade of Berlin and create
German Democratic Republic (1949)

NATO is created (1949)

Soviets explode an atomic bomb (1949)

Communists led by Mao Tse-tung win civil
war in China; Nationalists under Chiang
Kai-shek flee to Formosa (1949)

Korean War (1950–1953)

U.S. helps overthrow governments of Iran
(1953) and Guatemala (1954)

Communist Viet Minh defeats French at
Dien Bien Phu; Geneva Accords create
North Vietnam and South Vietnam (1954)

U.S. sends funds and military advisers to
South Vietnam (1954)

Warsaw Pact confirms military alliance of
communist Eastern European countries
with the Soviet Union (1955)

Egypt nationalizes the Suez Canal Company,
causing the Suez War (1956)

Soviet forces crush a liberation movement in
Hungary (1956)

Soviets launch *Sputnik*
(1957); U.S. launches
Explorer-I (1958)

Fidel Castro leads a successful revolution in
Cuba (1959)

Soviet Yuri Gagarin orbits
the earth; American Alan
Shepard reaches outer
space (1961)

U.S. launches Alliance for Progress and the
Peace Corps (1961)

Plot to overthrow Castro fails at Bay of Pigs
in Cuba (1961)

Cuban missile crisis (1962)

U.S. presence in Vietnam escalates after
Tonkin Gulf resolution (1964)

Cultural Revolution takes place in China
(1966–1976)

Women leave the workforce to make room for returning soldiers (1945)

College enrollment quadruples (1945–1970)

Proportion of homeowners increases by 50 percent in the United States (1945–1960)

Benjamin Spock publishes *Common Sense Book of Baby and Child Care* (1946)

Baby boom increases U.S. population by 30 percent (40 million) (1946–1960)

Number of television sets in the U.S. increases from 7,000 to 50 million (1946–1960)

Jackie Robinson becomes first black player in major-league baseball (1947)

Truman bans racial discrimination in federal hiring and orders desegregation of the armed forces (1948)

Rise of the suburbs (1950s)

Religious revival casts prosperity and conformity in a moral light (1950s)

Beat poets rebel against middle-class life and conformity (1950s)

Arthur Miller, Edward Albee, and Tennessee Williams write plays portraying alienation (1950s–1960s)

Brown v. Board of Education prohibits segregation in public schools, overruling "separate-but-equal" doctrine (1954)

Rosa Parks inspires Montgomery bus boycott (1955)

Martin Luther King establishes SCLC to combat racism (1957)

Arkansas prevents blacks from entering Little Rock's Central High School; Eisenhower sends federal troops to enforce desegregation (1957)

Cesar Chavez organizes the United Farm Workers (1962)

Betty Friedan's *The Feminine Mystique* is published (1963)

200,000 demonstrators take part in the March on Washington (1963)

Bracero program ends (1964)

Returning servicemen use GI Bill to pay for college or job training or to buy homes (1944–1949)

Strikes by auto and steel workers lead to wage and price increases, fueling inflation and leading to a 6 percent rise in the cost of living (1945–1946)

Auto production soars from 2 million to 8 million (1946–1950s)

Greater availability of discretionary income and credit fuels purchases of homes, cars, televisions, and washing machines (1946–1950s)

Technological advances lead to agricultural surpluses (1940s–1970s)

Taft-Hartley Act curbs power of labor unions (1947)

Congress funds construction of 79,000 miles of highways (1947–1956)

Gap between blacks' and whites' income continues to increase (1950s)

Eisenhower approves joint U.S.-Canadian development of St. Lawrence Seaway (1954)

Amendments to Social Security Act extend benefits to professionals (1954, 1956)

Government raises minimum wage from 75¢ to $1 per hour (1955)

Eisenhower submits to Congress largest peacetime budget in history (1957)

Government makes agriculture surpluses available to poor Americans through use of food stamps (1959)

Social Security benefits increase 7 percent (1959)

Area Redevelopment Act earmarks $400 million for "distressed areas" (1961)

Kennedy makes $4.9 billion available to cities for mass transit and housing (1962)

Trade Expansion Act leads to tariff cuts between U.S. and Common Market (1962)

Federal allocation of billions of dollars for education, medical care, and housing fuels economic growth (1964)

1945

1950

1960

Richard Nixon serves as president (1969–1974)

1970

Twenty-sixth Amendment gives 18-year-olds the right to vote in all elections (1971)

Watergate break-in occurs (1972)

War Powers Act passes (1973)

Spiro Agnew resigns vice presidency after accepting bribes (1973)

House impeaches Nixon for his role in the Watergate affair (1974)

Nixon resigns (1974); Gerald Ford serves as president (1974–1977)

1980

Gerald Ford pardons Nixon (1974)

Jimmy Carter serves as president (1977–1981)

Moral Majority becomes a political force (1980s)

Ronald Reagan serves as president (1981–1989)

Iran-Contra scandal cripples Reagan's presidency (1986)

George H. W. Bush serves as president (1989–1993)

1990

William J. Clinton serves as president (1993–2001)

1999

Republican-dominated Congress attempts to enact Contract with America, passing 26 bills, only 4 of which become law (1995)

House impeaches Clinton as a result of Monica Lewinsky scandal; Senate votes not to convict him (1999)

George W. Bush serves as president (2001–)

Tet offensive turns U.S. public opinion against the war in Vietnam (1968)

Soviets occupy Czechoslovakia, ending Prague Spring (1968)

Neil Armstrong becomes the first man to walk on the moon (1969)

Nixon travels to China (1972)

U.S. and Soviets sign SALT and begin détente (1972)

Last U.S. combat troops leave Vietnam (April 1973)

South Vietnam falls to Communists (1975)

Mao Tse-tung dies (1976)

Panama Canal treaties are ratified (1977)

Israel and Egypt sign Camp David accords (1978)

U.S. and Soviets sign SALT II (1979)

Soviets invade Afghanistan (1979)

Iranian hostage crisis unfolds (1979–1980)

Iran-Iraq War (1980–1988)

U.S. supports Contras and anti-Communist regimes in Central America (1980s)

U.S. begins development of Strategic Defense Initiative ("Star Wars") (1983)

Mikhail Gorbachev promotes glasnost and perestroika in Soviet Union (1985–1989)

U.S. and Soviets sign treaty eliminating intermediate-range missiles (1987)

Soviets pull out of Afghanistan; Berlin Wall falls; Soviet Empire collapses (1989)

Chinese government kills student protesters in Tiananmen Square (1989)

Germany is reunited (1990)

U.S. and Soviets sign agreement to reduce the number of long-range missiles (1991)

Soviet Union dissolves into 15 autonomous republics (1991)

Operation Desert Storm is put into effect in Iraq (1991)

Former Yugoslavia erupts in violent ethnic conflict among Serbs, Croats, and Bosnian Muslims (1991–1995)

Apartheid ends in South Africa (1991)

NATO intervention in Yugoslavia restores Muslim refugees to Kosovo (1999)

September 11 terrorist attacks (2001)

Civil Rights Act outlaws segregation in public facilities and discriminatory employment practices (1964)

LBJ's "war on poverty" leads to Great Society legislation (1964–1965)

Student activists protest Vietnam War (1964–1970s)

Immigration and Nationality Services Act liberalizes immigration policies (1965)

Separatist black power movement leads to founding of Black Panthers (1966)

Affirmative-action programs encourage hiring of women and members of racial minorities (1960s–1980s)

Evangelical religion experiences national revival (1970s–1980s)

In *Roe v. Wade,* Supreme Court legalizes abortions during first trimester (1973)

Percentage of Americans living below poverty level increases (1979–1983)

90 percent of nation's population growth occurs in sunbelt states (1980s)

Culture of consumerism is characterized by rampant spending and less personal savings (1980s)

Most immigrants to U.S. come from Asia and Latin America (1980s–1990s)

Computer technology revolutionizes the way people live and work (1980s–1990s)

Right-to-life movement emerges (1980s–1990s)

Militia movements spread, culminating in tragedies at Ruby Ridge, Waco, and Oklahoma City (1992–1995)

Federal courts limit affirmative-action programs (1995–1996)

Internet and e-mail spark commercial and communications revolutions (1990s)

Department of Housing and Urban Development is established (1966)

Inflation rises from 3 percent to 12 percent (1967–1974)

Clean Air Act allocates funds for cleaning up air pollution (1970)

1970

Stock-market contraction leads to "Nixon recession"; Nixon freezes wages and prices (1971)

Energy crisis in U.S. occurs because of Arab oil boycott and OPEC price increases (1973)

Inflation reaches 18 percent; mortgage rates reach 15 percent; interest rates peak at 20 percent (1980)

1980

Economic Recovery Tax Act lowers taxes and leads to mounting deficit (1981)

Unemployment reaches 10.4 percent in worst recession since the 1930s (1981–1982)

Federal deficit for 1983 is higher than all previous deficits combined (1983)

Labor union participation decreases (1980s)

Federal debt soars to $1.4 trillion (1987)

Stock market drops 22.6 percent (1987)

Savings-and-Loan crisis is resolved by a $500-billion federal bailout (1989)

NAFTA links economies of Mexico, the U.S., and Canada (1992)

1990

Major federal welfare programs are turned over to the states (1996)

Productivity and profits set records; gap between rich and poor widens (1990s)

Federal government has first surplus in 30 years (1998)

Dow Jones industrial average increases from 3,500 to over 11,000 (1993–1999)

1999

The United States emerged from World War II the preeminent military and economic power in the world. While much of Europe and Asia struggled to recover from the physical devastation of the war, the United States was virtually unscathed, its economic infrastructure intact and operating at peak efficiency. By 1955 the United States, with only 6 percent of the world's population, was producing half the world's goods. In Europe, Japan, and elsewhere, American products and popular culture attracted excited attention.

Yet the specter of a "cold war" cast a pall over the buoyant revival of the economy. The ideological contest with the Soviet Union and Communist China produced numerous foreign crises and sparked a domestic witch hunt for American Communists that far surpassed earlier episodes of political and social repression in the nation's history. Both major political parties accepted the geopolitical assumptions embedded in the ideological cold war with international communism. Both Republican and Democratic presidents affirmed the need to "contain" the spread of Communist influence around the world.

This bedrock assumption eventually embroiled the United States in a costly war in Southeast Asia, which destroyed Lyndon Johnson's presidency and revived isolationist sentiments. The Vietnam War was also the catalyst for a countercultural movement in which young idealists of the "baby-boom" generation promoted many overdue social reforms, including the civil rights and environmental movements. But the youth revolt also contributed to an array of social ills, from street riots to drug abuse to sexual promiscuity. The social upheavals of the 1960s and early 1970s provoked a conservative backlash. Richard Nixon's paranoid reaction to his critics led to the Watergate affair and the destruction of his presidency.

Through all of this turmoil, however, the basic premises of welfare-state capitalism that Franklin Roosevelt had instituted with his New Deal programs remained essentially intact. With only a few exceptions, both Republicans and Democrats after 1945 came to accept the notion that the federal government must assume greater responsibility for the welfare of individuals than had heretofore been the case. Even Ronald Reagan, a sharp critic of liberal social-welfare programs, recognized the need for the federal government to provide a "safety net" for those who could not help themselves.

This fragile consensus on public policy began to disintegrate in the late 1980s amid stunning international events and less visible domestic changes. The internal collapse of the Soviet Union and the disintegration of European communism surprised observers and sent policy makers scurrying to respond to a post–cold war world, in which the United States remained the only legitimate superpower. After forty-five years, American foreign policy was no longer centered on a single adversary, and world politics lost its bipolar quality. During the early 1990s the two Germanys reunited, apartheid in South Africa ended, and Israel and the Palestinians signed a previously unimaginable peace treaty.

At the same time, American foreign policy began to focus less on military power and more on economic competition and technological development. In those arenas, Japan and a reunited Germany challenged the United States for preeminence. By reducing the public's fear of nuclear annihilation, the end of the cold war also reduced American interest in foreign affairs. The presidential election of 1992 was the first since 1936 in which foreign-policy issues played virtually no role. This was an unfortunate development, for post–cold war world affairs remained volatile and dangerous. The implosion of Soviet communism after 1989 unleashed a series of ethnic, nationalist, and separatist conflicts throughout Eurasia. Responding to pleas for assistance, the United States found itself drawn into crises in faraway locations, such as Bosnia, Somalia, Kosovo, Afghanistan, and Iraq.

31

THE FAIR DEAL AND CONTAINMENT

FOCUS QUESTIONS

- What was the economic, social, and political aftermath of World War II?
- What were the origins and early manifestations of the cold war?
- What was Truman's Fair Deal?
- What was the extent of U.S. involvement in the Korean War?
- What were the roots of McCarthyism and the second Red Scare?

To answer these questions and access additional review material, please visit www.wwnorton.com/studyspace.

No sooner did the Second World War end than a "cold war" began. The uneasy wartime alliance between the United States and the Soviet Union had collapsed by the fall of 1945. The two strongest nations to emerge from the carnage of World War II could not bridge their ideological differences over such basic issues as human rights, individual liberties, and religious beliefs. Mutual suspicion and a race to gain influence and control over the so-called third world countries further polarized the two nations. The defeat of Japan and Germany had created power vacuums that sucked the United States and the Soviet Union into an unrelenting war of words fed by clashing geopolitical interests. At the same time the devastation wrought by the war in western Europe and the exhaustion of its peoples led to anti-colonial uprisings in Asia and Africa that threatened to strip Britain and France of their empires. The postwar world was thus an unstable one in which international tensions shaped the contours of domestic politics and culture as well as foreign relations.

DEMOBILIZATION UNDER TRUMAN

TRUMAN'S UNEASY START "Who the hell is Harry Truman?" Roosevelt's chief of staff asked the president in the summer of 1944. The question was on more lips when, after less than twelve weeks as vice president, Harry Truman took the presidential oath on April 12, 1945. Clearly he was not as charismatic or as magisterial as Franklin Roosevelt, and that was one of the burdens he would bear. Roosevelt and Truman came from quite different backgrounds. For Truman there had been no inherited wealth, no early contact with the great and near great, no European travel, no Harvard—indeed, no college at all. Born in 1884 in western Missouri, Truman grew up in Independence, outside Kansas City. Too nearsighted to join in the activities of other boys, Truman became bookish and introverted. After high school, however, he spent a few years working in Kansas City banks and grew into an outgoing young man.

During World War I, Truman served in France as captain of an artillery battery. Afterward he opened a clothing business, but it failed during the recession of 1922, and Truman then entered politics. In 1934 Missouri sent him to the U.S. Senate, where he remained fairly obscure until he chaired a committee investigating corruption in defense industries during World War II.

Something about Harry Truman evoked the spirit of Andrew Jackson: his decisiveness, his feistiness, his family loyalty. But that was a side of the man the people came to know only as he settled into the presidency. On his first full day as president, as the war in Asia ground on, he remained awestruck. "Boys, if you ever pray, pray for me now," he told a group of reporters. "I don't know whether you fellows ever had a load of hay fall on you, but when they told me yesterday what had happened, I felt like the moon, the stars and all the planets had fallen on me."

Truman favored much of the New Deal and was even prepared to extend its scope, but he was uneasy with many of the most ardent New Deal reformers. Within ninety days of taking office, he had replaced much of the Roosevelt cabinet with his own choices. On the whole his cabinet was more conservative in outlook and included several mediocrities. Truman suffered the further handicap of seeming to be a caretaker for the remainder of Roosevelt's term. Few expected him to run on his own in 1948.

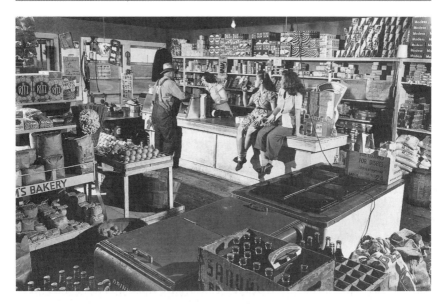

The Eldridge General Store, Fayette County, Illinois

Postwar America quickly demobilized, turning its attention to the pursuit of abundance.

The new president gave a significant clue to his domestic policies on September 6, 1945, when he sent Congress a comprehensive peacetime program that in effect proposed to enlarge the New Deal. Its twenty-one points included expansion of unemployment insurance, a higher minimum wage, a permanent Fair Employment Practices Committee, slum clearance and low-rent housing, regional development of the nation's river valleys, and a public-works program. "Not even President Roosevelt asked for so much at one sitting," charged the House Republican leader. "It's just a plain case of out-dealing the New Deal." But Truman did not have the same success as Roosevelt in getting his legislation through Congress. Beset by other problems, Truman soon saw his new domestic proposals mired in disputes over the transition to a peacetime economy.

CONVERTING TO PEACE The raucous celebrations that greeted Japan's surrender signaled the habitual American response to military victory: a rapid demobilization of the armed forces and a return to more carefree pursuits. The public demanded that the president and Congress bring the troops home as soon as possible. By 1947 the total armed forces had shrunk to 1.5 million from a wartime high of 12 million. By early 1950 the army had been reduced to 600,000 troops.

The military veterans returned to colleges, jobs, wives, and babies. Population growth, which had dropped off sharply in the Depression decade, now soared. Americans born during this postwar period composed what came to be known as the baby-boom generation, an oversize population cohort that would become a dominant force shaping the nation's social and economic life.

The end of the war, with its sudden demobilization and conversion to a peacetime economy, generated labor unrest and strikes but not the postwar depression that many had feared. Several shock absorbers cushioned the economic impact of demobilization: unemployment insurance and other Social Security benefits; the Servicemen's Readjustment Act of 1944, known as the GI Bill of Rights, under which $13 billion was spent for military veterans on education, vocational training, medical treatment, unemployment insurance, and loans for building houses and going into business; and most important, the pent-up demand for consumer goods that was fueled by wartime shortages. Instead of sinking into depression after the war, the economy enjoyed a spurt of private investment in new production facilities and equipment.

CONTROLLING INFLATION   The most acute economic problem facing postwar America was not depression but inflation. Released from wartime restraints, businesses demanded higher prices, and workers demanded higher wages, thereby conspiring to frustrate Truman's efforts to maintain stabilization of the economy. The president endorsed "reasonable" wage increases, which he thought businesses could absorb without raising prices, and he considered necessary to sustain consumer purchasing power. Management, however, did not agree. Within six weeks of the war's end, corporations had refused union demands for higher wages and better benefits, and a series of strikes followed in the automotive, steel, mining, petroleum, and railroad industries.

President Truman, miffed at what he considered to be excessive union demands, including a 30 percent wage boost, used powers granted the chief executive during wartime to seize the coal mines and threaten to draft striking railroad workers into the armed forces. A strike in the steel industry finally provided a formula for settling most of the disputes. Truman suggested a pay raise of 18.5¢ per hour, which the Steel Workers accepted but management refused. To break the logjam, the administration in 1946 agreed to let the steel companies increase their prices. That sequence of events became the pattern for settlements in other industries and set a dangerous precedent of price-wage spirals that would plague consumers in the postwar world.

The wartime Office of Price Administration maintained some restraint on price increases while gradually ending the rationing of most goods, and Truman asked for a one-year renewal of its powers. During the winter and spring of 1946, however, business lobbyists campaigned against price controls. Congress extended controls in July, but by then the cost of living had risen by 6 percent. After the 1946 congressional elections, Truman gave up the battle, ending all price controls except those on rent, sugar, and rice.

PARTISAN CONFLICT   Before the 1946 congressional elections, public discontent ran high, with most of it directed against the administration. Labor union supporters tagged Truman "the No. 1 strikebreaker," while much of the public, angry at striking unions, blamed the White House for the strikes. Critics of the administration had a field day coining campaign slogans. The most effective was the simple "Had enough?" attributed to a Boston ad agency: the message was that the Democrats had simply been in power too long. In the end, Republicans won majorities in both houses of Congress for the first time since 1928.

The rising public criticism of organized labor spurred the new Republican Congress to pass the Taft-Hartley Labor Act of 1947 to curb the power of the unions. It banned the closed shop (in which nonunion workers could not be hired) but permitted a union shop (in which workers newly hired were required to join the union) except where banned by state law. The antiunion legislation included provisions forbidding "unfair" union practices such as "featherbedding" (paying for work not done), refusing to bargain in good faith, and contributing to political campaigns. Unions' political action committees were allowed to function only on a voluntary basis, and union leaders had to take oaths declaring that they were not members of the Communist party. Employers were permitted to sue unions for breaking contracts and to speak freely during union campaigns. The act forbade strikes by federal employees and imposed a "cooling-off" period of eighty days on any strike that the president found to be dangerous to the national health or safety.

Truman's veto of the Taft-Hartley bill, which unions called the slave-labor act, restored his credit with labor and brought many unionists who had voted Republican in 1946 back to the Democratic fold. But the bill passed over the president's veto. Its most severe impact was probably on the CIO's Operation Dixie, a drive to win unions a more secure foothold in the South. By 1954 fifteen states, mainly in the South, had used the Taft-Hartley Act's authority to pass "right-to-work" laws forbidding the union shop. Those laws also eroded union strength in the North as many firms began to migrate to right-to-work southern states.

Yet the conflicts between Truman and Congress obscured the high degree of bipartisan cooperation marking matters of government reorganization and foreign policy. In 1947 a bipartisan majority in Congress passed the National Security Act, which created a National Military Establishment, headed by the secretary of defense with subcabinet departments of army, navy, and air force, and the National Security Council (NSC), which included the president, heads of the defense departments, and the secretary of state, among others. The act made permanent the Joint Chiefs of Staff, a wartime innovation, and established the Central Intelligence Agency (CIA) to coordinate global intelligence gathering.

THE COLD WAR

BUILDING THE UN   The hope that the wartime military alliance between the Soviet Union and the United States would carry over into the postwar world proved but another great illusion. The pragmatic Roosevelt had shared no such illusion. He expected that the great powers in the postwar world would have separate geographic spheres of influence but felt he had to temper such realpolitik with an organization "which would satisfy widespread demand in the United States for new idealistic or universalist arrangements for assuring the peace."

On April 25, 1945, two weeks after Roosevelt's death and two weeks before the German surrender, delegates from fifty nations at war with the Axis met in San Francisco to draw up the Charter of the United Nations. Additional members would be admitted by a two-thirds vote of the General Assembly. This body, one of the two major agencies set up by the charter, included delegates from all member nations and was to meet annually in regular session to approve the budget, receive annual reports from UN agencies, and choose members of the Security Council and other bodies.

The Security Council, the other major charter agency, would remain in permanent session and would have "primary responsibility for the maintenance of international peace and security." Its eleven members (fifteen after 1965) included six (later ten) members elected for two-year terms and five permanent members: the United States, the Soviet Union, Britain, France, and China. Each permanent member could veto any question of substance. The Security Council might investigate any dispute, recommend settlement or reference to another UN body—the International Court of Justice at The

Hague, in the Netherlands—and take measures, including the use of military force. The U.S. Senate, in sharp contrast to the reception it gave the League of Nations, ratified the UN charter by a vote of eighty-nine to two.

DIFFERENCES WITH THE SOVIETS   There were signs of trouble in the wartime alliance linking Britain, the Soviet Union, and the United States as early as the spring of 1945, as the Soviet Union set up compliant governments in the nations of Eastern Europe, violating the Yalta promises of democratic elections. Protests against such actions led to Soviet counter-protests that the British and the Americans were negotiating a German surrender in Italy "behind the back of the Soviet Union."

Such was the atmosphere when Truman entered the White House. A few days before the San Francisco conference to organize the United Nations, the president gave Soviet foreign minister Vyacheslav Molotov a tongue lashing in Washington on the Polish situation. "I have never been talked to like that in my life," Molotov protested. "Carry out your agreements," Truman snapped, "and you won't get talked to like that."

On May 12, 1945, four days after victory in Europe, Winston Churchill sent Truman a telegram: "What is to happen about Europe? An iron curtain is drawn down upon [the Russian] front. We do not know what is going on behind [it]. . . . Surely it is vital now to come to an understanding with Russia, or see where we are with her, before we weaken our armies mortally." Neverthe-less, as a gesture of goodwill, and over Churchill's protest, the U.S. forces with-drew from the occupation zone in Germany that had been assigned to the Soviet Union at Yalta. Americans still hoped that the Yalta agreements would be carried out, and they were even more eager to have Soviet help in defeating Japan.

Although the Soviets admitted British and American observers to their sectors of Eastern Europe, there was little the Western powers could have done to prevent Soviet control of the region even if they had kept up their military strength. The presence of Soviet armed forces frustrated the efforts of non-Communists to gain political influence in Eastern European coun-tries. Opposition leaders were exiled, silenced, executed, or imprisoned.

Secretary of State James F. Byrnes, who took office in 1945, struggled through 1946 with the problems of postwar treaties. In early 1947 the Coun-cil of Foreign Ministers finally produced treaties for Italy, Hungary, Romania, Bulgaria, and Finland that confirmed Soviet control over Eastern Europe, which in Russian eyes seemed but a parallel to American control over Japan and Western control over most of Germany and all of Italy. The Yalta Conference's guarantees of democracy in Eastern Europe had turned out much like the Open Door policy in China, little more than pious rhetoric sugarcoating the realities of power and national interest.

CONTAINMENT   By the beginning of 1947, relations with the Soviet Union had become even more troubled. The year before, Stalin had pronounced international peace impossible "under the present capitalistic development of the world economy." His statement impelled George F. Kennan, counselor of the U.S. embassy in Moscow, to send an 8,000-word dispatch to the State Department, in which he sketched the roots of Soviet policy.

More than a year later Kennan, back at the State Department in Washington, spelled out his ideas for a proper response to the Soviets. In a 1947 article published anonymously in *Foreign Affairs,* he provided a brilliant historical and psychological analysis of Soviet insecurity and postwar intentions. He predicted that the Soviets would try to fill "every nook and cranny available . . . in the basin of world power." Therefore, he insisted, the United States must pursue "a long-term, patient but firm and vigilant *containment* of Russian expansive tendencies."

Kennan's "containment" concept dovetailed with the outlook of Truman and his advisers. They all harbored a growing fear that Soviet aims reached beyond Eastern Europe, posing dangers in the eastern Mediterranean, the Middle East, and western Europe itself. The Soviet Union especially sought access to the Mediterranean region, long important to Russia for purposes of trade and defense. After the war the Soviet Union pressed Turkey for territorial concessions and the right to build naval bases on the Bosporus, an important gateway between the Black Sea and the Mediterranean. In 1946 civil war broke out in neighboring Greece between a British-backed government and a Communist-led faction that held the northern part of the country. In 1947 the British ambassador informed the U.S. government that the British could no longer bear the economic and military burden of aiding Greece and suggested that the United States assume the responsibility.

THE TRUMAN DOCTRINE AND THE MARSHALL PLAN   On March 12, 1947, Truman asked Congress for $400 million in economic and military aid to Greece and Turkey. In his speech to Congress, the president announced what quickly became known as the Truman Doctrine. Although intended as a response to a specific crisis, its rhetoric was universal. "I believe," Truman declared, "that it must be the policy of the United States to support free peoples who are resisting attempted subjugation by armed minorities or by outside pressures." In 1947 Congress passed the Greek-Turkish aid bill and by 1950 had spent $659 million on the program. Turkey achieved economic stability, and Greece defeated the Communist insurrection in 1949.

Such immediate gains created long-term problems, however. The Truman Doctrine marked the beginning of a contest that people began to call a "cold war." Greece and Turkey were but the front lines in an ideological struggle between East and West for world power and influence. That struggle quickly focused on western Europe, where wartime damage had devastated factory production and a severe drought in 1947, followed by a harsh winter, had destroyed crops. Coal shortages in London left only enough fuel to heat and light homes for a few hours each day. In Berlin, people were freezing or starving to death. The transportation system in Europe was in shambles: bridges were out, canals clogged, and rail networks destroyed. Amid the chaos the Communist parties of France and Italy were flourishing.

In the spring of 1947, former general George C. Marshall, who had replaced James Byrnes as secretary of state, called for a program of massive aid to rescue western Europe from disaster and possible Communist subversion. "Our policy," he pledged, "is directed not against country or doctrine, but against hunger, poverty, desperation, and chaos." Marshall offered aid to all European countries, including the Soviet Union, but Moscow refused to participate in the "imperialist" scheme.

In late 1947 Truman submitted his proposal for the European Recovery Program to Congress. Soon thereafter a Communist coup d'état in Czechoslovakia ended the last remaining coalition government in Eastern Europe. The Communist seizure of power in Prague assured congressional passage of the Marshall Plan, which from 1948 until 1951 provided $13 billion to promote European economic recovery.

DIVIDING GERMANY   The Marshall Plan drew the nations of western Europe closer together, but the breakdown of the wartime alliance with the Soviet Union left the problem of postwar Germany unsettled. The German economy had stagnated, requiring the U.S. Army to carry a staggering burden of relief to prevent civilians from starving. Slowly occupation zones evolved into functioning governments. In 1948 the British, French, and Americans merged their zones, and the "West Germans" elected delegates to a federal constitutional convention.

Soviet resentment of the Marshall Plan and the political unification of West Germany led the Soviets, in April 1948, to restrict road and rail traffic into West Berlin; on June 23 they stopped all traffic. The next day, the Soviets cut off electricity to the western sector of the divided city. The Soviets hoped the blockade would force the Allies to give up either Berlin or the plan to unify Germany. It was war by starvation and intimidation, but Truman stood firm. After considering the use of armed convoys to supply West Berlin, he opted for a massive airlift. At the time it seemed like an impossible task. But

How did the Allies divide Germany and Austria at the Yalta Conference (see page 854)? What was the "iron curtain"? Why did Truman airlift supplies to Berlin?

the Allied air forces quickly brought in planes from around the world, and soon they were flying in up to 13,000 tons of food, coal, and other supplies a day.

The massive airlift went on for months. Finally, on May 12, 1949, after extended talks, the Soviets lifted the blockade. Before the end of the year, the Federal Republic of Germany had a functioning government. At the end of May 1949, an independent German "Democratic" Republic arose in the Soviet-dominated eastern zone, dividing Germany into two independent states.

BUILDING NATO   As relations between the Soviets and western Europe chilled, transatlantic unity ripened into a formal military alliance. On April 4, 1949, diplomats signed the North Atlantic Treaty. Twelve nations were represented: the United States, Britain, France, Belgium, the Netherlands, Luxembourg, Canada, Denmark, Iceland, Italy, Norway, and Portugal. Greece and Turkey joined the alliance in 1952, West Germany in 1955,

NATO

NATO is depicted as a symbol of renewed strength for a battered Europe.

and Spain in 1982. The treaty pledged that an attack against any one of the members would be considered an attack against all. A council of the North Atlantic Treaty Organization (NATO) would govern the alliance. In 1950 the council voted to create an integrated defense force for western Europe. Five years later the Warsaw Treaty Organization appeared as the Eastern European counterpoint to NATO.

The eventful year of 1948 produced another foreign-policy decision with long-term consequences. Late in 1947 the UN General Assembly voted to partition Palestine into Jewish and Arab states. Despite fierce Arab opposition, Jewish leaders proclaimed the independence of the new State of Israel on May 14, 1948. President Truman, who had been in close touch with Jewish leaders at home and abroad, ordered immediate recognition of the new state; the United States was the first nation to do so.

The neighboring Arab states thereupon attacked Israel, which held its own. UN mediators gradually worked out truce agreements with Israel's Arab neighbors, restoring an uneasy peace by May 11, 1949, when Israel joined the United Nations. But the mutual hatred and intermittent warfare between Israel and the Arab states have festered ever since, complicating U.S. foreign policy, which has aimed to maintain friendship with both sides while insisting on the legitimacy of the Israeli nation.

CIVIL RIGHTS DURING THE 1940S

The social tremors triggered by World War II and the onset of the cold war transformed America's racial landscape. The government-sponsored racism of the German Nazis, the Italian Fascists, and the Japanese imperialists focused attention on the need for the United States to improve its own race relations and to provide for equal rights under the law.

For most of his political career, Harry Truman had shown little concern with the plight of African Americans. He had grown up in western Missouri assuming that blacks and whites preferred to be segregated from one another. As president, however, he began to reassess his convictions. In the fall of 1946, Truman hosted a delegation of civil rights activists who urged the president to condemn the resurgence of the Ku Klux Klan and the lynching of African Americans. Truman soon appointed a Committee on Civil Rights to investigate racist violence and recommend preventive measures. In its report the committee urged the renewal of the Fair Employment Practices Committee and the creation of a permanent civil rights commission to investigate abuses. It also argued that federal aid be denied to any state that mandated segregated schools and public facilities.

On July 26, 1948, Truman banned racial discrimination in the hiring of federal employees. Four days later he issued an executive order ending racial segregation in the armed forces. The air force and navy quickly complied, but the army dragged its feet until the early 1950s. By 1960 the armed forces were the most racially integrated of all organizations.

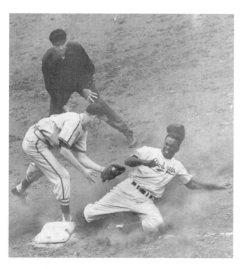

Jackie Robinson, 1949

Racial discrimination remained widespread throughout the postwar period. In 1947 Jackie Robinson of the Brooklyn Dodgers became the first black to play major-league baseball.

JACKIE ROBINSON Meanwhile, racial segregation was being confronted in a much more public field of endeavor: professional baseball. In April 1947, as the baseball season opened, the National League's Brooklyn Dodgers included the first black player to cross the color line in major-league baseball: Jackie Robinson. Born in Georgia and raised in California, Robinson was an army veteran and baseball player in the Negro leagues. Branch Rickey, president of the Dodgers, selected Robinson to integrate professional baseball not only for his athletic potential but because of his willingness to control his temper in the face of virulent racism. Teammates and opposing players viciously baited Robinson, pitchers threw at him, base runners spiked him, and spectators booed and taunted him in every city. Hotels refused him rooms, and restaurants denied him service. Hate mail arrived by the bucket load. On the other hand, black spectators were electrified by Robinson's courageous example; they turned out in droves to see him play.

As time passed, Robinson won over many racist fans and opposing players through his quiet courage, self-deprecating wit, and determined performance. Soon other teams signed black players. Baseball's pathbreaking efforts also stimulated the integration of football and basketball teams. Jackie Robinson vividly demonstrated that racism, not inferiority, impeded African-American advancement in the postwar era and that segregation need not be a permanent condition of American life.

SHAPING THE FAIR DEAL   As the 1948 election approached, the issue of civil rights presented daunting political challenges. While some Americans applauded Truman's efforts to desegregate the federal workforce, others were appalled. Liberals thought that his efforts were not bold enough. Southern conservative Democrats found him too radical. Truman's chances for winning the election of 1948 seemed bleak.

The president had a game plan for 1948, however. His advisers knew that to win another presidential term he needed the midwestern and western farm belts. In metropolitan areas he needed to carry the union and African-American vote, which Truman wooed by working closely with unions and pressing the cause of civil rights. Truman's advisers counted on the Solid South to stay in the Democratic column. With the South and the West, Truman could afford to lose some New Deal strongholds in the East and still win. This strategy erred chiefly in underrating the rebellion that would take four Deep South states out of Truman's camp because of his support for civil rights.

Truman used his State of the Union message to set the agenda for an election year. The 1948 speech offered something to nearly every group the Democrats hoped to win over. The first goal, Truman remarked, was "to secure fully the essential human rights of our citizens," and he promised a special message later on civil rights. "To protect human resources," he proposed federal aid to education, increased and extended unemployment and retirement benefits, a comprehensive system of health insurance, more federal support for public housing, and extension of rent controls. As one senator put it, the speech "raised all the ghosts of the old New Deal."

THE ELECTION OF 1948   The Republican majority in Congress for the most part spurned the Truman program, an action it would later regret. Scenting victory in November, Republican delegates again nominated Thomas Dewey, the former New York governor. The platform endorsed most of the New Deal reforms as an accomplished fact and approved the administration's bipartisan foreign policy; Dewey promised to run things more efficiently, however.

In July a glum Democratic Convention gathered in Philadelphia expecting to do little more than go through the motions but found itself surprised by a fierce debate over civil rights. To keep from stirring southern hostility, the administration sought a platform plank that opposed racial discrimination only in general terms. Activists, however, sponsored a plank that called on Congress to take action. Minneapolis mayor Hubert H. Humphrey electrified the delegates and set off a ten-minute demonstration when he declared, "The time has arrived for the Democratic party to get out of the shadow of states' rights and walk forthrightly into the bright sunshine of human rights." Segregationist delegates from Alabama and Mississippi instead walked out of the convention.

A group of rebellious southern Democrats, miffed by Truman's progressive civil rights plank, met later in Birmingham, Alabama, and nominated South Carolina governor Strom Thurmond on a States' Rights ticket, which was quickly dubbed the Dixiecrat party. The Dixiecrats sought to draw enough electoral votes to preclude a majority for either major party, throwing the election into the House of Representatives, where they might strike a sectional bargain. A few days later the left wing of the Democratic party gathered in Philadelphia to name Henry A. Wallace on a Progressive party ticket. These splits in the Democratic ranks seemed to spell the final blow to Truman.

"I Stand Pat!"

Truman's support of civil rights for African Americans had its political costs, as this 1948 cartoon suggests.

"Dewey Defeats Truman"

Truman's victory in 1948 was a huge upset, so much so that even the early edition of the *Chicago Daily Tribune* was caught off guard, running this premature headline.

But Truman, undaunted, set out on a 31,000-mile "whistle-stop" train tour, during which he castigated the "do-nothing" Eightieth Congress, provoking cries from his audiences to "Pour it on, Harry!" and "Give 'em hell, Harry." Truman responded, "I don't give 'em hell. I just tell the truth and they think it's hell." Dewey, in contrast, ran a restrained campaign designed to avoid controversy. By so doing, he may have snatched defeat from the jaws of victory.

The polls and the pundits predicted a sure win for Dewey, but on election day Truman chalked up the biggest upset in history, taking 24.2 million votes (49.5 percent) to Dewey's 22 million (45.1 percent) and winning by a thumping margin of 303 to 189 in the Electoral College. Thurmond and Wallace each got more than 1 million votes, but the revolt of right and left had worked to Truman's advantage. The Dixiecrat rebellion backfired by angering black voters, while the Progressive party's radicalism made it hard to tag Truman soft on communism. Thurmond carried four Deep South states, and his success hastened a momentous disruption of the Democratic Solid South. But Truman's victory carried Democratic majorities into Congress.

Truman viewed his upset victory as a vindication for the New Deal and a mandate for moderate liberalism. His 1949 State of the Union message repeated the agenda he had set forth the year before. "Every segment of our

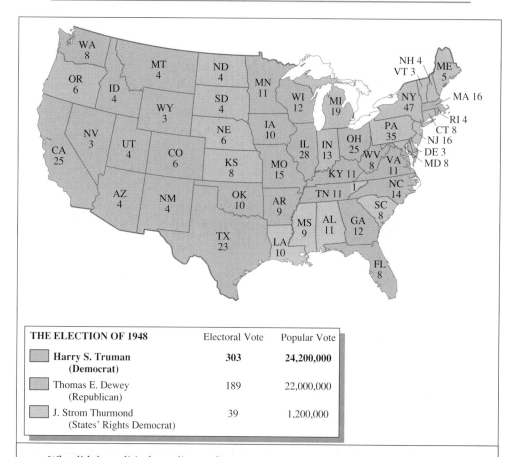

THE ELECTION OF 1948	Electoral Vote	Popular Vote
Harry S. Truman (Democrat)	**303**	**24,200,000**
Thomas E. Dewey (Republican)	189	22,000,000
J. Strom Thurmond (States' Rights Democrat)	39	1,200,000

Why did the political pundits predict a Dewey victory? Why was civil rights a divisive issue at the Democratic Convention? How did the candidacies of Thurmond and Wallace help Truman?

population and every individual," he stressed, "has a right to expect from his government a fair deal." Whether deliberately or not, he had invented a tag, the Fair Deal, to distinguish his program from the New Deal.

Some of Truman's Fair Deal proposals became law, but most of them were extensions or enlargements of New Deal programs already in place: a higher minimum wage, expanded Social Security coverage, extension of rent controls, increased farm subsidies, and a sizable slum-clearance and public-housing program. Despite Democratic majorities in Congress, however, the conservative coalition of Southern Democrats and Republicans disdained any drastic departures in domestic policy. Congress balked at civil rights bills, national health insurance, federal aid to education, and a plan to provide subsidies that would support farm income rather than farm prices. Congress also turned down Truman's demand for repeal of the Taft-Hartley Act.

THE COLD WAR HEATS UP

Global concerns, never far from center stage in the postwar world, plagued Truman's second term, as they had his first. Americans began to fear that Communists were infiltrating their society. In his inaugural address, Truman called for an anti-Communist foreign policy resting on four pillars: the United Nations, the Marshall Plan, NATO, and a "bold new plan" for technical assistance to underdeveloped parts of the world, a global Marshall Plan that came to be known as Point Four. This program to aid the postwar world never accomplished its goals, in part because other international problems soon diverted Truman's attention.

"LOSING" CHINA   One of the most intractable problems, the China tangle, was fast unraveling in 1949. The Chinese Nationalists, led by Chiang Kai-shek, had been fighting Mao Tse-tung (Mao Zedong)* and the Communists since the 1920s. The outbreak of war with Japan in 1937 halted the civil war, and both Roosevelt and Stalin believed that the Nationalists would control China after the war.

The commanders of U.S. forces in China during World War II, however, concluded that Chiang's government had become hopelessly corrupt, tyrannical, and inefficient. U.S. policy during and immediately after the war promoted peace between the factions in China. But when the civil war resumed in 1945, American forces ferried Nationalist armies back into the eastern and northern provinces as the Japanese withdrew.

It soon became a losing fight for the Nationalists as the Communists won over the land-hungry peasantry. By late 1949 the Nationalist government had fled to the island of Formosa, which it renamed Taiwan. Truman's critics asked bitterly: "Who lost China?" and a State Department report blamed Chiang for his failure to hold on to the support of the Chinese people. In fact it is hard to imagine how the U.S. government could have prevented a

---

*The traditional (Wade-Giles) transliterations of Chinese with pinyin in parentheses are used in this text up to 1976. After Mao's death the Chinese government adopted the pinyin translations that are widely used today: Mao Tse-tung became Mao Zedong; Peking became Beijing.

"It's the Same Thing."

The Marshall Plan, which distributed aid throughout Europe, is represented in this 1949 cartoon as a modern tractor driven by a prosperous farmer. In the foreground a poor, overworked man is yoked to an old-fashioned "Soviet" plow, forced to go over the ground of the "Marshal Stalin Plan," while Stalin himself tries to persuade others that "it's the same thing without mechanical problems."

Communist victory short of undertaking a massive military intervention, which would have been risky, costly, and unpopular. After 1949, the United States continued to recognize the Nationalist government on Taiwan as the rightful government of China, delaying formal relations with Communist China for thirty years. In an effort to shore up friendly governments in Asia, the United States in 1950 recognized the French-supported government of Emperor Bao Dai in Vietnam and shortly afterward extended aid to the French in their battle against Ho Chi Minh's Vietnamese guerrillas.

As the Communists were securing control in China, U.S. intelligence discovered that the Soviets had set off an atomic explosion. News of the Soviet bomb in 1949 provoked an intense reappraisal of the strategic balance of power in the world, causing Truman in 1950 to order the construction of a hydrogen bomb, a weapon far more powerful than the atomic bomb, lest the Soviets make one first. In addition, the National Security Council recommended rebuilding conventional military forces to provide options other than nuclear war. Such a plan represented a major departure from America's time-honored aversion to keeping large standing armies in peacetime. It was also an expensive proposition. But the American public was growing more receptive to the nation's role as world leader, and an invasion of South Korea by Communist forces from the north clinched the issue for most Americans.

WAR IN KOREA   The Japanese had occupied Korea since 1910, and after their defeat and withdrawal in 1945 the victorious Allies faced the difficult task of creating a new Korean nation. Complicating that task was the fact that Soviet troops had advanced into northern Korea and accepted the surrender of Japanese forces above the 38th parallel, while U.S. forces had done the same south of that line. The Soviets quickly organized a Korean government along Stalinist lines, while the Americans set up a Western-style regime in the south.

Like the postwar division of Germany, the victors' decision to divide Korea at the 38th parallel began as a temporary expedient and ended as a permanent fact. With the onset of the cold war, it became clear that Soviet-American agreement on unification was no more likely in Korea than in Germany. By the end of 1948, separate Korean regimes had appeared in the two sectors, and occupation forces had withdrawn. The weakened state of the demobilizing American military contributed to the impression that South Korea was vulnerable to a Communist assault. A growing body of evidence in Soviet archives reveals that Stalin encouraged the North Koreans to use force to unify their country and oust the Americans from the peninsula. The Soviets helped design a war plan that called for North Korean forces to seize Seoul within three days and all of South Korea within a week. Stalin apparently assumed the United States would not intervene.

Over 80,000 North Korean soldiers crossed the boundary on June 25, 1950, and swept down the peninsula. President Truman responded decisively. He and his advisers assumed that the North Korean attack was directed by Moscow and was a brazen indication of the aggressive designs of Soviet communism. Truman made two critical decisions. First, he decided to wage war under the auspices of the United Nations rather than unilaterally. Second, he decided to send troops without asking Congress for a formal declaration of war.

An emergency meeting of the UN Security Council quickly censured the North Korean "breach of peace." The Soviet delegate, who held veto power, was at the time boycotting the council because it would not seat Communist China in place of Nationalist China. On June 27, its first resolution having been ignored, the Security Council called on UN members to "furnish such assistance to the Republic of Korea as may be necessary to repel the armed attack and to restore international peace and security in the area."

Truman ordered American air, naval, and ground forces into action. Eventually U.S. units numbered over 350,000, while the South Koreans contributed 500,000. In all, some fourteen other nations sent another 50,000 men. Later the UN authorized a unified command and put General Douglas MacArthur in charge. The defense of South Korea remained chiefly an American affair and one that set a precedent of profound consequence: war by order of a president rather than by vote of Congress. Yet it had the sanction of the UN Security Council and could technically be considered a "police action," not a war. Other presidents had ordered U.S. troops into action without a declaration of war, but never on such a scale.

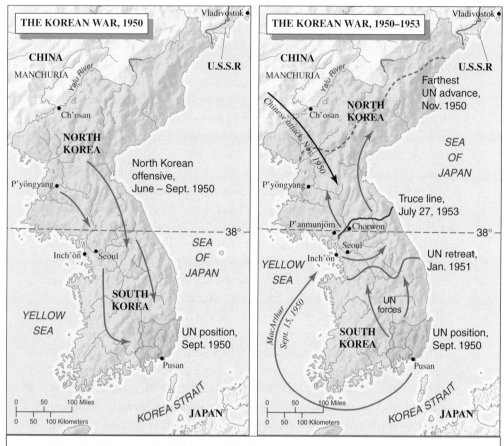

THE KOREAN WAR, 1950

CHINA

MANCHURIA · Yalu River

U.S.S.R

Vladivostok

Ch'osan

NORTH
KOREA

P'yŏngyang

North Korean
offensive,
June – Sept. 1950

SEA
OF
JAPAN

— — — — 38°

Inch'ŏn · Seoul

SOUTH
KOREA

YELLOW
SEA

UN position,
Sept. 1950

Pusan

0   50   100 Miles
0   50   100 Kilometers

KOREA STRAIT   JAPAN

THE KOREAN WAR, 1950–1953

CHINA

MANCHURIA · Yalu River

U.S.S.R

Vladivostok

Chinese attack, Nov. 1950

Ch'osan

NORTH
KOREA

Farthest
UN advance,
Nov. 1950

P'yŏngyang

SEA
OF
JAPAN

P'anmunjŏm · Chorwon

Truce line,
July 27, 1953

Inch'ŏn · Seoul

— — — — 38°

YELLOW
SEA

MacArthur Sept. 15, 1950

SOUTH
KOREA

UN
forces

UN retreat,
Jan. 1951

UN position,
Sept. 1950

Pusan

0   50   100 Miles
0   50   100 Kilometers

KOREA STRAIT   JAPAN

How did the surrender of the Japanese in Korea set up the conflict between Soviet-influenced North Korea and U.S.-influenced South Korea? What was MacArthur's strategy for retaking Korea? Why did Truman remove MacArthur from command?

Truman's conviction that the invasion of South Korea was orchestrated by Stalin led to two other decisions that had far-reaching consequences. First, Truman decided that the Korean conflict was actually a diversion for a Soviet invasion of western Europe, so he began a major expansion of American forces in NATO. Second, while dispatching U.S. military units to Korea and Europe, Truman increased assistance to the French troops in Indochina, creating the Military Assistance Advisory Group for Indochina—the start of America's deepening military involvement in Vietnam.

For three months the fighting went badly for the South Korean and UN forces. By September they were barely hanging on to the Pusan perimeter in the southeast corner of Korea. Then, in a brilliant maneuver on September 15, 1950, General MacArthur landed a new force to the North Korean rear at Inch'ŏn. Synchronized with a breakout from Pusan, the sudden blow stampeded the enemy back across the border.

At that point, MacArthur persuaded Truman to allow him to push north and seek to reunify Korea. The Soviet delegate was now back in the Security Council, wielding his veto, so on October 7 the United States got approval for this course from the UN General Assembly, where the veto did not apply. U.S. forces had crossed the North Korean boundary by October 1 and continued northward. President Truman, concerned about broad hints of Communist Chinese intervention, flew 7,000 miles to Wake Island for a conference with General MacArthur on October 15. There the general discounted chances that the Chinese Red Army would act, but if it did, he confidently predicted, "there would be the greatest slaughter."

That same day, Peking announced that Communist China "cannot stand idly by." On October 26 UN units reached the Yalu River, Korea's border with China. MacArthur predicted total victory by Christmas, but on the night of November 25, several hundred thousand Chinese "volunteers" counterattacked. Massive "human-wave" attacks, with the support of tanks and planes, turned the tables on the UN forces, sending them into a desperate retreat just at the onset of winter. It had become "an entirely new war," MacArthur concluded. Soon he was reporting that the war was dragging on because the administration refused to let him blockade the Chinese mainland.

Truman opposed leading the United States into the "gigantic booby trap" of a ground war with China, and the UN forces soon rallied. By January 1951 over 900,000 UN troops under General Matthew Ridgway finally secured their lines below Seoul and then launched a counterattack that in some places carried them back across the 38th parallel in March. When Truman seized the chance and offered negotiations to restore the boundary and end the war, General MacArthur undermined the move by issuing an ultimatum for China to make peace or suffer an attack. Truman decided then that he had no choice but to accept MacArthur's aggressive policy or fire him. Civilian control of the military was at stake, Truman later asserted. On April 11, 1951, the president removed MacArthur, whom he called Mr. Prima Donna, from all his commands and replaced him with Ridgway.

Truman's action set off an uproar across the country, and a tumultuous reception greeted MacArthur upon his first return home since 1937. MacArthur's dramatic speech to a joint session of Congress provided the climactic event. A Senate investigation showcased the administration's arguments, best summarized by General Omar Bradley, chairman of the Joint Chiefs of Staff. The MacArthur strategy, he said, "would involve us in the

September 1950

Soldiers engaged in the recapture of Seoul from the North Koreans.

wrong war at the wrong place at the wrong time and with the wrong enemy." Most Americans found Bradley's logic persuasive.

On June 24, 1951, the Soviet representative at the United Nations proposed a cease-fire in Korea along the 38th parallel, which Secretary of State Dean Acheson accepted in principle a few days later. China and North Korea responded favorably—at the time, General Ridgway's "meat-grinder" offensive was inflicting severe losses. Truce talks started in July, only to drag on for two years while the fighting continued. The chief snags were exchanges of prisoners and the South Korean president's insistence on unification.

By the time a truce was finally reached, on July 27, 1953, Truman had relinquished the White House to Dwight D. Eisenhower. The truce line followed the front at that time, mostly a little north of the 38th parallel, with a demilitarized zone separating the forces; repatriation of prisoners would be voluntary, supervised by a neutral commission. No final peace conference ever took place, and Korea, like Germany, remained divided. The war had cost the United States more than 33,000 deaths and 103,000 wounded or missing. South Korean casualties, all told, were about 1 million, and North Korean and Chinese casualties totaled an estimated 1.5 million.

ANOTHER RED SCARE   The costs of the Korean War included the far-reaching consequences of a second Red Scare, which had grown since 1945 as the domestic counterpart to the cold war abroad and reached a climax during the Korean conflict. Since 1938 the House Un-American Activities Committee (HUAC) had kept up a barrage of accusations about supposed subversives in the federal government.

In 1947 the HUAC subpoenaed nineteen prominent Hollywood writers, producers, and actors, intending to prove that Communist party members dominated the Screen Writers Guild, that they injected subversive propaganda into motion pictures, and that President Roosevelt had brought improper pressure to bear upon the industry to produce pro-Soviet films during the war. Ten of the witnesses, the so-called Hollywood Ten, jointly decided to use the First Amendment as a defense, and each of them refused to answer the question "Are you now or have you ever been a member of the Communist party?" All ten had been members of the party, but they would not answer the question as a matter of principle, claiming that party identification was their business, especially since membership in the Communist party at that time was not illegal in the United States. They were all judged to be in contempt and were sentenced to up to a year in prison. But greater punishment awaited them. The movie industry blacklisted the Hollywood Ten, denying them further work.

In the charged atmosphere of the postwar years, Truman decided that he, too, must become more vigilant in rooting out Communists from the government. On March 21, 1947, therefore, just nine days after he announced the Truman Doctrine, the president signed an executive order setting up procedures for an employee loyalty program in the federal government. Designed partly to protect the president's political flank, it failed to do so mainly because of disclosures of earlier Communist penetrations of the government that were few in number but sensational in character.

The case most embarrassing to the administration involved Alger Hiss, president of the Carnegie Endowment for International Peace, who had served in several government departments, including the State Department. Whittaker Chambers, a former Soviet agent and later an editor of *Time* magazine, told the HUAC in 1948 that Hiss had given him secret documents ten years earlier, when Chambers was spying for the Soviets. Hiss sued for libel, and Chambers produced microfilms of the State Department documents that he claimed Hiss had passed to him. Hiss denied the accusation, whereupon he was indicted and, after one mistrial, convicted in 1950. The charge was perjury, but he was convicted of lying about espionage, for which he could not be tried because the statute of limitations on that crime had expired.

President Truman, taking at face value the many testimonials to Hiss's integrity, had called the charges against him a "red herring." Secretary of State Dean Acheson compounded the damage when, meaning to express compassion, he pledged not "to turn my back on Alger Hiss." The Hiss affair had another political consequence: it raised to national prominence a young California congressman, Richard M. Nixon, who doggedly insisted on pursuing the case and then exploited an anti-Communist stance to win election to the Senate in 1950.

More cases of Communist infiltration surfaced. In 1950 the government disclosed the existence of a British-American spy network that had fed information about the development of the atomic bomb to the Soviet Union. These disclosures led to the arrest of, among others, Julius and Ethel Rosenberg.

JOSEPH MCCARTHY'S WITCH HUNT   Revelations of Soviet spying encouraged politicians in both parties to exploit the public's fears. If a man of such respectability as Hiss was guilty, many wondered, who could be trusted? Early in 1950 a little-known Republican senator from Wisconsin, Joseph R. McCarthy, surfaced as the shrewdest and most ruthless exploiter of the nation's anxieties. He took up the cause of anti-communism with a vengeance, claiming that the State Department was infested with Communists and that he possessed a list of their names. Later there was confusion as to whether he had said there were 205, 81, 57, or "a lot" of names on the list

Joseph McCarthy

Senator McCarthy (left) and his aide Roy Cohn (right) exchange comments during testimony.

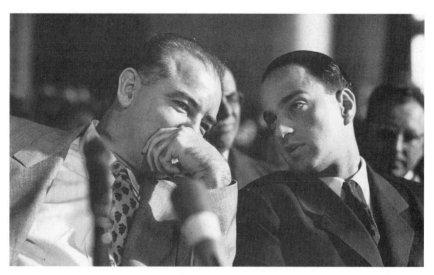

and even whether the sheet of paper he brandished contained any such list. Confusion would typically surround McCarthy's charges.

McCarthy never uncovered a single Communist agent in the government. But with the United States at war with Korean Communists in mid-1950, he continued to mobilize true believers behind his crusade. Republicans encouraged him to keep up the game. In 1951 he listed Generals George Marshall and Dwight Eisenhower among the disloyal. He kept up his outrageous campaign without successful challenge until the end of the Korean War.

Fears of Communist espionage led Congress in 1950 to pass the McCarran Internal Security Act over President Truman's veto, requiring Communist and Communist-front organizations to register with the attorney general. Aliens who had belonged to totalitarian parties were barred from admission to the United States. Documents recently uncovered in Russian archives and U.S. security agencies reveal that the Soviets did indeed operate an extensive espionage ring in the United States after World War II. Russian agents recruited several hundred American spies to ferret out secrets regarding atomic weapons, defense systems, and military intelligence.

ASSESSING THE COLD WAR   In retrospect the onset of the cold war takes on an appearance of terrible inevitability. America's preference for international principles such as self-determination and democracy conflicted with the Soviet Union's preference for international spheres of influence and totalitarian control. Russia, after all, had suffered two German invasions in the first half of the twentieth century, and Soviet leaders wanted tame buffer states on their borders for protection.

The people of Eastern Europe were again caught in the middle. But the Communists themselves held to a universal principle: world revolution. And since the time of President James Monroe, Americans had bristled at the thought of foreign intervention in their sphere of influence, the Western Hemisphere. Thus, to create a defensive shield against the spread of communism, the United States signed mutual defense treaties. Under the 1947 Treaty of Rio de Janeiro, the nations of the Western Hemisphere agreed to aid any country in the region that was attacked. In 1951 the United States and Japan signed a treaty that permitted the United States to maintain military forces in Japan. That same year American negotiators signed other mutual defense treaties with the Philippines, Australia, and New Zealand.

The policy initiatives of the Truman years led the country to abandon its long-standing aversion to peacetime alliances. It was a far cry from the world of 1796, when George Washington in his farewell address warned against "those overgrown military establishments which . . . are inauspicious to liberty" and advised his country "to steer clear of permanent alliances with any portion of the foreign world." But then Washington had warned only against participation in the "ordinary" combinations and collusions of Europe, and surely the postwar years had seen extraordinary events and unprecedented new alliances.

MAKING CONNECTIONS

- The cold war had a major impact on American society: among other things, it helped create the "conforming culture" described in the next chapter.

- The New Frontier and Great Society programs of Presidents Kennedy and Johnson, discussed in Chapter 34, accomplished much of what Truman tried to do through his Fair Deal policies.

- The world seemed a dangerous place at the height of the cold war, but when seen from the perspective of the post–cold war world of the 1990s (discussed in Chapters 36 and 37), it had a certain stability that discouraged political violence.

FURTHER READING

The cold war remains a hotly debated topic. The traditional interpretation is best reflected in John Lewis Gaddis's *The United States and the Origins of the Cold War, 1941–1947* (1972) and *We Now Know: Rethinking Cold War History* (1997). Both superpowers, Gaddis argues, were responsible for causing the cold war, but the Soviet Union was more culpable. The revisionist perspective is represented by Gar Alperovitz's *Atomic Diplomacy: Hiroshima and Potsdam: The Use of the Atomic Bomb and the American Confrontation with Soviet Power*, 2nd ed. (1994). Alperovitz places primary responsibility for the conflict on the United States. Also see H. W. Brands's *The Devil We Knew: Americans and the Cold War* (1993) and Melvyn P. Leffler's *A Preponderance of Power: National Security, the Truman Administration, and the Cold War* (1992). On the architect of containment, see David Mayers's *George Kennan and the Dilemmas of U.S. Foreign Policy* (1988).

Arnold A. Offner indicts Truman for clumsy statesmanship in *Another Such Victory: President Truman and the Cold War, 1945–1953* (2002). For a positive assessment of Truman's leadership, see Alonzo L. Hamby's *Beyond the New Deal: Harry S. Truman and American Liberalism* (1973). The domestic policies of the Fair Deal are treated in William C. Berman's *The Politics of Civil Rights in the Truman Administration* (1970), Richard M. Dalfiumes's *Desegregation of the U.S. Armed Forces: Fighting on Two Fronts, 1939–1953* (1969), and Maeva Marcus's *Truman and the Steel Seizure Case: The Limits of Presidential Power* (1977). The most comprehensive biography of Truman is David McCullough's *Truman* (1992).

For an introduction to the tensions in Asia, see Akira Iriye's *The Cold War in Asia: A Historical Introduction* (1974). For the Korean conflict, see Callum A. MacDonald's *Korea: The War before Vietnam* (1986) and Max Hasting's *The Korean War* (1987).

The anti-Communist syndrome is surveyed in David Caute's *The Great Fear: The Anti-Communist Purge under Truman and Eisenhower* (1978). Arthur Herman's *Joseph McCarthy: Reexamining the Life and Legacy of America's Most Hated Senator* (2000) covers McCarthy himself. For a well-documented account of how the cold war was sustained by superpatriotism, intolerance, and suspicion, see Stephen J. Whitfield's *The Culture of the Cold War,* 2nd ed. (1996).

32

THROUGH THE PICTURE WINDOW: SOCIETY AND CULTURE, 1945–1960

FOCUS QUESTIONS

· Why did the U.S. economy expand so rapidly in the postwar period?

· How did strains of conformity and innovation characterize the culture of the 1950s?

· What were the characteristics of America's burgeoning consumer culture?

To answer these questions and access additional review material, please visit www.wwnorton.com/studyspace.

Americans emerged from World War II elated, proud of their military strength and industrial might, and eager to enjoy peacetime prosperity. As the editors of *Fortune* magazine proclaimed in 1946, "This is a dream era, this is what everyone was waiting through the blackouts for. The Great American Boom is on." So it was. An American public that had known deprivation and sacrifice for a decade and a half began to enjoy unprecedented economic growth and seeming social contentment—at least on the surface.

Amid the rising affluence and optimism, however, many social critics, writers, and artists expressed a growing sense of unease. Was postwar society becoming too complacent, too conformist, too materialistic? These questions reflected the perennial tension in American life between idealism and materialism, a tension that arrived with the first settlers and remains with us today. Americans have always struggled to accumulate goods and cultivate goodness. During the postwar era the nation tried to do both. For a while, at least, it appeared to succeed.

PEOPLE OF PLENTY

The dominant feature of post–World War II society was its remarkable prosperity. After a surprisingly brief postwar recession, the economy soared to record heights. The gross national product nearly doubled between 1945 and 1960, and the 1960s witnessed an even more spectacular expansion of the economy. By 1970 the gap between the living standard in the United States and in the rest of the world had become a chasm: with 6 percent of the world's population, Americans produced and consumed nearly two thirds of its goods.

Several factors contributed to this sustained economic surge. The massive federal expenditures to meet military needs during the war had catapulted the economy out of the Depression. High government spending continued to drive the postwar economy, thanks to the tensions generated by the cold war. Military-related research also helped spawn the new glamour industries of the postwar era: chemicals, electronics, and aviation.

Most of the other major industrial nations of the world—England, France, Germany, Japan, the Soviet Union—had been physically devastated during the war, which meant that American manufacturers enjoyed a virtual monopoly on international trade. In addition, the widespread use of new and more efficient machinery and computers led to a 35 percent jump in the productivity of American workers between 1945 and 1955.

The major catalyst in promoting economic expansion after 1945, however, was the unleashing of pent-up consumer demand. During the war, civilians had postponed purchases of major items such as cars and houses and in the process had saved over $150 billion. Now they were eager to buy. The United States after World War II experienced a purchasing frenzy.

THE GI BILL OF RIGHTS   Part of that frenzy was indirectly financed by the federal government. People feared that a sharp postwar drop in military spending and the sudden influx of veterans into the civilian workforce would send the economy into a downward spiral and produce widespread unemployment. Those concerns led Congress to pass the Servicemen's Readjustment Act of 1944. Popularly known as the GI Bill of Rights (*GI* meaning "government issue," a phrase that was stamped on military uniforms and was slang for "serviceman"), it led to the creation of a new government agency, the Veterans Administration. The GI Bill also provided unemployment pay for veterans for one year, preference for veterans seeking government jobs, loans for home construction, access to government hospitals, and generous subsidies for college or professional training.

The infusion of funds into the economy provided by the GI Bill helped fuel the prosperity. Between 1944 and 1956 almost 8 million veterans took advantage of $14.5 billion in GI Bill subsidies to attend college or enroll in job-training programs. Some 5 million veterans bought new homes using GI Bill benefits. These two programs combined to produce a social revolution.

The GI Bill enabled millions of veterans to receive higher education. Before World War II approximately 160,000 Americans graduated from college each year. By 1950 the figure had more than tripled. In 1949 veterans accounted for 40 percent of all college enrollments, and the United States could boast the world's best-educated workforce.

The GI Bill democratized higher education. It provided a generation of working-class Americans with an opportunity to earn a college degree for the first time. In turn a college education served as a lever into the middle class and fostered economic security. But while the GI Bill helped erode class barriers, it was less successful in dismantling racial barriers. Many African-American veterans could not take equal advantage of the education benefits. Most colleges and universities after the war remained racially segregated, by regulation or by practice.

The historically black colleges, most of which were in the South, could not expand quickly enough to meet the demand. In 1940 African-American colleges enrolled 43,000 students; in 1950 the number had soared to 77,000. Yet over 20,000 others were denied admission because of overcrowded facilities. In 1946 only one fifth of the 100,000 African Americans who had applied for education benefits had enrolled.

The return of some 12 million veterans to private life also helped generate the postwar baby boom, which peaked in 1957. Between 1946 and 1960 the population grew by almost 40 million, a whopping 30 percent increase. Such a dramatic growth rate had a host of reverberating effects. Indeed, much of America's social history since the 1940s has been the story of the unusually large baby-boom generation and its progress through the stages of life.

AN EXPANDING CONSUMER CULTURE   The baby boom was accompanied by a postwar construction boom. The proportion of homeowners in the population increased by 50 percent between 1945 and 1960. And

The Baby Boom

Much of America's social history since the 1940s has been the story of the baby-boom generation.

those new homes were increasingly filled with the latest electrical appliances: refrigerators, washing machines, sewing machines, vacuum cleaners, freezers, mixers, and television sets. By far the most popular new household product was the TV set. In 1946 there were only 7,000 primitive black-and-white TV sets in the country; by 1960 there were 50 million high-quality sets. Nine out of ten homes had one, and by 1970, 38 percent of homes had the new color sets.

What differentiated the affluence of the post–World War II era from earlier periods of prosperity was its ever-widening dispersion. Although pockets of rural and urban poverty persisted, few noticed such exceptions to the prevailing prosperity during the 1950s. In 1955 union leader George Meany proclaimed that "American labor never had it so good."

On the surface many blacks were also beneficiaries of the wave of prosperity that swept over postwar society. By 1950 African Americans were earning on average more than four times their 1940 wages. While gains had been made, however, African Americans and other minority groups lagged behind whites in their rate of improvement. Indeed, the gap between the average yearly income of whites and blacks widened during the 1950s. Yet the desire to present a united front against communism led commentators to ignore or gloss over issues of racial and economic injustice. Such corrosive neglect would fester and explode during the 1960s, but for now the emphasis was on consensus, conformity, and economic growth.

To perpetuate the postwar prosperity, economists repeated the basic marketing strategy of the 1920s: the public must be taught to consume more and expect more. Economists knew that Americans had more money than ever before. The average adult had twice as much *real* income in 1955 as in the rosy days of the late 1920s before the crash. Still, many people who had undergone the severities of the Depression and the rationing required for the war effort had to be weaned from a decade and a half of imposed frugality in order to nourish the growing consumer culture.

Advertising became a more crucial component of the consumer culture than ever before. Expenditures for TV ads increased 1,000 percent during the 1950s. Such startling growth rates led the president of NBC to claim in 1956 that the primary reason for the postwar economic boom was that "advertising has created an American frame of mind that makes people want more things, better things and newer things." Paying for such "things" was no problem; the age of the credit card had arrived. Between 1945 and 1957 consumer credit soared 800 percent. Whereas families in other industrialized nations were typically saving 10 to 20 percent of their income, American families by the 1960s were saving only 5 percent.

Young Americans especially participated in the consumer culture. By the late 1950s the baby-boom generation was entering its teens, and the disproportionate number of affluent adolescents generated a vast new specialized market for youth-oriented goods ranging from transistor radios, Hula-Hoops, and rock-and-roll records to cameras, surfboards, *Seventeen* magazine, and Pat Boone movies. Most teenagers had far more discretionary income and free time than previous generations had had. Teens in the postwar era knew nothing of depressions or rationing; they were immersed in abundance from an early age and took for granted the notion of carefree consumption.

THE SUBURBAN FRONTIER   The population increase of the 1950s and 1960s was an urban as well as a suburban phenomenon. Dramatic new technological advances in agricultural production reduced the need for manual laborers. Almost 20 million Americans left the land for the city between 1940 and 1970. Much of the urban population growth occurred in the South, the Southwest, and the West, in an arc that stretched from the

Suburban Life

A woman vacuums her living room in Queens, New York, 1953, illustrating the 1950s ideal of domestic contentment facilitated by electrical appliances.

Carolinas to California, regions that by the 1970s were being lumped together and called the sunbelt. The dispersion of air-conditioning throughout these warm regions dramatically enhanced their attractiveness to northerners. But the Northeast remained the most densely populated area; by the early 1960s, 20 percent of the nation's population lived in the corridor that stretched south from Boston to Norfolk, Virginia.

While more people concentrated in cities, Americans after World War II were simultaneously spreading out within the metropolitan areas. During the 1950s suburbs grew six times faster than cities. By 1970 more people lived in suburbs (76 million) than in central cities (64 million). Suburban development required cars, highways, and government-backed home mortgages. It also required bold entrepreneurs.

William Levitt, a brassy New York developer, led the suburban revolution. In 1947, on 1,200 acres of Long Island farmland, he built 10,600 houses that were inhabited by more than 40,000 people, mostly adults under thirty-five and their children. Within a few years there were similar Levittowns in Pennsylvania and New Jersey, and other developers soon followed suit around the country. Expanded automobile production and highway construction facilitated the rush to the suburbs as more and more people were able to commute longer distances to work. Car production soared, and a car-dependent culture soon emerged. Widespread car ownership necessitated an improved road network. Local and state governments built many new roads, but the guiding force was the federal government. In 1947 Congress authorized the construction of 37,000 miles of federal highways, and nine years later it funded 42,000 additional miles of interstate expressways.

The federal government also fostered the suburban revolution through loans to developers and consumers. By insuring loans for up to 95 percent of the value of a house, the Federal Housing Administration made it easy for a builder to borrow money to construct low-cost homes. In addition, military veterans were given substantial assistance with home ownership. A veteran could buy a Levitt house with no down payment and monthly installments of $56. African Americans and other racial minorities, however, were often discriminated against. Contracts for homes in Levittown, Long Island, for example, specifically excluded "members of other than the Caucasian race." Such discrimination, whether explicit or implicit, was widespread; the nation's suburban population in 1970 was 95 percent white.

THE GREAT BLACK MIGRATION   World War II, like World War I, spurred a mass migration of rural southern blacks to the cities of other regions. This second migration was much larger in scope than the first, and its social consequences were much more dramatic. After 1945 more than 5 million southern blacks, mostly farm folk, left their native regions in search of better jobs, higher wages, decent housing, and greater social equality. During the 1950s, for example, the African-American population of Chicago more than doubled. The South Side of Chicago soon became known as the capital of black America. It remains the neighborhood with the largest concentration of African Americans in the nation.

Most black migrants were sharecroppers and farm laborers from the Mississippi Delta, the richest cotton-producing land in the world. For over a century the Delta cotton culture had been dependent upon African-American workers, first as slaves and then as sharecroppers and wage laborers. But a more efficient mechanical cotton picker invented in 1944 changed all that. The new machine could do the work of fifty people, making many farm-workers superfluous. Displaced southern blacks, many of them illiterate and provincial, streamed northward in search of a new promised land only to see many of their dreams dashed. In northern cities such as Chicago, Philadelphia, Newark, Detroit, New York, Boston, and Washington, D.C., African Americans from the rural South confronted harsh new realities. Slumlords often gouged them for rent, employers refused to hire them, and some union bosses denied them membership. Soon the promised land had become for many an ugly nightmare of slum housing, joblessness, illiteracy, dysfunctional families, welfare dependency, street gangs, pervasive crime, and racism.

The unexpected tidal wave of African-American migrants severely taxed the resources of urban governments and the tolerance of white racists. Throughout the North angry whites attacked blacks who dared move into their neighborhoods. Northern cities sought to deal with the migrants and alleviate racial stress by constructing massive all-black public-housing projects to accommodate the newcomers. These overcrowded racial enclaves were essentially segregated prisons. To be sure, many African-American migrants and their children did manage through extraordinary determination and ingenuity to "clear"—to climb out of the teeming ghettos and into the middle class. But most did not. As a consequence the great black migration produced a web of complex social problems in northern cities that in the 1960s would erupt into a crisis.

A CONFORMING CULTURE

In the 1950s social commentators mostly ignored people and cultures outside the mainstream. As evidenced in many of the new look-alike suburbs sprouting up across the land, much of white middle-class social life during the two decades after World War II exhibited an increasingly homogenized character. While fears generated by the cold war initially played a key role in encouraging orthodoxy, corporations and advertisers also came to play an increasingly important role in promoting homogeneity. Suburban life itself encouraged uniformity, since people felt a need for companionship and a sense of belonging as they moved into communities of strangers. "Conformity," predicted a journalist in 1954, "may very well become the central social problem of this age."

CORPORATE LIFE   During World War II big business had grown bigger. The government had relaxed its anti-trust activity, and huge defense contracts promoted corporate concentration and consolidation. In 1940, for example, the 100 largest companies were responsible for 30 percent of all manufacturing output; three years later they were producing 70 percent. After the war fewer and fewer people were self-employed; many now worked for large corporations, with manual labor giving way to mental labor for a large part of the workforce. In the huge companies as well as in similarly large government agencies and universities, the working atmosphere promoted conformity and regimentation rather than individualism.

WOMEN'S "PLACE" Increasing conformity in middle-class business and corporate life was mirrored in the middle-class home. A special issue of *Life* magazine in 1956 featured the "ideal" middle-class woman, a thirty-two-year-old "pretty and popular" white suburban housewife, mother of four, who had married at age sixteen. Described as an excellent wife, mother, volunteer, and "home manager," she hosted dozens of dinner parties each year, sang in her church choir, worked with the PTA and the Campfire Girls, and was devoted to her husband. "In her daily round," *Life* reported, "she attends club or charity meetings, drives the children to school, does the weekly grocery shopping, makes ceramics, and is planning to study French." *Life*'s ideal of the middle-class woman reflected a veritable cult of feminine domesticity that witnessed a dramatic revival in the postwar era. The soaring birthrate reinforced the deeply embedded notion that a woman's place was in the home. "Of all the accomplishments of the American woman," the *Life* cover story proclaimed, "the one she brings off with the most spectacular success is having babies."

Even though millions of women had responded to wartime appeals and joined the traditionally male workforce, afterward they were encouraged—and even forced—to turn their jobs over to the returning veterans and resume

The New Household

A Tupperware party in a middle-class suburban home.

their full-time commitment to home and family. Throughout the postwar era, educators, politicians, ministers, advertisers, and other commentators exalted the cult of domesticity and castigated the few feminists who were encouraging women to broaden their horizons beyond crib and kitchen. Women were to forget any thoughts of continuing their own careers in the workplace and return to their traditional domestic roles. Nonetheless, despite the ideal of women remaining in the home and the stigma associated with violating this norm, the percentage of women working outside the home increased overall during the 1950s.

THE SEARCH FOR COMMUNITY   In several respects, Americans were on the move after World War II. Some 20 percent of the population changed their place of residence each year. One cause of the mobility was the largest corporations' standard policy of relocating their sales and managerial employees. As they moved from central city to suburb, from suburb to suburb, from farm to city, from state to state, people searched for a sense of community and rootedness. Hence Americans, even more than usual, became joiners: they joined civic clubs, garden clubs, car pools, and babysitting groups.

Billy Graham Preaches to Thousands, 1955

The Baptist evangelist used radio and television to promote his huge crusades, as droves of Americans, encouraged by the president, Congress, and billboard advertising, joined churches and attended revival meetings.

Americans also joined churches and synagogues in record numbers. The postwar era witnessed a massive renewal of religious participation. In 1940 less than half the adult population belonged to a church; by 1960 over 65 percent were official communicants. Bible sales soared, and books, movies, and songs with religious themes were stunning commercial successes. The prevailing tone of the popular religious revival of the 1950s was upbeat and soothing. Most ministers assumed that people were not interested in "fire-and-brimstone" harangues from the pulpit; congregants did not want their conscience overburdened with a sense of personal sin or social guilt about issues such as segregation and inner-city poverty. Instead, they wanted to be reassured that their own comfortable way of life was indeed God's will.

CRACKS IN THE PICTURE WINDOW

Yet despite widespread prosperity, all was not well in postwar America. The widely publicized affluence masked festering poverty in rural areas and urban ghettos. People were also profoundly anxious about the meaning of their lives and of life in general in the nuclear age. That tranquilizers were the fastest growing medication suggested that considerable anxiety accompanied the nation's much-trumpeted affluence. Thus one of the most striking aspects of postwar American life was the sharp contrast between the prevailing sentiment that everything was fine and for the best as long as people believed in God, the "American way," and themselves and the increasingly bitter criticism of social life coming from artists, intellectuals, and other commentators.

THE LONELY CROWD   The criticism of postwar life and values began in the early 1950s and quickly gathered momentum. In *The Affluent Society* (1958), for example, the economist John Kenneth Galbraith warned that sustained economic growth would not necessarily solve chronic social problems. He reminded readers that for all of America's vaunted postwar prosperity, the nation had yet to confront, much less eradicate, the chronic poverty plaguing the nation's inner cities and rural hamlets. Postwar cultural critics also questioned the supposed bliss offered by middle-class suburban life. John Keats, in *The Crack in the Picture Window* (1956), launched a savage assault on life in the huge new suburban developments. Suburbanites, he concluded, were locked into a deadly routine, hounded by financial insecurity, engulfed by mass mediocrity, and living, in short, in a "homogeneous, postwar Hell."

Social critics in the 1950s repeatedly cited the huge modern corporation as an important source of regimentation in American life. The most provocative analysis of the docile new corporate character was David Riesman's *The Lonely Crowd* (1950). Riesman, a social psychologist, detected a fundamental shift in the dominant American personality from what he called the "inner-directed" type to the "other-directed" type. Inner-directed people, Riesman argued, possess a deeply internalized set of basic values implanted by strong-minded parents or other elders. Such an assured, self-reliant personality, Riesman claimed, had prevailed in nineteenth-century life. But during the mid–twentieth century a new, other-directed personality had displaced it. In the huge hierarchical corporations that abounded in postwar America, employees who could win friends and influence people thrived; rugged individualists indifferent to personal popularity did not. The other-directed people who adapted to the corporate culture had few internal convictions and standards; they did not follow their conscience so much as adapt to the prevailing standards of the moment. They were concerned more with being well liked than with being independent.

Riesman amassed considerable evidence to show that the other-directed personality was not just an aspect of the business world; its characteristics were widely dispersed throughout middle-class life. One of its sources, Riesman suggested, may have been Dr. Benjamin Spock's influential advice on raising children. Spock's popular manual, *The Common Sense Book of Baby and Child Care,* sold 1 million copies a year between its first appearance in 1946 and 1960. Spock stressed that parents should foster in their children qualities and skills that would enhance their chances in what Riesman called the "popularity market."

YOUTH CULTURE AND DELINQUENCY   Heeding Dr. Spock's advice, most parents of the 1950s tended to be permissive with their children, who occupied a distinctive place in postwar life. One commentator described the American family in 1957 as a "child-centered anarchy." As the baby boomers were reaching adolescence during the 1950s, a distinctive "teen" subculture began to emerge. And as most adults in postwar society were striving to get along and to conform to the values of the club or civic group or corporation, so too were most young people during the 1950s embracing the values of their parents and the capitalist system.

Yet such conformity and striving for popularity masked a great deal of turbulence. During the 1950s a wave of juvenile delinquency swept across middle-class society. By 1956 over 1 million teens a year were being arrested. Car theft was the leading offense, but larceny, rape, and murder were not

Youth Culture

A drugstore soda fountain, a popular outlet for teenagers' consumerism in the 1950s.

uncommon. A Boston judge announced that the entire city was being "terrorized" by juvenile gangs. What was causing the delinquency? J. Edgar Hoover, head of the Federal Bureau of Investigation, insisted that the root of the problem was a lack of religious training in more and more households. Others pointed to the growing number of urban slums, whose "brutish" environment could lead to criminality. Yet those factors failed to explain why so many middle-class kids from God-fearing families were becoming delinquents. One explanation may have been the unprecedented mobility of young people. Access to automobiles enabled teens to escape parental control, and in the words of one journalist, cars provided "a private lounge for drinking and for petting or sex episodes."

ROCK AND ROLL   Many concerned observers blamed the delinquency on a new form of music that emerged during the postwar era: rock and roll. In 1955 *Life* magazine published a long article about a mysterious new "frenzied teenage music craze" that was creating "a big fuss." Alan Freed, a Cleveland disc jockey, had coined the term *rock and roll* in 1951. At a record store he had noticed white teenagers buying rhythm and blues (R&B) records that had heretofore been purchased only by African Americans and Hispanic Americans. Freed began playing R&B records on the air but labeled the music rock and roll (a phrase used in African-American communities to refer to dancing and sex) to surmount the racial barrier.

Freed's radio program was an immediate success, and its popularity helped bridge the gap between "white" and "black" music. African-American singers such as Chuck Berry, Little Richard, and Ray Charles and Hispanic-American performers such as Ritchie Valens (Richard Valenzuela) were suddenly the rage among young white middle-class audiences eager to claim their own cultural style and message.

At the same time, Elvis Presley, a young white truck driver and aspiring singer from Memphis, Tennessee, began experimenting with "rockabilly" music, his unique blend of gospel, country-and-western, and R&B rhythms and lyrics. In 1956 the twenty-one-year-old Presley released "Heartbreak Hotel," and over the next two years the sensual baritone won fourteen gold records and emerged as the most popular entertainer in history. His sexually suggestive stage performances, featuring twisting hips and a gyrating pelvis, drove teenagers wild.

Such hysterics prompted cultural conservatives to urge parents to confiscate and destroy Presley's records because they promoted "a pagan concept of life." A Catholic cardinal denounced Presley as a vile symptom of a new teen "creed of dishonesty, violence, lust and degeneration." Patriotic groups claimed that rock-and-roll music was a tool of Communist insurgents designed to corrupt American youth.

Yet rock and roll survived the assaults and in the process gave

Elvis Presley, 1956

The teenage children of middle-class America made rock and roll a thriving industry in the 1950s and Elvis its first star. The strong beat of rock music combined with the electric guitar, its signature instrument, produced a distinctive new sound.

adolescents a self-conscious sense of belonging to a unique social group with distinctive characteristics and tastes. It also represented an unprecedented intermingling of racial, ethnic, and class identities.

ALIENATION IN THE ARTS   Dissatisfaction with the conventions and conformity of American society surfaced not only in rock and roll; it was manifested also in literature as well as in some of the artwork of the times. Many of the best novels and plays of the postwar period reinforced David Riesman's image of modern American society as a "lonely crowd" of individuals, hollow at the core, groping for a sense of belonging and affection. Arthur Miller's much-celebrated play *Death of a Salesman* (1949) explored this theme powerfully. Willy Loman, an aging, confused traveling salesman in decline, centers his life and that of his family on the notion of material success through personal popularity, only to be abruptly told by his boss that he is in fact a failure. Willy, for all his puffery about being well liked, admits that he is "terribly lonely." He has no real friends; even his relations with his family are neither honest nor intimate. When Willy finally realizes that he has been leading a counterfeit existence, he yearns for a life in which "a man is not a piece of fruit," but eventually he is so dumbfounded by his predicament that he decides he can endow his life with meaning only by ending it.

Nor are there many happy endings in the best novels of the postwar period. A brooding sense of resigned alienation dominated literary fiction in the two decades after 1945. The characters in novels such as James Jones's *From Here to Eternity* (1951), Ralph Ellison's *Invisible Man* (1952), Saul Bellow's *Dangling Man* (1944) and *Seize the Day* (1956), William Styron's *Lie Down in Darkness* (1951), and John Updike's *Rabbit, Run* (1961), among many others, tend to be like Willy Loman: restless, tormented, impotent individuals who are unable to fasten on a satisfying self-image and therefore can find neither contentment nor respect in an overpowering or impersonal world.

Many visual artists also explored the theme of desolate loneliness in urban-industrial American life. Virtually all of Edward Hopper's paintings, for example, depict isolated individuals, melancholy, anonymous, and motionless. The silence of his scenes is deafening, the monotony striking, the alienation absorbing.

A group of younger painters in New York City felt that postwar society was so chaotic that it denied any attempt at literal representation. Their anarchic technique came to be called abstract expressionism, and during the late 1940s and 1950s it dominated not only the American art scene but the international field as well. Abstract expressionists included Jackson Pollock,

Robert Motherwell, Willem de Kooning, Arshile Gorky, Clyfford Still, Adolph Gottlieb, and Mark Rothko. "Abstract art," Motherwell declared, "is an effort to close the void that modern men feel."

In practice this meant that the *act* of painting was as important as the result and that art no longer had to represent one's visual surroundings. Instead, it could unapologetically represent the painter's personal thoughts and actions. Wyoming-born Pollock, for example, placed his huge canvases flat on the floor and then walked around each side, pouring and dripping his paint in an effort to "literally be *in* the painting." Such action paintings, with their commanding size, bold form, powerful color contrasts, and rough texture, were vibrant, frenzied, meditative, disorienting, and provocative.

THE BEATS   The desire to liberate self-expression and reject middle-class conventions also animated a small but highly visible and controversial group of young writers, poets, painters, and musicians known as the Beats. These young men—Jack Kerouac, Allen Ginsberg, Gary Snyder, William Burroughs, and Gregory Corso, among others—rebelled against the mundane horrors of middle-class life. The Beats were not lost in despair, however; they strenuously embraced life. But it was life on their own terms, and their terms were shocking to most observers.

The self-described Beats grew out of the bohemian underground in New York's Greenwich Village. Essentially apolitical throughout the 1950s, the Beats sought personal rather than social solutions to their hopes and anxieties. As Jack Kerouac insisted, his friends were not beat in the sense of beaten; they were "mad to live, mad to talk, mad to be saved." Their road to salvation lay in hallucinogenic drugs and alcohol, sex, a penchant for jazz and the street life of urban ghettos, an affinity for Buddhism, and a restless, vagabond spirit that took them speeding back and forth across the country between San Francisco and New York.

This existential mania for intense experience and frantic motion provided the subject matter for the Beats' writing. Ginsberg's long prose poem *Howl*, published in 1956, features an explicit sensuality as well as an impressionistic attempt to catch the color, movement, and dynamism of modern life. Kerouac published his autobiographical novel *On the Road* a year later. In frenzied prose it portrays the Beats' life of "bursting ecstasies" and maniacal traveling. *Howl* and *On the Road* elicited angry sarcasm from many reviewers, but the books enjoyed brisk sales, especially among young people. *On the Road* made the best-seller list, and soon the term *Beat generation* or *beatnik* referred to almost any young rebel who openly dissented from the comfortable ethos of middle-class life.

Allen Ginsberg

Ginsberg, considered the poet laureate of the Beat generation, reads his uncensored poetry to a crowd in Washington Square Park in New York City.

A PARADOXICAL ERA

For all their eccentricities and vitality the Beats had little impact on the prevailing patterns of postwar social and cultural life. The same held true for most of the critics who attacked the smug conformity and excessive materialism they saw pervading their society. The public had become weary of larger social or political concerns in the aftermath of the Depression and the war. Instead, Americans eagerly focused on personal and family goals and material achievements.

Yet those achievements, considerable as they were, eventually created a new set of problems. The benefits of abundance were by no means equally distributed during the 1950s, and millions of people still lived in poverty. For those more fortunate, unprecedented affluence and security fostered greater leisure and independence, which in turn provided opportunities for pursuing more diverse notions of what the good life entailed. Yet the conformist mentality of the cold war era discouraged experimentation. By the mid-1960s tensions between innovation and convention would erupt into open conflict. Many members of the baby-boom generation would become the leaders of the 1960s rebellion against the corporate and consumer cultures and the militarism excited by the cold war. Ironically, the person who would warn Americans of the 1960s of the mounting dangers of the burgeoning "military-industrial complex" was the president who had long symbolized its growth: Dwight D. Eisenhower.

MAKING CONNECTIONS

- The culture of the 1950s laid the groundwork for the counterculture of the 1960s, discussed in Chapters 34 and 35.

- Fruitful comparisons may be made between American culture in the 1950s and the earlier postwar period, the 1920s, which was described in Chapter 26.

- The women's movement of the 1970s, discussed in Chapter 35, was led by women who rejected the cult of domesticity that is described in this chapter.

- The baby boom of the postwar period would have continuing economic, social, political, and cultural significance as its members moved through the life cycle. Follow along in the coming chapters.

FURTHER READING

Two excellent overviews of social and cultural trends in the postwar era are William H. Chafe's *The Unfinished Journey: America since World War II,* 5th ed. (2003) and William E. Leuchtenburg's *A Troubled Feast: America since 1945* (1973). For insights into the cultural life of the 1950s, see Jeffrey Hart's *When the Going Was Good!: American Life in the Fifties* (1982) and David Halberstam's *The Fifties* (1993).

The baby-boom generation and its impact are vividly described in Paul C. Light's *Baby Boomers* (1988). The emergence of the television industry is discussed in Erik Barnouw's *Tube of Plenty: The Evolution of American Television* (1975) and Ella Taylor's *Prime-Time Families: Television Culture in Postwar America* (1989).

A comprehensive account of the process of suburban development is Kenneth T. Jackson's *Crabgrass Frontier: The Suburbanization of the United States*

(1985). Equally good is Tom Martinson's *American Dreamscape: The Pursuit of Happiness in Postwar America* (2000).

The middle-class ideal of family life in the 1950s is examined in Elaine Tyler May's *Homeward Bound: American Families in the Cold War Era* (1988). Thorough accounts of women's issues are found in Wini Breines's *Young, White, and Miserable: Growing up Female in the Fifties* (1992). For an overview of the resurgence of religion in the 1950s, see George M. Marsden's *Religion and American Culture* (1990).

A lively discussion of movies of the 1950s can be found in Peter Biskind's *Seeing Is Believing: How Hollywood Taught Us to Stop Worrying and Love the Fifties* (1983). The origins and growth of rock and roll are surveyed in Carl Belz's *The Story of Rock*, 2nd ed. (1972). Thoughtful interpretive surveys of postwar American literature include Josephine Hendin's *Vulnerable People: A View of American Fiction since 1945* (1978) and Malcolm Bradbury's *The Modern American Novel* (1983). The colorful Beats are brought to life in Steven Watson's *The Birth of the Beat Generation: Visionaries, Rebels, and Hipsters, 1944–1960* (1995).

33

CONFLICT AND DEADLOCK: THE EISENHOWER YEARS

FOCUS QUESTIONS

- What characterized Eisenhower's "dynamic conservatism"?
- What were the central terms of American foreign policy in the 1950s?
- How did the civil rights movement emerge in the 1950s?
- What events led up to the Vietnam War?

To answer these questions and access additional review material, please visit www.wwnorton.com/studyspace.

The New Deal political coalition established by Franklin Roosevelt and sustained by Harry Truman posed a formidable challenge to Republicans after World War II. To counter the potent combination of Solid South white Democrats, African Americans, and members of other minority groups, and organized labor, the Grand Old Party turned to General Dwight David Eisenhower, a military hero capable of attracting independent voters as well as some Democrats. Eisenhower's commitment to a "moderate Republicanism" promised to slow the rate of government expansion while retaining many of the cherished social programs established by Roosevelt and Truman. Eisenhower's two terms as president are often characterized as a lull between two eras of Democratic activism. In Eisenhower's view, however, his administration would restore the authority of state and local governments and restrain the executive branch from political and social "engineering." In the process the former general sought to reinforce traditional virtues and inspire Americans with a vision of a brighter future.

"TIME FOR A CHANGE"

By 1952 the Truman administration had piled up a heavy burden of political liabilities: a bloody stalemate in Korea, renewed wage and price controls at home, reckless charges of subversion and disloyalty among federal employees, and the exposure of corrupt lobbyists and influence peddlers who rigged favors in Washington. The disclosure of government corruption led Truman to fire nearly 250 employees of the Internal Revenue Service. But doubts lingered that he would ever finish the housecleaning.

THE POLITICAL RISE OF EISENHOWER   It was, in a slogan of the day, "time for a change," and Republicans saw public sentiment turning their way as the 1952 election approached. Republican leaders recruited General Dwight D. Eisenhower to be their candidate. Despite his Kansas roots in Republican conservatism, Eisenhower had initially supported Roosevelt and the New Deal, and he admired Roosevelt's wartime leadership. During the Truman years, however, Eisenhower reverted to the political party of his youth. In early 1952 he affirmed that he was a Republican and permitted his name to be entered in party primaries. He won the nomination on the first ballot, then balanced the ticket by selecting as his running mate a youthful Californian, the thirty-nine-year-old senator Richard M. Nixon, who had built a career on strenuous opposition to domestic "subversives."

THE ELECTION OF 1952   The Twenty-second Amendment, ratified in 1951, forbade any president from serving more than two terms. The amendment exempted the current incumbent, Harry Truman, but weary of the war in Korea and harassed by charges of subversion and corruption in his administration, Truman chose to withdraw. In a wide-open Democratic race he supported Illinois governor Adlai E. Stevenson, who roused the Democratic Convention delegates with an eloquent speech welcoming them to Chicago.

The 1952 campaign matched two of the most magnetic personalities ever pitted against each other in a presidential contest, but the race was uneven from the start. Eisenhower, though a political novice, was a world hero who had been in the public eye for a decade. Stevenson was hardly known outside Illinois. The genial Eisenhower, who disliked politics and politicians, pledged to clean up "the mess in Washington." To this he added a promise, late in the campaign, that as president-elect he would secure "an early and honorable" peace in Korea. Stevenson offered a keen intellect spiced with a quick wit, but his resolve to "talk sense" and "tell the truth to the American

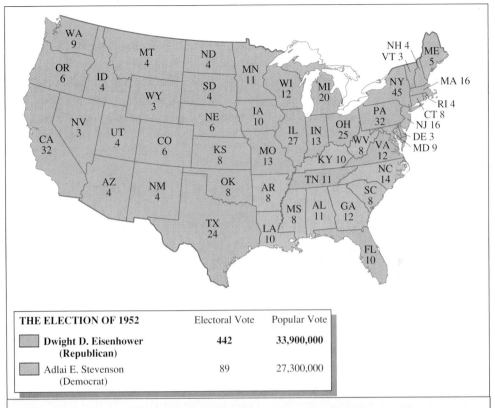

THE ELECTION OF 1952	Electoral Vote	Popular Vote
Dwight D. Eisenhower (Republican)	442	33,900,000
Adlai E. Stevenson (Democrat)	89	27,300,000

Why was the contest between Stevenson and Eisenhower so lopsided? Why was Eisenhower's victory in the South remarkable? Did Eisenhower's broad appeal help congressional Republicans win more seats?

people" came across as too aloof, a shade too intellectual. The Republicans labeled him an egghead in contrast to Eisenhower, the folksy man of the people, the man of decisive action.

In the end, Stevenson's humor and intellect were no match for Eisenhower's popularity. The war hero triumphed in a landslide of 34 million votes to 27 million. The election marked a turning point in Republican fortunes in the South: for the first time since the 1850s, the South was moving toward a two-party system. Stevenson carried only eight southern states plus West Virginia; Eisenhower picked up five states on the periphery of the Deep South: Florida, Oklahoma, Tennessee, Texas, and Virginia. The "nonpolitical" Eisenhower had made it respectable, even fashionable, to vote Republican in the South. Elsewhere, too, the general made inroads into the New Deal coalition, attracting supporters among the ethnic and religious minorities in the major cities who had long identified with the Democratic party.

The voters, it turned out, liked Ike better than they liked his party. In the 1952 election, Democrats retained most of the governorships, lost control of the House by only eight votes, and broke even in the Senate. The congressional elections two years later would weaken the Republican grip on Congress, and Eisenhower would have to work with a Democratic Congress until he left office.

Eisenhower's "Hidden-Hand" Presidency

IKE   Born in Denison, Texas, in 1890, Dwight David Eisenhower grew up in Abilene, Kansas, and attended the U.S. Military Academy at West Point, New York. As a general during World War II, he took command of American forces in the European theater and directed the invasion of North Africa in 1942. In 1944 he assumed the post of supreme commander of Allied forces in preparation for the invasion of German-controlled Europe. After the war, by then the five-star general of the army, Eisenhower became chief of staff and supreme commander of NATO forces, with a brief interlude as president of Columbia University.

Far from being a "do-nothing" president, as some have charged, Eisenhower was an effective leader. The art of leadership, he once explained, did not require "hitting people over the head. Any damn fool can do that. . . . It's persuasion—and conciliation—and education—and patience. That's the only kind of leadership I know—or believe in—or will practice." The public image of Ike was warm, sincere, and unpretentious, a man who rose above partisan politics. Those who were close to him have presented another side, however. When provoked, the genial general could show a fiery temper and release a stream of scalding profanity. One student of Eisenhower's leadership techniques has spoken of a "hidden-hand presidency," in which Ike deliberately cultivated a public image of passivity to hide his active involvement in policy decisions.

"DYNAMIC CONSERVATISM" AT HOME   Eisenhower called his domestic program dynamic conservatism, which meant being "conservative when it comes to money and liberal when it comes to human beings." Budget cutting was a high priority. Eisenhower warned repeatedly against the dangers of "creeping socialism," "huge bureaucracies," and budget deficits. His administration ended wage and price controls and reduced federal farm-price subsidies.

But though Eisenhower chipped away at New Deal programs, his presidency in the end served rather to legitimate the New Deal by keeping its basic structure and premises intact during an era of prosperity. In some ways the administration expanded the New Deal, especially after 1954, when it had the help of Democratic Congresses. Amendments to the Social Security Act in 1954 and 1956 brought coverage to millions in categories formerly excluded: professional people, domestic and clerical workers, farmworkers, and members of the armed forces. The federal minimum wage rose in 1955 from 75¢ to $1 an hour. Federal expenditures for public health rose steadily in the Eisenhower years, and low-income housing continued to be built, although on a much reduced scale. Some farm-related aid programs were actually expanded.

Despite Eisenhower's disapproval of federal electric-power programs, he continued to support government public works projects that served the national interest. Two such programs left major monuments to his presidency: the St. Lawrence Seaway and the interstate highways. The St. Lawrence Seaway, opened in 1959 as a joint venture with Canada, allowed oceangoing ships to reach the Great Lakes. The Federal-Aid Highway Act of 1956 authorized the federal government to contribute 90 percent of the cost of building 42,500 miles of limited-access interstate highways to serve the needs of commerce and defense, as well as the convenience of private citizens. The states provided the remaining 10 percent.

CONCLUDING AN ARMISTICE   America's new global responsibilities in the postwar world continued to absorb Eisenhower's attention. The most pressing problem when he entered office was the painful deadlock in the Korean peace talks. To break the stalemate, Eisenhower took a bold stand. In mid-May 1953 he stepped up aerial bombardment of North Korea, then had Secretary of State John Foster Dulles warn the Chinese of his willingness to use atomic bombs. Whether for that reason or others, negotiations moved quickly toward an armistice along the established border just above the 38th parallel and toward a complicated arrangement for an exchange of prisoners that allowed captives to decide whether to accept or refuse repatriation.

On July 26, 1953, Eisenhower announced the conclusion of the Korean armistice agreement. No one knows if he actually would have forced the issue with atomic weapons. Perhaps the more decisive factors in bringing about a settlement were the mounting Chinese losses and the spirit of uncertainty and caution felt by the Russian Communists after the death of Joseph Stalin on March 5, 1953, six weeks after Ike's inauguration.

The Army-McCarthy Hearings, June 1954

The attorney Joseph Welch (hand on head) listening incredulously to Senator Mc-Carthy's claims of Communist infiltration of the U.S. Army.

CONCLUDING A WITCH HUNT   The Korean armistice helped to end the meteoric career of Senator Joseph McCarthy. Convinced that the government was thoroughly infested with Communists and spies, the Wisconsin senator launched a one-man crusade to root them out. Eventually the logic of McCarthy's unscrupulous tactics led to his self-destruction, but not before he had left many careers and reputations in ruins. The Eisenhower Republicans thought their victory in 1952 would curb McCarthy's recklessness, but the senator grew more outlandish in both his charges and his investigative methods.

McCarthy finally overreached himself in the spring of 1954, when as chairman of the Senate's Government Operations Committee he made the absurd charge that the U.S. Army itself was "soft" on communism. The televised Army-McCarthy hearings displayed McCarthy at his worst, scowling at critics, bullying witnesses, repeatedly calling "point of order." He became the perfect foil for the Army's gentle but unflappable counsel, Joseph Welch, whose rapier wit repeatedly drew blood. On December 2, 1954, the Senate voted sixty-seven to twenty-two to "condemn" McCarthy for contempt of the Senate. McCarthy's political career collapsed. For all his attacks and inquiries he had never uncovered one Communist in the government. McCarthyism, Eisenhower joked, had become McCarthywasm. To the end, Eisenhower refused to "get down in the gutter with that guy" and sully the dignity of the presidency. He did work resolutely against McCarthy behind the scenes, but some scholars consider his "hidden-hand" approach to have been ineffective at best and cowardly at worst.

Eisenhower believed that espionage posed a real danger to national security. He denied clemency to Julius and Ethel Rosenberg, who had been convicted of passing atomic secrets to the Russians, on the grounds that they "may have condemned to death tens of millions of innocent people." The Rosenbergs were electrocuted in 1953.

INTERNAL SECURITY   The anti-Communist crusade survived McCarthy's downfall. Even before 1954 Eisenhower stiffened the government security program that Truman had set up in 1947. In 1953 he issued an executive order broadening the basis for firing subversive government workers, replacing Truman's criterion of "disloyalty" with the new category of "security risk." Under the new edict federal workers could lose their jobs because of dubious political associations or personal behavior that might make them careless or vulnerable to blackmail. However, the Supreme Court modified some of the more extreme expressions of this continuation of the Red Scare. In 1953 Eisenhower appointed as chief justice of the Supreme Court former governor Earl Warren of California, a decision he later pronounced the "biggest damnfool mistake I ever made." Warren, who had seemed safely conservative while in electoral politics, led an active Court on issues of civil rights and civil liberties. The Warren Court (1953–1969), under the chief justice's influence, became an important agent of social and political change through the 1960s. In connection with security programs and loyalty requirements, the Court veered back in the direction of traditional individual rights.

FOREIGN INTERVENTION

DULLES AND FOREIGN POLICY   The Eisenhower administration promised new foreign-policy departures under the direction of Secretary of State John Foster Dulles. Grandson of one secretary of state and nephew of another, Dulles pursued a lifetime career as an international lawyer and sometime diplomat. Son of a minister and himself an earnest Presbyterian, Dulles, in the words of the British ambassador, resembled those old zealots of the wars of religion who "saw the world as an arena in which the forces of good and evil were continuously at war." But he was also a man of immense energy, intelligence, and experience.

The foreign-policy planks of the 1952 Republican platform, which Dulles wrote, showed both the moralist and the tactician at work. Truman's policy of containment was needlessly defensive, Dulles thought. Americans instead should promote the "liberation" of sovereign nations from Soviet domination.

"Don't Be Afraid—I Can Always Pull You Back."

Secretary of State John Foster Dulles pushes a reluctant America to the brink of war.

Eisenhower was quick to explain, however, that liberating Eastern Europe from Soviet control would not involve military force. He would promote independence "by every peaceful means, but only by peaceful means."

Yet for all his talk of liberating Eastern Europe, Dulles made no significant departure from the containment strategy created under Truman. Instead, he institutionalized containment in the rigid mold of his cold war rhetoric and extended it to the military strategy of deterrence. Dulles's endorsement of "massive retaliation" was an effort to get, in the slogan soon current, "more bang for the buck." By this time both the United States and the Soviet Union had exploded hydrogen bombs. With the new policy of deterrence, what Winston Churchill called a balance of terror had replaced the old balance of power. The threat of nuclear holocaust was terrifying, but the notion that the United States would risk such a disaster in response to local wars had little credibility.

Dulles's policy of "brinksmanship" depended for its strategic effect upon those very fears of nuclear disaster. He argued in 1956 that in following a tough policy of confronting communism, a nation sometimes had to "go to the brink" of war. Such a firm stand had halted aggression in Korea when America threatened in 1953 to use atomic weapons. Dulles also employed brinksmanship in Indochina in 1954, when U.S. aircraft carriers moved into the South China Sea "both to deter any Red Chinese attack against Indochina and to provide weapons for instant retaliation."

INDOCHINA: THE BACKGROUND TO WAR Like the rest of the old colonial world of Asia and Africa, French Indochina experienced a wave of nationalism after World War II, damaging both the power and the prestige of France. By the early 1950s most of British Asia was independent or on its way to independence: India, Pakistan, Ceylon (now Sri Lanka), Burma (now Myanmar), and the Malay States (now Malaysia). The Dutch and French, however, were less willing to give up their colonies, a situation that created a dilemma for U.S. policy makers. Americans sympathized with the colonial nationalists but wanted Dutch and French help fending off the spread of communism. For the Dutch and the French to maintain control of their colonial empires, they had to reconquer areas that had passed from Japanese occupation into the hands of local patriots. The Truman administration had felt obliged to comply with the Dutch and French pleas for aid.

French Indochina, created in the nineteenth century out of the old kingdoms of Cambodia, Laos, and Vietnam, offered a variation on colonial nationalism. During World War II, opposition to the Japanese occupation of Indochina was led by the Viet Minh (League for the Independence of Vietnam), nationalists who fell under the influence of Communists led by the magnetic rebel Ho Chi Minh. At the end of the war, the Viet Minh controlled part of northern Vietnam, and on September 2, 1945, Ho Chi Minh proclaimed a Democratic Republic of Vietnam, with its capital in Hanoi. Ho had secretly received American help against the Japanese during the war, but his bids for further aid after the war went unanswered. Vietnam was a low priority in U.S. diplomatic concerns, which at the time were focused on restoring western Europe and containing the spread of communism there.

In 1946 the French government recognized Ho's new government as a "free state" within the French colonial union. Before the year was out, however, Ho had opposed French efforts to establish another regime in the southern provinces, and their clash soon expanded into the First Indochina War. This was a troubling development for the U.S. government. On the one hand, the United States resented France's determination to restore colonial rule. Yet Truman was even more determined to see France become a bulwark against communism

Ho Chi Minh

A seasoned revolutionary, Ho Chi Minh cultivated a humble, proletarian image of himself as Uncle Ho, a man of the people.

in Europe. As a result, the American government acquiesced in France's efforts to crush Vietnamese nationalism.

The Viet Minh movement thereafter became more dependent upon the Soviet Union and Communist China for help. In 1950, with the outbreak of fighting in Korea, the struggle in Vietnam took on the appearance of a battleground in the cold war. When the Korean War ended, American aid to the French in Vietnam, begun by the Truman administration, escalated dramatically. By the end of 1953, the Eisenhower administration was paying about two thirds of the cost of the French war effort in Indochina.

But even with lavish U.S. aid the French were unable to suppress the well-organized and tenacious Viet Minh. In 1954 a major French force had been sent to Dien Bien Phu, in the northwest corner of Vietnam, near the Laos border, in the hope of luring Viet Minh guerrillas into the open and overwhelming them with superior firepower. The French instead found themselves surrounded by a superior force that laid siege to their stronghold.

In March 1954 the French government requested an American air strike to relieve the pressure on Dien Bien Phu. Eisenhower seemed to endorse forceful action when he advanced his "domino theory" at a news conference on April 7. He implied that if Indochina fell to the Communists, the rest of Asia would be next. Eisenhower, however, opposed direct U.S. military action unless the British lent support. When they refused, Eisenhower backed away from unilateral action, explaining that it would be a "tragic error to go in alone as a partner of France."

America's decision not to intervene sealed the fate of the besieged French garrison at Dien Bien Phu. On May 7, 1954, the Viet Minh overwhelmed the courageous but vastly outnumbered French resistance. It was the very eve of the day on which an international conference at Geneva took up the question of Indochina. Six weeks later, as French forces continued to suffer defeats in Vietnam, a new French government promised an early settlement. On July 20 representatives of France, Britain, the Soviet Union, the People's Republic of China, and the Viet Minh signed the Geneva Accords and the next day produced their Final Declaration, which proposed to make Laos and Cambodia independent and divide Vietnam at the 17th parallel. The Viet Minh would take power in the north, and the French would remain south of the line until elections in 1956 would reunify Vietnam. American and South Vietnamese representatives refused to join in the accord or to sign the Final Declaration.

Eisenhower announced that although the United States "had not itself been party to or bound by the decision taken at the Conference," any renewal of Communist aggression in Vietnam "would be viewed by us as a matter of grave concern." (He failed to note that the United States had agreed at

Geneva to "refrain from the threat or use of force to disturb" the agreements.) Ho Chi Minh and his government in Hanoi quickly sought to consolidate control throughout the north. In the hinterlands local Communists held kangaroo courts that tried and executed landowners and confiscated their land. Residents of the north who wished to leave for the south did so with American aid. Over 900,000 refugees, most of them Catholics, relocated in the south, causing staggering logistical problems for the struggling new government there.

Power in the south gravitated to a new premier, Ngo Dinh Diem, a Catholic nationalist who had opposed both the French and the Viet Minh. Diem took office during the Geneva talks, after returning from exile at a seminary in New Jersey. In 1954 Eisenhower offered to assist Diem if he would enact democratic reforms and distribute land to the peasants. U.S. aid took the form of CIA and military advisers charged with training Diem's armed forces and police. Eisenhower remained opposed to the use of U.S. combat troops. He was convinced that such military intervention would bog down into a costly stalemate—as it eventually did.

Instead of instituting comprehensive reforms, however, Diem suppressed his political opponents on both the right and the left, offering little or no land distribution and permitting widespread corruption. In 1956 he refused to join in the elections to reunify Vietnam, and the United States endorsed his decision. But Diem's efforts to eliminate all opposition only played into the hands of the Communists, who found more and more recruits among the discontented peasantry. By 1957 guerrilla forces in the south, known as the Viet Cong, had begun attacks on the Diem government, and in 1960 the resistance formed its own political arm, the National Liberation Front. As guerrilla warfare gradually disrupted South Vietnam, Eisenhower was helpless to do anything but "sink or swim with Ngo Dinh Diem."

REELECTION AND FOREIGN CRISES

As the United States continued to forge postwar alliances and bring pressure to bear on foreign governments by practicing brinksmanship, a new presidential campaign unfolded. Despite having suffered a coronary seizure in the fall of 1955 and undergoing an operation for ileitis (an intestinal inflammation) in early 1956, Eisenhower decided to run for reelection. He retained widespread public support, although the Democrats controlled Congress. Meanwhile, new crises in foreign and domestic affairs required him to take decisive action.

A LANDSLIDE FOR IKE   In 1956 the Republican Convention renominated Eisenhower by acclamation and again named Nixon the vice-presidential candidate. The party platform endorsed Eisenhower's "modern Republicanism." The Democrats turned again to Adlai Stevenson, with a platform that revived party issues: less "favoritism" to big business, repeal of the Taft-Hartley Act, increased aid to farmers, and tax relief for those in low-income brackets.

Neither candidate generated much excitement. The Democrats focused their fire on the heir apparent, Richard Nixon, a "man of many masks." Stevenson roused little enthusiasm for two controversial proposals: to replace military conscription with an all-volunteer army and to ban hydrogen-bomb tests by international agreement. Both involved military questions that put Stevenson at a disadvantage by pitting his judgment against that of a successful former general. Voters handed Eisenhower a landslide victory. He lost one border state, Missouri, but in carrying Louisiana became the first Republican to win a Deep South state since Reconstruction; nationally, he carried all but seven states.

CRISIS IN THE MIDDLE EAST   To forestall Soviet penetration in the Middle East, the Eisenhower-Dulles foreign policy cultivated Arab friendship, and in 1955 Dulles had completed his line of alliances across the "northern tier" of the Middle East. Under American sponsorship, Britain had joined Turkey, Iraq, Iran, and Pakistan in the Middle East Treaty Organization (METO), or the Baghdad Pact Organization, as the treaty was commonly called. But after Iraq, the only Arab member, withdrew in 1959, the alliance lost its cohesion and credibility. The Arab states remained aloof from the organization. These were the states of the Arab League (Egypt, Iraq, Jordan, Lebanon, Saudi Arabia, Syria, and Yemen), which had warred on Israel in 1948–1949 and remained committed to its destruction.

The most fateful developments in the Middle East turned on the rise of the Egyptian general Gamal Abdel Nasser, who overthrew King Farouk in 1952. Nasser's nationalist regime soon pressed for the withdrawal of British forces guarding the Suez Canal, the crucial link between the Mediterranean Sea and the Indian Ocean. Eisenhower and Dulles supported Nasser's demand, and in 1954 an Anglo-Egyptian treaty provided for British withdrawal within twenty months. Ownership of the canal remained with the Anglo-French Suez Canal Company, however.

Nasser, like other leaders of the third world, remained unaligned in the cold war and sought to play both sides off against each other. The United States in turn courted Egyptian support by offering a loan to build a huge hydroelectric plant at Aswān on the Nile River. From the outset the administration's proposal

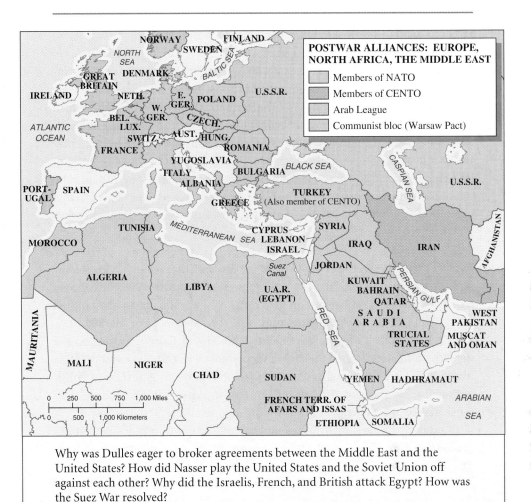

POSTWAR ALLIANCES: EUROPE, NORTH AFRICA, THE MIDDLE EAST

Members of NATO
Members of CENTO
Arab League
Communist bloc (Warsaw Pact)

Why was Dulles eager to broker agreements between the Middle East and the United States? How did Nasser play the United States and the Soviet Union off against each other? Why did the Israelis, French, and British attack Egypt? How was the Suez War resolved?

was opposed by Jewish constituencies concerned with Egyptian threats to Israel and by southern congressmen who feared the competition from Egyptian cotton. In 1956, when Nasser increased trade with the Soviet bloc and recognized Communist China, Dulles abruptly canceled the loan offer.

The outcome was far from a triumph of American diplomacy. The chief victims, it turned out, were Anglo-French interests in the Suez. Unable to retaliate against the United States, Nasser took control of the Suez Canal Company. The British and the French were furious. While negotiations dragged on, Israeli forces invaded the Gaza Strip and Sinai peninsula. Ostensibly their aim was to root out Arab guerrillas, but actually it was to synchronize with the British and the French, who began bombing Egyptian air bases and occupied Port Said.

The Suez War put the United States in a quandary. Either the administration could support its Western allies and see the troublesome Nasser crushed, or it could defend the UN charter and champion Arab nationalism against imperialist aggression. Eisenhower opted for the latter course, with the unusual result that the Soviet Union sided with the United States. Once the threat of American embargoes had forced the Anglo-French-Israeli to halt their advance against Egypt, the Soviets capitalized on the situation by threatening to use missiles against the Western aggressors. This belated bravado won for the Soviet Union in the Arab world some of the credit actually owed the United States.

REPRESSION IN HUNGARY   In the Soviet Union, Nikita Khrushchev had come out on top in the post-Stalin power struggles. In 1956 Khrushchev had delivered a "secret" speech on the crimes of the Stalin era and had hinted at relaxed policies in neighboring countries. This new policy of "de-Stalinization" put Stalinist leaders in the satellite countries of Eastern Europe on the defensive and emboldened the more independent leaders to take action. Riots in the Polish city of Poznan led to the rise of Wladyslaw Gomulka, a Polish nationalist, as leader of the Polish Communist party. Gomulka managed to win a degree of independence by avoiding an open break with the Soviets.

In Hungary, however, a similar movement got out of hand. On October 23, 1956, fighting broke out in Budapest, followed by the installation of Imre Nagy, a moderate Communist, as head of the government. Again the Soviets seemed content to let de-Stalinization follow its course, and on October 28 they withdrew their forces from Budapest. But Nagy's announcement three days later that Hungary would withdraw from the Warsaw Pact (a military alliance linking the Eastern European countries under Soviet control) brought Soviet tanks back into Budapest. Although Khrushchev was willing to relax relations with the Eastern European satellites, he refused to allow them to break with the Soviet Union or abandon their mutual defense obligations. The Soviets installed a more compliant leader in Hungary, János Kádár, and hauled Nagy off to Moscow, where a firing squad executed him in 1958. It was a tragic ending to an independence movement that at the outset promised the sort of moderation that might have vindicated George Kennan's policy of containment, if not Dulles's notion of liberation.

SPUTNIK   On October 4, 1957, the Soviets launched the first satellite, called *Sputnik*. Americans, until then complacent about their technical superiority, suddenly discovered an apparent "missile gap." If the Soviets were so advanced in rocketry, then perhaps they could hit American cities with missiles. All along Eisenhower had known that the "missile gap" was more illusory than real, but he could not reveal that high-altitude American U-2 spy planes were gathering that information.

Soviet success with *Sputnik* thus frightened the United States, prompting it to increase defense spending, offer NATO allies intermediate-range ballistic missiles pending development of long-range intercontinental ballistic missiles (ICBMs), set up a new agency to coordinate space efforts, and establish a crash program in science education and military research. In 1958 Congress created the National Aeronautics and Space Administration (NASA) to coordinate research and development in the space program. Before the end of the year, NASA had unveiled a program to put a manned craft in orbit, but the first manned U.S. flight, by Commander Alan B. Shepard Jr., did not take place until May 5, 1961. Finally, in 1958 Congress enacted the National Defense Education Act, which authorized federal grants, especially for training in mathematics, science, and modern languages, as well as for student loans and fellowships.

FESTERING PROBLEMS ABROAD

Once the Suez and Hungary crises had faded from the front pages, Eisenhower enjoyed eighteen months of smooth sailing in foreign affairs. Nonetheless, a brief flurry occurred in 1958 over hostile demonstrations in Peru and Venezuela against Vice President Richard Nixon, who was on a goodwill tour of eight Latin American countries. Meanwhile, problems in the Middle East and Europe continued to fester, only to reemerge with new force in 1958. The cold war would again be played out in the Middle East and in Eastern Europe, as well as at America's back door, in Cuba.

THE MIDDLE EAST By 1958 Congress had approved what came to be called the Eisenhower Doctrine, a resolution that promised to extend economic and military aid to Middle East nations and to use armed forces if necessary to assist any such nation against military aggression by Communist country.

Egypt's president Nasser, meanwhile, had emerged from the Suez crisis with heightened prestige, and in 1958 he created the United Arab Republic by (a short-lived) merger with Syria. Then a leftist coup in Iraq, supposedly inspired by Nasser and the Soviets, threw out the pro-Western government there. Lebanon, already unsettled by internal conflict, appealed to the United States for support to fend off a similar fate. Eisenhower immediately ordered 5,000 marines into Lebanon, limiting them to the capital, Beirut, and its airfield. He proposed to go no farther because, he said later, if the government was not strong enough to hold out with such protection, then "we probably should not be there." In October 1958, once the situation had stabilized and the Lebanese factions had reached a compromise, the U.S. forces withdrew.

BERLIN   The problem of Berlin, an island of Western capitalism deep in Soviet-controlled East Germany, continued to fester with little chance of a resolution. Soviet premier Nikita Khrushchev called it a "bone in his throat." West Berlin served as a "showplace" of Western democracy and prosperity in the middle of Communist East Germany, a listening post for Western intelligence gathering, and a funnel through which news and propaganda from the West penetrated what the British leader Winston Churchill had called the iron curtain. Although East Germany had sealed its western frontiers, refugees could still pass from East to West Berlin. On November 10, 1958, however, Khrushchev threatened to give East Germany control of East Berlin and the air lanes into West Berlin. After the deadline he set, May 27, 1959, Western occupation authorities would have to deal with the East German government, in effect recognizing it, or face the possibility of another blockade.

Eisenhower refused to budge from his position on Berlin. At the same time he refused to engage in saber-rattling or even to cancel existing plans to reduce the overall size of the army. Khrushchev, it turned out, was no more eager for confrontation than Eisenhower. Khrushchev's deadline passed almost unnoticed. In September 1959 Khrushchev visited the United States, stopping in New York, Washington D.C., Los Angeles, San Francisco, and Iowa. In talks with Eisenhower, he endorsed "peaceful coexistence," and Eisenhower admitted that the Berlin situation was "abnormal." They agreed to discuss the problem at a summit meeting in the spring.

THE U-2 SUMMIT   The planned summit meeting blew up in Eisenhower's face, however. On May 1, 1960, a Soviet rocket brought down an American U-2 spy plane over the Soviet Union. After a period of international jousting with Khrushchev, Eisenhower took personal responsibility for the incident—an unprecedented action for a head of state—and justified it on grounds of national security. At a summit meeting in Paris five days later, Khrushchev called upon the president to repudiate the U-2 flights, which had been going on for more than three years, and "pass severe judgment on those responsible." When Eisenhower refused, Khrushchev left the meeting.

Fidel Castro

Castro (center) became Cuba's Communist premier in 1959, following years of guerrilla warfare against the Batista regime. He planned a
social and agrarian revolution and opposed foreign control of the
Cuban economy.

CASTRO'S CUBA   Among all of Eisenhower's foreign crises, the greatest
thorn in his side was the regime of Fidel Castro, which took power in Cuba
on January 1, 1959, after two years of guerrilla warfare against a right-wing
dictator. Castro's forces had the support of many Americans who hoped for
a new day of democratic government in Cuba. But those hopes were dashed
when American television reported unfair trials and summary executions
conducted by the victorious leader. When Castro instituted programs of
land reform and nationalization of foreign-owned property, relations with
the United States worsened. Some observers believed, however, that by rejecting Castro's requests for loans and other help, the U.S. government lost a
chance to influence the direction of the Cuban revolution. Some thought,
too, that by acting upon the assumption that Communists had the upper
hand in his movement, the administration may have ensured that fact.

   Castro, on the other hand, eagerly accepted Soviet support. In 1960 he entered a trade agreement to swap Cuban sugar for Soviet oil and machinery.
One of Eisenhower's last acts as president, on January 3, 1961, was to suspend diplomatic relations with Cuba. The president also secretly authorized

the CIA to begin training a force of Cuban refugees for a new revolution. But the final decision on the use of that force would rest with the next president, John F. Kennedy.

THE EARLY YEARS OF THE CIVIL RIGHTS MOVEMENT

While the cold war had produced a tense stalemate by the mid-1950s, race relations in the United States threatened to destroy the domestic tranquility masking years of injustice. Eisenhower entered office committed to civil rights in principle. During his first three years, public services in Washington, D.C., were desegregated, as were navy yards and veterans' hospitals. Beyond that, however, two aspects of the president's philosophy inhibited vigorous action in enforcing the principle of civil rights: his preference for state or local action over federal involvement and his doubt that laws could change deeply embedded racial attitudes. "I don't believe you can change the hearts of men with laws or decisions," he said. Eisenhower's passive stance meant that leadership in the civil rights field came from the judiciary more than the executive or legislative branch of the government.

In the mid-1930s the NAACP had resolved to test the separate-but-equal doctrine that had upheld racial segregation since the *Plessy* decision in 1896. Charles H. Houston, dean of the Howard University Law School, laid the plans, and his former student Thurgood Marshall served as chief NAACP lawyer. They decided to begin their efforts to integrate society by focusing on higher education. But it took almost fifteen years to persuade the courts that segregated schooling must end. In *Sweatt v. Painter* (1950), the Supreme Court ruled that a separate black law school in Texas was not equal in quality to the state's whites-only schools. The Court ordered the state to remedy the situation.

THE *BROWN* DECISION   By the early 1950s challenges to state laws mandating segregation in the public schools were rising through the appellate courts. Five such cases, from Kansas, Delaware, South Carolina, Virgina, and the District of Columbia—usually cited by reference to the first, *Brown v. Board of Education of Topeka, Kansas*—came to the Supreme Court for joint argument by NAACP attorneys in 1952. Chief Justice Earl Warren wrote the opinion, handed down on May 17, 1954, in which a unanimous Court declared that "in the field of public education the doctrine of 'separate but equal' has no place." In support of its opinion, the Court cited sociological and psychological findings, demonstrating that even if separate facilities were

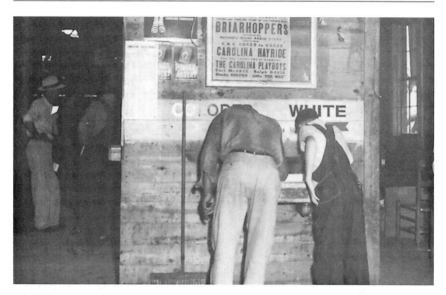

Civil Rights Stirrings

In the late 1930s the NAACP began to test the constitutionality of racial segregation.

equal in quality, the mere fact of separating people by race engendered feelings of inferiority. A year later, after further argument, the Court directed that the process of racial integration should move "with all deliberate speed."

But Eisenhower refused to force states to comply with the Court's decisions. Privately he maintained "that the Supreme Court decision *set back* progress in the South *at least fifteen years.* The fellow who tries to tell me you can do these things by *force* is just plain *nuts.*" While token integration began as early as 1954 in the border states, hostility mounted in the Deep South and Virginia, led by the newly formed Citizens' Councils. The Citizens' Councils were middle- and upper-class versions of the Ku Klux Klan that spread quickly across the region and eventually included 250,000 members. Instead of physical violence and intimidation, the Councils used economic coercion to discipline blacks who crossed racial boundaries. African Americans who defied white supremacy would lose their jobs, have their insurance policies canceled, or be denied personal loans or home mortgages. The Citizens' Councils grew so powerful in many communities that membership became almost a prerequisite for an aspiring white politician.

Before the end of 1955, opponents of court-ordered interaction grew dangerously belligerent. Virginia senator Harry F. Byrd supplied a rallying cry: "Massive Resistance." In 1956, 101 members of Congress signed a "Southern Manifesto" denouncing the Court's decision in the *Brown* case as "a clear abuse of judicial power." In six southern states at the end of 1956, not a single black child attended school with whites.

THE MONTGOMERY BUS BOYCOTT   The essential role played by the NAACP and the courts in providing a legal lever for the civil rights movement often overshadows the courageous contributions of individual African Americans who took great personal risks to challenge segregation. In Montgomery, Alabama, for example, on December 1, 1955, Rosa Parks, a black seamstress committed to gaining equal rights, was arrested for refusing to give up her seat on a city bus to a white man. As was the case in many southern communities, Montgomery had a local ordinance that required blacks to give up their bus or train seat to a white when asked. The next night black community leaders met in the Dexter Avenue Baptist Church to organize a massive bus boycott.

In Dexter Avenue's twenty-six-year-old pastor, Martin Luther King Jr., the movement found a charismatic leader. Born in Atlanta, the grandson of a slave and the son of a minister, King possessed intelligence, courage, and eloquence. After graduating from Morehouse College in Atlanta, he attended divinity school and earned a doctorate in philosophy from Boston University before accepting a call to preach in Montgomery. He inspired the civil-rights movement with a compelling call for nonviolent disobedience based upon the Gospels, the writings of Henry David Thoreau, and the example of Mahatma Gandhi in India. To his antagonists he said, "We will soon wear you down by our capacity to suffer, and in winning our freedom we will so appeal to your heart and conscience that we will win you in the process."

The Montgomery bus boycott achieved a remarkable solidarity. For months, blacks formed carpools, hitchhiked, or simply walked. But the white civic leaders held out against the boycott and against the pleas of a bus company tired of losing money. The boycotters finally won a federal case they had initiated against bus segregation, and in 1956 the Supreme Court affirmed that "the separate but equal doctrine can no longer be safely followed as a correct statement of the law." The next day, King and other African Americans boarded the buses.

To keep alive the spirit of the boycott, King and a group of associates in 1957 organized the Southern Christian Leadership Conference. Several days later King found an unexploded dynamite bomb on his front porch. Two hours later he addressed his congregation:

> I'm not afraid of anybody this morning. Tell Montgomery they can keep shooting and I'm going to stand up to them; tell Montgomery they can keep bombing and I'm going to stand up to them. If I had to die tomorrow morning I would die happy because I've been to the mountain top and I've seen the promised land and it's going to be here in Montgomery.

Montgomery, Alabama

Martin Luther King Jr., here facing arrest for leading a civil rights march, advocated nonviolent resistance to racial segregation.

THE CIVIL RIGHTS ACT   Despite President Eisenhower's reluctance to take the lead in desegregating schools, he supported the right of African Americans to vote. In 1956, hoping to exploit divisions between northern and southern Democrats and to reclaim some of the black vote for the Republicans, Eisenhower proposed legislation that became the Civil Rights Act of 1957, the first civil rights law passed since Reconstruction. It finally got through the Senate, after a year's delay, with the help of majority leader Lyndon B. Johnson, a Texas Democrat who won southern acceptance by watering it down. The Civil Rights Act established the Civil Rights Commission and a new Civil Rights Division in the Justice Department, which could seek injunctions to prevent interference with the right to vote. Yet by 1959 the Civil Rights Act had not added a single southern black to the voting rolls. Neither did the Civil Rights Act of 1960, which provided for federal court referees to register African Americans where a court found a "pattern and practice" of discrimination. This act, too, lacked teeth and depended upon vigorous presidential enforcement to achieve any real results.

DESEGREGATION IN LITTLE ROCK   A few weeks after passage of the Civil Rights Act of 1957, Arkansas governor Orval Faubus called out the

National Guard to prevent nine African-American students from entering Little Rock's Central High School under a federal court order. A conference between the president and the governor proved fruitless, but on court order Governor Faubus withdrew the National Guard. When the students tried to enter the school, a hysterical white mob forced local authorities to remove them. At that point, Eisenhower, who had said two months before that he could not "imagine any set of circumstances that would ever induce me to send federal troops," ordered 1,000 paratroopers to Little Rock to protect the black students, and he placed the National Guard on federal service. The soldiers stayed through the school year.

In the summer of 1958, Faubus decided to close the high schools of Little Rock rather than allow integration, and court proceedings dragged on into 1959 before the schools could be reopened. In that year massive resistance to integration in Virginia collapsed when both state and federal courts struck down state laws that had cut off funds to integrated schools. Thereafter, "massive resistance" for the most part was confined to the Deep South, where five states—from South Carolina west through Louisiana—still opposed even token integration.

ASSESSING THE EISENHOWER YEARS

Dwight Eisenhower entered office in 1953 after being elected in a landslide and held high approval ratings for ending the Korean War and his strong handling of foreign crises. He won a second landslide election in 1956. Yet support for the president did not translate into support for his party. Eisenhower's decisive win failed to swing a congressional majority for Republicans in either house, leaving the country in the hands of a Republican president and a Democratic Congress. Eisenhower was thus the first president to face three successive Congresses controlled by the opposition party. This meant that he could manage few initiatives in domestic policy, although he did oversee the admission of the first states that are not contiguous to the continental forty-eight: Alaska became the forty-ninth state on January 3, 1959, and Hawaii became the fiftieth on August 21, 1959.

During Eisenhower's second term the country experienced an economic slump, a drop in tax revenues, and a large federal deficit. The country also suffered the embarrassments of the U-2 spy-plane incident and Cuba's falling into the Communist orbit. Emotional issues such as civil rights, defense policy, and corrupt aides compounded Eisenhower's troubles. The president's reluctance to enforce civil rights rulings and his unwillingness to speak out on behalf of racial equality undermined his efforts to promote the general welfare. One observer called the Eisenhower years "the time of the great postponement," during which the president left domestic and foreign policies "about where he found them in 1953."

Yet opinion of Eisenhower's presidency has improved with time. Even critics now grant that Eisenhower succeeded in ending the war in Korea and settling the dust raised by Senator Joseph McCarthy. Although Eisenhower failed to end the cold war and in fact institutionalized global confrontation, he did sense the limits of American power and kept its application to low-risk situations. He also tried to restrain the arms race. Although he took few initiatives in addressing social and racial issues, he did sustain the major innovations of the New Deal. Although he tolerated unemployment of as much as 7 percent, he saw to it that inflation remained minimal during his two terms.

Eisenhower's January 17, 1961, farewell address to the American people showed his remarkable foresight in his own area of expertise, the military. He highlighted, perhaps better than anyone else could have, the dangers of a huge military establishment in a time of peace: "In the councils of government we must guard against the acquisition of unwarranted influence, whether sought or unsought, by the military-industrial complex. The potential for the disastrous rise of misplaced power exists and will persist." Eisenhower confessed that his great disappointment was that he could affirm only that "war has been avoided," not that "a lasting peace is in sight."

MAKING CONNECTIONS

- The civil rights movement of the 1950s aimed to achieve the racial integration of public services and equal access to political rights. This struggle would continue into the 1960s and then move in several new directions, as discussed in Chapter 34.

- American involvement in Vietnam grew in the 1950s but remained limited to an advisory role. Escalation to an active fighting role came under Lyndon Johnson in 1965, a topic also covered in Chapter 34.

- Eisenhower's hands-off approach to the presidency was reminiscent of the Gilded Age presidencies and those of the 1920s. See Chapters 18, 22, and 27.

FURTHER READING

Scholarship on the Eisenhower years is extensive. A carefully balanced overview of the period is Chester J. Pach Jr. and Elmo Richardson's *The Presidency of Dwight D. Eisenhower,* rev. ed. (1991). For the manner in which Eisenhower conducted foreign policy, see Robert A. Divine's *Eisenhower and the Cold War* (1981). Tom Wicker deems Eisenhower a better person than a president in *Dwight D. Eisenhower* (2002).

For the buildup of American involvement in Indochina, consult Lloyd C. Gardner's *Approaching Vietnam: From World War II through Dien Bien Phu, 1941–1954* (1988) and David L. Anderson's *Trapped by Success: The Eisenhower Administration and Vietnam, 1953–1961* (1991). How the Eisenhower Doctrine came to be implemented is traced in Stephen E. Ambrose and Douglas G. Brinkley's *Rise to Globalism: American Foreign Policy since 1938,* 8th ed. (1997).

The impact of the Supreme Court during the 1950s is the focus of Archibald Cox's *The Warren Court: Constitutional Decision as an Instrument of Reform* (1968). A masterful study of the important Warren Court decision on school desegregation is James T. Patterson's *Brown v. Board of Education: A Civil Rights Milestone and Its Troubled Legacy* (2001).

For the story of the early years of the civil rights movement, see Taylor Branch's *Parting the Waters: America in the King Years, 1954–1963* (1988) and Robert Weisbrot's *Freedom Bound: A History of America's Civil Rights Movement* (1990).

34

NEW FRONTIERS: POLITICS AND SOCIAL CHANGE IN THE 1960s

FOCUS QUESTIONS

· What were the goals of Kennedy's New Frontier and Johnson's Great Society?

· What were the achievements of the civil rights movement and the ensuing splinter movements?

· What factors led to America's growing involvement in Vietnam and the rising opposition to it?

· How did Kennedy try to combat communism in Cuba?

To answer these questions and access additional review material, please visit www.wwnorton.com/studyspace.

For those pundits who considered the social and political climate of the 1950s dull, the following decade would provide a striking contrast. The 1960s were years of extraordinary turbulence and innovation in public affairs—as well as tragedy and trauma. Many social ills that had been simmering for decades suddenly forced their way onto the national agenda. At the same time the deeply entrenched assumptions of cold war ideology led the country into the longest, most controversial, and least successful war in its history.

THE NEW FRONTIER

KENNEDY VERSUS NIXON   In 1960 there was little sense of dramatic change on the horizon. The presidential election that year featured two candidates—Richard M. Nixon and John F. Kennedy—who initially symbolized the bland politics of the 1950s. Though better known than Kennedy because of his eight years as Eisenhower's vice president, Nixon had developed the reputation of a cunning chameleon, the Tricky Dick who concealed his duplicity behind a series of masks.

Nixon possessed great ability, however, as well as tenacious energy and a compulsive love for politics, the more combative the better. Born in suburban Los Angeles in 1913, he grew up in a Quaker family that struggled to make ends meet. After law school and military service in the Pacific during World War II, Nixon jumped into the political arena in 1946 as a Republican and surprised observers by unseating a popular congressman in southern California. He arrived in Washington eager to reverse the tide of New Deal liberalism. Four years later he won election to the Senate. In his campaigns, Nixon unleashed scurrilous personal attacks on his opponents, shrewdly manipulating the growing anti-Communist hysteria. Yet Nixon became a respected, effective legislator, and by 1950 he was the most requested Republican speaker in the country. His rapid rise to political stardom led to his being offered the vice-presidential nomination in 1952 and 1956. He was an active, highly visible vice president.

Kennedy lacked such experience and exposure. He boasted an abundance of assets, including a widely publicized record of heroism in World War II, a glamorous young wife, a Harvard education, and a large, wealthy family. Yet the handsome forty-three-year-old candidate lacked national prominence and political distinction. Kennedy's record in the Senate was mediocre.

During his campaign for the Democratic nomination, however, Kennedy had shown that he had energy, grace, and ambition. As the first Catholic to run for the presidency since Al Smith in 1928, he strove to dispel the impression that his religion was a major political liability. In his acceptance speech at the Democratic Convention, Kennedy found the stirring rhetoric that would stamp the rest of his campaign and his presidency: "We stand today on the edge of a New Frontier—the frontier of unknown opportunities and perils—a frontier of unfulfilled hopes and threats."

The turning point in the presidential campaign came when Richard Nixon agreed to debate his less prominent opponent on television. During the first of four debates, some 70 million viewers saw Nixon, still weak from a recent illness, perspiring heavily and looking haggard, uneasy, and even

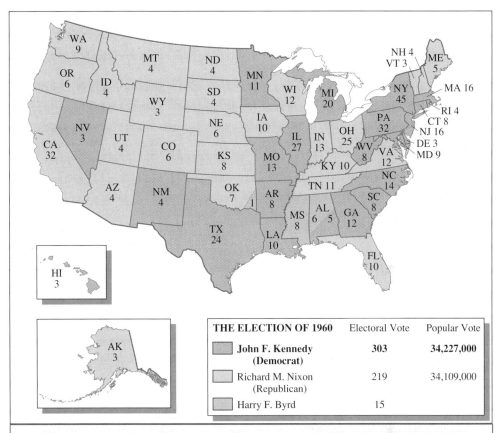

THE ELECTION OF 1960	Electoral Vote	Popular Vote
John F. Kennedy (Democrat)	303	34,227,000
Richard M. Nixon (Republican)	219	34,109,000
Harry F. Byrd	15	

How did the election of 1960 represent a sea change in American presidential politics? What three events shaped the campaign? How did Kennedy win the election in spite of winning fewer states than Nixon?

sinister before the camera. Kennedy, on the other hand, projected a cool poise that made him seem equal, if not superior, in his fitness for the office. Kennedy's popularity immediately shot up in the polls.

When the votes were counted, Kennedy and his running-mate, Lyndon Johnson of Texas, had won the closest presidential election since 1888. The winning margin was only 118,574 votes out of the 68 million cast. Kennedy's wide lead in the electoral vote, 303 to 219, belied the paper-thin margin in several key states.

THE NEW ADMINISTRATION   John F. Kennedy was the youngest person ever elected president, and his cabinet appointments highlighted youth. He sought to attract the "best and the brightest" minds, men who would inject a tough, dispassionate, pragmatic, and vigorous outlook into government affairs. To that end he asked Robert McNamara, one of the whiz kids who had reorganized the Ford Motor Company, to bring his managerial magic to bear on the Department of Defense. Kennedy appointed Harvard professor McGeorge Bundy, whom he called "the second smartest man I know," as special assistant for national security affairs and chose as his secretary of state Dean Rusk, a career diplomat and former Rhodes scholar. When critics attacked the appointment of Kennedy's thirty-five-year-old brother Robert as attorney general, the president quipped, "I don't see what's wrong with giving Bobby a little experience before he goes into law practice."

The inaugural ceremonies set the tone of elegance and youthful vigor that would come to be called the Kennedy style. After the poet Robert Frost paid tribute to the administration in verse, Kennedy dazzled listeners with his uplifting rhetoric. "Let every nation know," he proclaimed, ". . . that we shall pay any price, bear any burden, meet any hardship, support any friend, oppose any foe, to assure the survival and success of liberty. And so, my fellow Americans: ask not what your country can do for you—ask what you can do for your country." Spines tingled; the glittering atmosphere and inspiring language of the inauguration seemed to herald an era of fresh promise and youthful energy.

THE KENNEDY RECORD   Despite his idealistic rhetoric, however, Kennedy had a difficult time launching his New Frontier domestic program. Elected by a razor-thin margin, he did not have a popular mandate. Nor did he show much skill in dealing with a Democratic majority in a Congress controlled by conservative southerners. Congress blocked his efforts to increase federal aid to education, provide health insurance for the aged, and create a Department of Urban Affairs.

Administration proposals did nevertheless win some notable victories in Congress. They included a new Housing Act that appropriated nearly $5 billion for urban renewal over four years, an increase in the minimum wage, and enhanced Social Security benefits. Just two months into his administration, Kennedy launched the celebrated Peace Corps to supply volunteers for educational and technical service in underdeveloped countries. Kennedy also won support for an accelerated program to land astronauts on the moon before the end of the decade. Congress readily approved a series of broad foreign-aid programs to help Latin American nations, dubbed the Alliance for Progress. Another important initiative was a bold tax-reduction bill intended to accelerate economic growth. Passed in 1964, after Kennedy's death, it

Kennedy versus Nixon

John Kennedy's poise and precision in the debates with Richard Nixon impressed viewers and voters.

provided a surprisingly potent boost to the economy. Perhaps Kennedy's most significant legislative accomplishment was the Trade Expansion Act of 1962, which eventually led to tariff cuts averaging 35 percent on goods traded between the United States and the European Economic Community (the Common Market).

THE WARREN COURT   Under Chief Justice Earl Warren the Supreme Court continued to be a decisive influence on domestic life during the 1960s. In *Gideon v. Wainwright* (1963), the Court required that every felony defendant be provided a lawyer regardless of the defendant's ability to pay. In 1964 the Court ruled in *Escobedo v. Illinois* that a person accused of a crime must also be allowed to consult a lawyer before being interrogated by police. Two years later, in *Miranda v. Arizona,* the Court issued perhaps its most bitterly criticized ruling when it ordered that an accused person in police custody be informed of certain basic rights: the right to remain silent; the right to know that anything said can be used against the individual in court; and the right to have a defense attorney present during interrogation. In addition, the Court established rules for police to follow in informing suspects of their legal rights before questioning could begin.

EXPANSION OF THE CIVIL RIGHTS MOVEMENT

The most important developments in domestic life during the 1960s occurred in civil rights. John F. Kennedy was initially reluctant to challenge conservative southern Democrats on the race issue. He also was never as personally committed to civil rights as his brother Robert, the attorney general. Despite a few dramatic gestures of support for African-American leaders, President Kennedy only belatedly grasped the moral and emotional significance of what would become the most widespread reform movement of the decade. Eventually, however, his conscience was pricked by the grassroots civil rights movement led by Martin Luther King Jr., a movement that would profoundly change the contours of American life.

SIT-INS AND FREEDOM RIDES   After the Montgomery bus boycott of 1955–1956, King's philosophy of "militant nonviolence" inspired thousands to challenge segregation and discrimination with direct action. At the same time, lawsuits to desegregate the schools activated thousands of parents and young people. The momentum generated a genuine mass movement when four black college students courageously sat down and demanded service at a "whites-only" Woolworth's lunch counter in Greensboro, North Carolina, on February 1, 1960. Within a week the "sit-in" movement had spread to six more towns in the state, and within two months demonstrations had occurred in fifty-four cities in nine states.

In 1960 student activists, black and white, formed the Student Nonviolent Coordinating Committee (SNCC), which worked with King's Southern Christian Leadership Conference to spread the civil rights movement. The sit-ins became "kneel-ins" at churches and "wade-ins" at segregated public swimming pools. During the year after the Greensboro sit-ins, over 3,600 black and white activists spent time in jail. In many communities they were struck with clubs, poked with cattle prods, pelted with rocks, burned with cigarettes, and subjected to unending verbal abuse. Nonetheless, the protesters refused to retaliate.

In May 1961 the Congress of Racial Equality sent a group of black and white "freedom riders" on buses to test a federal ruling that had banned segregation on buses and trains and in their depots. In Alabama, mobs attacked the young travelers with fists and pipes, burned one of the buses, and assaulted Justice Department observers, but the demonstrators persisted, drawing national attention and generating new support for their cause. Yet President Kennedy was not inspired by the courageous freedom riders. Preoccupied with the Berlin crisis, he ordered an aide to tell them to "call it off."

Former president Harry Truman called the bus activists northern "busybodies." It fell to Attorney General Robert Kennedy to use federal marshals to protect the freedom riders during the summer of 1961.

FEDERAL INTERVENTION   In 1962 Governor Ross Barnett of Mississippi, a rabid racist who believed that God made "the Negro different to punish him," defied a court order and refused to allow James Meredith, an African-American student, to enroll at the University of Mississippi. Attorney General Robert Kennedy intervened again, but a violent white mob prevented the federal marshals he dispatched from enforcing the law. Federal troops had to intervene, and Meredith was registered at Ole Miss, but only after two deaths and many injuries.

Everywhere, it seemed, African-American activists and white supporters were challenging deeply entrenched patterns of segregation and prejudice. In 1963 Martin Luther King launched a series of demonstrations in Birmingham, Alabama, where Police Commissioner Eugene "Bull" Connor proved the perfect foil for King's tactic of nonviolent civil disobedience. Connor's policemen used dogs, tear gas, electric cattle prods, and fire hoses

Birmingham, Alabama, May 1963

Eugene "Bull" Connor's police unleash dogs on civil rights demonstrators.

on the protesters while millions of outraged Americans watched the confrontations on television.

King, who was arrested and jailed during the demonstrations, wrote his now-famous Letter from a Birmingham City Jail, a stirring defense of his non-violent strategy that became a classic of the civil rights movement. "One who breaks an unjust law," he stressed, "must do so openly, lovingly, and with a willingness to accept the penalty." In his letter, King signaled a shift in his strategy for social change. Heretofore he had emphasized the need to educate southern whites about the injustice of segregation and other patterns of discrimination. Now he focused more on gaining federal enforcement of the law and new legislation by provoking racists to display their violent hatred in public.

Southern traditionalists defied efforts to promote racial integration. In 1963 Governor George Wallace dramatically stood in the doorway of a building at the University of Alabama to block the enrollment of African-American students, but he stepped aside in the face of insistent federal marshals. Later that night NAACP official Medgar Evers was shot to death as he returned to his home in Jackson, Mississippi.

The high point of the integrationist phase of the civil rights movement occurred on August 28, 1963, when over 200,000 blacks and whites marched down the Mall in Washington, D.C., toward the Lincoln Memorial, singing "We Shall Overcome." The March on Washington for Jobs and Freedom was the largest civil rights demonstration in American history. Standing in front of Lincoln's statue, Martin Luther King delivered one of the century's memorable speeches: "Even though we face the difficulties of today and tomorrow, I still have a dream. It is a dream chiefly rooted in the American dream . . . one day . . . the sons of former slaves and the sons of former slave-owners will be able to sit together at the table of brotherhood." Such racial harmony had not yet arrived, however. Two weeks later a bomb exploded in a Birmingham church, killing four African-American girls who had arrived early for Sunday school.

Yet King's dream—shared and promoted by thousands of other activists—survived. The intransigence and violence that civil rights workers encountered won converts to their cause across the country and forced whites nationwide to confront the myths of their own virtue and innocence with the brutal facts of racial hatred. Persuaded by his brother Robert, a man of greater conviction, compassion, and vision, and by the pressure of events, President Kennedy finally decided that enforcement of existing statutes was not enough; new legislation was needed to deal with the race question. In 1963 he told the nation that racial discrimination "has no place in American life or law," and he endorsed an ambitious civil rights bill intended to end

"I Have a Dream," August 28, 1963

Protesters in the March on Washington make their way to the Lincoln Memorial, where Martin Luther King Jr. delivered his now-famous speech.

discrimination in public facilities, desegregate public schools, and protect black voters. Southern conservatives, however, quickly blocked the bill in Congress. The backlash that had surfaced in the South in the 1930s in response to the expansion of Franklin Roosevelt's New Deal continued to shape Democratic politics in the region.

Although Kennedy saw his support among southern voters plummet, he remained committed to the bill. As he told Martin Luther King: "This is a very serious fight. We're in this up to the neck. The worst trouble would be to lose the fight in Congress. . . . A good many programs I care about may go down the drain as a result of this [bill]—We may all go down the drain . . . so we are putting a lot on the line."

FOREIGN FRONTIERS

EARLY SETBACKS   John F. Kennedy's record in foreign affairs was mixed, more spectacularly so than his domestic record. Upon taking office, he discovered that there was in the works a secret CIA operation designed to prepare 1,500 anti-Castro Cubans for an invasion of their homeland. The Joint Chiefs of Staff endorsed the plan; analysts reported that the invasion would inspire Cubans on the island to rebel against Castro. But the scheme, poorly conceived and poorly executed, had little chance of succeeding. When the invasion force landed at Cuba's Bay of Pigs on April 17, 1961, it was brutally subdued in two days, and over 1,000 men were captured.

Two months after the Bay of Pigs disaster, Kennedy met Soviet premier Nikita Khrushchev in Vienna. The volatile Khrushchev tried to bully the inexperienced Kennedy. He threatened to limit Western access to Berlin, the divided city located 100 miles within Communist East Germany. Kennedy was shaken by the aggressive Soviet stand. Upon his return home he demonstrated his resolve by mobilizing army reserve and national guard units. The Soviets responded by erecting the Berlin Wall, cutting off movement between East and West Berlin.

THE CUBAN MISSILE CRISIS   A year later, in the fall of 1962, Khrushchev and the Soviets posed another serious challenge, this time just ninety miles south of Florida. Khrushchev granted Fidel Castro's request for nuclear missiles in Cuba to protect the island from future American-sponsored invasions and to redress the strategic imbalance caused by the presence of U.S. missiles in Turkey aimed at the Soviet Union. While such missiles would hardly alter the worldwide military balance, they would be placed in areas not covered by American radar systems and, if launched, would go undetected, arriving without warning. More important to Kennedy was the psychological effect of American acquiescence to a Soviet presence on its doorstep. Khrushchev's apparent purpose was to demonstrate his toughness to both Chinese and Soviet critics of his earlier advocacy of peaceful coexistence. But he misjudged the American response.

On October 14, 1962, U.S. intelligence flights discovered Soviet missile sites under construction in Cuba. Although the Soviet actions violated no law or treaty, the administration immediately decided that the missiles had to be removed; the only question was how. In a series of secret meetings, the Executive Committee of the National Security Council debated whether to launch a "surgical" air strike or a naval blockade of Cuba. President Kennedy wisely opted for a blockade, but since that would technically represent an act of war, it was called a *quarantine*. It offered the advantage of forcing the Soviets to shoot first, if matters came to that, and it left open options of stronger action. Monday, October 22, began the most perilous week in world history. On that day the president announced the discovery of the missile sites in Cuba and the U.S. naval quarantine of the island nation.

Tensions grew as Khrushchev blustered that Kennedy had pushed humankind "to the abyss of a world nuclear-missile war." Soviet ships, he declared, would ignore the quarantine. But on Wednesday, October 24, five Soviet supply ships stopped short of the American ships. Two days later the Soviets offered to withdraw the missiles in return for a public pledge by the United States not to invade Cuba.

In the aftermath of the crisis, the United States took several symbolic steps to relax tensions: an agreement to sell surplus wheat to the Soviets, the installation of a "hot-line" telephone between Washington and Moscow to provide instant contact between the heads of government, and the removal of obsolete American missiles from Turkey, Italy, and Britain. The United States also negotiated a treaty with Soviet and British representatives to end nuclear testing in the atmosphere. The treaty, ratified in September 1963, was an important move toward greater international cooperation on nuclear proliferation.

KENNEDY AND VIETNAM   As tensions with the Soviet Union were easing, a crisis was developing in Southeast Asia. Events there would lead to the greatest American foreign-policy debacle of the century. During John Kennedy's "thousand days" in office, the turmoil of Indochina never preoccupied public attention for any extended period, but it dominated international diplomatic debates from the time the administration entered office.

In South Vietnam Premier Ngo Dinh Diem had failed to deliver promised social and economic reforms. His repressive tactics, directed not only against Communists but also against the Buddhist majority and other critics, played into the hands of his enemies. In 1961 White House assistant Walt Rostow and General Maxwell Taylor, the first in a long line of presidential emissaries to South Vietnam's capital, Saigon, proposed a major increase in the U.S. military presence, but Kennedy instead dispatched more military "advisers." When he took office, there had been 2,000 U.S. troops in South Vietnam; by the end of 1963, there were 16,000, none of whom had been officially committed to battle.

But the American-supported Diem regime continued to be its own worst enemy. By mid-1963 growing Buddhist demonstrations against Diem ignited the public discontent in South Vietnam and created consternation abroad. The spectacle of Buddhist monks setting themselves on fire on Saigon streets in protest of Diem's iron-fisted rule shocked Americans but brought from the Diem regime only a sarcastic comment by the premier's sister-in-law about "barbecued monks."

By the fall of 1963, the Kennedy administration had decided that Diem was a lost cause. When dissident Vietnamese generals proposed a coup d'état, the

U.S. ambassador assured them that the Kennedy administration would not stand in the way. On November 1 the insurgent military leaders seized the government and murdered Diem. Yet the generals provided no more stability than had earlier regimes, and successive coups set South Vietnam's government spinning from one military leader to another.

KENNEDY'S ASSASSINATION   By the fall of 1963, President Kennedy seemed to recognize the intractability of the situation in Vietnam. Some of his aides later argued that Kennedy would never have allowed a dramatic escalation of U.S. military involvement in Vietnam. Others strongly disagreed. The question is endless because it is unanswerable, and it is unanswerable because on November 22, 1963, while visiting Dallas, Texas, Kennedy was shot twice in the throat and head and died almost immediately. A few hours later Dallas police arrested Lee Harvey Oswald, a twenty-four-year-old ex-marine drifter who had worked in the Texas School Book Depository, from which the shots had been fired at Kennedy. Yet before Oswald could be thoroughly interrogated, he, too, was killed. Two days after his arrest, as television cameras covered his transfer to another jail, Jack Ruby, a Dallas nightclub owner, stepped from the crowd of onlookers and fatally shot Oswald in the abdomen.

Oswald's death ignited a controversy over the assassination that still simmers. In December 1963 President Johnson appointed a commission to investigate Kennedy's murder. Headed by Chief Justice Earl Warren, it concluded that Oswald had acted alone. Yet many people were (and are) not convinced, and since 1963 dozens of conspiracy theories have been proposed. Some blame the CIA or the Mafia; others point at Fidel Castro, whom the CIA had once tried to assassinate. Still others insist that Cuban exiles in Miami, angered by Kennedy's failure to rescue their comrades during the Bay of Pigs fiasco, were behind the assassination. Whatever the actual story of the assassination, Kennedy's tragic death enshrined him in the public imagination as a martyred leader cut down in the prime of his career.

Lyndon Johnson and the Great Society

Lyndon Johnson took the presidential oath of office on board the plane that brought John F. Kennedy's body back to Washington from Dallas. Fifty-five years old, Johnson had spent twenty-six years on the Washington scene and had served nearly a decade as Senate Democratic leader, where he had displayed the greatest gift for compromise since Henry Clay. Johnson brought to the White House a marked change of style from his predecessor.

A self-made and self-centered man, he had used gritty determination and shrewd manipulation to work his way out of a hardscrabble rural Texas homeland to become one of Washington's most powerful figures. He had none of Kennedy's elegance. He was a bundle of conflicting elements: earthy, idealistic, domineering, insecure, gregarious, ruthless, and compassionate. His ego was as huge as his ambition.

Those who viewed Johnson as a stereotypical southern conservative ignored his long-standing admiration for Franklin Roosevelt, the depth of his concern for the poor, and his heartfelt commitment to the cause of civil rights. Though a novice in foreign affairs in the domestic arena during the 1950s, Johnson had been unsurpassed in his ability to shepherd legislation through the gauntlet of special-interest lobbyists and Congress. He had once bragged that "Ike couldn't pass the Lord's Prayer in Congress without me." Johnson wanted to be the greatest president, the one who did the most good for the most people. And he would let nothing stand in the way of his grand ambition. He ended up promising far more than he could accomplish, raising false hopes and stoking fiery resentments.

POLITICS AND POVERTY

Domestic policy was Johnson's first priority. He exploited the nation's grief after the assassination by declaring that Kennedy's legislative program, stymied in congressional committees, would be passed. Johnson loved the political infighting and legislative detail that Kennedy had loathed. The logjam in Congress that had blocked Kennedy's program broke under Johnson's forceful leadership, and a torrent of legislation poured through. At the top of Johnson's agenda were the stalled measures for tax reduction and civil rights. In 1962 Kennedy had announced an unusual plan to jump-start the sluggish economy: a tax cut designed to stimulate consumer spending.

The Johnson Treatment

Lyndon Johnson used powerful body language to intimidate and manipulate anyone who dared disagree with him.

Congressional Republicans opposed the idea because it would increase the federal budget deficit. And polls showed that public opinion was also skeptical. So Kennedy postponed the proposed tax cut for a year; it was still bogged down in Congress when the president was assassinated. Johnson broke the logjam, and the Revenue Act of 1964 provided a needed boost to the economy.

Likewise, the Civil Rights Act that Kennedy had presented to Congress in 1963 was brought to fruition in 1964 by Johnson's forceful leadership. The bill prohibited racial segregation in public facilities such as bus terminals, restaurants, theaters, and hotels. And it outlawed long-standing racial discrimination in the registration of voters and the hiring of employees. President Johnson revived bipartisan efforts on its behalf, and the bill passed the House in February 1964. In the Senate, however, southern legislators launched a filibuster that lasted two months. Johnson finally prevailed, and the civil rights bill became law on July 2. But the new president knew it had come at a political price. On the night after signing it, Johnson told an aide that "we have just delivered the South to the Republican Party for a long time to come."

In addition to fulfilling Kennedy's major promises, Johnson launched an ambitious legislative program of his own. In his 1964 State of the Union address, he added to his must-do list a bold new idea that bore the Johnson brand: "This Administration today, here and now, declares unconditional war on poverty in America." The particulars of this "war on poverty" were to come later, the product of a task force at work before Johnson took office.

Americans had rediscovered poverty in 1962, when the social critic Michael Harrington published a powerful exposé titled *The Other America*. Harrington argued that more than 40 million people were mired in a "culture of poverty." Unlike the upwardly mobile immigrant poor at the turn of the century, the modern poor were impervious to hope. President Kennedy had learned of *The Other America* in 1963 and asked his advisers to investigate the problem and suggest solutions. Upon taking office, Lyndon Johnson announced that he wanted an anti-poverty package that was "big and bold, that would hit the nation with real impact." Money for the program would come from the economic growth expected from the tax reduction of more than $10 billion that had passed in 1964.

The administration's war on poverty was embodied in an economic-opportunity bill that incorporated a wide range of programs: a Job Corps for inner-city youths, a Head Start program for disadvantaged preschoolers, work-study programs for college students, grants to farmers and rural businesses, loans to employers willing to hire the chronically unemployed, the Volunteers in Service to America (a domestic Peace Corps), and the Community Action Program, which would provide "maximum feasible participation" of the poor in directing neighborhood programs designed for their benefit. Speaking at Ann Arbor, Michigan, Johnson called for a "Great Society" resting on "abundance and liberty for all. The Great Society demands an end to poverty and racial injustice, to which we are fully committed in our time." In theory it was liberalism triumphant; in practice its considerable achievements were accompanied by administrative bungling, corruption, and misguided idealism.

THE ELECTION OF 1964   As the 1964 election approached, Johnson was conceded the Democratic nomination from the start. He chose as his running mate Hubert H. Humphrey of Minnesota, the prominent liberal senator with the seemingly permanent smile and inexhaustible supply of optimism and energy.

The Republicans, meeting in San Francisco, were determined to offer an alternative to Johnson's liberalism. By 1960 Arizona senator Barry Goldwater, a millionaire department-store owner, had emerged as the leader of the party's conservative wing. A movement to nominate Goldwater had begun as early as 1961, mobilizing conservative activists to capture party caucuses and contest primaries. In 1964 they took an early lead, and Goldwater swept the all-important California primary. Thus his forces controlled the Republican Convention.

Goldwater displayed an unusual gift for frightening voters. Accusing the administration of waging a "no-win" war in Vietnam, he urged wholesale bombing of North Vietnam and left the impression of being trigger-happy. He also savaged Johnson's war on poverty and the New Deal tradition. At times he was foolishly candid. In Tennessee he proposed the sale of the Tennessee Valley Authority; in St. Petersburg, Florida, a major retirement community, he questioned the value of Social Security. He had voted against both the nuclear test ban and the 1964 Civil Rights Act. Republican campaign buttons claimed, "In your heart, you know he's right." Democrats responded, "In your guts, you know he's nuts."

Johnson, on the other hand, appealed to the middle of the political spectrum. In contrast to Goldwater's bellicose rhetoric on Vietnam, he made a pledge that won great applause at the time and much comment later: "We are not about to send American boys nine or ten thousand miles from home to do what Asian boys ought to be doing for themselves."

The election was a landslide. Johnson polled 61 percent of the total vote; Goldwater carried only Arizona and five states in the Deep South. Johnson won the electoral vote by a whopping 486 to 52. In the Senate the Democrats increased their majority by two (68 to 32) and in the House by thirty-seven (295 to 140).

LANDMARK LEGISLATION   In 1965 Johnson took advantage of his electoral mandate to launch his Great Society program. It would, he promised, end poverty, renovate the decaying central cities, provide every young American with the chance to attend college, protect the health of the elderly, enhance cultural life, clean up the air and water, and make the highways safer and prettier.

To accomplish those goals, the Johnson administration pushed legislation through the Congress at a pace unseen since Franklin Roosevelt's Hundred Days. Priority went to health insurance and aid to education, proposals that had languished since President Truman had proposed them in 1945. The proposal for a comprehensive medical-insurance plan had long been stalled by the American Medical Association's ardent opposition. But now that Johnson had the votes, the AMA joined Republicans in supporting a bill serving those over age sixty-five. The act not only created the Medicare insurance program for the aged but also included another program, Medicaid, which provided states with federal grants to help cover medical payments for the indigent.

Five days after Johnson submitted his Medicare program, he sent to Congress his proposal for a massive increase in federal aid to elementary and secondary education. Such proposals had been ignored since the 1940s, blocked alternately by issues of segregation and separation of church and state. Now Johnson and congressional leaders devised a means of extending aid to "poverty-impacted" school districts regardless of their public or parochial character.

The momentum generated by these measures had already begun to carry others along, and it continued through the following year. Altogether the tide of Great Society legislation carried 435 bills through the Congress. Among them was the Appalachian Regional Development Act of 1966, which allocated federal funds for programs to enhance the standard of living in remote mountain areas that had long been pockets of desperate poverty. The Housing and Urban Development Act of 1965 provided for construction of 240,000 housing units. Rent supplements for low-income families followed in 1966, and in that year there began a new Department of Housing and Urban Development, headed by Robert C. Weaver, the first African-American cabinet member.

THE IMMIGRATION ACT   Little noticed among the legislation flowing from Congress was a major new immigration bill that had originated in the Kennedy White House. President Johnson signed the Immigration and Nationality Services Act of 1965 in a ceremony held on Liberty Island in New York Harbor. In his speech, Johnson stressed that the new law would redress the wrong done to those "from southern and eastern Europe" and the "developing continents" of Asia, Africa, and Latin America. It would do so by abolishing the discriminatory quotas based on national origins that had governed immigration policy since the 1920s.

The new law treated all nationalities and races equally. In place of national quotas, it created hemispheric ceilings on visas issued: 170,000 for persons from outside the Western Hemisphere, 120,000 for persons from within. It also stipulated that no more than 20,000 people could come from any one country each year. The new act allowed the entry of immediate family members of American residents without limit. Most of the annual visas were to be given on a first-come, first-served basis to "other relatives" of American residents, and only a small proportion (about 10 percent) were allocated to those with special talents or job skills. During the 1960s became the largest contingent of new Americans.

ASSESSING THE GREAT SOCIETY   The Great Society programs included several successes. The Highway Safety Act and the Traffic Safety Act established safety standards for automobile manufacturers and highway design, and the scholarships provided for college students under the Higher Education Act were quite popular. Many Great Society initiatives aimed at improving the health, nutrition, and education of poor Americans, young and old, made headway. So, too, did efforts to clean up air and water pollution. Some of Johnson's ambitious programs were hastily designed or mismanaged, however, and others were vastly underfunded. Medicare, for example, removed incentives for hospitals to control costs, and medical bills skyrocketed. The Great Society helped reduce the number of people living in poverty, but it did so largely by providing federal welfare payments, not by finding them productive jobs. The war on poverty ended up being as disappointing as the war in Vietnam. Often funds appropriated for various programs never made it through the tangled bureaucracy to the needy. Widely publicized cases of welfare fraud placed a powerful weapon in the hands of those opposed to liberal social programs. By 1966 middle-class resentment over the cost and waste of the Great Society programs helped generate a strong conservative backlash that fueled a Republican resurgence at the polls.

FROM CIVIL RIGHTS TO BLACK POWER

CIVIL RIGHTS LEGISLATION   Among the successes of the Great Society was a landmark piece of civil rights legislation: the Civil Rights Act of

1964, the most far-reaching civil rights measure ever enacted. It outlawed racial discrimination in hotels, restaurants, and other public accommodations. In addition, its provisions enabled the attorney general to bring suits to end school desegregation, relieving parents of that painful burden. Federally assisted programs and private employers alike were required to eliminate discrimination. An Equal Employment Opportunity Commission administered a ban on job discrimination by race, religion, national origin, or sex.

The Civil Rights Act increased the momentum of the movement. Early in 1965 Martin Luther King announced a voter-registration drive aimed at the 3 million unregistered African Americans in the South. On March 7 civil rights protesters began a march for voting rights from Selma, Alabama, to Montgomery, only to be violently dispersed by state troopers and a mounted posse. A federal judge then agreed to allow the march, and President Johnson provided federal troops for protection. By March 25, when the demonstrators reached Montgomery, they numbered 35,000, and King delivered a rousing address from the steps of the state capitol.

Several days before the march, President Johnson went before Congress with a moving plea for voting rights legislation. The resulting Voting Rights Act of 1965 ensured all citizens the right to vote. It authorized the attorney general to dispatch federal examiners to register voters. In states or counties where fewer than half the adults had voted in 1964, the act suspended literacy tests and other devices commonly used to defraud citizens of the vote. By the end of the year, some 250,000 African Americans were newly registered.

BLACK POWER   Amid this success, however, the civil rights movement began to fragment. On August 11, 1965, less than a week after the passage of the Voting Rights Act, Watts, a predominantly black and poor neighborhood in Los Angeles, exploded in a frenzy of riots and looting. When the uprising ended, thirty-four were dead, almost 4,000 rioters were in jail, and property damage exceeded $35 million. The Watts upheaval marked the beginning of four long hot summers of racial conflagration. Riots in 1966 erupted in Chicago and Cleveland and in forty other American cities. The following summer, Newark and Detroit burst into flames. Detroit provided the most graphic instance of urban violence as tanks rolled through the streets to restore order.

In retrospect, it was understandable that the civil rights movement would shift its focus to the plight of urban blacks. By the mid-1960s about 70 percent of African Americans lived in metropolitan areas, most of them in central-city ghettos that had been bypassed by the postwar prosperity. It seems clear, also in retrospect, that the nonviolent tactics that had worked in the rural South would not work in the northern cities. In the North racial problems resulted from segregated residential patterns not amenable to changes in the law. Moreover, northern white ethnic groups did not have the cultural heritage that southern whites shared with blacks by virtue of their living together in the South for so many generations. A special Commission on Civil Disorders noted that, unlike earlier race riots, which had been started by whites, the urban upheavals of the middle 1960s were initiated by African Americans themselves in an effort to destroy what they could not stomach and what civil rights legislation seemed unable to change.

In the midst of the violence, a new philosophy of racial separatism began to emerge. By 1966 "black power" had become the rallying cry of young activists. Radical members of SNCC had become estranged from Martin Luther King's theories of nonviolence. When Stokely Carmichael, a twenty-five-year-old graduate of Howard University, became head of SNCC in 1966, he adopted a separatist philosophy of black power and ousted whites from the organization. "We reject an American dream defined by white people and must work to construct an American reality defined by Afro-Americans," said a SNCC position paper. H. Rap Brown, who succeeded Carmichael as head of SNCC in 1967, even urged blacks to "get you some guns" and "kill the honkies." Meanwhile, Carmichael had moved on to the Black Panther party, founded in Oakland, California, in 1966. Headed by Huey P. Newton, Bobby Seale, and Eldridge Cleaver, the self-professed urban revolutionaries terrified the public. Eventually the Panthers fragmented in spasms of violence, much of which the FBI and local police officials helped to provoke.

The most articulate spokesman for black power was one of the earliest, Malcolm X (formerly Malcolm Little, with the X denoting his lost African surname). Malcolm had risen from a ghetto childhood involving narcotics and crime to become the chief disciple of Elijah Muhammad, a Black Muslim prophet who rejected Christianity as "the religion of white devils" and encouraged black culture and black pride. By 1964 Malcolm had broken with Elijah Muhammad and founded an organization committed to fostering alliances between African

Malcolm X

Malcolm X was the black power movement's most influential spokesman.

Americans blacks and the nonwhite peoples of the world. He had also begun to abandon his earlier separatist agenda and violent tactics. But Malcolm was gunned down in Harlem by Black Muslim assassins in early 1965. With him went the most effective voice for urban black militancy. What made the assassination especially tragic was that just months before Malcolm had begun to abandon his strident anti-white rhetoric and preach a biracial message of social change.

Although widely publicized and highly visible, the black power movement never attracted more than a small minority of African Americans. Only about 15 percent of blacks labeled themselves separatists. The preponderant majority continued to identify with the philosophy of nonviolent integration promoted by Martin Luther King and organizations such as the NAACP.

Yet the black power movement, despite its strident language and violence, had two positive effects upon the civil rights movement. First, it prompted African Americans to take greater pride in their racial heritage. As Malcolm X often pointed out, prolonged slavery and institutionalized racism had eroded the self-esteem of many blacks in the United States. "The worst crime the white man has committed," he declared, "has been to teach us to hate ourselves." He and others helped blacks appreciate their African roots and their American accomplishments. It was Malcolm X who insisted that blacks call themselves African Americans as a symbol of pride in their roots and as a spur to learning more about their history as a people.

Second, the black power phenomenon forced King and other mainstream African-American leaders and organizations to launch a new stage in the civil rights movement, focusing attention on the economic plight of poor inner-city blacks. Legal access to restaurants, schools, and other public accommodations, King pointed out, meant little to people mired in a culture of urban poverty. They needed jobs and decent housing as much as they needed legal rights. The time had come for radical measures "to provide jobs and income for the poor." Yet as King and others sought to escalate the war on poverty at home, the war in Vietnam was consuming more and more of America's resources and energies.

THE TRAGEDY OF VIETNAM

As domestic violence was escalating in America's inner cities, the war in Vietnam reached new levels of intensity and destruction. At the time of President Kennedy's death, there were 16,000 American military advisers in Vietnam. Lyndon Johnson inherited a commitment to prevent a Communist takeover in South Vietnam along with a reluctance to assume the military burden for fighting the war. One president after another had done just enough to avoid being charged with having lost Vietnam. Johnson did the same, fearing that any other course would undermine his influence and endanger his Great Society programs in Congress. But this path took him and the United States deeper into intervention in Southeast Asia. Early on Johnson doubted that Vietnam was worth American military involvement. In May 1964 he told his national security adviser, McGeorge Bundy, that he had spent a sleepless night worrying about Vietnam: "It looks to me like we are getting into another Korea. . . . I don't think we can fight them 10,000 miles away from home. . . . I don't think it's worth fighting for. And I don't think we can get out. It's just the biggest damned mess that I ever saw."

ESCALATION   The official sanction for America's "escalation"—a Defense Department term favored in the Vietnam era—was the Tonkin Gulf resolution, approved by Congress on August 7, 1964. On that day, Johnson reported in a national television address that two American destroyers had been attacked by North Vietnamese vessels on August 2 and 4 in the Gulf of Tonkin, off the coast of North Vietnam. Although he described the attacks as unprovoked, in truth the destroyers had been monitoring South Vietnamese raids against two North Vietnamese islands—raids planned by American advisers. Even though there was no tangible evidence of an attack on the American ships, the Tonkin Gulf resolution authorized the president to "take all necessary measures to repel any armed attack against the forces of the United States and to prevent further aggression."

Three months after his landslide victory over Goldwater, Johnson made the crucial decisions that would shape American policy in Vietnam for the next four years. Viet Cong guerrilla attacks on American forces in February 1965 led Johnson to launch Operation Rolling Thunder, the first sustained bombing of North Vietnam, which was intended to stop the flow of soldiers and supplies into the south. Six months later analysts concluded that the bombing had had little effect on the supplies pouring down the Ho Chi Minh Trail from North Vietnam through Laos into South Vietnam. Still, the bombing continued.

In March 1965 the new U.S. army commander in Vietnam, General William C. Westmoreland, requested and got the first installment of combat troops, ostensibly to defend American airfields. By the end of 1965, there were 184,000 U.S. troops in Vietnam; in 1966 there were 385,000. As combat operations increased throughout South Vietnam, so did American casualties, announced each week on the nightly news, along with the "body count" of alleged enemy dead.

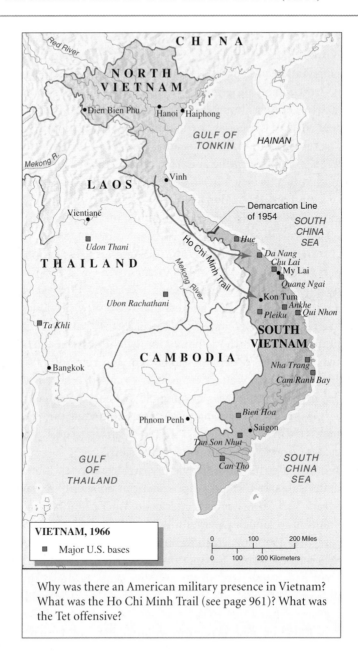

Why was there an American military presence in Vietnam? What was the Ho Chi Minh Trail (see page 961)? What was the Tet offensive?

THE CONTEXT FOR POLICY   Lyndon Johnson's decision to "Americanize" the Vietnam War, so ill-starred in retrospect, was entirely consistent with the foreign-policy principles pursued by all presidents after World War II. The version of the containment theory articulated in the Truman Doctrine, endorsed by Dwight Eisenhower, and reaffirmed by John Kennedy, pledged

The Tet Offensive

Many Vietnamese were driven from their homes during the bloody street battles of the 1968 Tet offensive. Here, following a lull in the fighting, civilians carrying a white flag approach U.S. Marines.

opposition to the advance of communism anywhere in the world. Secretary of State Dean Rusk frequently warned that Thailand, Burma, and the rest of Southeast Asia would fall "like dominoes" to communism if American forces withdrew from Vietnam. Military intervention was thus a logical culmination of the assumptions widely shared by the foreign-policy establishment and leaders of both political parties since the early days of the cold war.

Nor did the United States "stumble into a quagmire" blindly in Vietnam, as some commentators maintained. Johnson insisted from the start that military involvement must not reach levels that would provoke the Chinese or Soviets to intervene with their own forces. He therefore exercised a tight rein over the bombing campaign, once boasting that "they can't even bomb an outhouse without my approval." Such a restrictive policy meant, in effect, that military victory was never possible. America's goal was not to win the war in a conventional sense by capturing enemy territory but to prevent the North Vietnamese and the Viet Cong from winning and, eventually, to force

"How Deep Do You Figure We'll Get Involved, Sir?"

Although U.S. soldiers were first sent to Vietnam as noncombatant advisers, they soon found themselves involved in a quagmire of fighting.

a negotiated settlement with the North Vietnamese. This meant that America would have to maintain a military presence as long as the enemy retained the will to fight.

As it turned out, American public support for the war eroded faster than the will of the North Vietnamese leaders to tolerate devastating casualties and destruction. Systematic opposition to the war broke out on college campuses with the escalation of 1965. By 1967 anti-war demonstrations in New York City and at the Pentagon were attracting massive support. Nightly television accounts of the fighting—Vietnam was the first war to receive extended television coverage and hence was dubbed the living-room war—contradicted the official optimism.

In a war of political will, North Vietnam had the advantage. Johnson and his advisers grievously underestimated the tenacity of North Vietnam's commitment to unify Vietnam and expel the United States. While the United States fought a limited war for limited objectives, the Vietnamese Communists fought a total war for their survival. Just as General Westmoreland was assuring Johnson and the American public that his forces in early 1968 were on the verge of gaining the upper hand, the Communists again displayed their cunning and tenacity.

THE TURNING POINT   On January 31, 1968, the first day of the Vietnamese New Year (Tet), the Viet Cong and the North Vietnamese defied a holiday truce to launch a wave of surprise assaults on American and South Vietnamese forces throughout South Vietnam. The old capital city of Hue fell to the Communists, and Viet Cong units temporarily occupied the grounds of the U.S. embassy in Saigon. Within a few days, however, American and South Vietnamese forces organized a devastating counterattack. General Westmoreland justifiably proclaimed the Tet offensive a major defeat for the

Viet Cong. But while Viet Cong casualties were enormous, the psychological impact of the surprise attacks on the American public was more telling. The scope and intensity of the offensive contradicted upbeat claims by commanders that the war was going well. *Time* and *Newsweek* soon ran anti-war editorials urging American withdrawal. Polls showed that Johnson's popularity had declined to 35 percent, lower than that of any president in polling history. In 1968 the United States was spending $322,000 on every enemy soldier killed in Vietnam; the poverty programs at home received only $53 per person.

During 1968 Lyndon Johnson grew increasingly isolated. He suffered from depression and bouts of paranoia. The secretary of defense reported that a task force of prominent soldiers and civilians saw no prospect for a military victory; the stalemated war was undermining the Great Society programs. The Democratic party was also fragmenting. Robert Kennedy, now a senator from New York, was considering a run for the presidency in order to challenge Johnson's Vietnam policy. Senator Eugene McCarthy of Minnesota had already decided to oppose Johnson in the Democratic primaries. With anti-war students rallying to his candidacy, McCarthy polled 42 percent of the vote to Johnson's 48 percent in New Hampshire's March primary. It was a remarkable showing for a little-known senator. Each presidential primary now promised to become a referendum on Johnson's Vietnam policy.

On March 31 Johnson made a dramatic decision. He announced a limited halt to the bombing of North Vietnam and fresh initiatives for a negotiated cease-fire. Then he added a stunning postscript: "I shall not seek, and I will not accept, the nomination of my party for another term as your President." Although American combat troops would remain in Vietnam for seven more years and the casualties would mount, the quest for military victory had ended. Now the question was how the most powerful nation in the world could extricate itself from Vietnam with a minimum of damage to its prestige. It would not be easy. When direct negotiations with the North Vietnamese finally began in Paris in May 1968, they immediately bogged down over North Vietnam's demand for a halt to the bombing by the United States as a precondition for further discussion.

SIXTIES CRESCENDO

A TRAUMATIC YEAR   Change moved at a fearful pace throughout the 1960s, but 1968 was the most turbulent and the most traumatic year of all. On April 4, only four days after Johnson's withdrawal from the presidential race, Martin Luther King was gunned down in Memphis, Tennessee. The assassin, James Earl Ray, had expressed hostility toward African Americans, but Americans continue to debate whether he was a pawn in an organized conspiracy. King's death set off an outpouring of grief among whites and blacks. It also set off riots in over sixty American cities.

Two months later, on June 5, Robert Kennedy was shot in the head by a young Palestinian who resented Kennedy's strong support of Israel. Kennedy died on the day after he had convincingly defeated Eugene McCarthy in the California Democratic primary, thereby momentarily assuming leadership of the anti-war forces in the race for the nomination for president.

CHICAGO AND MIAMI   In August 1968 Democratic delegates gathered inside a Chicago convention hall to nominate Vice President Hubert Humphrey, while almost 20,000 police and national guardsmen and a small army of television reporters stood watch over several thousand diverse protesters herded together miles away in a public park. Chicago mayor Richard J. Daley, who had given "shoot-to-kill" orders to police during the April riots following the King assassination, warned that he would not tolerate disruptions. Nonetheless, riots broke out and were televised nationwide. As demonstrators chanted "The whole world is watching," police attacked the crowds with tear gas and billy clubs.

The Democratic party's liberal tradition was clearly in disarray, a fact that gave heart to the Republicans, who gathered in Miami Beach to nominate Richard Nixon and celebrate a remarkable political comeback. Nixon's narrow loss to Kennedy in 1960 had been followed by a disastrous defeat in the California gubernatorial race two years later. In what he labeled his "last press conference," he vowed never again to run for office. Yet Nixon displayed his remarkable resilience by returning to national politics in 1964, when he crisscrossed the nation in support of Goldwater's candidacy. For the next several years he remained active in politics, and in 1968 he was ready to take advantage of Johnson's crumbling popularity. He offered a vision of stability and order that appealed to a majority of Americans, soon to be called the silent majority.

But others were ready as well to challenge the Democratic party regulars. George Wallace, the Democratic governor of Alabama, ran as a third candidate in the campaign, on the American Independent party ticket. Wallace had made his political reputation as a brazen defender of segregation, but in his campaign for national office in 1968 he moderated his position on the race issue. And he appealed even more candidly than Nixon to the fears generated by rioting anti-war protesters, the welfare system, and the growth of

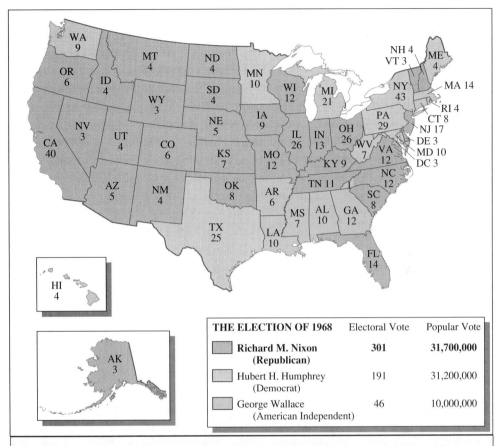

THE ELECTION OF 1968	Electoral Vote	Popular Vote
Richard M. Nixon (Republican)	**301**	**31,700,000**
Hubert H. Humphrey (Democrat)	191	31,200,000
George Wallace (American Independent)	46	10,000,000

How did the riots at the Chicago Democratic Convention affect the 1968 presidential campaign? How did Nixon engineer his political comeback? What was Wallace's appeal to over 10 million voters?

the federal government. Wallace's platform was compelling in its simplicity: rioters would be shot, the war in Vietnam won, states' rights and law and order restored, open-housing laws repealed, and welfare cheats jailed.

Wallace's reactionary candidacy generated considerable appeal outside his native South, especially in white working-class communities, where resentment of Johnson's Great Society liberalism was rife. Although never a possible winner, Wallace had to be taken seriously: he could deny Humphrey or Nixon an electoral majority and thereby throw the choice into the House of Representatives, which could provide an appropriate climax to a chaotic year.

NIXON AGAIN   It did not happen that way. Richard Nixon enjoyed an enormous early lead in the polls, which narrowed as the 1968 election approached. George Wallace's campaign was hurt by his outspoken running mate, retired air force general Curtis LeMay, who suggested using nuclear weapons in Vietnam. In October 1968 Hubert Humphrey infuriated Johnson and the party bosses when he announced that, if elected, he would stop bombing North Vietnam "as an acceptable risk for peace."

In the end, Nixon and his running mate, Governor Spiro Agnew of Maryland, eked out a narrow victory of about 500,000 votes, a margin of about 1 percentage point. The electoral vote was more decisive, 301 to 191. Wallace won 10 million votes, 13.5 percent of the total, the best showing by a third-party candidate since Robert La Follette headed the Progressive ticket in 1924. All but one of Wallace's 46 electoral votes were from the Deep South. Nixon swept all but four of the states west of the Mississippi, while Humphrey's support came almost exclusively from the Northeast.

So at the end of a turbulent year, near the end of a traumatic decade, a nation on the verge of violent chaos looked to Richard Nixon to provide what he had promised in the campaign: "peace with honor" in Vietnam and a middle ground on which a majority of Americans, silent or otherwise, could come together.

MAKING CONNECTIONS

- The reform movements of the 1960s galvanized the baby-boom generation into a new youth movement, described in the next chapter, that continued through the early 1970s.

- The conflict in Vietnam, America's longest war, would come to a bitter end for U.S. forces, but the divisions it spawned still echo today.

- The Immigration and Nationality Act of 1965 would have profound and unexpected consequences on American society, described in Chapter 37.

- The success of the civil rights movement in the 1960s led to similar movements by women, gays, Native Americans, and Latinos, as we will see in the next chapter.

Further Reading

A dispassionate analysis of Kennedy's life is Thomas C. Reeves's *A Question of Character: A Life of John F. Kennedy* (1991). The best study of the Kennedy administration's domestic policies is Irving Bernstein's *Promises Kept: John F. Kennedy's New Frontier* (1991). For details on the assassination, see David W. Belin's *Final Disclosure: The Full Truth about the Assassination of President Kennedy* (1988).

The most comprehensive biography of LBJ is Robert Dallek's two-volume work, *Lone Star Rising: Lyndon Johnson and His Times, 1908–1960* (1991) and *Flawed Giant: Lyndon B. Johnson and His Times, 1960–1973* (1998). On the Johnson administration, see Vaughn Davis Bornet's *The Presidency of Lyndon B. Johnson* (1984).

Among the works that interpret liberal social policy during the 1960s, John Schwarz's *America's Hidden Success: A Reassessment of Twenty Years of Public Policy* (1983) offers a glowing endorsement of Democratic programs. For a contrasting perspective, see Charles Murray's *Losing Ground: American Social Policy, 1950–1980,* rev. ed. (1994).

On foreign policy, see *Kennedy's Quest for Victory: American Foreign Policy, 1961–1963* (1989), edited by Thomas G. Paterson. To learn more about Kennedy's problems in Cuba, see Mark White's *Missiles in Cuba: Kennedy, Khrushchev, Castro and the 1962 Crisis* (1997). See also Aleksandr Fursenko and Timothy Naftali's *"One Hell of a Gamble": Khrushchev, Castro and Kennedy, 1958–1964* (1997).

American involvement in Vietnam has received voluminous treatment from all political perspectives. For an excellent overview, see Larry Berman's *Planning a Tragedy: The Americanization of the War in Vietnam* (1982) and *Lyndon Johnson's War: The Road to Stalemate in Vietnam* (1989), as well as Stanley Karnow's *Vietnam: A History,* rev. ed. (1991). An excellent analysis of policy making concerning the Vietnam War is David M. Barrett's *Uncertain Warriors: Lyndon Johnson and His Vietnam Advisors* (1993). An excellent account of the military involvement is Robert D. Schulzinger's *A Time for War: The United States and Vietnam, 1941–1975* (1997). On the legacy of the Vietnam War, see Arnold R. Isaacs's *Vietnam Shadows: The War, Its Ghosts, and Its Legacy* (1997).

Many scholars have dealt with various aspects of the civil rights movement and race relations in the 1960s. See especially Carl M. Brauer's *John F. Kennedy and the Second Reconstruction* (1977), David Garrow's *Bearing the Cross: Martin Luther King, Jr., and the Southern Christian Leadership Conference*

(1986), Adam Fairclough's *To Redeem the Soul of America: The Southern Christian Leadership Conference and Martin Luther King, Jr.* (1987). William H. Chafe's *Civilities and Civil Rights: Greensboro, North Carolina, and the Black Struggle for Freedom* (1980) details the original sit-ins. An award-winning study of racial and economic inequality in a representative American city is Thomas J. Sugrue's *The Origins of the Urban Crisis: Race and Inequality in Postwar Detroit* (1996).

35

REBELLION AND REACTION IN THE 1960s AND 1970s

FOCUS QUESTIONS

- What characterized the rebellion and struggles for rights in the 1970s?
- How did the war in Vietnam end?
- What was the Watergate incident, and how did it lead to Nixon's resignation?
- How did the Carter administration deal with the Middle East?

To answer these questions and access additional review material, please visit www.wwnorton.com/studyspace.

As Richard Nixon entered the White House in early 1969, he faced a nation whose social fabric was in tatters. Everywhere, it seemed, traditional institutions and notions of authority were under attack. The traumatic events of 1968 revealed how deeply divided American society had become and how difficult a task Nixon faced in carrying out his pledge to restore social harmony. The stability he promised proved elusive. His policies and his combative temperament served to heighten rather than reduce societal tensions. Those tensions reflected profound fissures in the postwar consensus promoted by Eisenhower and inherited by Kennedy and Johnson. Ironically, many of the same forces that had promoted the flush times of the Eisenhower years—the baby boom, the containment doctrine of anti-communism, and the superficial focus on the consumer culture—helped generate the social upheaval of the 1960s and 1970s.

The Roots of Rebellion

YOUTH REVOLT   By the early 1960s the postwar baby boomers were maturing. Now young adults, they differed from their elders in that they had experienced neither economic depression nor a major war. In record numbers they were attending colleges and universities: college enrollment quadrupled between 1945 and 1970. Many universities had become sprawling institutions increasingly dependent upon research contracts from giant corporations and the federal government. As these "multiversities" grew more bureaucratic and hierarchical, they unwittingly invited resistance from students wary of involvement in what President Eisenhower had called the military-industrial complex.

The Greensboro student sit-ins in 1960 not only precipitated a decade of civil rights activism but also signaled an end to the supposed apathy that had enveloped college campuses and social life during the 1950s. Although primarily concerned with the rights and status of black people, the sit-ins, marches, protests, principles, and sacrifices associated with the civil rights movement provided inspiring models and rhetoric for other groups demanding justice, freedom, and equality.

During 1960–1961 a small but significant number of white students joined the sit-in movement. They and many others were also inspired by President Kennedy's direct appeals to their youthful idealism. Soon, however, it became clear that politics was mixed with principle in the president's position on civil rights. Later, as criticism of escalating American involvement in Vietnam mounted, more and more young people grew disillusioned with the government, corporations, and parental authority. By the mid-1960s a full-fledged youth revolt had erupted across the country, and rebels began to flow into two distinct yet frequently overlapping movements: the New Left and the counterculture.

THE NEW LEFT   The explicitly political strain of the youth revolt coalesced when Tom Hayden and Al Haber, two student radicals at the University of Michigan, formed Students for a Democratic Society (SDS) in 1960. Two years later Hayden drafted what became known as the Port Huron Statement: "We are the people of this generation, bred in at least moderate comfort, housed in universities, looking uncomfortably to the world we inherit."

Hayden's manifesto focused on the absence of individual freedom in modern life. The country, he insisted, was dominated by huge organizational structures—governments, corporations, universities—all of which conspired to oppress and alienate the individual. Inspired by the example of African-American activism in the South, Hayden declared that students had the power to restore "participatory democracy" to American life by wresting "control of the educational process from the administrative bureaucracy" and then forging links with other dissident movements. He and others adopted the term New Left to distinguish their efforts at grassroots democracy from those of the Old Left of the 1930s, which had espoused an orthodox version of Marxism.

In the fall of 1964, students at the University of California at Berkeley took Hayden's program to heart. When the university's chancellor announced that sidewalk solicitations for political causes would no longer be allowed, several hundred students staged a sit-in. Over 2,000 more joined in and after a tense standoff the administration relented.

The program and tactics of the SDS soon spread to universities across the country, but the focus changed as escalating involvement in Vietnam brought a dramatic expansion of the military draft and millions of young men faced the grim prospect of participating in an increasingly unpopular war. In fact, however, Vietnam, like virtually every other war, was a poor man's fight. In 1965–1966, thanks to deferments and exemptions, college students made up only 2 percent of all military inductees. Yet several thousand male collegians would flee to Canada or Sweden to escape the draft, while hundreds of thousands engaged in various protests against a war they considered immoral.

During the eventful spring of 1968—when Lyndon Johnson announced he would not run for reelection and Martin Luther King was assassinated—campus unrest reached a climax with the disruption of Columbia University in New York City. Mark Rudd, an SDS leader, and a small group of radicals protested the university's insensitive decision to disrupt a neighboring African-American community in order to build a new gymnasium. The students occupied some campus buildings, and the protest quickly spread. During the following week more buildings were occupied, faculty and administrative offices were ransacked, and classes were canceled. University officials finally called in the New York City police. While arresting the protesters, officers injured a number of innocent bystanders. Their excessive force angered many unaligned students, who then joined militants in staging a strike that shut down the university for the remainder of the semester. That spring similar clashes among students, administrators, and police occurred

Upheaval in Chicago

The violence that accompanied the 1968 Democratic National Convention in Chicago seared the nation.

at Harvard, Cornell, and San Francisco State.

At the 1968 Democratic Convention in Chicago, the polarization of American society reached a bizarre climax. Inside the tightly guarded convention hall, Democrats were nominating Lyndon Johnson's faithful vice-president, Hubert Humphrey, while Chicago's streets roiled with anti-war dissenters. The outlandish behavior of the anarchic protesters provoked an equally outlandish response from Chicago's Mayor Richard Daley and his army of police. As a national television audience watched, many police officers went berserk, clubbing and gassing demonstrators as well as bystanders caught up in the chaotic scene. The televised spectacle lasted three days and generated a wave of anger among many middle-class Americans, anger that Richard Nixon and the Republicans shrewdly exploited at their nominating convention in Miami Beach. At the same time, the Chicago riots helped fragment the anti-war movement.

During 1968 the SDS fractured into rival factions, the most extreme of which called itself the Weathermen, a name derived from a lyric by Bob Dylan: "You don't need a weatherman to know which way the wind blows." These hardened young activists launched a campaign of violence and disruption, firebombing university and government buildings and killing innocent people, as well as several of their own. Government forces arrested most of them, and the rest went into hiding. By 1971 the New Left was dead as a political movement. In large measure it had committed suicide by abandoning the democratic and pacifist principles that had inspired participants and given the movement its moral legitimacy. The larger anti-war movement also began to fade. There would be a wave of student protests against the Nixon administration in 1970–1971, but thereafter campus unrest virtually disappeared as American troops returned home from Vietnam and the draft ended.

If the social mood was changing during Richard Nixon's presidency, a large segment of the public persisted in the quest for social justice. A *New York Times* survey of college campuses in 1969 revealed that many students were refocusing their attention on the environment. This new ecological awareness would blossom in the 1970s into one of the most compelling items on the nation's social agenda.

THE COUNTER CULTURE   The numbing events of 1968 led other disaffected activists away from radical politics altogether, toward another manifestation of the sixties youth revolt: the counterculture. Long hair, blue jeans, tie-dyed shirts, sandals, mind-altering drugs, rock music, and group living arrangements were more important than revolutionary ideology or mass protest to the hippies, the direct descendants of the Beats of the 1950s. These advocates of the counterculture were, like their New Left peers, primarily young whites alienated by the Vietnam War, racism, political corruption and parental demands, runaway technology, and a crass corporate mentality that equated the good life with material goods. Disillusioned with organized political action, they embraced the credo announced by the zany Harvard professor Timothy Leary, "Turn on to the scene, tune in to what's happening, and drop out."

For some the counterculture entailed the study and practice of Asian religions, such as Buddhism. For others it centered on the frequent use of hallucinogenic drugs such as LSD. Collective living in urban enclaves such as San Francisco's Haight-Ashbury district and New York's East Village was the rage for a while, until conditions grew so crowded and violent that residents migrated elsewhere. Rural communes also attracted bourgeois rebels. During the 1960s and early 1970s thousands of inexperienced romantics flocked to the countryside, eager to liberate themselves from parental and institutional restraints, live in harmony with nature, and coexist in an atmosphere of love and openness. Only a handful of their utopian homesteads survived more than a few months, however.

Huge outdoor rock-music concerts were also a popular source of community for hippies. The largest of these was the Woodstock Music and Art Fair, held in 1969 on a 600-acre farm near the tiny rural town of Bethel, New York. For three days some 500,000 "flower children" reveled in good music and cheap marijuana. But the carefree spirit of the Woodstock festival was short-lived. When promoters tried to replicate the scene four months later, this time at a Rolling Stones concert at the Altamont speedway, near San Francisco, members of the Hell's Angels motorcycle gang beat a man to death in front of the stage.

Just as the 1968 Democratic Convention in Chicago marked the end of the New Left as a vital political force, the violence at Altamont sharply diminished the appeal of the counterculture. Moreover, many of the flower children grew tired of their riches-to-rags existence and returned to college to become lawyers, doctors, politicians, or accountants. The search on the part of alienated youth for a better society and a good life was strewn with both comic and tragic aspects, and it reflected the deep social ills that had been allowed to fester throughout the post–World War II period.

FEMINISM   The ideal of liberation spawned during the 1960s helped accelerate a powerful women's rights crusade. Like the New Left the new feminism drew much of its inspiration and many of its initial tactics from the civil rights movement. Its aim was to challenge the cult of domesticity that had been touted as the ideal during the 1950s.

Woodstock

The Woodstock music festival drew nearly half a million people to a farm in Bethel, New York. The concert was billed as three days of "peace, music, . . . and love."

The mainstream women's movement was led by Betty Friedan. Her influential book *The Feminine Mystique* (1963) launched a new phase of female protest on a national level. Women, Friedan wrote, had actually lost ground during the years after World War II, when many left wartime jobs and settled down in suburbia to care for their children. Advertisers and women's magazines promoted the "feminine mystique" of blissful domesticity. In Friedan's view the middle-class home had become "a comfortable concentration camp" where women saw their individual potential suffocated in an atmosphere of mindless materialism, daytime TV, and neighborhood gossip.

The Feminine Mystique inspired many women who felt trapped in a domestic rut. In 1966 Friedan and other activists founded the National Organization for Women (NOW), whose membership grew rapidly. NOW spearheaded efforts to end job discrimination on the basis of sex, legalize abortion, and obtain federal and state support for child-care centers.

Pressured by NOW, Congress and the Supreme Court in the early 1970s advanced the cause of sexual equality. Under Title IX of the Educational Amendments Act of 1972, colleges were required to institute "affirmative-action" programs to ensure equal opportunities for women in such areas as admissions, faculty and staff hiring, and athletics. In the same year, Congress overwhelmingly approved the equal-rights amendment to the Constitution. And in 1973 the Supreme Court, in *Roe v. Wade*, struck down state laws forbidding abortions during the first three months of pregnancy, a ruling based on the constitutional right to privacy. Meanwhile, many bastions of male education, including Yale and Princeton, led a new movement for coeducation that swept the nation.

By the end of the 1970s, however, sharp disputes between moderate and radical feminists

Feminist Awakenings

In 1967 Syracuse University student Kathy Switzer challenged the Boston Marathon's tradition of excluding women. Officials tried to pull Switzer from the course, but with the aid of fellow runners she completed the race. Women did not become official entrants until 1971.

had fragmented the women's movement. The movement's failure to broaden its appeal much beyond the confines of the white middle class caused reform efforts to stagnate. In 1982 the equal-rights amendment died, several states short of ratification. The very success of NOW's efforts to liberalize state abortion laws helped generate a powerful backlash, especially among Catholics and fundamentalist Protestants, who mounted a "right-to-life" crusade that remains a potent political force.

Yet the success of the women's movement endured despite setbacks. The growing political power of women and their expanding presence in the workforce combined to become one of the most significant developments of the era. By 1976 over half the married women in America and nine out of ten female college graduates were employed outside the home, a development that one economist called "the single most outstanding phenomenon of this century." Many career women, however, did not regard themselves as feminists; they took jobs because they and their families needed the money to achieve higher levels of material comfort. Whatever the motives, women were changing traditional sex roles and child-rearing practices to accommodate the two-career family, which had replaced the established pattern of male breadwinner and female housekeeper as the new American norm.

HISPANIC RIGHTS   The activism that animated the crusade for women's rights also spread to various ethnic minority groups. The labor shortages during World War II had led defense industries to offer Hispanic Americans their first significant access to skilled-labor jobs. As was the case with African Americans, service in the military during the war years helped to heighten an American identity among Hispanic Americans and increase their desire for equal rights and opportunities.

But equality was elusive. After World War II, Hispanic Americans still faced widespread discrimination in hiring, housing, and education. Poverty was widespread. In 1960, for example, the median income of a Mexican-American family was only 62 percent of that of a family in the general population. Hispanic-American activists during the 1950s and 1960s mirrored the efforts of black civil rights leaders. They, too, denounced segregation, promoted efforts to improve the quality of public education, and struggled to increase Hispanic-American political influence and economic opportunities.

One of the most popular initiatives was the use of the term *Chicano* as an inclusive label for all Mexican immigrants, Spanish Americans in New Mexico, old Californios (descendants of the inhabitants of California before it was seized by the United States, most of whom were Indians or of mixed ancestry), and Tejanos (descendants of the inhabitants of Texas before it became independent).* In southern California, students formed Young Chicanos for Community Action, a social-service group designed to promote self-reliance and local involvement within Hispanic-American neighborhoods. Wearing brown berets, the members protested the disproportionate number of Hispanics being killed in the Vietnam War and demanded improvements in their neighborhood schools.

Unlike their African-American counterparts, however, Hispanic-American leaders faced an awkward dilemma: what should they do about the continuing stream of undocumented Mexicans flowing across the border? Many Mexican Americans argued that their hopes for economic advancement and social equality were put at risk by the daily influx of Mexican laborers willing to accept low-paying jobs in the United States. Mexican-American leaders thus helped end the bracero program in 1964 (which trucked in day laborers, from Mexico) and in 1962 formed the United Farm Workers (UFW, originally the National Farm Workers Association) to represent Mexican-American migrant workers.

The founder of the UFW was Cesar Chavez. Born in 1927 in Yuma, Arizona, to Mexican immigrant parents, Chavez moved with his family to California in 1939. There they joined thousands of other migrant farmworkers traversing the state, moving from job to job, living in tents, cars, or ramshackle cabins. In 1944, at age seventeen, Chavez joined the navy. After the war he married and found work, first as a sharecropper raising strawberries and then as a migrant laborer in apricot orchards. In 1952 Chavez joined the Community Service Organization (CSO), a social-service group that sought to educate and organize the migrant poor so that they could become self-reliant. He founded new CSO chapters and was named general director in 1958.

Chavez left the organization in 1962 when it refused to back his proposal to establish a union for farmworkers. Other CSO leaders believed that it was impossible to organize migrant workers into an effective union. They thought the migrant workers were too mobile, too poor, too illiterate, too ethnically diverse, and too easily replaced by braceros. Moreover, farmworkers did not enjoy protected status under the National Labor Relations Act of 1935 (the Wagner Act). Unlike industrial laborers they were not guaranteed

---

Hispanic, a term used in the United States to refer to people who are from, or trace their ancestry to, Spanish-speaking Latin America or Spain, came to be used increasingly after 1945 in conjunction with growing efforts to promote economic and social justice for those people.(Although frequently used as a synonym for *Hispanic,* the term *Latino* technically refers only to people of Latin American descent.)

the right to organize or the right to receive a minimum wage. Nor did federal regulations govern the safety of their workplace.

Despite such obstacles, Chavez resolved to organize the migrant farmworkers. His fledgling Farm Workers Association gained national attention in 1965 when it joined a strike by Filipino farmworkers against the corporate grape farmers in California's San Joaquin Valley. Chavez's charisma and Catholic piety, his insistence upon nonviolent tactics, his reliance upon college-student volunteers, his skillful alliance with organized labor and religious groups—all combined to attract media interest and popular support.

Still, the grape strike itself brought no tangible gains. So Chavez organized a nationwide consumer boycott of grapes. Two years later, in 1970, the grape strike and consumer boycott finally succeeded in bringing twenty-six grape growers to the bargaining table. They signed formal contracts recognizing the UFW, and soon migrant workers throughout the West were benefiting from Chavez's strenuous efforts on their behalf. Wages increased, and working conditions improved. In 1975 the California state legislature passed a bill that required growers to bargain collectively with the elected representatives of the farmworkers.

The chief strength of the Hispanic movement lay less in the duplication of the civil rights strategies than in the rapid growth of the Hispanic population. In 1960 Hispanics in the United States numbered slightly more than 3 million; by 1970 they had increased to 9 million, and by 2006 they numbered over 40 million, making them the largest minority in the country.

United Farm Workers

Cesar Chavez (center) with organizers of the grape boycott. In 1968 Chavez ended a three-week fast by taking communion and breaking bread with Senator Robert Kennedy.

NATIVE AMERICAN RIGHTS

American Indians—many of whom had begun calling themselves Native Americans—also emerged as a political force in the late 1960s. Two conditions combined to make Indian rights a priority: first, white Americans felt a persistent sense of guilt for the destructive policies of their ancestors toward a people who had, after all, first settled the continent; second, the plight of the Native American minority was more desperate than that of any other group in the country. Indian unemployment was 10 times the national rate, life expectancy was 20 years lower than the national average, and the suicide rate was 100 times higher than that for whites.

Although President Lyndon Johnson recognized the poverty of the Native Americans and attempted to funnel federal anti-poverty-program funds into reservations, militants within the Indian community became impatient with the pace of change. They organized protests and demonstrations against local, state, and federal agencies. In 1963 two Chippewas (Ojibwas) living in Minneapolis, George Mitchell and Dennis Banks, founded the American Indian Movement (AIM) to promote "red power." The leaders of AIM occupied Alcatraz Island in San Francisco Bay in 1969, claiming the site "by right of discovery." And in 1972 a sit-in at the Department of the Interior's Bureau of Indian Affairs (BIA) in Washington attracted national attention to their cause. The BIA was then—and still is—widely viewed as the worst-managed federal agency. Instead of finding creative ways to promote tribal autonomy and economic self-sufficiency, the BIA has served as a classic example of government paternalism gone awry.

Indian protesters subsequently discovered a more effective tactic than direct action and sit-ins: they went into federal courts armed with copies of old treaties and demanded that these become the basis for restitution. In Alaska, Maine, and Massachusetts they won significant settlements that provided legal recognition of their tribal rights and financial compensation at levels that upgraded the standard of living on several reservations.

GAY RIGHTS   The liberationist impulses of the 1960s also encouraged homosexuals to organize and assert their right to equal treatment. On June 27, 1969, New York City police raided the Stonewall Inn, a Greenwich Village bar popular with gay men. The patrons fought back, and the struggle spilled into the streets. Hundreds of other gays and their supporters joined the fracas against the police. Rioting lasted throughout the weekend. When it ended, homosexuals had forged a new sense of solidarity and a new organization, the Gay Liberation Front.

As news of the Stonewall riots spread across the country, the gay rights movement assumed national proportions. One of its main tactics was to encourage people to "come out," to make public their homosexuality. This was by no means an easy decision. By professing their homosexuality, gays faced social ostracism, physical assault, exclusion from the military and civil service, and discrimination in the workplace. Yet despite the risks, thousands of homosexuals did come out. By 1973 almost 800 gay and lesbian organizations had been formed across the country, and every major city had a visible gay community and cultural life.

Like the civil rights crusade and the women's movement, however, the campaign for gay rights soon suffered from internal divisions and aroused a conservative backlash. Gay activists engaged in fractious disputes over tactics and objectives, and conservative moralists and Christian fundamentalists launched a nationwide counterattack and succeeded in repealing new local laws banning discrimination against homosexuals. By the end of the 1970s, the gay movement had lost its initial momentum and was struggling to salvage many of its hard-won gains.

Nixon and Vietnam

The numerous liberation movements of the 1960s fundamentally changed the tone and texture of American social life. By the early 1970s, however, the national mood was swinging back toward conservatism. The election of Richard Nixon in 1968 and the rise of George Wallace as a serious political force on the right reflected the emergence of the "silent majority," those white working-class and middle-class citizens who were determined to regain control of a society they feared was awash in permissiveness. Large as the gap was between the "silent majority" and the varied forces of dissent, the two sides agreed on one thing: that the Vietnam War remained the dominant event of the time. Until the war was ended and all American troops were returned home, the nation would find it difficult to achieve the equilibrium that the new president had promised.

GRADUAL WITHDRAWAL Nixon and his special assistant for national security, Dr. Henry Kissinger, claimed to have a plan to achieve "peace with honor" in Vietnam. Peace, however, was long in coming and not very honorable when it arrived. The Nixon administration, even while withdrawing U.S. forces, held to a policy that refused to let the North Vietnamese dominate Indochina. By the time a settlement was reached, in 1973, another 20,000 Americans had died, the morale of the American army had been shattered, millions of Asians had been killed or wounded, and fighting was continuing in Southeast Asia. In the end, Nixon's policy gained little that the president could not have accomplished in 1969.

The administration's new strategy in Vietnam moved along three fronts. The first front was the deadlocked Paris peace talks, where American negotiators demanded the withdrawal of North Vietnamese forces from South Vietnam and the preservation of the U.S.-supported regime of President Nguyen Van Thieu. The North Vietnamese and Viet Cong negotiators insisted on retaining a Communist military presence in the south, however, and on reunifying the Vietnamese people under a Communist-dominated government. There was no common ground on which to come together. Hidden from public awareness and from America's South Vietnamese allies were secret meetings between Henry Kissinger and the North Vietnamese.

On the second front, Nixon tried to defuse domestic unrest generated by the war. To this end he sought to "Vietnamize" the conflict by turning over most of the combat missions to Vietnamese units and sharply reducing the number of U.S. ground forces. To assuage the South Vietnamese, he provided more equipment and training for their troops. From a peak of 560,000 in 1969, U.S. combat units were withdrawn at a steady pace. By 1973 only 50,000 troops remained in Vietnam. In late 1969 Nixon also established a lottery system that clarified the likelihood of being drafted: only those with low lottery numbers would have to go. Nixon was more successful in reducing anti-war activity than in forcing concessions from the North Vietnamese in Paris.

On the third front, while reducing the number of troops in Vietnam, Nixon and Kissinger secretly expanded the air war in an effort to persuade the enemy to come to terms. On March 18, 1969, U.S. planes began Operation Menu, a fourteen-month-long bombing of Communist forces in Cambodia. Over 100,000 tons of bombs were dropped, four times the tonnage dropped on Japan during World War II. Congress did not learn of those raids until 1970, when Nixon announced what he called an "incursion" by U.S. troops into supposedly "neutral" Cambodia to "clean out" North Vietnamese staging areas.

DIVISIONS AT HOME   News of the Cambodia "incursion" came on the heels of another incident that rekindled public indignation against the war. Late in 1969 the story of the My Lai Massacre broke. During the next two years the public learned the gruesome tale of Lieutenant William Calley, who in 1968 had ordered the murder of over 300 Vietnamese civilians in the village of My Lai. Twenty-five officers were charged with complicity in the massacre and subsequent cover-up, but only Calley was convicted of murder. Nixon then granted him parole.

The loudest public outcry against Nixon's Indochina policy occurred in the wake of the Cambodian "incursion," in the spring of 1970. Campuses across the country witnessed a new wave of protests that closed hundreds of colleges and universities. At Kent State University, the Ohio National Guard was called in to quell rioting, during which the campus Reserve Officers' Training Corps (ROTC) building was burned down by anti-war protesters. Pelted by rocks and verbal taunts, the poorly trained guardsmen panicked and opened fire on the demonstrators, killing four bystanders. Eleven days later, on May 15, Mississippi highway patrolmen riddled a dormitory at Jackson State College with bullets, killing two African-American students. Although an official investigation of the Kent State episode condemned the "casual and indiscriminate shooting," polls indicated that the public supported the national guard; students had "got what they were asking for."

The following year, 1971, the *New York Times* began publishing excerpts from a secret Defense Department study on the Vietnam War. The so-called Pentagon Papers, leaked to the press by a former Pentagon official, Daniel

Kent State University

National guardsmen shot and killed four bystanders during antiwar demonstrations on the campus of Kent State University in Ohio.

Ellsberg, confirmed what many critics of the war had long suspected: Congress and the public had not received the full story on the Gulf of Tonkin incident of 1964. Contingency plans for American entry into the war were being drawn up even while President Johnson was promising that combat troops would never be sent to Vietnam. The Nixon administration attempted to block publication of the Pentagon Papers, arguing that it would endanger national security and prolong the war. By a vote of six to three, the Supreme Court ruled against the government. Newspapers throughout the country began publication the next day.

WAR WITHOUT END   Although Nixon's decision in the spring of 1970 to use American forces to root out Communist bases in Cambodia did bring a tactical victory, it also served to widen a war he had promised to end. Moreover, his hopes that the South Vietnamese units replacing U.S. forces could hold their own against the North Vietnamese were dashed when they suffered repeated defeats in 1971 and 1972. Disorganized, poorly led, and lacking tenacity, the South Vietnamese soldiers had to call upon U.S. airpower to fend off North Vietnamese offensives.

The deteriorating ground war along with mounting divisions at home and the approach of the 1972 presidential elections combined to produce a shift in the American negotiating position in Paris. In the summer of 1972, Henry Kissinger dropped his insistence upon the removal of all North Vietnamese troops from the south before the withdrawal of the remaining U.S. troops. On October 26, only a week before the presidential election, he announced, "Peace is at hand." But the Thieu regime in South Vietnam objected to the plan for a cease-fire, fearful that the continued presence of North Vietnamese troops in the south virtually guaranteed an eventual Communist victory. Hanoi then stiffened its position by demanding that Thieu resign.

The Paris peace talks broke off on December 16, 1972, and Nixon told his military advisers that only a massive show of American airpower would make the North Vietnamese more cooperative at the negotiating table. Two days later the reelected Nixon unleashed furious B-52 raids on Hanoi and Haiphong. The so-called Christmas bombings aroused worldwide protest, but Henry Kissinger claimed Nixon's "jugular diplomacy" worked, for the talks in Paris soon resumed.

On January 27, 1973, the United States, North and South Vietnam, and the Viet Cong signed an "agreement on ending the war and restoring peace in Vietnam." The agreement showed that despite the Christmas bombings, the North Vietnamese never altered their basic stance: they kept 150,000 troops in the south and remained committed to the reunification of Vietnam under one government. What had changed since the previous fall was the willingness of the South Vietnamese, who were never allowed to participate in the negotiations, to accept these terms, albeit reluctantly, on the basis of Nixon's promise that the United States would respond "with full force" to any Communist violation of the agreement.

On March 29, 1973, the last U.S. combat troops left Vietnam. On that same day 587 American prisoners of war, most of them downed pilots, were released from Hanoi. Within a period of months, however, the war between north and south resumed, and the Communist forces gained the advantage. In Cambodia and Laos, where fighting had been more sporadic, Communist victory also seemed inevitable.

In 1975 the North Vietnamese launched a full-scale armored invasion against the south. President Thieu appealed to Washington for assistance, but the Democratic majority in Congress refused, and on April 30, 1975, Americans watched on television as North Vietnamese tanks rolled into Saigon, soon to be renamed Ho Chi Minh City. The scene at the U.S. embassy in Saigon, where thousands of terrified Vietnamese fought to board the last departing helicopters, was a poignant and tragic ending to America's greatest foreign-policy disaster.

The longest war in U.S. history was finally over, leaving in its wake a bitter legacy. The Vietnam war, described as a noble crusade on behalf of democratic ideals, instead suggested that democracy was not easily transferable to third world regions lacking experience with civil liberties and representative government. The war eroded respect for the military so thoroughly that many young Americans came to regard military service as inherently corrupting and ignoble. The war, fought to show the world that the United States was united in its anti-communist convictions, divided Americans more drastically than any event since the Civil War. The Vietnam War cost the nation some 58,000 deaths and $150 billion. Little wonder the dominant public reaction to the war's end was the urge to "put Vietnam behind us" and revert to a noninterventionist foreign policy.

NIXON AND MIDDLE AMERICA

Richard Nixon had been elected in 1968 as the representative of Middle America, those middle-class citizens fed up with the liberal politics and cultural radicalism of the 1960s. Nixon selected men for his cabinet and White House staff who would restore conservative values and carry out his orders with blind obedience. John Mitchell, the gruff attorney general who had been a senior partner in Nixon's New York law firm, was the new president's closest confidant. H. R. "Bob" Haldeman, an imperious former advertising executive, served as Nixon's chief of staff. As Haldeman explained, "Every President needs a son of a bitch, and I'm Nixon's. I'm his buffer, I'm his bastard." He was succeeded in 1973 by General Alexander Haig, whom Nixon described as "the meanest, toughest, most ambitious son of a bitch I ever knew." John Ehrlichman, a Seattle attorney and college schoolmate of Haldeman's, served as chief domestic policy adviser. As secretary of state, Nixon tapped his old friend William Rogers, who had served as attorney general under Eisenhower. Rogers's control over foreign policy was quickly preempted by Henry Kissinger, a distinguished Harvard political scientist who served as national security adviser before becoming secretary of state in 1973. Kissinger came to dominate the Nixon administration's diplomatic planning and emerged as one of the most respected and internationally famous members of the staff. Nixon often had to mediate the tensions between Rogers and Kissinger, noting that the secretary of state considered the German-born Kissinger "Machiavellian, deceitful, egotistical, arrogant, and insulting," while Kissinger viewed Rogers as "vain, emotional, unable to keep a secret, and hopelessly dominated by the State Department bureaucracy."

DOMESTIC AFFAIRS   A major reason for Richard Nixon's election in 1968 was the effective "southern strategy" fashioned by his campaign staffers. To garner support among Republican delegates from the South and then win over southern voters in the election, Nixon had assured southern conservatives that he would slow federal enforcement of civil rights laws and appoint pro-southern justices to the Supreme Court. Once in office, Nixon strove to follow through on his pledges. He appointed no African Americans to his cabinet and refused to meet with the Congressional Black Caucus. In 1970 he launched a concerted effort to block congressional renewal of the Voting Rights Act of 1965 and to delay implementation of court orders requiring the desegregation of school districts in Mississippi. The Democratic-controlled Congress then extended the Voting Rights Act over Nixon's veto. The Supreme Court, in the first decision made under the new chief justice, Warren Burger—a Nixon appointee—ordered the integration of the Mississippi public schools. During Nixon's first term, and despite his wishes, affirmative action made major inroads, and more schools were desegregated than in all the Kennedy-Johnson years combined.

Nixon's attempts to block desegregation efforts in urban areas also failed. The Burger Court ruled unanimously in *Swann v. Charlotte-Mecklenburg*

Board of Education (1971) that school systems must bus students out of their neighborhood if necessary to achieve racial integration. Protests over desegregation now occurred more in the North and the West than in the South as white families in Boston, Denver, and other cities denounced the destruction of "the neighborhood school." Busing opponents won a limited victory when the Supreme Court ruled in 1974 that requiring the transfer of students from the inner city to the suburbs was unconstitutional. That ruling, along with the *Board of Regents of the University of California v. Bakke* (1978) decision, which restricted the use of quotas to achieve racial balance in university classrooms, marked the transition of desegregation from an issue of simple justice to a more tangled thicket of conflicting group and individual rights.

It also reflected the growing conservatism of the Supreme Court, a trend encouraged by Nixon. The litany of liberal decisions during the 1960s had made the Warren Court a prime target for conservatives who resented what they regarded as the federal government's excessive protection of the "undeserving." Fate and the aging of the justices on the Warren Court gave Nixon the chance to make four new appointments. Only one, William Rehnquist, would consistently support Nixon's conservative interpretation of the Constitution, but overall the tenor of the Court did shift toward a more moderate stance.

Nixon also fervently desired to reverse the welfare-state policies of his Democratic predecessors. But the administration never succeeded in developing a comprehensive domestic agenda acceptable to Congress. Meanwhile, the Democratic Congress moved forward with new legislation: the right of eighteen-year-olds to vote in national elections (1970) and, under the Twenty-sixth Amendment (1971), in state and local elections as well; increases in Social Security benefits tied to the inflation rate; a rise in food-stamp funding; the Occupational Safety and Health Act (1970); and the Federal Election Campaign Act (1972). Moreover, in response to Nixon's proposal to decentralize responsibility for various programs, Congress passed a five-year revenue-sharing plan in 1972 that would distribute $30 billion of federal revenues to the states for use as they saw fit.

During Nixon's first term, Americans in large numbers began to lobby for government action to protect and improve the natural environment. In 1970 hundreds of thousands of activists rallied across the country in support of the first annual Earth Day. In response, Congress established new programs to control water pollution and passed the Clean Air Act (1970) over Nixon's veto. Congress also created the Environmental Protection Agency (EPA) to oversee federal guidelines for controlling air pollution, toxic wastes, and water quality. The EPA began requiring developers to perform environmental-impact studies before new construction could begin. The agency also set fuel-efficiency standards for automobiles and required manufacturers to reduce the level of carbon monoxide emissions from car engines.

ECONOMIC MALAISE   The major domestic development during the Nixon years was a floundering economy. Exacerbated by the expense of the Vietnam War, the annual inflation rate began to rise in 1967, when it was at 3 percent. By 1973 it had reached 9 percent; a year later it was at 12 percent, and it remained in double digits for most of the 1970s. Unemployment, at a low of 3.3 percent when Nixon took office, climbed to 6 percent by the end of 1970 and threatened to keep rising. Somehow the American economy was undergoing a recession and an inflation at the same time. Economists coined the term *stagflation* to describe the syndrome that defied the orthodox laws of economics.

The economic malaise had at least three deep-rooted causes. First, the Johnson administration had attempted to pay for both the Great Society's social-welfare programs and the war in Vietnam without a major tax increase, thereby generating larger federal deficits, a major expansion of the money supply, and rapid price inflation. Second and more important, by the late 1960s American goods faced stiff competition in international markets from West Germany, Japan, and other emerging industrial powers. This development sharply reduced the export of American goods and generated a growing trade deficit. Third, the economy had grown heavily dependent upon cheap sources of energy.

Just as domestic petroleum reserves began to dwindle and dependence upon foreign sources increased, the nations in the Organization of Petroleum Exporting Countries (OPEC), centered in the Middle East, resolved to use their oil as a political and economic weapon. In 1973, after the United States sent massive aid to Israel during the Yom Kippur War, OPEC announced that it would not sell oil to nations supporting Israel and that it was raising its prices by 400 percent. American motorists thereafter faced long lines at gas stations, schools and offices closed temporarily, factories cut production, and the inflation rate soared.

Another condition leading to stagflation was the flood of new workers—mainly baby boomers and women—entering the labor market. From 1965 to 1980, the workforce grew by 40 percent, almost 30 million workers, a figure greater than the total labor force of France or West Germany. The number of new jobs created could not keep up, leaving many unemployed. At the same time, worker productivity declined, further increasing prices in the face of rising demand.

Stagflation posed a new set of economic problems, but the Nixon administration responded with old remedies. First it tried to reduce the federal deficit by raising taxes and cutting the budget. When the Democratic Congress refused to cooperate with that approach, the White House encouraged the Federal Reserve Board to reduce the money supply by raising interest rates. But that move backfired when the stock market quickly collapsed, plunging the economy into the "Nixon recession." A sense of desperation seized the White House. In 1969, when asked about government restrictions on wages and prices, Nixon had been adamant: "Controls. Oh, my God, no! . . . We'll never go to controls." On August 15, 1971, however, he reversed himself. He froze all wages and prices for ninety days, yet the economy still floundered. By 1973 the wage and price guidelines were made voluntary and were therefore almost entirely ineffective. Stagflation continued to plague the economy for the rest of the decade.

NIXON TRIUMPHANT

Confronting a Congress controlled by Democrats, Richard Nixon focused his energies on foreign policy, where presidential initiatives were less restricted and where he, in tandem with Henry Kissinger, achieved several

Race to the Moon

In July 1969 a program begun by President Kennedy reached its goal: putting a man on the moon.

major breakthroughs. He also continued to support the American space program and the efforts to beat the Soviets to the moon. In July 1969 astronaut Neil Armstrong became the first person to walk on the moon. This extraordinary achievement buoyed American spirits at a time when troops were still mired in Vietnam, cities were boiling over with racial unrest, and the economy was languishing. Similarly, Nixon's foreign-policy successes gave Americans new confidence in their government. His administration managed to improve U.S. relations with the major powers of the Communist world—China and the Soviet Union—and fundamentally shift the pattern of the cold war.

By 1969 Nixon had perceived that a new multipolar world order was emerging to replace the conventional cold war confrontation between the United States and the Soviet Union. Since 1945 the United States had lost its monopoly on nuclear weapons and its overwhelming economic dominance and geopolitical influence. The rapid rise of competing power centers in Europe, China, and Japan complicated international relations—China had replaced the United States as the Soviet Union's most threatening competitor—but also provided strategic opportunities, which Nixon and Kissinger seized.

In early 1970 Nixon announced a significant alteration in American foreign policy. The United States could no longer be the world's policeman against communism; the long-standing containment policy developed by President Truman must be revised: "America cannot—and will not—conceive *all* the plans, design *all* the programs, execute *all* the decisions, and undertake *all* the defense of the free nations of the world." In explaining what became known as the Nixon Doctrine, the president declared that "our interests must shape our commitments, rather than the other way around." The United States, he

The United States and China

With President Richard Nixon's visit to China in 1972, the United States formally recognized China's Communist government. Here Nixon and Chinese premier Chou En-lai drink a toast.

and Kissinger stressed, must become more strategic and more realistic in its commitments, and it would begin to establish selected partnerships with Communist countries in areas of mutual interest.

CHINA   In 1971 Henry Kissinger made a secret trip to Peking to explore the possibility of U.S. recognition of China. In 1972 Nixon himself arrived in Peking and made recognition an official and public fact. The irony of the event was overwhelming. Richard Nixon, the former anti-Communist crusader who had condemned the State Department for "losing" China in 1949, had accomplished a diplomatic feat that his Democratic predecessors could not. Yet it was because Nixon had been such an ardent anti-Communist that he could pull off the recognition of China: he could not be accused of going soft on communism.

DÉTENTE   China sought the breakthrough in relations with the United States because its festering rivalry with the Soviet Union, with which it shares a long border, had become increasingly bitter. Soviet leaders, troubled by the Sino-American agreements, were also eager to ease tensions with the United States now that they had, as the result of a huge arms buildup following the Cuban missile crisis, achieved virtual parity with the United States in nuclear weapons. Once again Nixon surprised the world, announcing that he would visit Moscow in 1972 for discussions with Leonid Brezhnev, the Soviet premier.

What became known as détente with the Soviets offered the promise of a more orderly and restrained competition between the two superpowers. Nixon and Brezhnev signed the Strategic Arms Limitation Talks (SALT) agreement, which set ceilings on the number of long-range nuclear missiles each nation could possess and limited the construction of antiballistic missile systems. In effect the Soviets were allowed to retain a greater number of missiles with greater destructive power while the United States retained a lead in the total number of warheads. No limitations were placed on new weapons systems, though each side agreed to work toward a permanent freeze on all nuclear weapons.

SHUTTLE DIPLOMACY   The Nixon-Kissinger initiatives in the Middle East were less dramatic and less conclusive than the agreements with China and the Soviet Union, but they did show that America recognized Arab power in the region and its own dependence upon oil from Islamic states, which were fundamentally opposed to the existence of Israel. After Israel recovered from the initial shock of the Arab attacks that triggered the Yom Kippur War of 1973, it recaptured the Golan Heights and seized additional Syrian territory. Henry Kissinger initiated the negotiations leading to a cease-fire and exerted pressure to prevent Israel from taking more Arab territory. American reliance upon Arab oil led to closer ties with Egypt and its president, Anwar el-Sadat, and more restrained support for Israel. Although Kissinger's "shuttle diplomacy," involving numerous visits to the capitals of the Middle East, won acclaim from all sides, it failed to find a comprehensive peace formula for the troubled region. It also ignored the problem of establishing a homeland for Palestinian refugees. But Kissinger's efforts did lay groundwork for the accord between Israel and Egypt in 1977.

THE ELECTION OF 1972 Nixon's foreign-policy achievements allowed him to stage the presidential campaign of 1972 as a triumphal procession. The first threat to his reelection came from the Democratic governor of Alabama, George Wallace, who had the potential to deprive the Republicans of conservative votes. But on May 15, 1972, Wallace was shot by a deranged man. Paralyzed below the waist, Wallace was forced to withdraw from the campaign. Meanwhile, the Democrats were further ensuring Nixon's victory by nominating Senator George S. McGovern of South Dakota, a steadfast liberal who embodied anti-war principles and embraced progressive social-welfare policies. At the Democratic Convention, party reforms contributed to McGovern's nomination by increasing the representation of women, African Americans, and other minorities, but those reforms alienated the party regulars.

In 1972 Nixon won the greatest victory of any Republican presidential candidate in history, capturing 520 electoral votes to only 17 for McGovern. During the course of the campaign, McGovern complained about the "dirty tricks" of the Nixon administration, most especially the curious incident during the summer of 1972 in which burglars were caught breaking into the headquaters of the Democratic National Committee in the Watergate apartment complex in Washington, D.C. McGovern's accusations seemed shrill and biased at the time. Nixon and his staff made plans for "four more years" as the investigation of the fateful Watergate break-in unfolded.

WATERGATE

During the trial of the accused Watergate burglars in January 1973, the relentless prodding of Judge John J. Sirica led one of the accused to tell the full story of the Nixon administration's complicity in the episode. James McCord, a former CIA agent and security chief of the Committee to Re-elect the President (CREEP), was the first of many informers in a melodrama that unfolded over two years. It ended in the first resignation of a president in American history, the conviction and imprisonment of twenty-five officials of the Nixon administration, including four cabinet members, and the most serious constitutional crisis since the impeachment trial of President Andrew Johnson.

UNCOVERING THE COVER-UP   The trail of evidence pursued by Judge Sirica, a grand jury, several special prosecutors, and a televised Senate investigatory committee headed by Democrat Samuel J. Ervin Jr. of North Carolina led directly to the White House. No evidence surfaced that Nixon had ordered the break-in or that he had been aware of plans to burglarize the Democratic National Committee headquarters. From the start, however, Nixon participated in the cover-up, using his presidential powers to discredit and block the investigation. Perhaps most alarming was that the Watergate burglary proved to be just one small part of a larger pattern of corruption and criminality sanctioned by the Nixon White House. Having developed a compulsive view of his presidency as being above the law, Nixon had ordered intelligence agencies to spy on his most outspoken opponents, open their mail, and even burglarize their homes in an effort to uncover compromising information.

The Watergate cover-up began to unravel as various people, including John Dean, legal counsel to the president, began to cooperate with prosecuters. It unraveled further in 1973 when L. Patrick Gray, acting director of the FBI, resigned after confessing that he had destroyed several incriminating documents. On April 30 top Nixon aides John Ehrlichman and Bob Haldeman resigned, together with Attorney General Richard Kleindienst. A few days later Nixon nervously assured the public in a television address, "I'm not a crook." New evidence suggested otherwise. John Dean, whom Nixon had dismissed, testified before the Ervin committee and a rapt television audience that Nixon had approved the cover-up. In another bombshell disclosure, a White House aide told the committee that Nixon had installed a taping system in the White House and that many of the conversations about Watergate had been recorded.

A year-long legal battle for the "Nixon tapes" began. Pleading "executive privilege," Nixon refused to release them. On July 24, 1974, in *United States v. Richard M. Nixon,* the Supreme Court ruled unanimously that the president must surrender all of the tapes. A few days later the House Judiciary Committee voted to recommend three articles of impeachment: obstruction of justice through the payment of "hush money" to witnesses and the withholding of evidence, abuse of power through the use of federal agencies to deprive citizens of their constitutional rights, and defiance of Congress by withholding the tapes. Before the House of Representatives could meet to vote on impeachment, however, Nixon handed over the complete set of White House tapes. On August 9, 1974, fully aware that the evidence on the tapes implicated him in the cover-up, Richard Nixon resigned from office, the only president ever to do so.

Nixon's Resignation

Having resigned his office, Richard Nixon waves farewell outside the White House on August 9, 1974.

THE EFFECTS OF WATERGATE Vice President Spiro Agnew did not succeed Nixon because Agnew had been forced to resign in October 1973 for accepting bribes from contractors before and during his term as vice president. The vice president at the time of Nixon's resignation was Gerald Ford, the former Michigan congressman and House minority leader, whom Nixon had appointed, with congressional approval, under the provisions of the Twenty-fifth Amendment (ratified in 1967). President Ford insisted that he had no intention of pardoning Nixon, who was still liable for criminal prosecution. But a month after Nixon's resignation, on September 8, the new president issued the pardon, explaining that it was necessary to end the national obsession with the Watergate scandals. Many Americans suspected that Nixon and Ford had made a deal, though there was no evidence to confirm the speculation.

If there was a silver lining in Watergate's dark cloud, it was the vigor and resilience of the institutions that had brought a president down: the press, Congress, the courts, and an aroused public opinion. The Watergate revelations led Congress to pass several pieces of legislation designed to curb executive power in the future. The War Powers Act (1973) requires a president to inform Congress within forty-eight hours if U.S. troops are deployed in combat abroad and to withdraw troops after sixty days unless Congress specifically approves their stay. In an effort to correct abuses of campaign funds, Congress enacted legislation in 1974 that set new ceilings on political contributions and expenditures. In reaction to the Nixon claim of "executive privilege" as a means of withholding evidence, Congress strengthened the 1966 Freedom of Information Act to require prompt responses to requests for information from government files and to place on government agencies the burden of proof for classifying information as secret.

An Unelected President

While the Watergate crisis dominated the Washington scene, major domestic and foreign problems received little executive attention. Stagflation, the perplexing combination of inflation and recession, worsened, as did the oil crisis. At the same time, Henry Kissinger, who assumed control over the management of foreign policy, watched helplessly as the South Vietnamese forces began to crumble before North Vietnamese attacks, attempted with limited success to establish a framework for peace in the Middle East, and supported a CIA role in the overthrow of the popularly elected Marxist president of Chile.

THE FORD YEARS   Gerald Ford inherited those simmering problems, as well as the burden of being an unelected president. An amiable, honest man, Ford enjoyed widespread popular support for only a short time. "I am a Ford, not a Lincoln," he candidly recognized upon becoming vice president. His pardon of Nixon generated a storm of criticism. The *New York Times* called it "an unconscionable act."

As president, Ford adopted the posture he had developed as a conservative minority leader in the House: a nay-saying leader of the opposition who believed that the federal government exercised too much power over domestic affairs. In his fifteen months as president, Ford vetoed thirty-nine bills, outstripping Herbert Hoover's record in less than half the time. By resisting congressional pressure to reduce taxes and increase federal spending, he succeeded in plummeting the economy into the deepest recession since the Great Depression. Unemployment jumped to 9 percent in 1975, and the federal deficit hit a record the next year. Ford rejected wage and price controls to curb inflation, preferring voluntary restraints.

In foreign policy, Ford retained Henry Kissinger as secretary of state and attempted to pursue Nixon's goals of stability in the Middle East, rapprochement with China, and détente with the Soviet Union. Late in 1974 Ford met with Soviet leader Leonid Brezhnev and accepted the framework for another arms-control agreement that was to serve as the basis for SALT II. Meanwhile, Kissinger's tireless shuttling between Cairo and Tel Aviv produced an agreement: Israel promised to return to Egypt most of the Sinai territory captured in the 1967 war, and the two nations agreed to rely upon negotiations rather than force to settle future disagreements.

These limited but significant achievements should have enhanced Ford's image, but they were drowned in the sea of criticism and carping that followed the loss of South Vietnam to North Vietnam in the spring of 1975. Not only had a decade of American effort in Vietnam proved futile, but the Khmer Rouge, the Cambodian Communist movement, had also won a resounding victory, plunging Cambodia into a fanatic bloodbath. And the OPEC oil cartel was threatening another worldwide boycott while other third world nations denounced the United States as a depraved imperialistic power.

THE ELECTION OF 1976   In the midst of the turmoil, the Democrats could hardly wait for the 1976 election. At the Republican Convention, Ford managed to thwart a powerful challenge for the nomination from the former California governor and Hollywood actor Ronald Reagan. The Democrats chose Jimmy Carter, a former naval officer and engineer turned peanut farmer who had served one term as governor of Georgia. Carter capitalized on the post-Watergate cynicism by promising never to "tell a lie to the American people" and by citing his independence from traditional Washington power politics.

To the surprise of many pundits, the little-known Carter revived the New Deal coalition of southern whites, blacks, urban labor, and ethnic groups to win the election, with 41 million votes to Ford's 39 million. Polls showed that the Carter victory benefited from a heavy turnout of African Americans in the South, where Carter swept every state but Virginia. Minnesota senator Walter F. Mondale, Carter's liberal running mate and a favorite among blue-collar workers and the urban poor, also gave the ticket a big boost. The real story of the election, however, was the low voter turnout. Almost half of America's eligible voters, apparently alienated by Watergate and the lackluster candidates, chose to sit out the election.

THE CARTER INTERREGNUM

EARLY SUCCESSES   During the first two years of his term, Jimmy Carter enjoyed several successes. His administration included more African Americans, Hispanics, and women than any before. He offered amnesty to the thousands of young men who had fled the country rather than serve in Vietnam, closing one of the remaining open wounds of that traumatic event.

He reformed the civil service to provide rewards for meritorious performance, and he created new cabinet-level Departments of Energy and Education. Carter also pushed through Congress significant environmental initiatives, including a bill to regulate strip mining and a "superfund" to clean up chemical-waste sites.

His success was short-lived, however. In the summer of 1979, when renewed violence in the Middle East produced a second fuel shortage, motorists were again forced to wait in long lines for limited supplies of gasoline that they regarded as excessively expensive. Soon they directed their frustration at the White House. Opinion polls showed Carter with an approval rating of only 26 percent, lower than Nixon's during the worst moments of the Watergate crisis.

Several of Carter's early foreign-policy initiatives also got caught in political crossfires. Soon after his inauguration, Carter vowed that "the soul of our foreign policy" should be the defense of human rights abroad. But the human rights campaign aroused opposition from two sides: those who feared that it sacrificed a detached appraisal of national interest for high-level moralizing and those who believed that human rights were important but that the administration was applying the standard inconsistently.

THE CAMP DAVID ACCORDS   Carter's crowning diplomatic achievement was the arrangement of a peace agreement between Israel and Egypt. In 1978 Carter invited Egypt's president Anwar el-Sadat and Israel's prime minister Menachem Begin to Camp David, the presidential retreat in Maryland, for two weeks of difficult negotiations. The first part of the eventual agreement required Israel to return all land in the Sinai peninsula in exchange for Egyptian recognition of Israel's sovereignty. This agreement was successfully implemented in 1982, when the last Israeli settler vacated the peninsula. But the second part of the agreement, calling for Israel to negotiate with Sadat a resolution to the Palestinian refugee dilemma, began to unravel soon after the Camp David summit. Still, Carter and Secretary of State Cyrus Vance had orchestrated a dramatic display of high-level diplomacy that, whatever its limitations, made an all-out war between Israel and the Arab world less likely. It also represented a significant first step toward a comprehensive settlement of the region's volatile tensions.

MOUNTING TROUBLES   Carter's crowning failure was his mismanagement of the economy. In effect he inherited a bad situation and let it worsen. Carter employed the same economic policies as Nixon and Ford to fight stagflation, but he reversed the order of the federal "cure," preferring to fight unemployment first with a tax cut and increased public spending.

The Camp David Accords

Egyptian president Anwar el-Sadat (left), Jimmy Carter (center), and Israeli prime minister Menachem Begin (right) at the announcement of the Camp David Accords, September 1978.

Unemployment declined slightly, from 8 to 7 percent in 1977, but inflation soared; at 5 percent when he took office, it reached 10 percent in 1978 and kept rising. During one month in 1980, it measured an annual rate of 18 percent. Like previous presidents, Carter then reversed himself to fight the other side of the economic malaise. By midterm he was delaying tax reductions and vetoing government spending programs that he had proposed in his first year. The result was the worst of all possible worlds—a deepened recession and inflation averaging between 12 and 13 percent per year.

IRAN   Then the Iranian crisis exploded, producing a year-long barrage of unwelcome events that epitomized the inability of the United States to control world affairs. The crisis began in 1979 with the overthrow of the shah of Iran, long a staunch American ally and right-wing dictator. The revolutionaries who toppled the shah's government rallied around Ayatollah Ruhollah Khomeini, a fundamentalist Muslim leader who symbolized the militant Islamic values the shah had tried to replace with Western ways. Khomeini's hatred of the United States dated back to 1953, when the CIA had sponsored the overthrow of Iran's prime minister, Mohammed Mossadegh, an ardent nationalist who sought to rid his country of Western influence and interests. The 1953 coup had restored the shah's regime to power.

Late in 1979 Carter allowed the exiled shah to enter the United States to undergo cancer treatment. A few days later, on November 4, a frenzied mob stormed the U.S. embassy in Tehran and seized the staff. Khomeini applauded the mob action and demanded the shah's return, along with all his wealth, in exchange for the release of the fifty-two American hostages still held captive.

Carter was furious, but his options were limited. He appealed to the United Nations, but Khomeini scoffed at UN requests for the release of the hostages. Carter then froze all Iranian assets in the United States and appealed to American allies to organize a trade embargo of Iran. The trade restrictions were only partially effective—even America's most loyal European allies did not want to lose access to Iranian oil.

So a frustrated Carter, hounded by a public and press demanding "action," authorized a rescue attempt by U.S. commandos in April 1980. The raid was aborted in the Iranian desert because of helicopter malfunctions, however, and it ended with eight fatalities when a U.S. helicopter collided with a transport plane. Carter's presidency died with the failed raid. Secretary of State Cyrus Vance resigned in protest against the risky venture. Meanwhile, nightly television coverage of the taunting Iranian rebels generated a near obsession with the seeming impotence of the United States and the fate of the hostages. On January 20, 1981, the crisis ended after 444 days of captivity when Carter released several billion dollars of Iranian assets to ransom the kidnapped hostages. By then, however, Ronald Reagan had been elected president, and Carter was headed into retirement.

The turbulent and often tragic events of the 1970s—the Communist conquest of South Vietnam, the Watergate scandal and Nixon's resignation, the energy shortage and stagflation, and the Iranian hostage episode—provoked among Americans what Carter labeled a "crisis of confidence." By 1980 American power and prestige seemed to be on the decline, the economy remained in a shambles, and the sexual revolution launched in the 1960s, with the questions it raised for the family and other basic social and political institutions, had sparked a backlash of resentment in Middle America. With theatrical timing, Ronald Reagan emerged to tap the growing reservoir of public frustration and transform his political career into a crusade to make America "stand tall again." He told his supporters that there was "a hunger in this land for a spiritual revival, a return to a belief in moral absolutes." The United States, he declared, remained the "greatest country in the world. We have the talent, we have the drive, we have the imagination. Now all we need is the leadership."

MAKING CONNECTIONS

- Foreign affairs in the 1970s showed the changing patterns of the cold war. The next chapter details the end of both the cold war and the Soviet Union.

- Presidents Nixon and Ford tried, with limited success, to decrease the power of the federal government over domestic affairs. President Reagan was much more successful at advancing the conservative agenda, another topic covered in the next chapter.

- The rebellion and turbulence of the 1960s and 1970s became less apparent in the following decade; as Chapter 37 shows, however, that turbulence reappeared, in a somewhat different form, in the 1990s.

FURTHER READING

An engaging overview of the cultural trends of the 1960s is Maurice Isserman and Michael Kazin's *America Divided: The Civil War of the 1960s* (1999). The New Left is assessed in Irwin Unger's *The Movement: A History of the American New Left, 1959–1972* (1974). On the Students for a Democratic Society, see Kirkpatrick Sale's *SDS* (1973) and Allen J. Matusow's *The Unraveling of America: A History of Liberalism in the 1960s* (1984). Also useful is Todd Gitlin's *The Sixties: Years of Hope, Days of Rage,* rev. ed. (1993).

Two influential assessments of the counterculture by sympathetic commentators are Theodore Roszak's *The Making of a Counterculture: Reflections on the Technocratic Society and Its Youthful Opposition* (1969) and Charles A. Reich's *The Greening of America* (1970). A good scholarly analysis of the hippies that takes them seriously is Timothy Miller's *The Hippies and American Values* (1991).

The best study of the women's liberation movement is Ruth Rosen's *The World Split Open: How the Modern Women's Movement Changed America* (2000). The organizing efforts of Cesar Chavez are detailed in Ronald B. Taylor's *Chavez and the Farm Workers* (1975). The struggles of Native Americans for recognition and power are sympathetically described in Stan Steiner's *The New Indians* (1968).

On Nixon, see Melvin Small's *The Presidency of Richard Nixon* (1999). For a solid overview of the Watergate scandal, see Stanley I. Kutler's *The Wars of Watergate: The Last Crisis of Richard Nixon* (1990). For the way the Republicans handled foreign affairs, consult Tad Szulc's *The Illusion of Peace: Foreign Policy in the Nixon Years* (1978).

The loss of Vietnam and the end of American involvement there are traced in Larry Berman's *No Peace, No Honor: Nixon, Kissinger, and Betrayal in Vietnam* (2001). William Shawcross's *Sideshow: Kissinger, Nixon and the Destruction of Cambodia*, rev. ed. (2002), deals with the broadening of the war, while Larry Berman's *Planning a Tragedy: The Americanization of the War in Vietnam* (1982) assesses the final impact of American involvement. The most comprehensive treatment of the anti-war movement in the United States is Tom Wells's *The War Within: America's Battle over Vietnam* (1994).

A comprehensive treatment of the Ford administration is contained in John Robert Greene's *The Presidency of Gerald R. Ford* (1995). The best overview of the Carter administration is Burton I. Kaufman's *The Presidency of James Earl Carter, Jr.* (1993). A work more sympathetic to the Carter administration is John Dumbrell's *The Carter Presidency: A Re-evaluation* (1993). Gaddis Smith's *Morality, Reason, and Power: American Diplomacy in the Carter Years* (1986) provides an overview. Background on how the Middle East came to dominate much of American policy is found in William B. Quandt's *Decade of Decisions: American Policy toward the Arab-Israeli Conflict, 1967–1976* (1977).

36

A CONSERVATIVE INSURGENCY

FOCUS QUESTIONS

- What were the demographic, social, and economic reasons for the rise of Ronald Reagan and Republican conservatism?
- How did changing relations between the United States and the Soviet Union lead to the end of the cold war?
- What characterized the economy and the society of the 1980s?
- What were the causes and the aftermath of the Gulf War?

To answer these questions and access additional review material, please visit www.wwnorton.com/studyspace.

President Jimmy Carter and his embattled Democratic administration hobbled through 1979. The economy remained sluggish, double-digit inflation continued unabated, and failed efforts to free the hostages in Iran made the administration appear indecisive. Carter's inability to persuade the nation to embrace his energy conservation program revealed mortal flaws in his reading of the public mood and his understanding of legislative politics.

While the lackluster Carter administration was foundering, Republican conservatives were forging an aggressive plan to win the White House in 1980 and to assault the New Deal welfare-state mentality in Washington. Those plans centered on the popularity and charisma of Ronald Reagan, the Hollywood actor turned California governor and prominent political commentator. Reagan was not a deep thinker, but he was a superb analyst of the public mood, an unabashed patriot, and a committed champion of conservative

The Great Communicator

Ronald Reagan in 1980, shortly before his election.

principles. He was also charming and cheerful, a likable politician renowned for his folksy anecdotes and optimistic outlook. Where the dour Carter denounced the evils of free-enterprise capitalism and scolded Americans in an attempt to get them to revive long-forgotten virtues of frugality, a sunny Reagan promised a "revolution of ideas" designed to unleash the capitalist spirit, restore national pride, and regain international respect.

During the late 1970s Reagan's simple message promoting a restoration of American pride and prosperity offered an uplifting alternative to Carter's vision of a constrained future. Reagan wanted to increase military spending, dismantle the "bloated" federal bureaucracy, reduce taxes and regulations, and in general, shrink the role of the government. He also wanted to affirm old-time morality by banning abortions and reinstituting prayer in public schools. Reagan's appeal derived from his remarkable skills as a public speaker and his dogmatic commitment to a few overarching ideas and simple themes. As a true believer and an able compromiser, he combined the fervor of a revolutionary with the pragmatism of a diplomat.

Such attributes won Reagan two presidential terms, in 1980 and 1984, and ensured the election of his successor, George H. W. Bush, in 1988. Just how revolutionary the Reagan era was remains a subject of intense partisan debate. What cannot be denied, however, is that Reagan's actions and beliefs set the tone for the decade's political and economic life.

THE REAGAN REVOLUTION

THE MAKING OF A PRESIDENT   As the 1980 election approached, the Republicans eagerly anticipated the contest with a struggling Jimmy Carter. Their candidate, Ronald Reagan, had initially appeared as an even more improbable presidential possibility than Carter had four years earlier.

Born in Illinois in 1911, Reagan graduated from tiny Eureka College and then worked as a radio announcer and sportscaster before heading to Hollywood in 1937. In 1964 Reagan entered the political limelight when he delivered a rousing speech on behalf of Barry Goldwater at the Republican Convention. During two terms as governor of California (1967–1975), he displayed a commitment to conservative principles as well as a political realism and an openness to compromise. Nevertheless, by the middle 1970s Reagan's brand of free-enterprise conservatism still appeared too extreme for a national audience.

THE MOVE TO REAGAN   By the eve of the 1980 election, however, Reagan had become the beneficiary of three developments that made his conservative vision of America much more viable. First, the 1980 census revealed that the population was aging, and large numbers of retirees were moving from the liberal Northeast to the conservative sunbelt states of the South and the West. This development meant that demographic forces were carrying the electorate toward Reagan's conservative position.

Second, in the 1970s the country experienced a major revival of evangelical religion. No longer simply a local or provincial phenomenon, Christian evangelicals and fundamentalists had bought television and radio stations and were operating schools and universities. The Reverend Jerry Falwell's Moral Majority expressed the major goals of the religious right wing: free enterprise should remain free, big government should be shrunk, abortion should be outlawed, prayer in public schools should be reinstated, Darwinian evolution should be replaced in schoolbooks by the biblical story of creation, and Soviet communism should be opposed as a form of pagan totalitarianism. The moralistic zeal and financial resources of the religious right made its adherents effective opponents of liberal political candidates and programs. They rallied to Reagan's call for the strengthening of traditional values and local government.

A third factor contributing to the conservative resurgence was a well-organized and well-financed backlash against the feminist movement. During the 1970s women who opposed the social goals of feminism formed counterorganizations with names like Women Who Want to Be Women and Females Opposed to Equality. Spearheading those efforts was Phyllis Schlafly, a right-wing Republican activist from Illinois. Schlafly orchestrated the campaign to defeat the equal-rights amendment and thereafter served as the galvanizing force behind a growing anti-feminist movement. She characterized feminists as a "bunch of bitter women seeking a constitutional cure for their personal problems," and she urged women to embrace their "God-given" roles as wives and mothers. Feminists, she charged, were "anti-family, anti-children, and pro-abortion."

Many of Schlafly's supporters also participated in a mushrooming anti-abortion, or "pro-life," movement. By 1980 the National Right to Life Committee, supported by the National Conference of Catholic Bishops, boasted 11 million members representing all religious denominations. The intensity of its members' commitment made it a powerful political force in its own right, and the Reagan campaign was quick to highlight its own support for traditional "family values," gender roles, and the "rights" of the unborn. Such hot-button cultural issues helped persuade many northern Democrats to support Reagan. Whites alienated by the increasingly liberal social agenda of the Democratic party became a crucial element in Reagan's electoral strategy.

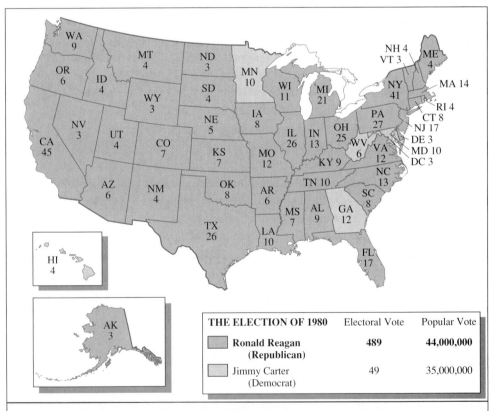

THE ELECTION OF 1980	Electoral Vote	Popular Vote
Ronald Reagan (Republican)	489	44,000,000
Jimmy Carter (Democrat)	49	35,000,000

Why was Reagan such an appealing candidate in 1980? What was the impact of "nonvoting"? Why was there so much voter apathy?

THE ELECTION OF 1980 By 1980 voters were flocking to Reagan's cheery promises of a new era of less government, lower taxes, renewed prosperity, waning inflation, and revived military strength and national pride. His "supply-side" economic proposals, soon dubbed Reaganomics by supporters and voodoo economics by critics, suggested that the stagflation of the 1970s had resulted from excessive taxes that weakened the incentive to work, save, and reinvest. The solution was to slash tax rates. For a long-suffering nation it was, in theory, an alluring economic panacea.

On election day, Reagan swept to a decisive victory, with 489 electoral votes to 49 for Carter, who carried only six states. The popular vote proved equally lopsided: 44 million (51 percent) to 35 million (41 percent), with 7 percent going to John Anderson, a moderate Republican who had bolted the party after Reagan's nomination and ran on an independent ticket.

In addition to affirming Reagan's conservative agenda, the 1980 election reflected the triumph of what one political scientist called the "largest mass movement of our time"—nonvoting. Almost as striking as Reagan's one-sided victory was the fact that his total votes represented only 28 percent of registered voters. Only 53 percent of eligible voters cast ballots in the 1980 election.

There were various explanations for the high level of voter apathy among working-class Americans. Some observers stressed the disillusionment with government that grew out of the Watergate affair. Others believed that the Democratic party had alienated its traditional blocs of support among common folk. Democratic leaders no longer spoke eloquently on behalf of those at the bottom of America's social scale. By embracing a fiscal conservatism indistinguishable from that of the Republicans, as Carter had done, Democrats had lost their appeal among blue-collar workers and the urban poor. When viewed in this light, Reagan's lopsided triumph represented both a resounding victory for conservative Republicans and a self-inflicted defeat by a fractured Democratic party. Flush with a sense of power and destiny, President-elect Ronald Reagan headed toward Washington with a blueprint for dismantling the welfare state.

REAGAN'S FIRST TERM

REAGANOMICS Ronald Reagan brought to Washington a simple conservative philosophy. "Government is not the solution to our problem," he insisted; "government is the problem." Reagan credited Calvin Coolidge and Coolidge's Treasury secretary, Andrew Mellon, with demonstrating that by reducing taxes and easing government regulation of business, free-market capitalism would revive the economy. By cutting taxes and domestic federal spending and by following a supply-side economic program, he claimed, a surging economy would produce *more* government revenues, which in turn would help reduce the budget deficit.

Unlike Carter, Reagan increased defense spending, reduced social spending, and persuaded Congress to pass a sweeping tax-reform proposal. Enough Democrats—mostly sympathetic southern conservatives dubbed boll weevils—supported the measures to pass them by overwhelming majorities. On August 1, 1981, Reagan signed the Economic Recovery Tax Act, which cut personal income taxes by 25 percent, lowered the maximum rate from 70 to 50 percent for 1982, cut the capital gains tax by one third, and offered a broad array of other tax concessions.

The new legislation embodied an idea that went back to Alexander Hamilton, George Washington's Treasury secretary: more money in the hands of the affluent would benefit society at large, since the wealthy would engage in productive consumption and investment. A closer parallel was Treasury Secretary Andrew Mellon's tax-reduction program of the 1920s. The difference was that the Reagan tax cuts were accompanied by massive increases in defense spending, which generated ever-mounting federal deficits. Reagan's advisers insisted that the unbalanced budgets were only temporary; the new tax plan would fuel economic growth and thereby boost tax revenues as personal income and corporate profits skyrocketed. But it did not work out that way. By the summer of 1983, a major economic recovery was under way, but the federal deficits had grown ever larger, so much so that the president, who in 1980 had pledged to balance the federal budget by 1983, had in fact run up debts larger than those of all his predecessors combined.

Bankers and investors feared that the rising federal debt would send interest rates soaring, a fear expressed in sagging bond and stock markets. A business slump and rising unemployment continued through most of 1982. That year the federal deficit doubled. Aides finally convinced Reagan that to reassure the public about deficits and the threat of inflation, the government needed "revenue enhancements," a euphemism for tax increases. With Reagan's support, Congress passed a new tax bill in 1982 that would raise almost $100 billion. During the midterm elections of 1982, Reagan urged voters to "stay the course" and appealed for more time to let his economic program take effect. Meanwhile, the economic slump persisted through 1982, with unemployment standing at 10.4 percent, and the congressional Republicans experienced moderate losses in the elections.

THE DEFENSE BUILDUP   Reagan's conduct of foreign policy reflected his belief that trouble in the world stemmed mainly from Moscow. He charged that the Soviets were "prepared to commit any crime, to lie, to cheat" and do anything necessary to promote world communism. Reagan and Secretary of Defense Caspar Weinberger embarked on a major buildup of nuclear and conventional weapons to close the gap that they claimed had developed between Soviet and U.S. military forces.

In 1983 Reagan escalated the nuclear arms race by authorizing the Defense Department to develop a Strategic Defense Initiative, a complex defense system meant to destroy enemy missiles in outer space well before they reached their targets. Despite skepticism among the media and many scientists that such a "Star Wars"defense system could be built, it forced the Soviets to launch an expensive research and development program of their own to keep pace.

Reagan borrowed the rhetoric of Harry Truman, John Foster Dulles, and John F. Kennedy's inaugural address to express American resolve in the face of "Communist aggression anywhere in the world." Détente deteriorated even further when the Soviets imposed martial law in Poland during the winter of 1981. The crackdown came after Polish workers, united under the banner of an independent union called Solidarity, challenged the Communist monopoly of power. As with the Soviet interventions in Hungary in 1956 and Czechoslovakia in 1968, there was little the United States could do except register protest and impose economic sanctions against Poland's Communist government.

THE AMERICAS   Reagan's foremost international concern, however, was in Central America, where he detected the most serious Communist threat. The tiny nation of El Salvador, caught up since 1980 in a brutal struggle between Communist-supported revolutionaries and right-wing extremists, received U.S. economic and military assistance. Reagan stopped short of sending troops, but he did increase the number of military advisers and the amount of financial aid to the Salvadoran government.

Even more troubling was the situation in Nicaragua. The State Department claimed that the Cuban-sponsored Sandinista government, which had only recently taken control of the country after ousting a corrupt dictator, was funneling Soviet and Cuban arms to leftist Salvadoran rebels. In response the Reagan administration ordered the CIA to train and supply guerrilla bands of disgruntled Nicaraguans, tagged Contras, who staged attacks on Sandinista bases and officials from sanctuaries in Honduras. In supporting these "freedom fighters," Reagan sought not only to impede the

"Shhhhhh. It's Top Secret."

A comment on the Reagan administration's covert operations in Nicaragua.

traffic in arms to Salvadoran rebels but also to overthrow the Communist Sandinistas.

Critics of Reagan's anti-Sandinista policy accused the Contras of being mostly right-wing fanatics who indiscriminately killed civilians as well as Sandinista soldiers. They also feared that the United States might eventually commit its own combat forces, thus threatening another Vietnam-like intervention.

THE MIDDLE EAST   The Middle East remained a tinderbox of geopolitical conflict throughout the 1980s. No peaceable end seemed possible in the bloody Iran-Iraq War, which had erupted in 1980, entangled as it was with the passions of Islamic fundamentalism. In 1984 both sides began to attack tankers in the Persian Gulf, a major source of the world's oil. Although the Reagan administration harbored no affection for either nation, it viewed Iranian fundamentalism as the greater threat and funneled aid to Iraq, a policy with unforeseen and grave consequences.

American diplomats continued to see Israel as the strongest ally in the region, all the while seeking to encourage moderate Arab groups and anti-Communist governments. Continuing chaos in Lebanon, where ethnic and religious tensions erupted into near anarchy, threatened both Israel's borders and America's goals for the region. The capital, Beirut, became a battleground for rival Muslim and Christian factions, the army of the Palestine Liberation Organization (PLO), Syrian invaders cast as peacekeepers, and Israelis responding to PLO attacks.

French, Italian, and U.S. forces moved into Beirut as "peacekeepers," but in such small numbers as to become targets themselves. On October 23, 1983, an Islamic suicide bomber drove a truck laden with explosives into the U.S. Marine headquarters at the Beirut airport. The explosion left 241 Americans dead. On February 7, 1984, Reagan announced that the marines would be redeployed on warships offshore. The Israeli forces pulled back to southern Lebanon, while the Syrians remained in eastern Lebanon and imposed a tenuous peace upon the faction-ridden country.

GRENADA   In a fortunate turn for the Reagan administration, an easy military triumph closer to home eclipsed news of the debacle in Lebanon. On the tiny Caribbean island of Grenada, a leftist government had admitted Cuban workers to build a new airfield and had signed military agreements with several Communist-bloc countries. Appeals from the governments of neighboring islands led Reagan in 1983 to order 1,900 soldiers to invade the island, depose the radical regime, and evacuate a group of American students at Grenada's medical school. The UN General Assembly condemned the action, but most Grenadans and their neighbors applauded it, and the intervention was immensely popular in the United States.

REAGAN'S SECOND TERM

By 1983 prosperity had returned, and inflation had subsided; the Reagan economic program seemed to be working as touted. A dramatic fall in oil prices following the fragmentation of the OPEC cartel helped fuel the economic expansion.

THE ELECTION OF 1984   By 1984 Reagan had restored strength and vitality to the White House and the nation. His prospects for reelection were bright. The Democratic nominee, former Monnesota senator and vice president Walter Mondale, faced an uphill struggle. Mondale won a lot of media attention by choosing as his running mate a woman, New York representative Geraldine Ferraro. Attention soon turned to Ferraro's husband's dubious business finances, however. In any case, Reagan's skill and confidence at campaigning outshone Mondale, and the economic recovery made it difficult for the Democratic nominee to attract interest, much less generate enthusiasm. In the end, Reagan won almost 59 percent of the popular vote and lost only Minnesota and the District of Columbia. His coattails were not as long as they had been in 1980, however. Republicans gained only fifteen seats in the House, leaving them still greatly outnumbered by Democrats, 253 to 182. They also lost two Senate seats, creating a margin of only 53 to 47.

THE REAGAN DOCTRINE   In his 1985 State of the Union message, the reelected president clarified what had come to be called the Reagan Doctrine in foreign affairs. The United States, he proclaimed, would support anti-Communist forces around the world seeking to "defy Soviet-supported aggression." In effect, he was challenging the isolationism that followed the nation's humbling experience in Vietnam. America, he promised, would not hesitate to intervene in the world's hot spots.

Yet for all his stern talk about the Soviet Union being "an evil empire," Reagan was determined to reach an arms-control agreement with the Soviets. In Geneva in 1985, he met with Mikhail Gorbachev, the innovative

Foreign Relations

A light moment at a meeting between U.S. president Ronald Reagan (left) and Soviet premier Mikhail Gorbachev (right).

new leader of the Soviet Union. The two signed several cultural and scientific agreements and issued a statement on arms-limitations talks, but no treaty was in the offing. Nearly a year after the Geneva summit, on sudden notice and with limited preparation, Gorbachev and Reagan met in Iceland for two days to discuss arms reductions. Early reports predicted a major breakthrough, including a total ban on nuclear weapons, but the talks collapsed over disagreement on Reagan's commitment to the Strategic Defense Initiative. After the Iceland meeting the two nations reduced the scope of their discussions in order to break the impasse.

The logjam impeding the arms negotiations suddenly broke when Gorbachev announced that he was willing to deal separately on a medium-range missile treaty. After nine months of strenuous negotiations, Reagan and Gorbachev met amid much fanfare in Washington on December 9, 1987, and signed a treaty to eliminate intermediate-range (300- to 3,000-mile) nuclear forces. It was an epochal event, not only because it marked the first time that the two nations had agreed to destroy a whole class of weapons systems but also because it represented a key first step toward the eventual end of the arms race altogether. Under the terms of the treaty, the United States would destroy 859 missiles, and the Soviets would eliminate 1,752. Provision was also made for on-site inspections by each side to verify compliance. Still, this winnowing of weapons would represent only 4 percent of the total number of nuclear missiles on both sides. Arms-control advocates thus looked toward a second and more comprehensive treaty that would eliminate long-range strategic missiles.

THE IRAN-CONTRA AFFAIR   During the fall of 1986, the Reagan administration suffered a double blow. In the midterm elections, Democrats regained control of the Senate by fifty-five to forty-five. For his final two years in office, Reagan would face an opposition Congress. What was worse, on election day reports surfaced that the United States, with Israeli assistance, had been secretly selling arms to Iran in the hope of securing the release of American hostages held in Lebanon by extremist Islamic groups with close ties to Iran. Such action contradicted Reagan's repeated public insistence that his administration would never negotiate with terrorists.

There was more to the story. Over the next several months, revelations reminiscent of the Watergate affair disclosed a more complicated series of covert activities carried out by administration officials. At the center of what came to be dubbed Irangate was the much-decorated marine lieutenant colonel Oliver North. An aide to the National Security Council who specialized in counterterrorism, North had been scheming to use the profits from the secret sale of military weapons to Iran to subsidize the

Contra rebels fighting in Nicaragua even though Congress had voted to ban such aid.

Under increasing criticism and amid growing doubts about his credibility and his ability, Reagan appointed both an independent counsel and a three-man commission, led by former Republican senator John Tower, to investigate the scandal. The Tower Commission issued a report early in 1987 that placed much of the responsibility for the bungled Iran-Contra affair on Reagan's loose management style. He seemed unaware of what his staffers were doing.

The investigations of the independent counsel led to six indictments in 1988. A Washington jury found Oliver North guilty of three relatively minor charges but innocent of nine more serious counts, apparently reflecting the jury's reasoning that he had acted as an agent of higher-ups. His conviction was later overturned on appeal. The Iran-Contra affair left support for the Nicaraguan Contras badly eroded in Congress, and it undermined much of Reagan's popularity.

THE POOR, THE HOMELESS, AND THE VICTIMS OF AIDS

The 1980s were years of vivid contrast. Despite unprecedented affluence there were countless beggars in the streets and homeless people sleeping in door-ways, in cardboard boxes, and on ventilation grates. A variety of factors caused the shortage of low-cost housing: the government had given up on building public housing, urban-renewal programs had demolished blighted areas but provided no housing for those they displaced, and owners had abandoned un-profitable buildings in poor neighborhoods or converted them into expensive condominiums, a process called gentrification.

After new medications enabled the deinstitutionalization of the mentally ill, many individuals ended up on the streets because the promised commu-nity mental-health services failed to materialize. By the summer of 1988, the *New York Times* estimated, more than 45 percent of New York's adults were living in poverty, totally outside the labor force, for lack of skills, drug use, and other problems.

Still another group cast aside were those suffering from the frightening new malady that had come to be known as AIDS (acquired immuno defi-ciency syndrome). At the beginning of the decade, public health officials had begun to report that gay men and intravenous drug users were especially at risk for contracting AIDS. Those infected with the virus that causes AIDS showed signs of fatigue, developed a strange combination of infections, and eventually died; people contracted the virus (HIV) by coming into contact with the blood or body fluids of an infected person. The Reagan administra-tion showed little interest in AIDS in part because it initially was viewed as a "gay" disease. Patrick Buchanan, the conservative spokesman who served as White House director of communications, said that homosexuals had "declared war on nature, and now nature is extracting an awful retribution."

THE REAGAN LEGACY   Although Ronald Reagan had declared in 1981 his intention to "curb the size and influence of the federal establishment," the welfare state remained intact when Reagan left office. Neither the Social Security system nor Medicare was dismantled or overhauled, nor were any other major welfare programs. And the federal agencies that Reagan had threatened to abolish, such as the Department of Education, not only remained in place in 1989 but saw their budgets grow. The federal budget as a percentage of the gross domestic product was actually higher when Reagan left office than when he had entered. Moreover, he did not try to push through Congress the incendiary social issues championed by the religious right, such as allowing prayer in public schools and a ban on abortions.

Yet Ronald Reagan succeeded in redefining the national political agenda and accelerated the conservative insurgency that had been developing for over twenty years. Reagan's critics highlighted his lack of intellectual sophistication and his indifference to day-to-day administrative details. His greatest successes were in renewing America's soaring sense of possibilities, bringing inflation under control, stimulating the longest sustained period of peacetime prosperity in history, and helping to light the fuse of democratic freedom in Eastern Europe. The fact that Reagan's tax policies widened the gap between the rich and the poor and created huge budget deficits for future presidents to confront did not diminish the popularity of the Great Communicator.

THE ELECTION OF 1988   As a new presidential election unfolded, eight Democratic presidential candidates engaged in a wild scramble for their party's nomination. As the primary season progressed, however, it soon became a two-man race, between Massachusetts governor Michael Dukakis and Jesse Jackson, the African-American civil rights activist who had been one of Martin Luther King's chief lieutenants. Dukakis eventually won out and managed a difficult reconciliation with the Jackson forces that left the Democrats unified and confident as the fall campaign began.

The Republicans nominated Reagan's two-term vice president, George H. W. Bush, who after a bumpy start had easily cast aside his rivals in the primaries. As Reagan's handpicked heir, Bush claimed credit for the administration's successes, but like all vice presidents he also faced the challenge of defining his own political identity. Yet at the Republican Convention, Bush delivered a forceful address that sharply enhanced his stature. The most

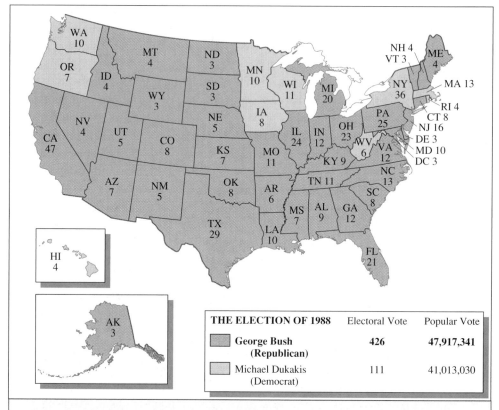

THE ELECTION OF 1988	Electoral Vote	Popular Vote
George Bush (Republican)	**426**	**47,917,341**
Michael Dukakis (Democrat)	111	41,013,030

How did George H. W. Bush overtake Dukakis's lead in the polls? What was the role of race and class in the election results? Who didn't vote in the election of 1988?

memorable line was a defiant statement on taxes: "Congress will push me to raise taxes, and I'll say no, and they'll push, and I'll say no, and they'll push again. And I'll say to them: Read my lips: *no new taxes.*"

In a campaign given over to mudslinging, the Bush partisans attacked Dukakis as a camouflaged liberal who would increase federal spending, raise taxes, gut the defense budget, and refuse to intervene to prevent Communist aggression abroad. The Republican onslaught took its toll against the less or-ganized, less focused Dukakis campaign. Moreover, the Republicans contin-ued to benefit from the population growth in the sunbelt states, the shift of population from the Democratic cities to the Republican suburbs, and from the votes of many moderate and conservative Democrats and independents. Dukakis captured only ten states plus the District of Columbia, with clusters in the Northeast, Midwest, and Northwest. Bush carried the rest, with a margin of about 54 percent to 46 percent in the popular vote and 426 to 111 in the Electoral College.

THE BUSH ADMINISTRATION

George H. W. Bush viewed himself as a guardian president rather than an activist. He lacked Reagan's visionary outlook and skill as a speaker. Bush was a pragmatic caretaker eager to avoid "stupid mistakes" and to find a way to get along with the Democratic majority in Congress. "We don't need to remake society," he announced. Bush sought to consolidate the programs that Reagan had put in place rather than launch his own array of programs and policies.

THE DEMOCRACY MOVEMENT ABROAD   Bush entered the White House with more foreign-policy experience than most presidents, and he found the spotlight of the world stage more congenial than wrestling with the intractable problems of the inner cities and the deficit. Within two years of his inauguration, George Bush would lead the United States into two wars. Throughout most of 1989, however, he merely had to sit back and observe the dissolution of one totalitarian or authoritarian regime after another. For the first time in years, global democracy was suddenly on the march in a sequence of mostly bloodless revolutions that took the world by surprise.

Although in China a democracy movement came to a tragic end in 1989 when government forces mounted a deadly assault on demonstrators in Beijing's (Peking's) Tiananmen Square, Eastern Europe had an entirely different experience. Mikhail Gorbachev set events in motion by responding to Soviet economic problems with policies of perestroika (restructuring) and glasnost (openness), a loosening of central economic planning and censorship. His foreign policy sought rapprochement and trade with the West, and he aimed to relieve the Soviet economy of burdensome military costs.

Gorbachev backed off from Soviet imperial ambitions. Early in 1989 Soviet troops left Afghanistan after spending nine years bogged down in civil war there. Then in July in Paris, Gorbachev repudiated the Brezhnev Doctrine, which asserted the right of the Soviet Union to intervene in the internal affairs of other Communist countries. The days when Soviet tanks would roll through Warsaw and Prague were over, and leaders in the Eastern-bloc countries found themselves beset by demands for democratic reform. With opposition strength building, the old regimes fell with surprisingly little bloodshed. Communist party rule ended first in Poland and Hungary, then in Czechoslovakia and Bulgaria. In Romania the year of peaceful revolution ended in a bloodbath when the Romanian people were joined by the army in a bloody uprising against the brutal dictator Nicolae Ceauşescu. He and his wife were captured, tried, and then executed on Christmas Day.

The most spectacular event in the collapse of the Soviet Empire in Eastern Europe came on November 9, 1989, when the chief symbol of the cold war—the Berlin Wall—was torn down by Germans, and the East German government succumbed to popular pressures for change. With the borders to the West fully open, the Communist government of East Germany collapsed, a freely elected government came to power, and on October 3, 1990, the five states of East Germany were united with West Germany. The reunified German nation remained in NATO, and the Warsaw Pact alliance was dissolved.

The reform impulse that Gorbachev helped unleash in the Eastern-bloc countries careened out of control within the Soviet Union, however.

Dissolution of the Soviet Empire

West Germans hacking away at the Berlin Wall on November 11, 1989, two days after all crossings between East Germany and West Germany were opened.

Gorbachev proved unusually adept at political restructuring. While yielding to the Communist monopoly of government, he built a new presidential system that gave him, if anything, increased powers. His skills did not extend to an antiquated economy that resisted change, however. The revival of ethnic allegiances added to the instability. Although Russia proper included slightly over half the Soviet Union's population, it was only one of fifteen constituent republics, most of which began to seek autonomy, if not independence.

Gorbachev's popularity in the Soviet Union shrank as it grew abroad. It especially eroded among the Communist hard-liners, who saw in his reforms the unraveling of their bureaucratic and political empire. On August 18, 1991, a cabal of political and military leaders tried to seize the reins of power in Russia. They accosted Gorbachev at his vacation retreat in the Crimea and demanded that he sign a decree proclaiming a state of emergency and transferring his powers to them. He replied, "Go to hell," whereupon he was placed under house arrest. Twelve hours later the Soviet news agency reported to the world that Gorbachev was "ill" and had temporarily transferred his powers to his vice president and an eight-member emergency

Action against Gorbachev

In August 1991, one day after Mikhail Gorbachev was placed under house arrest by Communists planning a coup, Russian Federation president Boris Yeltsin (holding papers) makes a speech criticizing the plotters.

committee. Political parties were suspended, newspapers were silenced, a curfew was announced, and street demonstrations were banned. Tanks and armored vehicles surrounded government buildings in Moscow. The new leaders promised to end the "chaos and anarchy" they claimed were bedeviling the country.

But the coup was doomed from the start. Poorly planned and clumsily implemented, it lacked effective coordination. The plotters failed to arrest popular leaders such as Boris Yeltsin, the president of the Russian republic, and they neglected to close the airports or cut off telephone and television communications. Most important, the plotters failed to recognize the strength of the democratic idealism unleashed by Gorbachev's reforms.

As the political drama unfolded in the Soviet Union, foreign leaders spoke out against the coup. On August 20 President Bush, after a day of indecision, responded favorably to Yeltsin's request for support and convinced other leaders to join him in refusing to recognize the legitimacy of the new Soviet government. The next day, word began to seep out that the plotters had given up and were fleeing. Several committed suicide, and a newly released Gorbachev ordered the others arrested. But Gorbachev's freedom did not bring a restoration of his power. Boris Yeltsin emerged as the most popular political figure in the country. Gorbachev reclaimed the title of president, but he was forced to resign as head of the Communist party and admit that he had made a grave mistake in appointing the men who had turned against him.

What began as a reactionary coup turned into a powerful accelerant for stunning changes in the Soviet Union. Most of the fifteen republics proclaimed their independence, with the Baltic republics of Latvia, Lithuania, and Estonia regaining the status of independent nations. The Communist party apparatus was dismantled, prompting celebrating crowds to topple statues of Lenin and other Communist heroes.

The aborted coup accelerated Soviet and American efforts to reduce the stockpiles of nuclear weapons. In 1991 President Bush announced that the United States would destroy all its tactical nuclear weapons on land and at sea in Europe and Asia, take its long-range bombers off twenty-four-hour-alert status, and initiate discussions with the Soviet Union for the purpose of instituting sharp cuts in nuclear missiles with multiple warheads. Bush explained that the prospect of a Soviet invasion of western Europe was "no longer a realistic threat," and this transformation presented an unprecedented opportunity for reducing the threat of nuclear holocaust. The Soviets responded by announcing reciprocal cutbacks. As Colin Powell, Chairman of the Joint Chiefs of Staff, remarked, the cold war "has vaporized before our eyes."

By the end of 1991, the Soviet Union had dissolved into a new—and fragile—Commonwealth of Independent States made up of eleven autonomous republics (Georgia joined in 1993). Held together by little other than historic ties and contiguous borders, the federated republics soon suffered outbreaks of ethnic tensions and separatist movements. With the Communist party dissolved, the Soviet Union dismantled, and continuing economic woes creating obstacles to his leadership, Mikhail Gorbachev resigned as president at the end of 1991. Boris Yeltsin, now a national hero, replaced him.

The dilution of the Soviet military threat led the U.S. Defense Department in 1992 to withdraw large numbers of personnel from military bases in Asia and Europe. The Pentagon also announced a plan to shrink the armed forces by 500,000 troops over the next five years. In 1992 Bush and Yeltsin declared their intention to reduce their combined arsenals of nuclear weapons from about 22,500 to no more than 7,000 by 2003. All land-based multiple-warhead missiles were to be destroyed.

PANAMA   The end of the cold war did not spell the end of international tensions and conflicts, however. Indeed, in some respects the world became more unstable. Before the end of 1989, American troops were engaged in battle in Panama, where General Manuel Noriega, as chief of the Panamanian Defense Forces since 1983, was head of the government in fact if not in title. Years earlier Noriega had worked secretly with the CIA, providing information about developments in Central America. At the same time he got involved in the lucrative—and illegal—drug trade. In 1988 federal grand juries in Miami and Tampa indicted Noriega and fifteen others on charges of international drug smuggling, gunrunning, and laundering the profits through Panamanian banks.

In 1989 Panama's National Assembly named Noriega head of the government and proclaimed that Panama "is declared to be in a state of war" with the United States. The next day, December 16, 1989, an American marine in Panama was killed. President Bush ordered an invasion of Panama in order to capture Noriega, bring him to the United States so that he could face the charges against him, and install a government headed by opposition leaders.

The 12,000 U.S. military personnel already in Panama were quickly joined by 12,000 more, and in the early morning of December 20 five military task forces struck at strategic targets in the country. Twenty-three U.S. servicemen were killed in the action, and estimates of Panamanians killed and wounded were as high as 4,000, including many civilians. Noriega was captured, and he was detained in a U.S. federal prison for well over a year before his trial began in late 1991. He was convicted in 1992 on eight counts of racketeering and drug distribution.

THE GULF WAR   Months after Panama had moved to the background of public attention, Saddam Hussein, dictator of Iraq, focused attention on the Middle East when his army suddenly invaded neighboring Kuwait on August 2, 1990. Kuwait had raised its production of oil, contrary to agreements with OPEC. The resulting drop in oil prices offended the Iraqi regime, deep in debt and heavily dependent upon oil revenues.

Saddam Hussein did not expect the firestorm of world indignation his assault on Kuwait ignited. The UN Security Council quickly voted unanimously to condemn the invasion and demand withdrawal. American secretary of state James Baker and Soviet foreign minister Eduard Shevardnadze issued a joint statement of condemnation. The Security Council then endorsed Resolution 661, an embargo on trade with Iraq.

President Bush condemned Iraq's "naked aggression" and dispatched planes and troops to Saudi Arabia on a "wholly defensive" mission: to protect Saudi Arabia. British forces soon joined in, as did troops from a half

The Gulf War

U.S. soldiers adapt to desert conditions during Operation Desert Shield, December 1990.

dozen Arab nations. On August 22 Bush ordered the mobilization of American reserve forces for the operation, now dubbed Desert Shield.

A flurry of peace efforts sent diplomats scurrying, but without result. Iraq refused to yield. On January 10 Congress began to debate whether to authorize the use of U.S. armed forces. The outcome was uncertain to the end, but on January 12 a resolution for the use of force passed in the House, by a vote of 250 to 183, and in the Senate, by 52 to 47.

By January 1991 an allied force of over thirty nations was committed to Operation Desert Storm when the first missiles began to hit Iraq at about 2:30 A.M. on January 17, Baghdad time. Saddam Hussein concentrated his forces in Kuwait, expecting an allied attack northward into that country. But the Iraqis were outflanked when 200,000 allied troops, largely American, British, and French, turned up on the undefended Iraqi border with Saudi Arabia, far to the west. The allied ground assault began on February 24 and lasted only four days. Thousands of Iraqi soldiers surrendered, and there was a quick breakthrough into Kuwait.

On February 28, six weeks after the fighting began, President Bush called for a cease-fire, the Iraqis accepted, and the shooting ended. There were 137 American fatalities. The lowest estimate of Iraqi fatalities, civilian and military, was around 100,000. The coalition forces occupied about one fifth of Iraq. The consequences of the brief but intense Persian Gulf War, the "mother of all battles" in Saddam Hussein's words, would be played out in the future in ways no one predicted.

MAKING CONNECTIONS

- Much of what characterized the 1980s, from economic and social policy to presidential leadership style, was reminiscent of the late nineteenth century as well as the 1920s and 1950s.

- Another parallel between the late nineteenth century and the 1980s was a rise in immigration and a change in immigration patterns. These changes are discussed in Chapter 37.

- Chapter 37 also shows how the economic and political conservatism of the 1980s became much more ideological in the early 1990s.

FURTHER READING

Two brief accounts of Reagan's presidency are David Mervin's *Ronald Reagan and the American Presidency* (1990) and Michael Schaller's *Reckoning with Reagan: America and Its President in the 1980s* (1992).

On Reaganomics, see David A. Stockman's *The Triumph of Politics: How the Reagan Revolution Failed* (1986) and Robert Lekachman's *Greed Is Not Enough: Reaganomics* (1982). On the issue of arms control, see Strobe Talbott's *Deadly Gambits: The Reagan Administration and the Stalemate in Nuclear Arms Control* (1984).

For Reagan's foreign policy in Central America, see James Chace's *Endless War: How We Got Involved in Central America and What Can Be Done* (1984) and Walter LaFeber's *Inevitable Revolutions: The United States in Central America*, 2nd ed. (1993). Insider views of Reagan's foreign policy are offered in Alexander M. Haig Jr.'s *Caveat: Realism, Reagan, and Foreign Policy* (1984) and Caspar W. Weinberger's *Fighting for Peace: Seven Critical Years in the Pentagon* (1990).

On Reagan's second term, see Jane Mayer and Doyle McManus's *Landslide: The Unmaking of the President, 1984–1988* (1988). For a masterful work on the Iran-Contra affair, see Theodore Draper's *A Very Thin Line: The Iran Contra Affairs* (1991). Several collections of essays include varying assessments of the Reagan years. Among these are *The Reagan Revolution?* (1988), edited by B. B. Kymlicka and Jean V. Matthews; *The Reagan Presidency: An Incomplete Revolution?* (1990), edited by Dilys M. Hill, Raymond A. Moore, and Phil Williams, and *Looking Back on the Reagan Presidency* (1990), edited by Larry Berman.

On the 1988 campaign, see Jack W. Germond and Jules Witcover's *Whose Broad Stripes and Bright Stars? The Trivial Pursuit of the Presidency, 1988* (1989) and Sidney Blumenthal's *Pledging Allegiance: The Last Campaign of the Cold War* (1990). For a social history of the decade, see John Ehrman's *The Eighties: America in the Age of Reagan* (2005).

37

TRIUMPH AND TRAGEDY: AMERICA AT THE TURN OF THE CENTURY

FOCUS QUESTIONS

- How did demographic patterns change in the 1980s and 1990s?
- What led to the Democratic resurgence of the early 1990s and the Republican landslide of 1994?
- Why did the economy and stock market surge during the 1990s?
- What were the consequences of the rise of global terrorism and the terrorist assaults on the United States?

To answer these questions and access additional review material, please visit www.wwnorton.com/studyspace.

The United States entered the final decade of the twentieth century triumphant. American vigilance in the cold war had led to the stunning collapse of the Soviet Union and the birth of democratic capitalism in eastern Europe. The United States was now the world's only superpower. By the mid-1990s the American economy would become the marvel of the world as remarkable gains in productivity afforded by new technologies created the greatest period of prosperity in modern history. Yet no sooner did the century come to an end than America's comfortable sense of physical and material security was shattered by a shocking terrorist assault that would kill thousands, plummet the economy into recession, and call into question conventional notions of national security and personal safety.

America's Changing Mosaic

DEMOGRAPHIC SHIFTS   During the 1980s and 1990s the nation's population grew by 20 percent, or some 50 million people, boosting the total to over 296 million in 2006. The much-discussed baby-boom generation—the 43 million people born between 1946 and 1964—entered middle age. This generation's maturation and its preoccupation with practical concerns such as raising families, paying for college, and buying houses helped explain the surge of political conservatism during the 1980s.

During the last quarter of the twentieth century, the sunbelt states of the South and the West continued to lure residents from the Midwest and the Northeast. Fully 90 percent of the nation's total population growth during the 1980s occurred in southern or western states. These population shifts forced a massive redistricting of the House of Representatives, with Florida, California, and Texas gaining seats and states such as New York losing seats.

Americans at the end of the twentieth century tended to settle in large communities. This continuing move to urban areas largely reflected trends in the job market, as the "postindustrial" economy continued to shift from manufacturing to professional-service industries, particularly those specializing in telecommunications and information processing. By 2000 fewer than 2 million people out of a total population of 290 million worked on farms.

Women continued to enter the workforce in large numbers. In 1970, 38 percent of the workforce was female; in 2000 the figure was almost 50 percent. Women made up over one third of the new doctors (up from 4 percent in 1970), 40 percent of the new lawyers (up from 8 percent in 1970), and 23 percent of the new dentists (up from less than 1 percent in 1970).

The decline of the traditional family unit continued. In 2006 less than 65 percent of children lived with two parents, down from 85 percent in 1970. And more people were living alone than ever before, largely as a result of high divorce rates or a growing practice of delaying marriage until well into the twenties. The number of single mothers increased 35 percent during the decade. The rate was much higher for African Americans: in 2000 fewer than 32 percent of African-American children lived with both parents, down from 67 percent in 1960.

Young African Americans in particular faced shrinking economic opportunities at the start of the twenty-first century. The urban poor more than others were victimized by high rates of crime and violence, with young black men suffering the most. In 2000 the leading cause of death among African-American men between the ages of fifteen and twenty-four was homicide.

Over 25 percent of African-American men aged twenty to twenty-nine were in prison, on parole, or on probation, while only 4 percent were enrolled in college. Nearly 40 percent of African-American men were functionally illiterate.

THE NEW IMMIGRANTS The racial and ethnic composition of the country was also changing rapidly at the turn of the century. By 2006 the United States had more foreign-born and first-generation residents than ever before. Over 30 percent of Americans claimed African, Asian, Latino, or American Indian ancestry. Latinos represented 13 percent of the total population, African Americans 11 percent, Asians about 4 percent, and American Indians almost 1 percent. The rate of increase among those four groups was twice as fast as it had been during the 1970s.

The primary cause of this dramatic change in the nation's ethnic mix was a surge of immigration. During the 1990s legal immigration to the United States totaled over 10 million people, 40 percent higher than in the previous

Illegal Immigration

Increasing numbers of Chinese risked their savings and their lives trying to gain entry to the United States. These illegal immigrants are trying to keep warm after being forced to swim ashore when the freighter carrying them to the United States ran aground near Rockaway Beach in New York City in June 1993.

decade and more than in any other decade. These figures do not include the hundreds of thousands of undocumented aliens, mostly Mexicans and Haitians. In 2000 the United States welcomed more than twice as many immigrants as all other countries in the world combined. For the first time in the nation's history, the majority of immigrants came not from Europe but from other parts of the world: Asia, Latin America, and Africa. Among the legal immigrants, Mexicans made up the largest share, averaging over 100,000 a year.

THE COMPUTER REVOLUTION   While demographic shifts and immigration were changing the nation's appearance, technological changes were transforming its behavior. A dramatic revolution in information technology produced a surge in productivity and prosperity during the 1980s and 1990s. Cellular phones, laser printers, VCRs and then DVDs, fax machines, personal computers, and iPods became commonplace. The computer age had arrived.

The idea of a programmable machine that would rapidly perform mental tasks had been around since the eighteenth century, but it took the crisis of World War II to gather the intellectual and financial resources needed to develop such a "computer." A team of engineers at the University of Pennsylvania created ENIAC (electronic numerical integrator and computer), the first all-purpose, all-electronic digital computer. Unveiled in 1946, it could perform 5,000 operations per second. ENIAC took up 3,000 cubic feet of space and housed 18,000 vacuum tubes (glass canisters designed to amplify electric current), 70,000 resistors, 10,000 capacitors, and 6,000 switches.

With the invention in 1971 of the microprocessor—a computer on a silicon chip, the functions that had once been performed by computers taking up an entire room could be performed by a microchip circuit the size of a postage stamp. Engineers soon incorporated microchips into television sets, wristwatches, automobiles, kitchen appliances, and spacecraft.

The invention of the microchip made possible the personal computer. In 1975 an engineer named Ed Roberts developed the prototype of the so-called personal computer. The Altair 8800 was imperfect and cumbersome, with no display, no keyboard, and not enough memory to do anything useful. But its potential excited a Harvard sophomore named Bill Gates. Gates improved the software of the Altair 8800, dropped out of college, and formed a company called Microsoft to market the new system. By 1977 Gates and others had helped transform the personal computer from a machine for hobbyists to a mass consumer product.

By the end of the 1980s, there were 60 million personal computers in the United States, and people began to talk about an "information superhighway,"

The Computer Age

Beginning with the cumbersome electronic numerical integrator and computer (ENIAC), pictured here in 1946, computer technology flourished, leading to the development of personal computers in the 1980s and the popularization of the Internet in the 1990s.

a worldwide network of linked computers and databases connected by fiber-optic lines that facilitated high-speed transmission. During the 1990s the development of the Internet and electronic mail meant that anyone with a personal computer and a modem could travel on the information super-highway. Such advances enabled instantaneous communication across the continents.

CULTURAL CONSERVATISM

Cultural conservatives helped elect Ronald Reagan and George Bush in the 1980s, but they were disappointed with the results. Once in office, neither president had, in the eyes of those conservatives, adequately addressed their moral agenda, including a complete ban on abortions and the restoration of prayer in public schools. By the 1990s a new generation of young conservative activists, mostly political independents or Republicans, had emerged as a force to be reckoned with in national affairs. They were more ideological, more libertarian, more partisan, and more impatient than their predecessors.

THE RELIGIOUS RIGHT Although quite diverse, cultural conservatives tended to be evangelical Christians or orthodox Catholics who joined together to exert increasing religious pressure on the political process. In 1989 the television evangelist Pat Robertson organized the Christian Coalition to replace Jerry Falwell's Moral Majority as the flagship organization of the resurgent religious right. The Christian Coalition encouraged religious conservatives to vote, run for public office, and support only those candidates who shared the organization's views.

The Christian Coalition chose the Republican party, with its well-organized grassroots movement in every state, as the best vehicle for transforming the religious right's pro-family campaign into public policies. The Christian Coalition encouraged its supporters to withhold political support from any candidate who did not provide an ironclad promise to support the coalition's school-prayer, anti-abortion, anti–gay rights positions. In addition to promoting "traditional family values," it urged politicians to "radically downsize and delimit government."

As a centrist professional politician, George Bush initially tried to keep the cultural conservatives at arm's length, only to find himself the target of their attacks. His successor, the Democrat Bill Clinton, also underestimated the growing strength of organized groups such as the Christian Coalition. In the 1994 congressional elections, religious conservatives went to the polls in record numbers, and 70 percent of them voted Republican. One third of the voters identified themselves as "white, evangelical, born-again Christians." In many respects they took control of the political and social agendas in the 1990s.

Bush to Clinton

For months after the Persian Gulf War in 1991, George H. W. Bush seemed unbeatable. But the aftermath of Desert Storm was mixed, with Saddam Hussein's grip on Iraq still intact. Despite his image of strength abroad, Bush began to look weak even on foreign policy. The Soviet Union, meanwhile, stumbled on to its surprising end. On December 25, 1991, the Soviet flag over the Kremlin was replaced by the flag of the Russian Federation. The cold war had ended not just with the collapse of the Soviet Union but with the dismemberment of its fifteen constituent republics. As a result, the United States had become the world's only superpower.

"Containment" of the Soviet Union, the bedrock of American foreign policy for more than four decades, had lost its reason for being. Bush struggled to interpret the fluid new international scene. He spoke of a "new world order" but never defined it. By his own admission he had trouble with "the vision thing." The dynamic international situation, in fact, did not lend itself to a simple vision—unless the answer was to drift into isolation, a great temptation with foreign dangers seemingly on the decline. By the end of 1991, a listless Bush faced a challenge in the Republican primary from the feisty television commentator and former White House aide Patrick Buchanan.

RECESSION AND DOWNSIZING For the Bush administration and for the nation, the most devastating development in the early 1990s was a prolonged economic recession that began in 1990. The first major economic setback in more than eight years, it grew into the longest, if not the deepest, since the Great Depression. During 1991, 25 million workers—about 20 percent of the labor force—were unemployed at some point.

What made this recession unusual was that its victims included a large number of white-collar workers. In the corporate world, terms such as *restructuring* and *downsizing* ruled the day as companies began to reduce personnel, switch employees to part-time status to reduce the cost of benefits, and find other ways to cut labor costs. At the same time the country was experiencing a continuing imbalance in foreign trade and soaring expenditures on defense and public-entitlement programs. During 1991 a $150-billion annual deficit had become a $450-billion shortfall.

A Senate-committee analysis of the stagnant economy confirmed a chilling fact: under the Bush administration "the average standard of living has actually declined." The euphoria over the allied victory in the Gulf War quickly gave way to anxiety and resentment generated by the depressed economy. At the end of 1991, *Time* magazine declared that "no one, not even George Bush" could deny "that the economy was sputtering."

Whatever the reasons for the recession, the cure remained elusive. Although the Federal Reserve Board began cutting interest rates, the economy remained in the doldrums through 1992. The Democratic Congress and the Republican president squabbled over legislation to promote economic recovery but little was done to prod new growth or reduce the hemorrhaging deficits. With his domestic policies in disarray and his foreign policy abandoned, George Bush tried a clumsy balancing act in addressing the recession, on the one hand acknowledging that "people are hurting" while on the other urging Americans that "this is a good time to buy a car."

THE THOMAS HEARINGS AND THE WOMEN'S MOVEMENT Other developments contributed to the erosion of President Bush's popularity, among them the retirement in 1991 of the first African-American Supreme Court justice, Thurgood Marshall, after twenty-four years on the bench. To succeed him Bush named Clarence Thomas, an African-American federal judge whose views delighted conservative senators. Thomas questioned the wisdom of the minimum wage, the use of school busing to achieve desegregation, and affirmative-action hiring programs, and he preached "black self-help," once declaring that all civil rights leaders ever did was "bitch, bitch, bitch, moan, and whine."

Such opinions promised trouble for Thomas's confirmation hearings in the Democratic Senate, but an unexpected explosion occurred when Anita Hill, a soft-spoken law professor at the University of Oklahoma, charged that Thomas had sexually harassed her when she worked for him at a federal agency. Pro-Thomas senators orchestrated an often-savage and sometimes absurd cross-examination of Hill. The televised hearings revealed that either Hill or Thomas had lied, and the committee's tie vote reflected the doubt. The full Senate then confirmed Thomas by the margin of fifty-two to forty-eight.

The Thomas hearings sparked a resurgence in the women's movement. Many women grew incensed at the treatment of Anita Hill, and an unprecedented number of women ran for national and local offices in 1992. The Thomas confirmation struggle thus widened the gender gap for a Republican party already less popular with women than with men.

TAX TURMOIL President Bush had already set a political trap for himself when he declared at the 1988 Republican Convention: "Read my lips. No new taxes." Fourteen months into his presidency, he had decided that the growing federal budget deficit was a greater risk than violating his no-tax pledge. After intense negotiations with congressional Democrats, Bush had announced that reducing the federal deficit required "tax revenue increases." Bush's backsliding set off a revolt among House Republicans, but a bipartisan majority (with most Republicans still opposed) finally approved a tax increase, raising the top personal rate from 28 to 31 percent, disallowing certain deductions in the upper brackets, and raising various excise taxes. Conservative Republicans would not let George Bush forget his abandoned pledge.

DEMOCRATIC RESURGENCE As the Republicans divided over tax policy and social issues, the Democrats sought to present an image of centrist forces in control. For several years the Democratic Leadership Council, in which Arkansas governor William Jefferson Clinton figured prominently, had pushed the party from the liberal left to the center of the political spectrum. Clinton strove to move the Democrats closer to the mainstream of political opinion. A graduate of Georgetown University, he had won a Rhodes scholarship to Oxford and then earned a law degree from Yale, where he met and married Hillary Rodham. By 1979, at age thirty-two, he was back in his native Arkansas, serving as the youngest governor in the country. He served three more terms as governor and in the process emerged as a dynamic young leader committed to winning back the middle-class whites who had voted Republican during the 1980s. Democrats had grown so liberal, he argued, that they had alienated their key constituency, the "vital center."

A self-described moderate, Clinton promised to cut the defense budget, provide tax relief for the middle class, and create a massive economic-aid package for the former republics of the Soviet Union seeking to embrace democratic capitalism. Handsome, witty, intelligent, and a compelling speaker, Clinton projected an image of youthful energy and optimism, reminding many political observers of John F. Kennedy. But underneath the veneer of Clinton's charisma were several flaws. He often seemed so determined to become president that he was willing to sacrifice consistency and principle. He made extensive use of polls to shape his stance on issues, pandered to special-interest groups, and flip-flopped on controversial subjects, leading critics to

The 1992 Presidential Campaign

Presidential candidate Bill Clinton and his running mate, Al Gore, brought youthful enthusiasm to the campaign trail.

label him Slick Willie. Said one former opponent in Arkansas: "He'll be what people want him to be. He'll do or say what it will take to get elected." Even more enticing to the media and more embarrassing to Clinton were charges that he was a chronic adulterer and that he had manipulated the ROTC program during the Vietnam War to avoid the draft. Clinton's evasive denials of both allegations could not dispel a lingering distrust of his character.

Yet after a series of bruising party primaries, Clinton emerged as the front-runner by the time of the nominating convention in the summer of 1992. Once nominated, Clinton chose Senator Albert Gore Jr. of Tennessee as his running mate. So the candidates were two southern Baptists from adjoining states.

Flushed with their convention victory and sporting a ten-point lead in the polls, the Clinton-Gore team stressed economic issues to win over working-class white and African-American voters. Clinton won the election with 370 electoral votes and about 43 percent of the vote, Bush received 168 electoral votes and 39 percent of the vote, and off-and-on independent candidate H. Ross Perot of Texas garnered 18 percent of the popular vote but no electoral votes. A puckish billionaire, Perot found a big audience for his simplified explanations of public problems and his offers to just "get under the hood and fix them."

DOMESTIC POLICY IN CLINTON'S FIRST TERM

Clinton had run a brilliant campaign, portraying himself as an outsider untainted by Washington politics and inertia. Yet his inexperience in international affairs and congressional maneuvering led to several missteps in his first year as president. Like George Bush before him, Clinton reneged on several campaign promises. He abandoned his proposed middle-class tax cut in order to keep down the federal deficit. Nine days into office he backed down when the Pentagon and Congress strongly opposed his attempt to allow professed homosexuals to serve in the military; subsequently he announced an ambiguous policy concerning gays in the military that came to be known as don't ask, don't tell. In Clinton's first two weeks in office, his approval rating dropped 20 percent.

THE ECONOMY Clinton entered office determined to reduce the federal deficit without damaging the economy. To this end, on February 17, 1993, he proposed higher taxes for corporations and for individuals in higher tax brackets and called for an economic-stimulus package for "investment" in public works (transportation, utilities, and the like) and "human capital" (education, skills, health, and welfare). Clinton's hotly contested deficit-reduction package passed by 218 to 216 in the House and 51 to 50 in the Senate, with Vice President Gore breaking the tie.

Equally contested was the North American Free Trade Agreement (NAFTA), which the Bush administration had negotiated with Canada and Mexico. The debate over its congressional approval revived old arguments on the tariff, pro and con. Clinton stuck with his party's tradition of low tariffs and urged approval of NAFTA, which would make North America the largest free-trade area in the world. He and his supporters argued that tariff reductions would open up foreign markets to American industries. Opponents of the bill, including wealthy gadfly Ross Perot and organized labor, favored barriers that would discourage cheaper foreign products and believed that with NAFTA the country would hear a "giant sucking sound" of American jobs being drawn to Mexico. Yet Clinton prevailed, winning solid Republican support while losing a sizable minority of Democrats, mostly from the South, where executives predicted that textile mills would lose business to "cheap-labor" countries.

HEALTH-CARE REFORM Clinton's major public-policy initiative was a new federal health-care plan. Sentiment for health-care reform spread as annual medical costs skyrocketed and some 39 million Americans went without insurance either by choice or out of necessity. Universal medical coverage as proposed by Clinton would entitle every citizen and documented immigrant to health insurance. First Lady Hillary Clinton chaired the health-care-plan task force and became the administration's lead witness on the plan before congressional committees. The bill aroused intense opposition from the pharmaceutical and insurance industries, however. By the summer of 1994, Clinton's health-insurance plan was doomed. Republican senators began a filibuster to prevent a vote on the bill. Lacking the votes to stop the filibuster, the Democrats acknowledged defeat and gave up the fight for universal medical coverage.

MISTRUST OF GOVERNMENT AND THE MILITIA MOVEMENT While Clinton sparred with Republicans in Washington, a grassroots militia movement spread across the country in the 1990s, a manifestation of the paranoid and populist strain in cultural politics. In Waco, Texas, a confrontation between federal authorities and a cultlike militia group called the Branch Davidians sparked a tragedy. The Davidians, an apocalyptic religious sect headed by a charismatic loony named David Koresh, was found to be

Oklahoma City

The Alfred P. Murrah Federal Building in Oklahoma City after it was bombed on April 19, 1995, in what was then the deadliest terrorist act on U.S. soil.

stockpiling weapons, engaging in child abuse, and violating immigration laws. On February 28, 1993, agents from the Treasury Department's Bureau of Alcohol, Tobacco, and Firearms (BATF) entered the sect's compound, where they were met with gunfire. Four agents and two Branch Davidians were killed, and twenty people were injured. The next day the FBI took over the siege of the compound, waging fruitless psychological warfare against the Branch Davidians. On April 19, the fifty-first day of the televised siege, FBI agents recklessly attacked the compound with armored vehicles and tear gas. Amid the commotion the compound caught fire and quickly burned to the ground. At least seventy-seven people died in the inferno.

On the second anniversary of the Waco incident, April 19, 1995, a massive truck bomb exploded in front of the federal office building in Oklahoma City, Oklahoma. The entire front portion of the nine-story building collapsed, killing 168 people, 19 of them children in the building's day-care center. Six hundred others were injured. Within days the FBI had arrested Timothy McVeigh and Terry Nichols and charged them with the bombing. A third man pleaded guilty to separate charges of conspiring to produce explosives. All three men were militia members who hated the federal government and had been incensed by the way the BATF and the FBI had dealt with the Branch Davidians at Waco. The Oklahoma City bombing shocked and saddened the nation. It brought to public attention the rise of right-wing militia groups and revealed the depth of anti-government sentiment among those fringe groups.

REPUBLICAN INSURGENCY

During 1994 Bill Clinton began to see his presidency unravel. Unable to get either health-care reform or welfare-reform bills through the

Democratic Congress and having failed to carry out his campaign pledge for middle-class tax relief, he and his party found themselves on the defensive.

In the midterm elections of 1994, the Democrats suffered a humbling defeat. It was the first election since 1952 in which Republicans captured both houses of Congress. In both the majority was solid: 52 to 48 in the Senate, a majority that soon increased when two Democrats declared themselves Republicans, and 230 to 204 in the House. Not a single Republican incumbent was defeated. Republicans also won a net gain of eleven governorships and fifteen state legislatures.

THE CONTRACT WITH AMERICA   A Georgian named Newton Leroy Gingrich led the Republican insurgency in Congress. Gingrich, a brilliant former history professor with an oversize ego, had helped mobilize religious and social conservatives associated with the Christian Coalition. In early 1995 he became the first Republican Speaker of the House in forty-two years. Gingrich announced that "we are at the end of an era." Liberalism was dead, and the Democratic party was dying. He dismissed Bill and Hillary Clinton as "counterculture McGoverniks." Gingrich pledged to start a new reign of congressional Republican dominance that would dismantle the "corrupt liberal welfare state." He was aided by freshman Republicans promoting what he called the Contract with America. The ten-point contract outlined an anti-big-government program with less regulation, less environmental conservation, term limits for members of Congress, a line-item veto for the president, welfare reform, and a balanced-budget amendment.

By April 13, exactly 100 days after taking office, the congressional Republicans had passed twenty-six bills stemming from the Contract with America and had failed to pass only two. Nonetheless, only four of those twenty-six bills succeeded in becoming law. The much-ballyhooed GOP revolution and the Contract with America fizzled out. The revolution that the imperious Gingrich touted was far too ambitious to be carried out in so limited a time with so slim a majority and so little sense of crisis. What is more, many of the congressional Republican freshmen were scornful of compromise and were amateurs at legislative procedure, and they limited Gingrich's ability to maneuver. The Senate rejected many of the bills that had been passed in the House as senators were less under Gingrich's spell and not party to the Contract with America anyway. The "Republican revolution" of 1994 fizzled out, too, because Newt Gingrich became such an unpopular figure, both in Congress and among the electorate. He was too ambitious, too slick, too aggressive, too rambunctious. Clinton's lieutenants effectively portrayed him as an extremist. And beyond all those factors, a presidential veto stood in the path of the Contract with America. President Clinton shrewdly moved to the political center and co-opted much of the Republican agenda. His distinctive strength—at least in the eyes of his supporters—resided in his agile responsiveness to changing public moods. To Clinton the Republican victory in the 1994 congressional elections and in the passage of the Contract with America initiatives bore a simple message: he must recapture the political center by radically changing his own agenda.

LEGISLATIVE BREAKTHROUGH   In the late summer of 1996, as lawmakers were preparing to adjourn and participate in the presidential nominating conventions, the 104th Congress broke through its partisan gridlock and passed a flurry of important legislation that President Clinton quickly signed, including bills increasing the minimum wage and broadening access to health insurance.

Even more significant was a comprehensive welfare-reform measure that ended the federal government's open-ended guarantee of aid to the poor, a guarantee that had been in place since 1935. The Personal Responsibility and Work Opportunity Act of 1996 turned over the major federal welfare programs to the states, which would receive federal grants to fund them. The bill also limited the amount of time during which a person could receive welfare benefits funded by federal money and required that at least half of a state's welfare recipients have jobs or be enrolled in job-training programs by 2002. States failing to meet the deadline would have their federal funds cut.

The Republican-sponsored welfare-reform legislation passed the Senate by a vote of seventy-four to twenty-four. It had the effect of cutting $56 billion over six years from various welfare programs, several of which dated back to Franklin Roosevelt's New Deal. Liberals charged that Clinton was abdicating Democratic social principles in order to gain reelection amid the conservative climate of the times. Clinton and his centrist advisers, dismissed the criticism, however. With his reelection bid at stake, the president was determined to live up to his 1992 campaign pledge to "end welfare as we know it." Clinton also knew that most voters in both parties were eager to see major cuts in federal entitlement programs.

THE 1996 CAMPAIGN After clinching the Republican presidential nomination in 1996, Senate majority leader Bob Dole resigned his seat in order to devote his attention to defeating Bill Clinton. As the 1996 presidential campaign unfolded, however, Clinton maintained a large lead in the polls. With an improving economy and no major foreign-policy crises to confront, personal and partisan issues surged into prominence. Concern about Dole's age (seventy-three) and his acerbic manner, as well as rifts in the Republican party between economic and social conservatives over issues such as abortion and gun control, hampered Dole's efforts to generate widespread support.

On November 5, 1996, Clinton won again, with an electoral vote of 379 to 159 and 49 percent of the popular vote. Dole received 41 percent of the popular vote, and independent candidate Ross Perot got 8 percent. The Republicans lost eight seats in the House but retained a 227 to 207 advantage over the Democrats in the House; in the Senate, Republicans gained two seats for a 55 to 45 majority. The resulting deadlock reflected the conservative mood of the times.

ECONOMIC AND SOCIAL TRENDS OF THE 1990S

THE "NEW ECONOMY" As the twentieth century came to a close, the United States benefited from a prolonged period of unprecedented prosperity. Buoyed by low inflation, high employment, declining federal budget deficits, dramatic improvements in productivity, the rapid globalization of economic life, and the astute leadership of Federal Reserve Board chairman Alan Greenspan, business and industry witnessed record profits.

During the late 1990s the stock market soared. In 1993 the Dow Jones industrial average hit 3,500. By 1996 it had topped 6,000. During 1998 it reached 9,000, defying the predictions of experts that the economy could not sustain such performance. In 1998 unemployment was only 4.3 percent, the lowest since 1970. Inflation was a measly 1.7 percent. People talked of the onset of a new economy, one that was centered on high-tech companies and would defy the boom-and-bust cycles of the previous hundred years. "It is possible," Greenspan suggested, "that we have moved 'beyond history.'"

In the 1990s much of the growth in the economy resulted from efforts to promote favored free markets on a world scale: global markets without tariffs and other barriers to free trade. More and more gigantic corporations such as IBM and General Electric had become international in scope. This phenomenon encouraged free-trade agreements such as NAFTA as well as most-favored-nation treatment for Communist China and other countries. With such agreements in place, American companies could easily "outsource" much of their production to plants in countries with lower labor costs. Increasingly, therefore, blue-collar labor lost ground to cheap foreign labor in assembly plants or "sweatshops" elsewhere in the world.

RACE INITIATIVES After the triumphs of the civil rights movement in the 1960s, the momentum for minority advancement had run out—except for gains in college admissions and employment under the rubric of affirmative action. The conservative mood during the mid-1990s manifested itself in the Supreme Court. In 1995 the Court ruled against election districts redrawn to create African-American or Latino majorities and narrowed federal affirmative-action programs.

In 1996 two major steps were taken against affirmative action in college admissions. In *Hopwood v. Texas*, a federal court ruled that considering race to achieve a diverse student body at the University of Texas was "not a compelling interest under the Fourteenth Amendment." Later that year the state of California passed Proposition 209, an initiative that ruled out race, sex, ethnicity, and national origin as criteria for preferring any group. These rulings eviscerated affirmative-action programs and drastically reduced African-American enrollments, thereby prompting second thoughts. In addition, the nation still had not addressed intractable problems that lay beyond civil rights—that is, problems of dependency: illiteracy, poverty, unemployment, urban decay, and slums.

THE SCANDAL MACHINE During his first term, President Clinton was dogged by allegations of improper involvement in the Whitewater Development Corporation. In 1978, as governor of Arkansas, he had invested in a resort project on the White River in northern Arkansas. The project turned out to be a fraud and a failure, and the Clintons took a loss on their investment. In 1994 Kenneth Starr, a Republican, was appointed to serve as independent counsel in an investigation of the Whitewater case. Although Starr had a reputation for fairness, many observers believed that his unwillingness to end the investigation and his former position in the Bush administration suggested a taint of partisanship. While revealing that Hillary Clinton had handled some legal work for the Whitewater enterprise, Starr's investigation did not uncover evidence that the Clintons were directly involved in the fraud, although a number of their close associates had been caught in the web and convicted of various charges, some related to Whitewater and some not.

Besides Whitewater, Starr's team of investigators looked into the allegations of Paula Jones that Clinton had sexually harassed her while he was governor of Arkansas and she was a state employee. In the course of the investigation, it surfaced that the president may have had a sexual affair with a former White House intern, Monica Lewinsky, and may have pressed her to lie about it under oath. Clinton publicly denied the affair, but the tawdry scandal would not disappear. In August 1998 President Clinton agreed to testify before a grand jury convened to investigate the sexual allegations. He was the first president in history to testify before a grand jury. On August 17, with the nation anxiously awaiting the results, Clinton recanted his earlier denials and acknowledged having had "inappropriate intimate physical contact" with Monica Lewinsky. Public reaction to Clinton's stunning about-face was mixed. A majority of Americans expressed sympathy for the president because of his public humiliation and wanted the matter dropped. Clinton's credibility had suffered a serious blow on account of his reckless lack of self-discipline and his efforts to deny and then cover up the sordid scandal.

Meanwhile, Kenneth Starr continued his tenacious investigation. On September 9, 1998, he submitted to Congress a 445-page report and eighteen boxes of supporting material. The Starr Report found "substantial and creditable" evidence of presidential wrongdoing. Drawing upon the evidence, the Republican-controlled House Judiciary Committee voted 21 to 16 to recommend a full impeachment inquiry into the allegations of perjury and obstruction of justice by the president. On October 8 the House of Representatives voted 258 to 176 to begin a wide-ranging impeachment

Impeachment

Representative Edward Pease, a member of the House Judiciary Committee, covers his face during the vote on the third of four articles of impeachment charging President Clinton with "high crimes and misdemeanors," December 1998.

inquiry of President Clinton. Thirty-one Democrats joined the Republicans in supporting the investigation. On December 19, 1998, William Jefferson Clinton became the second president to be impeached by the House of Representatives. The House officially approved two articles of impeachment, charging Clinton with lying under oath to a federal grand jury and obstructing justice.

The Senate trial of President Clinton began on January 7, 1999, with the swearing in of Chief Justice William Rehnquist to preside and the senators as jurors. Five weeks later, on February 12, the Senate acquitted the president. Rejecting the first charge of perjury, ten Republicans and all forty-five Democrats voted "not guilty." On the charge of obstruction of justice, the Senate split fifty-fifty (which meant acquittal, since sixty-seven votes were needed for conviction). In both instances, senators had a hard time interpreting Clinton's philandering as constituting "high crimes and misdemeanors," the constitutional requirement for removal of a president from office. Clinton's supporters portrayed him as the victim of a puritanical special prosecutor and partisan conspiracy run amok. His critics lambasted him as a lecherous man without honor or integrity. Both characterizations were incomplete. Politically astute, charismatic, and well-informed, Clinton had as much ability and potential as any president. Yet he was also shamelessly self-indulgent. The result was a scandalous presidency punctuated by dramatic achievements in welfare reform, economic growth, and foreign policy.

FOREIGN-POLICY CHALLENGES

Like Woodrow Wilson, Lyndon Johnson, and Jimmy Carter before him, Bill Clinton was a Democratic president who came into office determined to focus on the nation's domestic problems only to find himself mired in foreign entanglements that had no easy resolution. Clinton continued the Bush administration's intervention in Somalia, on the northeastern horn of Africa, where collapse of the government early in 1991 had left the country in anarchy, prey to tribal marauders. President Bush in 1992 had gained UN sanction for a military force led by American troops to relieve hunger and restore peace. In early 1993 U.S. troop levels peaked and began to shrink with the arrival of international forces. The Somalian operation proved successful at its primary mission, but it never solved the political problems that lay at the root of the population's-starvation and civil strife.

Clinton and the Middle East

President Clinton presides as Israeli prime minister Yitzhak Rabin (left) and PLO leader Yasir Arafat (right), agree to a peace accord between Israel and the Palestinians, September 1993.

THE MIDDLE EAST   Clinton also continued George Bush's policy of sponsoring patient negotiations between the Arabs and the Israelis. A new development was the inclusion of the PLO in the negotiations. In 1993 a draft agreement between Israel and the PLO provided for the restoration of Palestinian self-rule in the occupied Gaza Strip and in Jericho, on the West Bank of the Jordan River, in an exchange of land for peace as provided in UN Security Council resolutions. A formal signing occurred at the White House on September 13, 1993. With President Clinton presiding, Israeli prime minister Yitzhak Rabin and PLO leader Yasir Arafat exchanged handshakes, and their foreign ministers signed the agreement.

The Middle East peace process suffered a terrible blow in early November 1995, however, when Yitzhak Rabin was assassinated at a peace rally in Tel Aviv by an Israeli Jewish zealot who resented Rabin's efforts to negotiate with the Palestinians. Some observers feared that the assassin had killed the peace process as well when seven months later conservative hard-liner Benjamin Netanyahu narrowly defeated the U.S.-backed Shimon Peres in the Israeli elections. Yet in October 1998 Clinton brought Arafat, King Hussein of Jordan, and Netanyahu together at a conference center in Wye Mills, Maryland, where they reached an agreement. Under the Wye River Accord, Israel surrendered land in return for security guarantees by the Palestinians. As hard-liners attempted to derail the tenuous peace process, Netanyahu called elections early, and the Israeli public swept into power former general Ehud Barak, who promised to jump-start the peace process.

THE BALKANS   Bill Clinton's foreign policy also addressed the chaotic transition in eastern Europe from Soviet domination to independence. With the collapse of Communist power, ethnic and religious hatreds resurfaced, often leading to violent clashes. When Yugoslavia imploded in 1991, fanatics and tyrants incited ethnic conflict as four of its six republics seceded. Serb minorities, backed by Serbia itself, stirred up civil wars in Croatia and Bosnia. In Bosnia especially the war involved "ethnic cleansing"—driving Muslims from their homes and towns. In 1995 American negotiators finally persuaded the foreign ministers of Croatia, Bosnia, and the new Federal Republic of Yugoslavia to agree to a comprehensive peace plan. To enforce the agreement, 60,000 NATO troops would be dispatched to Bosnia as part of a peacekeeping operation. A cease-fire went into effect in October 1995.

In 1998 the Balkan tinderbox flared up again, this time in the Yugoslav province of Kosovo, a region long considered sacred by Christian Serbs. By 1989, however, over 90 percent of the 2 million Kosovars were ethnic Albanian Muslims. In that year, Yugoslav president Slobodan Milošević decided to reassert Serbian control over the province. He stripped Kosovo of its autonomy and established de facto martial law. When the Albanian Kosovars resisted and large numbers of Muslim men began to join the Kosovo Liberation Army, Serbian soldiers and state police ruthlessly suppressed them and launched another program of "ethnic cleansing," burning Albanian villages, murdering men, raping women, and displacing hundreds of thousands of Muslim Albanian Kosovars.

On March 24, 1999, NATO, relying heavily upon American military resources and leadership, launched air strikes against Yugoslavia. After seventy-two days of unrelenting bombardment, Milošević sued for peace on NATO's terms. An agreement was reached on June 3, 1999. As the Albanian Kosovars began to return to Kosovo, however, large numbers of Serbs, fearful of Muslim retribution, began to leave, and some of them were killed. Members of the Kosovo Liberation Army stepped into the vacuum left by the departing Serbs and began to take control of the province.

GLOBALIZATION   The deepening involvement of the United States in the complex affairs of eastern Europe symbolized the broadening scope of globalization. As the proliferation of global-spanning information and communications technologies shrank time and distance, a cornucopia of consumer goods was produced, distributed, marketed, and purchased by multinational companies all over the world, not just in the United States. Unlike the 1950s and 1960s, when the United States enjoyed a near monopoly on international commerce because of the devastation of European and Asian economies during World War II, the rest of the world was now aggressively competing with American businesses. Yet as more nations entered the world economy and experienced prosperity, they benefited corporations in the United Stated by buying more American goods and sending more and better goods to the United States. U.S. exports rose dramatically in the last twenty years of the twentieth century. In 1970 American exports totaled $43 billion; in 2000 they totaled $1.2 trillion. Globalization benefited American consumers as well, by making available many more products–and at lower prices.

By the end of the twentieth century, the American economy had become global dependent; foreign trade had become central to American prosperity–and to American politics. "The global economy," said a leading bank executive, "is defined by capital, ideas, and energy, not by artificial, geographic or political boundaries." Foreign government and foreign investors had become the primary purchasers of U.S. government bonds. Driven by a ferocious desire to cut production costs, large corporations moved more and more of their production overseas. Outsourcing work "offshore" to developing countries, where wages were low, became the rage. By 2000 over one third of the production of American multinational companies was occurring abroad, compared with only 9 percent in 1980. Likewise, executives in multinational countries became more multinational themselves. A growing number of chief executive officers were of a different nationality than that of the company they headed. By the end of the twentieth century, the American economy had become internationalized to such a profound extent that global concerns exercised an overwhelming influence on American domestic and foreign policies.

THE ELECTION OF 2000

The election of 2000 revealed that American voters were split evenly along partisan lines. The two major-party candidates for president, Democratic vice president Al Gore and Texas Republican governor George W. Bush, son of the former president, presented sharply contrasting views on the role of the federal government, tax cuts, environmental policies, and the best way to preserve Social Security and Medicare. Gore, a Tennessee native and Harvard graduate whose father had been a senator, favored an active federal government that would preserve Social Security and subsidize prescription-medicine expenses for the elderly. He criticized proposed Republican tax cuts as catering to the wealthy. An environmental activist, Gore reaffirmed his support for the Environmental Protection Agency and the Interior Department.

Bush, on the other hand, sought to transfer power from the federal government to the states, particularly in regard to the environment and education. He promoted more drilling for oil on federal land, and he endorsed the use of vouchers (cash grants) to enable parents to send their children to private schools. In international affairs, Bush questioned the need to maintain U.S. peacekeeping forces in Bosnia and the continuing expense of other global military commitments.

In the end the election was the one of the closest—and most controversial—in history. The television networks initially reported that Gore had narrowly won the state of Florida and its decisive twenty-five electoral votes. Later in the evening, however, the networks reversed themselves, saying that Florida was too close to call. The final tally in Florida showed Bush with a razor-thin lead, but state law required a recount. For the first time in 125 years, the results of a presidential election remained in doubt for weeks after the voting.

As a painstaking hand count of presidential ballots proceeded in Florida, supporters of Bush and Gore pursued victory through legal maneuvers in the Florida courts and the U.S. Supreme Court; each side accused the other of trying to steal the election. The stalemated political drama continued for five weeks. At last, on December 12, 2000, the Supreme Court halted the statewide manual recounts in Florida. In the case known as *Bush v. Gore,* a bare five-to-four majority ruled that any new recount would clash with existing Florida law. Bush was deemed the winner in Florida by the slimmest of margins: 537 votes. Although Gore amassed a 540,000-vote lead nationwide, he lost in the Electoral College by two votes when he lost Florida.

The 2000 election revealed the remarkable balance that had emerged in national politics. Not since the 1880s had the two major parties been so evenly divided. Republicans retained a slim lead in the House, 49.2 percent to 47.9 percent. The number of senators was split down the middle, fifty-fifty. Some 71 percent of city residents voted for Gore while only 26 percent chose Bush. Conversely, 59 percent of rural voters cast ballots for Bush while only 37 percent opted for Gore. Gore won fewer than one third of the votes in the South and lost his home state of Tennessee. Bush won the mountain West and the South while Gore dominated the Northeast, the West Coast, and the industrial Midwest. Women favored Gore over Bush by 11 percentage points, exactly the reverse of the male voters.

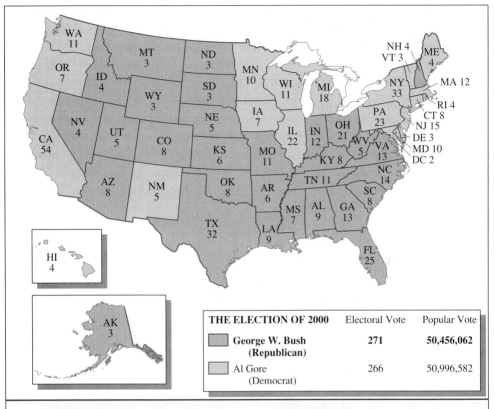

THE ELECTION OF 2000	Electoral Vote	Popular Vote
George W. Bush (Republican)	271	50,456,062
Al Gore (Democrat)	266	50,996,582

Why was the election so close? How was the conflict over the election results resolved? How were differences between urban and rural voters key to the outcome of the election?

COMPASSIONATE CONSERVATISM

THE SECOND BUSH PRESIDENCY During the 2000 election campaign, commentators criticized George W. Bush's political inexperience and lack of knowledge about world affairs. As president-elect he addressed those concerns by naming to his cabinet seasoned public figures. His vice-president, Richard "Dick" Cheney, is a former congressman from Wyoming who served as secretary of defense under the senior George Bush. Colin Powell, a former army general and chairman of the Joint Chiefs of Staff, became the first African-American secretary of state. Donald Rumsfeld, secretary of defense under Gerald Ford, returned to that position in the Bush administration. Bush named former Missouri senator John Ashcroft attorney general.

Bush not only arrived in the White House amid the controversy of a disputed election, but he also inherited a sputtering economy and a falling stock market. By the spring of 2000, the high-tech companies that had led the soaring stock market during the 1990s had begun to stall. Many of the dazzling new dot-com businesses declared bankruptcy. Greed fed by record profits and speculative excesses had led businesses, investors, and consumers to take dangerous risks; many leading corporate executives, it turned out, had engaged in unethical practices that undermined the economy. The Internet bubble burst in 2001. Stock values collapsed, stealing over $2 trillion from household wealth. Consumer confidence and capital investment plummeted with the stock market. By March 2001 the economy was in recession for the first time in over a decade.

Bush's disputed election and the political balance in Congress did not prevent the new president from launching an ambitious legislative agenda. Confident that he could win over Democrats, he promised within months of his inauguration to provide "an explosion of legislation" promoting his goal of "compassionate conservatism." The top item on Bush's wish list was a $1.6-trillion tax cut intended to stimulate the sagging economy. The Senate eventually trimmed the cut to $1.35 trillion over eleven years, and Bush signed it into law on June 7, 2001.

NO CHILD LEFT BEHIND In addition to tax reduction, one of President Bush's top priorities was education reform. In late 2001 Congress passed a comprehensive education-improvement plan called No Child Left Behind, and the president signed the bill in early 2002. It required states to set new learning standards and ensure that all students were "proficient" at reading and math by 2014. It also mandated that all teachers be "highly qualified" in their subject area by 2005, allowed children in low-performing schools to transfer to other schools, and required states to submit annual reports of students' scores on standardized tests. Schools and school districts that fell short of the new standards were eligible for financial and technical assistance, but if progress did not occur the federal government would issue a series of sanctions culminating in the state's taking over deficient school districts. States soon criticized the program, noting that it provided insufficient funds for remedial programs and that poor school districts, many of them in blighted inner cities or rural areas, would be especially hard pressed to meet the guidelines.

EXPLOITING THE ENVIRONMENT The Bush administration's environmental policies ignited a firestorm of controversy. The president refused to sign the Kyōto Protocol, an international agreement among dozens of nations setting limits on the emissions of carbon dioxide and other gases contributing to global climate change. Bush argued that the treaty would harm the economy. Administration officials also sought to roll back restrictions on economic development posed by long-standing environmental regulations. In addition, they wanted to allow more logging in national forests and open up more federal land, including wildlife sanctuaries, to exploration for energy sources in the face of dramatic increases in oil and gasoline prices. Like Ronald Reagan before him, Bush appointed former industry executives to federal agencies responsible for enforcing environmental regulations, and he exempted the Defense Department from many environmental restrictions. James Jeffords, a Republican turned independent and the ranking minority member of the Senate Environment and Public Works Committee, predicted that the Bush administration would "go down in history as the greatest disaster for public health and the environment in the history of the United States."

Yet the Bush administration did take several steps to protect the environment. The EPA ordered General Electric to spend hundreds of millions of dollars to remove toxic chemicals it had deposited into New York's Hudson River. It also established the first limits on diesel-fuel emissions for trucks and off-road vehicles. And Bush appropriated funds to begin chipping away at a huge deferred-maintenance backlog at the national parks.

GLOBAL TERRORISM

With the collapse of the Soviet Union and the end of the cold war, world politics had grown more unstable during the 1990s. The basic premise of American foreign policy was "unipolar": to maintain the nation's leadership role in global affairs. Yet a simmering mistrust of America's geopolitical and dominance economic glolaization festered internationally. Where ideologies such as capitalism and communism had earlier been the cause of conflict and tension in foreign relations, issues of religion, ethnicity, and clashing cultural values now divided peoples.

Nations were no longer the sole actors on the stage of world politics. Instead, nebulous multinational groups inspired by religious fanaticism and anti-American rage were using high-tech terrorism to gain notoriety and exact vengeance. The very rootlessness of the zealots—their alienation from their native societies and their ability to infiltrate other countries and cultures—proved to be an ironic strength. Well-financed and well-armed terrorists flourished in the cracks of foundering nations such as Sudan, Somalia, Pakistan, Yemen, and Afghanistan. Throughout the 1990s the United States had fought a losing secret war against organized terrorism. The ineffectiveness of Western intelligence agencies in tracking the movements and intentions of militant extremists became tragically evident in the late summer of 2001.

SEPTEMBER 11, 2001: A DAY OF INFAMY   At 8:45 on the morning of September 11, 2001, the world watched in horror as a commercial airliner hijacked by Islamic terrorists slammed into the north tower of the World Trade Center in New York City. A second hijacked jumbo jet, traveling at 500 miles per hour, hit the south tower eighteen minutes later. The fuel-laden planes turned the majestic buildings into infernos. The twin towers, both 110 stories tall and filled with thousands of people, collapsed from the intense heat. Surrounding buildings also crumpled. The entire southern end of Manhattan—ground zero—became a hellish scene of twisted steel, suffocating smoke, and wailing sirens.

While the catastrophic drama in New York was unfolding, a third hijacked plane crashed into the Pentagon in Washington, D.C. A fourth commandeered airliner, thought to be headed for the White House, missed its mark when passengers, who had heard reports of the earlier incidents via cell phones, assaulted the hijackers to prevent the plane from being used as a weapon. During the struggle in the cockpit, the plane went out of control and plummeted into the Pennsylvania countryside, killing all on board.

The hijackings represented the costliest terrorist assault on the United States in the nation's history. There were 266 passengers and crew members aboard the crashed jets. More than 100 civilians and military personnel were killed at the Pentagon. The death toll at the World Trade Center was over 2,600, with many firefighters, police officers, and rescue workers among the dead. Hundreds of those killed were foreign nationals working in the financial district; some eighty nations lost citizens in the attacks. The terrorists also destroyed a powerful symbol of America: the World Trade Center towers were the central offices of global capitalism.

The terrorist attacks of September 11 created shock and chaos, grief and anger. They also prompted an unprecedented display of national unity and patriotism. People rushed to donate blood, food, and money. Volunteers clogged military-recruiting centers. American flags were in evidence everywhere. Citizens around the world held vigils at U.S. embassies. World leaders offered condolences and support. For the first time in its history, NATO invoked Article V of its charter, which states that an attack on any member will be considered an attack on all.

September 11, 2001

Smoke pours out of the north tower of the World Trade Center as the south tower bursts into flames after being struck by a second hijacked airplane. Both towers collapsed about an hour later.

Within hours of the hijackings, officials had identified the nineteen terrorists as members of al Qaeda (the Base), a well-financed worldwide network of Islamic extremists led by a wealthy Saudi renegade, Osama bin Laden. Years before, bin Laden had declared holy war on the United States, Israel, and the Saudi monarchy. For several years he had been using remote bases in war-torn Afghanistan as terrorist training centers. Collaboring with bin Laden's terrorist agenda was Afghanistan's ruling Taliban, a coalition of radical Islamists that had emerged in the mid-1990s following the forced withdrawal of Soviet troops from Afghanistan. Taliban leaders provided bin Laden with a safe haven in exchange for his financial and military support against the Northern Alliance, a cluster of rebel groups opposed to Taliban rule. Bin Laden sought to mobilize Muslim militants into a global army energized by local causes. As many as 20,000 recruits from twenty countries circulated through his training camps. Most of the terrorists received religious indoctrination and basic infantry training to prepare them to fight for the Taliban. A smaller group was selected by al Qaeda for elite training to organize secret cells around the world and engage in urban warfare, assassination, demolition, and sabotage.

WAR ON TERRORISM The September 11 terrorist assault on the United States changed the course of the new presidency, the nation, and the world. The economy, already in decline, went into a free fall. With people world wide reluctant to fly, airlines laid off tens of thousands of employees. Insurance companies struggled to pay off an estimated $30 billion in claims resulting from the attacks. On Wall Street, markets plummeted in anticipation of a deeper recession combined with a war against terrorism.

President Bush, who had never professed to know much about international relations or world affairs and had shown only disdain for Bill Clinton's "multilateralism," was thrust onto center stage as commander in chief of a wounded nation eager for vengeance. The Bush administration immediately forged an international coalition to strike at terrorism worldwide. The coalition demanded that Afghanistan's Taliban government surrender the terrorists or risk military attack. In a televised address on September 20, Bush warned Americans that the war against terrorism would be a lengthy campaign involving covert action as well as conventional military forces, which would target not only terrorists but also the groups and governments that abet them. "Every nation in every region," he said, "now has a decision to make: either you are with us or you are with the terrorists."

On October 7, after the Taliban defiantly refused to turn over bin Laden, the United States and its allies launched a ferocious military campaign—Operation Enduring Freedom—to locate and punish terrorists or "those harboring terrorists." U.S. and British cruise missiles and bombers destroyed Afghan military installations and al Qaeda training camps. The coalition found key allies in neighboring Pakistan and in Afghanistan's Northern Alliance. U.S. military commanders used new high-tech weapons—precision-guided bombs, spy satellites, and laser-targeting devices—that enabled American forces to engage the enemy and occupy territory without risking soldiers' lives.

On December 9, only two months after the American-led military campaign in Afghanistan had begun, the Taliban regime collapsed. With its collapse, the war in Afghanistan devolved into a high-stakes manhunt for the elusive Osama bin Laden and an international network of terrorists operating in sixty countries.

In December 2001 Afghanistan's long-feuding factions, minus the Taliban, signed a UN-brokered peace agreement that created an interim government, led by Hamid Karzai, an exiled tribal leader who had reentered the country in October to rally opposition to the Taliban. While the American-led coalition forces continued to track down al Qaeda stragglers and search for bin Laden, the interim Afghan government faced the stern challenge of providing basic services and creating stability in a faction-ridden, war-torn country.

TERRORISM AT HOME While the military campaign continued in Afghanistan, officials in Washington worried that terrorists might launch additional attacks in the United States with biological, chemical, or even nuclear weapons. To address the threat and to help restore public confidence, President Bush created a new federal agency, the Office of Homeland Security, and a new federal agency, the Transportation Security Administration, assumed responsibility for screening airline passengers. At the same time, President Bush and a supportive Congress created new legislation, known as the USA Patriot Act, which gave government agencies the right to eavesdrop on confidential conversations between prison inmates and their lawyers and permitted terrorist suspects to be tried in military courts. Such tribunals would have less stringent standards regarding the burden of proof than civilian courts: they could be held in secret, they allowed for the admission of hearsay and illegally obtained information as evidence, and they required only a two-thirds majority for conviction. Civil liberties groups voiced grave concerns that the measures jeopardized constitutional rights and protections. But the crisis atmosphere after September 11 caused most people to support these extraordinary steps.

MIDDLE EAST TURMOIL The Middle East again exploded in violence in the new century. Seven years of relative calm ended when Israeli-Palestinian peace talks in Oslo collapsed in 2000. Disputes over the fate of Jerusalem, a holy city to Jews, Christians, and Muslims, undermined any new accords between the Israelis and the Palestinians. Frustrated by the collapse of negotiations, Palestinians again declared an intifada, or uprising. In October 2000 street demonstrations in the Israeli-controlled West Bank and Gaza Strip gave way to a series of suicide bombings against Israeli soldiers and civilians. Israeli troops retaliated. Hundreds of casualties resulted, many of them children.

In February 2001 Israeli voters, angry with the increasing violence, elected the party of Ariel Sharon, a militant conservative. As their prime minister, Sharon vowed that there would be no negotiating with the Palestinians as long as their intifada continued. Sharon's government responded to attacks with air strikes and armored assaults on Palestinian-controlled areas. Israeli

Bush and the Middle East

President George W. Bush addresses soldiers in July 2002 as part of an appeal to Congress to speed approval of increased defense spending after the September 11 terrorist attacks.

agents also assassinated leaders of Hamas and Islamic Jihad, two Palestinian terrorist organizations.

THE BUSH DOCTRINE In the fall of 2002, President Bush unveiled a new national security doctrine that marked a distinct shift from that of previous administrations. Containment and deterrence had been the guiding strategic concepts of the cold war. Now, President Bush declared, the growing menace posed by "shadowy networks" of terrorist groups and unstable rogue nations with "weapons of mass destruction," required a new doctrine of preemptive military action. "If we wait for threats to fully materialize," he explained, "we will have waited too long. In the world we have entered, the only path to safety is the path of action. And this nation will act."

A SECOND GULF WAR During 2002 and 2003 Iraq emerged as the focus of the Bush administration's new policy of "preemptive" military action to prevent terrorism and destroy weapons of mass destruction. Following the Persian Gulf War of 1991, UN inspectors had gone to Iraq to search for such biological and chemical weapons. Iraqi leader Saddam Hussein never accepted the legitimacy of those efforts, and in the fall of 1998 he had ordered the UN inspectors to leave. Thereafter, American officials grew increasingly concerned about Iraq's illegal possession of biological and chemical weapons as well as its support of global terrorism. In September 2002 President Bush urged the UN to confront the "grave and gathering danger" posed by Hussein's dictatorial regime in Iraq. He warned that the United States would act alone if the UN did not respond. In October, Congress approved a resolution proposed by Bush authorizing him to use "all means that he determines to be appropriate, including force" to defend the United States against the threat posed by Iraq. On November 8 the UN Security Council passed Resolution 1441 ordering Iraq to disarm immediately or face "serious consequences." Faced with growing international pressure, Hussein grudgingly allowed UN weapons inspectors to return to Iraq "without conditions."

As the UN inspectors resumed their efforts, however, the Iraqi government continued its partial cooperation and stalling tactics. President Bush gained the support of Great Britain and Spain in proposing a new UN resolution that would authorize military action to ensure that Iraq eliminated its weapons of mass destruction. "The United States," Bush insisted, "will not permit the world's most dangerous regimes to threaten us with the world's most destructive weapons."

During early 2003 American and British military units began to assemble in the Persian Gulf. France, China, Germany, and Russia opposed the American-led effort to use force against Iraq, arguing that the UN inspectors should be given more time to complete their task. Secretary of State Colin Powell's efforts to marshal international support for the forceful American stance proved fruitless. On March 17 the United States, Great Britain, and Spain withdrew their proposed Security Council resolution, announcing that diplomatic efforts had failed. President Bush issued an ultimatum to Saddam Hussein: he and his sons must leave Iraq within forty-eight hours or face a U.S.-led invasion. Hussein refused. Two days later, on March 19, American and British forces, supported by what George Bush called the "coalition of the willing," attacked Iraq.

Operation Iraqi Freedom involved a massive bombing campaign followed closely by a fast-moving invasion across the Iraqi desert from bases in Kuwait. Some 250,000 American soldiers, sailors, and marines were joined by 50,000 British troops as well as small contingents from other countries, including Australia and Poland. President Bush explained that the purpose of the invasion was to "disarm Iraq, to free its people, and defend the world from grave danger." Critics at home and abroad, however, saw the allied assault as an imperialist effort to control Iraqi oil and impose a capitalist democracy on an Arab country. On April 9, after only three weeks of intense

A Continued Presence in Iraq

U.S. military police patrol the market in Abu Ghraib, on the outskirts of Baghdad.

fighting amid sweltering heat and blinding sandstorms, allied forces occupied Baghdad, the capital of Iraq. Iraqis cheered as U.S. soldiers toppled an enormous statue of Saddam Hussein in the city center. Saddam's Baathist regime and his inept army collapsed and fled a week later. On May 1, 2003, an exuberant President Bush declared that the war was essentially over. "The battle of Iraq," he said, "is one victory in a war on terror that began on September 11, 2001, and still goes on."

The complicated Iraqi military campaign was a brilliantly orchestrated demonstration of intense firepower, daring maneuver, and complex logistical support. No one had predicted such a quick and decisive victory—or so few casualties among the allied forces. The six-week war came at a cost of fewer than 200 combat deaths among the 300,000 coalition troops. Over 2,000 Iraqi soldiers were killed; civilian casualties numbered in the tens of thousands.

Secretary of Defense Donald Rumsfeld saw the Iraq War as an opportunity to showcase America's new military strategy, with its focus on airpower, precision weaponry, sophisticated communications, and mobile ground forces adept at stealth and speed. Yet winning the peace proved far more difficult than winning the war. No sooner had Saddam Hussein's tyranny been destroyed than the allies faced the daunting task of restoring order and installing a democratic government in a chaotic Iraq torn by age-old religious feuds and ethnic tensions. Looting was rampant and basic services nonexistent. Saddam Hussein and many of his lieutenants evaded capture and organized insurgent attacks against the allied forces and the interim Iraqi government. Violence engulfed the war-torn country. Vengeful Islamic jihadists (holy warriors) from around the world streamed into Iraq to wage a merciless campaign of terror and sabotage against the coalition forces and their Iraqi allies.

Defense Department analysts had greatly underestimated the difficulty of pacifying and reconstructing postwar Iraq. As Secretary Rumsfeld told his staff in October 2003, the invasion of Iraq was the easy part. The allies now faced "a long, hard slog" in their effort to install a new Iraqi government and restore basic services in the midst of a growing guerrilla insurgency. By the fall of 2003, President Bush was forced to admit that substantial numbers of American troops (around 150,000) would remain in Iraq much longer than originally anticipated and that rebuilding the fractured nation would take much longer than expected. Victory on the battlefields of Iraq did not bring peace to the Middle East. Militant Islamic groups seething with hatred for the United States remained a constant global threat. In addition, the dispute over the Iraq War strained relations between the Anglo-American alliance and France, Germany, and Russia, all of which opposed the war.

Throughout 2003 and 2004 the Iraqi insurgency and its campaign of terror grew in scope and savagery. Near-daily suicide car bombings and roadside ambushes of U.S. military convoys wreaked havoc among Iraqi civilians and allied troops. Terrorists kidnapped foreign civilians and beheaded several of them in grisly rituals videotaped for the world to see. In the United States the euphoria of battlefield victory turned to dismay as the casualties and the expense of the Iraqi occupation soared. In the face of mounting criticism, President Bush urged Americans to "stay the course," insisting that a democratic Iraq would bring stability to the volatile Middle East and thereby blunt the momentum of Islamic terrorism.

But the president's credibility suffered a sharp blow in January 2004 when administration officials admitted that no weapons of mass destruction—the primary reason for launching the invasion—had been found in Iraq. The chief weapons inspector told Congress that the intelligence reports about Saddam's supposed secret weapons were "almost all wrong." Shocking revelations in April 2004 of American soldiers' torturing Iraqi prisoners further eroded public confidence in Bush's handling of the war and its aftermath.

By September 2004 American military deaths in Iraq had reached 1,000, and during 2006 they were well over 2,500. Although Saddam Hussein was captured in December 2003 and Iraqi citizens elected their first democratic government in January 2005 and approved a new constitution nine months later, Iraq seemed less secure than ever. The continuing guerrilla war in Afghanistan and the new one in Iraq strained American military resources and the federal budget. The Defense Department was forced to call up thousands of members of U.S. Army Reserve and National Guard units, and military recruiters found it increasingly difficult to meet their quotas.

THE ELECTION OF 2004 Growing public concern about the mayhem in Iraq complicated George Bush's campaign for a second term. Throughout 2004 his approval rating plummeted. And in the new century the electorate had become deeply polarized. A Gallup poll showed that Bush had the support of 91 percent of Republicans and only 17 percent of Democrats, the widest partisan gap in the poll's history. Visceral cultural issues such as abortion, school prayer, stem-cell research, and gay marriage continued to divide voters and inflame political discourse.

The 2004 Election

President George W. Bush (center) and Democratic candidate Senator John Kerry (left) participate in the second presidential debate, a town-hall style exchange held at Washington University in St. Louis, Missouri.

A ferocious partisanship dominated civic commentary in the early years of the century. Democrats still fumed over the contested election results of 2000. When asked about the intensity of his critics, a combative George Bush declared the furor "a compliment. It means I'm willing to take a stand." One of his advisers explained it more bluntly: "He likes being hated. It lets him know he's doing the right thing."

The 2004 presidential campaign was punctuated by negative attacks on each candidate as the two parties sought to galvanize their loyalists. Campaign rhetoric was especially caustic because both sides saw so much at stake. Democrats worried that the tide of Republican conservatism might sweep them into irrelevance. Republicans worried that the "jobless" economic recovery and deepening commitment in Iraq might derail their political momentum.

The Democratic nominee, Senator John Kerry of Massachusetts, was a decorated Vietnam War veteran who had helped organize the Vietnam Veterans against the War in the early 1970s. During the 2004 campaign, Kerry lambasted the Bush administration for misleading the nation on the issue of weapons of mass destruction in Iraq and for its inept handling of the Iraq occupation, implying that the United States was foundering in another Vietnam-like quagmire. Kerry charged that the Iraq War was hurting the war on global terror. He also highlighted the record budget deficits occurring under the Republican leadership. Bush countered that the tortuous efforts to create a democratic government in Iraq would enhance America's long-term security. The president also promised to continue his efforts to reform the Social Security pension program and the tax code and to reduce unemployment by restoring sustained economic growth.

On election day the exit polls suggested a Kerry victory, but in the end the election hinged on the crucial swing state of Ohio. No Republican had ever lost Ohio and still won the presidency. After an anxious night viewing returns from Ohio and even considering the contested ballots, Kerry conceded the election. "The outcome," he stressed, "should be decided by voters, not a protracted legal battle." By narrowly winning Ohio, Bush garnered 286 electoral votes to Kerry's 251. The 2004 election was remarkable for its high voter turnout. Almost 120 million people voted, some 15 million more than in the disputed 2000 election.

Bush won the popular vote by 50.73 to 48.27 percent, the narrowest margin won by any incumbent president. Yet in some respects the close election was not so close. Bush received 3.5 million more votes nationwide than Kerry, and Republicans increased their control of both the House and the Senate. As was true in the 2000 election, Bush and the Republicans dominated in the South, the Midwest, and the Rocky Mountain states while the

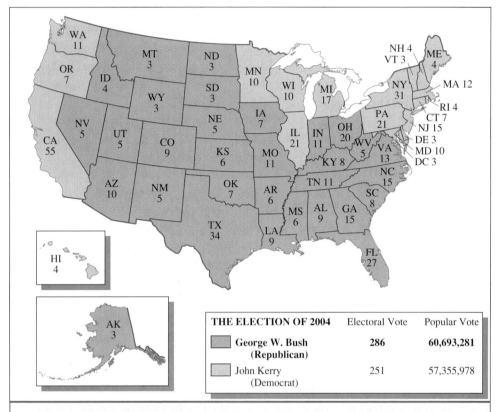

THE ELECTION OF 2004

	Electoral Vote	Popular Vote
George W. Bush (Republican)	286	60,693,281
John Kerry (Democrat)	251	57,355,978

How did the war in Iraq polarize the electorate? In what ways did the election of 2004 give Republicans a mandate?

Democrats controlled the West Coast, the Northeast, and the states border-ing the Great Lakes. Trumpeting "the will of the people at my back," Bush pledged to bring democracy and security to Iraq, overhaul the tax code and eliminate the estate tax, revamp Social Security, trim the federal budget deficit, limit awards for medical malpractice lawsuits, pass an energy bill, and create more jobs. "I earned capital in the campaign, political capital, and now I intend to spend it," he told reporters.

SECOND-TERM BLUES

Yet like many modern presidents, George Bush sputtered in his second term. In 2005 he pushed through Congress an energy bill and a Central

American Free Trade Act. But his effort to privatize Social Security retirement accounts went nowhere, and soaring budget deficits made repeal of the estate tax politically impossible.

The retirement of Sandra Day O'Connor from the Supreme Court in July 2005 ignited a fierce political debate over combustible issues such as abortion, gay marriage, and affirmative action. Militants on the left and on the right exerted unrelenting pressure on the White House, but Bush's shrewd decision to nominate John G. Roberts Jr., a socially conservative circuit court judge, stalemated critics because Roberts's legal credentials were impeccable. Yet the fractious cultural debates did not subside. No sooner had the Senate overwhelmingly confirmed Roberts (seventy-eight to twenty-two) than Chief Justice William Rehnquist died. Bush then named Roberts the new chief justice and nominated Harriet E. Miers, a longtime friend and former personal lawyer turned White House legal counsel, to replace O'Connor. Critics, many of them Republican conservatives, denounced Miers as a legal mediocrity and a presidential crony. The furor led Miers to withdraw her nomination in late October 2005, a humiliating development for President Bush that further hobbled his stalled legislative efforts. Her withdrawal coincided with the indictment of Vice President Richard Cheney's chief of staff, Lewis Libby, for perjury and obstruction of justice relating to an investigation of administration officials who purportedly had revealed the identity of a covert CIA agent in a supposed act of political revenge. To address concerns that the Bush administration was sputtering in its second term and heal the ruptures within the Republican coalition, Bush nominated to the Supreme Court Samuel Alito Jr., a federal judge and a favorite of conservatives.

HURRICANE KATRINA In the summer of 2005, President Bush's eroding public support suffered another blow, this time when a natural disaster turned into a political crisis. In late August a killer hurricane named Katrina slammed into the Gulf coast, devastating large areas of Alabama, Mississippi, and Louisiana. Coastal towns such as Gulfport and Biloxi, Mississippi, were blown away. The sultry metropolis of New Orleans was virtually destroyed as levees and flood walls holding back the Mississippi River and Lake Pontchartrain burst, inundating three quarters of the city, most of which is below sea level and below the Mississippi River.

New Orleans had always been at war with its environment. Since its founding in the early eighteenth century, the sodden city surrounded by mosquito-infested swamps and regularly visited by floods had placed its faith in engineering to keep back the surrounding water. This time nature

Hurricane Katrina

Cars and buildings are partially submerged on Canal Street, a central thoroughfare in New Orleans, September 3, 2005.

won. After Katrina roared through the city, whole neighborhoods lay underwater, often up to the roofline. Nearly 500,000 New Orleans residents were displaced, most of them poor and many of them African American. Looting was so widespread that officials declared martial law; the streets were awash with soldiers and police. Katrina's awful wake left over 1,000 people dead in three states and millions homeless and hopeless. "The magnitude of the situation is untenable," Louisiana's governor lamented. "It's just heartbreaking."

Local political officials and the Federal Emergency Management Agency (FEMA) were caught unprepared as the catastrophe unfolded. Disaster plans were incomplete; communication and coordination were sorely lacking; confusion and incompetence abounded. Evacuation plans proved faulty, and government red tape compounded the misery. A wave of public outrage crashed against the Bush administration. Republican senator David Vitter of Louisiana gave the federal relief effort "a failing grade, across the board." Already-high gasoline prices skyrocketed as the hurricane shut down refineries, oil platforms, and pipelines. In the face of blistering criticism,

President Bush accepted responsibility for the balky federal response to the disaster and accepted the resignation of the FEMA director. Rebuilding the Gulf coast would take a long time and a lot of money.

Hurricane Katrina was one of the worst natural disasters in American history. Although many thousands more people were killed in the hurricanes that destroyed Galveston, Texas, in 1900 and devastated the Lake Okeechobee area of Florida in 1928, the dollar cost of Katrina's fury was much greater. Experts predicted that it would take $200 billion to restore the Gulf coast. More worrisome were claims made by a growing number of scientists that the increasing frequency and potency of hurricanes were a dreadful manifestation of global warming, a controversial phenomenon supposedly caused by carbon dioxide emissions from industrial smokestacks and automobile exhaust rising into the atmosphere and depleting the earth's protective ozone layer. Depleted ozone causes the temperature of the earth and the oceans to rise, thereby affecting climate and, according to some scientists, making weather more extreme. Americans already insecure in the face of global terrorism wrestled with the anxiety of a planet suddenly turned unstable and unpredictable.

The havoc wreaked by Katrina was only partly the result of natural forces run amok, however. Environmental calamities usually expose human failings. And in washing away property and lives, Katrina revealed all the elements of a disaster waiting to happen: poor planning, social inequalities, embedded corruption, and racial injustice. The destruction of New Orleans could have been mitigated or avoided altogether if, for example, warnings about the weakness of the aging levees had been heeded. The failure of the levees revealed scandalous breaches in public policy and public leadership. New Orleans had come to depend upon the Army Corps of Engineers for its lifeline of levees and pumps designed to keep the Mississippi River and Lake Pontchartrain at bay. Yet the city's flood-control funding had been reduced by 44 percent since 2001. The weakening of wetlands protections to favor developers had also made the city far more vulnerable to the flood surge generated by hurricanes. Marshes absorb storm water, but much of the wetland surrounding New Orleans had disappeared as a result of strenuous efforts to reroute the Mississippi River in order to facilitate the passage of ships and, ironically, provide better flood control. Realigning the river had prevented silt from building up in the Delta and nourishing the wetlands. The natural calamity was made much worse by human action—and inaction.

A STALLED PRESIDENCY George Bush bore the brunt of public indignation over the federal response to the Katrina disaster. By the fall of 2006, the White House was beset by political problems, a sputtering economy, and growing public dissatisfaction with the president's performance. Bush's job-approval rating fell below 40 percent, an all-time low. Even his support among Republicans crumbled, and many social conservatives felt betrayed by his sporadic attention to their concerns. The editors of the *Economist*, an influential conservative newsmagazine, declared in June 2005 that Bush had become "the least popular re-elected president since Richard Nixon became embroiled in the Watergate fiasco." The skyrocketing gasoline prices and the federal budget deficit fueled public frustration. President Bush and Congress had overseen the largest increase in federal spending since Franklin Roosevelt. The president's efforts to reform the tax code, Social Security, and immigration laws languished during his second term, and the turmoil and violence in Iraq showed no signs of abating. Senator Chuck Hagel, a Nebraska Republican, declared in 2005 that "we're losing in Iraq." The drumbeat of disillusionment prompted President Bush to acknowledge "setbacks" in Iraq and flaws in the intelligence reports that provided the rationale for going to war. At the end of 2005, the embattled president visited the recovering Gulf coast. His purpose, explained an aide, was "to give people a sense of hope." George Bush might have done the same for his presidency. It, too, needed an infusion of hope and energy as he reached the midpoint of his second term.

FURTHER READING

On George H. W. Bush's presidency, see *Leadership and the Bush Presidency: Prudence or Drift in an Era of Change?* edited by Ryan J. Barilleaux and Mary E. Stuckey (1992) and Charles Tiefer's *The Semi-Sovereign Presidency: The Bush Administration's Strategy for Governing without Congress* (1994). Among the journalistic accounts of the presidential election of 1992, the best narrative is Jack W. Germond and Jules Witcover's *Mad as Hell: Revolt at the Ballot Box, 1992* (1993). The best scholarly study is Theodore J. Lowi and Benjamin Ginsberg's *Democrats Return to Power: Politics and Policy in the Clinton Era* (1994).

Analysis of the Clinton years can be found in Joe Klein's *The Natural: The Misunderstood Presidency of Bill Clinton* (2002). Clinton's impeachment is assessed in Richard A. Posner's *An Affair of State: The Investigation, Impeachment, and Trial of President Clinton* (1999).

On changing demographic trends, see Sam Roberts's *Who We Are Now: The Changing Face of America in the Twenty-First Century* (2004). On social and cultural life in the 1990s, see Haynes Johnson's *The Best of Times: Amer-*

ica in the Clinton Years (2001). The onset and growth of the AIDS epidemic are traced in *And the Band Played On: Politics, People, and the AIDS Epidemic* (1987) by Randy Shilts.

Aspects of fundamentalist and apocalyptic movements are the subject of Paul Boyer's *When Time Shall Be No More: Prophecy Belief in Modern American Culture* (1992), George M. Marsden's *Understanding Fundamentalism and Evangelicalism* (1991), and Ralph E. Reed's *Politically Incorrect: The Emerging Faith Factor in American Politics* (1994).

On the invention of the computer and the Internet, see Paul E. Ceruzzi's *A History of Modern Computing,* 2nd ed. (2003) and Janet Abbate's *Inventing the Internet* (1999). The booming economy of the 1990s is well analyzed in Joseph E. Stiglitz's *The Roaring Nineties: A New History of the World's Most Prosperous Decade* (2003). On the rising stress within the workplace, see Jill Andresky Fraser's *White-Collar Sweatshop: The Deterioration of Work and Its Rewards in Corporate America* (2001). Aspects of corporate restructuring and downsizing are the subject of Bennett Harrison's *Lean and Mean: The Changing Landscape of Corporate Power in the Age of Flexibility* (1994).

For further treatment of the end of the cold war, see Michael R. Beschloss's *At the Highest Levels: The Inside Story of the End of the Cold War* (1993) and Richard Crockatt's *The Fifty Years War: The United States and the Soviet Union in World Politics, 1941–1991* (1995). On the Persian Gulf conflict, see Lester H. Brune's *America and the Iraqi Crisis, 1990–1992: Origins and Aftermath* (1993). On the transformation of American foreign policy, see James Mann's *Rise of the Vulcans: The History of Bush's War Cabinet* (2004), Claes G. Ryn's *America the Virtuous: Crisis of Democracy and the Quest for Empire* (2003), and Stephen M. Walt's *Taming American Power: The Global Response to U.S. Primacy* (2005).

The disputed 2000 presidential election is the focus of Jeffrey Toobin's *Too Close to Call: The Thirty-Six-Day Battle to Decide the 2000 Election* (2001). On the attacks of September 11, 2001, and their aftermath, see *The Age of Terror: America and the World after September 11,* edited by Strobe Talbott and Nayan Chanda (2001).

GLOSSARY

Agricultural Adjustment Act (1933) New Deal legislation that established the Agricultural Adjustment Administration (AAA) to improve agricultural prices by limiting market supplies; declared unconstitutional in *United States v. Butler* (1936).

Alamo, Battle of the Siege in the Texas War for Independence, 1836, in which the San Antonio mission fell to the Mexicans, and Davy Crockett and Jim Bowie died.

***Alexander v. Holmes County Board of Education* (1969)** Case fifteen years after the *Brown* decision in which the U.S. Supreme Court ordered an immediate end to segregation in public schools.

Alien and Sedition Acts (1798) Four measures passed during the undeclared war with France that limited the freedoms of speech and press and restricted the liberty of noncitizens.

America First Committee Largely midwestern isolationist organization supported by many prominent citizens, 1940–41.

American Anti-Slavery Society National abolitionist organization founded in 1833 by New York philanthropists Arthur and Lewis Tappan, propagandist Theodore Dwight Weld, and others.

American Colonization Society Organized in 1816 to encourage colonization of free blacks to Africa; West African nation of Liberia founded in 1822 to serve as a homeland for them.

American Federation of Labor Founded in 1881 as a federation of trade unions, the AFL under president Samuel Gompers successfully pushed for the eight-hour workday.

American Protective Association Nativist, anti-Catholic secret society founded in Iowa in 1887 and active until the end of the century.

American System Program of internal improvements and protective tariffs promoted by Speaker of the House Henry Clay in his presidential campaign of 1824; his proposals formed the core of Whig ideology in the 1830s and 1840s.

Antietam, Battle of (Battle of Sharpsburg) One of the bloodiest battles of the Civil War, fought to a standoff on September 17, 1862, in western Maryland.

Anti-Federalists Forerunners of Thomas Jefferson's Democratic-Republican party; opposed the Constitution as a limitation on individual and states' rights, which led to the addition of a Bill of Rights to the document.

Appomattox Court House, Virginia Site of the surrender of Confederate general Robert E. Lee to Union general Ulysses S. Grant on April 9, 1865, marking the end of the Civil War.

Army-McCarthy hearings Televised U.S. Senate hearings in 1954 on Senator Joseph McCarthy's charges of disloyalty in the Army; his tactics contributed to his censure by the Senate.

Atlanta Compromise Speech to the Cotton States and International Exposition in 1895 by educator Booker T. Washington, the leading black spokesman of the day; black scholar W. E. B. Du Bois gave the speech its derisive name and criticized Washington for encouraging blacks to accommodate segregation and disenfranchisement.

Atlantic Charter Issued August 12, 1941, following meetings in Newfoundland between President Franklin D. Roosevelt and British prime minister Winston Churchill, the charter signaled the allies' cooperation and stated their war aims.

Atomic Energy Commission Created in 1946 to supervise peacetime uses of atomic energy.

Axis powers In World War II, the nations of Germany, Italy, and Japan.

Aztec Mesoamerican people who were conquered by the Spanish under Hernando Cortés, 1519–28.

baby boom Markedly higher birth rate in the years following World War II; led to the biggest demographic "bubble" in American history.

Bacon's Rebellion Unsuccessful 1676 revolt led by planter Nathaniel Bacon against Virginia governor William Berkeley's administration because it had failed to protect settlers from Indian raids.

***Bakke v. Board of Regents of California* (1978)** Case in which the U.S. Supreme Court ruled against the California university system's use of racial quotas in admissions.

balance of trade Ratio of imports to exports.

Bank of the United States Proposed by the first secretary of the treasury, Alexander Hamilton, the bank opened in 1791 and operated until 1811 to issue a uniform currency, make business loans, and collect tax monies. The Second Bank of the United States was chartered in 1816 but was not renewed by President Andrew Jackson twenty years later.

barbary pirates Plundering pirates off the Mediterranean coast of Africa; President Thomas Jefferson's refusal to pay them tribute to protect American ships sparked an undeclared naval war with North African nations, 1801–1805.

barbed wire First practical fencing material for the Great Plains was invented in 1873 and rapidly spelled the end of the open range.

Battle of the Currents Conflict in the late 1880s between inventors Thomas Edison and George Westinghouse over direct versus alternating electric current; Westinghouse's alternating current (AC), the winner, allowed electricity to travel over long distances.

Bay of Pigs Invasion Hoping to inspire a revolt against Fidel Castro, the CIA sent 1,500 Cuban exiles to invade their homeland on April 17, 1961, but the mission was a spectacular failure.

Bill of Rights First ten amendments to the U.S. Constitution, adopted in 1791 to guarantee individual rights and to help secure ratification of the Constitution by the states.

Black Codes (1865–66) Laws passed in southern states to restrict the rights of former slaves; to combat the codes, Congress passed the Civil Rights Act of 1866 and the Fourteenth Amendment and set up military governments in southern states that refused to ratify the amendment.

Black Power Post-1966 rallying cry of a more militant civil rights movement.

Bland-Allison Act (1878) Passed over President Rutherford B. Hayes's veto, the inflationary measure authorized the purchase each month of 2 to 4 million dollars' worth of silver for coinage.

"Bleeding" Kansas Violence between pro- and antislavery settlers in the Kansas Territory, 1856.

Bloody Shirt, Waving the Republican references to Reconstruction-era violence in the South, used effectively in northern political campaigns against Democrats.

Bonus Expeditionary Force Thousands of World War I veterans, who insisted on immediate payment of their bonus certificates, marched on Washington in 1932; violence ensued when President Herbert Hoover ordered their tent villages cleared.

Boston Massacre Clash between British soldiers and a Boston mob, March 5, 1770, in which five colonists were killed.

Boston Tea Party On December 16, 1773, the Sons of Liberty, dressed as Indians, dumped hundreds of chests of tea into Boston harbor to protest the Tea Act of 1773, under which the British exported to the colonies millions of pounds of cheap—but still taxed—tea, thereby undercutting the price of smuggled tea and forcing payment of the tea duty.

Boxer Rebellion Chinese nationalist protest against Western commercial domination and cultural influence, 1900; a coalition of American, European, and Japanese forces put down the rebellion and reclaimed captured embassies in Peking (Beijing) within the year.

brain trust Group of advisers—many of them academics—that Franklin D. Roosevelt assembled to recommend New Deal policies during the early months of his presidency.

Branch Davidians Religious cult that lived communally near Waco, Texas, and was involved in a fiery 1993 confrontation with federal authorities in which dozens of cult members died.

Brook Farm Transcendentalist commune in West Roxbury, Massachusetts, populated from 1841 to 1847 principally by writers (Nathaniel Hawthorne, for one) and other intellectuals.

***Brown v. Board of Education of Topeka* (1954)** U.S. Supreme Court decision that struck down racial segregation in public education and declared "separate but equal" unconstitutional.

Budget and Accounting Act of 1921 Created the Bureau of the Budget and the General Accounting Office.

Bull Run, Battles of (First and Second Manassas) First land engagement of the Civil War took place on July 21, 1861, at Manassas Junction, Virginia, at which surprised Union troops quickly retreated; one year later, on August 29–30, Confederates captured the federal supply depot and forced Union troops back to Washington.

Bunker Hill, Battle of First major battle of the Revolutionary War; it actually took place at nearby Breed's Hill, Massachusetts, on June 17, 1775.

"Burned-Over District" Area of western New York strongly influenced by the revivalist fervor of the Second Great Awakening; Disciples of Christ and Mormons are among the many sects that trace their roots to the phenomenon.

Burr conspiracy Scheme by Vice-President Aaron Burr to lead the secession of the Louisiana Territory from the United States; captured in 1807 and charged with treason, Burr was acquitted by the U.S. Supreme Court.

***Bush v. Gore* (2000)** U.S. Supreme Court case that determined the winner of the disputed 2000 presidential election.

Calhoun Resolutions In making the proslavery response to the Wilmot Proviso, Senator John C. Calhoun argued that barring slavery in Mexican acquisitions would violate the Fifth Amendment to the Constitution by depriving slaveholding settlers of their property.

Calvinism Doctrine of predestination expounded by Swiss theologian John Calvin in 1536; influenced the Puritan, Presbyterian, German and Dutch Reformed, and Huguenot churches in the colonies.

Camp David Accords Peace agreement between Israeli prime minister Menachem Begin and Egyptian president Anwar Sadat, brokered by President Jimmy Carter in 1978.

carpetbaggers Northern emigrants who participated in the Republican governments of the Reconstruction South.

Chancellorsville, Battle of Confederate general Robert E. Lee won his last major victory and General "Stonewall" Jackson died in this Civil War battle in northern Virginia on May 1–4, 1863.

Chattanooga, Battle of Union victory in eastern Tennessee on November 23–25, 1863; gave the North control of important rail lines and cleared the way for General William T. Sherman's march into Georgia.

Chinese Exclusion Act (1882) Halted Chinese immigration to the United States.

Civil Rights Act of 1866 Along with the Fourteenth Amendment, guaranteed the rights of citizenship to freedmen.

Civil Rights Act of 1957 First federal civil rights law since Reconstruction; established the Civil Rights Commission and the Civil Rights Division of the Department of Justice.

Civil Rights Act of 1964 Outlawed discrimination in public accommodations and employment.

clipper ships Superior oceangoing sailing ships of the 1840s to 1860s that cut travel time in half; the clipper ship route around Cape Horn was the fastest way to travel between the coasts of the United States.

closed shop Hiring requirement that all workers in a business must be union members.

Coercive Acts/Intolerable Acts (1774) Four parliamentary measures in reaction to the Boston Tea Party that forced payment for the tea, disallowed colonial trials of British soldiers, forced their quartering in private homes, and set up a military government.

cold war Term for tensions, 1945–89, between the Soviet Union and the United States, the two major world powers after World War II.

***Commonwealth v. Hunt* (1842)** Landmark ruling of the Massachusetts supreme court establishing the legality of labor unions.

Compromise of 1850 Complex compromise mediated by Senator Henry Clay that headed off southern secession over California statehood; to appease the South it included a stronger fugitive slave law and delayed determination of the slave status of the New Mexico and Utah territories.

Compromise of 1877 Deal made by a special congressional commission on March 2, 1877, to resolve the disputed presidential election of 1876; Republican Rutherford B. Hayes, who had lost the popular vote, was declared the winner in exchange for the withdrawal of federal troops from the South, marking the end of Reconstruction.

Congress of Industrial Organizations (CIO) Umbrella organization of semi-skilled industrial unions, formed in 1935 as the Committee for Industrial Organization and renamed in 1938.

Congress of Racial Equality (CORE) Civil rights organization started in 1944 and best known for its "freedom rides," bus journeys challenging racial segregation in the South in 1961.

conspicuous consumption Phrase referring to extravagant spending to raise social standing, coined by Thorstein Veblen in *The Theory of the Leisure Class* (1899).

Constitutional Convention Meeting in Philadelphia, May 25–September 17, 1787, of representatives from twelve colonies—excepting Rhode Island—to revise the existing Articles of Confederation; convention soon resolved to produce an entirely new constitution.

containment General U.S. strategy in the cold war that called for containing Soviet expansion; originally devised in 1947 by U.S. diplomat George F. Kennan.

Continental Army Army authorized by the Continental Congress, 1775–84, to fight the British; commanded by General George Washington.

Continental Congress Representatives of a loose confederation of colonies met first in Philadelphia in 1774 to formulate actions against British policies; the Second Continental Congress (1775–89) conducted the war and adopted the Declaration of Independence and the Articles of Confederation.

convict leasing System developed in the post–Civil War South that generated income for the states and satisfied planters' need for cheap labor by renting prisoners out; the convicts, however, were often treated poorly.

Copperheads Northerners opposed to the Civil War.

Coral Sea, Battle of the Fought on May 7–8, 1942, near the eastern coast of Australia, it was the first U.S. naval victory over Japan in World War II.

cotton gin Invented by Eli Whitney in 1793, the machine separated cotton seed from cotton fiber, speeding cotton processing and making profitable the cultivation of the more hardy, but difficult to clean, short-staple cotton; led directly to the dramatic nineteenth-century expansion of slavery in the South.

counterculture "Hippie" youth culture of the 1960s, which rejected the values of the dominant culture in favor of illicit drugs, communes, free sex, and rock music.

court-packing plan President Franklin D. Roosevelt's failed 1937 attempt to increase the number of U.S. Supreme Court justices from nine to fifteen in order to save his Second New Deal programs from constitutional challenges.

Credit Mobilier scandal Millions of dollars in overcharges for building the Union Pacific Railroad were exposed; high officials of the Ulysses S. Grant administration were implicated but never charged.

Cuban missile crisis Caused when the United States discovered Soviet offensive missile sites in Cuba in October 1962; the U.S.-Soviet confrontation was the cold war's closest brush with nuclear war.

crop-lien system Merchants extended credit to tenants based on their future crops, but high interest rates and the uncertainties of farming often led to inescapable debts (debt peonage).

D-Day June 6, 1944, when an Allied amphibious assault landed on the Normandy coast and established a foothold in Europe from which Hitler's defenses could not recover.

***Dartmouth College v. Woodward* (1819)** U.S. Supreme Court upheld the original charter of the college against New Hampshire's attempt to alter the board of trustees; set precedent of support of contracts against state interference.

Declaration of Independence Document adopted on July 4, 1776, that made the break with Britain official; drafted by a committee of the Second Continental Congress including principal writer Thomas Jefferson.

Deism Enlightenment thought applied to religion; emphasized reason, morality, and natural law.

Department of Homeland Security Created to coordinate federal antiterrorist activity following the 2001 terrorist attacks on the World Trade Center and Pentagon.

Depression of 1893 Worst depression of the century, set off by a railroad failure, too much speculation on Wall Street, and low agricultural prices.

Dixiecrats Deep South delegates who walked out of the 1948 Democratic National Convention in protest of the party's support for civil rights legislation and later formed the States' Rights (Dixiecrat) party, which nominated Strom Thurmond of South Carolina for president.

Dominion of New England Consolidation into a single colony of the New England colonies—and later New York and New Jersey—by royal governor Edmund Andros in 1686; dominion reverted to individual colonial governments three years later.

Donner Party Forty-seven surviving members of a group of migrants to California were forced to resort to cannibalism to survive a brutal winter trapped in the Sierra Nevadas, 1846–47; highest death toll of any group traveling the Overland Trail.

***Dred Scott v. Sandford* (1857)** U.S. Supreme Court decision in which Chief Justice Roger B. Taney ruled that slaves could not sue for freedom and that Congress could not prohibit slavery in the territories, on the grounds that such a prohibition would violate the Fifth Amendment rights of slaveholders.

due-process clause Clause in the Fifth and the Fourteenth amendments to the U.S. Constitution guaranteeing that states could not "deprive any person of life, liberty, or property, without due process of law."

Dust Bowl Great Plains counties where millions of tons of topsoil were blown away from parched farmland in the 1930s; massive migration of farm families followed.

Eighteenth Amendment (1919) Prohibition amendment that made illegal the manufacture, sale, or transportation of alcoholic beverages.

Ellis Island Reception center in New York Harbor through which most European immigrants to America were processed from 1892 to 1954.

Emancipation Proclamation (1863) President Abraham Lincoln issued a preliminary proclamation on September 22, 1862, freeing the slaves in the Confederate states as of January 1, 1863, the date of the final proclamation.

Embargo Act of 1807 Attempt to exert economic pressure instead of waging war in reaction to continued British impressment of American sailors; smugglers easily circumvented the embargo, and it was repealed two years later.

Emergency Banking Relief Act (1933) First New Deal measure that provided for reopening the banks under strict conditions and took the United States off the gold standard.

Emergency Immigration Act of 1921 Limited U.S. immigration to 3 percent of each foreign-born nationality in the 1910 census; three years later Congress restricted immigration even further.

encomienda System under which officers of the Spanish conquistadores gained ownership of Indian land.

ENIAC Electronic Numerical Integrator and Computer, built in 1944, the early, cumbersome ancestor of the modern computer.

Enlightenment Revolution in thought begun in the seventeenth century that emphasized reason and science over the authority of traditional religion.

Enola Gay American B-29 bomber that dropped the atomic bomb on Hiroshima, Japan, on August 6, 1945.

Environmental Protection Agency (EPA) Created in 1970 during the first administration of President Richard M. Nixon to oversee federal pollution control efforts.

Equal Rights Amendment Amendment to guarantee equal rights for women, introduced in 1923 but not passed by Congress until 1972; it failed to be ratified by the states.

Era of Good Feelings Contemporary characterization of the administration of popular Democratic-Republican president James Monroe, 1817–25.

Erie Canal Most important and profitable of the barge canals of the 1820s and 1830s; stretched from Buffalo to Albany, New York, connecting the Great Lakes to the East Coast and making New York City the nation's largest port.

Espionage and Sedition Acts (1917–18) Limited criticism of government leaders and policies by imposing fines and prison terms on those who acted out in opposition to in the First World War; the most repressive measures passed up to that time.

Fair Deal Domestic reform proposals of the second Truman administration (1949–53); included civil rights legislation and repeal of the Taft-Hartley Act, but only extensions of some New Deal programs were enacted.

Fair Employment Practices Commission Created in 1941 by executive order, the FEPC sought to eliminate racial discrimination in jobs; it possessed little power but represented a step toward civil rights for African Americans.

Family and Medical Leave Act (1993) Allowed certain workers to take twelve weeks of unpaid leave each year for family health problems, including birth or adoption of a child.

Farmers' Alliance Two separate organizations (Northwestern and Southern) of the 1880s and 1890s that took the place of the Grange, worked for similar causes, and attracted landless, as well as landed, farmers to their membership.

Federal Trade Commission Act (1914) Established the Federal Trade Commission to enforce existing antitrust laws that prohibited business combinations in restraint of trade.

The Federalist Collection of eighty-five essays that appeared in the New York press in 1787–88 in support of the Constitution; written by Alexander Hamilton, James Madison, and John Jay but published under the pseudonym "Publius."

Federalist party One of the two first national political parties, it favored a strong central government.

Fence-Cutters' War Violent conflict in Texas, 1883–84, between large and small cattle ranchers over access to grazing land.

"Fifty-four forty or fight" Democratic campaign slogan in the presidential election of 1844, urging that the northern border of Oregon be fixed at 54°40′ north latitude.

***Fletcher v. Peck* (1810)** U.S. Supreme Court decision in which Chief Justice John Marshall upheld the initial fraudulent sale contracts in the Yazoo Fraud cases; Congress paid $4.2 million to the original speculators in 1814.

Fort Laramie Treaty (1851) Restricted the Plains Indians from using the Overland Trail and permitted the building of government forts.

Fort McHenry Fort in Baltimore Harbor unsuccessfully bombarded by the British in September 1814; Francis Scott Key, a witness to the battle, was moved to write the words to "The Star-Spangled Banner."

Fort Sumter First battle of the Civil War, in which the federal fort in Charleston (South Carolina) Harbor was captured by the Confederates on April 14, 1861, after two days of shelling.

"forty-niners" Speculators who went to northern California following the discovery of gold in 1848; the first of several years of large-scale migration was 1849.

Fourteen Points President Woodrow Wilson's 1918 plan for peace after World War I; at the Versailles peace conference, however, he failed to incorporate all of the points into the treaty.

Fourteenth Amendment (1868) Guaranteed rights of citizenship to former slaves, in words similar to those of the Civil Rights Act of 1866.

franchise The right to vote.

"free person of color" Negro or mulatto person not held in slavery; immediately before the Civil War, there were nearly a half million in the United States, split almost evenly between North and South.

Free Soil party Formed in 1848 to oppose slavery in the territory acquired in the Mexican War; nominated Martin Van Buren for president in 1848, but by 1854 most of the party's members had joined the Republican party.

Free Speech Movement Founded in 1964 at the University of California at Berkeley by student radicals protesting restrictions on their right to demonstrate.

Freedmen's Bureau Reconstruction agency established in 1865 to protect the legal rights of former slaves and to assist with their education, jobs, health care, and landowning.

French and Indian War Known in Europe as the Seven Years' War, the last (1755–63) of four colonial wars fought between England and France for control of North America east of the Mississippi River.

Fugitive Slave Act of 1850 Gave federal government authority in cases involving runaway slaves; so much more punitive and prejudiced in favor of slaveholders than the 1793 Fugitive Slave Act had been that Harriet Beecher Stowe was inspired to write *Uncle Tom's Cabin* in protest; the new law was part of the Compromise of 1850, included to appease the South over the admission of California as a free state.

Fundamentalism Anti-modernist Protestant movement started in the early twentieth century that proclaimed the literal truth of the Bible; the name came from *The Fundamentals*, published by conservative leaders.

Gadsden Purchase (1853) Thirty thousand square miles in present-day Arizona and New Mexico bought by Congress from Mexico primarily for the Southern Pacific Railroad's transcontinental route.

Gentlemen's Agreement (1907) United States would not exclude Japanese immigrants if Japan would voluntarily limit the number of immigrants coming to the United States.

Gettysburg, Battle of Fought in southern Pennsylvania, July 1–3, 1863; the Confederate defeat and the simultaneous loss at Vicksburg spelled the end of the South's chances in the Civil War.

***Gibbons v. Ogden* (1824)** U.S. Supreme Court decision reinforcing the "commerce clause" (the federal government's right to regulate interstate commerce) of the Constitution; Chief Justice John Marshall ruled against the State of New York's granting of steamboat monopolies.

***Gideon v. Wainwright* (1963)** U.S. Supreme Court decision guaranteeing legal counsel for indigent felony defendants.

The Gilded Age Mark Twain and Charles Dudley Warner's 1873 novel, the title of which became the popular name for the period from the end of the Civil War to the turn of the century.

Glass-Owen Federal Reserve Act (1913) Created a Federal Reserve System of regional banks and a Federal Reserve Board to stabilize the economy by regulating the supply of currency and controlling credit.

Glass-Steagall Act (Banking Act of 1933) Established the Federal Deposit Insurance Corporation and included banking reforms, some designed to control speculation. A banking act of the Hoover administration, passed in 1932 and also known as the Glass-Steagall Act, was designed to expand credit.

Good Neighbor Policy Proclaimed by President Franklin D. Roosevelt in his first inaugural address in 1933, it sought improved diplomatic relations between the United States and its Latin American neighbors.

grandfather clause Loophole created by southern disfranchising legislatures of the 1890s for illiterate white males whose grandfathers had been eligible to vote in 1867.

Granger movement Political movement that grew out of the Patrons of Husbandry, an educational and social organization for farmers founded in 1867; the Grange had its greatest success in the Midwest of the 1870s, lobbying for government control of railroad and grain elevator rates and establishing farmers' cooperatives.

Great Awakening Fervent religious revival movement in the 1720s through the 1740s that was spread throughout the colonies by ministers like New England Congregationalist Jonathan Edwards and English revivalist George Whitefield.

Great Compromise (Connecticut Compromise) Mediated the differences between the New Jersey and Virginia delegations to the Constitutional Convention by providing for a bicameral legislature, the upper house of which would have equal representation and the lower house of which would be apportioned by population.

Great Depression Worst economic depression in American history; it was spurred by the stock market crash of 1929 and lasted until World War II.

Great Migration Large-scale migration of southern blacks during and after World War I to the North, where jobs had become available during the labor shortage of the war years.

Great Society Term coined by President Lyndon B. Johnson in his 1965 State of the Union address, in which he proposed legislation to address problems of voting rights, poverty, diseases, education, immigration, and the environment.

Greenback party Formed in 1876 in reaction to economic depression, the party favored issuance of unsecured paper money to help farmers repay debts; the movement for free coinage of silver took the place of the greenback movement by the 1880s.

habeas corpus, writ of An essential component of English common law and of the U.S. Constitution that guarantees that citizens may not be imprisoned without due process of law; literally means, "you must have the body."

Half-Breeds During the presidency of Rutherford B. Hayes, 1877–81, a moderate Republican party faction led by Senator James G. Blaine that favored some reforms of the civil service system and a restrained policy toward the defeated South.

Harlem Renaissance African-American literary and artistic movement of the 1920s and 1930s centered in New York City's Harlem district; writers Langston Hughes, Jean Toomer, Zora Neale Hurston, and Countee Cullen were among those active in the movement.

Harpers Ferry, Virginia Site of abolitionist John Brown's failed raid on the federal arsenal, October 16–17, 1859; he intended to arm the slaves, but ten of his compatriots were killed, and Brown became a martyr to his cause after his capture and execution.

Hartford Convention Meeting of New England Federalists on December 15, 1814, to protest the War of 1812; proposed seven constitutional amendments (limiting embargoes and changing requirements for officeholding, declaration of war, and admission of new states), but the war ended before Congress could respond.

Hawley-Smoot Tariff Act (1930) Raised tariffs to an unprecedented level and worsened the depression by raising prices and discouraging foreign trade.

Haymarket Affair Riot during an anarchist protest at Haymarket Square in Chicago on May 4, 1886, over violence during the McCormick Harvester Company strike; the deaths of eleven, including seven policemen, helped hasten the demise of the Knights of Labor, even though they were not responsible for the riot.

Hessians German soldiers, most from Hesse-Cassel principality (hence the name), paid to fight for the British in the Revolutionary War.

holding company Investment company that holds controlling interest in the securities of other companies.

Homestead Act (1862) Authorized Congress to grant 160 acres of public land to a western settler, who had only to live on the land for five years to establish title.

Homestead Strike Violent strike at the Carnegie Steel Company near Pittsburgh in 1892 that culminated in the disintegration of the Amalgamated Association of Iron and Steel Workers, the first steelworkers' union.

House Un-American Activities Committee (HUAC) Formed in 1938 to investigate subversives in the government; best-known investigations were of Hollywood no tables and of former State Department official Alger Hiss, who was accused in 1948 of espionage and Communist party membership.

Hundred Days Extraordinarily productive first three months of President Franklin D. Roosevelt's administration in which a special session of Congress enacted fifteen of his New Deal proposals.

impeachment Bringing charges against a public official; for example, the House of Representatives can impeach a president for "treason, bribery, or other high crimes and misdemeanors" by majority vote, and after the trial the Senate can remove the president by a vote of two-thirds.

implied powers Federal powers beyond those specifically enumerated in the U.S. Constitution; the Federalists argued that the "elastic clause" of Article I, Section 8, of the Constitution implicitly gave the federal government broad powers, while the Antifederalists held that the federal government's powers were explicitly limited by the Constitution.

"In God We Trust" Phrase placed on all new U.S. currency as of 1954.

indentured servant Settler who signed on for a temporary period of servitude to a master in exchange for passage to the New World; Virginia and Pennsylvania were largely peopled in the seventeenth and eighteenth centuries by English indentured servants.

Independent Treasury Act (1840) Promoted by President Martin Van Buren, the measure sought to stabilize the economy by preventing state banks from printing unsecured paper currency and establishing an independent treasury based on specie.

Indian Peace Commission Established in 1867 to end the Indian wars in the West, the commission's solution was to contain the Indians in a system of reservations.

Indian Removal Act (1830) Signed by President Andrew Jackson, the law permitted the negotiation of treaties to obtain the Indians' lands in exchange for their relocation to what would become Oklahoma.

Industrial Workers of the World Radical union organized in Chicago in 1905 and nicknamed the Wobblies; its opposition to World War I led to its destruction by the federal government under the Espionage Act.

internal improvements In the early national period the phrase referred to road building and the development of water transportation.

Interstate Commerce Commission Reacting to the U.S. Supreme Court's ruling in *Wabash Railroad* v. *Illinois* (1886), Congress established the ICC to curb abuses in the railroad industry by regulating rates.

Iran-Contra affair Scandal of the second Reagan administration involving sale of arms to Iran in partial exchange for release of hostages in Lebanon and use of the arms money to aid the Contras in Nicaragua, which had been expressly forbidden by Congress.

Iron Curtain Term coined by Winston Churchill to describe the cold war divide between western Europe and the Soviet Union's eastern European satellites.

Irreconcilables Group of isolationist U.S. senators who fought ratification of the Treaty of Versailles, 1919–20, because of their opposition to American membership in the League of Nations.

Jamestown, Virginia Site in 1607 of the first permanent English settlement in the New World.

Jay's Treaty Treaty with Britain negotiated in 1794 by Chief Justice John Jay; Britain agreed to vacate forts in the Northwest Territories, and festering disagreements (border with Canada, prewar debts, shipping claims) would be settled by commission.

Jim Crow Minstrel show character whose name became synonymous with post-Reconstruction laws revoking civil rights for freedmen and with racial segregation generally.

Judiciary Act of 1801 Enacted by the lame duck Congress to allow the Federalists, the losing party in the presidential election, to reorganize the judiciary and fill the open judgeships with Federalists.

Kansas-Nebraska Act (1854) Law sponsored by Illinois senator Stephen A. Douglas to allow settlers in newly organized territories north of the Missouri border to decide the slavery issue for themselves; fury over the resulting nullification of the Missouri Compromise of 1820 led to violence in Kansas and to the formation of the Republican party.

Kellogg-Briand Pact Representatives of sixty-two nations in 1928 signed the pact (also called the Pact of Paris) to outlaw war.

Kentucky and Virginia Resolutions (1798–99) Passed in response to the Alien and Sedition Acts, the resolutions advanced the state-compact theory that held states could nullify an act of Congress if they deemed it unconstitutional.

King William's War (War of the League of Augsburg) First (1689–97) of four colonial wars between England and France.

King's Mountain, Battle of Upcountry South Carolina irregulars defeated British troops under Patrick Ferguson on October 7, 1780, in what proved to be the turning point of the Revolutionary War in the South.

Knights of Labor Founded in 1869, the first national union picked up many members after the disastrous 1877 railroad strike but lasted, under the leadership of Terence V. Powderly, only into the 1890s; supplanted by the American Federation of Labor.

Know-Nothing (American) party Nativist, anti-Catholic third party organized in 1854 in reaction to large-scale German and Irish immigration; the party's only presidential candidate was Millard Fillmore in 1856.

Korean War Conflict touched off in 1950 when Communist North Korea invaded South Korea, which had been under U.S. control since the end of World War II; fighting largely by U.S. forces continued until 1953.

Ku Klux Klan Organized in Pulaski, Tennessee, in 1866 to terrorize former slaves who voted and held political offices during Reconstruction; a revived organization in the 1910s and 1920s stressed white, Anglo-Saxon, fundamentalist Protestant supremacy; the Klan revived a third time to fight the civil rights movement of the 1950s and 1960s in the South.

Land Ordinance of 1785 Directed surveying of the Northwest Territory into townships of thirty-six sections (square miles) each, the sale of the sixteenth section of which was to be used to finance public education.

League of Nations Organization of nations to mediate disputes and avoid war established after World War I as part of the Treaty of Versailles; President Woodrow Wilson's "Fourteen Points" speech to Congress in 1918 proposed the formation of the league.

Lecompton Constitution Controversial constitution drawn up in 1857 by proslavery Kansas delegates seeking statehood; rejected in 1858 by an overwhelmingly antislavery electorate.

Legal Tender Act (1862) Helped the U.S. government pay for the Civil War by authorizing the printing of paper currency.

Lend-Lease Act (1941) Permitted the United States to lend or lease arms and other supplies to the Allies, signifying increasing likelihood of American involvement in World War II.

Levittown Low-cost, mass-produced development of suburban tract housing built by William Levitt on Long Island in 1947.

Lexington and Concord, Battle of The first shots fired in the Revolutionary War, on April 19, 1775, near Boston; approximately 100 minutemen and 250 British soldiers were killed.

Leyte Gulf, Battle of Largest sea battle in history, fought on October 25, 1944, and won by the United States off the Philippine island of Leyte; Japanese losses were so great that they could not rebound.

Liberty party Abolitionist political party that nominated James G. Birney for president in 1840 and 1844; merged with the Free Soil party in 1848.

Lincoln-Douglas debates Series of senatorial campaign debates in 1858 focusing on the issue of slavery in the territories; held in Illinois between Republican Abraham Lincoln, who made a national reputation for himself, and incumbent Democratic senator Stephen A. Douglas, who managed to hold onto his seat.

Little Bighorn, Battle of Most famous battle of the Great Sioux War took place in 1876 in the Montana Territory; combined Sioux and Cheyenne warriors massacred a vastly outnumbered U.S. Cavalry commanded by Lieutenant Colonel George Armstrong Custer.

Lost Colony English expedition of 117 settlers, including Virginia Dare, the first English child born in the New World; colony disappeared from Roanoke Island in the Outer Banks sometime between 1587 and 1590.

Louisiana Purchase President Thomas Jefferson's 1803 purchase from France of the important port of New Orleans and 828,000 square miles west of the Mississippi River to the Rocky Mountains; it more than doubled the territory of the United States at a cost of only $15 million.

Lusitania British passenger liner sunk by a German U-boat, May 7, 1915, creating a diplomatic crisis and public outrage at the loss of 128 Americans (roughly 10 percent of the total aboard); Germany agreed to pay reparations, and the United States waited two more years to enter World War I.

Lyceum movement Founded in 1826, the movement promoted adult public education through lectures and performances.

maize Indian corn, native to the New World.

Manhattan Project Secret American plan during World War II to develop an atomic bomb; J. Robert Oppenheimer led the team of physicists at Los Alamos, New Mexico.

Manifest Destiny Imperialist phrase first used in 1845 to urge annexation of Texas; used thereafter to encourage American settlement of European colonial and Indian lands in the Great Plains and Far West.

Marbury v. Madison **(1803)** First U.S. Supreme Court decision to declare a federal law—the Judiciary Act of 1801—unconstitutional; President John Adams's "midnight appointment" of Federalist judges prompted the suit.

March on Washington Civil rights demonstration on August 28, 1963, where the Reverend Martin Luther King, Jr., gave his "I Have a Dream" speech on the steps of the Lincoln Memorial.

Marshall Plan U.S. program for the reconstruction of post–World War II Europe through massive aid to former enemy nations as well as allies; proposed by General George C. Marshall in 1947.

massive resistance In reaction to the *Brown* decision of 1954, U.S. senator Harry Byrd encouraged southern states to defy federally mandated school integration.

Maya Pre-Columbian society in Mesoamerica before about A.D. 900.

Mayflower Compact Signed in 1620 aboard the *Mayflower* before the Pilgrims landed at Plymouth, the document committed the group to majority-rule government; remained in effect until 1691.

Maysville Road Bill Federal funding for a Kentucky road, vetoed by President Andrew Jackson in 1830.

McCarran Internal Security Act (1950) Passed over President Harry S. Truman's veto, the law required registration of American Communist party members, denied them passports, and allowed them to be detained as suspected subversives.

McCulloch v. Maryland **(1819)** U.S. Supreme Court decision in which Chief Justice John Marshall, holding that Maryland could not tax the Second Bank of the United States, supported the authority of the federal government versus the states.

McNary-Haugen Bill Vetoed by President Calvin Coolidge in 1927 and 1928, the bill to aid farmers would have artificially raised agricultural prices by selling surpluses overseas for low prices and selling the reduced supply in the United States for higher prices.

Meat Inspection Act (1906) Passed largely in reaction to Upton Sinclair's *The Jungle,* the law set strict standards of cleanliness in the meatpacking industry.

mercantilism Limitation and exploitation of colonial trade by an imperial power.

Mestizo Person of mixed Native American and European ancestry.

Mexican War Controversial war with Mexico for control of California and New Mexico, 1846–48; the Treaty of Guadalupe Hidalgo fixed the border at the Rio Grande and extended the United States to the Pacific coast, annexing more than a half-million square miles of potential slave territory.

Midway, Battle of Decisive American victory near Midway Island in the South Pacific on June 4, 1942; the Japanese navy never recovered its superiority over the U.S. navy.

Military Reconstruction Act (1867) Established military governments in ten Confederate states—excepting Tennessee—and required that the states ratify the Fourteenth Amendment and permit freedmen to vote.

minstrel show Blackface vaudeville entertainment popular in the decades surrounding the Civil War.

Miranda v. Arizona **(1966)** U.S. Supreme Court decision required police to advise persons in custody of their rights to legal counsel and against self-incrimination.

Missouri Compromise Deal proposed by Kentucky senator Henry Clay to resolve the slave/free imbalance in Congress that would result from Missouri's admission as a slave state; in the compromise of March 20, 1820, Maine's admission as a free state offset Missouri, and slavery was prohibited in the remainder of the Louisiana Territory north of the southern border of Missouri.

Molly Maguires Secret organization of Irish coal miners that used violence to intimidate mine officials in the 1870s.

Monitor **and** *Merrimack,* **Battle of the** First engagement between ironclad ships; fought at Hampton Roads, Virginia, on March 9, 1862.

Monroe Doctrine President James Monroe's declaration to Congress on December 2, 1823, that the American continents would be thenceforth closed to colonization but that the United States would honor existing colonies of European nations.

Moral Majority Televangelist Jerry Falwell's political lobbying organization, the name of which became synonymous with the religious right—conservative evangelical Protestants who helped ensure President Ronald Reagan's 1980 victory.

Mormons Founded in 1830 by Joseph Smith, the sect (officially, the Church of Jesus Christ of Latter-Day Saints) was a product of the intense revivalism of the "Burned-Over District" of New York; Smith's successor Brigham Young led 15,000 followers to Utah in 1847 to escape persecution.

Montgomery bus boycott Sparked by Rosa Parks's arrest on December 1, 1955, a successful year-long boycott protesting segregation on city buses; led by the Reverend Martin Luther King.

Muckrakers Writers who exposed corruption and abuses in politics, business, meat-packing, child labor, and more, primarily in the first decade of the twentieth century; their popular books and magazine articles spurred public interest in progressive reform.

Mugwumps Reform wing of the Republican party which supported Democrat Grover Cleveland for president in 1884 over Republican James G. Blaine, whose influence peddling had been revealed in the Mulligan letters of 1876.

Munn v. Illinois (1877) U.S. Supreme Court ruling that upheld a Granger law allowing the state to regulate grain elevators.

NAFTA Approved in 1993, the North American Free Trade Agreement with Canada and Mexico allowed goods to travel across their borders free of tariffs; critics argued that American workers would lose their jobs to cheaper Mexican labor.

National Aeronautics and Space Administration (NASA) In response to the Soviet Union's launching of *Sputnik*, Congress created this federal agency in 1957 to coordinate research and administer the space program.

National Association for the Advancement of Colored People (NAACP) Founded in 1910, this civil rights organization brought lawsuits against discriminatory practices and published *The Crisis*, a journal edited by African-American scholar W. E. B. Du Bois.

National Defense Education Act (1958) Passed in reaction to America's perceived inferiority in the space race, the appropriation encouraged education in science and modern languages through student loans, university research grants, and aid to public schools.

National Industrial Recovery Act (1933) Passed on the last of the Hundred Days, it created public-works jobs through the Federal Emergency Relief Administration and established a system of self-regulation for industry through the National Recovery Administration, which was ruled unconstitutional in 1935.

National Organization for Women Founded in 1966 by writer Betty Friedan and other feminists, NOW pushed for abortion rights and nondiscrimination in the workplace, but within a decade it became radicalized and lost much of its constituency.

National Road First federal interstate road, built between 1811 and 1838 and stretching from Cumberland, Maryland, to Vandalia, Illinois.

National Security Act (1947) Authorized the reorganization of government to coordinate military branches and security agencies; created the

National Security Council, the Central Intelligence Agency, and the National Military Establishment (later renamed the Department of Defense).

National Youth Administration Created in 1935 as part of the Works Progress Administration, it employed millions of youths who had left school.

nativism Anti-immigrant and anti-Catholic feeling in the 1830s through the 1850s; the largest group was New York's Order of the Star-Spangled Banner, which expanded into the American, or Know-Nothing, party in 1854.

naval stores Tar, pitch, and turpentine made from pine resin and used in shipbuilding; an important industry in the southern colonies, especially North Carolina.

Navigation Acts Passed by the English Parliament to control colonial trade and bolster the mercantile system, 1650–1775; enforcement of the acts led to growing resentment by colonists.

Neutrality Acts Series of laws passed between 1935 and 1939 to keep the United States from becoming involved in war by prohibiting American trade and travel to warring nations.

New Deal Franklin D. Roosevelt's campaign promise, in his speech to the Democratic National Convention of 1932, to combat the Great Depression with a "new deal for the American people"; the phrase became a catchword for his ambitious plan of economic programs.

New England Anti-Slavery Society Abolitionist organization founded in 1832 by William Lloyd Garrison of Massachusetts, publisher of the *Liberator.*

New Freedom Democrat Woodrow Wilson's political slogan in the presidential campaign of 1912; Wilson wanted to improve the banking system, lower tariffs, and, by breaking up monopolies, give small businesses freedom to compete.

New Frontier John F. Kennedy's program, stymied by a Republican Congress and his abbreviated term; his successor Lyndon B. Johnson had greater success with many of the same concepts.

New Harmony Founded in Indiana by British industrialist Robert Owen in 1825, the short-lived New Harmony Community of Equality was one of the few nineteenth-century communal experiments not based on religious ideology.

New Left Radical youth protest movement of the 1960s, named by leader Tom Hayden to distinguish it from the Old (Marxist-Leninist) Left of the 1930s.

New Nationalism Platform of the Progressive party and slogan of former president Theodore Roosevelt in the presidential campaign of 1912; stressed government activism, including regulation of trusts, conservation, and recall of state court decisions that had nullified progressive programs.

New Orleans, Battle of Last battle of the War of 1812, fought on January 8, 1815, weeks after the peace treaty was signed but prior to its ratification; General Andrew Jackson led the victorious American troops.

New South *Atlanta Constitution* editor Henry W. Grady's 1886 term for the prosperous post–Civil War South he envisioned: democratic, industrial, urban, and free of nostalgia for the defeated plantation South.

Nineteenth Amendment (1920) Granted women the right to vote.

Nisei Japanese Americans; literally, "second generation."

normalcy Word coined by future president Warren G. Harding as part of a 1920 campaign speech—"not nostrums, but normalcy"—signifying his awareness that the public was tired of progressivism, war, and sacrifice.

North Atlantic Treaty Organization (NATO) Defensive alliance founded in 1949 by ten western European nations, the United States, and Canada to deter Soviet expansion in Europe.

Northwest Ordinance of 1787 Created the Northwest Territory (area north of the Ohio River and west of Pennsylvania), established conditions for self-government and statehood, included a Bill of Rights, and permanently prohibited slavery.

nullification Concept of invalidation of a federal law within the borders of a state; first expounded in the Kentucky and Virginia Resolutions (1798), cited by South Carolina in its Ordinance of Nullification (1832) of the Tariff of Abominations, used by southern states to explain their secession from the Union (1861), and cited again by southern states to oppose the *Brown* v. *Board of Education* decision (1954).

Nullification Proclamation President Andrew Jackson's strong criticism of South Carolina's Ordinance of Nullification (1832) as disunionist and potentially treasonous.

Office of Price Administration Created in 1941 to control wartime inflation and price fixing resulting from shortages of many consumer goods, the OPA imposed wage and price freezes and administered a rationing system.

Okies Displaced farm families from the Oklahoma dust bowl who migrated to California during the 1930s in search of jobs.

Old Southwest In the antebellum period, the states of Alabama, Mississippi, Louisiana, Texas, Arkansas, and parts of Tennessee, Kentucky, and Florida.

Oneida Community Utopian community founded in 1848; the Perfectionist religious group practiced universal marriage until leader John Humphrey Noyes, fearing prosecution, escaped to Canada in 1879.

OPEC Organization of Petroleum Exporting Countries.

Open Door Policy In hopes of protecting the Chinese market for U.S. exports, Secretary of State John Hay unilaterally announced in 1899 that Chinese trade would be open to all nations.

Operation Desert Storm Multinational allied force that defeated Iraq in the Gulf War of January 1991.

Operation Dixie CIO's largely ineffective post–World War II campaign to unionize southern workers.

Oregon fever Enthusiasm for emigration to the Oregon Country in the late 1830s and early 1840s.

Ostend Manifesto Memorandum written in 1854 from Ostend, Belgium, by the U.S. ministers to England, France, and Spain recommending purchase or seizure of Cuba in order to increase the United States' slaveholding territory.

Overland (Oregon) Trail Route of wagon trains bearing settlers from Independence, Missouri, to the Oregon Country in the 1840s through the 1860s.

overseer Manager of slave labor on a plantation.

Panic of 1819 Financial collapse brought on by sharply falling cotton prices, declining demand for American exports, and reckless western land speculation.

Panic of 1837 Major economic depression lasting about six years; touched off by a British financial crisis and made worse by falling cotton prices, credit and currency problems, and speculation in land, canals, and railroads.

Panic of 1857 Economic depression lasting about two years and brought on by falling grain prices and a weak financial system; the South was largely protected by international demand for its cotton.

Panic of 1873 Severe six-year depression marked by bank failures and railroad and insurance bankruptcies.

Peace of Paris Signed on September 3, 1783, the treaty ending the Revolutionary War and recognizing American independence from Britain also established the border between Canada and the United States, fixed the western border at the Mississippi River, and ceded Florida to Spain.

Pendleton Civil Service Act (1883) Established the Civil Service Commission and marked the end of the spoils system.

Pentagon Papers Informal name for the Defense Department's secret history of the Vietnam conflict; leaked to the press by former official Daniel Ellsberg and published in the *New York Times* in 1971.

Pequot War Massacre in 1637 and subsequent dissolution of the Pequot Nation by Puritan settlers, who seized the Indians' lands.

Personal Responsibility and Work Opportunity Act (1996) Welfare reform measure that mandated state administration of federal aid to the poor.

Philippine Sea, Battle of the Costly Japanese defeat of June 19–20, 1944; led to the resignation of Premier Tojo and his cabinet.

Pilgrims Puritan Separatists who broke completely with the Church of England and sailed to the New World aboard the *Mayflower*, founding Plymouth Colony on Cape Cod in 1620.

Pinckney's Treaty Treaty with Spain negotiated by Thomas Pinckney in 1795; established United States boundaries at the Mississippi River and the thirty-first parallel and allowed open transportation on the Mississippi.

planter In the antebellum South, the owner of a large farm worked by twenty or more slaves.

Platt Amendment (1901) Reserved the United States' right to intervene in Cuban affairs and forced newly independent Cuba to host American naval bases on the island.

Plessy v. Ferguson **(1896)** U.S. Supreme Court decision supporting the legality of Jim Crow laws that permitted or required "separate but equal" facilities for blacks and whites.

poll tax Tax that must be paid in order to be eligible to vote; used as an effective means of disenfranchising black citizens after Reconstruction, since they often could not afford even a modest fee.

popular sovereignty Allowed settlers in a disputed territory to decide the slavery issue for themselves.

Populist party Political success of Farmers' Alliance candidates encouraged the formation in 1892 of the National People's party (later renamed the Populist party); active until 1912, it advocated a variety of reform issues, including free coinage of silver, income tax, postal savings, regulation of railroads, and direct election of U.S. senators.

Pottawatomie Massacre Murder of five proslavery settlers in eastern Kansas led by abolitionist John Brown on May 24–25, 1856.

Potsdam Conference Last meeting of the major Allied powers, the conference took place outside Berlin from July 17 to August 2, 1945; United States president Harry Truman, Soviet dictator Joseph Stalin, and British prime minister Clement Atlee finalized plans begun at Yalta.

Proclamation of Amnesty and Reconstruction President Lincoln's plan for reconstruction, issued in 1863, allowed southern states to rejoin the Union if 10 percent of the 1860 electorate signed loyalty pledges, accepted emancipation, and had received presidential pardons.

Proclamation of 1763 Royal directive issued after the French and Indian War prohibiting settlement, surveys, and land grants west of the Appalachian Mountains; although it was soon overridden by treaties, colonists continued to harbor resentment.

Progressive party Created when former president Theodore Roosevelt broke away from the Republican party to run for president again in

1912; the party supported progressive reforms similar to the Democrats but stopped short of seeking to eliminate trusts.

Progressivism Broad-based reform movement, 1900–17, that sought governmental help in solving problems in many areas of American life, including education, public health, the economy, the environment, labor, transportation, and politics.

Protestant Reformation Reform movement that resulted in the establishment of Protestant denominations; begun by German monk Martin Luther when he posted his "Ninety-five Theses" (complaints of abuses in the Catholic church) in 1517.

Pullman Strike Strike against the Pullman Palace Car Company in the company town of Pullman, Illinois, on May 11, 1894, by the American Railway Union under Eugene V. Debs; the strike was crushed by court injunctions and federal troops two months later.

Pure Food and Drug Act (1906) First law to regulate manufacturing of food and medicines; prohibited dangerous additives and inaccurate labeling.

Puritans English religious group that sought to purify the Church of England; founded the Massachusetts Bay Colony under John Winthrop in 1630.

Quartering Act (1765) Parliamentary act requiring colonies to house and provision British troops.

Radical Republicans Senators and congressmen who, strictly identifying the Civil War with the abolitionist cause, sought swift emancipation of the slaves, punishment of the rebels, and tight controls over the former Confederate states after the war.

Railroad Strike of 1877 Violent but ultimately unsuccessful interstate strike, which resulted in extensive property damage and many deaths.

Reaganomics Popular name for President Ronald Reagan's philosophy of "supply side" economics, which combined tax cuts, less government spending, and a balanced budget with an unregulated marketplace.

Reconstruction Finance Corporation Federal program established in 1932 under President Herbert Hoover to loan money to banks and other institutions to help them avert bankruptcy.

Red Scare Fear among many Americans after World War I of Communists in particular and noncitizens in general, a reaction to the Russian Revolution, mail bombs, strikes, and riots.

Redcoats Nickname for British soldiers, after their red uniform jackets.

Redeemers/Bourbons Conservative white Democrats, many of whom had been planters or businessmen before the Civil War, who reclaimed control of the South following the end of Reconstruction.

Regulators Groups of backcountry Carolina settlers who protested colonial policies; North Carolina royal governor William Tryon retaliated at the Battle of Alamance on May 17, 1771.

Report on Manufactures First secretary of the treasury Alexander Hamilton's 1791 analysis that accurately foretold the future of American industry and proposed tariffs and subsidies to promote it.

Republican party Organized in 1854 by antislavery Whigs, Democrats, and Free Soilers in response to the passage of the Kansas-Nebraska Act; nominated John C. Frémont for president in 1856 and Abraham Lincoln in 1860.

Republicans Political faction that succeeded the Anti-Federalists after ratification of the Constitution; led by Thomas Jefferson and James Madison, it soon developed into the Democratic-Republican party.

Reservationists Group of U.S. senators led by Majority Leader Henry Cabot Lodge who would only agree to ratification of the Treaty of Versailles subject to certain reservations, most notably the removal of Article X of the League of Nations Covenant.

Revolution of 1800 First time that an American political party surrendered power to the opposition party; Jefferson, a Democratic-Republican, had defeated incumbent Adams, a Federalist, for president.

right-to-work State laws enacted to prevent imposition of the closed shop; any worker, whether or not a union member, could be hired.

***Roe v. Wade* (1973)** U.S. Supreme Court decision requiring states to permit first-trimester abortions.

Roosevelt Corollary (1904) President Theodore Roosevelt announced in what was essentially a corollary to the Monroe Doctrine that the United States could intervene militarily to prevent interference from European powers in the Western Hemisphere.

Romanticism Philosophical, literary, and artistic movement of the nineteenth century that was largely a reaction to the rationalism of the previous century; romantics valued emotion, mysticism, and individualism.

Rough Riders The 1st U.S. Volunteer Cavalry, led in battle in the Spanish-American War by Theodore Roosevelt; they were victorious in their only battle near Santiago, Cuba, and Roosevelt used the notoriety to aid his political career.

Santa Fe Trail Beginning in the 1820s, a major trade route from St. Louis, Missouri, to Santa Fe, New Mexico Territory.

Saratoga, Battle of Major defeat of British general John Burgoyne and more than 5,000 British troops at Saratoga, New York, on October 17, 1777.

Scalawags Southern white Republicans—some former Unionists—who served in Reconstruction governments.

***Schenck v. U.S.* (1919)** U.S. Supreme Court decision upholding the wartime Espionage and Sedition Acts; in the opinion he wrote for the case, Justice Oliver Wendell Holmes set the now-familiar "clear and present danger" standard.

scientific management Analysis of worker efficiency using measurements like "time and motion" studies to achieve greater productivity; introduced by Frederick Winslow Taylor in 1911.

Scottsboro case (1931) In overturning verdicts against nine black youths accused of raping two white women, the U.S. Supreme Court established precedents in *Powell* v. *Alabama* (1932), that adequate counsel must be appointed in capital cases, and in *Norris* v. *Alabama* (1935), that African Americans cannot be excluded from juries.

Second Great Awakening Religious revival movement of the early decades of the nineteenth century, in reaction to the growth of secularism and rationalist religion; began the predominance of the Baptist and Methodist churches.

Second Red Scare Post–World War II Red Scare focused on the fear of Communists in U.S. government positions; peaked during the Korean War and declined soon thereafter, when the U.S. Senate censured Joseph McCarthy, who had been a major instigator of the hysteria.

Seneca Falls Convention First women's rights meeting and the genesis of the women's suffrage movement; held in July 1848 in a church in Seneca Falls, New York, by Elizabeth Cady Stanton and Lucretia Coffin Mott.

"separate but equal" Principle underlying legal racial segregation, which was upheld in *Plessy* v. *Ferguson* (1896) and struck down in *Brown* v. *Board of Education* (1954).

Servicemen's Readjustment Act (1944) The "GI Bill of Rights" provided money for education and other benefits to military personnel returning from World War II.

settlement houses Product of the late nineteenth-century movement to offer a broad array of social services in urban immigrant neighborhoods; Chicago's Hull House was one of hundreds of settlement houses that operated by the early twentieth century.

Seventeenth Amendment (1913) Progressive reform that required U.S. senators to be elected directly by voters; previously, senators were chosen by state legislatures.

Seward's Folly Secretary of State William H. Seward's negotiation of the purchase of Alaska from Russia in 1867.

Shakers Founded by Mother Ann Lee Stanley in England, the United Society of Believers in Christ's Second Appearing settled in Watervliet, New York, in 1774 and subsequently established eighteen additional communes in the Northeast, Indiana, and Kentucky.

sharecropping Type of farm tenancy that developed after the Civil War in which landless workers—often former slaves—farmed land in exchange for farm supplies and a share of the crop; differed from tenancy in that the terms were generally less favorable.

Shays's Rebellion Massachusetts farmer Daniel Shays and 1,200 compatriots, seeking debt relief through issuance of paper currency and lower taxes, stormed the federal arsenal at Springfield in the winter of 1787 but were quickly repulsed.

Sherman Anti-Trust Act (1890) First law to restrict monopolistic trusts and business combinations; extended by the Clayton Anti-Trust Act of 1914.

Sherman Silver Purchase Act (1890) In replacing and extending the provisions of the Bland-Allison Act of 1878, it increased the amount of silver periodically bought for coinage.

Shiloh, Battle of At the time it was fought (April 6–7, 1862), Shiloh, in western Tennessee, was the bloodiest battle in American history; afterward, General Ulysses S. Grant was temporarily removed from command.

single tax Concept of taxing only landowners as a remedy for poverty, promulgated by Henry George in *Progress and Poverty* (1879).

Sixteenth Amendment (1913) Legalized the federal income tax.

Smith-Connally War Labor Disputes Act (1943) Outlawed labor strikes in wartime and allowed the president to take over industries threatened by labor disputes.

***Smith v. Allwright* (1944)** U.S. Supreme Court decision that outlawed all-white Democratic party primaries in Texas.

Social Darwinism Application of Charles Darwin's theory of natural selection to society; used the concept of the "survival of the fittest" to justify class distinctions and to explain poverty.

social gospel Preached by liberal Protestant clergymen in the late nineteenth and early twentieth centuries; advocated the application of Christian principles to social problems generated by industrialization.

Social Security Act (1935) Created the Social Security system with provisions for a retirement pension, unemployment insurance, disability insurance, and public assistance (welfare).

Sons of Liberty Secret organizations formed by Samuel Adams, John Hancock, and other radicals in response to the Stamp Act; they impeded British officials and planned such harassments as the Boston Tea Party.

South Carolina Exposition and Protest Written in 1828 by Vice-President John C. Calhoun of South Carolina to protest the so-called Tariff of Abominations, which seemed to favor northern industry; introduced the concept of state interposition and became the basis for South Carolina's Nullification Doctrine of 1833.

Southeast Asia Treaty Organization (SEATO) Pact among mostly western nations signed in 1954; designed to deter Communist expansion and cited as a justification for U.S. involvement in Vietnam.

Southern Christian Leadership Conference (SCLC) Civil rights organization founded in 1957 by the Reverend Martin Luther King, Jr., and other civil rights leaders.

Southern renaissance Literary movement of the 1920s and 1930s that included such writers as William Faulkner, Thomas Wolfe, and Robert Penn Warren.

Spanish flu Unprecedentedly lethal influenza epidemic of 1918 that killed more than 22 million people worldwide.

spoils system The term—meaning the filling of federal government jobs with persons loyal to the party of the president—originated in Andrew Jackson's first term; the system was replaced in the Progressive Era by civil service.

Sputnik First artificial satellite to orbit the earth; launched October 4, 1957, by the Soviet Union.

Stalwarts Conservative Republican party faction during the presidency of Rutherford B. Hayes, 1877–81; led by Senator Roscoe B. Conkling of New York, Stalwarts opposed civil service reform and favored a third term for President Ulysses S. Grant.

Stamp Act (1765) Parliament required that revenue stamps be affixed to all colonial printed matter, documents, dice, and playing cards; the Stamp Act Congress met to formulate a response, and the act was repealed the following year.

Standard Oil Company Founded in 1870 by John D. Rockefeller in Cleveland, Ohio, it soon grew into the nation's first industry-dominating trust; the Sherman Anti-Trust Act (1890) was enacted in part to combat abuses by Standard Oil.

staple crop Important cash crop, for example, cotton or tobacco.

steamboats Paddlewheelers that could travel both up- and down-river in deep or shallow waters; they became commercially viable early in the nineteenth century and soon developed into America's first inland freight and passenger service network.

Stimson Doctrine In reaction to Japan's 1932 occupation of Manchuria, Secretary of State Henry Stimson declared that the United States would not recognize territories acquired by force.

Strategic Defense Initiative ("Star Wars") Defense Department's plan during the Reagan administration to build a system to destroy incoming missiles in space.

Student Non-violent Coordinating Committee Founded in 1960 to coordinate civil rights sit-ins and other forms of grassroots protest.

Students for a Democratic Society (SDS) Major organization of the New Left, founded at the University of Michigan in 1960 by Tom Hayden and Al Haber.

Sugar Act (Revenue Act of 1764) Parliament's tax on refined sugar and many other colonial products; the first tax designed solely to raise revenue for Britain.

Taft-Hartley Act (1947) Passed over President Harry Truman's veto, the law contained a number of provisions to control labor unions, including the banning of closed shops.

tariff Federal tax on imported goods.

Tariff of Abominations (Tariff of 1828) Taxed imported goods at a very high rate; the South hated the tariff because it feared it would provoke Britain to reject American cotton.

Tariff of 1816 First true protective tariff, intended strictly to protect American goods against foreign competition.

Tax Reform Act (1986) Lowered federal income tax rates to 1920s levels and eliminated many loopholes.

Teapot Dome Harding administration scandal in which Secretary of the Interior Albert B. Fall profited from secret leasing to private oil companies of government oil reserves at Teapot Dome, Wyoming, and Elk Hills, California.

tenancy Renting of farmland by workers who owned their own equipment; tenant farmers kept a larger percentage of the crop than did sharecroppers.

Tennessee Valley Authority Created in 1933 to control flooding in the Tennessee River Valley, provide work for the region's unemployed, and produce inexpensive electric power for the region.

Tenure of Office Act (1867) Required the president to obtain Senate approval to remove any official whose appointment had also required Senate approval; President Andrew Johnson's violation of the law by firing Secretary of War Edwin Stanton led to the Radical Republicans retaliating with Johnson's impeachment.

Tertium Quid Literally, the "third something": states' rights and strict constructionist Republicans under John Randolph who broke with President Thomas Jefferson but never managed to form a third political party.

Tet Offensive Surprise attack by the Viet Cong and North Vietnamese during the Vietnamese New Year of 1968; turned American public opinion strongly against the war in Vietnam.

Tippecanoe, Battle of On November 7, 1811, Indiana governor William Henry Harrison (later president) defeated the Shawnee Indians at the Tippecanoe River in northern Indiana; victory fomented war fever against the British, who were believed to be aiding the Indians.

Title IX Part of the Educational Amendments Act of 1972 that required colleges to engage in "affirmative action" for women.

Tonkin Gulf Resolution (1964) Passed by Congress in reaction to supposedly unprovoked attacks on American warships off the coast of North Vietnam; it gave the president unlimited authority to defend U.S. forces and members of SEATO.

Tories Term used by Patriots to refer to Loyalists, or colonists who supported the Crown after the Declaration of Independence.

Townshend Acts (1767) Parliamentary measures (named for the chancellor of the exchequer) that punished the New York Assembly for failing to house British soldiers, taxed tea and other commodities, and established a Board of Customs Commissioners and colonial vice-admiralty courts.

Trail of Tears Cherokees' own term for their forced march, 1838–39, from the southern Appalachians to Indian lands (later Oklahoma); of 15,000 forced to march, 4,000 died on the way.

Transcendentalism Philosophy of a small group of mid-nineteenth-century New England writers and thinkers, including Ralph Waldo Emerson, Henry David Thoreau, and Margaret Fuller; they stressed "plain living and high thinking."

Transcontinental railroad First line across the continent from Omaha, Nebraska, to Sacramento, California, established in 1869 with the linkage of the Union Pacific and Central Pacific railroads at Promontory, Utah.

Truman Doctrine President Harry S. Truman's program of post–World War II aid to European countries—particularly Greece and Turkey—in danger of being undermined by communism.

trust Companies combined to control competition.

Twenty-first Amendment (1933) Repealed prohibition on the manufacture, sale, and transportation of alcoholic beverages, effectively nullifying the Eighteenth Amendment.

Twenty-second Amendment (1951) Limited presidents to two full terms of office or two terms plus two years of an assumed term; passed in reaction to President Franklin D. Roosevelt's unprecedented four elected terms.

Twenty-sixth Amendment (1971) Lowered the voting age from twenty-one to eighteen.

U.S.S. *Maine* Battleship that exploded in Havana Harbor on February 15, 1898, resulting in 266 deaths; the American public, assuming that the Spanish had mined the ship, clamored for war, and the Spanish-American War was declared two months later.

Uncle Tom's Cabin Harriet Beecher Stowe's 1852 antislavery novel popularized the abolitionist position.

Underground Railroad Operating in the decades before the Civil War, the "railroad" was a clandestine system of routes and safehouses through which slaves were led to freedom in the North.

Understanding clause Added to state constitutions in the late nineteenth century, it allowed illiterate whites to circumvent literacy tests for voting by demonstrating that they understood a passage in the Constitution; black citizens would be judged by white registrars to have failed.

Underwood-Simmons Tariff (1913) In addition to lowering and even eliminating some tariffs, it included provisions for the first federal income tax, made legal the same year by the ratification of the Sixteenth Amendment.

Unitarianism Late eighteenth-century liberal offshoot of the New England Congregationalist church; rejecting the Trinity, Unitarianism professed the oneness of God and the goodness of rational man.

United Farm Workers Union for the predominantly Mexican-American migrant laborers of the Southwest, organized by César Chavez in 1962.

United Nations Organization of nations to maintain world peace, established in 1945 and headquartered in New York.

Universal Negro Improvement Association Black nationalist movement active in the United States from 1916 to 1923, when its leader Marcus Garvey went to prison for mail fraud.

Universalism Similar to Unitarianism, but putting more stress on the importance of social action, Universalism also originated in Massachusetts in the late eighteenth century.

V-E Day May 8, 1945, the day World War II officially ended in Europe.

vertical integration Company's avoidance of middlemen by producing its own supplies and providing for distribution of its product.

veto President's constitutional power to reject legislation passed by Congress; a two-thirds vote in both houses of Congress can override a veto.

Vicksburg, Battle of The fall of Vicksburg, Mississippi, to General Ulysses S. Grant's army on July 4, 1863, after two months of siege was a turning point in the war because it gave the Union control of the Mississippi River.

Virginia and New Jersey Plans Differing opinions of delegations to the Constitutional Convention: New Jersey wanted one legislative body with equal representation for each state; Virginia's plan called for a strong central government and a two-house legislature apportioned by population.

Volstead Act (1919) Enforced the prohibition amendment, beginning January 1920.

Voting Rights Act of 1965 Passed in the wake of Martin Luther King's Selma to Montgomery March, it authorized federal protection of the right to vote and permitted federal enforcement of minority voting rights in individual counties, mostly in the South.

Wabash Railroad v. Illinois **(1886)** Reversing the U.S. Supreme Court's ruling in *Munn* v. *Illinois*, the decision disallowed state regulation of interstate commerce.

Wade-Davis Bill (1864) Radical Republicans' plan for reconstruction that required loyalty oaths, abolition of slavery, repudiation of war debts, and denial of political rights to high-ranking Confederate officials; President Lincoln refused to sign the bill.

Wagner Act (National Labor Relations Act of 1935) Established the National Labor Relations Board and facilitated unionization by regulating employment and bargaining practices.

War Industries Board Run by financier Bernard Baruch, the board planned production and allocation of war materiel, supervised purchasing, and fixed prices, 1917–19.

War of 1812 Fought with Britain, 1812–14, over lingering conflicts that included impressment of American sailors, interference with shipping, and collusion with Northwest Territory Indians; settled by the Treaty of Ghent in 1814.

War on Poverty Announced by President Lyndon B. Johnson in his 1964 State of the Union address; under the Economic Opportunity Bill signed later that year, Head Start, VISTA, and the Jobs Corps were created, and grants and loans were extended to students, farmers, and businesses in efforts to eliminate poverty.

War Production Board Created in 1942 to coordinate industrial efforts in World War II; similar to the War Industries Board in World War I.

War Relocation Camps Internment camps where Japanese Americans were held against their will from 1942 to 1945.

Warren Court The U.S. Supreme Court under Chief Justice Earl Warren, 1953–69, decided such landmark cases as *Brown v. Board of Education* (school desegregation), *Baker v. Carr* (legislative redistricting), and *Gideon v. Wainwright* and *Miranda v. Arizona* (rights of criminal defendants).

Washington Armaments Conference Leaders of nine world powers met in 1921–22 to discuss the naval race; resulting treaties limited to a specific ratio the carrier and battleship tonnage of each nation (Five-Power Naval Treaty), formally ratified the Open Door to China (Nine–Power Treaty), and agreed to respect each other's Pacific territories (Four-Power Treaty).

Watergate Washington office and apartment complex that lent its name to the 1972–74 scandal of the Nixon administration; when his knowledge of the break-in at the Watergate and subsequent coverup was revealed, Nixon resigned the presidency under threat of impeachment.

Webster-Ashburton Treaty Settlement in 1842 of U.S.-Canadian border disputes in Maine, New York, Vermont, and in the Wisconsin Territory (now northern Minnesota).

Webster-Hayne debate U.S. Senate debate of January 1830 between Daniel Webster of Massachusetts and Robert Hayne of South Carolina over nullification and states' rights.

Whig Party Founded in 1834 to unite factions opposed to President Andrew Jackson, the party favored federal responsibility for internal improvements; the party ceased to exist by the late 1850s, when party members divided over the slavery issue.

Whigs Another name for revolutionary Patriots.

Whiskey Rebellion Violent protest by western Pennsylvania farmers against the federal excise tax on corn whiskey, 1794.

Whitewater Development Corporation Failed Arkansas real estate investment that kept President Bill Clinton and his wife Hillary under investigation by Independent Counsel Kenneth Starr throughout the Clinton presidency; no charges were ever brought against either of the Clintons.

Wilderness, Battle of the Second battle fought in the thickly wooded Wilderness area near Chancellorsville, Virginia; in the battle of May 5–6, 1864, no clear victor emerged, but the battle served to deplete the Army of Northern Virginia.

Wilderness Road Originally an Indian path through the Cumberland Gap, it was used by over 300,000 settlers who migrated westward to Kentucky in the last quarter of the eighteenth century.

Wilmot Proviso Proposal to prohibit slavery in any land acquired in the Mexican War, but southern senators, led by John C. Calhoun of South Carolina, defeated the measure in 1846 and 1847.

Works Progress Administration (WPA) Part of the Second New Deal, it provided jobs for millions of the unemployed on construction and arts projects.

Wounded Knee, Battle of Last incident of the Indians Wars took place in 1890 in the Dakota Territory, where the U.S. Cavalry killed over 200 Sioux men, women, and children who were in the process of surrender.

writs of assistance One of the colonies' main complaints against Britain, the writs allowed unlimited search warrants without cause to look for evidence of smuggling.

XYZ Affair French foreign minister Tallyrand's three anonymous agents demanded payments to stop French plundering of American ships in 1797; refusal to pay the bribe led to two years of sea war with France (1798–1800).

Yalta Conference Meeting of Franklin D. Roosevelt, Winston Churchill, and Joseph Stalin at a Crimean resort to discuss the postwar world on February 4–11, 1945; Soviet leader Joseph Stalin claimed large areas in eastern Europe for Soviet domination.

Yazoo Fraud Illegal sale of the Yazoo lands (much of present-day Alabama and Mississippi) by Georgia legislators; by 1802 it had become a tangle of conflicting claims that the U.S. Supreme Court settled in *Fletcher* v. *Peck* (1810).

yellow journalism Sensationalism in newspaper publishing that reached a peak in the circulation war between Joseph Pulitzer's *New York World* and William Randolph Hearst's *New York Journal* in the 1890s; the papers' accounts of events in Havana Harbor in 1898 led directly to the Spanish-American War.

yeoman farmers Small landowners (the majority of white families in the South) who farmed their own land and usually did not own slaves.

Yorktown, Battle of Last battle of the Revolutionary War; General Lord Charles Cornwallis along with over 7,000 British troops surrendered at Yorktown, Virginia, on October 17, 1781.

Zimmermann telegram From the German foreign secretary to the German minister in Mexico, February 1917, instructing him to offer to recover Texas, New Mexico, and Arizona for Mexico if it would fight the United States to divert attention from Germany in case of war.

APPENDIX

THE DECLARATION
OF INDEPENDENCE

WHEN IN THE COURSE OF HUMAN EVENTS, it becomes necessary for one people to dissolve the political bands which have connected them with another, and to assume the Powers of the earth, the separate and equal station to which the Laws of Nature and of Nature's God entitle them, a decent respect to the opinions of mankind requires that they should declare the causes which impel them to the separation.

We hold these truths to be self-evident, that all men are created equal, that they are endowed by their Creator with certain unalienable rights, that among these are Life, Liberty, and the pursuit of Happiness. That to secure these rights, Governments are instituted among Men, deriving their just powers from the consent of the governed. That whenever any Form of Government becomes destructive of these ends, it is the Right of the People to alter or to abolish it, and to institute new Government, laying its foundation on such principles and organizing its powers in such form, as to them shall seem most likely to effect their Safety and Happiness. Prudence, indeed, will dictate that Governments long established should not be changed for light and transient causes; and accordingly all experience hath shown, that mankind are more disposed to suffer, while evils are sufferable, than to right themselves by abolishing the forms to which they are accustomed. But when a long train of abuses and usurpations, pursuing invariably the same Object evinces a design to reduce them under absolute Despotism, it is their right, it is their duty, to throw off such Government, and to provide new Guards for their future security.—Such has been the patient sufferance of these Colonies; and such is now the necessity which constrains them to alter their former Systems of Government. The history of the present King of Great Britain is a history of repeated injuries and usurpations, all having in direct object the establishment of an absolute Tyranny over these States. To prove this, let Facts be submitted to a candid world.

He has refused his Assent to Laws, the most wholesome and necessary for the public good.

He has forbidden his Governors to pass Laws of immediate and pressing importance, unless suspended in their operation till his Assent should be obtained; and when so suspended, he has utterly neglected to attend to them.

He has refused to pass other Laws for the accommodation of large districts of people, unless those people would relinquish the right of Representation in the Legislature, a right inestimable to them and formidable to tyrants only.

He has called together legislative bodies at places unusual, uncomfortable, and distant from the depository of their public Records, for the sole purpose of fatiguing them into compliance with his measures.

He has dissolved Representative Houses repeatedly, for opposing with manly firmness his invasions on the rights of the people.

He has refused for a long time, after such dissolutions, to cause others to be elected; whereby the Legislative powers, incapable of Annihilation, have returned to the People at large for their exercise; the State remaining in the mean time exposed to all dangers of invasion from without, and convulsions within.

He has endeavoured to prevent the population of these States; for that purpose obstructing the Laws of Naturalization of Foreigners; refusing to pass others to encourage their migrations hither, and raising the conditions of new Appropriations of Lands.

He has obstructed the Administration of Justice, by refusing his Assent to Laws for establishing Judiciary powers.

He has made Judges dependent on his Will alone, for the tenure of their offices, and the amount and payment of their salaries.

He has erected a multitude of New Offices, and sent hither swarms of Officers to harass our People, and eat out their substance.

He has kept among us, in times of peace, Standing Armies without the Consent of our legislatures.

He has affected to render the Military independent of and superior to the Civil Power.

He has combined with others to subject us to a jurisdiction foreign to our constitution, and unacknowledged by our laws; giving his Assent to their Acts of pretended Legislation:

For quartering large bodies of armed troops among us:

For protecting them, by a mock Trial, from Punishment for any Murders which they should commit on the Inhabitants of these States:

For cutting off our Trade with all parts of the world:

For imposing taxes on us without our Consent:

For depriving us of many cases, of the benefits of Trial by jury:

For transporting us beyond Seas to be tried for pretended offences:

For abolishing the free System of English Laws in a neighbouring Province, establishing therein an Arbitrary government, and enlarging its

Boundaries so as to render it at once an example and fit instrument for introducing the same absolute rule into these Colonies:

For taking away our Charters, abolishing our most valuable Laws, and altering fundamentally the Forms of our Governments:

For suspending our own Legislatures, and declaring themselves in vested with Power to legislate for us in all cases whatsoever.

He has abdicated Government here, by declaring us out of his Protection and waging War against us.

He has plundered our seas, ravaged our Coasts, burnt our towns, and destroyed the lives of our people.

He is at this time transporting large armies of foreign mercenaries to compleat the works of death, desolation, and tyranny, already begun with circumstances of Cruelty & perfidy scarcely paralleled in the most barbarous ages, and totally unworthy the Head of a civilized nation.

He has constrained our fellow Citizens taken Captive on the high Seas to bear Arms against their Country, to become the executioners of their friends and Brethren, or to fall themselves by their Hands.

He has excited domestic insurrections amongst us, and has endeavoured to bring on the inhabitants of our frontiers, the merciless Indian Savages, whose known rule of warfare, is an undistinguished destruction of all ages, sexes, and conditions.

In every stage of these Oppressions We have Petitioned for Redress in the most humble terms: Our repeated Petitions have been answered only by repeated injury. A Prince, whose character is thus marked by every act which may define a Tyrant, is unfit to be the ruler of a free people.

Nor have We been wanting in attention to our British brethren. We have warned them from time to time of attempts by their legislature to extend an unwarrantable jurisdiction over us. We have reminded them of the circumstances of our emigration and settlement here. We have appealed to their native justice and magnanimity, and we have conjured them by the ties of our common kindred to disavow these usurpations, which, would inevitably interrupt our connections and correspondence. They too must have been deaf to the voice of justice and of consanguinity. We must, therefore, acquiesce in the necessity, which denounces our Separation, and hold them, as we hold the rest of mankind, Enemies in War, in Peace Friends.

WE, THEREFORE, the Representatives of the UNITED STATES OF AMERICA, in General Congress, Assembled, appealing to the Supreme Judge of the world for the rectitude of our intentions, do, in the Name, and by Authority of the good People of these Colonies, solemnly publish and declare, That these United Colonies are, and of Right ought to be FREE AND INDEPENDENT STATES; that they are Absolved from all Allegiance to the

British Crown, and that all political connection between them and the State of Great Britain, is and ought to be totally dissolved; and that as Free and Independent States, they have full Power to levy War, conclude Peace, contract Alliances, establish Commerce, and to do all other Acts and Things which Independent States may of right do. And for the support of this Declaration, with a firm reliance on the Protection of Divine Providence, we mutually pledge to each other our Lives, our Fortunes, and our sacred Honor.

The foregoing Declaration was, by order of Congress, engrossed, and signed by the following members:

John Hancock

NEW HAMPSHIRE
Josiah Bartlett
William Whipple
Matthew Thornton

MASSACHUSETTS BAY
Samuel Adams
John Adams
Robert Treat Paine
Elbridge Gerry

RHODE ISLAND
Stephen Hopkins
William Ellery

CONNECTICUT
Roger Sherman
Samuel Huntington
William Williams
Oliver Wolcott

NEW YORK
William Floyd
Philip Livingston
Francis Lewis
Lewis Morris

NEW JERSEY
Richard Stockton
John Witherspoon
Francis Hopkinson
John Hart
Abraham Clark

PENNSYLVANIA
Robert Morris
Benjamin Rush
Benjamin Franklin
John Morton
George Clymer
James Smith
George Taylor
James Wilson
George Ross

DELAWARE
Caesar Rodney
George Read
Thomas M'Kean

MARYLAND
Samuel Chase
William Paca
Thomas Stone
Charles Carroll, of Carrollton

VIRGINIA
George Wythe
Richard Henry Lee
Thomas Jefferson
Benjamin Harrison
Thomas Nelson, Jr.
Francis Lightfoot Lee
Carter Braxton

NORTH CAROLINA
William Hooper
Joseph Hewes
John Penn

SOUTH CAROLINA
Edward Rutledge
Thomas Heyward, Jr.
Thomas Lynch, Jr.
Arthur Middleton

GEORGIA
Button Gwinnett
Lyman Hall
George Walton

Resolved, that copies of the declaration be sent to the several assemblies, conventions, and committees, or councils of safety, and to the several commanding officers of the continental troops; that it be proclaimed in each of the united states, at the head of the army.

ARTICLES OF
CONFEDERATION

To all to whom these Presents shall come, we the undersigned Delegates of the States affixed to our Names send greeting.

Whereas the Delegates of the United States of America in Congress assembled did on the fifteenth day of November in the Year of our Lord One Thousand Seven Hundred and Seventy-seven, and in the Second Year of the Independence of America agree to certain articles of Confederation and perpetual Union between the States of Newhampshire, Massachusetts-bay, Rhodeisland and Providence Plantations, Connecticut, New York, New Jersey, Pennsylvania, Delaware, Maryland, Virginia, North-Carolina, South-Carolina and Georgia in the Words following, viz.

Articles of Confederation and perpetual Union between the States of Newhampshire, Massachusetts-bay, Rhodeisland and Providence Plantations, Connecticut, New-York, New-Jersey, Pennsylvania, Delaware, Maryland, Virginia, North-Carolina, South-Carolina and Georgia.

Article I. The stile of this confederacy shall be "The United States of America."

Article II. Each State retains its sovereignty, freedom and independence, and every power, jurisdiction and right, which is not by this confederation expressly delegated to the United States, in Congress assembled.

Article III. The said States hereby severally enter into a firm league of friendship with each other, for their common defence, the security of their liberties, and their mutual and general welfare, binding themselves to assist each other, against all force offered to, or attacks made upon them, or any of them, on account of religion, sovereignty, trade or any other pretence whatever.

ARTICLE IV. The better to secure and perpetuate mutual friendship and intercourse among the people of the different States in this Union, the free inhabitants of each of these States, paupers, vagabonds and fugitives from justice excepted, shall be entitled to all privileges and immunities of free citizens in the several States; and the people of each State shall have free ingress and regress to and from any other State, and shall enjoy therein all the privileges of trade and commerce, subject to the same duties, impositions and restrictions as the inhabitants thereof respectively, provided that such restrictions shall not extend so far as to prevent the removal of property imported into any State, to any other State of which the owner is an inhabitant; provided also that no imposition, duties or restriction shall be laid by any State, on the property of the United States, or either of them.

If any person guilty of, or charged with treason, felony, or other high misdemeanor in any State, shall flee from justice, and be found in any of the United States, he shall upon demand of the Governor or Executive power, of the State from which he fled, be delivered up and removed to the State having jurisdiction of his offence.

Full faith and credit shall be given in each of these States to the records, acts and judicial proceedings of the courts and magistrates of every other State.

ARTICLE V. For the more convenient management of the general interests of the United States, delegates shall be annually appointed in such manner as the legislature of each State shall direct, to meet in Congress on the first Monday in November, in every year, with a power reserved to each State, to recall its delegates, or any of them, at any time within the year, and to send others in their stead, for the remainder of the year.

No State shall be represented in Congress by less than two, nor by more than seven members; and no person shall be capable of being a delegate for more than three years in any term of six years; nor shall any person, being a delegate, be capable of holding any office under the United States, for which he, or another for his benefit receives any salary, fees or emolument of any kind.

Each State shall maintain its own delegates in a meeting of the States, and while they act as members of the committee of the States.

In determining questions in the United States, in Congress assembled, each State shall have one vote.

Freedom of speech and debate in Congress shall not be impeached or questioned in any court, or place out of Congress, and the members of Congress shall be protected in their persons from arrests and imprisonments, during the time of their going to and from, and attendance on Congress, except for treason, felony, or breach of the peace.

ARTICLE VI. No State without the consent of the United States in Congress assembled, shall send any embassy to, or receive any embassy from, or enter into any conference, agreement, alliance or treaty with any king, prince or state; nor shall any person holding any office of profit or trust under the United States, or any of them, accept of any present, emolument, office or title of any kind whatever from any king, prince or foreign state; nor shall the United States in Congress assembled, or any of them, grant any title of nobility.

No two or more States shall enter into any treaty, confederation or alliance whatever between them, without the consent of the United States in Congress assembled, specifying accurately the purposes for which the same is to be entered into, and how long it shall continue.

No State shall lay any imposts or duties, which may interfere with any stipulations in treaties, entered into by the United States in Congress assembled, with any king, prince or state, in pursuance of any treaties already proposed by Congress, to the courts of France and Spain.

No vessels of war shall be kept up in time of peace by any State, except such number only, as shall be deemed necessary by the United States in Congress assembled, for the defence of such State, or its trade; nor shall any body of forces be kept up by any State, in time of peace, except such number only, as in the judgment of the United States, in Congress assembled, shall be deemed requisite to garrison the forts necessary for the defence of such State; but every State shall always keep up a well regulated and disciplined militia, sufficiently armed and accoutred, and shall provide and constantly have ready for use, in public stores, a due number of field pieces and tents, and a proper quantity of arms, ammunition and camp equipage.

No State shall engage in any war without the consent of the United States in Congress assembled, unless such State be actually invaded by enemies, or shall have received certain advice of a resolution being formed by some nation of Indians to invade such State, and the danger is so imminent as not to admit of a delay, till the United States in Congress assembled can be consulted: nor shall any State grant commissions to any ships or vessels of war, nor letters of marque or reprisal, except it be after a declaration of war by the United States in Congress assembled, and then only against the kingdom or state and the subjects thereof, against which war has been so declared, and under such regulations as shall be established by the United States in Congress assembled, unless such State be infested by pirates, in which case vessels of war may be fitted out for that occasion, and kept so long as the danger shall continue, or until the United States in Congress assembled shall determine otherwise.

ARTICLE VII. When land-forces are raised by any State of the common defence, all officers of or under the rank of colonel, shall be appointed by the Legislature of each State respectively by whom such forces shall be raised, or in such manner as such State shall direct, and all vacancies shall be filled up by the State which first made the appointment.

ARTICLE VIII. All charges of war, and all other expenses that shall be incurred for the common defence or general welfare, and allowed by the United States in Congress assembled, shall be defrayed out of a common treasury, which shall be supplied by the several States, in proportion to the value of all land within each State, granted to or surveyed for any person, as such land and the buildings and improvements thereon shall be estimated according to such mode as the United States in Congress assembled, shall from time to time direct and appoint.

The taxes for paying that proportion shall be laid and levied by the authority and direction of the Legislatures of the several States within the time agreed upon by the United States in Congress assembled.

ARTICLE IX. The United States in Congress assembled, shall have the sole and exclusive right and power of determining on peace and war, except in the cases mentioned in the sixth article—of sending and receiving ambassadors—entering into treaties and alliances, provided that no treaty of commerce shall be made whereby the legislative power of the respective States shall be restrained from imposing such imposts and duties on foreigners, as their own people are subjected to, or from prohibiting the exportation or importation of and species of goods or commodities whatsoever—of establishing rules for deciding in all cases, what captures on land or water shall be legal, and in what manner prizes taken by land or naval forces in the service of the United States shall be divided or appropriated—of granting letters of marque and reprisal in times of peace—appointing courts for the trial of piracies and felonies committed on the high seas and establishing courts for receiving and determining finally appeals in all cases of captures, provided that no member of Congress shall be appointed a judge of any of the said courts.

The United States in Congress assembled shall also be the last resort on appeal in all disputes and differences now subsisting or that hereafter may arise between two or more States concerning boundary, jurisdiction or any other cause whatever; which authority shall always be exercised in the manner following. Whenever the legislative or executive authority or lawful agent of any State in controversy with another shall present a petition to Congress, stating the matter in question and praying for a hearing, notice thereof shall be given by order of Congress to the legislative or executive authority of the other State in controversy, and a day assigned for the appearance of the parties by their lawful agents, who shall then be directed to appoint by joint consent, commissioners or judges to constitute a court for hearing and determining the matter in question: but if they cannot agree, Congress shall name three persons out of each of the United States, and from the list of such persons each party shall alternately strike out one, the petitioners beginning, until the number shall be reduced to thirteen; and from that number not less than seven, nor more than nine names as Congress shall direct, shall in the presence of Congress be drawn out by lot, and the persons whose names shall be so drawn or any five of them, shall be commissioners or judges, to hear and finally determine the controversy, so always as a major part of the judges who shall hear the cause shall agree in the determination: and if either party shall neglect to attend at the day appointed, without reasons, which Congress shall judge sufficient, or being present shall refuse to strike, the Congress shall proceed to nominate three persons out of each State, and the Secretary of Congress shall strike in behalf of such party absent or refusing; and the judgment and sentence of the court to be appointed, in the manner before prescribed, shall be final and conclusive; and if any of the parties shall refuse to submit to the authority of such court, or to appear or defend their claim or cause, the court shall nevertheless proceed to pronounce sentence, or judgment, which shall in like manner be final and decisive, the judgment or sentence and other proceedings being in either case transmitted to Congress, and lodged among the acts of Congress for the security of the parties concerned: provided that every commissioner, before he sits in judgment, shall take an oath to be administered by one of the judges of the supreme or superior court of the State where the case shall be tried, "well and truly to hear and determine the matter in question, according to the best of his judgment, without favour, affection or hope of reward:" provided also that no State shall be deprived of territory for the benefit of the United States.

All controversies concerning the private right of soil claimed under different grants of two or more States, whose jurisdiction as they may respect such lands, and the states which passed such grants are adjusted, the said grants or either of them being at the same time claimed to have originated antecedent to such settlement of jurisdiction, shall on the petition of either party to the Congress of the United States, be finally determined as near as may be in the same manner as is before prescribed for deciding disputes respecting territorial jurisdiction between different States.

The United States in Congress assembled shall also have the sole and exclusive right and power of regulating the alloy and value of coin struck by their own authority, or by that of the respective States—fixing the standard of weights and measures throughout the United States—regulating the trade and managing all affairs with the Indians, not members of any of the States, provided that the legislative right of any State within its own limits be not infringed or violated—establishing and regulating post-offices from one State to another, throughout all of the United States, and exacting such postage on the papers passing thro' the same as may be requisite to defray the expenses of the said office—appointing all officers of the land forces, in the service of the United States, excepting regimental officers—appointing all the officers of the naval forces, and commissioning all officers whatever in the service of the United States—making rules for the government and regulation of the said land and naval forces, and directing their operations.

The United States in Congress assembled shall have authority to appoint a committee, to sit in the recess of Congress, to be denominated "a Committee of the States," and to consist of one delegate from each State; and to appoint such other committees and civil officers as may be necessary for managing the general affairs of the United States under their direction—to appoint one of their number to preside, provided that no person be allowed to serve in the office of president more than one year in any term of three years; to ascertain the necessary sums of money to be raised for the service of the United States, and to appropriate and apply the same for defraying the public expenses—to borrow money, or emit bills on the credit of the United States, transmitting every half year to the respective States an account of the sums of money so borrowed or emitted,—to build and equip a navy—to agree upon the number of land forces, and to make requisitions from each State for its quota, in proportion to the number of white inhabitants in such State; which requisition shall be binding, and thereupon the Legislature of each State shall appoint the regimental officers, raise the men and cloath, arm and equip them in a soldier like manner, at the expense of the United States; and the officers and men so cloathed, armed and equipped shall march to the place appointed, and within the time agreed on by the United States in Congress assembled: but if the United States in Congress assembled shall, on consideration of circumstances judge proper that any State should not raise men, or should raise a smaller number of men than the quota thereof, such extra number shall be raised, officered, cloathed, armed and equipped in the same manner as the quota of such State, unless the legislature of such State shall judge that such extra number cannot be safely spared out of the same, in which case they shall raise officer, cloath, arm and equip as many of such extra number as they judge can be safely spared. And the officers and men so cloathed, armed and equipped, shall march to the place appointed, and within the time agreed on by the United States in Congress assembled.

The United States in Congress assembled shall never engage in a war, nor grant letters of marque and reprisal in time of peace, nor enter into any treaties or alliances, nor coin money, nor regulate the value thereof, nor ascertain the sums and expenses necessary for the defence and welfare of the United States, or any of them, nor emit bills, nor borrow money on the credit of the United States, nor appropriate money, nor agree upon the number of vessels to be built or purchased, or the number of land or sea forces to be raised, nor appoint a commander in chief of the army or navy, unless nine States assent to the same: nor shall a question on any other point, except for adjourning from day to day be determined, unless by the votes of a majority of the United States in Congress assembled.

The Congress of the United States shall have power to adjourn to any time within the year, and to any place within the United States, so that no period of adjournment be for a longer duration than the space of six months, and shall publish the journal of their proceedings monthly, except such parts thereof relating to treaties, alliances or military operations, as in their judgment require secresy; and the yeas and nays of the delegates of each State on any question shall be entered on the Journal, when it is desired by any delegate; and the delegates of a State, or any of them, at his or their request shall be furnished with a transcript of the said journal, except such parts as are above excepted, to lay before the Legislatures of the several States.

ARTICLE X. The committee of the States, or any nine of them, shall be authorized to execute, in the recess of Congress, such of the powers of Congress as the United States in Congress assembled, by the consent of nine States, shall from time to time think expedient to vest them with; provided that no power be delegated to the said committee, for the exercise of which, by the articles of confederation, the voice of nine States in the Congress of the United States assembled is requisite.

ARTICLE XI. Canada acceding to this confederation, and joining in the measures of the United States, shall be admitted into, and entitled to all the advantages of this Union: but no other colony shall be admitted into the same, unless such admission be agreed to by nine States.

ARTICLE XII. All bills of credit emitted, monies borrowed and debts contracted by, or under the authority of Congress, before the assembling of the United States, in pursuance of the present confederation, shall be deemed and considered as a charge against the United States, for payment and satisfaction whereof the said United States, and the public faith are hereby solemnly pledged.

ARTICLE XIII. Every State shall abide by the determinations of the United States in Congress assembled, on all questions which by this confederation are submitted to them. And the articles of this confederation shall be inviolably observed by every State, and the Union shall be perpetual; nor shall any alteration at any time hereafter be made in any of them; unless such alteration be agreed to in a Congress of the United States, and be afterwards confirmed by the Legislatures of every State.

And whereas it has pleased the Great Governor of the world to incline the hearts of the Legislatures we respectively represent in Congress, to approve of, and to authorize us to ratify the said articles of confederation and perpetual union. Know ye that we the undersigned delegates, by virtue of the power and authority to us given for that purpose, do by these presents, in the name and in behalf of our respective constituents, fully and entirely ratify and confirm each and every of the said articles of confederation and perpetual union, and all and singular the matters and things therein contained: and we do further solemnly plight and engage the faith of our respective constituents, that they shall abide by the determinations of the United States in Congress assembled, on all questions, which by the said confederation are submitted to them. And that the articles thereof shall be inviolably observed by the States we respectively represent, and that the Union shall be perpetual.

In witness thereof we have hereunto set our hands in Congress. Done at Philadelphia in the State of Pennsylvania the ninth day of July in the year of our Lord one thousand seven hundred and seventy-eight, and in the third year of the independence of America.

THE CONSTITUTION OF
THE UNITED STATES

WE THE PEOPLE OF THE UNITED STATES, in order to form a more perfect Union, establish Justice, insure domestic Tranquility, provide for the common defence, promote the general Welfare, and secure the Blessings of Liberty to ourselves and our Posterity, do ordain and establish this Constitution for the United States of America.

ARTICLE. I.

Section. 1. All legislative Powers herein granted shall be vested in a Congress of the United States, which shall consist of a Senate and House of Representatives.

Section. 2. The House of Representatives shall be composed of Members chosen every second Year by the People of the several States, and the Electors in each State shall have the Qualifications requisite for Electors of the most numerous Branch of the State Legislature.

No Person shall be a Representative who shall not have attained to the Age of twenty five Years, and been seven Years a Citizen of the United States, and who shall not, when elected, be an Inhabitant of that State in which he shall be chosen.

Representatives and direct Taxes shall be apportioned among the several States which may be included within this Union, according to their respective Numbers, which shall be determined by adding to the whole Number of free Persons, including those bound to Service for a Term of Years, and excluding Indians not taxed, three fifths of all other Persons. The actual Enumeration shall be made within three Years after the first Meeting of the Congress of the United States, and within every subsequent Term of ten Years, in such Manner as they shall by Law direct. The Number of Representatives shall not exceed one for every thirty Thousand, but each State shall have at Least one Representative; and until such enumeration shall be made, the State of New Hampshire shall be entitled to chuse three, Massachusetts eight, Rhode-Island and Providence Plantations one, Connecticut five, New-York six, New Jersey four, Pennsylvania eight, Delaware one, Maryland six, Virginia ten, North Carolina five, South Carolina five, and Georgia three.

When vacancies happen in the Representation from any state, the Executive Authority thereof shall issue Writs of Election to fill such Vacancies.

The House of Representatives shall chuse their Speaker and other Officers; and shall have the sole Power of Impeachment.

Section. 3. The Senate of the United States shall be composed of two Senators from each State, chosen by the legislature thereof, for six Years; and each Senator shall have one Vote.

Immediately after they shall be assembled in Consequence of the first Election, they shall be divided as equally as may be into three Classes. The Seats of the Senators of the first Class shall be vacated at the Expiration of the second Year, of the second Class at the Expiration of the fourth Year, and of the third Class at the Expiration of the sixth Year, so that one third maybe chosen every second Year; and if Vacancies happen by Resignation, or otherwise, during the Recess of the Legislature of any State, the Executive thereof may make temporary Appointments until the next Meeting of the Legislature, which shall then fill such Vacancies.

No Person shall be a Senator who shall not have attained to the Age of thirty Years, and been nine Years a Citizen of the United States, and who shall not, when elected, be an Inhabitant of that State for which he shall be chosen.

The Vice President of the United States shall be President of the Senate, but shall have no Vote, unless they be equally divided.

The Senate shall chuse their other Officers, and also a President pro tempore, in the Absence of the Vice President, or when he shall exercise the Office of President of the United States.

The Senate shall have the sole Power to try all Impeachments. When sitting for that Purpose, they shall be on Oath or Affirmation. When the President of the United States is tried, the Chief Justice shall preside: And no Person shall be convicted without the Concurrence of two thirds of the Members present.

Judgment in Cases of Impeachment shall not extend further than to removal from Office, and disqualification to hold and enjoy any Office of honor, Trust or Profit under the United States: but the Party convicted shall nevertheless be liable and subject to Indictment, Trial, Judgment and Punishment, according to Law.

Section. 4. The Times, Places and Manner of holding Elections for Senators and Representatives, shall be prescribed in each State by the Legislature thereof; but the Congress may at any time by Law make or alter such Regulations, except as to the Places of chusing Senators.

The Congress shall assemble at least once in every Year, and such Meeting shall be on the first Monday in December, unless they shall by Law appoint a different Day.

Section. 5. Each House shall be the Judge of the Elections, Returns and Qualifications of its own Members, and a Majority of each shall constitute a Quorum to do Business; but a smaller Number may adjourn from day to day, and may be authorized to compel the Attendance of absent Members, in such Manner, and under such Penalties as each House may provide.

Each House may determine the Rules of its Proceedings, punish its Members for disorderly Behaviour, and, with the Concurrence of two thirds, expel a Member.

Each House shall keep a Journal of its Proceedings, and from time to time publish the same, excepting such Parts as may in their Judgment require Secrecy; and the Yeas and Nays of the Members of either House on any question shall, at the Desire of one fifth of those Present, be entered on the Journal.

Neither House, during the Session of Congress, shall, without the Consent of the other, adjourn for more than three days, not to any other Place than that in which the two Houses shall be sitting.

Section. 6. The Senators and Representatives shall receive a Compensation for their Services, to be ascertained by Law, and paid out of the Treasury of the United States. They shall in all Cases, except Treason, Felony and Breach of the Peace, be privileged from Arrest during their Attendance at the Session of their respective Houses, and in going to and returning from the same; and for any Speech or Debate in either House, they shall not be questioned in any other Place.

No Senator or Representative shall, during the Time for which he was elected, be appointed to any civil Office under the Authority of the United States, which shall have been created, or the Emoluments whereof shall have been increased during such time; and no Person holding any Office under the United States, shall be a Member of either House during his Continuance in Office.

Section. 7. All Bills for raising Revenue shall originate in the House of Representatives; but the Senate may propose or concur with Amendments as on other Bills.

Every Bill which shall have passed the House of Representatives and the Senate shall, before it become a Law, be presented to the President of the United States; If he approve he shall sign it, but if not he shall return it, with his Objections to that House in which it shall have originated, who shall enter the Objections at large on their Journal, and proceed to reconsider it. If after such Reconsideration two thirds of that House shall agree to pass the Bill, it shall be sent, together with the Objections, to the other House, by which it shall likewise be reconsidered, and if approved by two thirds of that House, it shall become a Law. But in all such Cases the Votes of both Houses shall be determined by yeas and Nays, and the Names of the Persons voting for and against the Bill shall be entered on the Journal of each House respectively. If any Bill shall not be returned by the President within ten Days (Sundays excepted) after it shall have been presented to him, the Same shall be a Law, in like Manner as if he had signed it, unless the Congress by their Adjournment prevent its Return, in which Case it shall not be a Law.

Every Order, Resolution, or Vote to which the Concurrence of the Senate and House of Representatives may be necessary (except on a question of Adjournment) shall be presented to the President of the United States; and before the Same shall take Effect, shall be approved by him, or being disapproved by him, shall be repassed by two thirds of the Senate and House of Representatives, according to the Rules and Limitations prescribed in the Case of a Bill.

Section. 8. The Congress shall have Power To lay and collect Taxes, Duties, Imposts and Excises, to pay the Debts and provide for the common Defence and general Welfare of the United States; but all Duties, Imposts and Excises shall be uniform throughout the United States;

To borrow Money on the credit of the United States;

To regulate Commerce with foreign Nations, and among the several States, and with the Indian Tribes;

To establish an uniform Rule of Naturalization, and uniform Laws on the subject of Bankruptcies throughout the United States;

To coin Money, regulate the Value thereof, and of foreign Coin, and fix the Standard of Weights and Measures;

To provide for the Punishment of counterfeiting the Securities and current Coin of the United States;

To establish Post Offices and Post Roads;

To promote the Progress of Science and useful Arts, by securing for limited Times to Authors and Inventors the exclusive Right to their respective Writings and Discoveries;

To constitute Tribunals inferior to the supreme Court;

To define and punish Piracies and Felonies committed on the high Seas, and Offences against the Law of Nations;

To declare War, grant Letters of Marque and Reprisal, and make Rules concerning Captures on land and Water;

To raise and support Armies, but no Appropriation of Money to that Use shall be for a longer Term than two Years;

To provide and maintain a Navy;

To make Rules for the Government and Regulation of the land and naval Forces;

To provide for calling forth the Militia to execute the Laws of the Union, suppress Insurrections and repel Invasions;

To provide for organizing, arming, and disciplining, the Militia, and for governing such Part of them as may be employed in the Service of the United States, reserving to the States respectively, the Appointment of the Officers, and the Authority of training the Militia according to the discipline prescribed by Congress.

To exercise exclusive Legislation in all Cases whatsoever, over such District (not exceeding ten Miles square) as may, by Cession of Particular States, and the Acceptance of Congress, become the Seat of the Government of the United States, and to exercise like Authority over all Places purchased by the Consent of the Legislature of the State in which the Same shall be, for the Erection of Forts, Magazines, Arsenals, dock-Yards, and other needful Buildings;—And

To make all Laws which shall be necessary and proper for carrying into Execution the foregoing Powers, and all other Powers vested by this Constitution in the Government of the United States, or in any Department or Officer thereof.

Section. 9. The Migration or Importation of such Persons as any of the States now existing shall think proper to admit, shall not be prohibited by the Congress prior to the Year one thousand eight hundred and eight, but a Tax or duty may be imposed on such Importation, not exceeding ten dollars for each Person.

The Privilege of the Writ of Habeas Corpus shall not be suspended, unless when in Cases of Rebellion or Invasion the public Safety may require it.

No Bill of Attainder or ex post facto Law shall be passed.

No Capitation, or other direct, Tax shall be laid, unless in Proportion to the Census or Enumeration herein before directed to be taken.

No Tax or Duty shall be laid on Articles exported from any State.

No Preference shall be given by any Regulation of Commerce or Revenue to the Ports of one State over those of another: nor shall Vessels bound to, or from, one State, be obliged to enter, clear, or pay Duties in another.

No Money shall be drawn from the Treasury, but in Consequence of Appropriations made by Law; and a regular Statement and Account of the Receipts and Expenditures of all public Money shall be published from time to time.

No Title of Nobility shall be granted by the United States: And no Person holding any Office of Profit or trust under them, shall, without the Consent of the Congress, accept of any present, Emolument, Office, or Title, of any kind whatever, from any King, Prince, or foreign State.

Section 10. No State shall enter into any Treaty, Alliance, or Confederation; grant Letters of Marque and Reprisal; coin Money; emit Bills of Credit; make any Thing but gold and silver Coin a Tender in Payment of Debts; pass any Bill of Attainder, ex post facto Law, or Law impairing the Obligation of Contracts, or grant any Title of Nobility.

No State shall, without the Consent of the Congress, lay any Imposts or Duties on Imports or Exports, except what may be absolutely necessary for executing its inspection Laws: and the net Produce of all Duties and Imposts, laid by any State on Imports or Exports, shall be for the Use of the Treasury of the United States; and all such Laws shall be subject to the Revision and Controul of the Congress.

No State shall, without the Consent of Congress, lay any Duty of Tonnage, keep Troops, or Ships of War in time of Peace, enter into any Agreement or Compact with another State, or with a foreign Power, or engage in War, unless actually invaded, or in such imminent Danger as will not admit of delay.

ARTICLE. II.

Section. 1. The executive Power shall be vested in a President of the United States of America. He shall hold his Office during the term of four Years, and, together with the Vice President, chosen for the same Term, be elected, as follows:

Each State shall appoint, in such Manner as the Legislature thereof may direct, a Number of Electors, equal to the whole Number of Senators and Representatives to which the State may be entitled in the Congress: but no Senator or Representative, or Person holding an Office of Trust or Profit under the United States, shall be appointed an Elector.

The Electors shall meet in their respective States, and vote by Ballot for two Persons, of whom one at least shall not be an Inhabitant of the same State with themselves. And they shall make a List of all the Persons voted for, and of the Number of Votes for each; which List they shall sign and certify, and transmit sealed to the Seat of the Government of the United States, directed to the President of the Senate. The President of the Senate shall, in the Presence of the Senate and House of Representatives, open all the Certificates, and the Votes shall then be counted. The Person having the greatest Number of Votes shall be the President, if such Number be a Majority of the whole Number of Electors appointed; and if there be more than one who have such Majority, and have an equal Number of Votes, then the House of Representatives shall immediately chuse by Ballot one of them for President; and if no Person have a Majority, then from the five highest on the List the said House shall in like Manner chuse the President. But in chusing the President, the Votes shall be taken by States, the Representation from each State having one Vote; A quorum for this Purpose shall consist of a Member or Members from two thirds of the States, and a Majority of all the States shall be necessary to a Choice. In every Case, after the Choice of the President, the Person having the greatest Number of Votes of the Electors shall be the Vice President. But if there should remain two or more who have equal Votes, the Senate shall chuse from them by Ballot the Vice President.

The Congress may determine the Time of chusing the Electors, and the Day on which they shall give their Votes; which Day shall be the same throughout the United States.

No Person except a natural born Citizen, or a Citizen of the United States, at the time of the Adoption of this Constitution, shall be eligible to the Office of President; neither shall any Person be eligible to that Office who shall not have attained to the Age of thirty five Years, and been fourteen Years a Resident within the United States.

In Case of the Removal of the President from Office, or of his Death, Resignation, or Inability to discharge the Powers and Duties of the said Office, the Same shall devolve on the Vice President, and the Congress may by Law provide for the Case of Removal, Death, Resignation or Inability, both of the President and Vice President, declaring what Officer shall then act as

President, and such Officer shall act accordingly, until the Disability be removed, or a President shall be elected.

The President shall, at stated Times, receive for his Services, a Compensation, which shall neither be encreased or diminished during the Period for which he shall have been elected, and he shall not receive within that Period any other Emolument from the United States, or any of them.

Before he enters on the Execution of his Office, he shall take the following Oath or Affirmation:—"I do solemnly swear (or affirm) that I will faithfully execute the Office of President of the United States, and will to the best of my Ability, preserve, protect and defend the Constitution of the United States."

Section. 2. The President shall be Commander in Chief of the Army and Navy of the United States, and of the Militia of the several States, when called into the actual Service of the United States; he may require the Opinion, in writing, of the principal Officer in each of the executive Departments, upon any Subject relating to the Duties of their respective Offices, and he shall have Power to grant Reprieves and Pardons for Offences against the United States, except in Cases of Impeachment.

He shall have Power, by and with the Advice and Consent of the Senate, to make Treaties, provided two thirds of the Senators present concur; and he shall nominate, and by and with the Advice and Consent of the Senate, shall appoint Ambassadors, other public Ministers and Consuls, Judges of the supreme Court, and all other Officers of the United States, whose Appointments are not herein otherwise provided for, and which shall be established by Law; but the Congress may by Law vest the Appointment of such inferior Officers, as they think proper, in the President alone, in the Courts of Law, or in the Heads of Departments.

The President shall have Power to fill up all Vacancies that may happen during the Recess of the Senate, by granting Commissions which shall expire at the End of their next Session.

Section. 3. He shall from time to time give to the Congress Information of the State of the Union, and recommend to their Consideration such Measures as he shall judge necessary and expedient; he may, on extraordinary Occasions, convene both Houses, or either of them, and in Case of Disagreement between them, with Respect to the Time of Adjournment, he may adjourn them to such Time as he shall think proper; he shall receive Ambassadors and other public Ministers; he shall take Care that the Laws be faithfully executed, and shall Commission all the Officers of the United States.

Section. 4. The President, Vice President and all civil Officers of the United States, shall be removed from Office on Impeachment for, and Conviction of, Treason, Bribery, or other high Crimes and Misdemeanors.

Article. III.

Section. 1. The judicial Power of the United States, shall be vested in one supreme Court, and in such inferior Courts as the Congress may from time to time ordain and establish. The Judges, both of the supreme and inferior Courts, shall hold their Offices during good Behavior, and shall, at stated Times, receive for their Services, a Compensation, which shall not be diminished during their Continuance in Office.

Section. 2. The judicial Power shall extend to all Cases, in Law and Equity, arising under this Constitution, the Laws of the United States, and Treaties made, or which shall be made, under their Authority;—to all Cases affecting Ambassadors, other public Ministers and Consuls;—to all Cases of admiralty and maritime Jurisdiction;—the Controversies to which the United States shall be a Party;—to Controversies between two or more States;—between a State and Citizens of another State;—between Citizens of different States;—between Citizens of the same State claiming Lands under Grants of different States, and between a State, or the Citizens thereof, and foreign States, Citizens or Subjects.

In all cases affecting Ambassadors, other public Ministers and Consuls, and those in which a State shall be Party, the supreme Court shall have original Jurisdiction. In all the other Cases before mentioned, the supreme Court shall have appellate Jurisdiction, both as to Law and Fact, with such Exceptions, and under such Regulations as the Congress shall make.

The Trial of all Crimes, except in Cases of Impeachment, shall be by Jury; and such Trial shall be held in the State where the said Crimes shall have been committed; but when not committed within any State, the Trial shall be at such Place or Places as the Congress may by Law have directed.

Section. 3. Treason against the United States, shall consist only in levying War against them, or in adhering to their Enemies, giving them Aid and Comfort. No Person shall be convicted of Treason unless on the Testimony of two Witnesses to the same overt Act, or on Confession in open Court.

The Congress shall have Power to declare the Punishment of Treason, but no Attainder of Treason shall work Corruption of Blood, or Forfeiture except during the Life of the Person attainted.

ARTICLE. IV.

Section. 1. Full Faith and Credit shall be given in each State to the public Acts, Records, and judicial Proceedings of every other State. And the Congress may by general Laws prescribe the Manner in which such Acts, Records and Proceedings shall be proved, and the Effect thereof.

Section. 2. The Citizens of each State shall be entitled to all Privileges and Immunities of Citizens in the several States.

A Person charged in any State with Treason, Felony, or other Crime, who shall flee from Justice, and be found in another State, shall on Demand of the executive Authority of the State from which he fled, be delivered up, to be removed to the State having Jurisdiction of the Crime.

No Person held to Service or Labour in one State, under the Laws thereof, escaping into another, shall, in Consequence of any Law or Regulation therein, be discharged from such Service or Labour, but shall be delivered up on Claim of the Party to whom such Service or Labour may be due.

Section. 3. New States may be admitted by the Congress into this Union; but no new State shall be formed or erected within the Jurisdiction of any other State; nor any State be formed by the Junction of two or more States, or Parts of States, without the consent of the Legislatures of the States concerned as well as of the Congress.

The Congress shall have Power to dispose of and make all needful Rules and Regulations respecting the Territory or other Property belonging to the United States; and nothing in this Constitution shall be so construed as to Prejudice any Claims of the United States, or of any particular States.

Section. 4. The United States shall guarantee to every State in this Union a Republican Form of Government, and shall protect each of them against Invasion; and on Application of the Legislature, or of the Executive (when the Legislature cannot be convened) against domestic Violence.

ARTICLE. V.

The Congress, whenever two thirds of both Houses shall deem it necessary, shall propose Amendments to this Constitution, or, on the Application of the

Legislatures of two thirds of the several States, shall call a Convention for proposing Amendments, which, in either Case, shall be valid to all Intents and Purposes, as Part of this Constitution, when ratified by the Legislatures of three fourths of the several States, or by Conventions in three fourths thereof, as the one or the other Mode of Ratification may be proposed by the Congress; Provided that no Amendment which may be made prior to the Year One thousand eight hundred and eight shall in any Manner affect the first and fourth Clauses in the Ninth Section of the first Article; and that no State, without its Consent, shall be deprived of its equal Suffrage in the Senate.

ARTICLE. VI.

All Debts contracted and Engagements entered into, before the Adoption of this Constitution, shall be as valid against the United States under this Constitution, as under the Confederation.

This Constitution, and the Laws of the United States which shall be made in Pursuance thereof; and all Treaties made, or which shall be made, under the Authority of the United States, shall be the supreme Law of the Land; and the Judges in every State shall be bound thereby, any Thing in the Constitution or Laws of any State to the Contrary notwithstanding.

The Senators and Representatives before mentioned, and the Members of the several State Legislatures, and all executive and judicial Officers, both of the United States and of the several States, shall be bound by Oath or Affirmation, to support this Constitution; but no religious Test shall ever be required as a Qualification to any Office or public Trust under the United States.

ARTICLE. VII.

The Ratification of the Conventions of nine States, shall be sufficient for the Establishment of this Constitution between the States so ratifying the Same.

Done in Convention by the Unanimous Consent of the States present the Seventeenth Day of September in the Year of our Lord one thousand seven hundred and Eighty seven and of the Independence of the United States of America the Twelfth. In witness thereof We have hereunto subscribed our Names,

G⁰. WASHINGTON—Presdt.
and deputy from Virginia.

New Hampshire	John Langdon Nicholas Gilman			Geo: Read
		Delaware		Gunning Bedford jun John Dickinson
Massachusetts	Nathaniel Gorham Rufus King			Richard Bassett Jaco: Broom
Connecticut	Wm Saml Johnson Roger Sherman	Maryland		James McHenry Dan of St Thos Jenifer Danl Carroll
New York: . . .	Alexander Hamilton			
		Virginia		John Blair— James Madison Jr.
New Jersey	Wil: Livingston David A. Brearley. Wm Paterson. Jona: Dayton	North Carolina		Wm Blount Richd Dobbs Spaight. Hu Williamson
Pennsylvania	B Franklin Thomas Mifflin Robt Morris Geo. Clymer Thos FitzSimons Jared Ingersoll James Wilson Gouv Morris	South Carolina		J. Rutledge Charles Cotesworth Pinckney Charles Pinckney Pierce Butler.
		Georgia		William Few Abr Baldwin

AMENDMENTS TO THE CONSTITUTION

ARTICLES IN ADDITION TO, and Amendment of the Constitution of the United States of America, proposed by Congress, and ratified by the Legislatures of the several States, pursuant to the fifth Article of the original Constitution.

AMENDMENT I.

Congress shall make no law respecting an establishment of religion, or prohibiting the free exercise thereof; or abridging the freedom of speech, or of the press; or the right of the people peaceably to assemble, and to petition the Government for a redress of grievances.

Amendment II.

A well regulated Militia, being necessary to the security of a free State, the right of the people to keep and bear Arms, shall not be infringed.

Amendment III.

No Soldier shall, in time of peace be quartered in any house, without the consent of the Owner, nor in time of war, but in a manner to be prescribed by law.

Amendment IV.

The right of the people to be secure in their persons, houses, papers, and effects, against unreasonable searches and seizures, shall not be violated, and no Warrants shall issue, but upon probable cause, supported by Oath or affirmation, and particularly describing the place to be searched, and the persons or things to be seized.

Amendment V.

No person shall be held to answer for a capital, or otherwise infamous crime, unless on a presentment or indictment of a Grand Jury, except in cases arising in the land or naval forces, or in the Militia, when in actual service in time of War or public danger; nor shall any person be subject for the same offence to be twice put in jeopardy of life or limb; nor shall be compelled in any criminal case to be a witness against himself, nor be deprived of life, liberty, or property, without due process of law; nor shall private property be taken for public use, without just compensation.

Amendment VI.

In all criminal prosecutions, the accused shall enjoy the right to a speedy and public trial, by an impartial jury of the State and district wherein the crime shall have been committed, which district shall have been previously ascertained by law, and to be informed of the nature and cause of the accusation;

to be confronted with the witnesses against him; to have compulsory process for obtaining witnesses in his favor, and to have the Assistance of Counsel for his defence.

AMENDMENT VII.

In Suits at common law, where the value in controversy shall exceed twenty dollars, the right of trial by jury shall be preserved, and no fact tried by a jury, shall be otherwise re-examined in any Court of the United States, than according to the rules of the common law.

AMENDMENT VIII.

Excessive bail shall not be required, nor excessive fines imposed, nor cruel and unusual punishments inflicted.

AMENDMENT IX.

The enumeration in the Constitution, of certain rights, shall not be construed to deny or disparage others retained by the people.

AMENDMENT X.

The powers not delegated to the United States by the Constitution, nor prohibited by it to the States, are reserved to the States respectively, or to the people. [The first ten amendments went into effect December 15, 1791.]

AMENDMENT XI.

The Judicial power of the United States shall not be construed to extend to any suit in law or equity, commenced or prosecuted against one of the United States by Citizens of another State, or by Citizens or Subjects of any Foreign State. [January 8, 1798.]

AMENDMENT XII.

The Electors shall meet in their respective states, and vote by ballot for President and Vice-President, one of whom, at least, shall not be an inhabitant of the same state with themselves; they shall name in their ballots the person voted for as President, and in distinct ballots the person voted for as Vice-President, and they shall make distinct lists of all persons voted for as President, and of all persons voted for as Vice President, and of the number of votes for each, which lists they shall sign and certify, and transmit sealed to the seat of the government of the United States, directed to the President of the Senate;—The President of the Senate shall, in the presence of the Senate and House of Representatives, open all the certificates and the votes shall then be counted;—The person having the greatest number of votes for President, shall be the President, if such number be a majority of the whole number of Electors appointed; and if no person have such majority, then from the persons having the highest numbers not exceeding three on the list of those voted for as President, the House of Representatives shall choose immediately, by ballot, the President. But in choosing the President, the votes shall be taken by states, the representation from each state having one vote; a quorum for this purpose shall consist of a member or members from two-thirds of the states, and a majority of all the states shall be necessary to a choice. And if the House of Representatives shall not choose a President whenever the right of choice shall devolve upon them, before the fourth day of March next following, then the Vice-President shall act as President, as in the case of the death or other constitutional disability of the President.—The person having the greatest number of votes as Vice-President, shall be the Vice-President, if such number be a majority of the whole number of Electors appointed, and if no person have a majority, then from the two highest numbers on the list, the Senate shall choose the Vice-President; a quorum for the purpose shall consist of two-thirds of the whole number of Senators, and a majority of the whole number shall be necessary to a choice. But no person constitutionally ineligible to the office of President shall be eligible to that of Vice-President of the United States. [September 25, 1804.]

AMENDMENT XIII.

Section 1. Neither slavery nor involuntary servitude, except as a punishment for crime whereof the party shall have been duly convicted, shall exist within the United States, or any place subject to their jurisdiction.

Section 2. Congress shall have power to enforce this article by appropriate legislation. [December 18, 1865.]

AMENDMENT XIV.

Section 1. All persons born or naturalized in the United States, and subject to the jurisdiction thereof, are citizens of the United States and of the State wherein they reside. No State shall make or enforce any law which shall abridge the privileges or immunities of citizens of the United States; nor shall any State deprive any person of life, liberty, or property, without due process of law; nor deny to any person within its jurisdiction the equal protection of the laws.

Section 2. Representatives shall be apportioned among the several States according to their respective numbers, counting the whole number of persons in each State, excluding Indians not taxed. But when the right to vote at any election for the choice of electors for President and Vice President of the United States, Representatives in Congress, the Executive and Judicial officers of a State, or the members of the Legislature thereof, is denied to any of the male inhabitants of such State, being twenty-one years of age, and citizens of the United States, or in any way abridged, except for participation in rebellion, or other crime, the basis of representation therein shall be reduced in the proportion which the number of such male citizens shall bear to the whole number of male citizens twenty-one years of age in such State.

Section 3. No person shall be a Senator or Representative in Congress, or elector of President and Vice President, or hold any office, civil or military, under the United States, or under any State, who, having previously taken an oath, as a member of Congress, or as an officer of the United States, or as a member of any State legislature, or as an executive or judicial officer of any State, to support the Constitution of the United States, shall have engaged in insurrection or rebellion against the same, or given aid or comfort to the enemies thereof. But Congress may by a vote of two-thirds of each House, remove such disability.

Section 4. The validity of the public debt of the United States, authorized by law, including debts incurred for payment of pensions and bounties for services in suppressing insurrection or rebellion, shall not be questioned. But neither the United States nor any State shall assume or pay any debt or obligation incurred in aid of insurrection or rebellion against the United States, or any claim for the loss or emancipation of any slave; but all such debts, obligations and claims shall be held illegal and void.

Section 5. The Congress shall have power to enforce, by appropriate legislation, the provisions of this article. [July 28, 1868.]

AMENDMENT XV.

Section 1. The right of citizens of the United States to vote shall not be denied or abridged by the United States or by any State on account of race, color, or previous condition of servitude—

Section 2. The Congress shall have power to enforce this article by appropriate legislation.—[March 30, 1870.]

AMENDMENT XVI.

The Congress shall have power to lay and collect taxes on incomes, from whatever source derived, without apportionment among the several States, and without regard to any census or enumeration. [February 25, 1913.]

AMENDMENT XVII.

The Senate of the United States shall be composed of two senators from each State, elected by the people thereof, for six years; and each Senator shall have one vote. The electors in each State shall have the qualifications requisite for electors of the most numerous branch of the State legislature.

When vacancies happen in the representation of any State in the Senate, the executive authority of such State shall issue writs of election to fill such vacancies: *Provided,* That the legislature of any State may empower the executive thereof to make temporary appointments until the people fill the vacancies by election as the legislature may direct.

This amendment shall not be so construed as to affect the election or term of any senator chosen before it becomes valid as part of the Constitution. [May 31, 1913.]

Amendment XVIII.

After one year from the ratification of this article, the manufacture, sale, or transportation of intoxicating liquors within, the importation thereof into, or the exportation thereof from the United States and all territory subject to the jurisdiction thereof for beverage purposes is hereby prohibited.

The Congress and the several States shall have concurrent power to enforce this article by appropriate legislation.

This article shall be inoperative unless it shall have been ratified as an amendment to the Constitution by the legislatures of the several States, as provided in the Constitution, within seven years from the date of the submission thereof to the States by Congress. [January 29, 1919.]

Amendment XIX.

The right of citizens of the United States to vote shall not be denied or abridged by the United States or by any State on account of sex.

The Congress shall have power by appropriate legislation to enforce the provisions of this article. [August 26, 1920.]

Amendment XX.

Section 1. The terms of the President and Vice-President shall end at noon on the twentieth day of January, and the terms of Senators and Representatives at noon on the third day of January, of the years in which such terms would have ended if this article had not been ratified; and the terms of their successors shall then begin.

Section 2. The Congress shall assemble at least once in every year, and such meeting shall begin at noon on the third day of January, unless they shall by law appoint a different day.

Section 3. If, at the time fixed for the beginning of the term of the President, the President-elect shall have died, the Vice-President-elect shall become President. If a President shall not have been chosen before the time fixed for the beginning of his term, or if the President-elect shall have failed to qualify, then the Vice-President-elect shall act as President until a President shall have qualified; and the Congress may by law provide for the case wherein neither a President-elect nor a Vice-President-elect shall have qualified, declaring who shall then act as President, or the manner in which one who is to act shall be selected, and such person shall act accordingly until a President or Vice-President shall have qualified.

Section 4. The Congress may by law provide for the case of the death of any of the persons from whom the House of Representatives may choose a President whenever the right of choice shall have devolved upon them, and for the case of the death of any of the persons from whom the Senate may choose a Vice-President whenever the right of choice shall have devolved upon them.

Section 5. Sections 1 and 2 shall take effect on the 15th day of October following the ratification of this article.

Section 6. This article shall be inoperative unless it shall have been ratified as an amendment to the Constitution by the legislatures of three-fourths of the several States within seven years from the date of its submission. [February 6, 1933.]

AMENDMENT XXI.

Section 1. The eighteenth article of amendment to the Constitution of the United States is hereby repealed.

Section 2. The transportation or importation into any State, Territory or possession of the United States for delivery or use therein of intoxicating liquors, in violation of the laws thereof, is hereby prohibited.

Section 3. This article shall be inoperative unless it shall have been ratified as an amendment to the Constitution by convention in the several States, as provided in the Constitution, within seven years from the date of the submission thereof to the States by the Congress. [December 5, 1933.]

AMENDMENT XXII.

Section 1. No person shall be elected to the office of the President more than twice, and no person who has held the office of President, or acted as President, for more than two years of a term to which some other person was elected President shall be elected to the office of the President more than once. But this Article shall not apply to any person holding the office of President when this Article was proposed by the Congress, and shall not prevent any person who may be holding the office of President, or acting as President, during the term within which this Article becomes operative from holding the office of President or acting as President during the remainder of such term.

Section 2. This article shall be inoperative unless it shall have been ratified as an amendment to the Constitution by the legislatures of three-fourths of the several states within seven years from the date of its submission to the States by the Congress. [February 27, 1951.]

AMENDMENT XXIII.

Section 1. The District constituting the seat of government of the United States shall appoint in such manner as the Congress may direct:

A number of electors of President and Vice-President equal to the whole number of Senators and Representatives in Congress to which the District would be entitled if it were a State, but in no event more than the least populous State; they shall be in addition to those appointed by the States, but they shall be considered, for the purposes of the election of President and Vice-President, to be electors appointed by a State; and they shall meet in the District and perform such duties as provided by the twelfth article of amendment.

Section 2. The Congress shall have the power to enforce this article by appropriate legislation. [March 29, 1961.]

AMENDMENT XXIV.

Section 1. The right of citizens of the United States to vote in any primary or other election for President or Vice President, for electors for President or Vice President, or for Senator or Representative in Congress, shall not be denied or abridged by the United States or any State by reason of failure to pay any poll tax or other tax.

Section 2. The Congress shall have power to enforce this article by appropriate legislation. [January 23, 1964.]

Amendment XXV.

Section 1. In case of the removal of the President from office or of his death or resignation, the Vice President shall become President.

Section 2. Whenever there is a vacancy in the office of Vice President, the President shall nominate a Vice President who shall take office upon confirmation by a majority vote of both Houses of Congress.

Section 3. Whenever the President transmits to the President pro tempore of the Senate and the Speaker of the House of Representatives his written declaration that he is unable to discharge the powers and duties of his office, and until he transmits to them a written declaration to the contrary, such powers and duties shall be discharged by the Vice President as Acting President.

Section 4. Whenever the Vice President and a majority of either the principal officers of the executive departments or of such other body as Congress may by law provide, transmit to the President pro tempore of the Senate and the Speaker of the House of Representatives their written declaration that the President is unable to discharge the powers and duties of his office, the Vice President shall immediately assume the powers and duties of the office as Acting President.

Thereafter, when the President transmits to the President pro tempore of the Senate and the Speaker of the House of Representatives his written declaration that no inability exists, he shall resume the powers and duties of his office unless the Vice President and a majority of either the principal officers of the executive departments or of such other body as Congress may by law provide, transmit within four days to the President pro tempore of the Senate and the Speaker of the House of Representatives their written declaration that the President is unable to discharge the powers and duties of his office. Thereupon Congress shall decide the issue, assembling within forty-eight hours for that purpose if not in session. If the Congress, within twenty-one days after receipt of the latter written declaration, or, if Congress is not in session, within twenty-one days after Congress is required to assemble, determines by two-thirds vote of both Houses that the President is unable to discharge the powers and duties of his office, the Vice President shall continue to discharge the same as Acting President; otherwise, the President shall resume the powers and duties of his office. [February 10, 1967.]

Amendment XXVI.

Section 1. The right of citizens of the United States, who are eighteen years of age or older, to vote shall not be denied or abridged by the United States or by any State on account of age.

Section 2. The Congress shall have power to enforce this article by appropriate legislation [June 30, 1971.]

Amendment XXVII.

No law, varying the compensation for the services of the Senators and Representatives shall take effect, until an election of Representatives shall have intervened. [May 8, 1992.]

PRESIDENTIAL ELECTIONS

Year	Number of States	Candidates	Parties	Popular Vote	% of Popular Vote	Electoral Vote	% Voter Participation
1789	11	**GEORGE WASHINGTON**	No party designations			69	
		John Adams				34	
		Other candidates				35	
1792	15	**GEORGE WASHINGTON**	No party designations			132	
		John Adams				77	
		George Clinton				50	
		Other candidates				5	
1796	16	**JOHN ADAMS**	Federalist			71	
		Thomas Jefferson	Democratic-Republican			68	
		Thomas Pinckney	Federalist			59	
		Aaron Burr	Democratic-Republican			30	
		Other candidates				48	
1800	16	**THOMAS JEFFERSON**	Democratic-Republican			73	
		Aaron Burr	Democratic-Republican			73	
		John Adams	Federalist			65	
		Charles C. Pinckney	Federalist			64	
		John Jay	Federalist			1	
1804	17	**THOMAS JEFFERSON**	Democratic-Republican			162	
		Charles C. Pinckney	Federalist			14	

Year	Number of States	Candidates	Parties	Popular Vote	% of Popular Vote	Electoral Vote	% Voter Participation
1808	17	**JAMES MADISON**	Democratic-Republican			122	
		Charles C. Pinckney	Federalist			47	
		George Clinton	Democratic-Republican			6	
1812	18	**JAMES MADISON**	Democratic-Republican			128	
		DeWitt Clinton	Federalist			89	
1816	19	**JAMES MONROE**	Democratic-Republican			183	
		Rufus King	Federalist			34	
1820	24	**JAMES MONROE**	Democratic-Republican			231	
		John Quincy Adams	Independent			1	
1824	24	**JOHN QUINCY ADAMS**	Democratic-Republican	108,740	30.5	84	26.9
		Andrew Jackson	Democratic-Republican	153,544	43.1	99	
		Henry Clay	Democratic-Republican	47,136	13.2	37	
		William H. Crawford	Democratic-Republican	46,618	13.1	41	
1828	24	**ANDREW JACKSON**	Democratic	647,286	56.0	178	57.6
		John Quincy Adams	National-Republican	508,064	44.0	83	

Year	Number of States	Candidates	Parties	Popular Vote	% of Popular Vote	Electoral Vote	% Voter Participation
1832	24	**ANDREW JACKSON**	Democratic	688,242	54.5	219	55.4
		Henry Clay	National-Republican	473,462	37.5	49	
		William Wirt	Anti-Masonic	101,051	8.0	7	
		John Floyd	Democratic			11	
1836	26	**MARTIN VAN BUREN**	Democratic	765,483	50.9	170	57.8
		William H. Harrison	Whig			73	
		Hugh L. White	Whig	739,795	49.1	26	
		Daniel Webster	Whig			14	
		W. P. Mangum	Whig			11	
1840	26	**WILLIAM H. HARRISON**	Whig	1,274,624	53.1	234	80.2
		Martin Van Buren	Democratic	1,127,781	46.9	60	
1844	26	**JAMES K. POLK**	Democratic	1,338,464	49.6	170	78.9
		Henry Clay	Whig	1,300,097	48.1	105	
		James G. Birney	Liberty	62,300	2.3		
1848	30	**ZACHARY TAYLOR**	Whig	1,360,967	47.4	163	72.7
		Lewis Cass	Democratic	1,222,342	42.5	127	
		Martin Van Buren	Free Soil	291,263	10.1		
1852	31	**FRANKLIN PIERCE**	Democratic	1,601,117	50.9	254	69.6
		Winfield Scott	Whig	1,385,453	44.1	42	
		John P. Hale	Free Soil	155,825	5.0		
1856	31	**JAMES BUCHANAN**	Democratic	1,832,955	45.3	174	78.9
		John C. Frémont	Republican	1,339,932	33.1	114	
		Millard Fillmore	American	871,731	21.6	8	

Year	Number of States	Candidates	Parties	Popular Vote	% of Popular Vote	Electoral Vote	% Voter Participation
1860	33	**ABRAHAM LINCOLN**	Republican	1,865,593	39.8	180	81.2
		Stephen A. Douglas	Democratic	1,382,713	29.5	12	
		John C. Breckinridge	Democratic	848,356	18.1	72	
		John Bell	Constitutional Union	592,906	12.6	39	
1864	36	**ABRAHAM LINCOLN**	Republican	2,206,938	55.0	212	73.8
		George B. McClellan	Democratic	1,803,787	45.0	21	
1868	37	**ULYSSES S. GRANT**	Republican	3,013,421	52.7	214	78.1
		Horatio Seymour	Democratic	2,706,829	47.3	80	
1872	37	**ULYSSES S. GRANT**	Republican	3,596,745	55.6	286	71.3
		Horace Greeley	Democratic	2,843,446	43.9	66	
1876	38	Rutherford B. Hayes	Republican	4,036,572	48.0	185	81.8
		Samuel J. Tilden	Democratic	4,284,020	51.0	184	
1880	38	**JAMES A. GARFIELD**	Republican	4,453,295	48.5	214	79.4
		Winfield S. Hancock	Democratic	4,414,082	48.1	155	
		James B. Weaver	Greenback-Labor	308,578	3.4		
1884	38	**GROVER CLEVELAND**	Democratic	4,879,507	48.5	219	77.5
		James G. Blaine	Republican	4,850,293	48.2	182	
		Benjamin F. Butler	Greenback-Labor	175,370	1.8		
		John P. St. John	Prohibition	150,369	1.5		
1888	38	**BENJAMIN HARRISON**	Republican	5,477,129	47.9	233	79.3
		Grover Cleveland	Democratic	5,537,857	48.6	168	
		Clinton B. Fisk	Prohibition	249,506	2.2		
		Anson J. Streeter	Union Labor	146,935	1.3		

Year	Number of States	Candidates	Parties	Popular Vote	% of Popular Vote	Electoral Vote	% Voter Partici- pation
1892	44	**GROVER CLEVELAND**	Democratic	5,555,426	46.1	277	74.7
		Benjamin Harrison	Republican	5,182,690	43.0	145	
		James B. Weaver	People's	1,029,846	8.5	22	
		John Bidwell	Prohibition	264,133	2.2		
1896	45	**WILLIAM MCKINLEY**	Republican	7,102,246	51.1	271	79.3
		William J. Bryan	Democratic	6,492,559	47.7	176	
1900	45	**WILLIAM MCKINLEY**	Republican	7,218,491	51.7	292	73.2
		William J. Bryan	Democratic; Populist	6,356,734	45.5	155	
		John C. Wooley	Prohibition	208,914	1.5		
1904	45	**THEODORE ROOSEVELT**	Republican	7,628,461	57.4	336	65.2
		Alton B. Parker	Democratic	5,084,223	37.6	140	
		Eugene V. Debs	Socialist	402,283	3.0		
		Silas C. Swallow	Prohibition	258,536	1.9		
1908	46	**WILLIAM H. TAFT**	Republican	7,675,320	51.6	321	65.4
		William J. Bryan	Democratic	6,412,294	43.1	162	
		Eugene V. Debs	Socialist	420,793	2.8		
		Eugene W. Chafin	Prohibition	253,840	1.7		
1912	48	**WOODROW WILSON**	Democratic	6,296,547	41.9	435	58.8
		Theodore Roosevelt	Progressive	4,118,571	27.4	88	
		William H. Taft	Republican	3,486,720	23.2	8	
		Eugene V. Debs	Socialist	900,672	6.0		
		Eugene W. Chafin	Prohibition	206,275	1.4		

Year	Number of States	Candidates	Parties	Popular Vote	% of Popular Vote	Electoral Vote	% Voter Participation
1916	48	**WOODROW WILSON**	Democratic	9,127,695	49.4	277	61.6
		Charles E. Hughes	Republican	8,533,507	46.2	254	
		A. L. Benson	Socialist	585,113	3.2		
		J. Frank Hanly	Prohibition	220,506	1.2		
1920	48	**WARREN G. HARDING**	Republican	16,143,407	60.4	404	49.2
		James M. Cox	Democratic	9,130,328	34.2	127	
		Eugene V. Debs	Socialist	919,799	3.4		
		P. P. Christensen	Farmer-Labor	265,411	1.0		
1924	48	**CALVIN COOLIDGE**	Republican	15,718,211	54.0	382	48.9
		John W. Davis	Democratic	8,385,283	28.8	136	
		Robert M. La Follette	Progressive	4,831,289	16.6	13	
1928	48	**HERBERT C. HOOVER**	Republican	21,391,993	58.2	444	56.9
		Alfred E. Smith	Democratic	15,016,169	40.9	87	
1932	48	**FRANKLIN D. ROOSEVELT**	Democratic	22,809,638	57.4	472	56.9
		Herbert C. Hoover	Republican	15,758,901	39.7	59	
		Norman Thomas	Socialist	881,951	2.2		
1936	48	**FRANKLIN D. ROOSEVELT**	Democratic	27,752,869	60.8	523	61.0
		Alfred M. Landon	Republican	16,674,665	36.5	8	
		William Lemke	Union	882,479	1.9		
1940	48	**FRANKLIN D. ROOSEVELT**	Democratic	27,307,819	54.8	449	62.5
		Wendell L. Willkie	Republican	22,321,018	44.8	82	
1944	48	**FRANKLIN D. ROOSEVELT**	Democratic	25,606,585	53.5	432	55.9
		Thomas E. Dewey	Republican	22,014,745	46.0	99	

Year	Number of States	Candidates	Parties	Popular Vote	% of Popular Vote	Electoral Vote	% Voter Participation
1948	48	**HARRY S. TRUMAN**	Democratic	24,179,345	49.6	303	53.0
		Thomas E. Dewey	Republican	21,991,291	45.1	189	
		J. Strom Thurmond	States' Rights	1,176,125	2.4	39	
		Henry A. Wallace	Progressive	1,157,326	2.4		
1952	48	**DWIGHT D. EISENHOWER**	Republican	33,936,234	55.1	442	63.3
		Adlai E. Stevenson	Democratic	27,314,992	44.4	89	
1956	48	**DWIGHT D. EISENHOWER**	Republican	35,590,472	57.6	457	60.6
		Adlai E. Stevenson	Democratic	26,022,752	42.1	73	
1960	50	**JOHN F. KENNEDY**	Democratic	34,226,731	49.7	303	62.8
		Richard M. Nixon	Republican	34,108,157	49.5	219	
1964	50	**LYNDON B. JOHNSON**	Democratic	43,129,566	61.1	486	61.9
		Barry M. Goldwater	Republican	27,178,188	38.5	52	
1968	50	**RICHARD M. NIXON**	Republican	31,785,480	43.4	301	60.9
		Hubert H. Humphrey	Democratic	31,275,166	42.7	191	
		George C. Wallace	American Independent	9,906,473	13.5	46	
1972	50	**RICHARD M. NIXON**	Republican	47,169,911	60.7	520	55.2
		George S. McGovern	Democratic	29,170,383	37.5	17	
		John G. Schmitz	American	1,099,482	1.4		

Year	Number of States	Candidates	Parties	Popular Vote	% of Popular Vote	Electoral Vote	% Voter Participation
1976	50	**JIMMY CARTER** Gerald R. Ford	Democratic Republican	40,830,763 39,147,793	50.1 48.0	297 240	53.5
1980	50	**RONALD REAGAN** Jimmy Carter John B. Anderson Ed Clark	Republican Democratic Independent Libertarian	43,901,812 35,483,820 5,719,437 921,188	50.7 41.0 6.6 1.1	489 49	52.6
1984	50	**RONALD REAGAN** Walter F. Mondale	Republican Democratic	54,451,521 37,565,334	58.8 40.6	525 13	53.1
1988	50	**GEORGE H. W. BUSH** Michael Dukakis	Republican Democratic	47,917,341 41,013,030	53.4 45.6	426 111	50.1
1992	50	**BILL CLINTON** George H. W. Bush H. Ross Perot	Democratic Republican Independent	44,908,254 39,102,343 19,741,065	43.0 37.4 18.9	370 168	55.0
1996	50	**BILL CLINTON** Bob Dole H. Ross Perot	Democratic Republican Independent	47,401,185 39,197,469 8,085,295	49.0 41.0 8.0	379 159	49.0
2000	50	**GEORGE W. BUSH** Al Gore Ralph Nader	Republican Democrat Green	50,455,156 50,997,335 2,882,897	47.9 48.4 2.7	271 266	50.4
2004	50	**GEORGE W. BUSH** John F. Kerry	Republican Democrat	62,040,610 59,028,444	50.7 48.3	286 251	60.7

Candidates receiving less than 1 percent of the popular vote have been omitted. Thus the percentage of popular vote given for any election year may not total 100 percent.

Before the passage of the Twelfth Amendment in 1804, the electoral college voted for two presidential candidates; the runner-up became vice-president.

ADMISSION OF STATES

Order of Admission	State	Date of Admission	Order of Admission	State	Date of Admission
1	Delaware	December 7, 1787	26	Michigan	January 26, 1837
2	Pennsylvania	December 12, 1787	27	Florida	March 3, 1845
3	New Jersey	December 18, 1787	28	Texas	December 29, 1845
4	Georgia	January 2, 1788	29	Iowa	December 28, 1846
5	Connecticut	January 9, 1788	30	Wisconsin	May 29, 1848
6	Massachusetts	February 7, 1788	31	California	September 9, 1850
7	Maryland	April 28, 1788	32	Minnesota	May 11, 1858
8	South Carolina	May 23, 1788	33	Oregon	February 14, 1859
9	New Hampshire	June 21, 1788	34	Kansas	January 29, 1861
10	Virginia	June 25, 1788	35	West Virginia	June 30, 1863
11	New York	July 26, 1788	36	Nevada	October 31, 1864
12	North Carolina	November 21, 1789	37	Nebraska	March 1, 1867
13	Rhode Island	May 29, 1790	38	Colorado	August 1, 1876
14	Vermont	March 4, 1791	39	North Dakota	November 2, 1889
15	Kentucky	June 1, 1792	40	South Dakota	November 2, 1889
16	Tennessee	June 1, 1796	41	Montana	November 8, 1889
17	Ohio	March 1, 1803	42	Washington	November 11, 1889
18	Louisiana	April 30, 1812	43	Idaho	July 3, 1890
19	Indiana	December 11, 1816	44	Wyoming	July 10, 1890
20	Mississippi	December 10, 1817	45	Utah	January 4, 1896
21	Illinois	December 3, 1818	46	Oklahoma	November 16, 1907
22	Alabama	December 14, 1819	47	New Mexico	January 6, 1912
23	Maine	March 15, 1820	48	Arizona	February 14, 1912
24	Missouri	August 10, 1821	49	Alaska	January 3, 1959
25	Arkansas	June 15, 1836	50	Hawaii	August 21, 1959

POPULATION OF THE UNITED STATES

Year	Number of States	Population	% Increase	Population per Square Mile
1790	13	3,929,214		4.5
1800	16	5,308,483	35.1	6.1
1810	17	7,239,881	36.4	4.3
1820	23	9,638,453	33.1	5.5
1830	24	12,866,020	33.5	7.4
1840	26	17,069,453	32.7	9.8
1850	31	23,191,876	35.9	7.9
1860	33	31,443,321	35.6	10.6
1870	37	39,818,449	26.6	13.4
1880	38	50,155,783	26.0	16.9
1890	44	62,947,714	25.5	21.1
1900	45	75,994,575	20.7	25.6
1910	46	91,972,266	21.0	31.0
1920	48	105,710,620	14.9	35.6
1930	48	122,775,046	16.1	41.2
1940	48	131,669,275	7.2	44.2
1950	48	150,697,361	14.5	50.7
1960	50	179,323,175	19.0	50.6
1970	50	203,235,298	13.3	57.5
1980	50	226,504,825	11.4	64.0
1985	50	237,839,000	5.0	67.2
1990	50	250,122,000	5.2	70.6
1995	50	263,411,707	5.3	74.4
2000	50	281,421,906	6.8	77.0

IMMIGRATION TO THE UNITED STATES, FISCAL YEARS 1820–2005

Year	Number	Year	Number	Year	Number	Year	Number
1820–1989	55,457,531	1871–80	2,812,191	1921–30	4,107,209	1971–80	4,493,314
1820	8,385	1871	321,350	1921	805,228	1971	370,478
1821–30	143,439	1872	404,806	1922	309,556	1972	384,685
1821	9,127	1873	459,803	1923	522,919	1973	400,063
1822	6,911	1874	313,339	1924	706,896	1974	394,861
1823	6,354	1875	227,498	1925	294,314	1975	386,914
1824	7,912	1876	169,986	1926	304,488	1976	398,613
1825	10,199	1877	141,857	1927	335,175	1976 TQ	103,676
1826	10,837	1878	138,469	1928	307,255	1977	462,315
1827	18,875	1879	177,826	1929	279,678	1978	601,442
1828	27,382	1880	457,257	1930	241,700	1979	460,348
1829	22,520	1881–90	5,246,613	1931–40	528,431	1980	530,639
1830	23,322	1881	669,431	1931	97,139	1981–90	7,338,062
1831–40	599,125	1882	788,992	1932	35,576	1981	596,600
1831	22,633	1883	603,322	1933	23,068	1982	594,131
1832	60,482	1884	518,592	1934	29,470	1983	559,763
1833	58,640	1885	395,346	1935	34,956	1984	543,903
1834	65,365	1886	334,203	1936	36,329	1985	570,009
1835	45,374	1887	490,109	1937	50,244	1986	601,708
1836	76,242	1888	546,889	1938	67,895	1987	601,516
1837	79,340	1889	444,427	1939	82,998	1988	643,025
1838	38,914	1890	455,302	1940	70,756	1989	1,090,924
1839	68,069	1891–1900	3,687,564	1941–50	1,035,039	1990	1,536,483
1840	84,066	1891	560,319	1941	51,776	1991–2000	9,090,857
1841–50	1,713,251	1892	579,663	1942	28,781	1991	1,827,167
1841	80,289	1893	439,730	1943	23,725	1992	973,977
1842	104,565	1894	285,631	1944	28,551	1993	904,292
		1895	258,536	1945	38,119	1994	804,416
		1896	343,267	1946	108,721		

Year	Number	Year	Number	Year	Number	Year	Number
1843	52,496	1897	230,832	1947	147,292	1995	720,461
1844	78,615	1898	229,299	1948	170,570	1996	915,900
1845	114,371	1899	311,715	1949	188,317	1997	798,378
1846	154,416	1900	448,572	1950	249,187	1998	660,477
1847	234,968					1999	644,787
1848	226,527	**1901–10**	**8,795,386**	**1951–60**	**2,515,479**	2000	841,002
1849	297,024	1901	487,918	1951	205,717	**2001–5**	**4,904,341**
1850	369,980	1902	648,743	1952	265,520	2001	1,058,902
		1903	857,046	1953	170,434	2002	1,059,356
1851–60	**2,598,214**	1904	812,870	1954	208,177	2003	705,827
1851	379,466	1905	1,026,499	1955	237,790	2004	957,883
1852	371,603	1906	1,100,735	1956	321,625	2005	1,122,373
1853	368,645	1907	1,285,349	1957	326,867		
1854	427,833	1908	782,870	1958	253,265		
1855	200,877	1909	751,786	1959	260,686		
1856	200,436	1910	1,041,570	1960	265,398		
1857	251,306						
1858	123,126	**1911–20**	**5,735,811**	**1961–70**	**3,321,677**		
1859	121,282	1911	878,587	1961	271,344		
1860	153,640	1912	838,172	1962	283,763		
		1913	1,197,892	1963	306,260		
1861–70	**2,314,824**	1914	1,218,480	1964	292,248		
1861	91,918	1915	326,700	1965	296,697		
1862	91,985	1916	298,826	1966	323,040		
1863	176,282	1917	295,403	1967	361,972		
1864	193,418	1918	110,618	1968	454,448		
1865	248,120	1919	141,132	1969	358,579		
1866	318,568	1920	430,001	1970	373,326		
1867	315,722						
1868	138,840						
1869	352,768						
1870	387,203						

Source: U.S. Immigration and Naturalization Service, 2006.

IMMIGRATION BY REGION AND SELECTED COUNTRY OF LAST RESIDENCE, FISCAL YEARS 1820–2004

Region and Country of Last Residence[1]	1820	1821–30	1831–40	1841–50	1851–60	1861–70	1871–80	1881–90
All countries	8,385	143,439	599,125	1,713,251	2,598,214	2,314,824	2,812,191	5,246,613
Europe	7,690	98,797	495,681	1,597,442	2,452,577	2,065,141	2,271,925	4,735,484
Austria-Hungary	—[2]	—[2]	—[2]	—[2]	—[2]	7,800	72,969	353,719
Austria	—[2]	—[2]	—[2]	—[2]	—[2]	484[3]	63,009	226,038
Hungary	—[2]	—[2]	—[2]	—[2]	—[2]	7,124[3]	9,960	127,681
Belgium	1	27	22	5,074	4,738	6,734	7,221	20,177
Czechoslovakia	—[4]	—[4]	—[4]	—[4]	—[4]	—[4]	—[4]	—[4]
Denmark	20	169	1,063	539	3,749	17,094	31,771	88,132
France	371	8,497	45,575	77,262	76,358	35,986	72,206	50,464
Germany	968	6,761	152,454	434,626	951,667	787,468	718,182	1,452,970
Greece	—	20	49	16	31	72	210	2,308
Ireland[5]	3,614	50,724	207,381	780,719	914,119	435,778	436,871	655,482
Italy	30	409	2,253	1,870	9,231	11,725	55,759	307,309
Netherlands	49	1,078	1,412	8,251	10,789	9,102	16,541	53,701
Norway-Sweden	3	91	1,201	13,903	20,931	109,298	211,245	568,362
Norway	—[6]	—[6]	—[6]	—[6]	—[6]	—[6]	95,323	176,586
Sweden	—[6]	—[6]	—[6]	—[6]	—[6]	—[6]	115,922	391,776
Poland	5	16	369	105	1,164	2,027	12,970	51,806
Portugal	35	145	829	550	1,055	2,658	14,082	16,978
Romania	—[7]	—[7]	—[7]	—[7]	—[7]	—[7]	11	6,348
Soviet Union	14	75	277	551	457	2,512	39,284	213,282
Spain	139	2,477	2,125	2,209	9,298	6,697	5,266	4,419
Switzerland	31	3,226	4,821	4,644	25,011	23,286	28,293	81,988
United Kingdom[5,8]	2,410	25,079	75,810	267,044	423,974	606,896	548,043	807,357
Yugoslavia	—[9]	—[9]	—[9]	—[9]	—[9]	—[9]	—[9]	—[9]
Other Europe	—	3	40	79	5	8	1,001	682

Asia	6	30	55	141	41,538	64,759	124,160	69,942
China[10]	1	2	8	35	41,397	64,301	123,201	61,711
Hong Kong	—[11]	—[11]	—[11]	—[11]	—[11]	—[11]	—[11]	—[11]
India	1	8	39	36	43	69	163	269
Iran	—[12]	—[12]	—[12]	—[12]	—[12]	—[12]	—[12]	—[12]
Israel	—[13]	—[13]	—[13]	—[13]	—[13]	—[13]	—[13]	—[13]
Japan	—[14]	—[14]	—[14]	—[14]	—[14]	186	149	2,270
Korea	—[15]	—[15]	—[15]	—[15]	—[15]	—[15]	—[15]	—[15]
Philippines	—[16]	—[16]	—[16]	—[16]	—[16]	—[16]	—[16]	—[16]
Turkey	1	20	7	59	83	131	404	3,782
Vietnam	—[11]	—[11]	—[11]	—[11]	—[11]	—[11]	—[11]	—[11]
Other Asia	3	—	1	11	15	72	243	1,910
America	387	11,564	33,424	62,469	74,720	166,607	404,044	426,967
Canada & Newfoundland[17,18]	209	2,277	13,624	41,723	59,309	153,878	383,640	393,304
Mexico[18]	1	4,817	6,599	3,271	3,078	2,191	5,162	191,319
Caribbean	164	3,834	12,301	13,528	10,660	9,046	13,957	29,042
Cuba	—[12]	—[12]	—[12]	—[12]	—[12]	—[12]	—[12]	—[12]
Dominican Republic	—[20]	—[20]	—[20]	—[20]	—[20]	—[20]	—[20]	—[20]
Haiti	—[20]	—[20]	—[20]	—[20]	—[20]	—[20]	—[20]	—[20]
Jamaica	—[21]	—[21]	—[21]	—[21]	—[21]	—[21]	—[21]	—[21]
Other Caribbean	164	3,834	12,301	13,528	10,660	9,046	13,957	29,042
Central America	2	105	44	368	449	95	157	404
El Salvador	—[20]	—[20]	—[20]	—[20]	—[20]	—[20]	—[20]	—[20]
Other Central America	2	105	44	368	449	95	157	404
South America	11	531	856	3,579	1,224	1,397	1,128	2,304
Argentina	—[20]	—[20]	—[20]	—[20]	—[20]	—[20]	—[20]	—[20]
Colombia	—[20]	—[20]	—[20]	—[20]	—[20]	—[20]	—[20]	—[20]
Ecuador	—[20]	—[20]	—[20]	—[20]	—[20]	—[20]	—[20]	—[20]
Other South America	11	531	856	3,579	1,224	1,397	1,128	2,304
Other America	—[22]	—[22]	—[22]	—[22]	—[22]	—[22]	—[22]	—[22]
Africa	1	16	54	55	210	312	358	857
Oceania	1	2	9	29	158	214	10,914	12,574
Not specified[22]	300	33,030	69,902	53,115	29,011	17,791	790	789

Region and Country of Last Residence[1]	1891–1900	1901–10	1911–20	1921–30	1931–40	1941–50	1951–60	1961–70
All countries	3,687,564	8,795,386	5,735,811	4,107,209	528,431	1,035,039	2,515,479	3,321,677
Europe	3,555,352	8,056,040	4,321,887	2,463,194	347,566	621,147	1,325,727	1,123,492
Austria-Hungary	592,707[23]	2,145,266[23]	896,342[23]	63,548	11,424	28,329	103,743	26,022
Austria	234,081[3]	668,209[3]	453,649	32,868	3,563[24]	24,860[24]	67,106	20,621
Hungary	181,288[3]	808,511[3]	442,693	30,680	7,861	3,469	36,637	5,401
Belgium	18,167	41,635	33,746	15,846	4,817	12,189	18,575	9,192
Czechoslovakia	—[4]	—[4]	3,426[4]	102,194	14,393	8,347	918	3,273
Denmark	50,231	65,285	41,983	32,430	2,559	5,393	10,984	9,201
France	30,770	73,379	61,897	49,610	12,623	38,809	51,121	45,237
Germany	505,152[23]	341,498[23]	143,945[23]	412,202	114,058[24]	226,578[24]	477,765	190,796
Greece	15,979	167,519	184,201	51,084	9,119	8,973	47,608	85,969
Ireland[5]	388,416	339,065	146,181	211,234	10,973	19,789	48,362	32,966
Italy	651,893	2,045,877	1,109,524	455,315	68,028	57,661	185,491	214,111
Netherlands	26,758	48,262	43,718	26,948	7,150	14,860	52,277	30,606
Norway-Sweden	321,281	440,039	161,469	165,780	8,700	20,765	44,632	32,600
Norway	95,015	190,505	66,395	68,531	4,740	10,100	22,935	15,484
Sweden	226,266	249,534	95,074	97,249	3,960	10,665	21,697	17,116
Poland	96,720[23]	—[23]	4,813[23]	227,734	17,026	7,571	9,985	53,539
Portugal	27,508	69,149	89,732	29,994	3,329	7,423	19,588	76,065
Romania	12,750	53,008	13,311	67,646	3,871	1,076	1,039	2,531
Soviet Union	505,290[23]	1,597,306[23]	921,201[23]	61,742	1,370	571	671	2,465
Spain	8,731	27,935	68,611	28,958	3,258	2,898	7,894	44,659
Switzerland	31,179	34,922	23,091	29,676	5,512	10,547	17,675	18,453
United Kingdom[5,8]	271,538	525,950	341,408	339,570	31,572	139,306	202,824	213,822
Yugoslavia	—[9]	—[9]	1,888[9]	49,064	5,835	1,576	8,225	20,381
Other Europe	282	39,945	31,400	42,619	11,949	8,486	16,350	11,604

Asia	74,862	323,543	247,236	112,059	16,595	37,028	153,249	427,642
China[10]	14,799	20,605	21,278	29,907	4,928	16,709	9,657	34,764
Hong Kong	—[11]	—[11]	—[11]	—[11]	—[11]	—[11]	15,541[11]	75,007
India	68	4,713	2,082	1,886	496	1,761	1,973	27,189
Iran	—[12]	—[12]	—[12]	241[12]	195	1,380	3,388	10,339
Israel	—[13]	—[13]	—[13]	—[13]	—[13]	476[13]	25,476	29,602
Japan	25,942	129,797	83,837	33,462	1,948	1,555	46,250	39,988
Korea	—[15]	—[15]	—[15]	—[15]	—[15]	107[15]	6,231	34,526
Philippines	—[16]	—[16]	—[16]	—[16]	528[16]	4,691	19,307	98,376
Turkey	30,425	157,369	134,066	33,824	1,065	798	3,519	10,142
Vietnam	—[11]	—[11]	—[11]	—[11]	—[11]	—[11]	335[11]	4,340
Other Asia	3,628	11,059	5,973	12,739	7,435	9,551	21,572	63,369
America	38,972	361,888	1,143,671	1,516,716	160,037	354,804	996,944	1,716,374
Canada & Newfoundland[17,18]	3,311	179,226	742,185	924,515	108,527	171,718	377,952	413,310
Mexico[18]	971[19]	49,642	219,004	459,287	22,319	60,589	299,811	453,937
Caribbean	33,066	107,548	123,424	74,899	15,502	49,725	123,091	470,213
Cuba	—[12]	—[12]	—[12]	15,901[12]	9,571	26,313	78,948	208,536
Dominican Republic	—[20]	—[20]	—[20]	—[20]	1,150[20]	5,627	9,897	93,292
Haiti	—[20]	—[20]	—[20]	—[20]	191[20]	911	4,442	34,499
Jamaica	—[21]	—[21]	—[21]	—[21]	—[21]	—[21]	8,869[21]	74,906
Other Caribbean	33,066	107,548	123,424	58,998	4,590	16,874	20,935[21]	58,980
Central America	549	8,192	17,159	15,769	5,861	21,665	44,751	101,330
El Salvador	—[20]	—[20]	—[20]	—[20]	673[20]	5,132	5,895	14,992
Other Central America	549	8,192	17,159	15,769	5,188	16,533	38,856	86,338
South America	1,075	17,280	41,899	42,215	7,803	21,831	91,628	257,954
Argentina	—[20]	—[20]	—[20]	—[20]	1,349[20]	3,338	19,486	49,721
Colombia	—[20]	—[20]	—[20]	—[20]	1,223[20]	3,858	18,048	72,028
Ecuador	—[20]	—[20]	—[20]	—[20]	337[20]	2,417	9,841	36,780
Other South America	1,075	17,280	41,899	42,215	4,894	12,218	44,253	99,425
Other America	—[22]	—[22]	—[22]	31[22]	25	29,276	59,711	19,630
Africa	350	7,368	8,443	6,286	1,750	7,367	14,092	28,954
Oceania	3,965	13,024	13,427	8,726	2,483	14,551	12,976	25,122
Not specified[22]	14,063	33,523[25]	1,147	228	—	142	12,491	93

Region and Country of Last Residence[1]	1971–80	1981–89	1990–99	1991–2000	2001	2002	2003	2004	Total 184 Years 1820–2004
All countries	4,493,314	5,801,579	9,781,496	9,095,417	1,064,318	1,063,732	705,827	946,142	69,869,450
Europe	800,368	637,524	1,291,299	1,359,737	177,833	177,652	102,843	130,151	39,049,276
Austria-Hungary	16,028	20,152	N/A	24,882	2,318	4,016	2,181	3,683	4,379,862
Austria	9,478	14,566	5,094	15,500	1,004	2,657	1,163	2,442	1,851,712
Hungary	6,550	5,586	11,003	9,382	1,314	1,359	1,018	1,241	1,682,074
Belgium	5,329	6,239	5,783	7,090	1,002	842	518	746	220,754
Czechoslovakia[27]	6,023	6,649	7,597	9,816	1,921	1,862	1,474	1,870	162,744
Czech Republic	N/A	N/A	723	N/A	N/A	N/A	N/A	N/A	N/A
Slovak Republic	N/A	N/A	3,010	N/A	N/A	N/A	N/A	N/A	N/A
Denmark	4,439	4,696	5,785	6,079	741	655	436	568	378,891
France	25,069	28,088	26,879	35,820	5,431	4,596	2,933	4,209	840,576
Germany	74,414	79,809	60,082	92,606	22,093	21,058	8,102	10,270	7,237,594
Germany, East	N/A	N/A	105	N/A	N/A	N/A	N/A	N/A	N/A
Germany, West	N/A	N/A	7,338	N/A	N/A	N/A	N/A	N/A	N/A
Greece	92,369	34,490	15,403	26,759	1,966	1,516	914	1,213	736,272
Ireland	11,490	22,229	67,975	56,950	1,550	1,419	1,010	1,518	4,787,580
Italy	129,368	51,008	23,365	62,722	3,377	2,837	1,904	2,495	5,446,443
Netherlands	10,492	10,723	12,334	13,308	1,895	2,305	1,329	1,713	394,782
Norway-Sweden	10,472	13,252	15,720	17,893	2,561	2,097	1,520	2,011	2,172,036
Norway	3,941	3,612	4,618	5,178	588	464	386	457	760,792
Sweden	6,531	9,640	11,102	12,715	1,973	1,633	1,134	1,554	1,265,817
Poland	37,234	64,888	180,035	163,747	12,355	13,304	11,016	13,972	820,730
Portugal	101,710	36,365	25,428	22,916	1,654	1,320	821	1,062	529,034
Romania	12,393	27,361	55,303	51,203	6,224	4,525	3,311	4,064	274,168
Russia	N/A	N/A	110,921						
Soviet Union[28]	38,961	42,898	126,115	462,874	55,099	55,464	33,563	36,646	4,087,352
Former Soviet Republics[29]	N/A	N/A	255,552						
Spain	39,141	17,689	14,310	17,157	1,889	1,603	1,107	1,453	308,357
Switzerland	8,235	7,561	8,840	11,841	1,796	1,503	867	1,193	376,639
United Kingdom	137,374	140,119	138,380	151,866	20,258	18,057	11,220	16,680	5,337,231
Yugoslavia[28]	30,540	15,984	25,923	66,557	21,937	28,100	8,296	13,211	274,372

Former Yugoslavian States	N/A	N/A	61,389						
Other Europe	9,287	7,324	822,161	57,651	11,766	10,573	10,321	11,574	283,859
Asia	1,588,178	2,416,278	2,965,360	2,795,672	337,566	326,871	236,039	314,489	10,029,817
China, People's Republic	124,326	306,108	410,736	419,114	50,821	55,974	37,395	45,942	1,523,622
Hong Kong	113,467	83,848	78,016	109,779	10,307	7,952	5,020	5,421	440,709
India	164,134	221,977	371,925	363,060	65,916	66,864	47,157	65,472	1,064,185
Iran	45,136	101,267	129,055	68,556	8,063	7,730	4,709	5,898	271,807
Israel	37,713	38,367	33,814	39,397	4,925	4,938	3,719	5,206	195,725
Japan	49,775	40,654	60,112	67,942	10,464	9,150	6,724	8,652	565,176
Korea	267,638	302,782	187,794	164,166	19,933	20,114	12,177	19,441	878,079
Philippines	354,987	477,485	526,835	503,945	50,870	48,674	43,258	54,632	1,728,032
Taiwan	N/A	N/A	112,464	N/A	N/A	N/A	N/A	N/A	N/A
Turkey	13,399	20,028	26,178	38,212	3,477	3,934	3,332	4,489	465,771
Vietnam	172,820	266,027	443,173	286,145	34,648	32,425	21,270	30,064	862,829
Other Asia	244,783	557,735	769,425	735,356	78,142	69,116	51,278	69,272	2,033,882
Africa	80,779	144,096	374,149	354,939	50,209	56,135	45,640	62,510	903,578
Oceania	41,242	38,401	49,040	55,845	7,253	6,536	5,102	6,929	286,287
America	1,982,735	2,564,698	4,529,512	4,486,806	473,351	478,777	306,793	407,471	19,220,746
Canada	169,939	132,296	138,165	191,987	30,203	27,299	16,555	22,437	4,584,066
Mexico	640,294	975,657	2,756,513	2,249,421	204,844	217,318	114,984	173,664	6,848,960
Caribbean	741,126	759,416	1,023,237	978,787	96,958	94,240	67,660	81,893	4,022,715
Cuba	264,863	135,142	170,675	169,322	26,073	27,520	8,722	15,385	995,732
Dominican Republic	148,135	209,899	365,598	335,251	21,256	22,474	26,157	30,049	945,323
Haiti	56,335	118,510	179,725	179,644	22,535	19,189	11,942	13,502	481,569
Jamaica	137,577	184,481	182,552	169,227	15,099	14,567	13,082	13,565	655,040
Other Caribbean	134,216	111,384	124,687	125,343	11,995	10,490	7,757	9,392	945,051
Central America	134,640	321,845	611,597	526,915	73,063	66,520	53,435	60,299	1,599,860
El Salvador	34,436	133,938	274,989	215,798	31,054	30,539	27,915	29,285	609,258
Other Central America	100,204	187,907	336,608	311,117	42,009	35,981	25,520	31,014	990,602
South America	295,741	375,026	569,650	539,656	68,279	73,400	54,155	69,177	2,054,956
Argentina	29,897	21,374	27,431	26,644	3,459	3,811	3,217	4,672	172,921
Colombia	77,347	99,066	140,685	128,499	16,333	18,488	14,455	17,887	491,015
Ecuador	50,077	43,841	81,204	76,592	9,694	10,564	7,040	8,351	268,008
Other South America	138,420	210,745	320,330	307,921	38,793	40,537	29,443	38,267	1,123,012
Other America	995	458	595	40	4	3	4	1	110,189
Unknown or not reported	N/A	N/A	2,486	42,418	18,106	17,761	9,410	24,592	379,746

Source: U.S. Immigration and Naturalization Service, 2006.

[1]Data for years prior to 1906 relate to country whence alien came; data from 1906–79 and 1984–89 are for country of last permanent residence; and data for 1980–99 refer to country of birth. Because of changes in boundaries, changes in lists of countries, and lack of data for specified countries for various periods, data for certain countries, especially for the total period 1820–2004, are not comparable throughout. Data for specified countries are included with countries to which they belonged prior to World War I.

[2]Data for Austria and Hungary not reported until 1861.

[3]Data for Austria and Hungary not reported separately for all years during the period.

[4]No data available for Czechoslovakia until 1920.

[5]Prior to 1926, data for Northern Ireland included in Ireland.

[6]Data for Norway and Sweden not reported separately until 1871.

[7]No data available for Romania until 1880.

[8]Since 1925, data for United Kingdom refer to England, Scotland, Wales, and Northern Ireland.

[9]In 1920, a separate enumeration was made for the Kingdom of Serbs, Croats, and Slovenes. Since 1922, the Serb, Croat, and Slovene Kingdom recorded as Yugoslavia.

[10]Beginning in 1957, China includes Taiwan.

[11]Data not reported separately until 1952.

[12]Data not reported separately until 1925.

[13]Data not reported separately until 1949.

[14]No data available for Japan until 1861.

[15]Data not reported separately until 1948.

[16]Prior to 1934, Philippines recorded as insular travel.

[17]Prior to 1920, Canada and Newfoundland recorded as British North America. From 1820 to 1898, figures include all British North America possessions.

[18]Land arrivals not completely enumerated until 1908.

[19]No data available for Mexico from 1886 to 1893.

[20]Data not reported separately until 1932.

[21]Data for Jamaica not collected until 1953. In prior years, consolidated under British West Indies, which is included in "Other Caribbean."

[22]Included in countries "Not specified" until 1925.

[23]From 1899 to 1919, data for Poland included in Austria-Hungary, Germany, and the Soviet Union.

[24]From 1938 to 1945, data for Austria included in Germany.

[25]Includes 32,897 persons returning in 1906 to their homes in the United States.

[26]Data for fiscal year 1998 have been revised due to changes in the count for asylees and cancellation of removal. The previously reported total was 660,477.

[27]Prior to 1993, data include independent republics; beginning in 1993, data are for unknown republic only.

[28]Prior to 1992, data include independent republic; beginning in 1992, data are for Yugoslavia only.

[29]Prior to 1992, data include previously independent republics only; beginning in 1992, data are for all former republics except Russia.

— represents zero.

NOTE: From 1820 to 1867, figures represent alien passengers arrived at seaports; from 1868 to 1891 and 1895 to 1897, immigrant aliens arrived; from 1892 to 1894 and 1898 to 1989, immigrant aliens admitted for permanent residence. From 1892 to 1903, aliens entering by cabin class were not counted as immigrants. Land arrivals were not completely enumerated until 1908. For this table, fiscal year 1843 covers 9 months ending September 1843; fiscal years 1832 and 1850 cover 15 months ending December 31 of the respective years; and fiscal year 1868 covers 6 months ending June 30, 1868.

PRESIDENTS, VICE-PRESIDENTS, AND SECRETARIES OF STATE

	President	*Vice-President*	*Secretary of State*
1.	George Washington, Federalist 1789	John Adams, Federalist 1789	Thomas Jefferson 1789 Edmund Randolph 1794 Timothy Pickering 1795
2.	John Adams, Federalist 1797	Thomas Jefferson, Dem.-Rep. 1797	Timothy Pickering 1797 John Marshall 1800
3.	Thomas Jefferson, Dem.-Rep. 1801	Aaron Burr, Dem.-Rep. 1801 George Clinton, Dem.-Rep. 1805	James Madison 1801
4.	James Madison, Dem.-Rep. 1809	George Clinton, Dem.-Rep. 1809 Elbridge Gerry, Dem.-Rep. 1813	Robert Smith 1809 James Monroe 1811
5.	James Monroe, Dem.-Rep. 1817	Daniel D. Tompkins, Dem.-Rep. 1817	John Q. Adams 1817
6.	John Quincy Adams, Dem.-Rep. 1825	John C. Calhoun, Dem.-Rep. 1825	Henry Clay 1825
7.	Andrew Jackson, Democratic 1829	John C. Calhoun, Democratic 1829 Martin Van Buren, Democratic 1833	Martin Van Buren 1829 Edward Livingston 1831 Louis McLane 1833 John Forsyth 1834
8.	Martin Van Buren, Democratic 1837	Richard M. Johnson, Democratic 1837	John Forsyth 1837
9.	William H. Harrison, Whig 1841	John Tyler, Whig 1841	Daniel Webster 1841

	President	Vice-President	Secretary of State
10.	John Tyler, Whig and Democratic 1841	None	Daniel Webster 1841 Hugh S. Legaré 1843 Abel P. Upshur 1843 John C. Calhoun 1844
11.	James K. Polk, Democratic 1845	George M. Dallas, Democratic 1845	James Buchanan 1845
12.	Zachary Taylor, Whig 1849	Millard Fillmore, Whig 1848	John M. Clayton 1849
13.	Millard Fillmore, Whig 1850	None	Daniel Webster 1850 Edward Everett 1852
14.	Franklin Pierce, Democratic 1853	William R. King, Democratic 1853	William L. Marcy 1853
15.	James Buchanan, Democratic 1857	John C. Breckinridge, Democratic 1857	Lewis Cass 1857 Jeremiah S. Black 1860
16.	Abraham Lincoln, Republican 1861	Hannibal Hamlin, Republican 1861 Andrew Johnson, Unionist 1865	William H. Seward 1861
17.	Andrew Johnson, Unionist 1865	None	William H. Seward 1865
18.	Ulysses S. Grant, Republican 1869	Schuyler Colfax, Republican 1869 Henry Wilson, Republican 1873	Elihu B. Washburne 1869 Hamilton Fish 1869
19.	Rutherford B. Hayes, Republican 1877	William A. Wheeler, Republican 1877	William M. Evarts 1877

	President	Vice-President	Secretary of State
20.	James A. Garfield, Republican 1881	Chester A. Arthur, Republican 1881	James G. Blaine 1881
21.	Chester A. Arthur, Republican 1881	None	Frederick T. Frelinghuysen 1881
22.	Grover Cleveland, Democratic 1885	Thomas A. Hendricks, Democratic 1885	Thomas F. Bayard 1885
23.	Benjamin Harrison, Republican 1889	Levi P. Morton, Republican 1889	James G. Blaine 1889 John W. Foster 1892
24.	Grover Cleveland, Democratic 1893	Adlai E. Stevenson, Democratic 1893	Walter Q. Gresham 1893 Richard Olney 1895
25.	William McKinley, Republican 1897	Garret A. Hobart, Republican 1897 Theodore Roosevelt, Republican 1901	John Sherman 1897 William R. Day 1898 John Hay 1898
26.	Theodore Roosevelt, Republican 1901	Charles Fairbanks, Republican 1905	John Hay 1901 Elihu Root 1905 Robert Bacon 1909
27.	William H. Taft, Republican 1909	James S. Sherman, Republican 1909	Philander C. Knox 1909
28.	Woodrow Wilson, Democratic 1913	Thomas R. Marshall, Democratic 1913	William J. Bryan 1913 Robert Lansing 1915 Bainbridge Colby 1920
29.	Warren G. Harding, Republican 1921	Calvin Coolidge, Republican 1921	Charles E. Hughes 1921
30.	Calvin Coolidge, Republican 1923	Charles G. Dawes, Republican 1925	Charles E. Hughes 1923 Frank B. Kellogg 1925

	President	Vice-President	Secretary of State
31.	Herbert Hoover, Republican 1929	Charles Curtis, Republican 1929	Henry L. Stimson 1929
32.	Franklin D. Roosevelt, Democratic 1933	John Nance Garner, Democratic 1933 Henry A. Wallace, Democratic 1941 Harry S. Truman, Democratic 1945	Cordell Hull 1933 Edward R. Stettinius, Jr. 1944
33.	Harry S. Truman, Democratic 1945	Alben W. Barkley, Democratic 1949	Edward R. Stettinius, Jr. 1945 James F. Byrnes 1945 George C. Marshall 1947 Dean G. Acheson 1949
34.	Dwight D. Eisenhower, Republican 1953	Richard M. Nixon, Republican 1953	John F. Dulles 1953 Christian A. Herter 1959
35.	John F. Kennedy, Democratic 1961	Lyndon B. Johnson, Democratic 1961	Dean Rusk 1961
36.	Lyndon B. Johnson, Democratic 1963	Hubert H. Humphrey, Democratic 1965	Dean Rusk 1963
37.	Richard M. Nixon, Republican 1969	Spiro T. Agnew, Republican 1969 Gerald R. Ford, Republican 1973	William P. Rogers 1969 Henry Kissinger 1973
38.	Gerald R. Ford, Republican 1974	Nelson Rockefeller, Republican 1974	Henry Kissinger 1974
39.	Jimmy Carter, Democratic 1977	Walter Mondale, Democratic 1977	Cyrus Vance 1977 Edmund Muskie 1980

	President	Vice-President	Secretary of State
40.	Ronald Reagan, Republican 1981	George H. W. Bush, Republican 1981	Alexander Haig 1981 George Schultz 1982
41.	George H. W. Bush, Republican 1989	J. Danforth Quayle, Republican 1989	James A. Baker 1989 Lawrence Eagleburger 1992
42.	William J. Clinton, Democrat 1993	Albert Gore, Jr., Democrat 1993	Warren Christopher 1993 Madeleine Albright 1997
43.	George W. Bush, Republican 2001	Richard B. Cheney, Republican 2001	Colin L. Powell 2001 Condoleezza Rice 2005

CREDITS

CHAPTER 18: **p. 488,** Library of Congress; **p. 490,** Library of Congress; **p. 492,** Library of Congress; **p. 495,** Library of Congress; **p. 499,** Library of Congress; **p. 507,** Bettmann/Corbis; **p. 512,** Library of Congress; **p. 515,** Library of Congress.

PART 5: **p. 521,** The Granger Collection; **p. 522,** The Granger Collection, Bettmann/Corbis; **p. 523,** The Granger Collection; **p. 524,** Library of Congress and Library of Congress; **p. 525,** Warder Collection and The Granger Collection; **p. 526,** The Granger Collection.

CHAPTER 19: **p. 527,** Library of Congress; **p. 533,** The Granger Collection; **p. 539,** Library of Congress; **p. 540,** Warder Collection; **p. 542,** Kansas State Historical Society; **p. 547,** Warder Collection; **p. 550,** Bettmann/Corbis; **p. 554,** Western Historical Collections, University of Oklahoma Library.

CHAPTER 20: **p. 558,** Library of Congress; **p. 560,** Alfred Stieglitz, *The Hand of Man,* 1902, photogravure, P.1978.112, Amon Carter Museum; **p. 562,** Union Pacific Museum; **p. 567,** Warder Collection; **p. 569,** Carnegie Library of Pittsburgh; **p. 570,** Pierpont Morgan Library; **p. 571,** The Granger Collection; **p. 576,** T.V. Powderly Photographic Collection, The American Catholic History Research Center and University Archives, The Catholic University of America, Washington, D.C.; **p. 580,** Walter P. Reuther Library, Wayne State University.

CHAPTER 21: **p. 585,** Library of Congress; **p. 589,** Culver Pictures; **p. 590,** Bettmann/Corbis; **p. 594,** The Byron Collection, Museum of the City of New York; **p. 595,** William Williams Papers, Manuscripts and Archives Division, The New York Public Library, Astor, Lenox and Tilden Foundations; **p. 598,** Brown Brothers; **p. 601,** Old York Library; **p. 602,** Library of Congress; **p. 610,** The Salvation Army National Archives; **p. 611,** University of Illinois at Chicago.

CHAPTER 22: **p. 616,** Library of Congress; **p. 620,** Library of Congress; **p. 623,** Warder Collection; **p. 626,** Bettmann/Corbis; **p. 631,** Library of Congress; **p. 634,** Kansas State Historical Society; **p. 638,** Library of Congress.

CHAPTER 31: **p. 871,** Bettmann/Corbis; **p. 873,** University of Louisville; **p. 881,** Hartford Courant; **p. 882,** Hy Peskin/Getty Images; **p. 884,** © 1948, The Washington Post. Reprinted with permission; **p. 885,** Bettmann/Corbis; **p. 888,** Library of Congress; **p. 892,** Bettmann/Corbis; **p. 894,** Yale Joel/Getty Images.

CHAPTER 32: **p. 898,** Hulton Archive; **p. 901,** AP/Wide World Photos; **p. 903,** Bettmann/Corbis; **p. 906,** Fogg Art Museum, Harvard University; **p. 907,** PNI/Archive Photos; **p. 910,** Hulton Archive; **p. 911,** AP/Wide World Photos; **p. 914,** AP/Wide World Photos.

CHAPTER 33: **p. 917,** Bettmann/Corbis; **p. 922,** Bettmann/Corbis; **p. 924,** "Don't Be Afraid—I Can Always Pull You Back," from Herblock's Special for Today (Simon & Schuster, 1958); **p. 925,** Photoworld; **p. 933,** AP/Wide World Photos; **p. 935,** University of Louisville; **p. 937,** Black Star/Stock Photo.

CHAPTER 34: **p. 941,** Bettmann/Corbis; **p. 945,** National Archives; **p. 947,** National Archives; **p. 949,** Hulton Archive; **p. 953,** Time & Life Pictures; **p. 959,** National Archives; **p. 963,** Bettmann/Corbis; **p. 964,** The Newark Star-Ledger.

CHAPTER 35: **p. 971,** Bettmann/Corbis; **p. 974,** Magnum Photos; **p. 976,** John Dominis/Getty Images; **p. 977,** Bettmann/Corbis; **p. 980,** AP/Wide World Photos; **p. 984,** Valley News Dispatch; **p. 990,** NASA Kennedy Space Center; **p. 991,** John Dominis/Getty Images; **p. 995,** AP/Wide World Photos; **p. 999,** AP/Wide World Photos.

CHAPTER 36: **p. 1003,** Bettmann/Corbis; **p. 1004,** Bettmann/Corbis; **p. 1010,** Los Angeles Times Syndicate; **p. 1012,** AP/Wide World Photos; **p. 1018,** Woodfin Camp; **p. 1019,** AP/Wide World Photos; **p. 1022,** Bettmann/Corbis.

CHAPTER 37: **p. 1025,** Bettmann/Corbis; **p. 1027,** AP/Wide World Photos; **p. 1029,** Library of Congress; **p. 1033,** Chris Wilkins/Getty Images; **p. 1036,** AP/Wide World Photos; **p. 1041,** AP/Wide World Photos; **p. 1043,** AP/Wide World Photos; **p. 1051,** Bettmann/Corbis; **p. 1054,** Bettmann/Corbis; **p. 1056,** Bettmann/Corbis; **p. 1058,** Bettmann/Corbis; **p. 1062,** Bettmann/Corbis.

INDEX

Page numbers in *italics* refer to illustrations.

Czech Americans, 593
Czechoslovakia, 1018
  Communist takeover of, 879
  creation of, 725
  German occupation of, 817–18, 820
  Soviet crackdown of 1968 in, 1009
Czolgosz, Leon, 666–67

Dakota territory, 546
Daley, Richard, 966, 974
Dallas, Tex., 952
dance halls, 600
Dangling Man (Bellow), 912
Daniels, Jonathan, 750
Darling, J. N. "Ding," 727
Darrow, Clarence, 737–38
Darwin, Charles, 605–6, 748
Darwinism, 605–6, 648, 1005
  reform, 606
  social, 605–6, 609, 653–54, 690
Daugherty, Harry M., 754, 756
Davis, John W., 759, 797
Dawes General Allotment Act (1887), 793
Dawes Severalty Act (1887), 549
Daylight Saving Time, 716
D-Day invasion (1944), 843, 846–48, *846, 847*
Dean, John, 994
Death of a Salesman (Miller), 912
Debs, Eugene V., 579–81, *580,* 689, 693, 694,
  719, 757
debt, national, 755
Declaration of Cairo (1943), 846
Defense Department, U.S., 876
deficit, federal, 989, 990, 996, 1008, 1015,
  1031, 1032, 1034, 1061, 1064
de Kooning, Willem, 913
DeLeon, Daniel, 581
de Lôme, Depuy, 657
Democratic Leadership Council, 1032
Democratic party, 534, 536
  African Americans and, 802–3
  in election of 1880, 621–22
  in election of 1884, 623–24
  in election of 1888, 626–27
  in election of 1890, 628–29
  in election of 1892, 634–35
  in election of 1894, 637
  in election of 1896, 637–40
  in election of 1900, 666
  in election of 1904, 684
  in election of 1908, 689
  in election of 1910, 691
  in election of 1912, 693–95
  in election of 1916, 712–13
  in election of 1918, 723–24
  in election of 1920, 754

in election of 1924, 759
in election of 1928, 766–67
in election of 1930, 772
in election of 1932, 778, 779–80
in election of 1936, 802–3
in election of 1938, 807
in election of 1940, 823
in election of 1942, 835
in election of 1944, 852
in election of 1946, 875
in election of 1948, 883–85
in election of 1952, 918–20
in election of 1956, 927–28
in election of 1960, 942–43
in election of 1964, 955
in election of 1968, 966–68
in election of 1972, 993
in election of 1976, 997
in election of 1980, 1007
in election of 1984, 1011–12
in election of 1986, 1013
in election of 1988, 1015–17
in election of 1992, 1034
in election of 1994, 1036–37
in election of 1996, 1038–39
in election of 2000, 1045–46
in election of 2004, 1058–60
in Gilded Age, 616–19
as party of progressive reform, 640
and welfare state, 868
World War II and, 860
see also specific candidates
Denmark, 821, 881
Denver, Colo., 586
Dependent Pension Act (1890), 627
Depression, Great, 649, 769–75
  agriculture in, 770, 771, 773–74, 782, 783,
    786–87, 790–92
  banking industry in, 769, 770, 771, 773,
    777, 780–81, 782–83
  congressional initiatives in, 772–73
  farmers and, 770, 771, 773–74
  Hoover's recovery efforts in, 771–72
  human toll of, 771, 789–93
  Social Security Act and, 799–801
  stock market and, 768–70
  totalitarianism and, 778
  unemployment in, 769–70, 771, 777, 780,
    789, 797
  war debts and reparations and, 811
  World War II and, 833, 860
  see also New Deal; Roosevelt, Franklin D.
depressions, 526
  of 1893, 579, 636–37
  see also Depression, Great; recessions
desegregation: